Introducing
3ds Max® 2008

Introducing
3ds Max® 2008

DARIUSH DERAKHSHANI

RANDI LORENE MUNN

WILEY PUBLISHING, INC.

Acquisitions Editor: Mariann Barsolo
Development Editor: Laurene Sorensen
Technical Editor: Mark Gerhard
Production Editor: Debra Banninger
Copy Editor: Kathy Carlyle
Production Manager: Tim Tate
Vice President and Executive Group Publisher: Richard Swadley
Vice President and Executive Publisher: Joseph B. Wikert
Vice President and Publisher: Neil Edde
Media Associate Project Manager: Laura Atkinson
Media Assistant Producer: Josh Frank
Media Quality Assurance: Kit Malone
Compositor: Happenstance Type-O-Rama
Proofreader: Nancy Carrasco
Indexer: Ted Laux
Cover Designer: Ryan Sneed
Cover Images: Dariush Derakhshani, Randi L. Munn, the Game Wizards Production Team at the Art Institute of California–Los Angeles, and Sean Dunny.

Library of Congress Cataloging-in-Publication Data

Derakhshani, Dariush.

  Introducing 3ds max 2008 / Dariush Derakhshani. — 1st ed.

    p. cm.

  ISBN 978-0-470-18494-3 (paper/cd-rom)

  1. Computer animation. 2. 3ds max (Computer file) 3. Three-dimensional display systems. I. Title.

  TR897.7.D47 2008

  006.6'96—dc22

                    2007044837

Dear Reader

Thank you for choosing *Introducing 3ds Max 2008*. This book is part of a family of premium quality Sybex books, all written by outstanding authors who combine practical experience with a gift for teaching.

Sybex was founded in 1976. More than thirty years later, we're still committed to producing consistently exceptional books. With each of our titles we're working hard to set a new standard for the industry. From the paper we print on, to the authors we work with, our goal is to bring you the best books available.

I hope you see all that reflected in these pages. I'd be very interested to hear your comments and get your feedback on how we're doing. Feel free to let me know what you think about this or any other Sybex book by sending me an email at nedde@wiley.com, or if you think you've found a technical error in this book, please visit http://sybex.custhelp.com. Customer feedback is critical to our efforts at Sybex.

Best regards,

Neil Edde
Vice President and Publisher
Sybex, an Imprint of Wiley

Dedication

To Max Henry

Acknowledgments

We are thrilled to be updating *Introducing 3ds Max* for version 2008. Education is an all-important goal in life and should always be approached with eagerness and earnestness. We would like to show appreciation to the teachers who inspired us; you can always remember the teachers who touched your life, and to them we say thanks. We would also like to thank all of our students, who taught us a lot during the course of our many combined academic years. Equally, we would like to extend many thanks to the student artists who contributed to this book; many of them are our own students from The Art Institute of California at Los Angeles. Thanks to the AI faculty for their help in gathering the inspiring work for the color insert and for their support in writing this book.

Having a good computer system is important with this type of work; so a special thank you goes to Dell for keeping us on the cutting edge of workstation hardware. Special thanks go to Mariann Barsolo, Laurene Sorensen, Debra Banninger, and Kathy Carlyle, our editors at Wiley who have been professional, courteous, and ever patient. Our appreciation also goes to technical editor Mark Gerhard, who worked hard to make sure this book is of the utmost quality.

Tremendous gratitude goes to Jon McFarland for his fantastic contributions to the previous edition of this book, some of which have carried over to this edition. Finally, thanks to Dariush's mother and brother for their love and support, not to mention the life-saving babysitting services.

About the Authors

Dariush Derakhshani is a Creative Director with Radium, a creative design and VFX boutique, and a writer & educator in Los Angeles, California. Dariush used Autodesk's AutoCAD software in his architectural days and migrated to using 3D programs when his firm's principal architects needed to visualize architectural designs in 3D on the computer. Dariush started using Alias PowerAnimator version 6 when he enrolled in USC Film School's Animation program, and he has been using Alias/Autodesk animation software for the past 11 years. He received an M.F.A. in Film, Video, and Computer Animation from the USC Film School in 1997. He also holds a B.A. in Architecture and Theatre from Lehigh University in Pennsylvania. He worked at a New Jersey architectural firm before moving to Los Angeles for film school. He has worked on feature films, music videos, and countless commercials as a 3D animator, as a CG supervisor, and sometimes as a compositor. Dariush also serves as a contributing editor and on the Advisory Board of *HDRI3d,* a professional computer graphics (CG) magazine from DMG Publishing.

Randi Lorene Munn is a staff instructor with The Art Institute of California at Los Angeles. She began working with computer graphics in 1992, and she was hired by her instructor to work at Sony Pictures Imageworks, where she developed her skills with 3ds Max and Shake, among many other programs. A teacher since 1999, Randi enjoys sharing her wisdom with young talent and watching them develop at The Art Institute, as well as at the UCLA Extension. Currently, she teaches a wide range of classes from Autodesk 3ds Max to compositing with Apple Shake and Adobe After Effects. Juggling her teaching activities with caring for a little baby boy makes Randi a pretty busy lady.

CONTENTS AT A GLANCE

Introduction ■ **xv**

Chapter 1 ■ Basic Concepts **1**

Chapter 2 ■ Your First 3ds Max Animation **31**

Chapter 3 ■ The 3ds Max Interface **61**

Chapter 4 ■ Modeling in 3ds Max: Part I **107**

Chapter 5 ■ Modeling in 3ds Max: Part II **183**

Chapter 6 ■ Character Poly Modeling **239**

Chapter 7 ■ Materials and Mapping **295**

Chapter 8 ■ Introduction to Animation **369**

Chapter 9 ■ Character Studio and IK Animation **411**

Chapter 10 ■ 3ds Max Lighting **455**

Chapter 11 ■ 3ds Max Rendering **501**

Chapter 12 ■ Particles and Dynamics **545**

Appendix ■ About the Companion CD **583**

Index ■ **587**

Contents

Introduction   xv

Chapter 1 ▪ Basic Concepts   **1**

How to Read This Book   2

What Is CGI?   2

Production Workflow   4

CG Workflow   8

CG Specialties   13

Core Concepts   14

Coordinate Systems   23

Basic Animation Concepts   24

Basic 3ds Max Terms and Concepts   27

Summary   30

Chapter 2 ▪ Your First 3ds Max Animation   **31**

Getting Around in 3ds Max   32

Project and File Management Workflow   32

The 3ds Max Interface   35

Jumping Headlong into Animation   40

Setting Up the Hierarchy   51

Ready, Set, Animate!   58

Summary   60

Chapter 3 ▪ The 3ds Max Interface   **61**

What Am I Looking At?   62

Screen Layout   62

Command Panels   72

Controls at the Bottom of the UI   79

The Viewports   89

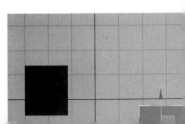

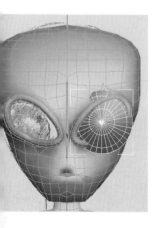

Managing Scene Objects	97
Scene Explorer	105
Summary	106
Chapter 4 ▪ Modeling in 3ds Max: Part I	**107**
Planning Your Model	108
Modeling Concepts	109
Modifiers and the Modifier Stack	115
Look at the Mesh You Got Us Into!	121
Editable Poly Tools	131
Modeling a Chest of Drawers	139
Modeling a Hand	167
Summary	181
Chapter 5 ▪ Modeling in 3ds Max: Part II	**183**
Building the Red Rocket	184
Summary	237
Chapter 6 ▪ Character Poly Modeling	**239**
Setting Up the Scene	240
Creating the Basic Form	246
Adding Detail	271
Final Touches	290
Summary	293
Chapter 7 ▪ Materials and Mapping	**295**
Materials	296
The Material Editor	298
Mapping a Pool Ball	314
Mapping, Just a Little Bit More	323
Maps	326
Using Opacity Maps	331
Mapping the Rocket	333
Summary	366

Chapter 8 ■ Introduction to Animation   369

   Hierarchy in Animation: The Mobile Redux   370

   Using Dummy Objects   374

   The Bouncing Ball   378

   Using the Track Editor–Curve Editor   379

   Track View   394

   Anticipation and Momentum in
Knife Throwing   398

   Summary   409

Chapter 9 ■ Character Studio and IK Animation   411

   Character Animation   412

   Character Studio Workflow   412

   Creating a Biped   415

   Animating a Biped   424

   Associating a Biped to a Character   438

   Using Inverse Kinematics   448

   Summary   452

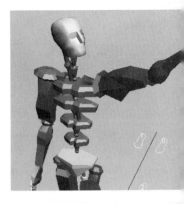

Chapter 10 ■ 3ds Max Lighting   455

   Basic Lighting Concepts   456

   Three-Point Lighting   458

   3ds Max Lights   461

   Common Light Parameters   474

   Ambient Light   482

   Lighting the Red Rocket   483

   Atmospheres and Effects   493

   Light Lister   498

   Summary   499

Chapter 11 ■ 3ds Max Rendering   501

   Rendering Setup   502

   Motion Blur   511

Previewing with ActiveShade 513

Cameras 513

Safe Frame 518

Render Elements 519

Rendering Effects 523

Raytraced Reflections and Refractions 526

Bringing It All Together:
Rendering the Rocket 534

Summary 542

Chapter 12 ■ Particles and Dynamics 545

Understanding Particle Systems 546

Setting Up a Particle System 550

Particle Systems and Space Warps 565

Using Rigid Body Dynamics 571

Using Soft Body Dynamics 578

Summary 581

So Long, and Thanks for All the Fish 581

Appendix ■ About the Companion CD 583

Index 587

Introduction

Welcome to *Introducing 3ds Max 2008*. The world of Computer Generated Imagery (CG) is fun and ever-changing. Whether you are new to CG in general or are a CG veteran new to 3ds Max, you'll find this book the perfect primer. It introduces you to Autodesk 3ds Max and shows how you can work with the program to create your art, whether it is animated or static in design.

This book exposes you to all facets of 3ds Max by introducing and plainly explaining its tools and functions to help you understand how the program operates—but it does not stop there. This book also explains the use of the tools and the ever-critical concepts behind the tools. You'll find hands-on examples and tutorials that give you firsthand experience with the toolsets. Working through these will develop your skills and the conceptual knowledge that will carry you to further study with confidence. These tutorials expose you to various ways to accomplish tasks with this intricate and comprehensive artistic tool.

Finally, this book explains the 3ds Max workflow. It explains how specific tasks are accomplished and why—that is, it explains how the tasks fit into the larger process of producing 3D animation. By doing that, these chapters should give you the confidence you need to venture deeper into 3ds Max's feature set, either on your own or by using any of 3ds Max's other learning tools and books as a guide.

Learning to use a powerful tool such as 3ds Max can be frustrating. You need to remember to pace yourself. The major complaints CG book readers have are that the pace is too fast and that the steps are too complicated or overwhelming. Addressing those complaints is a tough nut to crack, to be sure. No two readers are the same. However, this book offers the opportunity to run things at your own pace. The exercises and steps may seem confusing at times, but keep in mind that the more you try and the more you fail at some attempts, the more you will learn how to operate 3ds Max. Experience is king when learning the workflow necessary for *any* software program, and with experience comes failure and aggravation. But try and try again. You will find that further attempts will always be easier and more fruitful.

Above all, however, this book aims to inspire you to use 3ds Max as a creative tool to achieve and explore your own artistic vision.

What You Will Learn from This Book

You will learn how to work in CG with 3ds Max 2008, but moreover, you will learn how CG works and that you will be able to apply the basic techniques and concepts to any software package to accomplish anything you need from modeling to animation. The important thing to keep in mind is that this book is merely the beginning of your CG education. With the confidence you will gain from the exercises in this book and the peace of mind you can have by using this book as a reference, you can go on to create your own increasingly complex CG projects.

Who Should Read This Book

Anyone who is interested in learning 3ds Max should start with this book. No other series of books provides a better, more solid foundation than the Introducing series. *Introducing 3ds Max 2008* will give you more than just the basics of software operation; it will also explain how CG productions are accomplished.

If you are new to CG, or you are a veteran looking to pick up another program, *Introducing 3ds Max 2008* will give you the core foundation you will need to progress further into Autodesk's 3ds Max software.

If you are an educator, you will find a solid foundation on which to build a new course. You can also treat the book as a source of raw materials that you can adapt to fit an existing curriculum. Written in an open-ended style, *Introducing 3ds Max 2008* contains several self-help tutorials for home study as well as plenty of material to fit into any class.

How to Use This Book

Introducing 3ds Max 2008 approaches teaching CG by first giving you an informal look into the core concepts that make up this art form. The book aims to create a solid reference for you by showing you the commonly used toolsets and interfaces you will need to navigate to accomplish your goal. By following up the concepts and reference, *Introducing 3ds Max 2008* gives you hands-on recitations in the form of exercises and tutorials, letting you flex your muscles and giving you a chance to try for yourself.

The process can be a bit daunting when you begin to learn a CG program. In that light, it's best to explore the material in this book at your own pace, and allow yourself to digest not just the nuts and bolts, but also the workflow and concepts behind how *and* why 3ds Max artists work the way they do.

Once you have a firm grasp of the concepts introduced in this book, you will be ready to tackle more advanced material in the form of an intermediate class or even another book. Learning CG is a tough hurdle to get over, and you can rest easy knowing that this book is targeted to give you the tools you need to begin a longer, deeper study of the craft.

How This Book Is Organized

Chapter 1, "Basic Concepts," begins with an introduction to the basic concepts of CG production as well as its terminology and general workflows and pipelines. This chapter gives you an overview of how CG is created and how 3ds Max relates to the overall process.

Chapter 2, "Your First 3ds Max Animation," creates a simple animation to introduce you to 3ds Max's workflow and give you a taste of how things work. By animating a simple mobile, you will learn the basic concepts of creating and animating in 3ds Max.

Chapter 3, "The 3ds Max Interface," presents you with the entire 3ds Max interface and shows you how to access all the tools you will need for a CG production. Beginning with a roadmap of the 3ds Max screen, this chapter gives you a rundown of the icons and explains their uses. You can use this chapter as a reference to which you can return for UI refreshers whenever they're needed.

Chapter 4, "Modeling in 3ds Max: Part I," is an introduction to modeling concepts and workflows in general. It shows you how to model using 3ds Max tools with polygonal meshes and modifiers to create various objects, including a human hand and a bedroom dresser.

Chapter 5, "Modeling in 3ds Max: Part II," takes your modeling lesson a step further by showing you how to model a complex object. You will use and add to the tools you learned in Chapter 4 to create a toy rocket model. You will learn how to loft and lathe objects, as well as how to use Booleans.

Chapter 6, "Character Poly Modeling," rounds out your modeling lessons by showing you how to use subdivision surfaces to create organic models such as an alien character.

Chapter 7, "Materials and Mapping," shows you how to assign textures and materials to your models. You will learn to texture various objects, such as the toy rocket from Chapter 5, as you learn the basics of working with 3ds Max's materials and UVW mapping.

Chapter 8, "Introduction to Animation," covers the basics of animating a bouncing ball using keyframes and moves on to creating a more complex animation—throwing a knife at a target. You will also learn how to use the Track Editor to time, edit, and finesse your animation.

Chapter 9, "Character Studio and IK Animation," expands on Chapter 8 to show you how to use Character Studio to create and edit a walk cycle. You will also learn how to use 3ds Max's IK system to rig a tank model's gun.

Chapter 10, "3ds Max Lighting," begins by showing you how to light a 3D scene with the three-point lighting system. It then shows you how to use the tools to create and edit 3ds Max lights for illumination, shadows, and special lighting effects. You will light the toy rocket you added materials to in Chapter 7.

Chapter 11, "3ds Max Rendering," explains how to create image files from your 3ds Max scene and how to achieve the best look for your animation by using proper cameras and rendering settings. You'll also learn about different ways to implement raytracing, atmospheric effects, and motion blur when you render the toy rocket.

Chapter 12, "Particles and Dynamics," introduces you to 3ds Max's particle systems and space warps, as well as the reactor physics simulation system. You will animate dynamic objects colliding with one another using rigid body dynamics, and you will learn how to use soft body dynamics.

The companion CD to this book provides all the sample images, movies, and files that you will need to work through the projects in *Introducing 3ds Max 2008*, as well as a demo version of the program. See the Appendix at the back of the book for specific information.

Hardware and Software Considerations

Hardware changes constantly, and it evolves faster than publications can keep up. Having a good solid machine is important to a production, although simple home computers will be able to run 3ds Max quite well. Any laptop (with discrete graphics) or desktop PC running Windows XP Professional or Windows Vista (32 or 64 bit) with at least 1GB of RAM and an Intel Pentium Core Duo or AMD Athlon 64 or higher processor will work. Of course, having a good video card will help; you can use any hardware-accelerated OpenGL or Direct3D video card. Your computer system should have at least a 3GHz processor with 1GB of RAM, a few GBs of hard drive space available, and an Nvidia GeForceFX or ATI

Radeon video card. Professionals may want to opt for workstation graphics cards, such as the ATI FireGL or the Nvidia QuadroFX series of cards. The following systems would be good ones to use:

- Intel Pentium Core2Duo, 2GB RAM, nVidia Quadro FX1400, 400GB 7200 RPM hard disk
- AMD Opteron 2x, 2GB RAM, ATI FireGL V5000, 400GB hard disk

You can check the list of system requirements at Autodesk's website at www.autodesk.com/3dsmax.

The Next Step

The next step is really up to you. *Introducing 3ds Max 2008* is meant to give you a kick-start into learning CG. Your education beyond this primer can be from DVDs, classes, or more books—all bundled with a good amount of playing around and creating your own 3D productions. There is no better way to learn CG than to create something for yourself. Use these tools as a reference to help you get there.

You can contact the author at koosh3d.com.

CHAPTER 1

Basic Concepts

Any way you cut it, everyone learns in different ways, especially when they are learning about Autodesk 3ds Max 10 or any other computer graphics (CG) package. You should realize that the best education you'll get is through months or even years of working with the software in different capacities. Ask any successful student, and they will tell you one thing: There is no such thing as book smarts when it comes to good CG production—it all comes down to what you can achieve.

Achievement comes only from practice. You can't avoid the many pitfalls of production work without falling into and climbing out of them. Some readers may find this idea frustrating, but it is an intractable truth. The more you work with 3ds Max, the better you will become with it. And the more you struggle, fail, and recover, the more you will learn.

This chapter introduces you to basic concepts in computer graphics production.

Topics in this chapter include:

- **How to Read This Book**
- **What Is CGI?**
- **Production Workflow**
- **Core Concepts for Animation**

How to Read This Book

First and foremost, you don't need to read this book cover to cover and front to back to get the most from it. If you are the type who loves to jump right into the pool to learn to swim, then skip this chapter and jump into Chapter 2, "Your First 3ds Max Animation" to start working with the interface. If you already know how to navigate 3ds Max, you can begin with any of the other chapters. You can leave this chapter for bathroom reading when you're bored or the cable goes out.

If you like slowly dipping your toe in the water first, then by all means sit back, put on your bifocals, and have a long soak in this chapter. It will cover a lot of basic concepts and core topics with which you may or may not already be familiar. It will gently ease you into the powerful program that is Autodesk 3ds Max 10 and into computer graphics in general.

No matter how you choose to read this book, it is crucial that you approach the lessons as a way to *begin* the learning process. This book aims to give you a solid foundation in many aspects of 3ds Max, so that you can take this beginning and move on to more study. In keeping with that ideal, you will need to understand that you will not necessarily become proficient in any one aspect of 3ds Max *just by reading* this book. Instead, you'll gain an understanding of how it works and how you can work with the program to create animations and models.

Frequently, students are annoyed by tutorials that don't seem to lead them to perfection in the first go-around. This is the case for all tutorials, and indeed for all books that purport to teach anything. The key is to use the lessons as a guideline not just once, but repeatedly. Doing a lesson multiple times will help you understand the concepts better and give you opportunities to try out a few different methods, stray a little from the dictated steps, and try your own ideas on for size. Ideally, you will obtain a stronger education this way, but doing so will perhaps be slower and require you to be more patient. However, getting a good education always requires this sort of dedication.

What Is CGI?

In addition to standing for computer graphics, *CG* is sometimes used as an acronym for *computer generated*. You may have heard the term *CGI* (computer-generated imagery). These terms refer to any image or images that are created with the aid of a computer. In this day and age, you'd be hard-pressed to find anyone with any computer experience who hasn't messed around with electronic images such as scanned pictures or digital photos. Learning a CG package such as 3ds Max is just an extension of the simple concept of playing around with a digital photo. The obvious differences are that 3ds Max adds the dimension of depth as well as control over time.

Computer graphics is a more common toolset in the hands of the masses than it was just a few years ago. Within the next decade or so, 3D rendering will be as ubiquitous as "Photoshopping" a photo is today. Artists who are not in the 3D or CG industry are finding that programs such as 3ds Max are valuable tools for generating elements for their own work, digital or not. Let's take a look at the concepts behind 3D creation.

The following sections break down the fundamental concepts behind CG.

3D Space

3D space, the virtual canvas in which you create 3D objects, is a simulation of space that is divided into three axes, *X*, *Y*, and *Z*, representing (in loose terms) left/right, up/down, and in/out. Figure 1.1 shows 3D space in a Max window.

So what the heck do you with 3D space? In many ways, setting up a scene in CG is like setting up a photo shoot. With a photo shoot, you gather your subjects and pose them in your composition. You set up lights to illuminate them as dramatically or naturally as you need them to look and then take pictures with your camera, framing the composition as you like it. Next, you develop and fine-tune your photos or adjust them with tools such as Photoshop before you print them. Finally comes the happy part of showing them off and sharing your work with others.

Computer graphics production has much the same workflow, although with CG you create nearly everything from scratch in your 3D space. Instead of running out and hunting down the perfect models and all the props and settings you need for a photo, you create them. You model everything first and then apply colors and texture to the surfaces you created. Once you lay out your scene with all the settings and props you need, you set up your CG lights to illuminate the models. Lighting is perhaps the most important aspect of CG, as this stage of CG production really makes or breaks a scene.

Once your lighting is ready, you *render* the scene. This is akin to developing your photos. Knowing what the end result should be will dictate how you decide to render. You can choose several settings for quality and output, for example, so you can show off your scene to your friends (although a QuickTime movie can't be hung on the fridge the way a photo can).

Figure 1.1

3D space looks good enough to eat!

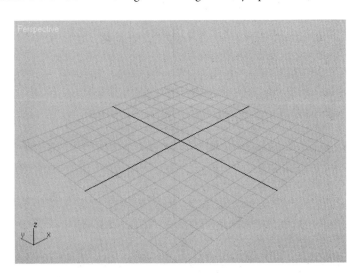

Of course, with CG you also have control over time, because you can animate your scene. The workflow we'll discuss in this chapter is best illustrated with a film production example. The next section will briefly describe a film production workflow and how it relates to CG production.

Production Workflow

There are three major stages to producing films: preproduction, production, and postproduction. In preproduction, the script is written, storyboards are drawn up to outline the action, costumes and sets are designed and built, the actors are cast and prepared, and a production crew is put together. During the production phase, the scenes are set up and shot according to a production schedule that lays everything out in the most efficient manner possible. Finally, in postproduction, everything else happens. The film is printed and edited, a score and soundtrack are laid, any digital effects are added, and scenes are colored to match an overall aesthetic. When all of this is finished, the film is distributed for people to see.

Although the specific tasks of CG are vastly different from those of live-action photography, understanding this framework is useful to understanding CG.

Preproduction

Preproduction for a CG workflow requires that the artist or artists gather together all the reference materials, motion tests, layout drawings, model sketches, and other components to make the actual CG production as uncomplicated as they can.

Because everything is essentially made from scratch, you have to formulate a strong plan of attack. You can't just take some actors into the park and begin shooting. With CG, you have to make it all from nothing, or at least acquire assets such as models from places such as TurboSquid.com. The time spent in preproduction planning is vital to smooth production and postproduction, and it helps the overall outcome of the project. Never underestimate how much time and planning you should put into a CG project.

> You will seriously sandbag your project if you don't plan it effectively. Although you may get sick of hearing this, it will always be true.

As you do the exercises in this book, you will work with sketches and other files supplied on the accompanying CD. These are your preproduction assets. Additionally, you are strongly encouraged to put together as much information as you possibly can about your intended project, no matter how short it may seem.

A poorly planned production will always fall short of its potential and give you many headaches throughout your project.

Writing a Script

Whether a CG project has a ton of dialogue or doesn't have a single spoken word, both the project and you will benefit from having at least a rudimentary script. Even abstract animations can benefit from a script that presents a highly detailed explanation of timings and colors, whether that script is typed neatly or scribbled on a cocktail napkin.

A script serves as your intention. Without having a clear intention of what you wish to say with your film, your production time may as well be spent lying on a lounge chair drinking iced tea; you will not get much done in either case.

Storyboards

A storyboard is the next step in defining the action laid out in the script. It shows the timing and framing for the camera, as well as the action and dialogue (if any). To create an effective storyboard, you should dissect your script into scenes, and further dissect the scenes into shots, with each shot presenting a distinct view from the camera or a distinct cut of action. Each storyboard panel describes what is happening in that shot. The panels show you the overall action of the project in a linear, shot-by-shot fashion, and how it should come together in editing.

Even if your storyboards are simple ones composed of stick figures, they are important to preproduction.

Concept Art

Conceptuals (also called *concept art*) are the design elements that are needed for a CG production. If you don't have concept art, whether it's your own drawings or photos or images grabbed from the Internet, you are in trouble. You must have an idea of how you want your CG to look; otherwise, you are just burning calories and not saying anything.

Figure 1.2

A character sheet

If you have CG characters, create *character sheets* for each character that show them in three different neutral poses: from the front, from the side, and from an angle called a ¾ *view*. You can even sculpt reference characters in clay or Play-Doh if you need to have a better idea of how they should look in 3D space. In Figure 1.2, you can see a character sheet generated for a student-produced short at The Art Institute of California at Los Angeles.

Sketch or download images of the props and sets you need in your scene. You should map out the "look" for everything that you need to have in your scene. When you are working on your project, you won't be limited to the things you picked out at this stage; however, you will find that knowing how things should look will help enormously in getting you to your final product. The better your concept art and research, the smoother the production and the better your end result will be.

Production

Production is the meat of any project. Film production begins when you start filming your project. In the case of CG, production begins when you start creating assets for your projects, such as models or textures, based on well-researched reference materials. The production phase lasts until the rendering phase, where you actualize your scene into image files.

Animation, texturing, and lighting are all performed between the modeling and rendering phases. Later in this chapter, we'll divide the CG production phase into more stages; however, most of the techniques you'll learn in this book are components of the production phase.

Postproduction

Postproduction begins when your scene elements and animation are all set up and raring to be completed. Postproduction for a CG project is very similar to postproduction for a film. When you click the Render button, you'll end up with several image files or movie files that are then edited and put together to make your project. You add sound, correct color, combine elements, and add any finishing touches in postproduction. Here is a quick rundown of the CG postproduction pipeline.

Rendering

All CG scenes need to be rendered to their final image or movie files. Again, this is the process by which the computer calculates how everything in the scene should look and displays it. Rendering makes your computer work hard. It usually requires the full attention of your PC and can take a lot of time. As you'll learn throughout this book, the decisions you make, such as how much detail you give the objects you create for a scene, can make a big difference in the rest of the process and can affect the rendering speed.

You can render one scene while another scene is in production, but working on a system that is rendering is not advisable unless you're using a dual-processor machine with plenty of memory. Once everything has been rendered properly, the final images will be sorted and the CG project assembly will begin. Rendering is the subject of Chapter 11, "3ds Max Rendering."

Compositing, editing, and adding sound are advanced postproduction activities, and a detailed discussion of them is beyond the scope of this book. However, a multitude of books are available on these topics for further study.

Compositing

CG is often rendered in different layers. These segments ultimately need to be put back together. For example, in a scene where multiple characters interact, each character can be rendered separately from the others and from the setting. *Compositing* is the process of bringing together rendered elements to form the final scene, usually using compositing software such as Autodesk's Combustion, Adobe's After Effects, or Apple's Shake.

Compositing can greatly affect the look of a CG project and professionals consider it to be an integral part of CG creation. Compositing programs allow you to compose CG elements together, but they also give you additional control over color, timing, and a host of other additions and alterations you can make to a scene.

> A lot of students assume that they need to render a scene in a single pass and create its intended look on the first try. This is not the case. CG has an inherently modular nature. You can render items separately and composite them in the finishing stage while retaining the ability to make changes in the project without rendering everything again. Rendering a project in different layers (sometimes called *passes*) also gives you much greater control over the project's look.

Editing

During editing, rendered and composited CG footage is collected and edited to fit the script and storyboards. This process is usually more straightforward for a CG film than for a live-action movie, provided that you made good storyboards during preproduction to follow when assembling the finished film.

With live-action shoots, you shoot much more footage than will ultimately end up in the film. You do this to make sure you have enough material for all your scenes and to leave extra room for creative editing. Additionally, you have to run through all the footage and choose which takes will be in the final product.

Because CG footage is generally much more time-consuming to generate than live action, scenes and shots should be tightly arranged in preproduction storyboards. The entire production can be edited beforehand in storyboards, so the scenes that are built and animated can match the story almost down to the frame. If your preproduction was done well, it can be just a matter of putting the shots together using an editing program such as Adobe's Premiere or even Apple's Final Cut Pro. (If you don't have an editing program, you can use the Video Post module in 3Ds Max.). This functionality is not covered in this introductory text, however.

Sound

Sound design can add an entirely new dimension of reality or mood to any CG. The audience needs to associate visuals with audio. Even a basic soundtrack adds a boost to a simple animation by enhancing realism, mood, narrative, and other aspects of its "feel." A good music soundtrack and well-placed sound effects can be very powerful.

Sound effects, such as footsteps, can be added to match the action in the animation; this type of sound effect is also known as *Foley sound*. Just as with any film, adding music to most animations can help with pacing as well as mood. In this case, music and live action sound design are pretty similar. Once you combine everything, you assess the sound needs.

The one glaring difference between CG and live action sound relates to dialogue. When you shoot live action, you generally capture the sound and dialogue live as you shoot. With CG, all dialogue needs to be recorded and edited at the beginning of the production phase. In other words, dialogue is a part of the CG preproduction and postproduction phases. This is because animators need to hear dialogue spoken so they can animate images to match the lips of the characters speaking (this is known as *lip-sync*). Recording the dialogue with actors also helps you animate the CG characters because you can imitate the gestures and actions of the live actors to help make your animation more real.

CG Workflow

CG is a collaborative effort in which all the stages of production work hand-in-hand to achieve your final images. Because of how CG comes together, following a structured production pipeline or workflow generally works best. The layout of this book and its exercises follow this overall workflow. You begin by modeling, texturing, animating, lighting, and then rendering. You can texture after you animate, if you wish; however, for most projects, the workflow described here is best. What is universally true is that you will go back and forth between these stages several times throughout the process as you assess and further define your needs. For example, you may have to change some textures once you see the lighting or change a model according to an unexpected animation need.

Modeling

Modeling is the topic of Chapters 4 through 6 of this book. Modeling is usually the first step in CG creation, and it can sometimes take the longest time. You probably already know that modeling and modeling tutorials are popular on the Internet, where you will also find a generous number of free and fee-based models. You might be able to find a lot of the props and characters you need for your scene there. Unless you enjoy modeling, take a look through Google (or another search engine) and see what's already available, especially at sites such as www.turbosquid.com.

When you model, of course, you'll be faced with many choices about how to proceed. Most Max modeling is done using *polygons* (geometric representations of surfaces and objects); however, the specific tools you use to create the models will depend on how you like to work. The process of modeling can be easier when you have a good idea of your whole story via a storyboard and copiously reference the object you are modeling. If you identify your project needs as fully as you can at the outset, you'll be able to fulfill them more easily when you start modeling or gathering models.

With forethought, you will know how detailed your models need to be. In many cases, you can add sufficient detail to a model through texture. If a park bench is shown in a wide shot from far away, there is no need for abundant detail or complicated surfacing. If you create a highly detailed model for that far-away shot, you will have wasted your time and will also increase your rendering time. However, if you have to show that park bench prominently in a close-up, it will need as much detail as possible. In such cases, viewers will see more of the bench and have more of an opportunity to question it. The more you use models in scenes, the better you will be at sensing exactly how much detail to give a specific model. As you begin with CG, however, it's better to give too much attention to detail than needed than to give too little. The detailing process will teach you a majority of what you need to learn about modeling. This in turn will benefit your overall speed and technique. With more experience, you will be able to discern the level of detail you really need and work more efficiently.

Here is a quick rundown of some different kinds of modeling.

Character Modeling

Character modeling includes the modeling of any characters in your scene, from humanoids to animals to ordinary objects that are animated to life. Most characters are organic forms, such as animals, humans, aliens, and so on. However, a talking cheese sandwich is just as much a character as the person holding it. As a good character modeler, you need to keep in mind the animation needs of a character when you're modeling. It's important to know what you need from your shot way ahead of time, so you can model appropriately.

Traditional characters, such as humans, need to appear seamless once they're modeled. Character animation usually requires the model to deform in some way, such as bending and warping at certain points like the elbows. The pieces that make up the model may tear apart if the character is not built to accommodate deformation and movement.

Like the park bench we talked about earlier, your character must be built with the level of detail required by the scene. As a matter of fact, you could wind up with multiple models for a single character that are built to account for differences in detail level. Using different versions of the same character can help keep the scene efficient and workable. A low-resolution model of a character (one that uses few polygonal faces) can easily be placed in wide shots, and a more detailed, higher-resolution model can be used in close-ups.

Architectural and Environmental Modeling

3ds Max is a natural tool for architectural and environmental modeling. In fact, architects and engineers use it to model and render designs for previsualizing. This type of modeling includes the generation of backgrounds for sets and environments. To do this, you model any buildings or interiors, as well as mountains and other required scenery, such as trees, roads, lampposts, and mailboxes.

Do not create overly detailed environments when they are far off in the background. The biggest common mistake new CG practitioners make is over-creating detail. Doing this adds more geometry to a scene, creates inefficiency, and can crash a scene. The more geometry that is used in a scene, the more slowly the computer will run and the more time you will need to render the scene.

You can create a good deal of the environment using clever textures on simple geometry. Detailed maps on bare surfaces are used frequently for game environments.

> Because your computer stores everything in a scene as vector math, the term *geometry* refers to all the surfaces and models in a scene.

Props Modeling

A *prop* is any object in a scene that is actively used by a character in his or her action. Props are useful to the narrative of the story. They help the characters' actions. A prop can be anything from a baseball bat that a character is swinging to a purse that a character is carrying.

Any objects not used by the characters as props are called *scenics*, as they are often used to add realism to the set by "setting the scene." Think about it. If your scene takes place in front of a desk, that desk will need scenics such as pens, notebooks, and papers to make it look more realistic. Just showing an empty desk may not be enough to make the scene believable. You usually can find the props and scenics you need on the Internet, frequently in a format for 3ds Max.

Texturing

Once you have created a model, you'll want to finish its look. You can apply materials to its surface(s) to make it look right, whether it is supposed to look "real" or not. *Texturing* is typically applied immediately after modeling and heavily tweaked when the scene is lighted. The process of texturing essentially applies colors and tactile feeling to models. 3ds Max automatically assigns simple colored materials to objects as you create them.

You don't need to finalize every texture at the beginning, because you'll be coming back and making adjustments all the time. Remember that the materials you create for your scene will probably look different when you light and animate everything.

You'll learn more about texturing in Chapter 7, "Materials and Mapping."

Animation

Animation puts your scene into action and adds life to your characters. *Animation is change over time.* Anything in a scene that needs to change from one second to another will need to be animated to do so.

Everyone has their own reflexive sense of how things move. This knowledge is gleaned through years of perception and observation. Therefore, your audience can be more critical of a CG scene's motion than lighting, coloring, or anything else. You know when something doesn't look right. So will your audience.

Animation takes quite a lot of setup, sometimes more than just modeling. For a character, you will need to create a *rig* (a character's setup or digital armature used to drive character animation, such as a Character Studio Biped) to attach to the model and then create controls to make animation easier to operate.

It's thrilling to see your hard work on a scene come to life with animation. On the flip side, it can be extremely aggravating to see your creation working improperly. Making mistakes is how you learn things, and your frustrations will ease over time. Your first several attempts at animating a scene will not look like Pixar films, but that should not dissuade you from working on more animations and scenes. You will get better with more practice.

Chapter 8, "Introduction to Animation," and Chapter 9, "Character Studio and IK Animation" cover animation techniques in 3ds Max.

Lighting

Lighting is the most important aspect of CG production. This area is where you get to see your models and textures, as well as set the mood of the project. During lighting, you set up virtual lights in 3D space that will illuminate the objects in your scene when it comes time to render. Lighting can drastically change how your scene looks. Using lighting wisely is a learned skill, and it takes tons of time to master; there are no shortcuts to becoming a good lighter. Not only are you dealing with the aesthetics of getting your shot to look great, but you are also dealing with rendering issues and bottlenecks that could make rendering your shot a nightmare. These issues come up with much larger scenes than the ones you will be using in the first years of your CG education; however, it's important to start learning how to use lighting efficiently as well as aesthetically.

Lighting can make or break all your hard work. You can use lighting to affect the believability of your models and textures as well as to create the proper mood and tone.

In this stage of the pipeline, the lighting workflow begins when you are texturing your objects. You need to light your scene initially to evaluate how your textures are progressing. However, the final lighting and look really happen after everything else is done, and you are left to go back and forth with the render to check and recheck, fix and refix issues that come up in the rendered images. You may even find, for example, that a model you've built needs to be altered because a lighting scheme works for everything but that model. Therefore, a back-and-forth workflow with lighting does not just apply to texturing.

The more experience you gain with lighting, the more you will start to notice that lighting affects every stage of CG creation. Once you start mastering the subtleties of lighting, and after years of modeling, you may change how you model to accommodate how you now light. Even your animation and texturing preferences may take a back seat to how a scene needs to be lighted.

CG is fundamentally all about light. Manipulating how light is created and reflected is what you're doing with CG.

Luckily, in 3ds Max, lighting is set up to mimic the behavior of real lights used in live action (at least in principle), making the lighting process easier to use. You will learn how to light in 3ds Max in Chapter 10, "3ds Max Lighting."

Rendering

You've modeled it all, textured it, and lit your scene like a pro. Hundreds of hours and several cases of Red Bull later, you are ready to render. *Rendering* is the stage where your computer makes all the computations necessary to create images from your 3D objects. Depending on how much stuff is in your scene, rendering may be super quick or painfully slow. The amount of geometry (the number of polygons) you used to model, the number and types of lights, the size of texture images, and the effects in your scene all affect render times. When time or resources are limited, you need to build your scene intelligently so that you don't spend hours rendering a single frame. The more efficient your scene is, the faster the rendering will go.

Having said that, there is really no magic formula to figure out how long is too long for a render. Some scenes require a massive amount of time to render, for whatever reason, and you are stuck with that—but most do not. In time you'll be able to ascertain for yourself how long is too long for your renders.

A good gauge for render times is to identify what computers you have to render with and how much time you have before a project has to be completed. With a little simple math, you can determine an acceptable render time for your scenes and adjust your quality and output settings, as well as your lighting setup, to fit within your constraints.

> The general rule in production is: You're always out of time. Therefore, the most efficient pipeline will be your savior, because eventually your producer or boss will tire of hearing, "But I'm still rendering…."

For now, go ahead and use as much geometry and lighting as you think is necessary. With more experience, you'll start pruning your scenes and getting more efficient renders. Right now, knowing *how* a scene is put together is more important than knowing how efficient it needs to be.

CG Specialties

As in most professions, CG professionals specialize in specific areas. Those areas coincide with the stages of CG production outlined earlier in this chapter.

Modelers create models for shows or projects. They need to have a keen eye for detail, as well as a sense of how objects come together. Environment modelers create settings, and character modelers specialize in creating organic surfaces for characters such as people. In all cases, professional modelers need to understand form and function and be experienced in lighting, rendering, and texturing to effectively model professionally.

Animators are artists who work directly with the animation of a project. Character animators specialize in character movement, ranging from mimicking human movement to outlandish cartoon animation. There are also animators who specialize in mechanical objects. Frequently, good animators can span the divide between character animation and other types of animation because they inherently understand motion and timing.

In some cases, great animators are also great *riggers*. Studios hire character TDs (technical directors) who specialize in rigging characters for motion. This usually includes creating skeleton structures, such as Bipeds or Bones, for the character as well as skinning the model to such a system before handing it off to the animator(s). Character TDs can also work with motion-capture systems to transfer motion to a character. They use recorded data from a live-action stage where actors are outfitted in special equipment that records their movements.

Effects TDs are specialists who generally animate special effects such as tornadoes, clouds, or explosions. These specialists generally rely on particles and dynamics, as well as textures, lights, and rendering tricks to perform their effects. This specialty requires a strong eye in all stages of CG production and a strong ability to troubleshoot and come up with solutions that are frequently not standard techniques in a program such as 3ds Max.

Lighters light and render a scene once it is completed. Lighters specialize in being able to *final* a shot; in other words, to complete a shot for final approval and output. A good lighter needs to understand how models and textures behave in a scene and sometimes must remodel or retexture an object to make it work. Good lighters also need to be good compositors, because so much of CG can be broken into elements that later need to be put back together. For example, the shadows in a scene may be rendered separately from the rest of the scene.

Compositing as a specialty requires much less knowledge of CG, although today's competitive compositors should know as much as they can cram in their brains about CG. Compositors not only have to assemble and *color time* (make final color decisions about) CG shots, but they also have to work with live-action footage that needs to be altered or affected. For example, a compositor will need to remove a green screen from behind an actor and "place" that actor into a virtual rendered set. With color correction and other tools at their disposal, the compositors must make sure everything looks as though it belongs in the shot. In many cases, the line between lighter and compositor is blurred, and the two specialties can become one.

Generalists are CG artists who can do everything. This is not to say they are the be-all and end-all of all things CG. Many studios and boutiques have short-term jobs that are small in scale (as compared to a production of the DreamWorks film *Madagascar,* for example). When a short turnaround is required, you need artists who can take a shot from beginning to end by modeling, texturing, lighting, animating, and rendering a scene. Generalists are more likely to work on commercials, for example, than feature films.

Core Concepts

CG touches many disciplines, and you will come across many different concepts as you learn CG. You'll need to understand something about physics, computer output, film, photography, sculpting, painting, and other disciplines. This section introduces several key concepts that will make it easier for you to understand how CG is created. Again, if you've been around the block a few times, you can skip large parts of this chapter. However, you never know when you might come across a little tidbit that fills in an educational gap you never thought you had.

Computer Graphics Basics

Here are some general terminologies and methodologies used in computer graphics. Understanding them will help you understand how 3ds Max works. First on our plate is the critical distinction between *raster* (bitmap) and *vector* graphics and how this distinction affects you as a 3ds Max user.

Raster Images

Raster images (also known as bitmap images or bitmaps) make up the world of computer images today. In raster images, colored pixels are arranged to display an image on a screen; these pixels come together to form the image like a tapestry. The same is true of printouts, where dots of ink serve as pixels to form the printed image. The printed dots, like each colored pixel, come together to form the overall image.

When you work in a program such as Photoshop, you are editing the pixels of an image directly by adjusting existing settings such as color, size, and position for all or part of an image. In this manner, you can bring a scanned photo or a digital picture of your house into Photoshop and paint one wall red just to see how it would look before you buy paint at the store.

Essentially, a raster or bitmap image is a mosaic of pixels, each pixel corresponding to a mosaic tile. The *resolution*—fineness of detail—of an image is defined by the number of pixels per inch (or other unit of measure) in the horizontal and vertical directions. Because raster images are based on a fixed grid, these images do not scale larger very well. The closer you zoom into a raster image (or the larger a raster image is scaled), the larger the pixels seem, which makes the zoomed or enlarged image blocky, or *pixelated*. To use larger raster images, you need to start with a higher resolution when the image is created. The higher the resolution, the larger the file size will be. Figure 1.3 shows what happens when you blow up a raster image.

Figure 1.3

A raster image does not scale up very well. Here is the front of a stereo receiver that has been blown up by several hundred per-cent. The pixels look blocky.

So why are raster images even used if you can't scale them well? Most common displays and output methods such as television or computer screens, or even printers, are actually raster displays. The display devices need raster images to display the pictures properly. The term *raster* originally referred to the display area of a television or computer monitor. To form an image, the electronics in these devices "paint" it as a grid of red, green, and blue pixels on a glowing screen. Every image generated by a computer, therefore, must either begin as a raster image or be *rasterized* as part of rendering for display.

Vector Images

Why does the interface for 3ds Max look so different from Photoshop's interface? Where is the original image that gets altered in 3ds Max? Autodesk 3ds Max and other 3D programs work with vectors. Vectors are created using mathematical algorithms and geometric functions. A vector program defines its images using coordinates and geometric formulas to plot points that define *areas, volumes,* and *shapes* instead of defining the color of each and every pixel in a grid of a raster image.

Popular vector-based image applications include Adobe Illustrator and Macromedia Flash, as well as practically all computer-aided design (CAD) programs, including Auto-CAD and SolidWorks. These programs let you define shapes and volumes and add color and texture to them through their toolsets.

Vector files store the scene in 3D space using coordinates and equations of points in space; and the color values are assigned through materials. Therefore, when a vector image is scaled, the image does not suffer from the same blocky limitations as a raster image would. As you can see in Figure 1.4, vectors can be scaled with no loss of quality. They will never pixelate because they always redraw at the new scale.

Motion in a raster movie, such as a QuickTime movie, is stored in a long sequence of image files that, when played back, show animation or movement. By contrast, motion in vector programs is stored in the changes in the coordinates of the geometry and in the math that defines the shapes and volumes.

When a Flash cartoon plays on a web page you are visiting, for example, the information for that cartoon is downloaded into your computer in vector form. The data contains the position, size, and shape of all the elements of the animation. The vector information is then converted into raster images (called *rasterization*) so you can view the final image or animation. Your computer *renders* this information on-the-fly, in real time, into a raster display that you can enjoy on your screen.

This is roughly how things are done with 3D programs such as 3ds Max. You begin your work in Max's 3D space in vectors. When you are ready to render, Max renders the scene contents into raster images or movie files that you can display. You use the tools in 3ds Max to change the geometric information, which in turn changes the scene, and then rerender to show the output. Changing a raster image, such as a digital photo, alters that original file (assuming you do not have a backup file) once you save your work because it directly affects the pixels of the image.

Figure 1.4

A vector image of a girl at its original size (left) and blown up to a few hundred percent (right) shows no loss in quality. The curves are not stepped or pixelated.

Image Output

When you're done with all your CG, you will probably want as many people to see your work as possible. To accomplish this, you will need to render the scene out to image files or a movie file. These files can be output and saved in many different ways. The kind of file output you will use will be determined by a combination of disk space, personal preference, project needs, and output requirements.

Color Depth

An image file stores the color of each pixel as three values, representing red, green, and blue. Image type depends on how much storage is allotted to each pixel (the *color depth*). These are the color depths common to image files in CG production:

Grayscale The image is black and white with varying degrees (typically 256) of gray in between. Grayscale images are good for rendering out black-and-white subjects because no extraneous color information is stored in the image file.

16-Bit Color Display or High-Color 5-Bit Image File Each color channel (red, green, blue) gets 5 bits of space to store its value, resulting in an image that can display a maximum of 32,768 colors. Each color channel has a limited range of shades, but still gives a nice color image. You might notice the gradation in the different shades of each color, which can result in *color banding* in the image. There is little use of these limited-color images in CG work, though you will find them used in web pages to maximize efficiency.

8-Bit Image File This format is referred to as 24-bit color display or True Color, especially in Microsoft Windows desktop settings. Each color channel is given 8 bits for a range of 256 shades of each red, green, and blue channel. A total of 16 million colors are available to use in the image. This color depth gives the best color quality for an image and is widely used in most animation applications. The human eye cannot see quite as many shades of color as there are in a True Color image. Most of your renders from 3ds Max will be 24-bit color files.

16-Bit Image File Used primarily in film work using such file types as TIFF16, this type of image file holds 16 bits of information for each color channel, resulting in an astounding number of color levels and ranges. Each file can exceed several megabytes even at low resolutions. These files are primarily used in the professional workplace and are more standard for film work because outputting CG to film can require high levels of color and brightness range in the image.

Floating Point/32-Bit Image File Thirty-two-bit floating-point images are commonly used in film production to give the utmost attention to color depth. Most computers are capable of rendering a huge range of tones and colors, and 32-bit floating-point images capture that range effectively. These files (such as EXR and HDR images) are not easy to work with and require a lot of tweaking in compositing to output properly.

EXR (based on the OpenEXR format pioneered by Industrial Light and Magic for high-end film work) and High Dynamic Range (HDR) images are usually in 32-bit float format and are incredibly detailed in the range of contrast they store. You should not worry about 32-bit images and high dynamic ranges such as this until you have gained a good amount of experience with lighting and rendering.

Color Channels

As mentioned, each image file holds the color information in channels. All color images have a red, green, and blue color channel. Each channel is a measurement of the amount of red, green, or blue in areas of the image. A fourth channel, called the *alpha* channel, is used as a transparency channel. This channel, also know as the matte channel, defines which portions of the image are transparent or opaque. Not all image files have alpha channels.

FILE FORMATS

In addition to image types, several image file formats are available today. The most common is probably JPEG (Joint Photographic Experts Group), which is widely used on the Internet for its small size and reasonable image quality. However, JPEGs are too compressed and lossy (meaning they lose color detail when compared to the original) to be used in most CG renders.

The main difference among file formats relates to how they store images. Some formats compress the file to reduce file size; however, the greater the compression, the poorer the image's color.

The popular formats to render into from 3ds Max are TIFF (Tagged Image File Format) and Targa (TGA). These file formats maintain a good 24-bit color depth using an 8-bit image file, are either uncompressed or hardly compressed (*lossless* compression), and are frequently used for broadcast or video work. These formats also have an alpha channel, giving you better control when you later composite images together.

To see an animation rendered in a file sequence of TIFFs, you will need to play them back using a frame player, such as 3ds Max's RAM Player, or you can compile them into a movie file, such as a QuickTime file.

Your final image output format will depend on the project's needs. If, for example, you need to composite your CG together, you will need to output in a format that can be used in your compositing or editing program. TIFF files are perhaps the best format to use as they are widely compatible, store uncompressed color, and have an alpha channel.

MOVIE FILES

Animations can also be output to movie files such as AVI or QuickTime. These usually large files are self-contained and hold all the images necessary for the animation that they play back as frames. Like image files, movie files can be compressed to keep their sizes to a minimum, but they suffer from quality loss as well.

3ds Max can render directly to an AVI or QuickTime movie file. This may seem like it saves you the hassle of rendering out large sequences of image files. In reality, you shouldn't render directly to a movie file, at least for your final output. It is best to render a sequence of files, because image sequences can easily be compiled into a movie file later using a program such as Autodesk Combustion, Adobe After Effects, Premiere, or even QuickTime Pro.

Rendering to images is less risky than rendering to a movie. In addition to having a sequence you can easily manipulate, you do not have to worry about crashing and losing rendering time. Sometimes, your render will crash or your machine will freeze. If you are rendering to a movie file when that happens, you'll need to restart rendering from the beginning, because you can't append content to a half-rendered QuickTime. With a file sequence render, you can simply pick up the render from the last good frame.

With a sequence, you also have the option of reordering the frames or easily adjusting a few individual frames' properties, such as hue or saturation, without affecting the entire movie file.

Color

Color is how we perceive the differences in the frequency of light. The wide range of colors that we see (the visible spectrum) results when any of three *primary colors* of light—red, green, and blue—are mixed together. Color can be mixed in two ways, subtractive and additive. These color definitions are most often displayed in *color wheels*, which place primary colors equally spaced around a ring and place the colors that result when the primaries are mixed in between the appropriate primaries.

Understanding how color works will help you gain more from your CG's color scheme and help you design your shots with greater flexibility and better outcomes.

SUBTRACTIVE AND ADDITIVE COLOR

Subtractive color mixing is used when an image will be seen with an external light source. It's based on the way reflected light creates color. Light rays bounce off colored surfaces and are tinted by the different pigments on the surface. These pigments absorb and reflect only certain frequencies of the light hitting them, in essence *subtracting* certain colors from the light before it gets to your eyes. Pile up enough different colors of paint and you'll get black; all the color is absorbed by the pigment and only black is reflected.

With subtractive color mixing for painting, the traditional color wheel's primary colors are *red*, *blue*, and *yellow*. These three pigments can be mixed together to form any other color pigment. This is the basis for the color wheel most people are exposed to in art education. However, in the world of print production, a CMYK (Cyan, Magenta, Yellow, and blacK) color wheel is used, which places cyan, yellow, and magenta ink colors as the primary colors used to mix all the other ink colors for print work.

Projected light, however, is mixed as *additive color*. Each light's frequency adds upon another's to form color. The additive primary colors are *red*, *green*, and *blue*. These three colors, when mixed in certain ratios, form the entire range of color. When all are equally mixed together, they form a white light.

A computer monitor uses only additive color, mixing each color with amounts of red, green, and blue (RGB). Output for print is converted to a CMYK color model.

Warm colors are those in the magenta to red to yellow range, and *cool colors* are those in the green to cyan to blue range of the additive color wheel. Warm colors seem to advance from the frame, and cool colors seem to recede into the frame.

HOW A COMPUTER DEFINES COLOR

Computers represent all information, including color, as sets of numeric values made up of binary 0s and 1s (bits). With a 24-bit RGB color depth, each pixel is represented by three 8-bit values corresponding to the red, green, and blue "channels" of the image. An 8-bit binary number can range from 0 to 255; therefore, you have 256 possible levels for each primary color. With three channels, you have $256 \times 256 \times 256$ (16.7 million) possible combinations of each primary color mixed to form the final color.

Color value need not be expressed in values for red, green, and blue. It can also be set on the hue, saturation, and value (HSV) channels of a color. Again, each channel holds a value from 0 to 255 (in an 8-bit image) that defines the final color. The hue value defines the actual tint (from red to green to violet) of the color. The saturation defines *how much* of that tint is present in the color. The higher the saturation value, the deeper the color. Finally, value defines the brightness of the color, from black to white. The higher the value, the brighter the color.

HSV and RGB give you different methods to control color, allowing you to use the method you prefer. All the colors available in 3ds Max, from textures to lights, are defined as either RGB or HSV values for the best flexibility. You can switch from HSV to RGB definition in 3ds Max at any time.

CMYK COLOR SPACE

A CMYK color wheel is used for print work. This is referred to as the four-color process. Color inkjet printers produce color printouts by mixing the appropriate levels of these inks onto the paper.

All output from a computer that is RGB-based to a printer goes through a CMYK conversion as it is being printed. For professional print work, specially calibrated monitors are used to better preview the CMYK color of an RGB image before it is printed. Fortunately, only print professionals need to worry about this conversion process because most of it is handled by graphics software to a fairly accurate degree.

VIEWING COLOR

The broadcast standard for North America is called *NTSC*, which stands for National Television Standards Committee. Industry folks sometimes refer to the acronym as Never The Same Color, calling attention to the fact that the color you see on one TV screen will inevitably look different on another TV. The same is true for computer monitors, especially flat panel displays. Unless made to do so, different screens are not calibrated to show the same color the same way, so what you see on one screen will display differently on another screen. If it is paramount that the color appear as you see it on a specific screen, it makes sense to finalize the work and show it on that screen. You can also download color bars from the Internet to display on monitors in an attempt to calibrate them to your eye. This is not the best way to go, but at least it will help a little, without exacting the costs and trouble of using color calibration equipment.

Resolution, Aspect Ratio, and Frame Rate

Resolution expresses the size of an image by the number of horizontal and vertical pixels it contains, and usually is stated as "$x \times y$"; an example of this would be 640 × 480. The higher the resolution, the finer the image detail will be.

You will adjust your final render size to suit the ultimate medium for which you are creating the animation. Table 1.1 lists some typical video resolutions.

Table 1.1

**Typical Video
Resolutions**

STANDARD	SIZE	NOTES
VGA (Video Graphics Array)	640 × 480	Formerly, the standard computing resolution and still a popular television resolution for tape output.
NTSC D1 (National Television System Committee)	720 × 486	The standard resolution for broadcast television in North America.
NTSC DV	720 × 480	Close to the NTSC D1 resolution, this is the typical resolution of digital video cameras.
PAL (Phase Alternation Line)	720 × 586	The standard broadcast resolution for most European countries.
HDTV (High Definition TV)	1920 × 1080	The emerging television standard, sometimes also referred to as 1080i.
1K Academy (1K refers to 1000 pixels across)	1024 × 768	Typically, the lowest allowable resolution for film production at Academy ratio. Because film is an optical format (whereas TV is a raster format), there is no real set defined resolution for film. Suffice it to say, the higher the better.
2K Academy (2K refers to 2000 pixels across)	2048 × 1556	Most studios output CG for film at this resolution, which gives the best size-to-performance ratio.
4K Academy (4K is 4000 pixels across)	4094 × 3072	A high resolution for film, used for highly detailed shots.

Any discussion of resolution must include the matter of *aspect ratio*. Aspect ratio is the ratio of the screen's *width* to its *height*. There are a variety of standard aspect ratios (Table 1.2).

Table 1.2

**Standard Aspect
Ratios**

STANDARD	SIZE	NOTES
Academy Standard	1.33:1 or 4:3	The most common aspect ratio. The width is 1.33 times the length of the height. This is the NTSC (National Television Standards Committee) television aspect ratio as well as the aspect ratio of 16mm films and some 35mm films, especially classics such as *Gone with the Wind*.
Widescreen TV	1.78:1 or 16:9	With HD and widescreen TVs gaining popularity, the 16:9 standard is commonplace now. This aspect is used in HD programming and is also the aspect ratio of many widescreen computer monitors and laptops. This aspect is very close to how most films are displayed (1.85:1, as seen below)
Widescreen Film (aka, Academy Flat)	1.85:1	The most often used 35mm film aspect today. When it's displayed on a television, horizontal black bars appear above and below the picture so that the edges are not cropped off (This is called *letterboxing*).
Anamorphic Ratio	2.35:1	Using a special lens (called an *anamorphic lens*), an image originally captured on 35mm film is squeezed. When played back with a projector with an anamorphic lens, the image is projected at a width 2.35 times its height. On a standard TV, the letterboxing would be more severe to avoid cropping the sides.

The number of frames that are played back per second determines the *frame rate* of an animation. This is denoted as *fps*, or frames per second. The three standard frame rates for media are:

- NTSC: 30fps
- PAL: 25fps
- Film: 24fps

Knowing what your final output medium is going to be before you begin your project is pretty important. It is not crucial by any means, but knowing what the screen will look like (i.e., whether it will be a small web window or a large television) will help you better compose your scenes. You can always change your frame rate and render resolution later, but it is much simpler to begin with it already worked out.

Playing back a 24fps animation at 30fps will yield a slower-moving animation and will either require repeating some frames to fill in the gaps or ending the animation early. Conversely, playing a 30fps animation at 24fps will create a faster-moving animation that will either skip some frames or end later than it should.

Games do not typically have a set playback rate for animation. When a scene is created for a game, the assets in the scene are rendered and played back on the user's computer system in real time; therefore, many factors contribute to the playback speed of scenes created for games.

On the Internet, typical playback speeds for animated content on websites average about 12 to 15 frames per second, about half of what you would see on a TV or film screen. This saves the viewer considerable download time because the files are much smaller.

Coordinate Systems

Coordinates are numerical representations of where an object is in 3D space. Every object in 3ds Max has a coordinate of where it exists. Without this coordinate, it would be gone— *poof*—into thin air! Max's 3D space is organized with the Cartesian coordinate system, which uses a three-pronged axis to define width, height, and depth as *X, Y,* and *Z,* respectively. The overall coordinate system in Max is called the *world coordinate system.* It is an absolute coordinate system that is fixed and unchangeable.

Objects in Max can have their own coordinate systems as well. When an object is created, it has its own width, height, and depth, again expressed as *X, Y,* and *Z.* Upon creation, the local coordinate system (belonging to the created object) and the world coordinate system are aligned. However, when the object is rotated, its Local Coordinate System rotates with it. Because of this, an object created in a Front viewport (for instance) will have a different Local axis than if it were created in the Top viewport.

Figure 1.5 shows a box. The *X*-, *Y*-, and *Z*-axes of the box are displayed in the center of the box and align with the axes of the home grid (which shows the World Space axes) displayed in the lower-left corner of the window.

When the box in the scene is rotated, Max retains them as Local space instead of substituting its own axes. The *X*-axis of the box does not change. Now the Local axis and the World Space axis are not aligned. This is a very good feature because it allows you to manipulate the box based on its original Local axes.

Basic Animation Concepts

A wealth of information regarding animation concepts and techniques is available on the Internet. There are tons of books out there that also teach the basics of animation. In this very brief section, you will be exposed to a few important concepts behind animation. These concepts will help you better understand what you're doing in 3ds Max.

Frames, Keyframes, and In-Betweens

Animation is based on change over time; so you need a unit of measure for time. In animation, time is almost always expressed in *frames*. One frame is a single rendered image in an animation, or a single drawing in a traditional animation. *Frame* also refers to a single unit of time in your animation. The exact length of that time depends on the final frame rate at which the animation will be played back. For example, at film rate (24fps), a single frame will last 1/24 of a second. At NTSC video rate (30fps), that same frame will last 1/30 of a second. Therefore, a video based output will require more frames for the same amount of time as would a film.

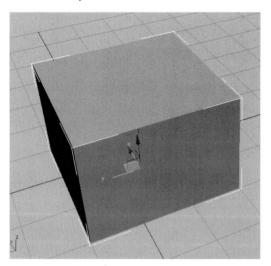

Figure 1.5

The Object space of the box aligns with the World Space.

Keyframes (or keys) are points at which the animator creates a pose for a character (or whatever is being animated). A keyframe, in CG terms, is a frame in which a pose, a position, or some other parameter's value has been saved in time. Animation is when the object travels or changes between keyframes. Because the change happens between *keys*, these frames are called *in-between* frames. The computer extrapolates what needs to happen to get the object from its state in keyframe 1 to its state in keyframe 2. You will have plenty to keyframe in the coming chapters of this book.

In 3ds Max, a keyframe can be set on almost *any* parameter of an object, such as its color, position, or size. In reality, you can set several keyframes on any one frame in CG animation. Figure 1.6 illustrates a keyframe sequence.

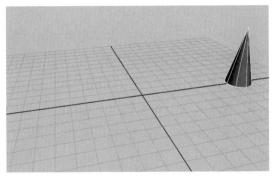

Keyframe at Frame 1

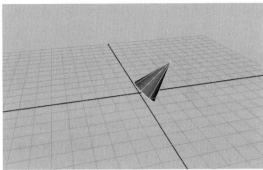

Frame 5

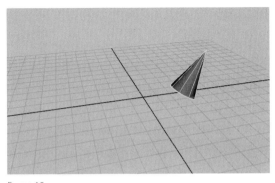

Frame 10

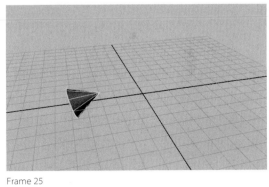

Frame 15

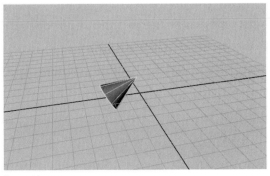

Frame 20

Frame 25

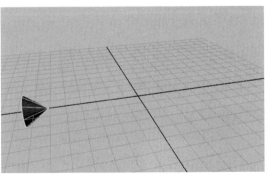

Keyframe at 30

Figure 1.6

In the first frame of this sequence, a keyframe is set on the position, rotation, and scale of the cone. On frame 30, the same properties are again keyframed. The computer calculates all the movement inbetween.

Weight

Weight is an implied facet of design and animation. Weight denotes the heaviness or presence of an element in a design. The more weight an element has, the more power it has in the composition. The weight of an object in a composition is affected by its color, its contrast, its background, its position in the frame, and other variables.

The weight of an object in animation roughly follows that idea, but more pragmatically denotes the actual weight of the object as it relates to its environment. Giving an object a good weight in animation is critical to the believability of the animation. You will have a chance to animate an object and edit the animation to give it weight in Chapter 8's Bouncing Ball and Knife exercises.

Weight in animation is a perception of mass. An object's movement and how it reacts in motion and to other objects are critical to conveying the feeling of weight. Otherwise, the animation will look bogus or "cartoonish."

Over the years, animators have created a set of techniques to give their subject weight in animation. Manipulating these concepts correctly in your work will greatly help your animations.

Squash and Stretch

"Squash and stretch" is a cartoon concept that allows a character to physically squash down when he is landing from a jump, or stretch out thin while he is jumping up. The overall mass of an object should never really change. When you squash an object down, you should also reduce its height to make it seem as if it's squashing down. Similarly, when you stretch an object up, you should also thin it. This technique will make a character seem to respond to gravity. You will see how this applies in the Bouncing Ball exercise in Chapter 8.

Ease-In and Ease-Out

Things in the real world don't immediately come to an abrupt stop. There is always a slowing before a stoppage, no matter how fast the stop may be. This is called *ease-out*.

Just as objects don't suddenly stop, they don't immediately start moving either. Pretty much everything needs to accelerate, no matter how fast it begins moving. This is called *ease-in*. The mechanics of *ease-in* and *ease-out* will also be illustrated in the Bouncing Ball exercise in Chapter 8.

Follow-Through and Anticipation

Exaggerating the weight of an object in animation is sometimes necessary. Objects ending an action usually have some type of *follow-through* motion. For example, a ponytail on a girl jumping down from a chair will continue to move after she lands on the floor. There should be a slight resting follow-through to her action. For example, she may bend slightly at the waist to center herself once she lands.

You can also create a small amount of movement before your action is in full swing. Before committing to an action, a character may "wind up" to a greater or lesser extent. Doing so will create a slight *anticipation* in the movement (for example, a hammer cocking back slightly before it strikes or a cartoon superhero that bends down before he jumps up to fly away). These concepts are covered in Chapter 8.

Basic 3ds Max Terms and Concepts

Any 3D program has terms and concepts you need to learn to become a good artist in that tool. Most of these concepts are fairly transferable, meaning they apply to more than one CG package, although their names may vary depending on which package you are using. Here are several terms and concepts you will encounter in the world of CG as they relate to 3ds Max. If you are not already familiar with 3ds Max's interface, running through this list before diving into the next chapter might be a good idea.

Objects An element in your 3ds Max scene is called an *object.* An object may be converted to a more easily editable mesh at any time. You will learn about this concept in Chapter 4, "Modeling in 3ds Max: Part I."

Primitives *Primitives* are basic Max objects such as spheres or boxes. Primitives can be shaped and altered to suit the needs of the model.

Sub-objects Many (though not all) objects are made up of components called *sub-objects.* You can select and manipulate sub-objects in 3ds Max to alter the look or function of an object. Kinds of sub-objects include vertices, faces, polygons, edges, gizmos, and centers. The types of sub-object you are able to manipulate depend on the type of object you are manipulating. See Chapter 4 for more on sub-objects.

Normals Each face of a polygon has a direction in which it points. A *normal* is a vector that defines which way a face points.

Spinners *Spinners* are a function of the user interface (UI) in Max. Spinners are the little arrows to the right of value readouts; they allow you to adjust the values by clicking up or down on them. A spinner for a sphere's radius value is shown here.

Radius: 0.0

Flyouts Another UI term, a *flyout* is an icon in 3ds Max that is actually several icons in one. If you press and hold a flyout icon, the other icons "fly out" and display themselves. Scroll to the icon you need and click to activate its flyout properties. A flyout icon has a black triangle in its lower-right corner (as here:). Flyouts are further covered in Chapter 3, "The 3ds Max Interface."

Figure 1.7

**The Home Grid in
the Perspective
viewport**

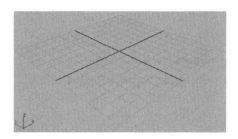

Home Grid The *Home Grid* is a gray grid that displays the origin (0,0,0). It is useful for grounding yourself in the viewports, and it helps with proportion and direction as well. A Perspective viewport Home Grid is shown in Figure 1.7.

Absolute/Relative *Absolute* refers to an adjustment on an object that is based on a fixed reference, such as World Space. An absolute scale of 2 will scale the object to a flat unit of 2. *Relative* refers to an adjustment made to an object that takes its current state into account. Scaling with a relative value of 2 will make that object twice its current size.

Track In 3ds Max a *track* is a display of animation data for an animated object. When an object has animation on several parameters, such as Translation *X* and *Y*, as well as Scale in *X* and *Z*, it is said to have four tracks. One track defines one animation on one parameter of that object on one axis.

SUGGESTED READING

The more you know about all the arts that are used in CG, the more confident you'll feel among your peers. To get started, check out the following excellent resources:

Art and Design

These books provide valuable insights into the mechanics and art of design. The more you understand design theory, the stronger your art will be.

Bowers, John. *Introduction to Two-Dimensional Design: Understanding Form and Function*. New York: John Wiley & Sons, 1999.

Itten, Johannes. *Design and Form: The Basic Course at the Bauhaus and Later*. New York: John Wiley & Sons, 1975.

Ocvirk, Otto G., and others. *Art Fundamentals: Theory and Practice*. New York: McGraw-Hill, 1997.

Wong, Wucius. *Principles of Form and Design*. New York: John Wiley & Sons, 1993.

CG

CG has an interesting history and is evolving at breakneck speeds. Acquiring a solid knowledge of this history and evolution is as important as keeping up with current trends.

Kerlow, Isaac Victor. *The Art of 3-D: Computer Animation and Imaging*. New York: John Wiley & Sons, 2000.

Derakhshani, Dariush. *Introducing Maya 9: 3D for Beginners*. San Francisco: Sybex, 2008.

Kuperberg, Marcia. *Guide to Computer Animation*. Burlington, MA: Focal Press, 2002.

Masson, Terrence. *CG 101: A Computer Graphics Industry Reference*. Indianapolis: New Riders Publishing, 1999.

Film

Block, Bruce. *The Visual Story: Seeing the Structure of Film, TV, and New Media*. Burlington, MA: Focal Press, 2001.

General

Myers, Dale K. *Computer Animation: Expert Advice on Breaking into the Business*. Milford, MI: Oak Cliff Press, 1999.

Periodicals

These magazines offer great topical insights into the industry and product reviews as well as offering some tutorials for further study.

Computer Graphics World (free subscription for those who qualify): `www.cgw.pennnet.com`

cinefex: `www.cinefex.com`

HDRI3D: `www.hdri3-D.com`

3D World: `www.3-Dworldmag.com`

Websites

You'll find a wealth of information at your finger tips at these websites.

`www.area.autodesk.com`

`www.animationartist.com`

`www.awn.com`

`www.highend3d.com`

`www.3dcafe.com`

Summary

In this chapter, you learned the basic concepts that drive the CG field. Starting with production workflow and moving into CG workflow, we discussed how productions are generally run. Next, you learned the different types of tasks used in CG production and the professional specialties that have arisen from them. After that, you learned about core computer concepts, color space, and output formats. Finally, you saw a preview of some of the key 3ds Max terms and concepts that are covered in depth in the following chapters.

No matter how you use this chapter—or even if you skip it entirely to get right to the action—there is a lot of background information here that can be useful in your overall knowledge of CG production. Although it takes some extra time to develop a good foundation, having one is an excellent idea because gaining true understanding of a subject is fundamental to its mastery. Having said this, take the rest of the book as it comes, enjoy the challenges of the exercises, and remember that *some* frustration with an exercise will inevitably help you learn the concepts better; so keep at it.

CHAPTER 2

Your First 3ds Max Animation

This chapter gets your engine revving right away. It begins with an overview of the user interface (UI) and starts you off with an exercise that will expose you to quite a few Autodesk 3ds Max workflows and practices. The goal of the chapter is to put some concepts from the previous chapter into production so you can get going quickly.

Topics in this chapter include:

- **Getting Around in 3ds Max**
- **Project and File Management Workflow**
- **The 3ds Max Interface**
- **Jumping Headlong into Animation**
- **Setting Up the Hierarchy**
- **Ready, Set, Animate**

Getting Around in 3ds Max

At this point, it's important not to get caught up in the details of this great machine. Don't worry about the steps, buttons, menus, switches, and levers; just allow yourself to become comfortable with the tools that you use to create your artwork. Creating art is never about which button to press; it's about what to create. Always remember that, and your studies will be a great deal more successful.

Jumping straight into an exercise without knowing how to get around the interface might seem a little weird. However, you'll find everything you ever wanted to know, and then some, in Chapter 3, "The 3ds Max Interface." Learning is an experimental art, and there's no better way to learn than to start experimenting as soon as you can. The overall goal of this chapter is to expose you to the UI and show you how to get some things done in Max. Then you can proceed to the next chapter for a debriefing. (If you prefer, you can skip ahead to Chapter 3, get a tour of the UI, and then come back to this chapter for your first experience.)

Project and File Management Workflow

Autodesk 3ds Max provides several subfolders automatically grouped into projects for you. Different kinds of files are saved in categorized folders under the Project folder. For example, scene files are saved in a Scenes folder and rendered images are saved in a Render Output folder in the Project folder. The projects are set up according to what types of files you are working on, so everything is neat and organized from the get-go. 3ds Max will automatically create this folder structure for you once you create a new project, and its default settings will keep the files organized in that manner.

The conventions followed in this book and on the accompanying CD will follow this project-based system so that you can grow accustomed to it and make it a part of your own workflow. File organization is extremely important for professional work. If you do a lot of CG for fun or profit, it pays to be organized.

The exercises in this book are organized into specific projects, such as the one you will tackle in this chapter, *Mobile*. The Mobile project will be on your hard drive, and the folders for your scene files and rendered images will be in it. Once you copy the appropriate projects to your hard drive, you can tell 3ds Max which project to work on by choosing File → Set Project Folder. This will send the current project to that project folder. For example, when you save your scene, Max will automatically take you to the Scenes folder of the current project.

Before we begin any project, we'll briefly explain the naming conventions and suggest a folder structure. Using these naming conventions and structures is a good habit to develop.

Naming Conventions

Every studio and professional production company worth its salt has an established *naming convention* for its files and folders. This is a documented procedure that dictates how to name files and (usually) where to store them. Most organizations have different conventions, but the point is to have a convention and stick to it.

Students, in particular, tend to forgo any semblance of organization in their file-naming procedures. A common mistake is to save files to the local disk on the school computer, only to have the files erased by the support teams during the school's weekly purge. Designating a specific place on your PC or server for all your project files is important.

In addition to finding a suitable place to store your files, you need to name the files following some sort of convention. Your files will not only look neat when you're browsing, but they'll make sense months later when you try to figure out where that finished scene file is that you need. Typically, you should name a scene file with a project name or an abbreviation of such, then a brief description of what the file is, and a version number.

For example, if you are working on a project about a castle, begin by setting a new project called *Castle*. Choose File → Set Project Folder. On your hard drive, click the Make New Folder button (Figure 2.1) to create a folder named Castle. 3ds Max will automatically create the project and its folders.

Once you save a scene, one of your scene filenames should look like this: `Castle_GateModel_v05.max`. This tells you right away it's a scene from your Castle project, and that it is a model of the gate. The version number tells you that it's the fifth iteration of the model and possibly the most recent version. Following a naming convention will save you oodles of time and aggravation.

Figure 2.1

Enter the folder name and click Make New Folder.

Version Up!

The naming convention just mentioned used a version number appended to the end of the filename. After you've spent a significant amount of time working on your scene, or after you've made a major change or big breakthrough in your work, you will want to *version up*. This means you save your file using the same name, but you increase the version number by one to tell yourself, or your colleagues, that there was a big change since the last version. Version numbers are also useful for keeping track of your progress.

Version numbers can also save your hide. If you start down a path on your scene, but discover after hours of work (and saving your work as you go along, versioning up as you went) that this was indeed the wrong way to go, you can simply close the scene and open one of the previous versions that you created before you started going in the wrong direction. This happens a lot more than you might think.

Disk space is cheap and scene files, even huge ones, aren't all that big in the face of the hundreds of gigabytes you can buy for less than $100. Keep a notebook and a pen next to your workstation so that you can take notes on your progress and record exactly what you did during your work sessions. Professionals do this regularly. They can't afford to waste time trying to figure out what file they should load to access a particular chunk of work.

The Basic Project Structure Used in This Book

Each exercise in this book will be its own 3ds Max project. Pick a place on your hard drive and start there. Create a folder called Max Projects on your C: drive (you can create one anywhere you want, including your My Documents folder). Place all of your projects in this folder. This will make it easy to find your files and back them up to CD or tape.

Let's create the first project we'll be working on, *Mobile*. Select File → Set Project Folder, navigate to your Max Projects folder (or My Documents folder), and then click Make New Folder. Name the folder Mobile. 3ds Max will create the subfolders for the project, as shown in Figure 2.2.

That's pretty much it. Having a naming convention is easy; sticking to it is not, especially when you're first starting out. Make sure you stick to it.

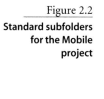

Figure 2.2

Standard subfolders for the Mobile project

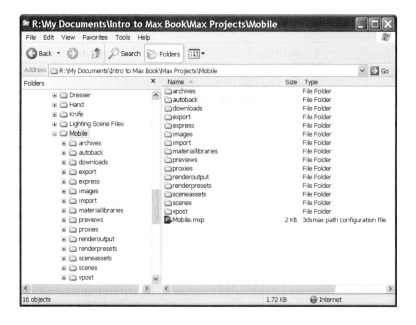

Saving Your Scenes in Max

Save your scene frequently to protect yourself from mistakes and from losing your work. Choosing File → Save updates the current scene by overwriting the last save of the scene. If no scene was previously saved, this command opens the Save File As dialog box. Using it, you can select where to save the scene and enter your scene's name. If you are working on a scene already, I recommend using Save As so you do not accidentally overwrite your current work. You can also use an incremental save function discussed shortly.

To "version up," you can save by using File → Save As and manually changing the version number appended to the end of the filename. Max also lets you do this automatically by using an increment feature in the Save As dialog box. Simply name your scene file and click the Increment button (the + icon) to the right of the filename text (Figure 2.3).

Clicking the Increment button will append the filename with 01, then 02, then 03, and so on as you keep saving your work using Save As and the Increment button. In the previous example, the scene's base filename was SceneName_v. Clicking the Increment button added the two-digit version number after the _v. Adding the _v is a personal preference, of course, but it keeps with the naming convention set up in this book. It looks nicer, and you can easily determine the version number for your file by reading the number after the _v.

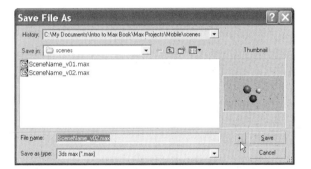

Figure 2.3

Click the Increment button to version up.

The 3ds Max Interface

Here is a brief rundown of what you need to know about the UI and how to navigate in Max's 3D space. We will cover the interface in more detail in the next chapter, so feel free to jump back and forth if you need to know more about the UI.

The menu bar running across the top of the UI gives you access to a ton of commands—from basic file operations, such as Save, to advanced tools you may need for a scene. Immediately below the main menu bar is the main toolbar. It contains several icons for functions such as Undo and the three Transform functions (Move, Rotate, and Scale). You will use some of these icons for the Mobile exercise. They are described more fully in Chapter 3.

The Undo and Redo functions are important, and you should be familiar with them. If you do something and then wish you hadn't, click the Undo icon (the icon on the left) or press Ctrl+Z. To redo a command or action that you just undid, click the Redo button (the icon on the right) or press Ctrl+Y.

The Command Panel

The Command panel is a vertical column or panel on the right side of the Max UI. It is segmented into tabs, as shown in Figure 2.4. Each tab displays the buttons and icons for a particular part of your workflow, such as creating objects, modifying objects, and animating objects. In each tab, the functions are grouped under headings that can be expanded or collapsed by clicking on the heading title. A plus next to the heading name means that you can expand the heading's view; a minus means that you can collapse the heading to save space.

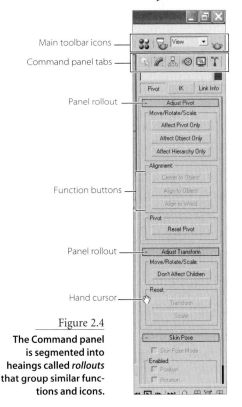

Main toolbar icons

Command panel tabs

Panel rollout

Function buttons

Panel rollout

Hand cursor

Figure 2.4

The Command panel is segmented into heaings called *rollouts* that group similar functions and icons.

If you mouse over the Command panel, the arrow pointer will change to a hand pointer, as shown in Figure 2.4, when it is not on a button or icon. While the pointer is a hand, you can click and drag to move the current panel up and down in the Command panel to see more functions in that space. You can also click on the far right side of the panel to scroll up and down if you don't want to use the hand.

As shown here, the viewport controls, which contain icons for various options for the 3D world windows (called *viewports*), are in the lower-right corner of the UI. These functions allow you to navigate the windows and their 3D space. However, you may find it easier to use hot keys rather than icons to invoke most of these functions. We will cover navigating 3D space and the appropriate hot keys next.

Viewports

You'll be doing most of your work in the viewports. These windows represent 3D space using a system based on *Cartesian coordinates*. That is a fancy way of saying "space in X-, Y-, and Z-axes." All CG programs, including 3ds Max, are based on this coordinate system.

You can visualize X as left–right, Y as up–down, and Z as in–out (into and out of the screen). The coordinates are expressed as a set of three numbers such as (0, 3,–7). These coordinates represent a point that is at 0 in the X-axis, three units up in the Y-axis, and seven units back in the Z-axis.

Four-Viewport Layout

3ds Max's viewports are the windows into your scene (Figure 2.5). By default, there are four main views: Front, Top, Left, and Perspective. The first three: Front, Top, and Left, are called Orthographic (2D) views. They are also referred to as *modeling windows.* These windows are good for expressing exact dimensions and size relationships, so they are a good tool for sizing up your scene objects and fine-tuning their layout.

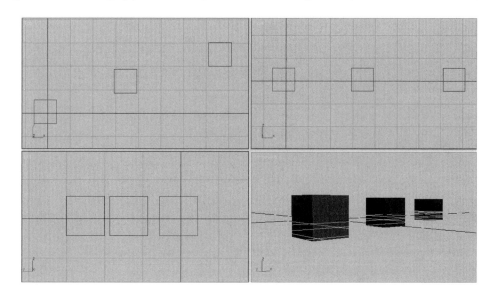

Figure 2.5

The 3ds Max viewports

The Perspective viewport displays objects in 3D space using a simulation of perspective. Notice in Figure 2.5 how the distant cubes seem to get smaller in the Perspective view. In actuality, they are the same size, as you can see in the Orthographic views. The Perspective view gives you the best representation of what your output will be.

To select a viewport, click in a blank part of the viewport (not on an object). If you do have something selected, it will be deselected when you click in the blank space. You can also right-click anywhere in an inactive viewport to activate it. When active, the view will have a yellow highlight around it. If you right-click in an already active viewport, you will get a pop-up context menu called the *Quad menu.* You can use this shortcut menu to access some basic commands for a faster workflow. We will cover this and other shortcut menus in the next chapter.

Display of Objects and Axes in a Viewport

Viewports can display your scene objects in a few different ways. If you right-click the viewport's name, the right-click Viewport menu will appear (Figure 2.6). The most common view modes are Wireframe mode and Smooth + Highlights mode. Wireframe mode displays the outlines of the object. It is the fastest to use because it requires less computation on your video card. The Smooth + Highlight mode is a shaded view where the objects in the scene appear solid. You will get the chance to experiment with different display modes in the upcoming Mobile exercise.

Figure 2.6

Right-click to see the viewport options.

Figure 2.7

The Home Grid in a Perspective viewport

Each viewport displays a ground plane grid (as shown in the Perspective viewport), called the *Home Grid* (Figure 2.7). This is the basic 3D space reference system. It's defined by three fixed planes on the coordinate axes (*X, Y, Z*). The center of all three axes is called the *origin*. This is where the coordinates are (0, 0, 0). The Home Grid is visible in 3ds Max's default settings when you start the software, but it can be turned off in the right-click Viewport menu. You can also toggle the grid by pressing G.

The Perspective viewport has a red, green, and blue axis marker in which the *X*-axis is red, the *Y*-axis is green, and the *Z*-axis is blue. Max uses this red, green, and blue color scheme to represent the *X*-, *Y*-, and *Z*-axes throughout the interface.

> Most 3D packages use red, green, and blue to represent *X*-, *Y*-, and *Z*-axes, respectively. It's not just a Max thing.

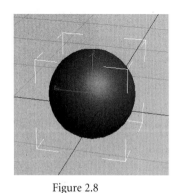

Figure 2.8

The white frame indicates the object is selected.

Selecting Objects in a Viewport

Selecting objects in a viewport is as easy as clicking them. If the object is displayed in Wireframe mode, its wireframe will turn white while it is selected. If the object is displayed in a Shaded mode, a white bracket will appear around the object as shown in Figure 2.8.

To select multiple objects, hold the Ctrl key down as you click additional objects to add to your selection. If you Ctrl+click an active object, you will deselect it. You can clear all of your active selections by clicking anywhere an empty area of the viewport.

> The Alt key can also be used to subtract objects from a selection set.

Changing/Maximizing the Viewports

To change the view in any given viewport—for example, to go from a Perspective view to a Front view—right-click the current viewport's name. From the context menu, select View and then select the view you want to have in this viewport, as shown in Figure 2.9.

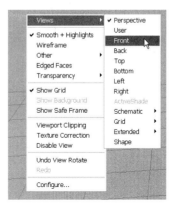

Figure 2.9

Right-click to change the view.

A faster way to change viewports is by using keyboard shortcuts. To switch from one view to another, press the appropriate key on the keyboard as shown in the following table:

VIEWPORT	KEYBOARD SHORTCUT
Top View	T
Bottom View	B
Front View	F
Left View	L
Camera View	C
Perspective View	P

If you want to have a larger view of the active viewport than is provided by the default four-viewport layout, press the Maximize Viewport Toggle icon (![icon]) in the lower-right corner of the Max window. You can also use the Alt+W keyboard shortcut to toggle between the maximized and four-viewport views.

Viewport Navigation

To work effectively, you will need to navigate in 3D space. Max allows you to move around its viewports either by using key/mouse combinations, which are highly preferable, or by using the viewport controls found in the lower-right corner of the Max UI. A full explanation of the viewport controls is in the next chapter. However, to navigate within the views, you should become familiar with the key/mouse combinations now.

Open a new, empty scene in Max. Experiment with the following controls to get a feel for moving around in 3D space. If you are new to 3D, this may seem odd at first, but it will become easier as you gain experience and should become second nature in no time. If you are coming to 3ds Max from another 3D package, such as Maya, you will notice several things that will take a little getting used to, but you will also notice similarities. With time and practice, you should be able to hop back and forth between packages with little confusion.

Pan Panning a viewport will slide the view around the screen. Using the middle mouse button (abbreviated in the remainder of this text as MM), click in the viewport and drag the mouse pointer to move the view.

Zoom Zooming will move your view in closer or farther away from your objects. To zoom, press Ctrl+Alt and MM+click in your viewport, and then drag the mouse up or down to zoom in or out, respectively. It is more common to use the scroll wheel to zoom, however.

> Zooming is sometimes called *dollying* in other packages; Max also has a dolly function, but it is active only when you are in a Camera viewport. Max differentiates between Camera viewports and Perspective viewports, unlike other packages).

Arc Rotate Arc rotate will rotate your view around your objects. To arc rotate, press Alt and MM+click and drag in the viewport. By default, Max will rotate (or *tumble*, as it's called in some other CG programs) about the center of the viewport to change your perspective.

> The arc rotate move is used primarily in the Perspective views and is not used in the Orthographic views. If you accidentally arc rotate in one of the Orthographic views, you will be given a new User view. This view will be similar to a perspective. However, it will remain orthographic, meaning that there will be no vanishing point or perspective shift in the view; it is not a real Camera view. You can reset the view back to your straight Orthogonal view by right-clicking the User viewport's name and selecting your original view.

Jumping Headlong into Animation

Let's get busy and dive right into 3ds Max and create an animation. You may not understand the reasons for all the things you're about to do, but you will get a quick trial by fire by getting into the program and following these steps, which will guide you through some of the basic workflows for Max.

For your first experience, we will create a simple mobile. This example will teach you the basics of object creation, hierarchies, setting keyframes to create animation, and general workflow.

Plan of Attack for Making Objects

It's always a good idea to go into something with a goal in mind. Knowing, even roughly, where you are headed will make things much easier. In production work, setting down a plan and having clear goals for your animation is very important. Without a good idea of where you need to go, you'll end up floundering and losing out on the whole experience. With that in mind, our goal in this chapter is to create a finished mobile, like the ones that hang over baby cribs. Because this is our first foray into Max, let's start with a simple object, so we won't be bogged down with the specifics of creating masterful models. Instead, we'll use simple objects that are easily created in Max.

Hierarchies

Once we model the mobile, we'll set up the pieces for animation. We will do this by creating proper hierarchies within the scene. The concept of *hierarchy* is a common feature in almost all CG packages. The hierarchy in a CG scene deals with how objects are arranged in a scene in relation to each other. *Parents* in a hierarchy lead *children*; where a parent goes, the children follow. When you *translate* (move) or rotate or scale a parent object, its children will move, turn, or scale along with it.

However, children retain the ability to move individually under their parent's supervision. The Mobile exercise is a perfect way to demonstrate the idea of hierarchies. Take a look at Figure 2.10, which displays the completed mobile. The top bar (the parent), from which the other bars hang, rotates and takes the lower bars (its children) with it. In this exercise, we will also animate the lower bars to rotate individually, just as a real mobile would.

The dangling shapes on the lower bars are the children of their respective bars. Those lower bars are children of the bars above them, and so on up to the top bar that controls the rotation of the entire mobile. Once you begin working on it, it will make more sense. As you can see now, hierarchy plays an important part in animation.

Don't get hung up on all the steps and what they mean. This is a quick dip in the pond to get your feet wet. In the next chapters, we will explain everything you did here.

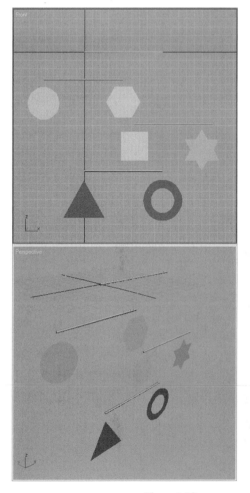

Figure 2.10

The completed mobile object

Making the Mobile's Bars

To begin, we'll create the simple objects that are the parts of the mobile. The mobile comprises horizontal bars and shapes that hang from the ends of each bar. We will forgo the strings used in an actual mobile and just make do with the bars and the shapes. To create the bars for the mobile, follow these steps:

1. In the Command panel, activate the Create panel (as shown in Figure 2.11) by clicking on the Create tab ( ) The Create panel is usually enabled by default. Click the Geometry button ( ) to display the Geometry Object Types; it is usually enabled by default. You will see a number of ways to create various objects. You will begin most, if not all, of your Max models in this panel.

Figure 2.11

The Create panel

Figure 2.12

Drag out a circle, then drag up a cylinder.

2. With Standard Primitives selected in the Create panel's pull-down menu, as shown in Figure 2.11, click the Create Cylinder button. The Cylinder button will turn orange, and your cursor will turn from the default arrow to a cross.

3. Go to the Perspective view. On the Home Grid, click and drag the mouse in any direction to begin the radius of the cylinder. Drag the mouse until it makes a circle, as shown in Figure 2.12, and release the mouse button.

   You'll notice that as you move the mouse up or down, Max will pull the circle into a cylinder. Settle on a height for the cylinder and right-click to create the cylinder (Figure 2.12). Don't worry about the size of the tube; we will modify it in the following steps to turn this cylinder into the top hanging bar for the mobile. Any size cylinder is fine for right now.

4. With the cylinder still selected in the Perspective panel, click the Modify tab (![icon]) in the Command panel to bring up all the nifty tools you can use to modify objects in Max.

   You will rename the cylinder and size it to be a bar for the mobile. At the top of the panel, you'll notice a text box with Cylinder01 and a colored square next to it, as shown in Figure 2.13. The color swatch is the Object Color, and it helps you organize your elements in a scene. The color is easily changed by clicking on the swatch and simply choosing another color from the window that pops up (as shown in Figure 2.14). This color is not necessarily the color your object will render in the final output of your animation (for more on rendering in Max, see Chapter 11, "3ds Max Rendering"). However, we are not too interested in the color of the bar right now, so you can leave the cylinder the way it is, or you can change it if you desire.

5. You do need to change the name of the cylinder, however. Click in the text box and change it from Cylinder01 to Main Parent. This name signifies that the cylinder will be the top bar of the mobile and the top parent to the rest of the objects in the scene. For more on hierarchies, see the "Hierarchies" section earlier in this chapter.

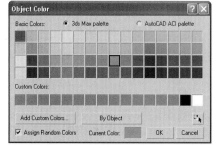

Figure 2.13

The Modify panel allows you to change the name of the selected object and color it in the scene.

Figure 2.14

The Object Color helps you organize the scene by letting you assign colors to your objects.

6. You need to size the cylinder (Main Parent) to make it a bar. Under the Parameters heading in the Modify panel, you'll notice a handful of parameters for Main Parent, as shown in Figure 2.15. If you don't see anything there, make sure the cylinder is selected. The Modify panel will display the parameters for the selected object only. To adjust the parameters for the bar, you can type values directly into the appropriate boxes. You can also use the Up and Down arrows on the right either by clicking the arrows or by clicking and dragging up or down on the arrows. Change the radius to 1, height to 100, and height segments to 1 (as shown in Figure 2.15). Your cylinder should look like a bar, as shown in Figure 2.16. For a quick explanation of the other cylinder parameters, see the note on the following page.

Every object in Max will have parameters that define it geometrically in the scene. The exact parameters that are available for editing depend on the object that is being edited. For this cylinder, for example, you've already seen what the Radius and Height parameters do. The Height Segments, Cap Segments, and Sides parameters determine how many polygons you will use to define the shape, and hence how smooth it appears. Because the bar will not bend, you do not need extra polygons along the length. Therefore, the Height Segment parameter was changed from the default of 5 to 1.

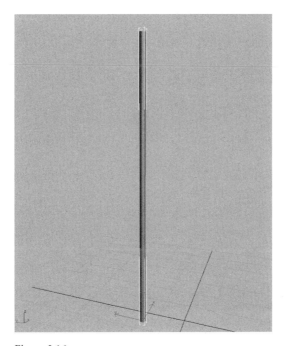

Figure 2.15

The parameters of a selected object (in this case the Main Parent cylinder) can be changed to suit your needs.

Figure 2.16

Your cylinder should be a thin bar.

NAMING OBJECTS AND KEEPING THE SCENE ORGANIZED

In 3ds Max, and in any CG package, it is incredibly important to keep things organized and as clean as possible. It's no fun to pick up a scene from a colleague and waste tons of time trying to figure out exactly what is in it. Many artists will touch the same digital files and assets through a production. This is why many professional studios have strict naming procedures and conventions to minimize the confusion their artists may have when working in a pipeline. Even if you are the only person who will ever see a scene in Max, it is still an incredibly good idea to name and organize your objects. Get into the habit of naming your objects and keeping a clean scene. You will waste a lot of time if you don't—not to mention the dirty looks you'll get from other artists handling your cluttered scenes.

Positioning the Bar

Now you need to position the first bar, and then create copies for the other bars of the mobile, as shown in the following steps:

1. Click the Select and Rotate icon ()—we'll call it the Rotate tool from now on—in the main toolbar just below the menu bar. (You can also use the hot key E to enable Select and Rotate.) Click on the Main Parent cylinder to select it and enable the Rotate tool. Notice that the Rotate gizmo appears at the base of the cylinder.

2. Clicking and dragging one of the axes will rotate the cylinder in that axis. For this step, click on the *Y*-axis rotate *handle*, which is the green circle, and drag the mouse to rotate the cylinder to the right of the screen as shown in Figure 2.17. The green *Y*-axis handle will turn yellow when you select it. (A gizmo's active axis handle is yellow.)

3. The bar needs to be rotated a perfect 90 degrees, and that is usually difficult to do by hand using the gizmo. Look at the bottom left of the Max UI, and you will see the orientation of the bar in three text boxes called the Transform Type-In boxes. You can enter a value of **90** in the *Y*-axis Transform Type-In box to set the bar to exactly 90 degrees, as shown in Figure 2.18.

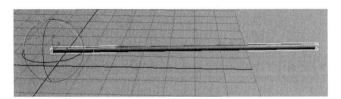

Figure 2.17

The Rotate gizmo allows you to rotate the selected object.

Figure 2.18

Set the rotation to exactly 90 degrees in the *Y*-axis in the Transform Type-In box.

Copying the Bar

In the next set of steps, you will copy the bar to make the other bars. Because the bar is already the size and orientation we need, it'll be much faster to copy three more bars and place them. Copying objects in Max is actually quite easy if you follow these steps:

1. Click the Select and Move Tool icon (⊕)—we'll call it the Move tool from now on— and select the bar. You can also invoke the Move tool with the hot key **W**.

> You can also access the Move/Rotate/Scale and Select tools easily by right-clicking on the intended object to transform and picking the tool from the Quad menu that appears.

2. With the bar selected, hold down the Shift key and move the bar down in the *Z*-axis. A second copy of the bar will form: Move it down in the *Z*-axis with your cursor. As soon as you release the mouse button, the Clone Options window will ask you what kind of copy you want to make (Figure 2.19). We will cover the different types of copies and what they mean in Chapter 4, "Modeling in 3ds Max: Part I."

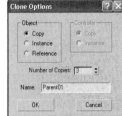

Figure 2.19

The Clone Options window asks you the type and number of copies to make.

3. In the Clone Options window (Figure 2.19), keep the Copy button checked, enter **3** for the number of copies, and change the Name to Parent01. Click OK. Max will create three copies for you and position them as far down in the *Z*-axis as you moved the original clone while you had the Shift key pressed.

4. Use the Move tool to position the lower bars as shown in Figure 2.20; just don't move the bars off the *Z*-axis by moving any of them in the *Y*-axis. (We will keep all the bars in the *Z*-axis for simplicity's sake. After all, this is your first Max animation; there will be plenty of time for confusion later.)

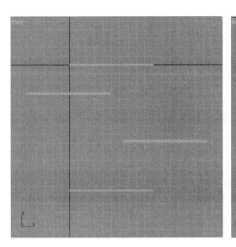
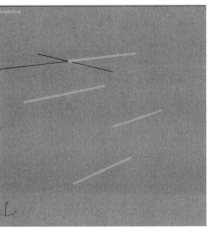

Figure 2.20

Position the bars for the mobile.

Figure 2.21

Creating spline-based shapes

Figure 2.22

Under the Keyboard Entry heading, you can enter the exact radius to use for the circle.

Try to position the bars so that the second bar's center lines up with the left end of the top bar. The third bar's center should be lined up with the top bar's right end. The fourth bar can line up with the top bar. Each level of the bars should be about five units down in the Z-axis from the last bar. Now you're ready to make the hanging objects.

Creating the Mobile's Objects

What kind of mobile has only four sticks hanging on a string? You'll have to make some objects to hang from the ends of the bars. These objects will be simple shapes you can create with the following steps:

1. Activate the Front viewport by right-clicking inside it (by right clicking, you will not affect any of your selections and still be able to activate the viewport). Maximize that viewport with the Maximize Viewport Toggle icon ( ) in the bottom-right corner of the Max UI.

2. In the Command panel, click the Create tab and then click the Shapes button ( ) to display the creation options for various shapes. The Splines option should appear in the Object Type menu, as shown in Figure 2.21.

3. Let's start with a circle. Click the Circle button. Your cursor will turn to a cross as it did when you created the cylinder. This time, expand the Keyboard Entry rollout. Enter a value of 20 for the Radius under the Keyboard Entry rollout in the Create panel, as you can see in Figure 2.22. Click the Create button. A circle with radius 20 should appear at the origin. This is a way to make objects with precise dimensions, as opposed to clicking and dragging as you did to create the cylinder.

4. Max has given the circle you created the name Circle01, which is fine, so there is no need to change its name. Use the Move tool to position it under the second bar, lining up its center with the left end of the second bar as shown in Figure 2.23. Splines, including the circle you just created, are not renderable shapes by default. This means they will not render when you output your scene unless you specify otherwise. The circle will be displayed as a wireframe, even when the viewport is in Smooth + Highlights mode (also called Shaded mode) when objects are shown as solid in the viewport. For more on display modes in viewports, see the following brief sidebar.

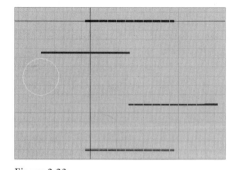

Figure 2.23

Position the circle under the second bar.

VIEWPORT MODES

In Smooth + Highlights mode, you see the objects in your scene as solid objects. This is the default mode for all the Max Perspective viewports, but not for the Modeling viewports such as the Front view. To switch from one view mode to another, right-click on the viewport name in the upper-left corner of the viewport. A menu will appear, as shown here. You can also use keyboard shortcuts to change from one viewport to the next.

You can select the view mode for that viewport by selecting it from the right-click menu. Additional display modes are listed under Other on the menu.

Spline shapes, such as our lovely circle, are curves that need to be given a surface to be able to render as solid objects. To make the circle solid, you will *extrude* it by following these steps:

Figure 2.24

The Modifier List

1. Select the `Circle01` object (the circle) and click the Modify tab in the Command panel ( ).

   In the Circle01 name text box, click the Modifier List pull-down menu to access the many *modifiers* you can add to the circle (Figure 2.24). Under the Object-Space Modifiers heading, select Extrude.

2. In the box below the Modifier List menu, a new entry called *Extrude* should appear above the existing Circle entry for the selected Circle01 object. This box, called the *Modifier Stack,* is shown in Figure 2.25. The Modifier Stack displays all the modifiers that are contributing to the selected object, in this case the circle. The Circle modifier entry holds the original parameters of Circle01, while the new Extrude modifier entry holds the parameters for the extrusion you just applied to the circle. The circle now has a surface and is solid in the Perspective viewport (Figure 2.26).

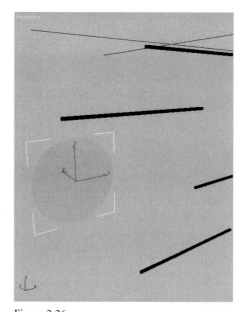

Figure 2.25

The Modifier Stack shows off the Extrude modifier you just applied.

Figure 2.26

The circle is now a flat disc.

In 3ds Max 2008, a flat object may display with one black side, whereas previous versions of 3ds Max displayed flat objects properly. This is due to Backface Culling, which is a display optimization toggle that is now turned off by default in 3ds Max 2008. If you notice that one side of your flat object turns black, don't fret. Simply select the object and go to the Display tab of the Command panel (🖳). Scroll down to the bottom of the panel under the Display Properties rollout and click to toggle on Backface Cull.

3. In the Modifier Stack, click the Extrude entry to bring up its parameters. Play with the Amount parameter to give the circle extrusion some depth and make a cylinder.

4. Let's go off topic just for a second to learn something a bit more general about Max. Go into Wireframe View mode in your Perspective window by right-clicking the Perspective viewport name in the upper-left corner and selecting Wireframe from the menu (you may also press F3). Make sure you right-click on the viewport name; right-clicking elsewhere in the viewport will bring up the Quad menu (which is explained in Chapter 3).

Now that you see the wireframe of the extruded circle, change the Segments of the Extrude modifier to see what happens. Figure 2.27 shows the extruded circle with Segments of 1 on the top, and Segments of 4 on the bottom. You'll see that now there are more geometry divisions (called *subdivisions*), which make the object smoother lengthwise. Because you don't need to bend this extruded cylinder, you do not need extra subdivisions along the length, so set the Segments back down to 1.

5. Back to the topic at hand, we need the circle to remain a flat disc, so set the Amount to 0.01 and keep the Segments at 1 as in the previous step.

6. Set the Perspective viewport back to Smooth + Highlights by right-clicking the viewport name, which is Perspective, and selecting Smooth + Highlights from the menu. You may also press F3 to toggle between the two display modes. You should now see a flat solid disc as shown in Figure 2.28.

7. Create a hexagon for the second shape. Go back to the Front viewport. In the Command panel, click the NGon button as shown in Figure 2.29. In the Parameters heading, set the Sides to 6 for a hexagon. An *NGon* is a polygon with *N* number of sides. In this case, *N* is 6 to make a hexagon. In the Front viewport, click and drag to create the hexagon to a radius of about 20.

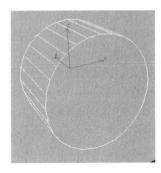

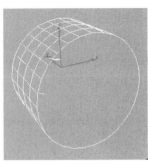

Figure 2.27

The extruded cylinder with a Segments value of 1 on the top, and a Segments value of 4 on the bottom.

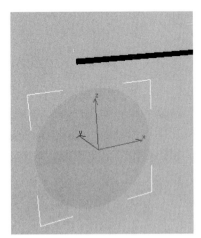

Figure 2.28

The flat disc in Smooth + Highlights mode

Figure 2.29

Setting parameters for the hexagon

8. In the same way you created the disc using an Extrusion modifier on the circle, make a hexagon into a solid shape by adding an Extrusion modifier to it. Select the hexagon (named NGon01). In the Modifier panel, click the Modifier List menu and select Extrude (as shown in Figure 2.25). The NGon01 object will now have its own Extrude modifier in the Modifier Stack.

9. Use the Move tool () to place the NGon01 hexagon below and lined up with the other end of the second bar. Figure 2.30 shows the solid NGon01 surface in position.

10. Create four more shapes and place them to line up under the ends of the remaining bars as shown in Figure 2.31. You will need to create and extrude the remaining four shapes all at about the same size (radius of 20). The following table shows you the remaining shapes and what Object Type button to use to create them and what their names will be in the scene. To avoid any confusion when we begin to set up the hierarchies for animation, keep the naming as shown here:

MOBILE OBJECT	CREATION TYPE	OBJECT NAME
Square	Use the Create Rectangle button	Rectangle01
Star	Use the Create Star button	Star01
Triangle	Use the Create NGon button with three sides	Ngon02
Donut	Use the Create Donut button	Donut01

You should already have created these first two shapes:

MOBILE OBJECT	CREATION TYPE	OBJECT NAME
Circle	Used the Create Circle button	Circle01
Hexagon	Used the Create NGon button with six sides	NGon01

Figure 2.30

The solid hexagon is in place.

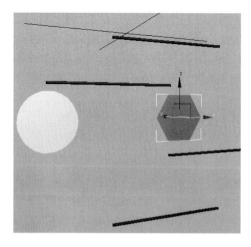

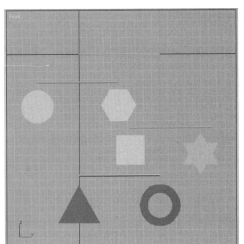 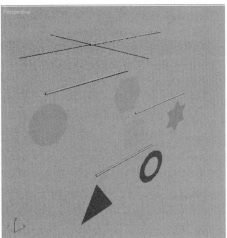

Figure 2.31

The shapes are now in position for the mobile.

If you click and drag to create a shape in the Perspective viewport and nothing happens, you will need to switch to one of the Orthographic views. In this Mobile example, make sure to create all the shapes in the Front viewport for simplicity's sake.

There you have it—a completed mobile model ready to set up and animate. The next sections of the chapter will take you through setting these objects up for animation in hierarchies so that when one bar rotates, its shapes and any bars beneath it also rotate with it. Go put your feet up and watch something dumb on TV for a little while; you've earned a break. It's actually important to take a break at this point, and make sure what you've gone through makes some sense. Feel free to go back and redo the exercise in part or in whole. In the next section, we will tackle hierarchies and setting up the mobile objects to animate properly.

Save your progress, making sure to version up so that you don't overwrite any previous scene files you might need later. You can check your work against the Mobile_v01.max scene file in the Mobile\Scenes folder on the CD.

Setting Up the Hierarchy

Before we continue with the next step in the Mobile exercise, let's take a look at hierarchies in action. Here is a quick introduction to how hierarchies work.

Parent and Child Objects

In the following steps, we will create a hierarchy of a few boxes to see how the relationship works when parents move, taking their children with them, and how children can move independently under their parents.

1. In a new scene, in the Create panel, click Box to create a new box. Click and drag in the Front viewport and draw out a box. Notice that when you drag the first time, a flat box is created. When you are happy with the size of the rectangle, click once and drag to "pull out" the third dimension of the box to give it depth. Click again when you are happy with the 3D box and Max will create it. Your cursor will still be active in the Create Box tool. Click and drag to create two more boxes of approximately the same size to the right of the first box, as shown in Figure 2.32.

2. You need to set up a hierarchy so that the box on the right is a child of the box in the middle, which in turn is a child of the box on the left, like a row of ducks. In the main toolbar across the top of the UI, click the Select and Link tool ( ). The Select and Link tool works upward, meaning you select the bottom of the hierarchy and work your way up.

Figure 2.32

Create three lined-up boxes.

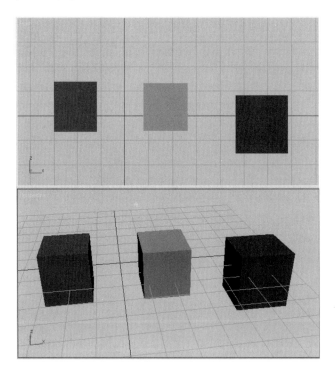

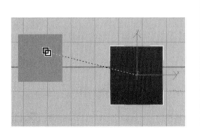

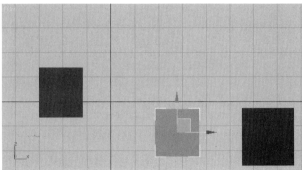

Figure 2.33

Notice the cursor cues.

Figure 2.34

The box follows as you drag it.

3. In either the Front or Perspective viewports, click the box on the right and then drag the mouse over to the box in the middle. A dashed line and a cursor will change while you do this, as shown in Figure 2.33. When you release the mouse button, the two boxes will flash a white outline. This indicates that the link worked. The box on the right is now a child of the box in the middle.

4. Click the Move tool (⊕) and select the middle box. Move it around in the viewport. The box on the right (the child) will now follow as shown in Figure 2.34. Click the child box on the right, and move it. Notice the child can move independently of its parent (the box in the middle).

5. Click the Select and Link tool (⬛) again. This time click on the box in the middle and drag to the box on the left. Select and move the box on the left, and all the boxes will follow.

Now let's set a few keyframes on these boxes to get our juices flowing.

Setting Keyframes

The Time slider is at the bottom of the screen, as shown in Figure 2.35. The Time slider is used to change your position in time, counted in *frames*. As you read in the previous chapter, frames are the common increment for denoting time in an animation. You'll read more about the Time slider in the next chapter.

Figure 2.35

The Time slider allows you to change your position in time and scrub your animation.

You can click and drag the horizontal bar to change the frame in your animation on the fly. This is called *scrubbing* animation. The bar displays the current frame/end frame (it should read 0/100 before you click and drag it). Click and drag the slider to the left so your current frame is 0. Now, in the lower-right corner of the UI, click the Auto Key button, as shown in the graphic. Both the Auto Key button and the Time slider will turn red. This means that any movement in the objects in your scene will be recorded as animation. How exciting!

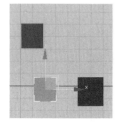

Move the Time slider to the right to frame 20. Select the box on the left (the top parent) and move it across the Front viewport to the left along the *X*-axis. Next, click and move the middle box down in the *Y*-axis in the viewport, as shown here.

Now scrub the timeline between 0 and 20, and you will see your animation. Even though you did not set any keyframes on the box to the right, it will follow along with both the left box and the middle box, doing a combination of their moves. The middle box goes with its parent, the left box, and its own animation, sliding down the viewport in the *Y*-axis. This is a simple hierarchy showing you how the relationships between objects build animation. You will use the same theory to build the animation for the Mobile exercise.

Before you continue on to the next exercise, make sure to turn off AutoKey.

Hierarchies for the Mobile

Let's start with a simple hierarchy scheme much like the Boxes exercise. Start with your own Mobile scene, or open the `Mobile_v01.max` scene file in the Mobile\Scenes folder on the CD.

You will create the hierarchies for animation of the mobile using the following steps:

1. Remember, the Select and Link tool works from the children up the hierarchy to the top parent. You will link the shapes to their respective bars up the mobile. Click the Select and Link tool (![icon]) and then select the triangle. Drag the cursor to its bar, as shown in Figure 2.36. The triangle is now linked to the bar above it.

2. With the Select and Link tool still active, click and drag from the donut shape to the bar above it, as shown in Figure 2.37.

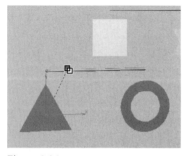

Figure 2.36

Drag from the triangle to link it to the bar.

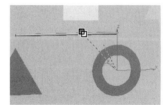

Figure 2.37

Link the donut to the bar.

3. With the Select and Link tool, click and drag from the bottom bar that holds the triangle and donut to the square shape above it, as shown in Figure 2.38. The bar is hanging from that square as if this were a real mobile, so you would link it as such. If you want to check your work, select and move the square and the bar. The shapes beneath it will move with the square. Just make sure to press Ctrl+Z to undo any moves you made to check the linking.

4. Now you just need to use the same steps to link the rest of the mobile:

   a. Click and drag with the Select and Link tool from the square to the bar above it.

   b. Link from the star to its bar.

   c. Link from the bar above the star and square to the top bar, as shown in Figure 2.39.

   d. Link from the hexagon to its bar.

   e. Link from the circle to its bar.

   f. Link from the bar above the circle and hexagon to the top bar, as shown in Figure 2.40.

You can refer to Figure 2.41 for a diagram of the linking order. It doesn't matter in what order you link the pieces, as long as you link from the bottom pieces up the chain.

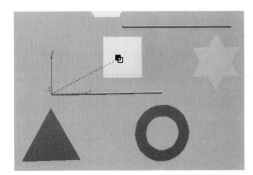

Figure 2.38
Link the bar to the square.

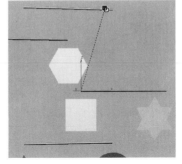

Figure 2.39
Link one bar to another.

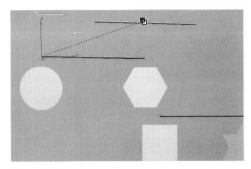

Figure 2.40
Link the circle's bar to the top one.

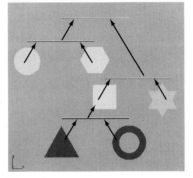

Figure 2.41
The linking order determines the hierarchy of the mobile.

Pivot Points

Now you've linked all the pieces of the mobile and created your first animation hierarchy. It's time to rotate parts of the mobile and test your handy work. This will be the last

step before you animate the mobile. To test the mobile, select the bottom bar and rotate it on the *Z*-axis in either direction. Figure 2.42 shows the rotation of the bottom bar. Notice that the Rotate gizmo is at one end of the bar and not in the middle. You should also notice that the bar (along with the triangle and donut) is rotating around the end of the bar, although it should rotate in the middle, where the string would be hanging it from the square right above it.

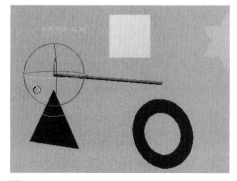

Figure 2.42

The bottom bar is rotating around one end instead of the middle.

Your results might be slightly different from what is shown here. Your bar might not rotate around the same end or it might rotate somewhere else along the cylinder. This is perfectly normal. The important thing is where the *pivot point* of the object is—and that pivot should be in the middle of the bar.

Simply put, the pivot point of an object in Max is the point about which it rotates. It is also the point on the object that defines the point in coordinate space where the object resides. So a coordinate of (2,6,0) for the position of a cube, for example, technically describes the pivot point of that cube to be at the location (2,6,0).

Because the pivot of the bottom bar is not in the middle of the bar, you will have to move the pivot to the middle. To do so, follow these steps:

Figure 2.43

The Hierarchy panel

1. Use Ctrl+Z to undo any rotations you have already put on the bottom bar. Click the Move tool (⊕) or press the hot key W for the Move tool, and select the bottom bar if it is not currently selected. In the Command panel, switch to the Hierarchy panel, as shown in Figure 2.43, by pressing the Hierarchy Panel tab (⬚).

2. At the top of the Hierarchy panel, make sure the Pivot button is active and then click the Affect Pivot Only button to activate it (the button will change color). This will tell Max to move only the pivot point of the currently selected object and not to move the entire object. Your gizmo icon will change, as shown in Figure 2.44.

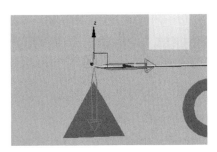

Figure 2.44

Again, the cursor cues you to what action is being taken: You're moving only the pivot point.

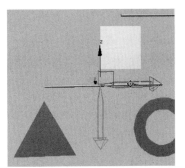

Figure 2.45

Move the pivot to the middle of the bar.

3. Click the *X*-axis Move handle (the small red arrow inside the larger outline of an arrow) and move the pivot along the length of the bar to the middle of the bar, as shown in Figure 2.45.

4. In the Hierarchy panel, click the Affect Pivot Only button again to turn it off. Your cursor will return to the normal Move Tool gizmo. Select the Rotate tool from the main toolbar ( ) and rotate the bottom bar again. It will now rotate around the middle of the bar as it should, with the triangle and donut in tow, as shown in Figure 2.46.

5. To make sure the pivot points are all in the middle of the respective bars, check the other bars in the mobile. If not, use the previous steps to relocate the pivots to their proper places.

You can check your work against the Mobile_v03.max scene file in the Mobile\Scenes folder on the CD. Once the pivot points are all placed properly on the mobile's bars, you are ready to animate. Grab a cold drink; you deserve it!

Figure 2.46

The bottom bar now rotates properly.

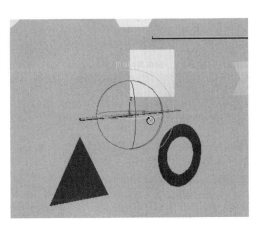

Ready, Set, Animate!

In this animation, we will rotate *only the bars* of the mobile. Don't worry about rotating or animating the shapes for now. We will revisit this exercise in Chapter 8, "Introduction to Animation."

You can use your own file, or you can load the Mobile_v03.max scene file in the Mobile\Scenes folder on the CD. In this file, the mobile is already linked properly for this animation and all the pivots are placed at the middle of each bar. To animate the mobile, follow these steps:

1. Scrub the Time slider to 0. If it is not already on, turn on the Auto Keyframe feature by clicking the Auto Key button (Auto Key). Both the Auto Key button and the Time slider will turn red.

2. Move the Time slider to frame 50. Click the Rotate tool (or press the hot key E for the Rotate tool), and select and rotate the bottom bar (which will also rotate the triangle and donut shapes beneath it). You can rotate the bar in either direction on the *Z*-axis, as shown in Figure 2.47. Give it a few full rotations all the way around. Don't be shy.

3. You can scrub the animation to check it out. The bottom bar and its shapes should be spinning. Make sure you go back to frame 50 in the Time slider. With the Rotate tool still active, select the second bar from the bottom (the bar with the square and the star shapes), and rotate it in either direction in the *Z*-axis. Figure 2.48 shows how the bottom bar follows along.

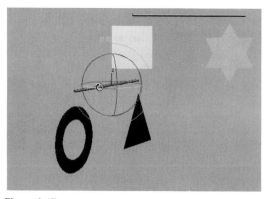

Figure 2.47

Rotate the bottom bar with gusto!

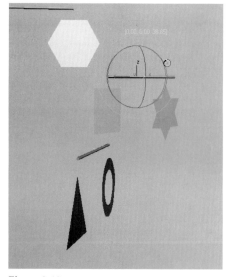

Figure 2.48

Rotate the second bar and the bottom bar follows.

4. While still at frame 50, select the third bar from the bottom (the bar with the circle and the hexagon) and rotate it in either direction on the *Z*-axis. The circle and hexagon rotate with the bar, as shown in Figure 2.49.

5. With the Rotate tool, select the top bar and rotate it in either direction on the *Z*-axis. The entire mobile will rotate along with it, because the top bar is the top parent of this hierarchy (Figure 2.50).

Scrub your animation, and you'll see that the mobile is in full swing! The bars rotate and carry with them the shapes and bars beneath them, according to the previously set hierarchy. If your shapes or child bars are not rotating with their parent bars, check your hierarchies or redo that portion of the exercise.

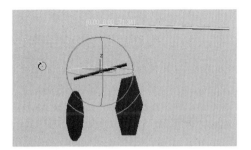

Figure 2.49

The shapes rotate properly.

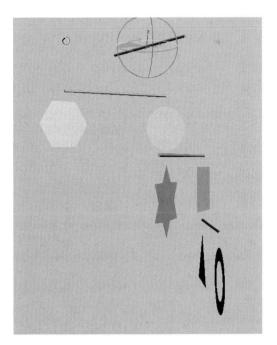

Figure 2.50

The whole mobile rotates with the top bar.

You may have noticed that this exercise asked you not to animate the rotation of the shapes linked under the bars. This was to avoid overloading you with information. If you animate the shapes under the bars to rotate, you will probably get some strange results when you play back the animation. The shapes and some of the bars linked below the animated shapes will not rotate properly. We will revisit this exercise to learn how to properly animate the shapes and the bars in Chapter 8.

Summary

Understanding the underlying technique used here is important, so doing the exercise more than once is not a bad idea. These things can be frustrating, so take it easy and when you get confused or stuck, back up and try again.

In this chapter, you learned how project management and file workflow help you keep things organized. You learned how to navigate the User Interface to create and manipulate objects in the viewports. You learned about hierarchies and how to link objects together to create a hierarchy useful for our mobile animation. Finally, you learned how pivot points are used, and you also learned how to create animation using the Auto Key function.

CHAPTER 3

The 3ds Max Interface

This chapter explains the 3ds Max interface and its most commonly used windows and panels. You already mucked about in the UI when you built your mobile in the previous chapter. This chapter will go into more depth regarding some of the tasks you performed, and it will give you a layout of where things are and what they do. Furthermore, we'll take a look at the commonly used windows and panels in 3ds Max and see how to operate them.

You can use this chapter as a reference as you work through the rest of this book. As you progress, you might want to check back here to review some of the information. It's important to be in front of your computer when you read this chapter, so you can try things out as we discuss them in the book.

Topics in this chapter include:

- **What Am I Looking At?**
- **Screen Layout**
- **Command Panels**
- **Controls at the Bottom of the UI**
- **The Viewports**
- **Managing Scene Objects**
- **Scene Explorer**

What Am I Looking At?

When you start up 3ds Max, you will be looking at a screen full of buttons, icons, menus, and panels and an empty work area—how daunting! Although it may seem that there is no end to the switches and levers in 3ds Max, you'll be able to master the UI with just a little experience. The more you use 3ds Max to create, the more comfortable you'll become with the UI and all of its nuances. Before you know it, the UI will be a nonissue for you—just give it time and patience.

As with many other 3d applications, almost any command or tool can be accessed at least a few different ways. For example, you can access some tools through icons in the Command panel by selecting them from the menu bar, by pressing a hot key, or by using context-sensitive Quad menus that appear when you right-click in the interface.

With so many different ways to perform any single function, how can you keep it all straight? Having a function or tool in several different places may seem like overload, but ultimately it gives users the most freedom to discover their preferred workflow. You may prefer to work mostly through the Command panel; others may find the menu bar easier to use. In either case, it's important to first experience the most common way to use 3ds Max and then branch out and find your own preference. In this book, we will first present the most obvious way to access a function; later we will give you alternative ways (such as hot keys) that you can use to access that feature.

Please don't obsess about all the information you're about to encounter. It's best to peruse this chapter at your own pace in front of your PC. Don't worry about memorizing all the information on every button and panel. Each of the exercises in this book contains short descriptions of the UI elements you'll use in that exercise. You can always refer back to this chapter for a more thorough explanation of a particular element. You should read through this chapter once to become familiar with where everything is and how everything works. Experience—and only experience—will show you how to make the tools work effectively; this chapter just shows you where they are.

In this chapter, you will find a fairly comprehensive explanation of 3ds Max's UI that expands on what you learned in Chapter 2, "Your First Max Animation." If you skipped Chapter 2, please go back to it now and read the section called "The Max Interface" for a run-through of how to work in 3ds Max's UI. Because experience will teach you so much more than just reading a text, it's wise to give the UI a whirl. Go ahead and click on things and move around in the UI using this and the previous chapter as a guide.

Screen Layout

Let's take a quick look at how the screen is laid out. Figure 3.1 shows the initial 3ds Max screen.

The menu bar runs across the top of the 3ds Max UI, just as with many other applications. Here you can access tons of features to help you with your scene creation and manipulation. Immediately under the menu bar is the main toolbar, which contains the most frequently accessed tool icons. Everything from Undo to Render is in the main toolbar for easy access.

Running down the right side of the 3ds Max UI is the Command panel. Object creation and manipulation tools are gathered here for your access. The Command panel, as you discovered in the previous chapter, is divided into tabs. Each tab has its own specific panel of tools, ranging from Create to Utilities.

The meat of the UI is in the viewports. These portals give you access to 3ds Max's 3D space through orthographic and perspective views. These viewports are where you'll do the bulk of your work. By using mouse and key combinations, as you saw in the previous chapter, you can navigate through 3D space and around your scenes quite easily.

Running across the bottom of the UI are the tools for changing time values (such as the Time slider, which you experienced in the previous chapter), viewport navigation controls, and controls for animating.

Each of these UI sections is explained in more detail in the following pages with a breakdown of the major components.

The following conventions are used throughout this book:

click - click with the left mouse button

MM click - click with the Middle Mouse button

RM click - click with the Right Mouse button

The Menu Bar

If you've ever played with a computer, you should be familiar with the layout of menu bars, so let's keep this brief. Here is a rundown of what to expect in each of the menus shown in Figure 3.2. Feel free to click along with the text to see for yourself what is in each menu.

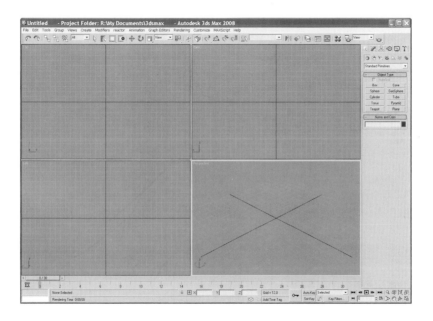

Figure 3.1

The default 3ds Max screen

Figure 3.2

The menu bar

⑤ **Untitled**   **- Project Folder: R:\My Documents\3dsmax**

File   Edit   Tools   Group   Views   Create   Modifiers   reactor   Animation   Graph Editors   Rendering   Customize   MAXScript   Help

File Menu Here you will find the familiar commands for file management, including commands for creating, opening, and saving scenes; importing/exporting outside formats; setting project folders; viewing images; displaying/changing scene properties; asset tracking; viewing an informational summary about your file, and exiting.

Edit Menu This contains the commands for editing and selecting objects in your scene. This is one of the areas where you will find the Undo/Redo functions, as well as easy selection methods such as Select All. Under the Select By submenu heading in the Edit menu, you can select objects in the scene using a certain criteria, such as by their color or name. Tools such as Move, Rotate, and Scale (transforms) are found here as well.

Tools This menu is where tools to manipulate your objects are located, such as Mirror or Align. Many of these tools and functions are found on the main toolbar and are also found in the Command panels. You'll see how several of these tools operate in the coming chapters.

Group Grouping lets you combine two or more objects into a single grouped object. Groups can be open or closed, depending on how you want the user to access objects inside the group. You can also permanently break up the group by ungrouping or exploding (a command that dissolves all nested groups).

Views Options to set up and control viewports. From here, for example, you can disable the view of your gizmos in the viewports or toggle your Home Grids on and off.

Create This menu gives tools for creating objects and is very extensive with many submenus. Everything that you would ever want to create for your 3D scene is found here. Some of the objects you created in the previous chapter for your mobile can be created through this menu as well as through the Command panel's Create panel, which you used in the mobile exercise.

Each of the main menus is divided into 15 categories. The main ones we will be using in this book are Standard Primitives, Extended Primitives, Shapes, Helpers, Lights, Camera, and Particles.

Modifiers A modifier is a type of 3ds Max object that controls and changes the basic structure of objects. Modifiers are used for modeling, animating, and adding special effects to objects. Through the Modifier menu you can apply modifiers to selected objects in the scene. Once applied, modifiers are edited through the Modify panel.

reactor This is a plug-in for 3ds Max that allows you to create complex dynamics such as cloth and fluid simulation and soft body dynamics. You will be introduced to reactor in Chapter 12, "Particles and Dynamics."

Animation This menu has features for animation, constraints, controllers, and Inverse Kinematics (IK), a feature that is used for character animation.

Graph Editors These are floating windows for managing a scene, hierarchy, and animation. Graph Editors give you access to scene components in graphical layout for easy use. Everything from nodes (a node represents an object in 3ds Max) to animation curves are displayed. Animation curves are animation expressed in mathematical graphs. It sounds harder than it is. You'll see plenty of curves later in the book.

Rendering These commands are for scene rendering, setting up an environment and render effects, accessing video post for in-program compositing, and using a RAM player. The Material Editor is also accessed under this menu, as is the Material/Map browser.

Customize This menu is for all things relating to user interface customization. This book will, for the most part, use the default layout for the 3ds Max UI, as that is most universal for the readers. Once you get a feeling for 3ds Max and are more comfortable with it, you'll find yourself customizing the UI to your tastes.

MAXScript These are commands for working with MAXScript, which is a scripting language for 3ds Max. MAXScript allows you to automate certain functions and program parts of your scene as needed. MAXScript will not be covered in this book because it is an advanced feature set.

Help This provides access to online references, tutorials, and online support, and it is perhaps the most important menu in the program.

Main Toolbar

The main toolbar puts the tools most commonly used in 3ds Max in a convenient location at the top of the interface. (See Figure 3.3) This toolbar can be rearranged as a floating palette or docked on the bottom, left, or right side of the interface. To do this, place your cursor to the far left side of the toolbar over the embossed vertical line. An icon of white boxes will appear next to your cursor. Click and drag to create a floating toolbar, or drag the toolbar to one side of the UI to dock it.

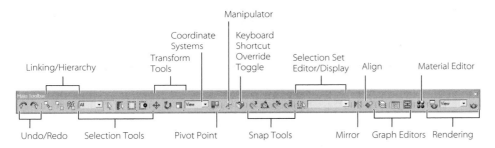

Figure 3.3

The main toolbar

You can also right-click on the embossed vertical line for a pop-up window, giving you options for docking and floating the toolbar, as shown in Figure 3.4. All palettes and bars in the 3ds Max interface can be rearranged in this fashion.

If your screen does not show all the icons shown in Figure 3.3, don't panic. Your display is probably set to a lower resolution than the width of the toolbar. In this case, you can scroll the toolbar left and right to expose the missing end of the toolbar. Place your cursor over an empty part of the toolbar (not on an icon) and it will turn into a hand icon,

as shown here. Click and drag to scroll the toolbar as needed.

The icons for the main toolbar are as shown in the following tables. You should use them as references while you use this book; you don't need to memorize everything here. For the most part, you will learn tools and functions in 3ds Max as you come across them in your work. Trying to memorize all the icons and their functions at the outset will just drive you nutty. Grab your mouse and click along through the examples in this chapter to get a feel for the icons.

Some icons, characterized by the small triangle in the lower-right corner have flyouts. *Flyouts* are additional options for the tool that appear as a context menu of new icons when you click and hold the icon, as shown here for the Scale tool.

Undo/Redo Icons

Undo and Redo are extremely useful in 3ds Max. You will find yourself painted into a corner many times—especially when you are first starting out—and Undo will let you back out of those corners. The icons are as follows:

ICON	NAME	FUNCTION
	Undo	Reverses the effect of the last action. Right-clicking the Undo button shows a list of the previous actions. You must select a continuous selection; you cannot skip over any items in the list.
	Redo	Cancels the last Undo. Right-clicking the Redo button shows a list of the previous actions. You must select a continuous selection; you cannot skip over any items in the list.

Figure 3.4
You can float menu bars easily in 3ds Max.

Linking and Hierarchy Icons

Linking and Hierarchy tools are used to parent objects for animation, as you saw with the Mobile exercise in Chapter 2. The icons are listed here:

ICON	NAME	FUNCTION
	Select and Link	Allows you to create a hierarchical link of child and parent between objects.
	Select and UnLink	Allows you to remove the hierarchical link of child and parent between objects.
	Select and Bind to Space Warp	Allows you to bind an object to a space warp effect (like gravity, wind, or displace).

Selection Tools Icons

Selection tools allow you to select objects in a scene using different methods. The icons are listed here:

ICON	NAME	FUNCTION
	Selection Filter List	Allows you to screen out certain objects that can be selected. For example, if you choose geometry from the list, you will not be able to select anything other than geometry. This is particularly helpful when you have a very crowded scene. You can also create combination filters such as cameras and lights together.
	Select Object	Allows you to select any object in your 3D scene.
	Select by Name	Allows you to select an object from a list within the Select from Scene dialog box, shown in Figure 3.5. The list contains objects currently in your scene and has filters for easy selection. For more on Select by Name, see below.
	Select Region flyout	Gives you different ways to select objects by defining a region, which is done by clicking and dragging in a viewport. There are five region selection methods: Rectangle (the default), Circular, Fence, Lasso, and Paint. These methods are similar to Photoshop's Marquee Selection and Lasso tools.
	Window/Crossing Selection	Switches between Window and Crossing modes when you select by region. If you are in Window mode, it will select only objects that are entirely inside the window's region. The default Crossing mode allows selection of objects that are touching the edge of the region. This tool will also work when you are selecting polygons in Sub-Object mode.

Figure 3.5

The Select by Name icon opens the Select from Scene window.

SELECT BY NAME ICON

When you click the Select by Name icon in the main toolbar, 3ds Max will bring up the Select from Scene dialog (Figure 3.5), which is an updated interface from previous versions of 3ds Max. With the Select from Scene dialog box, you can select any object in your scene, which is mighty handy if you have an extensive scene or need to select objects that are difficult to select through a viewport. While the window is open, you cannot edit anything in your scene until you click the Select button in the dialog to close the window. As you can see in Figure 3.5, the Select from Scene dialog box gives you information about the objects, such as their hierarchy and scene color.

This window is a trimmed down version of the more powerful Scene Explorer window, covered at the end of this chapter.

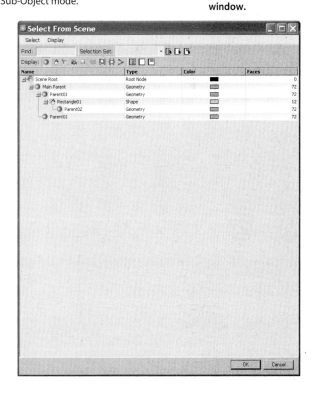

Transformation Tools Icons

As you saw in the previous chapter, transformation tools move, rotate, and scale your objects. Their icons are listed here:

ICON	NAME	FUNCTION
	Select and Move	Selects and moves objects. For all the transform tools (Move, Rotate, and Scale), you can click and drag a region box around the object or objects to select them. You can also invoke this tool with the W hot key.
	Select and Rotate	Selects and rotates objects. Clicking and dragging a region box around the object or objects selects them. You can also invoke this tool with the E hot key.
	Select and Scale	This icon leads to a flyout where you can access two other Scale tools. The default Scale tool is the Uniform Scale tool (left icon), which allows you to scale along all three axes evenly. The middle icon in the flyout is the Non-uniform Scale tool, which allows you to scale along the axis you choose. The right icon is the Squash Scale tool, which is a type of scale used mainly for the "squash and stretch" style of animation found in cartoons. When you are scaling down in one axis, it scales up in the other two, and vice versa. You can also invoke this tool with the R hot key.

Coordinate Systems, Center Pivots, and Manipulator Icons

As you saw in the first chapter, coordinate systems define the axes that you use. The icons for this section of the main toolbar are listed here:

ICON	NAME	FUNCTION
	Reference Coordinate System	Allows you to choose which coordinate system you want to use. Coordinate Systems are covered in depth at the end of Chapter 1, "Basic Concepts."
	Use Center flyout	The tools accessed through this flyout allow you to determine the pivot point of an object for its rotation and scale. The default setting, Use Pivot Point Center, is adequate for nearly all situations and is used throughout this book; however, this tool has a flyout that lets you relocate the center point of your transformation tool. You can use the tool if you have multiple objects selected.
	Select and Manipulate	Allows you to edit the parameters of certain objects, modifiers, and controllers by dragging manipulators in viewports. Manipulators are similar to the gizmos you've already used. Manipulators are an advanced way to edit and use objects in 3ds Max and are not covered in this book.
	Keyboard Shortcut Override	Determines which set of keyboard shortcuts are currently useable; when it is disabled, only the main UI shortcuts are recognized. When it is enabled, the main UI and the functional area shortcuts are recognized.

Snapping Icons

Snapping functions allow accurate placement of objects in your scene. When you enable a Snap function and then move an object, for example, 3ds Max will "snap" the object to points on the Home Grid or to other geometry in the scene. Because they let you snap to specific locations during creation and transformation of objects or sub-objects, Snaps give you control when you're creating, moving, rotating, and scaling objects.

There are several different types of snaps; you can snap to a grid, pivot, or vertex. You can turn snaps on and off by clicking their icons in the main toolbar or by pressing the S key while you are in the middle of a transform for an object. We will be using snaps in the following chapters. Right-clicking on a Snap function will open its Options window. In it, you can select exactly how you want to snap. Figure 3.6 shows the options for the Snaps toggle.

ICON	NAME	FUNCTION
	2D, 2.5D, and 3D Snap flyout	The 2D Snap (top) icon allows you to snap to the home or construction grid or to any shapes or geometry on the grid. This is the default Snap function.
		The 2.5D Snap (middle) icon allows you to snap to only vertices or edges of an object.
		The 3D Snap (bottom) icon will snap to any geometry in 3D space.
	Angle Snap	Allows you to set the increment of rotation for rotating an object in a given axis.
	Percent Snap	Allows you to define a set scaling increment when you are scaling an object. To set the increment you want to snap to, right-click the icon to open the Options window, as shown in Figure 3.7.
	Spinner Snap	Allows you to adjust numerical values. You will run into spinners constantly in 3ds Max. Use the Spinner Snap function to set the increment by which you want to increase or decrease a metric.

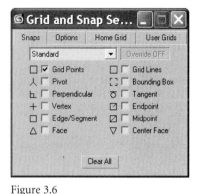

Figure 3.6

The Options window for the Snap functions

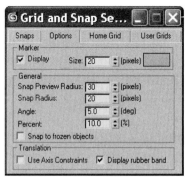

Figure 3.7

Right-clicking the Angle Snap or Percent Snap tool will open the Snap's Options window.

Named Selection Sets Icons

Selection sets are a way to easily select several objects at once. To create a selection set for your workflow, choose the objects you want it to contain, and then type a name for the set in the Named Selection Sets field. That name will be added to the drop-down menu so you can select all those objects in the set by selecting its name. Later in this book, we will further explore selection sets.

ICON	NAME	FUNCTION
	Named Selection sets	To create a named selection set, choose the objects for the selection set and enter a name for that set.
	Edit Named Selection Sets	Launches a menu that allows you to organize your selection sets and the objects that are members of those sets. Click the plus (+) or minus (–) to expand the object list for each set. The buttons along the top allow you to create or delete sets and add or remove objects. See Figure 3.8.

Figure 3.8

You can edit selection sets using this window.

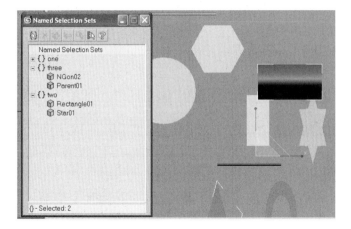

Align and Mirror Icons

The Align and Mirror icons are next up in this main toolbar discussion. The Mirror function (Figure 3.9) allows you to mirror an object's orientation. Click this icon to bring up the Mirror dialog box shown in Figure 3.9. In the dialog box, you can choose a mirror axis and offset the mirror amount. You can either mirror the object or create a clone that is mirrored by selecting the Copy option to duplicate the object mirrored.

ICON	NAME	FUNCTION
	Mirror	Mirrors the selected object in the chosen axis. Can also copy a mirror of the object.
	Align	The flyout gives you access to all the Align functions discussed in the following table. This Align icon is displayed by default.

Figure 3.9

The Mirror function

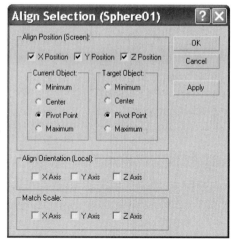

Figure 3.10

The Align options allow you to dictate how your objects are to be aligned.

The Align tools found in this flyout allow you to line up your object as discussed in the following table. Select the object you want to align, click the appropriate Align Tool icon from the flyout, and then click the target object to which the object is to be aligned. You will have a chance to see the Align and Mirror functions in action in Chapter 4, "Modeling in 3ds Max: Part I," and throughout the book.

ICON	NAME	FUNCTION
	Align	Once you click on the target object to align to, 3ds Max will open the Align dialog box shown in Figure 3.10. Here you can choose which axis to align your selected object to as a function of position, rotation, or even scale.
	Quick Align	Lets you instantly align the position of the current selection to that of a target object.
	Normal Align	Lets you align two objects based on the direction of the normal of a face or selection on each object. A *normal* is an imaginary line that is perpendicular to the surface of a geometry.
	Place Highlight	Lets you align a light or object to another object so that its highlight or reflection can be precisely positioned.
	Align Camera	Lets you align a camera to a selected face normal.
	Align to View	Lets you align an object with the current viewport.

Editing and Organizational Icons

Layers, the Curve Editor, and the Schematic View are three editing and organizational tools in 3ds Max. We will cover each of them later in this chapter. Their icons are explained in this table.

ICON	NAME	FUNCTION
	Layer Manager	Lets you manage sets of objects in layers. Very useful for large scenes and complicated setups.
	Curve Editor	Allows you to edit animation by manipulating mathematical curves.
	Schematic View	A node-based display of the objects in a scene that allows you to edit parameters as well as hierarchies.

The Material and Rendering Editors give you access to materials for shading and texturing, as well as options for rendering out your scene. These functions will be covered later in this chapter, along with other commonly used windows and panels. Their icons are as follows:

ICON	NAME	FUNCTION
	Material Editor	Accesses materials you can add to scene objects to give them their final look when rendered (also known as texturing or shading).
	Render Scene dialog box	Lets you create renderings and save them to files. The Render Scene dialog box has multiple panels.
	Quick Render (Production)	Lets you render the scene using the current production render settings without displaying the Render Scene dialog box.
	Quick Render (Active Shader)	Creates an ActiveShade rendering in a floating window. This icon is a flyout of the Quick Render (Production) icon.

Whoa! Did You Get All That?

That was a lot to take in!

Don't worry. There is absolutely no need to memorize all this material.

You will see most of these tools in action in the next few chapters, and before long, using them (and recognizing their icons) will be second nature to you. This part of the book is designed as a reference guide, so bookmark these pages for easy access later.

Command Panels

Everything you need to create, manipulate, and animate objects can be found here. As you saw in the previous chapter, the Command panel (shown here) is divided into tabs according to function. This lets you access several commands and functions through the different panels that comprise a quick workflow in 3ds Max.

The function or toolset you need to access will determine which panel you need to click. The division of panel tabs is very instinctive and easy to decipher.

You can scroll up and down a panel to access tools that are not visible on the screen because the panel is too long vertically. When you encounter a panel that is longer than your screen, 3ds Max will display a thin vertical scroll bar on the right side, as shown previously. Your pointer will also turn into a hand that lets you click and drag the panel up and down. Try it. It's fun!

You will be exposed to more panels as you progress through this book. Here is a rundown of the Command Panel functions and what they do. They are discussed in more detail in later sections of this chapter.

ICON	NAME	FUNCTION
	Create panel	Lets you create objects, lights, cameras, etc.
	Modify panel	Lets you apply and edit modifiers to objects
	Hierarchy panel	Lets you adjust hierarchy for objects and adjust their pivots
	Motion panel	Lets you access animation tools and functions
	Display panel	Lets you access display options for scene objects
	Utilities panel	Lets you access several functions of 3ds Max, such as motion capture utilities and the asset browser

Create Panel

The first panel, the Create panel, is used primarily for creating various objects for your scene. You can create seven categories of objects. The panels under the Create panel are listed here:

ICON	NAME	FUNCTION
	Geometry	Lets you create renderable objects, such as primitives or parametric objects
	Shapes	Lets you create 2D lines and splines of various shapes
	Lights	3ds Max lights simulate real-world lights to illuminate objects in the scene
	Camera	Lets you create cameras to view and render your 3D scene
	Helpers	Helper objects are aids to constructing a scene
	Space Warp	Objects that deform the appearance of other objects
	Systems	Catch-all panel containing functions such as Bones and Biped Animation tools, as well as lighting systems to simulate sun and daylight

Figure 3.11

The Create Geometry category for the Create panel

Figure 3.12

Creating shapes in the Create panel

Figure 3.13

Creating lights

Figure 3.14

Camera Creation category in the Creation panel

Geometry

The Geometry category in the Create panel is responsible for renderable objects, also known as primitives or *parametric objects* (objects whose parameters may be changed at any time to adjust their original shape or appearance). The default is Standard Primitives. Click on the drop-down window to access more object types, such as extended primitives, compound objects, and particles.

When you created the mobile in the previous chapter, you made several shapes and modified them. You can access many of these creation objects through the Create menu as well (Figure 3.11).

Shapes

Shapes are 2D lines or splines that can be used as is. You can also use them to create objects using modifiers, such as Extrude, as you saw in the Mobile exercise. You can use stock shapes, such as a circle or rectangle, or you can use the Line tool to create free-form shapes. Lines are used as components to create other objects. You can use splines to create motion paths, extrusions, lathes, lofts, and 3D objects. The drop-down menu will give you access to NURBS and extended splines. Figure 3.12 shows the Shapes Creation option.

Lights

Lights in 3ds Max, just like lights in the real world, are used to illuminate objects. You can create lights that simulate indoor lights (such as incandescent or florescent lights), outdoor lights (such as the sun or street lights), or lights that don't simulate anything but the look you need for your scene. 3D lights are designed to simulate lights in the real world. 3ds Max provides two types of lights: Standard and Photometric. The different light types are available in the drop-down menu. Standard lights simulate the basic light rigs used in film and stage, and Photometric lights are used to simulate *radiosity* (bounced light) within 3D environments. You will use both kinds of lights later in this book when you learn how to light and render your scenes (Figure 3.13).

Camera

Camera objects are designed to simulate real-world still and motion cameras. They are used to record the action you animate, and they output through rendering. Just like real-world cameras, 3ds Max's camera objects allow you to use a variety of lens types. There is a standard camera and there is a camera that has a target to make it easier to follow an object or action. You'll get to use cameras a lot in Chapter 11, "3ds Max Rendering." You can see the Camera Creation category in Figure 3.14.

Helpers

Helpers take care of the unglamorous and thankless jobs in 3ds Max. They help you construct scenes, but they aren't necessarily part of the scenes. Helpers help you position, measure, and animate a scene's renderable geometry. Figure 3.15 shows the various helpers you can create.

Space Warps

Space warps are objects that deform or animate objects in your scene. They are known as *deformers* in other animation packages, such as Maya. You can create ripples and waves and even blow up objects by applying Space Warp objects to them. In order for the space warp to work, it must be bound to the object using "bind to space warp." The drop-down menu shown in Figure 3.16 lists the different space warps available.

Systems

The Systems category holds some advanced functions of 3ds Max. This is where you'll go to set up Sun and Daylight lighting systems or Bones systems to animate a character or object rig. Figure 3.17 shows the various systems you can create.

Modify Panel

The Modify panel, as you saw with the Mobile project, houses all the modifiers you can apply to an object. It also houses a selected object's Modifier Stack. Using this stack, you can reorder or remove the modifiers for an object, which can be invaluable in creating precisely the right object for your scene.

This panel also allows you to change and animate the parameters for an existing object, such as the radius or length of a cylinder, even after it has been created.

Modifiers are the bread and butter of editing objects in 3ds Max. This form of workflow is terrific because you can stack modifiers on top of each other when creating an object and then go back and edit any of the modifiers in the stack (for the most part) to adjust the object at any point in its creation. This sort of workflow, where any stage of the creation process can be adjusted at any time, is akin to a *node-based* editing workflow. Figure 3.18 shows the Modify panel for a selected Sphere object.

Almost all the parameters in the Modify panel can be animated. For example, you can create a sphere and animate its radius. Then you can add a taper modifier and animate the taper amount. You can also go into the sub-object level of a modifier, such as an FFD (free-form deformation), select the control points, and animate the points on the lattice. This can give you layer upon layer of animation. The downside of this is that editing the animation can be a nightmare. For instance, with the FFD, each control point has its own track in the Curve Editor. So, if you have a lattice with 4 × 4 × 4, you would have to edit 64 potential tracks. Yikes!

Figure 3.15

Helpers help you create your scene.

Figure 3.16

Creating space warps

Figure 3.17

Systems creation

Figure 3.18

The Modify panel for a sphere

There are two types of modifiers. World Space modifiers attach to an object but use world space instead of local space. Object Space modifiers affect an object's geometry in local space. Figure 3.19 shows a Bend modifier applied to a box. The Bend modifier does what it says: It bends the geometry. It is an example of an Object Space modifier because it affects the entire object as one piece.

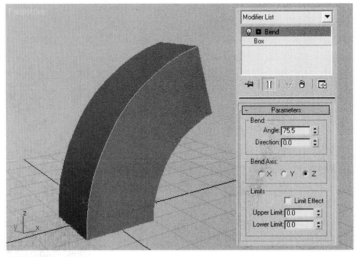

Figure 3.19

A Bend modifier is applied to a box through the Modify panel.

Hierarchy Panel

The Hierarchy panel is where you create and edit the hierarchies for your objects. As you saw in the Mobile project, creating parent-child relationships through linking allowed you to create complex animations—i.e., different rotations on different parts of the mobile. The children objects—or *nodes*—travel with their parents, but retain the ability to have their own motions once they inherit their parents' motion(s).

Pivot

In the Hierarchy panel, you can also adjust the position of an object's pivot point. As you've already seen, the pivot point plays a critical role in how an object moves, rotates, and scales. Having control of the pivot is important to setting up the proper animation for any given object. All objects have a *pivot point,* which is a center for all transforms. A pivot also defines the transform relationship of a hierarchy, sets the center location of an added modifier, and defines IK (Inverse Kinematics) joint locations.

In the Pivot category of the Hierarchy panel, you can adjust the pivot by moving it, centering it, or aligning it to another object or the world space, as shown in Figure 3.20.

Figure 3.20

The Hierarchy panel's Pivot category is a must for proper animation setup.

IK

Inverse Kinematics (IK) is a method often used in character animation; it provides an easier way to move the parts of a character's armature by using IK handles to place the limb's extremities, such as the feet. You simply animate the placement of the feet, and IK solves all the necessary rotations of the leg bones and animates the legs into the proper placement for the feet. The IK category gives you all the tools you need for adjusting hierarchical linkage between objects. The IK panel is shown in Figure 3.21. You will see how IK and bones work in Chapter 9, "Character Studio and IK Animation."

Link Info

Link Info is a great way to set limits for the motions of your objects. The Link Info section allows you to restrict the movement of objects in a hierarchy by limiting from which axes motion is inherited from parents.

Try this exercise:

1. In a new scene, create a box of any size and a Teapot object of similar size. You can find the teapot in the Create panel's Geometry Standard Primitive category.

2. Link the teapot to the box so that the box is the parent of the teapot, as shown here:

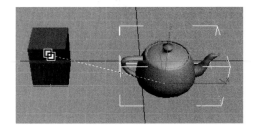

3. Press the W hotkey for the Move tool. Select and move the teapot first in the *X*-axis, then in the *Y*-axis, and then in the *Z*-axis. The teapot freely moves with the box (assuming the link was created successfully).

4. Select and move the teapot in all three axes as you did the box. The teapot moves in all directions.

5. Select the teapot and click on the Hierarchy panel. In the panel, select the Link Info section. Under the Locks heading rollout, check the box in the Move section for the *X*-axis. In the Inherit heading rollout, uncheck the box for Move in the *Y*-axis, as shown here.

Figure 3.21

The IK section of the Hierarchy panel

Figure 3.22

The Parameters in the Motion panel allow you to edit keyframes of an object's animation.

Figure 3.23

The Trajectories option in the Motion panel gives you a visual display of your animation's path.

6. Select and move the teapot separately in the three axes. You'll see that the teapot has been locked in the *X*-axis and will not move at all in *X*. This is what a lock does to an object, no matter where it is in a hierarchy.

7. Select the box and move it separately in all three axes. You'll see that the teapot, except the *Y*-axis, moves along with the box as it should. The teapot is restricted from inheriting any motion in the *Y*-axis from the box parent. This is what an inheritance lock does to a child under a moving parent.

Motion Panel

The Motion panel houses all the tools for controlling animated objects using keyframes editing and animation controllers. You will have a chance to play with keyframes and controllers in Chapter 8, "Introduction to Animation." The Parameters option allows you to edit keyframes without using the Curve Editor, which is usually the preferred and more powerful way to edit keyframes (Figure 3.22).

The Trajectories option in the Motion panel (Figure 3.23) allows you to display the path that an object travels in its animation. This way you can actually see the movement an object takes in its animation and adjust it visually to change its course.

Display Panel

The Display panel (Figure 3.24) allows you to choose how an object appears in your viewports. Use the Display panel to Hide/Unhide, Freeze/Unfreeze, and alter display characteristics of objects. This ability is extremely useful when you need to organize your scenes, no matter what their size.

The Hide by Category heading rollout allows you to turn off types of objects in 3ds Max to let you focus on certain objects. For example, if you have a scene replete with objects, but you only need to adjust your lights, you can easily turn off your geometry and shapes to better see where your lights are in the scene.

Hiding objects is useful for getting parts of your scene out of the way temporarily. Hiding, as it implies, turns offs the display of the hidden object. Similarly, freezing objects allows you to still see frozen objects, but not select or transform them. This feature is useful when you still need to reference a model but don't want to move it accidentally. When you freeze an object, its display in the viewports turns dark gray by default.

The larger and more complicated your scenes become, the more you can rely on the Display panel to help you with your scene.

You can also use the Layer toolbar, which is covered later in this chapter, to help you organize large scenes.

Utilities Panel

The Utilities panel (Figure 3.25) allows you to access different utility programs, or *plug-ins,* inside 3ds Max. Some plug-ins are already shipped with 3ds Max, and some are third-party applications from various software makers. One such utility is Motion Capture, which allows you to import and work with animation data captured using external devices, such as a joystick or a midi device configured to mimic puppetry animation. These utilities are all advanced and will not be covered in this book.

Controls at the Bottom of the UI

Time controls, animation controls, playback controls, and viewport controls are aligned at the bottom edge of the 3ds Max UI. This section covers the icons and functions.

Time Slider and Track Bar

Running across the bottom of the 3ds Max UI are the Time slider and the track bar, as shown in Figure 3.26.

The Time slider allows you to move through any frame in your scene by *scrubbing* (moving the slider back and forth). By scrubbing, you can also view your animation playback in the viewports. You can move through your animation one frame at a time by clicking on the arrows on either side of the Time slider or by pressing the < and > keys.

You can also use the Time slider to animate objects by setting keyframes. A right-click on the Time slider brings up a Create Key dialog box, which allows you to create transform keyframes for the selected object. Figure 3.27 shows the Create Key window.

The track bar is directly below the Time slider. The track bar is the timeline that displays the timeline format for your scene. More often than not, this is displayed in frames, with each tick mark representing frames. On the track bar, you can move and edit your animation properties for the selected object. When a keyframe is present, right-click it to reveal individual transform values; these values can be edited within the dialog box. From this pop-up menu, you can delete keyframes and filter the Track Bar display. You will have a chance to explore using these tools in the chapters on animation in this book.

Figure 3.24

The Display panel is important to keeping your scene organized.

Figure 3.25

The Utilities panel

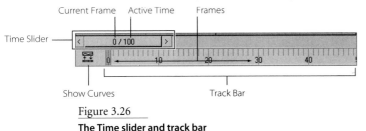

Figure 3.26

The Time slider and track bar

Figure 3.27

The Create Key window lets you set a keyframe for a selected object by right-clicking the Time slider.

The icon to the left of the track bar is the Mini Curve Editor icon. This toggle displays a version of the Track View Curve Editor. The Track View Curve Editor shows you your scene's animation as curves that you can edit.

The Status Bar

The status bar in 3ds Max gives you feedback and information as you work in your scene. The status bar runs across about two-thirds of the bottom of the screen as shown in Figure 3.28. Check it out, you'll love it.

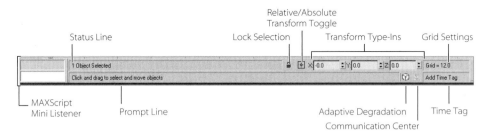

Figure 3.28

The status bar is full of useful information.

Here are the elements on the status bar.

MAXScript Mini Listener This is a command prompt used for entering and viewing feedback for MAXScript. MAXScript is the scripting language used in 3ds Max to automate actions and customize functions. This line displays a single line of the actual MAXScript Listener window, which gives you easier access in a window to MAXScript.

Status Line Displays the number and type of objects selected in your scene.

Lock Selection When your object is selected, Lock Selection lets you lock the object so you won't inadvertently deselect or select something else in your scene. The icon turns yellow when turned on. The keyboard shortcut for this tool is the spacebar.

Relative/Absolute Transform Toggle When you enter values in the Transform Type-In boxes (as you did with the Mobile exercise in the previous chapter), 3ds Max treats the values as *absolute*. If you set the toggle to *relative*, the values you enter will be used to offset the selected object from its current state.

Coordinate Display You can enter values in these boxes (delineated as *X, Y,* and *Z* values) to transform the selected object, whether it is moving, rotating, or scaling. The Coordinate Display allows you to specify exact values for transforms instead of using the gizmo. When nothing is selected and you are moving the cursor around in a viewport, the Coordinate Display area shows the coordinates of your cursor.

Grid Settings Shows the size of one grid square on the Home Grid in your viewport. To edit the size of your grid squares, go to the Grid and Snap Settings dialog box. This can be found by choosing Customize → Grid and Snap Settings (or by right-clicking the Snap Toggle tool) and clicking the Home Grid tab.

Prompt Line This line in the status bar is similar to a guy who stands behind you and taps you on the shoulder to tell you what you need to do next. Here, 3ds Max displays instructions that prompt you for the next action in a function, such as "Click and drag to select and move objects" when the Move tool is active. The Prompt Line gives you ongoing feedback as you work with a tool. It can be a good place to look when you're unsure of what to do next. In addition, Tool Tips are displayed here when you mouse over icons and buttons. Mousing around and checking icon names is a good way to become more familiar with the interface.

Adaptive Degradation This toggle helps improve performance in the viewports whenever you transform geometry, change your view, or play back an animation by decreasing the display quality of certain objects temporarily while you are making the transform or change. Only when your 3ds Max scenes become large, or your system's performance is low, will this toggle be truly handy. Right-click this icon to access the new Adaptive Degradation priority settings

Communication Center This notification system keeps you up to date on new service packs available for 3ds Max and provides information for members of the Autodesk Subscription Program. The Communication Center can give you information such as product tricks and tips and support info.

Time Tag Time Tag is an animation assistant that allows you to set up tags at a certain point in your animation that you can easily jump to by selecting the tag's name.

Animation Controls

The Animation controls are a selection of icons to the right of the status bar that are used in animation. Figure 3.29 shows the icons.

The functions of the Animation controls are covered in Chapter 8, "Introduction to Animation." The rundown on the icons is as follows:

Set Key Sets a keyframe for the selected object(s) at the current frame for all tracks of the object. A *track* is a specific translation type (move, rotate, and/or scale, or a parameter) on a specific axis. The keyboard hot key for Set Key is K.

Auto Key Animation Mode Toggles the Keyframing mode on and off. The icon turns red when Auto Key mode is on. Keyframes are automatically created when Auto Key icon is on and objects are transformed. You don't need to set a key manually while in the Auto Key mode.

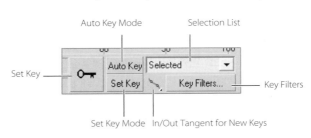

Figure 3.29

The Animation controls

Set Key Animation Mode You can create specific keyframes for a selected object by placing the object as you like and then setting a keyframe manually. This Animation mode, along with the Key Filters (discussed next), allows you to control exactly which tracks are keyed while you animate. With Set Key mode off, any keys you set will set for all tracks by default.

Key Filters Clicking this icon will open the Set Key Filters window shown in Figure 3.30. This window is where you can pick the tracks and the desired axis or axes you want to be keyframed as you animate. This keeps your scene free of extra keyframes you may not need.

Selection List Gives you quick access to named selection sets and track sets while you are working with Set Key. Lets you easily swap between different selection sets and track sets.

In/Out Tangent for New Keys Shortcut for setting up tangent types for keys on curves for animation created with Set Key or Auto Key. This is only for new keyframes. Curves and keyframes are covered in detail in Chapter 8.

Figure 3.30

The Set Key Filters window allows you to select the keyframes for which you want tracks set.

Animation Playback Controls

The Animation Playback controls (Figure 3.31) are similar to the ones you would find on a VCR (how old are you?) or DVD player.

Go to Start Moves the Time slider to the first frame in the active time segment.

Previous Frame/Key Moves the Time slider back one frame or one key, depending on the Key Mode toggle.

Play/Stop Plays your animation in the active viewport. The icon is a flyout that lets you access another icon (an outline of a play arrow instead of the filled black arrow) to play only the animation of selected objects instead of the entire scene.

Go to End Moves the Time slider to the last frame in the active time segments.

Next Frame/Key Moves the Time Slider forward one frame or one key, depending on the Key Mode Toggle.

Current Frame Also called *Go to Frame*, this field displays the current frame. It allows you to enter a frame number in the field to jump your Time slider to that frame. There is also a spinner that you can click/drag to change the frame number.

Figure 3.31

The Animation Playback controls run your playback.

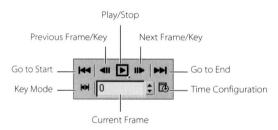

Key Mode This tool allows you to jump from one keyframe to another. In order for it to work, you must enable it and then use the Previous and Next Key icons to move from one frame to the next. When active, the Key Mode icon turns cyan, and the Previous Key and Next Key icons appear as shown in Figure 3.32.

Figure 3.32

Stepping keys instead of frames

Time Configuration A dialog (Figure 3.33) that allows control over frame rates, time display, playback, and animation. You can use this to scale your animation length so it goes faster or slower, or to add more frames to the start or end of your animation. This is covered further in Chapter 8.

Figure 3.33

The Time Configuration window

Viewport Navigation Controls

The tools for viewport navigation are extensive, and many of the icons have nested flyouts that give access to multiple tools. The available tools change depending on the viewport you have selected, such as Orthographic, User (a 3D view that is created when an orthographic view is rotated), Perspective, Camera, or Light. Working with the UI is the best way to learn what tools are associated with each viewport.

When a navigation tool is selected, it turns yellow and stays selected until you choose another tool, right-click in a viewport, or press Esc.

Viewports are used for orthographic and perspective views, and also for views through cameras and lights. By setting a viewport to a view from a camera or light, you can easily position the camera or light exactly as you need it using the Viewport Navigation controls, working interactively as you watch the result in that viewport. (We will experiment with cameras and lights in later chapters in this book.)

The Navigation controls, as they appear when the Perspective viewport is active, are as shown in Figure 3.34

Figure 3.35 shows how the icons appear while an Orthographic view is active.

Figures 3.36 and 3.37 show the default icons for a light and a camera, respectively.

In the following tables, all of the Navigation icons are laid out and briefly explained. The 3ds Max screen has a lot of icons, but experience will help you make sense of things very quickly. Take a look at these icons and click around to get a feel for how they work.

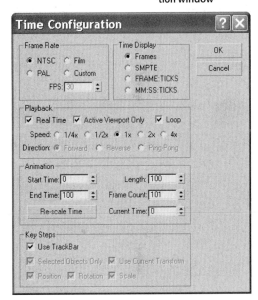

Figure 3.34

The default Viewport Navigation icons for a Perspective viewport

Figure 3.35

The default Viewport Navigation icons for the Orthographic viewports

Figure 3.36

The default Viewport Navigation icons for a light

Figure 3.37

The default Viewport Navigation icons for a camera

Create a few objects to have something to look at in your viewports, or open the Mobile exercise scene file. Spend some time poking around the viewports and looking at things. Use the Viewport Navigation controls and their key/mouse combinations to get used to navigating a bit more.

> The key to getting good at navigating 3ds Max, or any other 3d package, is to work on projects and get things done. You will gain the skills you need as you work toward a goal. As you will see, the exercises in the rest of this book will let you flex your muscles and give you a chance to become comfortable with 3ds Max.

The individual icons are explained in the following tables. Refer back to Figures 3.34 through 3.37 to see the icons' locations on the UI.

Tools Available in All Viewports

These icons are available in all of the viewports in Figures 3.34 through 3.37.

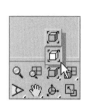

Keep in mind that some of the following icons are nested icons beneath flyouts; to reveal them you will need to click and hold the flyout icon. An example of a flyout for the Navigation controls is shown here:

ICON	NAME	FUNCTION
	Zoom Extends All	Works like the Zoom Extend tool, but lets you zoom in your scene in all four viewports. The keyboard shortcut for this tool is Z.
	Zoom Extends All Selected	Works like Zoom Extends All for objects that you have selected.
	Min/Max Viewport	Toggles between Normal and Full Screen viewport sizing. The keyboard shortcut is Alt+W.
	Pan View	Lets you move the selected viewport up, down, and side to side. The shortcut Ctrl+P; you can also click/drag the middle mouse button.

Tools Available in Perspective and Orthographic Viewports

These icons (refer back to Figures 3.34 and 3.35) appear available in the Perspective and Orthographic viewports. Keep in mind that some of the following icons are nested beneath flyouts.

ICON	NAME	FUNCTION
	Zoom	Zoom magnifies the objects in your viewport from big to small by moving the view in and out of 3D space in the scene. Zoom works the same way in both the Perspective and Orthographic viewports. The keyboard shortcut is Ctrl+Alt+MM. If your mouse has a middle dial, you can use it as a Zoom tool by centering your pointer in the selected viewport and rolling the dial to zoom in and out.
	Zoom All	Works like Zoom but lets you zoom all four viewports at once.

ICON	NAME	FUNCTION
	Zoom Extents	This flyout icon works like a "Fit to Window" function because it zooms all objects in your scene into the viewport. It only works for Orthographic and Perspective viewports.
	Zoom Extents Selected	This flyout icon is nested with Zoom Extents. It works like the Zoom Extents tool for selected objects only.
	Field-of-View (FOV)	This flyout icon nested with Zoom Region is available in the Perspective or Camera. FOV changes the amount of the scene that you can see in the viewport by adjusting the field of view. It zooms in and out like a camera lens. (This is not the same as Zoom, which moves the view in and out of the scene.)
	Zoom Region	This flyout icon nested with Field of View allows you to drag a rectangle marquee around the area you want to zoom in on. This tool is available only in Orthographic/User and Perspective viewports.
	Walkthrough	This flyout icon is nested with Pan View (the hand icon). This very cool tool lets you move through a viewport by pressing the arrow keys. It is similar to the Pan tool, but you use the arrow key for navigation instead of the mouse. When you enter the Walkthrough Navigation mode, the pointer changes to a hollow circle that shows a directional arrow while you are pressing one of the arrow keys. Walkthrough is available only for Perspective and Camera viewports.
	Arc Rotate	This flyout Icon is nested with Arc Rotate Selected and Arc Rotate SubObject. Arc Rotate lets you rotate a viewport by clicking and dragging a series of handles on the gizmo (shown in Figure 3.38). Uses the viewport center as the center for its rotation. The shortcuts are Alt+MM and Ctrl+R.
	Arc Rotate Selected	This flyout icon is nested with Arc Rotate and Arc Rotate SubObject. This icon has a white circle. It works like Arc Rotate but uses the selected object as the center for rotation. The object remains in the same position as the viewport rotates around the object.
	Arc Rotate SubObject	This flyout icon is nested with Arc Rotate and Arc Rotate Selected and has a yellow circle. It works similarly to Arc Rotate Selected, but it rotates about the current SubObject selection.

Camera Viewport Controls

A camera view shows your scene through the lens of a virtual camera. These tools control the Camera viewport. The specific tools available will change depending on whether you are using a Free or Target camera. (Cameras are covered in Chapter 11.)

Again, use this section as a reference, and click along with the descriptions. You don't need to memorize it all or understand everything at once. You can come back to this chapter when you need to look up something.

To access these navigation tools, you will need to create a camera and switch a viewport to its view. To create a camera, follow these steps in a new scene or a current scene:

1. Choose Create → Cameras → Free Camera, and click in one of your viewports to place the camera. You may also click in the Create panel under the Cameras category and click the Free icon. Figure 3.38 shows a camera placed in the scene.

Figure 3.38

A camera

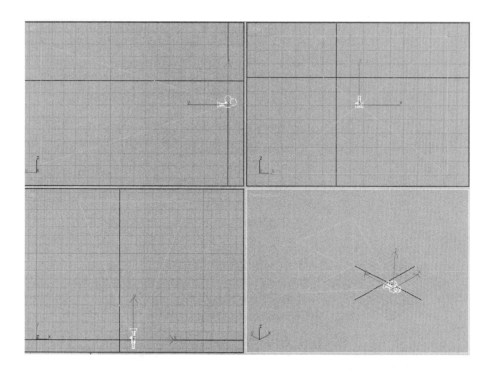

2. Right-click a viewport name in the upper-left corner of the viewport, and select Views → Camera01, as shown in Figure 3.39. This will change the viewport to the camera's view. You will now be able to access the Camera Viewport navigation tools shown in the following table.

Figure 3.39

Set your viewport to the new camera.

Now that you have created a Free Camera in your scene, click the following icons as you explore to see how they'll help you navigate in a Camera viewport. Some of these navigation icons apply to a Target camera only, and several of these icons are flyouts nested with other icons:

ICON	NAME	FUNCTION
↕	Dolly Camera	Moves the camera object to and from the object at which it is pointing.
↕	Dolly Target	Moves the camera's target to and from the object. This may not show any changes unless you use other camera tools, such as Orbit.

ICON	NAME	FUNCTION
	Dolly Camera + Target	Moves the camera and target to and from the object at which it is pointing. This is available only if the camera has a target.
	Perspective	Adjusts Field Of View (FOV) and Dolly. Acts like a zoom camera lens.
	Roll	Rolls the camera around the line of sight for a Target camera or (if it is a Free camera) around the local Z-axis.
	Truck	Moves the camera from side to side, parallel to your scene.
	Orbit	Rotates the camera around the target object selected in the scene. This is a flyout with the Pan Camera icon.
	Pan Camera	Rotates the target around the camera. This is a flyout with the Orbit icon.

Light Viewport Controls

This set of tools shows your scene through the perspective of a light. This may seem a bit unusual, but it can be very useful for exact positioning of your lights. Some tools for the light objects have the same names (Dolly, Roll, Truck, Orbit and Pan) and are used the same way as the Camera navigation tools. Therefore, their icons are not repeated here. However, the Light Viewport controls that are specific to lights are listed.

You will need to create a light in your scene to access these icons in the Viewport Controls section of the UI. To create a light in the scene, follow these steps:

1. Choose Create → Lights → Standard Lights → Free Spotlight and click in one of your viewports to place the camera. You may also click the Create panel under the Lights category, and click the Free Spot icon. Figure 3.40 shows a light placed in the scene.

2. Right-click a viewport name in the upper-left corner of the viewport, and select Views → Fspot01, as shown in Figure 3.41. This will change the viewport to the light's view. You will now be able top access the Camera Viewport navigation tools shown in the following table:

ICON	NAME	FUNCTION
	Light Hotspot	Lets you adjust the angle of the light's hotspot, which is the brightest part of the circle of light.
	Light Falloff	Lets you adjust the angle of the light's falloff, which is the light fading to the back of the circle of light.

Light Viewport controls help you place your lights just the way you want them. (You'll get more hands-on experience with lights in Chapter 10, "3ds Max Lighting.")

If you are getting sick of looking at icons, remember that nearly all viewport navigation tasks can be performed using the keyboard shortcuts and the mouse buttons. This rich set of navigation tools gives you many options for moving around in 3D space, but you needn't really worry about any of them until you are comfortable just getting around—and by now this should be coming easier to you.

Figure 3.40

A Free spotlight

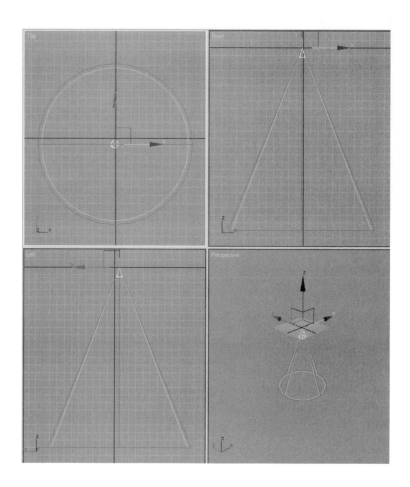

Figure 3.40

A Free spotlight

Navigating Viewports

The easiest way to navigate the viewports is to use the keyboard/mouse button combinations you used in the previous chapter while working on the Mobile exercise. Here is a review of these keyboard/mouse actions.

Figure 3.41

Set your viewport to the new light.

Pan Panning a viewport will "slide" the view around the screen. MM+click in the viewport and drag the mouse to move the view.

Zoom Zooming will move your view in closer or farther away from your objects. To zoom, use the middle wheel, or press Ctrl+Alt and MM+click in your viewport, and then drag the mouse up or down to zoom in or out, respectively. Zooming is called *dollying* in some other packages, and *zoom* sometimes is used to refer to the virtual camera's lens.

Arc Rotate and Arc Rotate Selected Arc Rotate and Arc Rotate Selected let you rotate your view around your objects. To use either of the two Arc Rotate tools, press Alt and MM+click and drag in the viewport. Use Shift+Alt+ MM for constrained rotation. By default, 3ds Max will rotate (or *tumble* as it's called in some other CG programs) about the center of the viewport to change your perspective. However, if an object is selected, 3ds Max will revert to Arc Rotate Selected, which will rotate about the center of the selected object instead of the center of the viewport. This way the object remains in the same position as the viewport rotates around the object.

The Viewports

Viewports are where 3D space is simulated. Viewports in 3ds Max are always set up with four equally sized views when you first start (Top, Front, Left, and Perspective viewport). One will have a yellow highlighted border, which shows that this viewport is the selected view. You can activate a view by working in it or by right-clicking in it. (Be careful about left-clicking because if something is selected, it will be deselected.)

You can also resize your viewports by centering the pointer over the splitter bars that separate the views. It will change to a four-sided arrow, and you can click/drag the viewports to the size desired. To switch the viewport layout back to the default, right-click over the center splitter bars. A pop-up tag with "Reset Layout" will allow you to go back to the default.

Let's not forget the Min/Max Viewport tool in the navigation area (its hot key is Alt+W). This will change the equally sized views into one full-screen view of the active viewport.

One way to change the default look of your viewports is to use the Viewport Configuration/Layout dialog box. You can find it by choosing Customize → Viewport Configuration and clicking the desired layout, as shown in Figure 3.42.

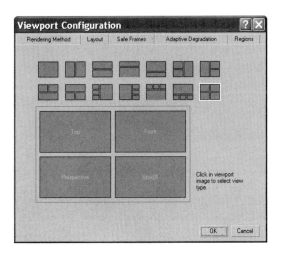

Figure 3.42

The Viewport Configuration window allows you to quickly change your viewport layouts.

In each of the viewports, the axes are displayed in the lower-left corner of the World Space tripod. The axes are always displayed in red, green, and blue format to represent the *X*-, *Y*-, and *Z*-axes respectively, as seen in the Perspective viewport. You have seen this familiar color scheme at work in the gizmos as well.

You've undoubtedly noticed the Home Grid in your views by now. This grid is a ground plane that centers around the Origin (0,0,0). The Home Grid tab lets you set the spacing of your Home Grid.

The Home Grid is a helper for construction of objects. When you create a new object, it is placed on the grid. The Home Grid's defaults can be edited for more effective scene creation, and they can be turned on and off easily by right-clicking the viewport name to access the pop-up menu. In that menu, you will see Show Grid. Click the grid to toggle it on and off. To use the keyboard shortcut to toggle the grid, press G.

The grid displays the units of your scene. The default is set up as Max Units where one unit equals 1 inch. Each grid division is 10 units. The best approach is to choose a grid spacing that matches your unit of measurement. For example, if you are using centimeters, make one grid square equal 1 centimeter. To access the Grid dialog box, choose Customize → Grid and Snap Settings, and click the Home Grid tab as shown here.

Changing Viewport Views

As you saw earlier, the viewports are flexible and can be changed to different displays by right-clicking on the viewport name and choosing the new viewport from the menu (Figure 3.43).

This lets you change which view you have in a viewport. You can also use keyboard shortcuts to access any of the viewports. In an active viewport, press the hotkey for the desired view. Hot keys are listed in this table:

HOTKEY	VIEW
T	Top
B	Bottom
F	Front
L	Left
C	Camera
P	Perspective
U	User or Axonometric—a 3D view without perspective

Figure 3.43

Changing viewports is easy.

These keys are extremely helpful when one viewport is maximized and you need to access different views quickly. For scenes that have more than one camera, press the C key to bring up a pop-up menu from which you can select the camera. With so many ways to change viewport views, you'll be able to find the way that works best for your workflow.

Because the R shortcut enables the Select and Scale tool, there is no keyboard shortcut for the Right viewport.

Viewport Rendering Levels

Viewports let you view your scene in a few different ways. For example, in the Mobile exercise, you saw how you can switch between Wireframe and Smooth + Highlight Shaded views. How you view objects in a viewport is referred to as *viewport rendering.* Again, you can access a different viewport rendering method by right-clicking the viewport's name, as shown in Figure 3.44. Depending on the size of your scene, your viewport may be more responsive and have a less-taxing rendering display level than the one shown here.

Figure 3.44

Selecting the viewport's rendering level

Each of the viewport rendering levels has specific properties.

Smooth+Highlights Displays scene objects with smooth shading and specular highlights from the scene lights. This gives the best feedback for your objects.

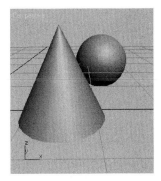

Smooth Displays objects with no highlights and only smooth shading.

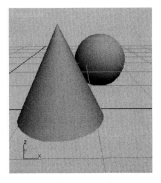

Facets+Highlights Displays scene objects with flat shading and displays specular highlights. This is a fast way to see your solid objects with highlights when Smooth+ Highlights is too taxing with heavy scenes.

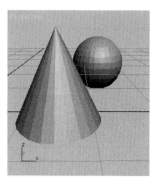

Facets Displays polygons as flat surfaces that are shaded, but includes no smoothing or scene highlights.

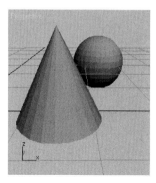

Flat Displays each polygon in its raw diffuse color, disregarding any scene lighting or light sources. This viewing method is useful when you need to see each polygon rather than to see their shading.

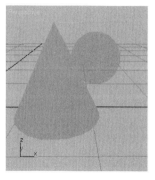

Hidden Line A Wireframe mode that allows you to use the Wireframe mode without seeing through every object. In this display mode only, the wireframe color is determined by choosing Customize → Customize User Interface in the Colors tab under Elements → Viewports and selecting Hidden Line Unselected rather than the object or material color.

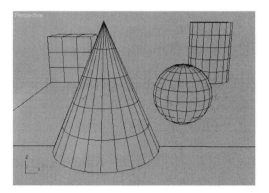

Lit Wireframes Displays objects as their wireframes with a flat shading for a sense of lighting.

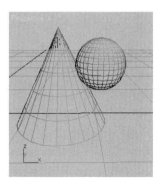

Wireframe Draws objects as wireframes only. This is the fastest viewing method that still lets you see an object's shape.

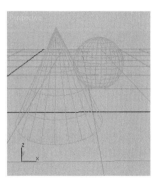

Bounding Box Displays objects as bounding boxes. *Bounding boxes* are approximations of the amount of volume a shape occupies. No shading is applied.

3ds Max 2008 will automatically degrade the display of certain objects variably (such as using bounding boxes) when the geometry in a complex scene is too much for the display to handle when the viewport is being moved. You probably will not encounter this feature, called Adaptive Degradation, until you begin dealing with very large scenes. You can disable Adaptive Degradation by pressing the keyboard shortcut O.

Edged Faces Edged Faces draws the wireframe of an object back onto its shape when it is displayed in one of the shaded modes (Smooth, Smooth+Highlights, Facets+Highlights, or Facets). Edged Faces lets you see the wireframe lines and faces of an object for easier editing, while still seeing it shaded.

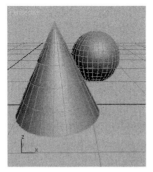

Setting the viewport rendering levels will help you with larger scenes. More often than not, viewing your scenes with the Smooth+Highlights mode will give you the best feedback.

With the new Adaptive Degradation features in 3ds Max 2008, you won't need to worry about which rendering level you choose. The levels are designed to automatically adapt when your systems responsiveness is slower because of a larger scene.

Gizmos

Using gizmos is a fast and effective way to transform your objects with interactive feedback. As you saw in the Mobile exercise in the previous chapter, gizmos let you manipulate objects in your viewports interactively to transform them—i.e., translate (move), rotate, and/or scale. Coordinate Display boxes at the bottom of the screen display coordinate or angular or percentage information on the position/rotation/scale of your object as you transform it. The gizmos appear in the viewport on the selected object at their pivot point as soon as you invoke one of the transformation tools.

After you invoke the Move tool by pressing W (or accessing it through the toolbar), your gizmo should look like this:

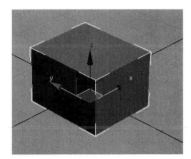

The *XYZ*-axis gives you handles to move an object on one specific axis. You can also click on the box between two axes to move the object in that plane, which is shown here as *YZ*:

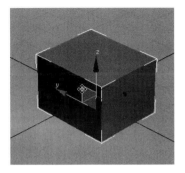

If you invoke the Rotate tool by pressing E, your gizmo will turn into three circles as shown. You can click on one of the circles to rotate the object on the axis only, or you can click anywhere between the circles to freely rotate the selected object in all three axes.

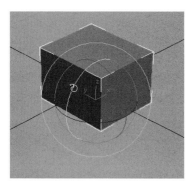

Invoke the Scale tool by pressing the R key, and your gizmo will turn into a triangle, as shown here:

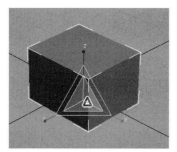

Clicking and dragging anywhere inside the yellow triangle will scale the object uniformly in all three axes. By selecting the red, green, or blue handles for the appropriate axis, you can scale along one axis only. You can also scale an object in a plane between two axes by selecting the side of the yellow triangle between two axes as shown here along the Y- and Z-axes:

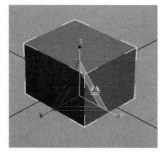

Keep in mind that the gizmos appear at an object's pivot point; therefore, if there is an object where you have relocated the pivot point away from the object itself, the gizmo will appear there and not on the object itself, as shown here where the rectangle's pivot is to the right of the object.

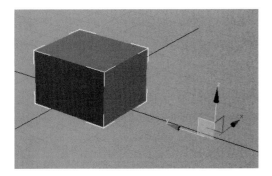

In the following graphic, a cube is being transformed in the *Y*-axis. The Coordinate Display box indicates how much it is being moved.

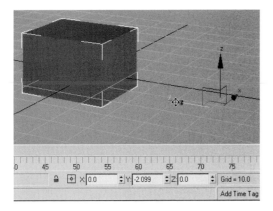

Managing Scene Objects

3ds Max has a few ways to organize and manage your scene elements to make working with things easier. These tools include the Layer Manager, the Schematic View, the Material Editor, and the Curve Editor/Dope Sheet. The Layer Manager works with objects to organize them in layers. The Schematic View allows you to view, manage, and edit your scene's hierarchies. The Layer Manager and Schematic View windows are outlined for you here, and they are used extensively throughout this book.

The Material Editor allows you to manage your scene's materials and textures. The Material Editor is covered in Chapter 7. "Materials and Mapping." The Curve Editor manages the animation in your scene by giving you access to animation curves. The Dope Sheet manages the animation in your scene by giving you access to animation ranges or sets of keys. The Curve Editor is covered in Chapter 8, and the Dope Sheet is covered in Chapter 9.

Layer Manager

The Layer Manager can be accessed through the main menu: Tools → Layer Manager or through the Main Toolbar icon 🗇 (Figure 3.45).

Figure 3.45

The Layer Manager

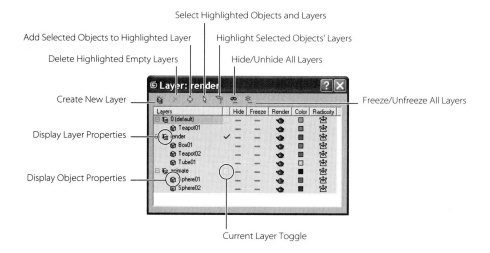

Layers can be used to organize scene objects. In 3ds Max, layers are organized similarly to Photoshop layers; you can organize different elements of an image in separate layers. Layers are mainly used to control object visibility, default color, selecting, freezing, and hiding. All of these functions help you organize your scene and make object management easier. You will use the Layer Manager in future exercises in this book.

The icons across the top of the Layer Manager are explained here.

Create New Layer   Creates a new layer when you have objects selected in your scene. The selected objects are assigned to the new layer.

Delete Highlighted Empty Layers   Deletes selected layers if they are empty.

Add Selected Objects to Highlighted Layer   Moves currently selected objects into the selected layer.

Select Highlighted Objects and Layers   Selects all highlighted objects, as well as all objects contained in any highlighted layers.

Highlight Selected Objects' Layers Highlights layers containing the currently selected objects and automatically scrolls so that highlighted layers are visible in the Layer Manager.

Hide/Unhide All Layers Enables the display of all layers.

Freeze/Unfreeze All Layers Enables the frozen state of all layers.

The columns in the Layer Manager window itself are the following:

Layers Displays the names of the layers/objects. To select or rename a layer, click its name. To display object or layer properties, click the object icon to open the Object Properties dialog box for all highlighted objects.

Current Layer Toggle The unlabeled column to the right of the layer name indicates the current layer. The check mark next to a layer means it is selected and current. This feature lets you make a different layer current.

Hide Hides and unhides layers. When a layer is hidden, it's invisible.

Freeze Freezes layers. Frozen layers can not be selected.

Render When this feature is enabled, objects appear in the rendered scene. Nonrendering objects won't cast shadows or affect the visual component of the rendered scene.

Color Changes the default color on highlighted objects.

Radiosity When this feature is enabled, objects are included in the radiosity solution.

Using the Layer Manager

The Layer Manager can be extremely useful for organizing and managing your scene objects. You will use the Layer Manager throughout the rest of this book. Let's take a quick look at how the Layer Manager can help you with a scene.

1. Open a new scene and create four new objects as shown here: a box, a sphere, a cone, and a torus.

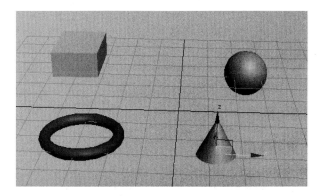

2. Open the Layer Manager by choosing Tools → Layer Manager or by clicking the Layer Manager icon (▤) in the main toolbar. Click the Create New Layer icon ▤ to create two new layers.

> To select more than one object in a viewport, press the Ctrl key as you click on additional objects to add to your selection. Many applications use the Shift key to add to a selection; however, 3ds Max uses Ctrl.

3. In the viewport, select the box and the sphere and assign them to Layer01 by selecting Layer01 and clicking the Add Selected Objects To Highlighted Layer icon ⊕ in the Layer Manager, as shown here.

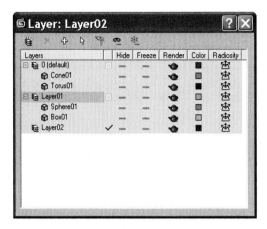

4. As you did in step 3, assign the cone to Layer02. Select Layer01 and turn on Freeze. The sphere and box will turn gray in the viewport and you will no longer be able to select them. Click Hide, and the box and sphere will disappear from the viewports.

Experiment with toggling Hide and Freeze for the objects or the layers so that you can see how your scene reacts when they are on and off.

Schematic View

The Schematic View is another way to organize and manage your scene, particularly object hierarchies. This window displays the objects in your scene in a flowchart scheme, allowing you to see how objects are linked or grouped together. Parents connect down the flowchart to their children. This method of viewing hierarchies is powerful, because you get an immediate visualization of how the objects in your scene work and relate to each other.

While we're talking about hierarchies, let's return to the Mobile exercise from the previous chapter and see how the Schematic View depicts the scene. Figure 3.46 shows the Mobile scene in the Schematic View.

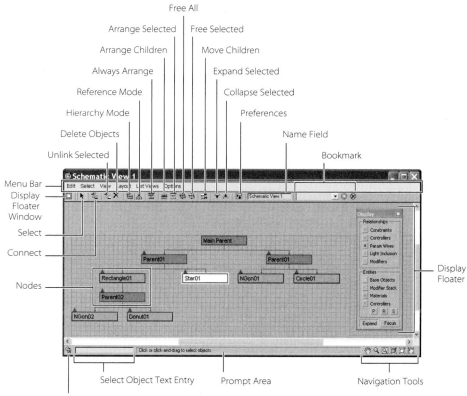

Figure 3.46

The Mobile scene broken down in the Schematic View immediately tells you how the objects are organized.

A scene can become so complicated that trying to select one object is impossible. The Schematic View makes editing character rigs easier, allowing you to view, create, and edit links between objects. The Schematic View simplifies the selection process by clearly displaying every object in the scene as a box with the object's name displayed in it. You can use the middle mouse button to pan around in the Schematic View, or you can use any of the familiar navigation icons found in the lower right-hand corner of the window, as shown in Figure 3.46.

When you select any object in the schematic, its parameter automatically appears in the Modify panel for easy editing. Because objects can have different states of being, different conventions are used to indicate an object's current state in the scene, with the more important states listed here:

Red Border The object is animated.

White Fill The object is currently selected in the Schematic View window.

White Border The object is currently selected in a viewport.

Up Arrow Used to simplify a view. Pressing the Up arrow collapses each node and its dependent child nodes up to the next highest parent, putting everything into one node for simpler display. This is useful for large characters and long hierarchy chains because you don't have to see all the child nodes in a large scene. This does not remove the hierarchy; it only affects the display.

Down Arrow Used to gain more information about a group of objects. Clicking the down arrow expands the next child down from that node to show you its immediate child node(s).

In the Mobile scene, you can see how the Main Parent node runs the show. It is the top bar of the mobile; the second row of bars hangs from it as its children with the shapes on the Mobile hung below them.

The toolbar across the top of the Schematic View is used for editing hierarchies in your scene. We will experiment with reordering the Mobile hierarchy in the Schematic View in just a moment. First, let's look at the tools as called out in Figure 3.46.

Display Floater Enables the Display Floater window, which gives you access to display toggles for certain object types in the Schematic View.

Select Allows you to select objects in the Schematic View. When you select an object in a viewport, its node in the Schematic View will be outlined in white. However, it will not necessarily be selected in the Schematic View. If you want to be able to select an object in either window once and have it selected in both the Schematic View and the viewports, choose Select → Sync Selection in the Schematic View window.

Connect To create links in the Schematic View, just as you created links between objects in the Mobile project, click the child object and drag it to the desired parent.

Unlink Selected To break links between objects, click the child to unlink and then click this icon.

Delete Objects Deletes the selected object(s) from the scene. If you make a mistake, you can press the Undo icon in the main toolbar or press Ctrl+Z to get the object(s) back.

Hierarchy Mode Lays out the Schematic View as an outline view, as shown here.

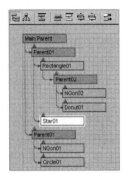

Reference Mode Lays out the view in the Schematic View, as shown here. This view is good for viewing object relationships and materials.

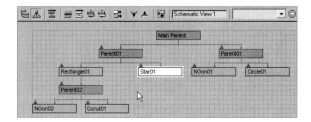

Always Arrange The Schematic View will keep the node display rigid. As you see in the Reference Mode graphic, you will not be able to freely move nodes around. Turning this Always Arrange mode off allows you to arrange the nodes any way you want, as shown here.

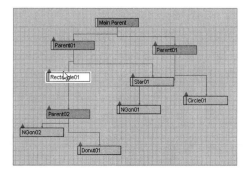

The next group of icons—Arrange Children, Arrange Selected, Free All, and Free Selected—all have to do with automatically arranging nodes when you turn off Always Arrange.

Move Children When you click and drag a node, all of its child nodes will follow it when this mode is enabled.

Expand/Collapse Selected Used to reveal or hide the child nodes of the selected node.

Preferences In the Preferences window for the Schematic View, you can filter certain object types (such as lights, cameras, objects, etc.) from displaying in the schematic.

Schematic View Name Field Lets you save certain views to recall later for easy access. When you have a heavy scene, with tons of nodes to view, getting to the right place in a complicated hierarchy can take some time. When you type a name for your current view into this text box, 3ds Max will save the view for you. To access that particular view again, in the main menu bar, select Graph Editors → Saved Schematic Views → Schematic View Name. See Figure 3.47.

Figure 3.47

**Accessing a saved
Schematic View**

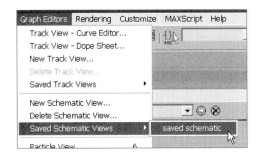

Bookmark Name Field Lets you define a selection of nodes in the Schematic View with bookmarks that you can later return to easily.

Using the Schematic View with the Mobile

Let's take a look at the Schematic View in action, and have another whack at the Mobile scene's hierarchy.

You can start with your own Mobile scene file, or load the scene Mobile_v04.max from the Scenes folder in the Mobile project on the companion CD. Just follow these steps:

1. With your Mobile scene loaded, open the Schematic View by choosing Graph Editors → New Schematic View or by clicking the Schematic View (Open) icon ⊞ in the main toolbar, as shown in Figure 3.48.

Figure 3.48

**The Schematic View
for the Mobile scene**

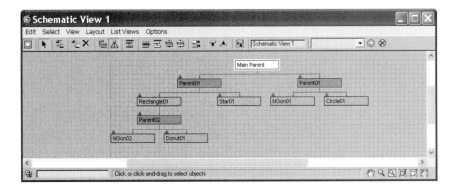

2. Unlink the Star object from the Mobile and relink it to the Circle object. To do this, click the Connect button and then select the Star01 node and drag it to the Circle01 node, as shown in Figure 3.49.

3. When you release the mouse button, notice that the Star01 node is linked under the Circle01 node, as shown in Figure 3.50. The Star has been automatically unlinked from its old parent.

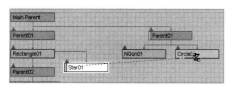

Figure 3.49

Reconnecting the Star to the Circle

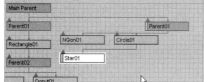

Figure 3.50

The Star is linked under the Circle.

You can see how easy it is to restructure your scene hierarchies using the Schematic View. All the controls for viewing and arranging nodes might be a bit much for one window. You probably won't need half those icons, but knowing how to use the Schematic View is important. It is an important tool in organizing and setting up your scenes for animation. You will continue to use the Schematic View throughout this book.

Scene Explorer

New to 3ds Max 2008 is the Scene Explorer dialog (Figure 3.51). This window is accessed through the Tools → New Scene Explorer and is an expanded version of the dialog opened with the Select by Name icon in the 3ds Max toolbar as discussed earlier in the chapter. Scene Explorer allows you to view the objects in your scene by name, as well as sort or filter them by type, view and edit their hierarchies, and generally manage the objects in your scene. Through the Scene Explorer you can rename, delete, hide, freeze, and edit some object properties en masse.

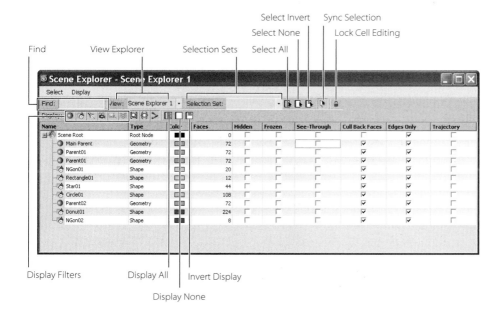

Figure 3.51

The Scene Explorer window

Two primary uses of the Scene Explorer are to select objects and edit their hierarchies. To select objects in your scene in Scene Explorer, enable Sync Selection by clicking its icon in the Scene Explorer toolbar, as shown in Figure 3.51. While it is enabled, if you select an object in your scene through a viewport, it is simultaneously selected in the Scene Explorer and vice versa.

You can link and unlink objects to edit hierarchies as well. If you drag an object's icon onto another object in the Scene Explorer dialog until you see a yellow arrow to the left of the target object, the dragged object will become a child of the target object. To unlink an object, drag its icon from the target object in the Scene Explorer to the Scene Root node at the top of the list.

You can have as many Scene Explorer windows open as you like because they persist in your scene as you work. You can toggle between different views of the Scene Explorer that you have opened previously through the window's View Explorer pull-down menu.

Summary

Wow! That was a lot of information. You've learned how to navigate the menus, toolbars, icons, panels, and windows in 3ds Max. Remember, don't worry about absorbing all that information. This chapter exists to give you a unified reference guide for 3ds Max UI issues. Come back to this chapter as you work with 3ds Max on the tutorials in this book and any other 3ds Max work you have.

If you've read all the way through this chapter, you've seen the icons and buttons you will come across most often, and have had a taste of everything on the main 3ds Max UI screen and a brief description of what each feature does.

Complete understanding of how to use 3ds Max comes with time and experience. To develop that understanding, you need to work on projects that further challenge you and get you moving around inside the UI. This book begins that ride and tries to give you a good push in the right direction. Take everything in this chapter with a grain of salt and head into the coming chapters.

CHAPTER 4

Modeling in 3ds Max: Part I

Modeling in 3D programs is akin to sculpting or carpentry; you essentially create objects out of shapes and forms. No matter how you look at it, even a complex model is just an amalgam of simpler parts. The successful modeler can dissect a form down to its components and translate them into surfaces and meshes.

3ds Max's modeling tools are incredibly strong for polygonal modeling. The focus of this book will be on polygonal modeling because the majority of 3ds Max models are created with polygons. In addition to mechanical models, in this book you will model an organic model—an alien creature—and use that model to animate a character using SubDivision surfaces.

In this chapter, you will learn modeling concepts and how to use 3ds Max modeling toolsets. You will also tackle two different models to get a sense of a workflow using 3ds Max.

Topics in this chapter include:

- **Planning Your Model**
- **Modeling Concepts**
- **Modifiers and the Modifier Stack**
- **Look at the Mesh You Got Us Into!**
- **Editable Poly Tools**
- **Modeling a Chest of Drawers**
- **Modeling a Hand**

Planning Your Model

The most important thing to know before you begin to model is exactly *what* you are going to model. That sounds obvious, but it's true. You need to think about your model and gather as many references as you can. The best training you can hope to gain is simply by observing the core elements and forms that make up objects in everyday life. Learn how to dissect things around you into component shapes that you can picture in a 3D window. When you look at a barbell, for example, you should see several cylinders connected to each other. When you see an office chair, you should see a few boxes and cylinders arranged and rounded at the edges. When you begin to see objects in this manner, the idea of modeling them may not seem quite as daunting.

"Yeah, but all my friends can sit down and model anything they want." Be that as it may, if you are a novice to 3D, surround yourself with references. Even if you are not new to 3D or to modeling, you should surround yourself with as many references as you can. Not having a clear picture in your head of where you need to go for your model will just aggravate the process and give you a slack result.

Take pictures all around the proposed object. Get the dimensions, sizes, angles, and slopes of the surfaces of your subject. You could even try to re-create the object in a different medium. Try sketching the subject, or grab some children's Play-Doh or a plate of mashed potatoes and make a rough sculpture. It may seem like a lot of effort to build something trivial, but it will pay off in the long run.

But enough of that old lecture.

Your first question should be, "How detailed should I make the model?" As you may have read in the first chapter, it's always a good idea to match the level of detail for a model to what is needed in the shot. If you are featuring the object up close and personal, then you should take care to build it with extra detail, adding as many polygons as it takes to make it look good and still render. If, however, the object is far away and half obscured, detailing the heck out of it would be a waste of time. In Figure 4.1 on the left, you can see a park bench in a far shot compared to a view of the bench up close on the right. It would be a waste of effort and time to detail the bench to exacting levels when the bench will be seen *only* in a far shot.

You should ask yourself what the model will be used for when you are deciding how best to detail it. If you are not sure how the model will be used in the end, it's generally best to create as much detail as you think necessary. You can always prune down the details later if, for example, your scene ends up very large and will not render.

Here's another thing to confuse you: You can always add detail to a model with texturing. Textures, when applied well, can really turn an otherwise ho-hum model into a spectacular object when rendered. You can easily add details such as grooves, dents, and engravings with special texture maps called *bump maps* or *displacement maps*. You will learn about

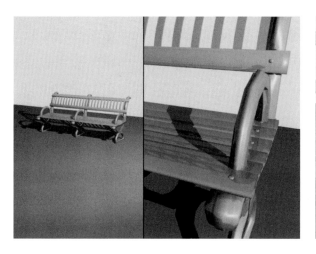

Figure 4.1
The level of detail in a model depends on how much of the model is seen.

these maps in Chapter 7, "Materials and Mapping." Don't worry about these things yet, though. Most people begin by putting all the details they can into their model, and as they gain more experience, they start to realize that some of the modeling work can be deferred until the texturing phase.

Modeling Concepts

To get a foothold in modeling, you will need to understand a number of things. If you are not new to CG or are desperate to get started, feel free to skip ahead and start modeling. However, you still might want to peruse this section for some concepts and terms that may make things easier for you in the coming exercises.

Polygons

A *polygon* is a surface created by connecting three or more points in 3D space. This flat surface connects to other polygons to form more intricate surfaces. In Figure 4.2, you see a sphere. The facets of the sphere are polygons, all connected at common *edges* at the correct angles and in the proper arrangement to make a sphere.

The points that generate a polygon are called *vertices*. The lines that connect the points are called *edges*. If the polygon has three vertices, its surface is called a *face*. Polygons are made up of triangular faces by design. In the example of the sphere in Figure 4.2, the polygon's facets all have four vertices.

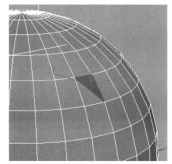

The graphic shows the same sphere with one face selected. See how the face is half of the polygon, using three of its vertices.

Figure 4.2

**A sphere is com-
posed of polygons.**

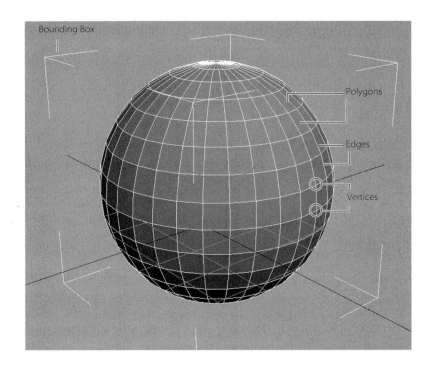

The more polygons you have in a model, the more detailed it becomes. However, greater numbers of polygons tax your system and take longer to render. This is where the term *low-poly modeling* originates. In computer or console games, the machine renders the scene on the fly, so its computation requirements are strict. The fewer the polygons in the scene, the faster the game can play back. Games frequently use low-poly models to maximize the effect in their game without sacrificing precious computational cycles.

Higher-resolution models are typically used in television and film, because the scenes are all rendered beforehand and then laid off to video tape or output to film. A computational ceiling is still dictated by the machines that are used in creating the TV or film animations, however, so it is always a good idea to be smart when creating models.

Primitives

Primitives are the basic 3D geometric shapes that are automatically generated by 3D modeling applications. As such, they do not need to be constructed from scratch. A considerable amount of modeling (perhaps most) begins with primitives, which are then edited and used with other primitives to create more complex objects. Use primitives as the core of your object. For example, to sculpt an apple, you might start out with a sphere primitive.

As you can see in Figure 4.3, 3ds Max affords you plenty of primitives to choose from for your original form. All of these primitives have their own parameters for customizing the form to your liking. You have already seen how to create some of these objects in the Mobile exercise in Chapter 2, "Your First Max Animation."

Figure 4.3

3ds Max standard and extended primitives

Objects such as the primitives would be useless in 3ds Max if you could not edit them to suit your needs. For example, you could sculpt a sphere into the shape of an apple. To sculpt a surface, you will need to convert your object (such as the sphere for the apple) into an editable object, frequently called a *mesh,* to get to the object's component level where you can move points and reshape faces that make up the object or primitive. We will look at that in the next section.

Meshes and Sub-Objects

Once you have chosen a primitive that will best work for your intended model, you begin the modeling process by changing the primitive into a mesh object to access the components of the object with which you will edit the model (such as vertices, faces, etc.).

In 3ds Max, *mesh* objects are defined by smaller component pieces that form the object as a whole. The smaller components (called *sub-objects*) can be manipulated to adjust the shape of the object or to form more complex models. Once you convert your object in 3ds Max to an editable object such as a mesh, you can edit using the sub-objects available for that object.

For instance, mesh models break down your object into a number of individual flat surfaces—polygons and faces. With meshes, you can select any of the sub-objects at different component levels such as the polygons, vertices, or faces of the mesh to make adjustments while sculpting your model.

In 3ds Max, there are two ways to create a mesh object: by applying a *modifier* to the base object or primitive or by *converting* the primitive to a mesh. Both methods give you access to the sub-object level for editing. The one big difference, however, can be critical if you need to edit the base object—for example, if you want to change the radius of a primitive sphere after you start editing it as a mesh. Instead of converting, you are better off using the modifier method because it preserves the original primitive object intact and allows you to modify the object's original parameters (such as radius for a sphere) even after you begin to edit the mesh.

In this exercise, you will create an object and turn it into a mesh. Follow these steps:

1. Create a sphere in a new scene using the Create panel. You will turn this object into a mesh to check out the sub-objects at your disposal.

2. With the sphere selected, switch to the Modify panel. Figure 4.4 shows the newly created sphere. Notice the Sphere heading in the Modifier List on the right.

Figure 4.4

The newly created sphere awaits your command.

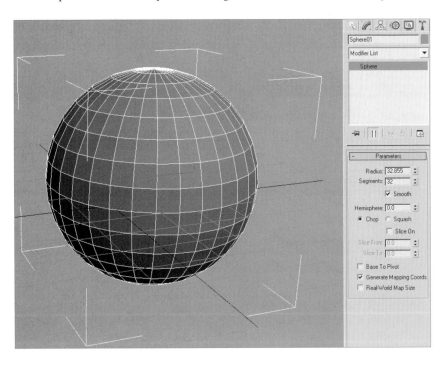

3. With the sphere selected, choose Modifiers → Mesh Editing → Edit Mesh. This will apply an Edit Mesh modifier to the sphere, giving you access to the sub-objects that a mesh affords you.

4. The Modifier Stack will display a heading called Edit Mesh. Highlight Edit Mesh in the Modifier Stack. You should see something like what is shown in Figure 4.5.

5. Under the Selection heading in the Modify panel, select the type of sub-object you would like to begin editing. Choose the first icon ( ) for Vertex.

6. As you can see in Figure 4.6, small dots appear on the sphere. They are the vertices you can now select. Choose the Move tool and select one of the vertices on the sphere. Click and drag to move the vertex anywhere to sculpt the surface of the sphere, as shown in Figure 4.6.

7. Change your sub-object selection to polygons by choosing the Polygon icon ( ) in the Modify panel. The vertices will disappear from the viewport. Change to Edged Faces display mode in the viewport either by right-clicking the viewport name and selecting Edged Faces or by pressing the F4 shortcut.

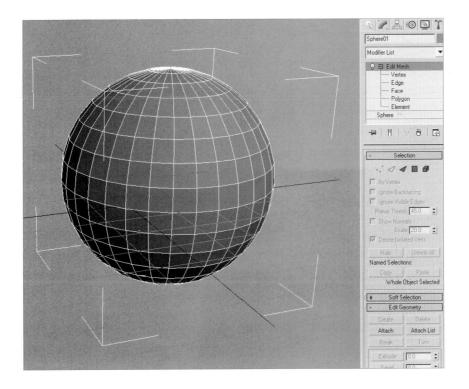

Figure 4.5

You now have access to the Edit Mesh's sub-objects.

8. Click on a polygon to select it. Notice that the polygon turns red in the viewport. Move the selected polygon around to see how the surface of the sphere mesh changes (Figure 4.7).

9. Try selecting the other sub-object types and changing the shape of the sphere.

10. In the Modifier Stack, click on the original sphere entry. You will still have access to changing the radius and other parameters of the original primitive. Changing any of these parameters does not negate the Edit Mesh modifier.

Figure 4.6

Adjusting sub-objects such as vertices allows you to sculpt your model.

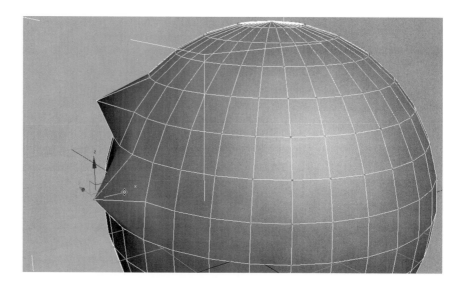

Figure 4.7

Selecting and playing around with a polygon sub-object on the sphere mesh

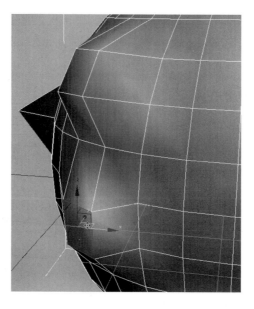

As you can see, you have greater control over the shape of your model once you access the sub-object levels of an Edit mesh. You'll see quite a bit of mesh editing in the exercises throughout this book. One exercise you can do now quickly is to try to sculpt a simple cartoon head using nothing but sub-object manipulation on a base sphere.

In some 3D packages, you have inherent access to a model's components (such as a vertex or face). However, with 3ds Max you will need to either convert created objects into meshes or add the appropriate modifier to create a mesh, as you did in the previous exercise, to manipulate the sub-objects. You will be modeling with meshes later in this chapter, and you will learn other ways to access sub-objects on a model.

Modifiers and the Modifier Stack

Modifiers, as you have already seen, are a way to edit your objects in 3ds Max. In almost all cases, you can apply several modifiers to an object to get the desired result. In the Modify panel's Modifier Stack, you can access any of those modifiers to change any of its parameters at any time in your modeling. This is perhaps one of the best aspects of modeling in 3ds Max.

3ds Max has tons of modifiers that accomplish any number of tasks. These tasks need not be limited to editing models, though; many modifiers work well in animation and dynamics chores as well. In this section, we will cover a few modeling-specific modifiers and more importantly, we will see how the Modifier Stack operates.

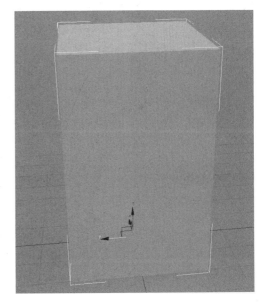

Figure 4.8

The Twist modifier is now applied to the box. You can still access the original parameters of the box.

Applying Modifiers

Let's take a quick look at how modifiers work on editing objects. In the following steps, you will apply a few modifiers to an object.

1. In a new scene, create a tall box in the Perspective viewport, as shown here. The box should have a height of at least 45, with a width and length of about 20.

2. With the box selected, choose Modifiers → Parametric Deformers → Twist. The box should now have an orange outline, and Twist should appear in the Modifier Stack. Go to the Modify panel to see the Modifier Stack, as shown in Figure 4.8. Click Twist in the Modifier Stack to access its parameters.

3. Click the Angle spinner and drag the mouse to increase the angle to 240 or so. As you can see in Figure 4.9, the box gets completely strange. You can see the box twist pretty nicely at first, but the higher the Angle on the Twist, the more shearing the box will undergo, to the point where it no longer resembles what a twisted box should look like.

4. The box is suffering from a case of low definition, meaning the box does not have enough *segments* to handle the twist deformation without turning inside out. You will need to add more segments to the box for a smoother twist effect. In the Modifier Stack, click **Box** to access the parameters for the box, before the Twist modifier.

5. To better see the effect of adding more segments to the box, enable Edged Faces in the viewport (right-click **Perspective**, which is the viewport name) and select **Edged Faces** from the menu.

6. Click the **Length Segs** parameter spinner and increase the value to **4**. Increase the **Width Segs** to **4** and the **Height Segs** to **16**. As you increase the segments in the original box, the Twist Modifier takes on a much nicer shape. Figure 4.10 shows the box with more segments.

7. You can increase the segments as much you prefer; however, it's best to use the fewest number of segments that will give you the desired result. Increasing the number of segments essentially increases the polygons in the surface.

Figure 4.9

The box is twisted out of shape.

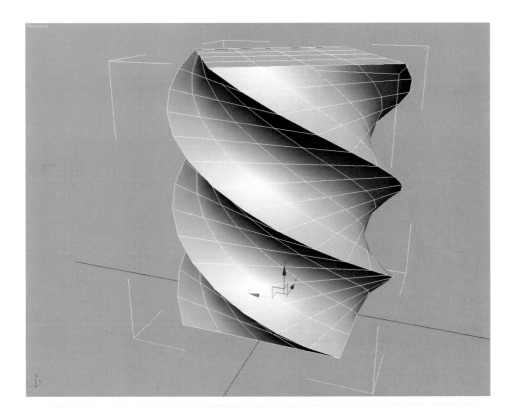

Figure 4.10
Adding more segments to the box makes the deformation from the Twist modifier smoother.

8. Now add another modifier to the box. Select the box and highlight the box entry in the Modifier Stack. Choose Modifier → Parametric Deformers → Spherify. Your box should look like a ball (Figure 4.11). Neat!

9. Play with the Spherify modifier's only parameter (Percentage) to see how the twisted box can turn into a sphere. Although this is kind of a neat trick, you don't really need this modifier, so go ahead and remove it from the stack. In the Modifier Stack, click the Spherify entry and click the Trash Can icon () at the bottom of the Modifier List, as shown here. This will remove the Spherify modifier without harming anything else, and it will return the box to its twisted state.

Modifiers are powerful editing and animation tools. Take some time to play around in a scene such as the one from the previous exercise. Apply different deformers to objects and see what they do. It's really best to learn by experience sometimes. The Parametric Deformer modifiers are especially fun to play with, as you can see.

You have not seen the last of modifiers in this book; they are an integral part of the 3ds Max workflow, and we will use them throughout this book. We will take another look at the Modifier Stack in the next section.

Figure 4.11

Spherify the box.

Modifier Stack with a Side of Maple Syrup

The Modifier Stack displays the modifiers added to any objects. It gives you access to any of the parameters for the modifiers applied to the object, as well as the original parameters of the object itself. When working with the Modifier Stack, you can access several options through the icons below the stack itself, as shown in Figure 4.12.

Pin Stack If you want to freeze the display on the Modify panel controls on the currently selected object, click this icon. Pin Stack locks the stack and all the controls in the panel so that you can see that object's stack even while you have other objects selected in the scene.

Show End Result When on, it shows the effect of the entire stack on the selected object. When off, it shows the effect of the stack only up to the currently highlighted modifier.

Make Unique With a certain type of object duplication (instancing), making any adjustments to the instanced copy also reflects in the original object. Make Unique separates the objects and disallows a shared adjustment, so if you apply a modifier to an instanced copy, it will not reflect in the original object when Make Unique is applied.

Remove Modifier This deletes the current modifier from the stack, eliminating all changes caused by that modifier.

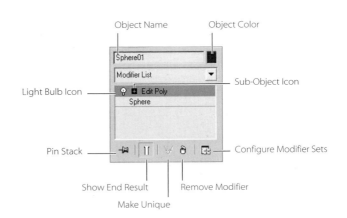

Figure 4.12

The Modifier Stack's controls

Configure Modifier Sets This displays a menu that allows you to configure the display of the Modify panel and choose which modifiers will be available to you directly from the Modify panel, without having to access the drop-down list.

Sub-Object Icon The plus or minus icon to the right of the Modifier name signifies that you have access to the sub-object (or sub-modifier) levels.

Light Bulb Icon This turns the effect of the modifier on and off. This is very useful for troubleshooting and verifying the effect of a particular modifier in a stack.

Order in the Stack

Unless changed, the Modifier Stack contains a history of an object's modifiers in the order they were applied. The Stack is read and applied to the object from the bottom going up, with the original object's entry at the very bottom. As you can imagine, the order in which you stack your modifiers is very important. You can get very different results from the same objects with the same modifiers in a different order.

Figure 4.13

A cylinder with the Bend modifier applied

Fortunately, changing the order of modifiers in the stack is very easy. In the Modifier Stack, click the modifier you want to move and drag it to its new position in the stack. Once you release the mouse button, a blue line will demarcate where in the stack the modifier will be placed.

For example, you can start with a cylinder and apply the Bend modifier (Modifiers → Parametric Deformers → Bend) to the cylinder first, as shown in Figure 4.13.

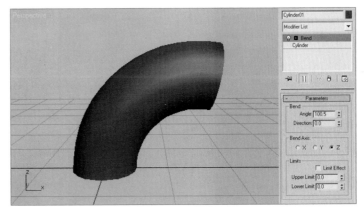

Now if you want to pinch in or taper the bent side of the cylinder, you can add a Taper modifier (Modifiers → Parametric Deformers → Taper) to the stack. The results won't look the way you would expect, as you can see in Figure 4.14.

Figure 4.14

Trying to taper the bent side of the cylinder does not work with the Taper modifier—yet.

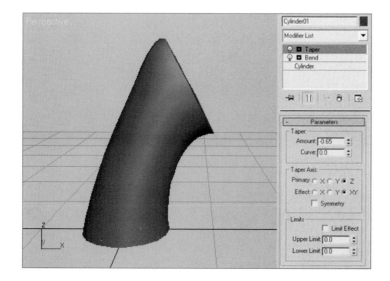

Now go to the Modifier Stack, click and drag the Taper modifier, and move it below the Bend modifier (Figure 4.15). These are the results you want to see. You want to bend the Taper, not taper the Bend. Using this principle will help you figure out how to order the modifiers in the stack.

Figure 4.15

This is the way it's supposed to look.

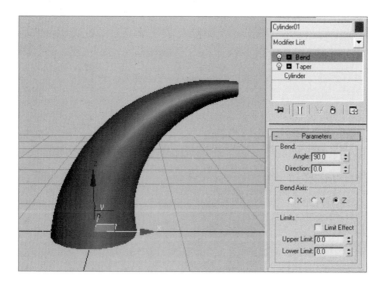

Look at the Mesh You Got Us Into!

As you saw earlier in this chapter, to access the sub-object level of objects, you will need to turn them into a mesh. You've seen how you can add an Edit Mesh modifier to an object so you can begin to sculpt the surface using vertices and faces. There are tons of editing tools inherent in meshes.

When you create a mesh from an object, you not only have access to the sub-objects of that object, but you also have access to a host of tools to allow you to edit the surface. How do you get into a mesh? There are at least four different ways.

Converting versus Adding a Modifier

You can *add* the Edit Mesh or Edit Poly modifiers to an object, or you can *convert* to an editable mesh or editable poly. Converting to an editable mesh or adding an Edit Mesh modifier is roughly the same; they both host the same toolset and allow you the same sub-object levels for the mesh. However, adding a modifier allows you to edit the parameters of the original object, as you may have seen earlier in the chapter.

To experiment with the modifiers, try this exercise:

1. Create two spheres in a new scene, and place them side by side, as shown in Figure 4.16.

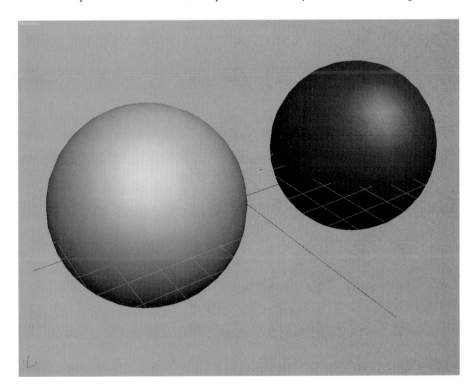

Figure 4.16

Two spheres side by side

2. Select the sphere on the left and apply an Edit Mesh modifier to it (choose Modifiers → Mesh Editing → Edit Mesh).

3. Select the sphere on the right and convert it to an editable mesh by right-clicking on the sphere's entry in the Modifier Stack. From the right-click menu, choose Editable Mesh under the Convert To: heading, as shown here.

4. Take turns clicking back and forth between the two spheres. You should notice very little difference in the toolsets in the Modify panel. Figure 4.17 shows the Modify panel for the sphere with the Edit Mesh modifier, and Figure 4.18 shows the Modify panel for the Editable Mesh sphere.

5. Notice that the Editable Mesh sphere no longer has the same Modifier Stack entries. This sphere now displays as Editable Mesh in the Modifier Stack. You should also note that the Editable Mesh sphere also has a rollout at the bottom of the Modifier panel called Surface Properties. Aside from those two issues, the modifier and the conversion are exactly the same.

The Convert method has its own advantages, however. Converting to an editable mesh, as opposed to applying the Edit Mesh modifier, saves memory and is more efficient because 3ds Max doesn't have to save the base object's parameter information. However, using the modifier gives you a little bit of comfort if you have commitment issues because you can always go back to the original object and remove the Edit Mesh modifier at any time. You cannot reconvert an editable mesh back to its original object.

Mesh versus Poly

How do you decide whether to use Edit Mesh or Edit Poly modifier, or editable mesh instead of editable poly? Which is better to use? Well, so far you have seen the Edit Mesh modifier and the Editable Mesh one. A more up-to-date toolset for sub-object tools is obtained through the Edit Poly modifier or Editable Poly, and it is the preferred way to go for many 3ds Max artists.

Why show the Edit Mesh modifier *and* Editable Mesh? They are both good to know, and you should understand the similarities and differences in how they function. Having said that, we'll concentrate on the Edit Poly modifier and Editable Poly for this chapter's exercises.

Edit Poly Modifier/Editable Poly

The Edit Poly modifier gives you plenty of controls to edit an object, just as the Edit Mesh modifier does. Figure 4.19 shows the Modify panel entries for the Edit Poly modifier on a sphere.

Figure 4.17

The sphere with the Edit Mesh modifier

Figure 4.18

The sphere converted to an editable mesh

Figure 4.19

Edit Poly modifier applied to a sphere

Figure 4.20

Polygon faces on this box have three edges or sides, making them triangular. A polygon on this box has four edges, or sides, making it a square.

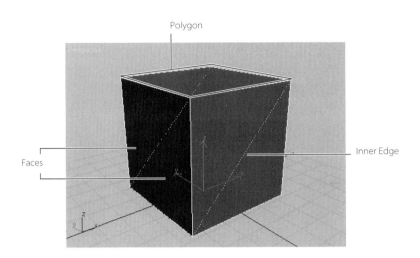

The differences between mesh and poly are few. Editable mesh gives you a sub-object level called *faces* that are polygons with just three edges (they have three vertices). Figure 4.20 shows you faces on a box object.

When modeling with an editable mesh (or through the Edit Mesh modifier), having faces gives you an inner edge where the faces meet along the center of the polygon. The inner edge can cause all kinds of problems even when you are working in Poly mode. An editable poly is similar to an editable mesh, but it gives you access to four-sided polygons instead of faces. It also hosts a slew of other, more refined tools and selection options.

In addition, the toolsets found in the Edit Poly/Editable Poly are more fleshed out than Edit Mesh/Editable Mesh and have been updated more, so they will give you slightly more options. The major difference between the toolsets in the Editable Poly and Edit Poly modifiers is that you have inherent access to SubDivision modeling on the editable poly.

In the next section, you will learn about the Edit Poly modifier and the editable poly.

Edit Poly/Editable Poly Tools

In this section, you will explore the actual toolsets in the Edit Poly/Editable Poly world. Most of these toolsets will also apply to the toolsets you will find in the Edit Mesh/Editable Mesh world as well, although some may be used slightly differently. In either case, using an Edit Poly modifier or an editable poly is preferred.

Similarly, the toolset in an editable poly is very similar to those found with the Edit Poly modifier; so here is a rundown on the rollouts and toolsets you will find for the editable poly. (Many cross over for the edit poly as well).

When you convert a primitive to an editable poly, you can see the controls for manipulating an object at sub-object levels in the Modify panel interface. They are very similar to the sub-objects you learned about earlier in the book with the Edit Mesh modifier. In all, there are six rollouts (as shown here). The main ones are Selection, Edit Geometry, and Subdivision Surface.

Selection Rollout

The Selection rollout contains tools used to access different levels of the object's sub-objects and their display in the viewport. You can also find information about the selected components in this rollout, as shown in Figure 4.21.

When you first create an editable poly and access the Modifier panel, you are in the Object level, meaning you will select the object. By clicking the different sub-object–level icons at the top of this rollout (see Figure 4.22), you can access the different selection levels as well as their relevant tools. Deselecting the icon will return you to the Object selection level.

You can also select the desired sub-object level by clicking the plus sign (+) next to the Editable Poly entry in the Modifier Stack and selecting one of the entries, as shown here.

Here are the different sub-object levels for an editable poly:

Vertex *Vertices* define the structure of other sub-objects that make up the poly. They are simply points in space. However, when a vertex is moved, the geometry that they form is changed accordingly. While your editable poly is selected, you can press 1 on the keyboard to select the Vertex level.

Edge The line connecting two vertices together is an *edge* and, therefore, creates the side of a polygon. Edges can be shared by only two polygons. Press 2 to enter Edge level selection.

Border A *border* is the edge of a hole. A surface's edge contains polygons that are not flanked by other polygons; in essence, they are on the edge of the surface. The row of edges on the perimeter of that surface is the border. You may invoke Border-level selection by pressing 3.

Polygon A *polygon* is a flat shape created by connecting three or more vertices, forming a closed shape. Polygons are what actually render when you output your scene in rendering. Press 4 to enter the Polygon level.

Element An *element* is one of two or more individual mesh objects (that is, groups of contiguous faces) grouped together into one larger object. For example, if you attach one box to another, you create one mesh object from the two boxes. Each box is now an element of the object. Any function you perform on that object affects all its elements. However, you can manipulate the elements independently at the Element sub-object

Figure 4.21

The Selection rollout for an editable poly

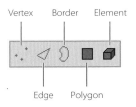

Figure 4.22

The sub-object icons for an editable poly

level. When you attach two or more meshes together, for example, the object becomes a larger single object in 3ds Max. However, the original meshes attached to each other are still accessible as Elements of the larger grouped object. Press **5** to enter the Element level.

The Selection modifier has a few options that will help you quickly alter your selection to better suit your needs. The following covers a few of the important selection options:

By Vertex When you click the check box, you can select sub-objects by selecting the vertex they are near. This feature is grayed out when you are in Vertex mode.

Ignore Backfacing When you click the check box you can select only the sub-objects that are facing you. With the default, which is *off,* you can select any sub-object(s) whether they are facing you or even visible. Think of it like selecting a dot on an orange. With Ignore Backfacing turned on, you can select a dot only on the side of the orange you can see. With Ignore Backfacing off, you can select any dot—even if it is on the side of the orange that's away from you.

By Angle When you select a polygon with By Angle enabled, 3ds Max will also select the neighboring polygons based on the value given for the angle in the text box next to this check box. This value determines the maximum angle between neighboring polygons that may be selected.

Shrink When you have made a sub-object selection, but you feel the selection is too wide, use Shrink. Shrink will deselect the outermost sub-objects to shrink your selection.

Grow Conversely, you can make a small selection of sub-objects and use Grow to increase the selection area outward in all available directions.

Loop Once you select an edge, you can propagate that selection to all the edges continuously around the mesh object by clicking the Loop icon. In the image on the left, a single edge is selected. The entire loop of edges is selected in the image on the right.

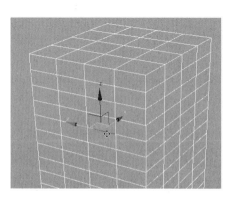
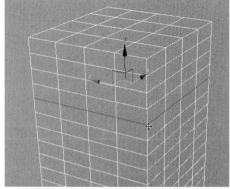

Ring Similar to the Loop function, Ring propagates an edge selection to the ring of edges perpendicular to the edge selected. In the following image on the left, there is a single edge selection. In the image on the right, the edges are selected with the Ring function.

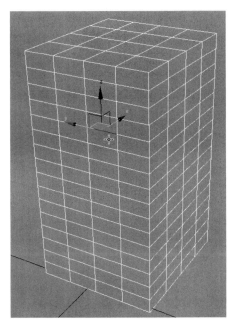 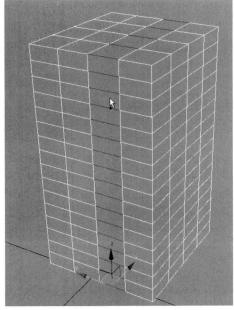

Soft Selection Rollout

As you already know, a regular selection selects only what you pick in the viewport for editing. You can, however, create a *soft* selection (shown in Figure 4.23), where a falloff effect emanates from your selection area toward the unselected sub-objects. In this case, the unselected sub-objects gain a partial selection value that is displayed in the viewports as a color gradient on the vertices or faces. When you apply a transformation—for example, if you move the soft selection—the actual selection will transform at a 1:1 ratio, while the falloff area of the soft selection will react at a lesser ratio according to the gradient falloff. This is similar to picking up a tablecloth with two fingers. The cloth between the two fingers is the full selection, while the cloth around the fingers falls off and does not lift up off the table as high as your fingers.

You can adjust the amount of falloff using the Falloff, Pinch, and Bubble parameters. In Figure 4.24, a sphere's vertices are being pulled outward with a soft selection. The area in the falloff, as you can see, is smoothly holding back as the main selection vertices are

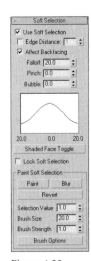

Figure 4.23
The Soft Selection rollout

pulling out. The sphere in the back of the viewport in Figure 4.24 has a vertex pulled out without the benefit of a soft selection.

Figure 4.24

Front sphere with Soft Selection enabled and back sphere without Soft Selection enabled

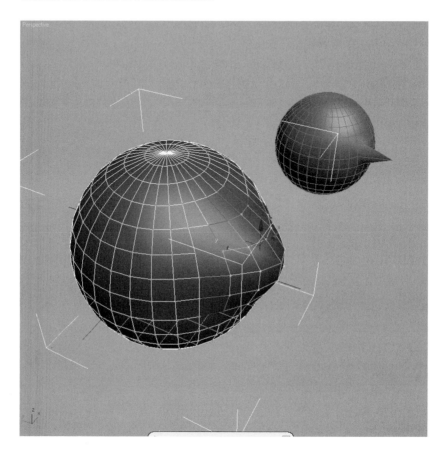

Figure 4.24

Front sphere with Soft Selection enabled and back sphere without Soft Selection enabled

Edit (Sub-Object) Rollout

These rollouts provide specific tools for editing the sub-object of your poly object. There are tools that are specific to the sub-object and ones that are the same for all sub-objects. The rollout heading name changes to reflect the sub-object level you are currently in and shows you the tools available for just that sub-object.

Try this exercise:

1. In a new scene, create a sphere. Convert the sphere to an editable poly.

2. Select the Poly sub-object level and select a single poly on the sphere, as shown here. Make sure Soft Selection is not enabled.

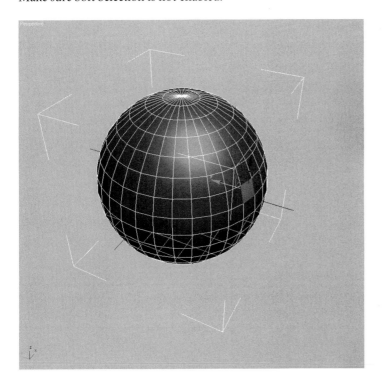

3. In the Edit Polygons rollout, choose Extrude, as shown here.

4. The appearance of your mouse pointer in the viewport will change. Click on the polygon you already have selected, and drag the mouse up to extrude the polygon out from the sphere. If you drag the mouse down, the polygon will extrude into the sphere, creating a square tunnel. Pull the polygon out as shown and release the mouse button.

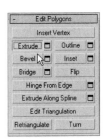

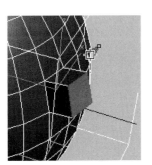

5. Select another polygon and extrude the face inward by dragging down on the cursor, as shown here.

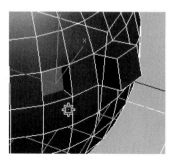

6. Select a third polygon on the sphere, and this time select the Bevel tool in the Modifier panel. Similar to an Extrude, Bevel allows you to taper the extruded polygon. Click the polygon, and drag the mouse to pull the polygon out. When you release the mouse button, 3ds Max allows you to select the taper amount by moving the mouse up or down. When you have the desired taper, as shown here, click once to exit the tool and set the bevel as you see it here.

Figure 4.25

The Edit Geometry rollout

Edit Geometry Rollout

This rollout (Figure 4.25) is the same for all the sub-objects. These tools allow you to edit your object. You will be using many of these tools in the upcoming Chest of Drawers and Hand exercises in this chapter.

Subdivision Surface Rollout

You have probably heard of *subdivision (SubD) surfaces* and SubD modeling. A SubD surface is a surface that has been divided to have more faces. However, the SubD surface retains the original object's general shape, which is sometimes called a *cage*. You subdivide to add more detail to a model, but you can still edit the original cage of the model to alter its overall shape and form.

The Subdivision Surface rollout lets you access tools specific to modeling with a subdivision surface, as shown in Figure 4.26.

You will be modeling with subdivision surfaces a little bit later in the Hand exercise in this chapter and then again in Chapter 6, "Character Poly Modeling."

The Edit rollout tools give you access to functions such as Extrude and Bevel to help you shape your model. The next section, "Editable Poly Tools," will give you some more experience with these toolsets. You will also use many of these tools in the Chest of Drawers exercise in this chapter.

Figure 4.26

The Subdivision Surface rollout

Editable Poly Tools

Let's experiment with some of the other Editable Poly tools. Dive right into the following exercises.

Extrude

When you *extrude* a vertex, 3ds Max moves it along a *normal*—that is, a line that is perpendicular to the surface in most cases. The extrusion creates new polygons that form the sides of the extrusion that also connect the vertex to the object.

We will start by extruding a vertex on a sphere:

1. Create a sphere by going to the Create panel and selecting **Sphere**. Create the sphere with about 20 units radius. Convert the sphere to an editable poly by right-clicking the sphere and choosing **Editable Poly** under the Convert To heading in the right-click menu. Go to Vertex mode, or press **1** on your keyboard. The vertices will appear as blue dots on your model.

2. Select a vertex on your sphere. The vertex will turn red. Go to the Edit Vertices rollout in the Modify panel, and press the **Settings** button (next to Extrude) to bring up the dialog box shown in Figure 4.27. Set an exact extrusion height and base width, and click **Apply** to create the extrusion. You can also click and drag to interactively pull out the vertex. Figure 4.28 shows a single extruded vertex.

Figure 4.27

The Extrude Vertices dialog box

Extrude acts the same in any of the sub-object modes—Vertex, Edge, or Poly. Figure 4.29 shows an extruded edge; you saw what an extruded polygon looks like earlier in the chapter.

You will be able to work with more extrude options in the Creating the Fingers exercise later in this chapter.

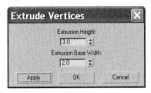

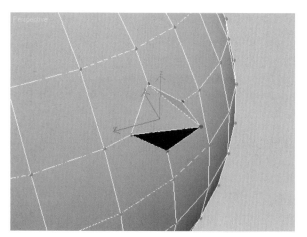

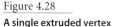
Figure 4.28

A single extruded vertex

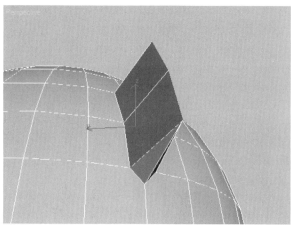

Figure 4.29

A single extruded edge

Chamfer

In the following steps, you will use a different tool, called *Chamfer*, to create extra detail on an editable poly:

1. Undo the vertex extrusion with Ctrl+Z, or start with a fresh sphere and select a vertex. Hold down the Ctrl key and select two more vertices on either side of the one already selected. Click the Chamfer Settings button in the Modify panel to open the Chamfer Settings dialog box, as shown here.

2. The new vertices are created around the ones you selected. You can dial in the exact value for your chamfer in the Options window as shown here and click **Apply** or **OK**. You can also simply click the **Chamfer** button (and not the Settings button), and click and drag in the viewport to interactively set your chamfer distance.

When you chamfer a sub-object, 3ds Max creates new faces around the area you have selected, complete with connecting edges, as you can see in Figure 4.30. Having been offset from the original vertex location, the three vertices are split into four new vertices each and arranged in a diamond formation. Chamfering, in this case, is good for creating some extra area of detail in your mesh or poly.

You can also use Chamfer to cut a hole in your surface. If you click the **Open** option box in the Chamfer Settings window, 3ds Max will cut a hole where the Chamfer exists, as shown in Figure 4.31.

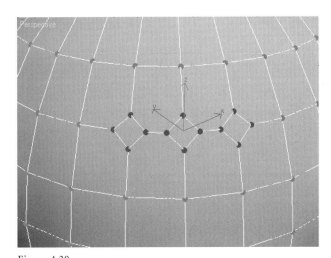

Figure 4.30

Chamfer three vertices next to each other.

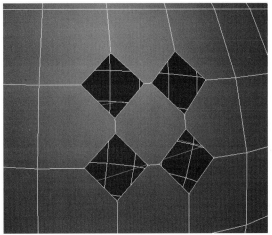

Figure 4.31

The Open option in the Chamfer Settings window will cut holes in your model.

When you are in the Edge sub-object level, you can chamfer edges. In this case, the chamfer splits an edge into more edges and offsets them from their original location. In Figure 4.32, the corner edge of a box (shown on the right) is selected and chamfered (shown on the left).

Use Chamfer with some caution, because you can create overlapping geometry without realizing it.

Figure 4.32

Chamfering an edge

Weld

Welding vertices helps you combine vertices on a poly or mesh that should occupy the same space. It helps simplify the model by taking out extra vertices that need not be there. Welding also can help shape your model. The following steps show you how to weld vertices together:

1. Start with a new Editable Poly sphere, in a new scene if you wish. Remember, to get an Editable Poly sphere, create a sphere and convert it to an editable poly by right-clicking on the Sphere entry in the Modifier Stack and selecting **Editable Poly.**

2. Select two vertices next to each other on the sphere. Select the **Weld Settings** button to open the window shown here.

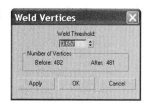

3. Use the Weld Threshold spinner in the Weld Settings window to weld the two vertices together, as shown in Figure 4.33. The Weld tool combines selected vertices that are within the threshold you set.

Weld is used a lot when detail is added to a model, such as with a chamfer, and some of the points need to be pulled together and combined into a single point.

Bevel

As you saw earlier in the chapter, a Bevel command creates a rounded edge for an extrusion. First, select the polygon, and then click **Bevel** in the Modify panel under the Edit Polygon rollout to create a bevel like the one shown in Figure 4.34.

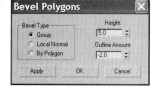

You can also click the **Settings** button next to Bevel to open the Bevel Settings window shown here.

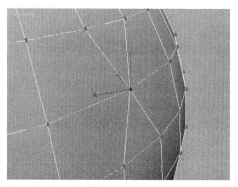

Figure 4.33
Welding two vertices together

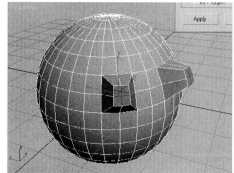

Figure 4.34
A pair of beveled polygons

Outline

The Outline function allows you to resize a polygon cleanly. Follow these steps to outline a polygon:

1. With a new Editable Poly sphere, go into Polygon level and select a polygon on the face of the sphere.

2. Select the **Outline Settings** button and set a desired Outline Amount value in the Settings window, as shown here.

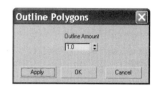

   Then click **OK** or **Apply**. The polygon will change size, and the edges of the polygons around it will shift to accommodate the newly outlined polygon, as shown in Figure 4.35.

   Outline lets you increase or decrease the size of the edges of a polygon. Using Outline is similar to selecting the polygon and scaling it with the Scale tool, but Outline is cleaner and easier to control.

> Clicking **OK** and clicking **Apply** in a dialog window are not the same. Clicking **OK** will perform the respective function and close the Settings window. Clicking **Apply** will perform the action but keep the window open.

Inset

Similar to the Outline function for a polygon, the Inset function creates a tapered version of the original polygon that is inset from its original location. An inset is similar to a bevel, but it doesn't add any height to the polygon. Select a polygon on your editable poly, and click **Inset** on the Modify panel's Edit Polygons rollout. You can click and drag in the viewport to set the Inset size, or click the **Settings** button next to the Inset button to open the Inset Settings window, as shown here. Figure 4.36 shows an Inset polygon on a sphere.

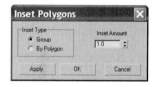

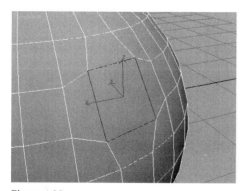

Figure 4.35
An Outlined Polygon on the sphere

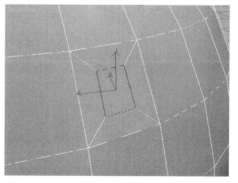

Figure 4.36
An Inset is similar to a beveled polygon, but without any height added to it.

Hinge from Edge

Now let's see some of the more involved tools in the Editable Poly toolset. The Hinge from Edge tool creates a series of new polygons that rotate along an edge on the surface of an existing poly, connecting it to the original object. You can think of it as an extrusion with a rotation.

Follow these steps to see Hinge from Edge in action:

1. Create a new sphere in a new scene, and convert it to an editable poly. Enter into Polygon-level selection.

2. Select a polygon and click the **Hinge from Edge** button, as shown here, to open the Hinge Polygons from Edge Settings window in Figure 4.37.

3. Select the edge that will be the hinge or the edge about which the polygons will extrude and rotate. To select the hinge edge, click the **Pick Hinge** button in the dialog box next to the Current Hinge parameter. Then, in the viewport, go to the selected polygon and choose which edge you want to use.

4. Once you select the hinge, the polygon will hinge out, rotating about that selected edge however many degrees are cited in the Angle parameter. You can use the spinner to select or you can enter the desired angle value for the hinge. The model will interactively hinge the polygon as you set the Angle value. Figure 4.38 shows a small hinge. Notice the hinge is flat, as it only has a Segments value of 1.

5. In the Settings window, change the Angle value to 90, and the Segments value to 5. Press OK to complete the function. Figure 4.39 shows the results.

The Hinge from Edge tool is an interesting way to extrude, and it can be handy in many instances, such as when you're creating an awning or a curved overhang. Remember, the smoother you need the hinge to be, the more segments you will need to add.

Figure 4.37

The Hinge Polygons from Edge Settings window

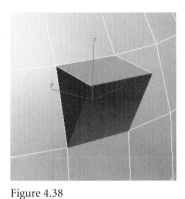

Figure 4.38

A hinged polygon on the sphere, but with only one segment

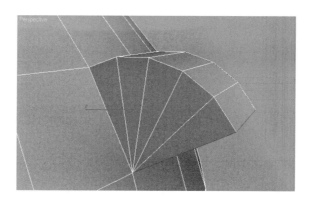

Figure 4.39

A smoother hinge is created when you increase the segments parameter.

Cap

The *Cap* function creates a new polygon to fill a hole on a surface. For this function, you'll need to be in the Border-level selection. To see a cap in action, follow these steps:

1. Create a new sphere and convert it to an editable poly.

2. Select a few polys that are next to each other, side by side, and delete them by pressing the **Delete** key. You should now have holes in your sphere, as shown.

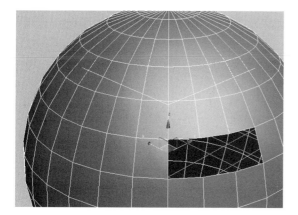

3. You may be wondering why you did that. You need to have a hole in the polygon surface for a Cap function and to check out the Border sub-object. As you may recall, a Border-level selection is the row of edges around a hole in a surface or on the edge of a surface, where only one side of the edge has a polygon. In the case of this sphere, the border is the line of edges surrounding the hole.

4. Now you need to cap the hole. Enter the Border-level selection by pressing the **Border** icon or pressing **3**. Under the Edit Borders rollout, select **Cap**. The hole should be filled with a single polygon, as shown in Figure 4.40.

Figure 4.40

The Cap function fills in a hole with a single polygon.

Figure 4.40

The Cap function fills in a hole with a single polygon.

This tool can be very convenient. If you have done something to a polygon but don't like it, you can delete that poly and use the Cap tool to create a new one. Keep in mind, however, that cap will use a flat polygon to fill the hole, so a complex surface hole will not be patched with the same surface contours as the original.

Extrude Along Spline

The *Extrude Along Spline* function works just as it sounds. It will extrude a polygon sub-object along a spline path, which is a curve drawn in 3ds Max. Splines will be introduced later in this chapter and covered more extensively in the following chapters.

To see the Extrude Along Spline function in action, open the Path Extrude.max file found in the Chapter 4 directory in its Scenes folder. This file has a sphere that has already been converted to an editable poly and a spline that will act as the path of extrusion. To continue, follow these steps:

1. Select the sphere and go into Poly mode (use shortcut 4, or select the Poly icon in the Modify panel's Selection rollout). Select a polygon; it doesn't matter which one.

2. Click the **Settings** button next to Extrude Polygons Along Spline to open the Settings window for the tool, as shown here.

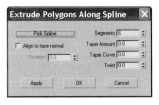

3. Click the Pick Spline button and click the spline next to the sphere.

4. Immediately, you will see an extruded element coming from the sphere. It probably doesn't look very good because you still need to work with the parameters.

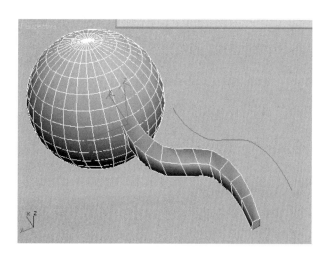

Figure 4.41

A polygon on this sphere is extruded along a spline path.

5. Start by adding more segments; 15 to 20 should give you a good-looking extrusion. The extrusion in Figure 4.41 is the result of 11 segments, –0.5 taper amount, and 2.0 taper curve.

Play around with some of the settings to get a good feel for what this tool can do. As a matter of fact, it's a really good idea to play around with all of the tool settings you have seen here and some of the ones you haven't. This is a good way, if not somewhat frustrating, to learn 3ds Max—or any 3D program for that matter. Use this sphere, or another editable poly you create, to experiment with the different tools available in this rollout for all the sub-object levels to get a basic idea of how things work. You can rely on the text in this book, as well as the online user reference dialog titled "Autodesk 3ds Max Reference," which you can launch from 3ds Max's Help menu.

Modeling a Chest of Drawers

Let's finally put some of your newfound knowledge into practice. If you skipped to this section from the beginning of the chapter or even from the beginning of the book, look at the previous sections in this chapter after you finish this model. Doing so will help fill in some of the gaps in your CG education and better explain how or why you've accomplished some of this exercise's topics.

In this section, you will model a chest of drawers (or dresser) to develop your editable-poly muscles. Why buy a chest of drawers when you can just make one in 3ds Max? Make sure you make it large enough for all your socks.

Ready, Set, Reference!

You're so close to modeling something! You'll want to get some sort of reference for what you're modeling. Study the photo in Figure 4.42 for a look at the desired result.

Figure 4.42

Modeling this chest of drawers

There are plenty of reference photos, and you will access them throughout this exercise to help build different parts of the chest. You may want to flip through the following pages to see the various photos to get a better idea of what you will be modeling.

Of course, if this were your chest of drawers, you could have captured tons of pictures already, right?

Ready, Set, Model!

Create a Project called Dresser, or copy the Dresser project from the companion CD directly to your hard drive.

> It's never a good idea to work from a CD. To learn how to create a new project, see Chapter 2, "Your First 3ds Max Animation."

Top of the Dresser

To begin the chest of drawers model, follow these steps:

1. Begin with a new scene (choose File → New, and click **New All** in the pop-up window). Select the **Perspective** viewport and enable Edged Faces mode in the view (right-click the viewport name and toggle on **Edged Faces** from the menu). Go to the Create panel. In the Geometry heading, click **Box**. You are going to create a box using the Keyboard Entry rollout shown here.

2. Using the Keyboard Entry rollout allows you to specify the exact size and location to create an object in your scene. Leave the *X*, *Y*, and *Z* values at 0, but enter these values: Length of **15**, Width of **30**, and Height of **40**. Click **Create** to create a box aligned in the center of the scene with the specified dimensions.

3. With the box still selected, go to the Modify panel. You can see the box's parameters here. You will need to add more height segments, so change the Height Segs parameter to 6. Your box should look like the box in Figure 4.43.

4. Add an Editable Poly modifier to the box by selecting the box and choosing Modifiers → Mesh Editing → Edit Poly. As shown in Figure 4.44, you can always go through the Modifier Stack to convert the box to the editable poly instead of using the menus.

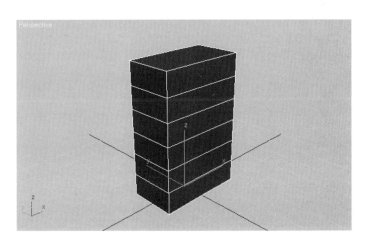

Figure 4.43

The box from which a beautiful chest of drawers will emerge.

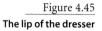

Figure 4.44

Add an Edit Poly modifier

Figure 4.45

The lip of the dresser

5. Press **4** on your keyboard to take you to the Polygon sub-object mode. Now select the polygon on the top of the box. As you can see in the viewport, the polygon is shaded red when it's selected.

6. Now go to the Edit Polygons rollout in the Modify panel and select **Settings** (the button next to Bevel). We are going to bevel several times to create the lip on the crown of the dresser shown in Figure 4.45.

7. Enter the following parameters: Height: **0.5** and Outline Amount: **1.3**. Keep the Bevel Type set to Group as shown. Bevel Type will be explained in the Hand Modeling exercise in the next section. For now, just know that when you bevel only one poly, the Bevel Type is irrelevant; it is only for multiple polygons. Click **Apply** (*not* the **OK** button), and 3ds Max will apply the specified settings without closing the window to give you results that should be similar to Figure 4.46.

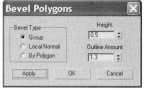

8. After the first bevel is applied, add more bevels to round out the crown. In the still-open Bevel Polygons window, input these parameters: Height: **0.1** and Outline Amount: **0.06**. Click **Apply** (you want to keep the Bevel window open because you'll need to bevel several times). This will bevel a very slight bit up, as shown in Figure 4.47.

9. For the third bevel, input the following values: Height: **0.1** and Outline Amount: **0.03**. Click Apply. Next, input these values: Height: **0.1** and Outline Amount: **0**. Click Apply. This creates a slight curve in the crown. Again enter new values: Height: **0.3** and Outline Amount: **0**. Click Apply. For the sixth bevel, change the values: Height: **0.1** and Outline Amount: **–0.06**. Click Apply. Finally, enter these values: Height: **0.1** and Outline Amount: **–0.08**. Click OK. Your dresser's top should resemble Figure 4.48 and Figure 4.49.

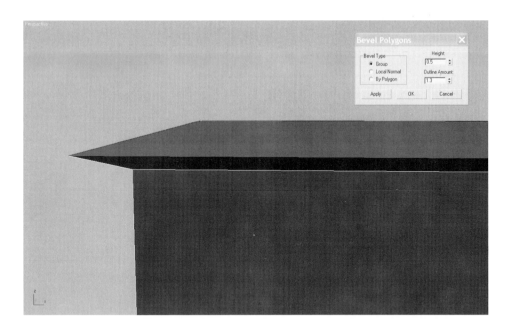

Figure 4.46

The first bevel for the crown of the dresser

Figure 4.47

The second bevel is hardly noticeable.

Figure 4.48

The crown lip of the dresser's top

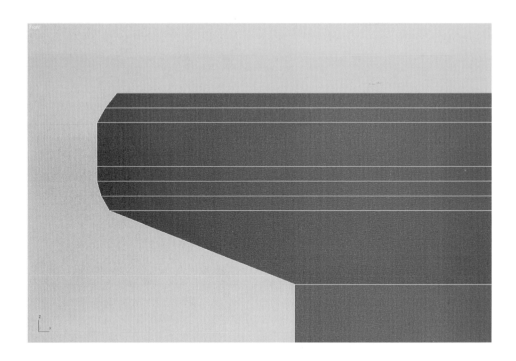

Figure 4.49

The dresser top is ready.

These bevel amounts are not necessarily set in stone. You can play around with the settings to get as close to the image as you can or to add your own design flair. You can load the Dresser01.max scene file from the Scenes folder in the Dresser project on the companion CD.

Bottom of the Dresser

Now it is time for the bottom of the dresser. This dresser doesn't have legs, but it has a nice detail at the bottom nonetheless, as you can see in Figures 4.50 and 4.51. To create this detail, you need to extrude a segment.

1. You should already be in Poly sub-object mode if you are continuing with your own file, so select the poly on the bottom of the dresser as shown here.

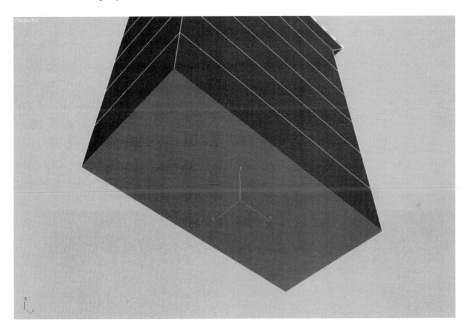

2. Go to the Edit Poly rollout, select the Extrude Settings button, change the Extrusion Height to **2.5** as shown, and click **OK**. This will extrude a polygon out from the bottom of the dresser, essentially adding a segment to the box as shown in Figure 4.52.

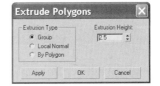

Figure 4.50

An angle view of the dresser's bottom corner

Figure 4.51

A straight view of the dresser's bottom corner

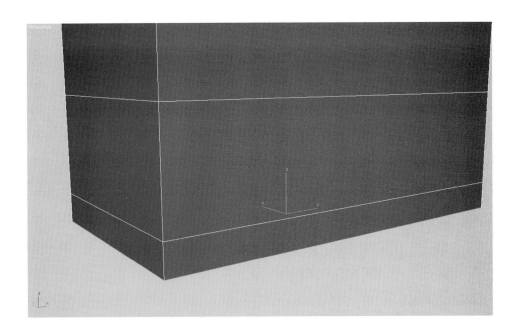

Figure 4.52

Extrude the bottom of the dresser.

3. The polygon will still be selected, so select the Inset button, change the Inset Amount to **0.6**, and click **OK**. This creates an inset poly, as shown here.

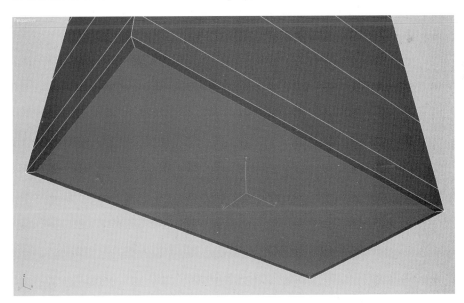

4. The poly is still selected, so select the Extrude Settings button, enter an Extrusion Height of **–2.0**, and click OK. Figure 4.53 shows how the bottom of the dresser has moved up into itself slightly.

Figure 4.53

The dresser's bottom lip

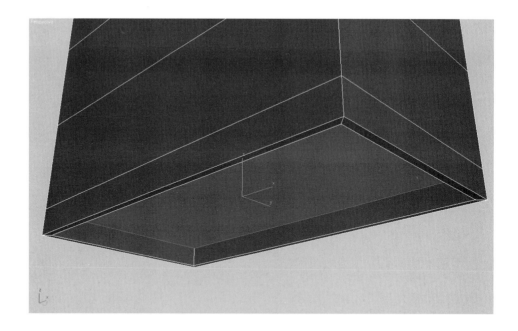

Figure 4.54

A mock-up of how the bottom lip needs to be cut

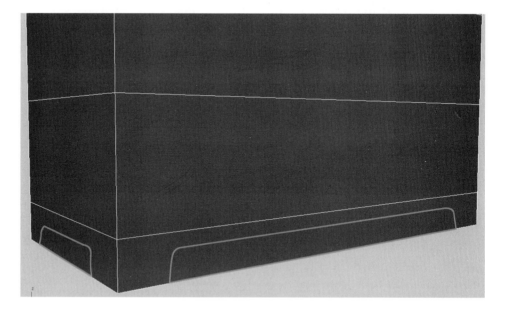

To create the detail on the bottom, you need to add more segments in the newly extruded polygons. Figure 4.54 shows a mock-up of how the bottom lip should be cut. To do this, you will use the Slice tool. The Slice tool works only when the polygons are selected. You will start by slicing into the extruded polygons on the front and back of the bottom lip.

1. Select all the polygons that make up the front and back lip of the bottom. Make sure you select the front, back, and bottom of the front and back lip as shown in the following graphic. The selections are marked darker in the graphic. It is also a good idea to lock your selection. The Lock icon  appears at the bottom of the interface. When that icon is highlighted yellow, whatever you have selected will be locked and will not be deselected until you disable the Selection Lock.

The keyboard shortcut for the Selection Lock toggle is the spacebar.

2. When all the necessary polygons are selected, go to the Edit Geometry rollout and click the Slice Plane tool as shown here. When you select the Slice Plane tool, a yellow wire box will surround the selected polygons; this is the Slice Plane gizmo. Position/rotate the gizmo where you want to slice your polygon, as shown in Figure 4.55.

3. Until now, when you have selected a polygon, it turned solid red in the viewport. You can change it to display as outline when a polygon is selected, and not as solid red. You will need to do this so you can see the new edges you are creating. To turn off Shaded Edge mode, press **F2**. Your selected polygons will now show red only around the edges.

4. With the Slice Plane tool still active, right-click in the viewport to bring up the Quad menu. Go to the Transform menu and select Rotate. Figure 4.56 shows this shortcut for the Transform tools.

Figure 4.55

The Slice Plane gizmo

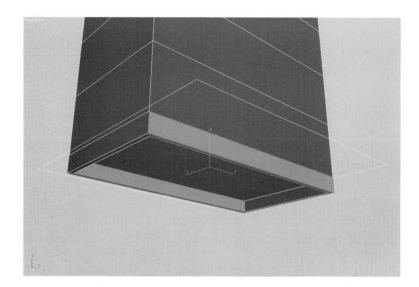

Figure 4.56

Rotate the Slice Plane gizmo.

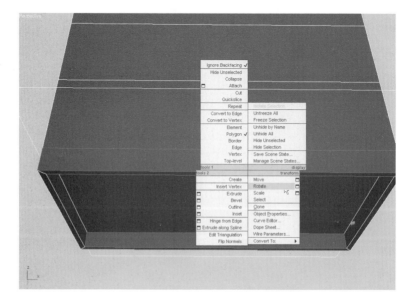

5. You need to rotate the Slice Plane gizmo 90 degrees along the *Y*-axis. Center the cursor over the Transform gizmo's *Y*-axis (green wire), and click/drag until the Transform type-in box at the bottom of the interface reads 90 in the *Y*-box, or enter the rotation amount for *Y* and press **Enter**. As you rotate, you will see the slice interactively displayed as a red line on the selected polygons.

6. Use the Move tool (W) to position the Slice Plane gizmo where you want the first slice. The movement will be along the *X*-axis or horizontal along the box. When the Slice Plane gizmo is positioned as shown in Figure 4.57, go to the Edit Geometry rollout and click **Slice**. Don't click Slice plane because that will deactivate only the Slice Plane tool. You must click the Slice button because it is like clicking an Apply button for the Slice Plane tool. Once you click Slice, the polygon will have a new segment at that location. The Slice Plane tool should still be active.

7. You need four slices at each end of the dresser bottom, as shown in Figure 4.58. Keep in mind that the polygons are selected on the front and back so that the Slice Plane tool will slice only polygons that are selected within the gizmo. Click the Slice Plane button to deactivate the tool when you have placed four vertical slices in all four corners of the front and back bottom lips of the dresser, as shown in Figure 4.58.

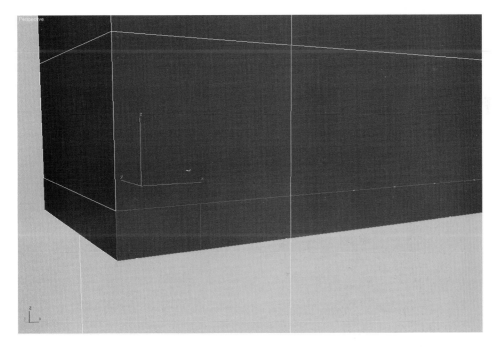

Figure 4.57

Place a slice in the corner for the foot of the dresser.

Figure 4.58

Place four vertical slices at each corner.

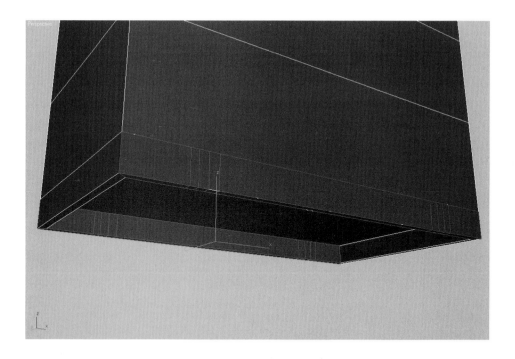

8. Press the spacebar to unlock your selection. You are going to use a combination of moving edges and polygons to create the detail on the bottom of the dresser as shown here.

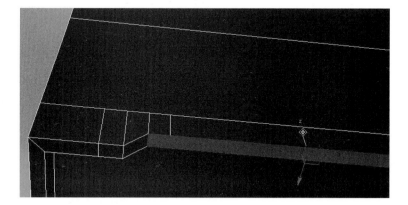

Select the relevant polygons, and use the Move tool to place them as shown in Figure 4.59.

Don't worry if your adjustments don't have a perfectly smooth curve. Unless the camera is right on top of the detail, it will look good from a distance. A perfect curve is not necessary, especially for our purposes.

You can use the same techniques in the steps 1 through 8 to create detail in the side bottom lip of the dresser, as shown in Figure 4.60. Make sure you save your work.

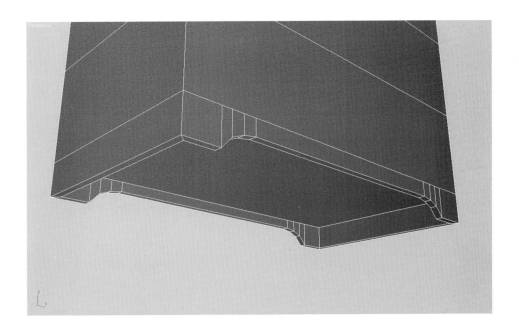

Figure 4.59

Move polygons to create detail in the dresser feet.

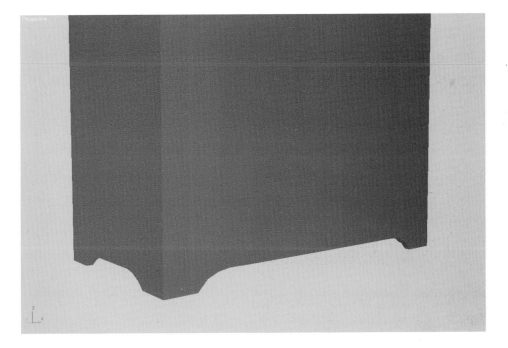

Figure 4.60

Use the same steps to create the details on the sides of the bottom.

I Can See Your Drawers

In the beginning of this exercise, you created a box with six segments on its height. You can use those segments to create the drawers. This is an example of thinking ahead and planning your model before you start an object. This was by far the easiest way to go; using the Slice Plane tool to add segments for the drawers after the box is made is doable, but much more laborious.

For simplicity's sake, you will not create drawers that can open and shut in this exercise. If this dresser were to be used in an animation in which the drawers would be opened, you would make them differently.

First, take a look at the drawers and see where you have to go. Figure 4.61 shows the drawers and an important detail we need to consider. Luckily, you needn't worry about the junk on top of the dresser.

Figure 4.61

Checking out the real dresser drawers

Gap Between Drawers and Dresser

To model the drawers, begin with these steps:

1. Create a small gap around the edge of the box. This gap will represent the space between the drawer and the main body of the dresser (Figure 4.61). Go to Polygon mode (press **4**), and select the six polygons on the front of the box that represent the drawers. Remember to hold the Ctrl key while selecting the additional polygons; this will allow you to make multiple polygon selections, as shown.

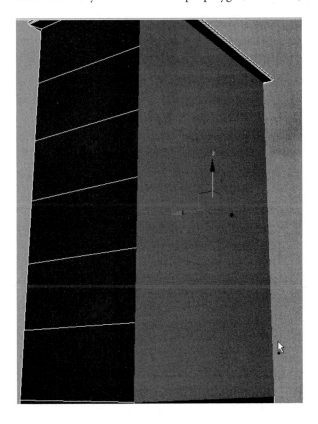

2. Go to the Edit Polygons rollout in the Modify panel, and click the Inset Settings button. Set the Inset Amount to **0.6** and keep the Inset Type to **Group**, as shown here. Click **OK**. Figure 4.62 shows the result of the Inset operation.

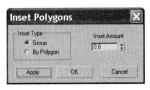

You can load the Dresser02.max scene file from the Scenes folder in the Dresser project on the companion CD to check your work or to begin the next series of steps.

Figure 4.62

The Inset creates the detail needed to make the drawers.

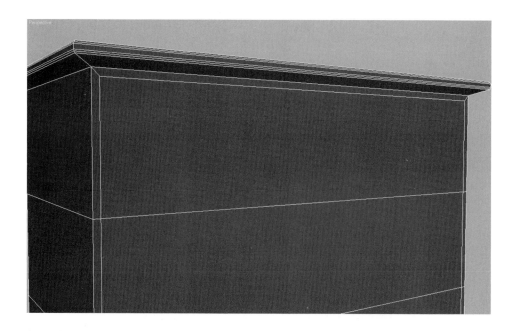

3. Keep those newly inset polygons selected, and go back to the Edit Polygons rollout to select the Extrude Settings button. Change the Extrusion Height to **–0.5**, keep Extrusion Type set to Group, and press **OK**. The faces will now extrude inward a little bit, as shown here.

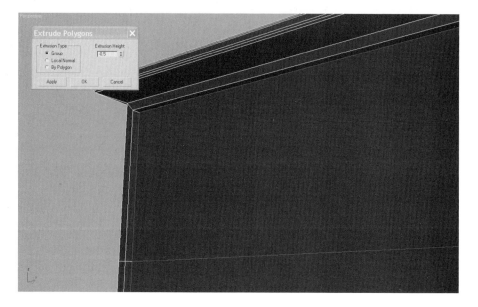

4. In the original reference picture (Figure 4.42), the top drawer of the dresser is split into two, so you need to slice that top-drawer polygon vertically to create two drawers. Make sure the selected polygons are displayed with the red outlines instead of the solid red color (you can toggle between these views with the **F2 key**). Switch your viewport to a front view.

5. Select the polygon that represents the top drawer, as shown in Figure 4.63. Select **Slice Plane** in the Edit Geometry rollout. Rotate and move the Slice Plane gizmo so that it is vertical and centered on the polygon as shown here, and click Slice. Click the Slice Plane button to release the tool.

6. The polygons are still selected after the Slice operation, so go back to the Edit Polygons rollout and click **Inset Settings**. Set the Inset Amount to **0.25**. This time we are going to change the Inset Type from Group to By Polygon, as shown here.

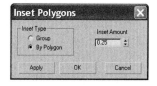

This setting insets each polygon individually, instead of performing this operation on multiple, contiguous polygons (which is what the Group option does). Click **OK** to run the Inset operation. Your polygons should resemble the ones in Figure 4.64.

Figure 4.63

**Select the top
drawer polygon.**

Figure 4.64

**The drawers are
inset separately.**

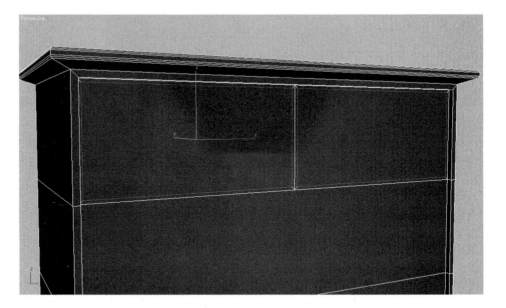

7. Perform the same inset operation on the remaining drawer polygons on the front of the box (as shown): Set the Inset Amount to **.25**, and set the Inset Type to **By Polygon**. This will inset the five lower, wide drawers.

8. Select all of the "drawer" polygons. Go to the Edit Polygons rollout and click **Extrude Settings**. Set the Extrude Amount to **0.7** as shown here. You don't need it to extrude very much; you just want the drawers to extrude a bit more than the body of the dresser.

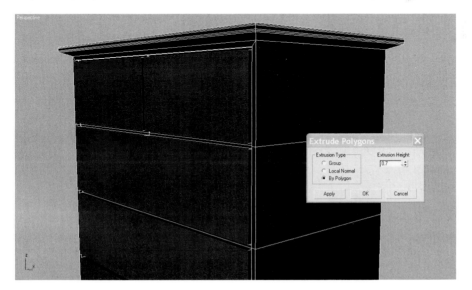

Go grab yourself a frosty beverage! The dresser is finished. Go ahead and name the dresser. You can even change the color of the dresser if you'd like. Go to the Name and Color type-in box (shown in Figure 4.65), change the name of the object to **Dresser**, and pick a nice light color.

The finished dresser body should look like the dresser in Figure 4.66. Remember to save this version of your file. You can also load the `Dresser03.max` scene file from the Scenes folder in the Dresser project on the companion CD to check your work or to skip to this part in the exercise.

Creating the Knobs

Figure 4.65

Name the dresser and pick a nice color.

Object Name Type-In   Object Default Color

Now that the body of the dresser is done, it's time to add the final bit of detail to make the dresser complete: knobs. We will use Splines and a few surface creation tools new to your workflow. Goose bumps, anyone? Take a look at the reference for the knobs in Figure 4.67. You are going to create a profile of the knob and then rotate the profile around its axis to form a surface. This technique is known as *Lathe*, not to be mistaken for *latte*, which is a whole different deal and not really covered in this book.

Here's a quick rundown of what a spline is. A spline is a group of vertices and connecting segments that form a line or curve. To create the knob profile, we are going to use the Line Spline, shaped in the outline of—you guessed it—a knob. The Line tool allows you to create a free-form spline.

Figure 4.66

The finished dresser body

Figure 4.67
Knobs

You can use your last file from the Dresser exercise, or you can load `Dresser03.max` from the Scenes folder of the Dresser project on the companion CD. To build the knobs, follow these steps:

1. Make sure you are in the Left viewport, so you can see which side of the dresser the drawers are on, as shown here. You are going to create a profile of half the knob, as shown in Figure 4.68. Don't worry about creating all the detail in the knob because detail won't be seen; a simple outline will be fine.

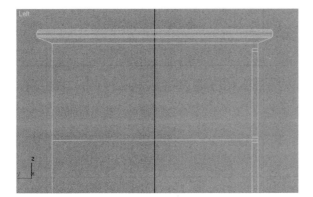

Figure 4.68

The intended profile curve for the knob

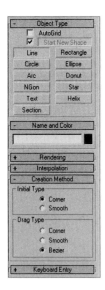

2. Go to the Create panel and choose Shapes . Click the Line button. Use the current default values in the Creation Method rollout, as shown here.

3. In the Left viewport, click once to lay down a vertex for this line, starting at the bottom of the intended profile for the knob. This is the starting point for the curve. When you are creating a line, every click lays down the next vertex for the line. In essence, the vertex controls the position of a point of the line. If you want to create a curve in the line, click once and drag the mouse in any direction to give the vertex a curvature of sorts. This curve vertex creates a curve in that part of the line. You will need to follow the rough outline of a knob, so click and drag where there is curvature in the line. Once you have laid down your first vertex, continue to click and drag more vertices for the line clockwise until you create the half-profile knob shape shown in Figure 4.68.

Figure 4.69 shows the profile line with the vertices numbered according to their creation order.

To create a straight line segment between two vertices, press and hold **Shift** to keep the next vertex to be laid down orthogonal to the last vertex, either horizontally or vertically.

4. Once you lay down your last vertex at the top, finish the spline by either right-clicking to release the Line tool or clicking the first vertex you created to close the spline. For this example, it really doesn't matter which method you choose. Either an open or closed spline will work; however, a closed spline is shown in Figure 4.69. Drawing splines entails a bit of a learning curve, so it might be helpful to delete the one you did first and try again for the practice. Once you get something resembling the spline in Figure 4.69, you can edit it. Don't drive yourself crazy; just get the spline as close as you can.

> When you are creating a line, you can click once to create a corner vertex for the line, but you need to click and drag to create a Bezier vertex if you want to put a curve into the line.

5. With the spline selected, go to the Modify panel. In the Modifier Stack window, you will see the entry Line with a plus sign in a black box next to it denoting that it has sub-object modes. Click the plus sign (+) to expand the list of sub-objects, as shown here.

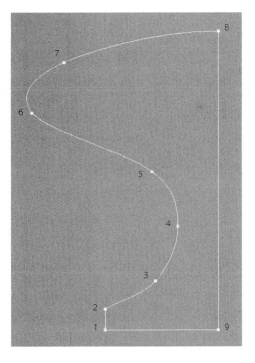

Figure 4.69

The knob's profile line's vertices are numbered according to the order in which they were created.

A LINE'S VERTEX TYPE

When you center your cursor over a line's vertex and right-click to bring up the shortcut menu shown, you will have access to several vertex controls. In that shortcut menu, under the Tools1 heading, you can choose a vertex type.

The vertex types are the following:

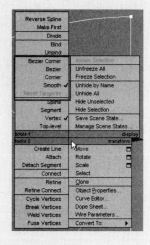

Smooth: A Smooth vertex creates a smooth continuous curve. The actual curvature at a smooth vertex depends on the spacing of the adjacent vertices. This is a nonadjustable vertex, meaning it has no handles with which you can control the curvature directly.

Corner: A Corner vertex is nonadjustable, which creates sharp corners.

Bezier: A Bezier vertex is a vertex that has locked continuous handles that create a smooth curve. You can directly adjust the curvature at a Bezier vertex by manipulating its handles. Adjusting a handle on one side of the vertex will also adjust the other side's handle, as they are continuous.

Bezier Corner: A Bezier Corner vertex creates a sharp corner like the Corner vertex, but it has discontinuous tangent handles with which you can control the curvature of the line at that vertex. The handle on one side of the vertex will not affect the handle on the other side.

In some ways, Line's sub-objects are similar to the Editable Poly sub-object modes. However, when you are working with a spline, you are working with a 2D nonrendering object. A spline is made up of three sub-objects: a vertex, a segment, and a spline. As you know, a *vertex* is a point in space. A *segment* is the line that connects two vertices. The Spline mode allows you to select and/or transform a single or multiple splines within a spline object. To continue with the project, follow these steps:

1. Choose the vertex sub-object for the line. Make sure you are still working in the Left viewport. When you're working with 2D splines, it is always best to work in Orthographic view. Use the Move tool to click on one of the vertices. The vertex has a Transform gizmo just like an object. Use the Move tool to edit the shape to better fit the outline of the knob.

   Be sure to read the sidebar in this section entitled "A Line's Vertex Type" to learn more about the types of vertices a line can have and how it can change the curvature of a line. If needed, you can change the vertex type of your line's vertices to control the curvature.

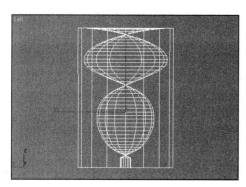

Figure 4.70

Eeek! That isn't a knob at all.

To catch up to this point, you can load the `Dresser04.max` file from the Scenes folder of the Dresser project on the companion CD.

2. The profile line is ready to turn into a 3D object. This is where the modifiers are used. Get out of sub-object mode for your line. Choose Modifiers → Patch/Spline Editing → Lathe. (You could also go to the Modifier List and choose **Lathe** from the alphabetical list of modifiers.) When you first put the Lathe modifier on your spline, it won't look anything like the knob (see Figure 4.70)—but don't panic! You need to futz with the parameters to get it right (Figure 4.71). Right now the object is turned inside out.

3. Go to the Parameters rollout and under the `Align` heading click the Max button. It's a knob! Now, that is more like it. You just had to change the alignment of the axis so the lathe revolution would be correct.

> If step 3 does not work properly for you, try clicking **Min** instead of **Max** under the `Align` heading. When you are creating a line, where you begin to create that line and in what order you place the vertices (clockwise or counterclockwise) are both important. This example drew the knob's profile line in a clockwise direction.

4. Rotate the perspective view so you can see the top of the knob. You should notice a strange artifact. To correct this, check the Weld Core box under the Parameters rollout for the lathe.

That's it! Check out Figure 4.72 for a look at the lathed knob. By using Splines and Lathe, you can create all sorts of surfaces for your models. In the next section, you will resize the knob, position it, and copy it to fit on the drawers.

Figure 4.71

The titillating parameters for the Lathe

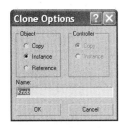

Figure 4.72

The lathe completes the knob.

Figure 4.73

Using an instance to copy the knob

Figure 4.74

The dresser, knobs, and all

Copying the Knob

Now that you have a knob, you may need to adjust it and make it the right size. If you still want to futz with the knob, go back down the stack to the line to edit your spline. For example, you may want to scale the knob a bit to better fit the drawer (refer to the reference photo in Figure 4.67). Select the Scale tool, and click and drag until the original line is about 40 percent smaller. The Lathe modifier will re-create the surface to fit the new size. You can also delete the knob and restart with another line for more practice. In the following steps, you will copy and position the knob for the drawers.

1. Position and rotate the knob to fit on to the front of a top drawer. Change its default color (if you want) and change its name to **Knob**.

2. You'll need a few copies of the original knob, one for each drawer. Choose Edit → Clone (Figure 4.73). You are going to use the Instance command. An instance is a copy, but is still connected to the original. If you edit the original or an instance, all of the instances change. Click **OK** to create an instance.

3. Position the instanced knob in the middle of the other top drawer.

4. Using additional instances of the original knob, place knobs in the middle of all the remaining drawers of your dresser, as shown in Figure 4.74.

As you saw with this exercise, there are plenty of tools for the Editable Poly object. Your model doesn't have to be all of the same type of modeling either. In this example, we created the dresser with *box modeling* techniques, where you begin with a single box and extrude your way into a model, and with surface creation techniques using splines.

You can compare your work to the scene file Dresser05.max from the Scenes folder of the Dresser project on the companion CD.

Modeling a Hand

Now that you've had some experience modeling in 3ds Max, you can tackle modeling a simple hand. The goal is to acquire experience with some other tools 3ds Max has to offer. Before you begin modeling, look at a reference. Luckily, you probably have one or two hands at the ends of your arms.

> If you have access to *Introducing Maya 2008: 3d for Beginners*, by this volume's author, you can also reference a similar hand modeling tutorial to see how modeling workflows compare between 3ds Max and Maya.

Starting the Palm

There are several ways to model a hand, but you'll start with the same modeling techniques you started with in the Dresser exercise. To begin box-modeling the hand, follow these steps:

1. Start a new 3ds Max file in a new project called Hand, or copy the Hand project from the companion CD to your hard drive.

2. Make sure the Perspective viewport is active. Create a box on the Home Grid in the Perspective viewport. You are going to use Keyboard Entry to create the box to certain specifications. In the Keyboard Entry rollout in the Create panel's parameters for the box, enter the following parameters: Length of **90**, Width of **150**, and Height of **30**, as shown in the graphic on the right. The *X*-, *Y*-, and *Z*-parameters in the Keyboard Entry rollout are used to place the object in your scene by using the coordinate you specify. Keep those values at **0** to create the box in the center of your scene. Choose the Create button at the bottom of the rollout to create the box as defined.

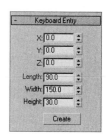

3. Go to the Modify panel, and you will see the parameters for the box. You need to subdivide the box so it has more polygons. Press **F4** to toggle on Edged Face mode in your viewport. In the Modify panel's Parameters rollout, set the box's Length Segs to **4**, Width Segs to **3**, and Height Segs to **1**, as you see here.

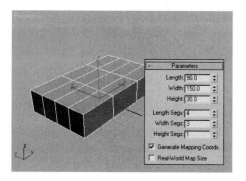

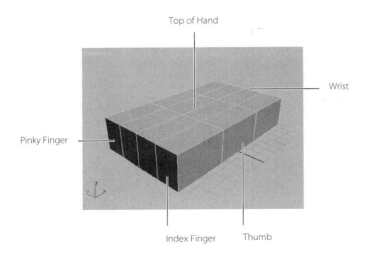

4. Look at the box and imagine that it is the palm of the hand. The polygons facing you in Figure 4.75 are going to be the fingers. The poly farthest from you will be the pinky finger, and the one nearest will be the index. This should help you get oriented.

5. Convert the box into an Editable Poly object (not the Edit Poly modifier). You can reference the Dresser exercise in this chapter if you have skipped to this section.

6. The fingers' polygons will need to be slightly splayed out, so they will not all stick together when you extrude them. Use the Edge sub-object mode to do this. In the Modifier Stack, click the plus (+) sign to reveal the sub-objects for the box.

7. Use the keyboard shortcut **2** to choose the Edge sub-object level. Select the edge closest to you (which will be the outer edge of the index finger), as shown in Figure 4.76.

Figure 4.76

Select the edge of the index finger.

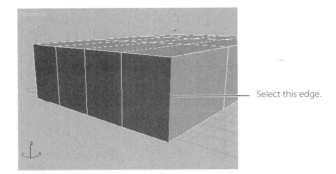

8. Click the Lock Selection icon ( ) or press the spacebar to lock this selection so you don't lose the selected edge. The Lock button will turn yellow, indicating it is in use.

9. Use the keyboard shortcut **W** to enable the Move tool. Move the edge along the X-axis. You might find it easier to use the Top viewport for the move. Use the Transform gizmo—center the pointer so that the X and the tail of the X-axis arrow are yellow.

Yellow indicates that the axis is active. This will confine the movement to the *X*-axis and no other, as shown here.

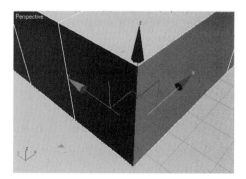

10. Switch to the Top viewport and move the edge, as shown here. Press the spacebar to release the selection Lock.

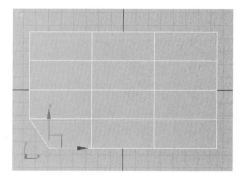

11. Move the other edges to create a slight arch where the top of the palm will be, as shown in the following graphic. This will ensure that when you extrude the polygons for the fingers, there will be space for the webbing in-between. If you don't want the fingers spread apart this much, make the arc less curved. This repositions the polygon to a different angle so it won't extrude straight.

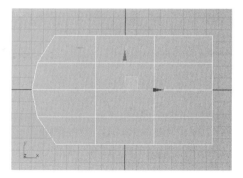

Now is a good time to save with File → Save As. Make sure you use the plus sign (+) instead of pressing the Save button, as this will add a number increment to the end of your filename (for instance, hand01.max) as shown in Figure 4.77. To catch up to this point or to check your own work, load the scene file Hand01.max from the Hand project on the companion CD.

Figure 4.77

Save!

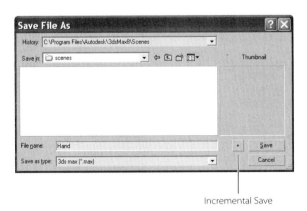

Incremental Save

Creating the Fingers

Now it is time to extrude the fingers.

1. With the box selected, select the Polygon sub-object mode or press **4** on your keyboard. Go to the perspective view. Click on the polygon that represents the index finger (closest to you), as you see here.

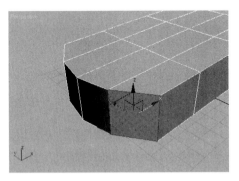

2. Go to the Modify panel under the Edit Polygons rollout. Click the Extrude Settings button (▢) (the Settings button is directly to the right of the extrude button) to bring up the Extrude Settings dialog box. See the sidebar entitled "Extrusion Options" for more about the parameters and options for the Extrude function.

EXTRUDE OPTIONS

Using the palm model of the hand for reference, the options for an extrude operation will behave as indicated here. All of the polygons on the front of the box are selected:

Group—The polygons are extruded out along their averaged normals, effectively extending the palm out, as shown here.

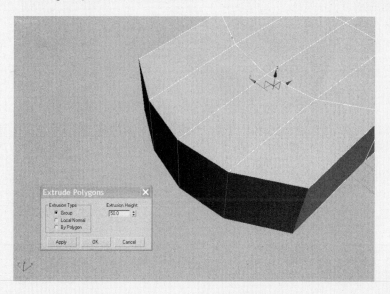

Local Normal—The polygons are extruded straight out along their normal (usually perpendicular to the polygon's face), creating a flare at the end of the palm.

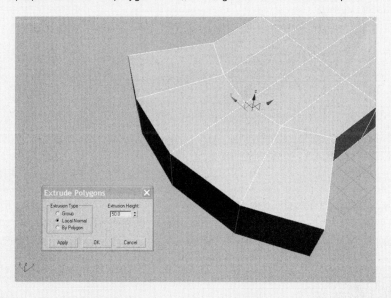

continued

EXTRUDE OPTIONS

By Polygon—Each polygon is extruded individually along its own normal.

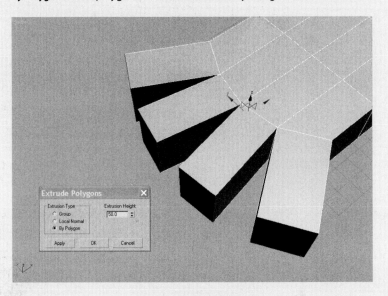

Extrusion Height—Specifies how much to extrude in scene units. As you've already seen, positive values extrude out away from the object, and negative values extrude into the object.

3. We are going to extrude the first finger so that it has three sections, so instead of doing one extrude, we are going to do three back to back. This will give the finger more segments with which to work. If you look at your own finger, you will notice the lower joint is the biggest joint, getting smaller toward the tip of the finger. In the Settings dialog box, set the first amount to **60**. The Setting dialog box allows you to interactively perform these functions so you can see the extrude before you apply it. The 60-unit extrude looks good, so click **Apply**. This keeps the Settings window open. Go to Extrusion Amount and enter **50**; this will change the extruded segment to 50 units. Click Apply again for the second extrusion. Change the extrude amount to **40**, and press **OK** for the last extrusion of the index finger. Figure 4.78 shows the first finger.

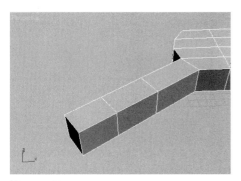

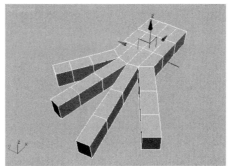

Figure 4.78

The index finger is extruded into place.

Figure 4.79

Fingers!

4. Using the same techniques and the following settings for the extrusion amounts, extrude the rest of the fingers.

FINGER	FIRST EXTRUDE	SECOND EXTRUDE	THIRD EXTRUDE
Middle Finger	70	60	50
Ring Finger	60	50	40
Pinky	50	40	30

Figure 4.79 shows all the fingers extruded. You can use other values as long as you have three segments in each finger. Use your own hand as a guide.

This is a good time to do another Save As; make sure you use the plus sign (+) instead of pressing the Save button. To catch up to this point or to check your own work, load the scene file Hand02.max from the Hand project on the companion CD.

Creating the Thumb

Now you will create the thumb, also using extrusions. Follow these steps:

1. Select the polygon in the middle of the side of the hand, as shown here.

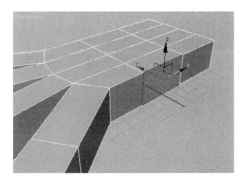

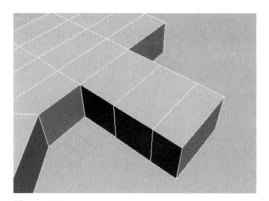

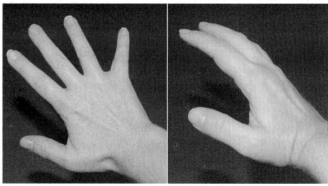

Figure 4.80

Extruding the thumb

Figure 4.81

Notice how the thumb extends from a hand.

As with the fingers, the thumb will have three segments. Select the Extrude Settings button and enter an extrude amount of **30**. With the value of **30**, click **Apply** twice for two 30-unit extrusions. Now enter an extrude amount of **20** and click once more. Click **OK**. Figure 4.80.

2. To shape the thumb, you will use a combination of adjusting edge and poly locations. Figure 4.81 shows a picture of a hand; notice how the thumb extrudes from the bottom of the hand. Using Edge mode, rearrange the edges in the extruded thumb to create a shape as shown in Figure 4.82.

Figure 4.82

Shape your thumb to match by moving and adjusting edges and polygons.

 Save an iteration of your scene. Now you should have the general shape for the hand. It is still very rough, with no detail. To catch up to this point or to check your own work, load the scene file Hand03.max from the Hand project on the companion CD.

Subdivision Surfaces

You may be wondering how to take this boxy thing and turn it into something more organic and realistic. By using Subdivision Surfaces (SubDs), you can take a relatively simple object with very few segments and subdivide the polygons. SubDs make a flat surface appear smoother.

Follow these steps to use Subdivision Surfaces for your hand:

1. To apply the SubD, with the hand selected, check the Use NURMS Subdivision box in the Subdivision Surface rollout in the Modify panel. Figure 4.83 shows the hand before and after you apply the NURMS Subdivision.

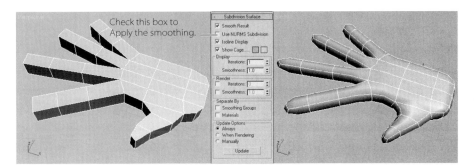

Figure 4.83

Using the NURMS subdivision to smooth out the hand

2. Once the smoothing is applied, you will see an orange cage surrounding the hand if you are in any sub-object mode, as shown here. This allows you to work with this low-res cage while the smoother version is updating at the same time.

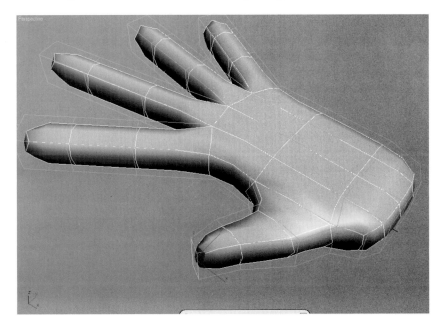

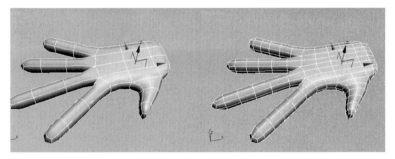

Figure 4.84

When Isoline Display is turned off, all of the faces added by the smoothing operation are shown.

Figure 4.85

You can mold the hand by moving polygons.

3. You can control how much smoothing applies to the hand using the Iterations parameter, which is by default set to 1. Be very careful how many iterations you add. The higher the number, the harder the computer has to work to process the information. You can leave Iterations set to 1 for the hand.

4. Uncheck **Isoline Display** in the Subdivision Surface rollout. When Isoline Display is off, 3ds Max displays all the faces added by the smoothing, as shown on the right in Figure 4.84. The default setting of On shows only the object's original edges, as shown on the left in Figure 4.84.

5. Make sure you are in Polygon sub-object mode. Press **F2** to toggle the Shaded Face mode, so that when you select a poly, it will be shaded in red and easier to see. Now, select a polygon on the hand and right-click to access the shortcuts menu. Select Transform → Move. Move the polygon in any direction. The polygon will pull the surrounding polygons with it, but the selection is softer (Figure 4.85). This makes it possible to model in a push and pull fashion, just as if molding clay.

You don't want to save what you have done with the SubDs, so either undo all the smoothing changes or reopen the last saved file. You will probably find it easier to work with the boxy hand before the NURMS smoothing. You can also just uncheck the Use NURMS Subdivision. You will come back to this later.

Adding Detail to the Hand

You are going to begin adding some simple detail to the hand. One of the easiest ways to do this is using the Cut tool, which is a part of the Cut and Slice Group. You will find the Cut tool in the Edit Geometry rollout, which is shown here.

The Cut tool allows you to divide an edge at any point. You then divide a second edge at any point, and the tool will create a new edge between the two points. To create more edges for detail on the hand, follow these steps:

1. With the hand selected, click the Cut Tool button. Now click the first edge (use Figure 4.86 as a reference) at the first knuckle on the index finger. A new vertex is created where you clicked. A dotted line will track along with your cursor until you click a second edge.

2. Click the opposite edge from your initial one to add a new edge next to the first segment on the index finger. Right-click to exit the tool.

3. Using the same sequence of commands, add new edges to the knuckle areas shown in Figure 4.86. You may want to add the new edges in a Nonperspective viewport.

Working with the Cut tool in a Perspective viewport may be a bit difficult; the newly created edges may appear to jump around the hand or won't place correctly. In the Orthogonal views, it is simpler to read where the Cut tool is placing edges. With the Cut tool, you can cut across any number of faces. Also, if you double-click on the first edge, 3ds Max will divide that edge at the point where you clicked by adding a vertex there. You need not click on a second edge if you double-click.

4. Right-click to exit the tool.

While working with the Cut tool, turn on Ignore Backfacing in the Selection rollout to avoid selecting edges on the back of the hand by accident.

 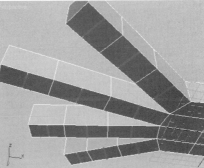

Figure 4.86

Add new edges where shown to add detail to the knuckles.

5. With all the new edges, use the Move tool to move those edges to create the knuckles and the fleshy area on the bottom of the fingers. You can also rearrange the edges at the tip of the finger to give the fingers a more tapered look. Click on Use NURMS Subdivision to see how the knuckles and fingers look with smoothing, as shown in Figure 4.87. You can see how the NURMS SubDs really smooth out the detail; so don't be afraid to exaggerate the detail so that it looks better when smoothed, as you can see on the right in Figure 4.87. Deselect **Use NURMS Subdivision** to return to the boxy hand.

Figure 4.87

See how the smoothing will affect the detail you are adding to the fingers.

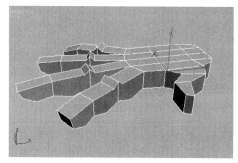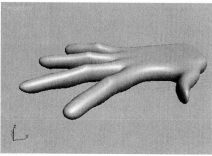

6. Let's add some knuckles at the end of the fingers. You are going to use a tool for adding detail that is another way of subdividing a polygon. Tessellate doesn't give you the control options the Cut tool does, but it can be more precise. The Tessellate button is under the Edit Geometry rollout in the Modify panel. Two Tessellate methods are available: Edge and Face (Figure 4.88).

Figure 4.88

The Tessellate Selection window

See the sidebar in this section titled "Tessellate Options" for more on Tessellate before you use it in the following steps.

Continue with these steps to add detail with the Tessellate function:

1. Before you tessellate any of the polygons on the hand, edit the poly size. The polygons are too long and they should be squarer. Select the lower edge of the polygons and move them closer to the base of the fingers, as you can see in Figure 4.89.

Figure 4.89

Move the edges to make the knuckle polygons squarer.

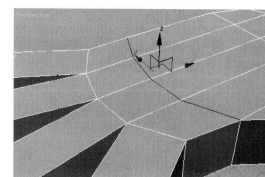

TESSELLATE OPTIONS

Edge—Vertices are inserted in the middle of each edge of the selected polygon, and a line is drawn connecting the new vertices to form new edges inside that polygon. The number of new polygons will be equal to the number of sides on the original polygon.

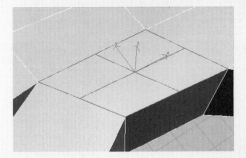

Face—A vertex is inserted into the middle of the selected polygon, and edges are drawn from the original vertices of the polygon to the new vertex. Again, the number of new polygons will be equal to the number of sides on the original polygon.

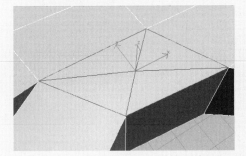

Tension—This parameter controls the Edge tension value, which essentially pulls vertices inward or outward from the plane, creating a concave or rounding effect, respectively. You can see how the edge is concave in this graphic.

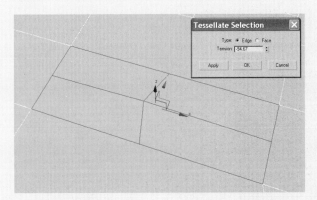

Figure 4.90

Select all four polygons where the fingers meet the hand.

2. Select the polygons at the base of the fingers and hold the Ctrl key down, which will allow you to select all four polygons, as shown in Figure 4.90. Select the Tessellate Settings button under the Edit Geometry rollout. You are going to use the Edge option with Tension set to **0**. Click **OK**, and your hand should tessellate as in Figure 4.91.

3. Switch to Vertex mode and select the vertices in the center of the subdivided polygons. Right-click to access the shortcut menu and choose **Move**. Move the vertices up away from the hand along the Z-axis, as shown in Figure 4.92. Check the Use NURMS Subdivision box to see the smoothing of the hand with the raised knuckles (as shown in Figure 4.93). You may want to go back to Vertex mode while in NURMS to use the SubDs cage to refine the changes. Continue to edit until you are satisfied with the look. Don't forget to save another iteration.

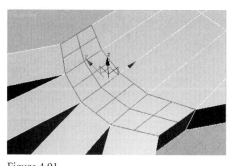

Figure 4.91

The polygons are tessellated to give you more detail.

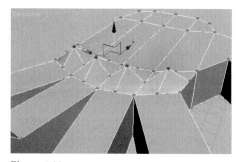

Figure 4.92

Raise the knuckles.

Now that you have created the basic shape for the hand, you should use the NURMS cage to refine and edit the look. Remember you have to be in a sub-object mode for the cage to appear.

To check your work, load the scene file Hand04.max from the Hand project on the companion CD.

Don't bog yourself down trying to model small details such as knuckle wrinkles or lines on the palm. Those details can be added using materials in texturing.

Summary

In this chapter, you learned how to model with 3ds Max. Through exploring the modeling toolsets to creating a dresser and a hand, you saw firsthand how the primary modeling tools in 3ds Max operate.

You began by first examining how to best plan a model. Then you learned some modeling concepts and how to use modifiers and the Modifier Stack effectively. You moved on to learning the differences between objects and meshes, and how to use sub-objects to edit your surfaces before you began a series of short exercises describing some of the poly editing tools. With that under your belt, you learned how to put these tools to use by making a dresser and finally modeling a simple hand.

Modeling is an artful craft. It is best to know where you are trying to go in your mind's eye, so you can effectively get there with your models. Becoming a good modeler takes time and patience; so stick with it.

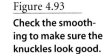

Figure 4.93

Check the smoothing to make sure the knuckles look good.

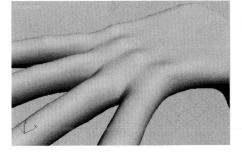

CHAPTER 5

Modeling in 3ds Max: Part II

Building models in 3D is as simple as building them out of clay, wood, or metal. Using 3ds Max to model something may not be as tactile as physically building it, but the same concepts apply: You have to identify how the model is shaped and figure out how to break it down into manageable parts that you can piece together into the final form.

Instead of using traditional tools to hammer or chisel or weld a shape into form, you will use the vertices of the geometry to shape the CG model. As you have seen, 3ds Max's Polygon toolset is quite robust.

In this chapter, we will tackle a more complex model with a children's Red Rocket toy. We will use the Editable Poly toolset, the Lathe and Bevel modifiers, and the Loft compound object to create the toy. We will also examine the use of QuickSlice (to add detail) and Booleans (to easily create interesting indentations on an existing surface).

Topics in this chapter include:

- **Building the Red Rocket**

Building the Red Rocket

Using reference materials will help you efficiently create your 3D model and achieve a good likeness in your end result. The temptation to just "wing it" and start building the objects is strong, especially when time is short and you're raring to go. This temptation should always be suppressed in deference to a well thought-out approach to the task. Sketches, photographs, and drawings can all be used as resources for the modeling process; you can place them in a scene as backdrop images and model over them. Not only are references useful for giving you a clear direction in which to head, but you can use references directly in 3ds Max to help you model. Photos, especially those taken from different sides of the intended model, can be added to a scene as background images to help you shape your model.

Creating Planes and Adding Materials

There are two common approaches to adding backdrop images for modeling in 3ds Max. You can use the viewport's Background Image feature or you can use the *crossing boxes* technique, which involves placing the reference images on crossing plane objects or thin boxes in the scene. In this exercise, we'll use the crossing boxes technique as the starting point to build a child's rocket ride-on toy, as shown in Figure 5.1.

Before you begin, copy the Red Rocket folder from the CD to your hard drive where you keep your other 3ds Max projects. Set your project folder to the Red Rocket project you just copied (File → Set Project Folder).

1. Open a new 3ds Max file by choosing File → New.

2. Go to the Customize menu → Units Setup. In the dialog box, set the units to Generic. Generic units are the 3ds Max's default units—one Max unit equals one inch.

Figure 5.1

A photograph of a child's Red Rocket flyer

3. Go to the Create panel to create a box (click the Geometry button () and, under Standard Primitives in the pull-down menu, click the Box button.

   Instead of creating the box with the click and drag method, we will use Keyboard Entry, as shown in Figure 5.2. Expand the Keyboard Entry rollout. Make sure the Perspective View is selected. Leave the *XYZ* parameters all set to 0; this will place the box at the origin point of your scene. Change the Length, Width, and Height parameters to the following and click Create:

   Length: 22

   Width: 0.05

   Height: 12

Figure 5.2

The Keyboard Entry panel for creating the box

4. When you click Create, 3ds Max will create the image plane we'll use for the side view. Rename the box01 object **Side View.**

5. Repeat steps 2 and 3 to create another flat box, which you'll use for the Top View image plane. Use the following parameters.

   Length: 22

   Width: 12

   Height: 0.05

   Rename the box **Top View.**

6. Activate the Front View, and then repeat steps 2 and 3 one last time to create the image plane for the front view of the rocket toy. Rename the box **Front View.**

   Length: 12

   Width: 12

   Height: 0.05

7. Move the Front View box up six units in the *Z*-axis to raise it so the bottom edge is directly on the Home Grid, as shown in Figure 5.3. Switch all the viewports to Smooth & Highlights (F3).

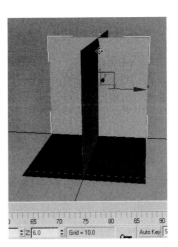

Figure 5.3

The Front View box is moved up.

8. Navigate to the SceneAssets\Images folder in the Red Rocket directory that you copied to your hard drive. In this folder, you will find three reference JPEG images, one for each of the three image plane views we just created in the scene. Select the Top View reference image (called `TOP VIEW.jpg`); drag it into the Top viewport in 3ds Max, and drop it onto the Top View image plane box. This will automatically place the image onto the box, so the image will be viewable in the viewport.

9. Repeat the previous step to place SIDE VIEW.jpg onto the Side View image plane in the Left viewport and place FRONT VIEW.jpg onto the Front View image plane in the Front viewport. Figure 5.4 shows the image planes with the reference images applied.

> If, for some reason, the image on your Top View object seems to be the reverse of what is shown in the book, simply rotate the Top View object to correctly line it up the way the images appear in this chapter. You may also have noticed black bars appearing in the images. They are intended to allow the images to better line up with each other.

10. If you need to, adjust the placement of the Front View image plane so the proportions of the rocket match up. The bottom of the wheels and the top of the handlebars should line up in all three images. Just move the box using the Select and Move tool. You will need to use the Arc Rotate Viewport Navigation tool to rotate the view so that the image planes can be viewed from different sides to get them aligned.

> If the rocket images do not show up in the viewport after you drop them onto the boxes, make sure the viewport is set to Smooth & Highlights and try again.

Figure 5.4

The image planes with the rocket views applied

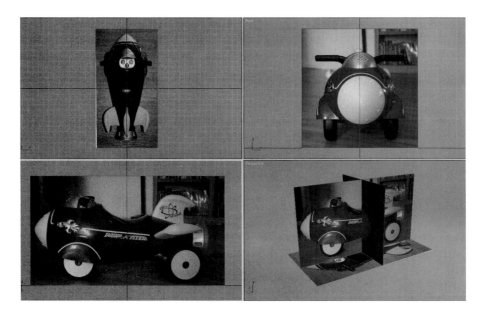

Organizing Your Scene File

The next step is to begin organizing your scene file. We are going to use the Layer Manager (shown in Figure 5.5), which is a floating dialog window where you can organize objects into layers (something like Adobe Photoshop layers but for 3D objects).The objects you create have common properties for their associated layer including color, renderability, and display settings. An object can assume these properties directly from the layer on which you create it. Using layers makes it easier to manage the information in your scenes. For example, layers are often used to control the visibility of objects in a populated scene so you can focus on certain objects without the clutter of having the entire scene all visible at once. Layers can also control the color of your objects' wireframes and the frozen and hidden state of objects to better help you organize your scene.

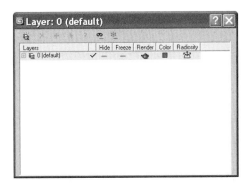

Figure 5.5

The Layer Manager

In the Layer Manager, when you create new layers, 3ds Max names them sequentially by default. These default names are Layer01, Layer02, and so on. After creating a layer, you should rename it something less generic so you can track your layers better. Click the layer in the Layer Manager to highlight the layer, and click again to change its name, as shown in Figure 5.6.

3ds Max assigns a random color to all new layers. You can accept the default settings or specify other colors by clicking on the little color swatch. For more on the Layer Manager see Chapter 3.

In the following steps, we will use the Layer Manager to organize our scene:

1. Select the image planes

2. On the main toolbar, click the Layer Manager icon ( ).

3. In the Layer Manager, click Create New Layer ( ) to create a new layer. Click Layer01 and enter **Image Planes** as its new name.

4. If you create the new layer with the objects you want in the layer selected, they automatically will be added to the layer.

5. Now when we work in the scene, we do not want to select the image planes. There is no need to adjust them as you model. In the Layer Manager, this is made very simple. Click the Freeze icon next to the layer, as shown in Figure 5.7. The layer will be frozen so its objects cannot be selected in the viewports. The frozen boxes will turn gray, and the images will disappear.

6. Open the layer by clicking the plus sign. You will see the objects listed. Select all three image planes by holding down the Ctrl key and clicking the objects. Click

Figure 5.6

Changing layer names

Figure 5.7

The Freeze icon

the cube symbol next to one of the image plane names. This will bring up the Object Properties dialog box for that image plane box for that layer, as shown in Figure 5.8. In the Display Properties list, uncheck the Show Frozen in Gray box. When you press OK, the image will show up on the plane. Because all three objects were selected, this option was applied to all three.

7. Any objects you create will automatically be assigned to the selected layer, so in the Layer Manager make sure to click on layer0 (default) to set it as the current layer.

As you continue modeling the rocket, you will frequently use the Layer Manager to help manage the scene.

Figure 5.8

Use the Object Properties list to turn on the image display for the frozen image planes.

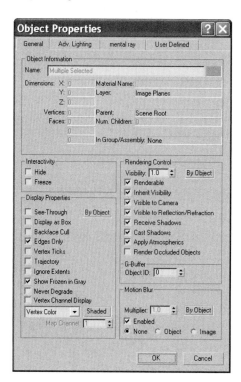

Creating the Body

To begin the body of the rocket, you can load the scene file Rocket_00.max from the Scenes folder of the Red Rocket project. In the following steps, we will begin the rocket model:

1. Start in the Front viewport. In the Create panel, click the Geometry icon ( ) and select Extended Primitives in the drop-down menu. Click to activate the Capsule tool, and then create a Capsule object with Keyboard Entry values set to a Radius of 3 and a Height of 21. Remember to use the Front viewport so that the capsule is created oriented as shown in Figure 5.9.

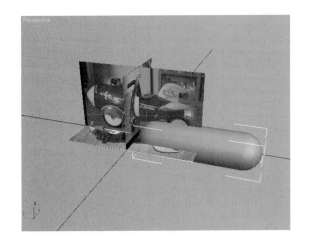

Figure 5.9

Capsule with Front viewport

2. In the Modify panel set the capsule's Sides to 8 and Height Segs to 6. Uncheck the Smooth option; we will do the smoothing later.

3. Rename the capsule **Rocket Body**. Make Rocket Body see-through in all the viewports by pressing Alt+X in any of the viewports. This way you will be able to see the image plane through the geometry.

4. Line up the rocket body to the Side, Top, and Front image planes, matching the rocket body to the front end of the image as shown in Figure 5.10.

Figure 5.10

Line up the Capsule object to the image plane views.

5. Center the pointer over the capsule to access the right-click menu, and choose Convert To → Convert to Editable Poly as shown in Figure 5.11.

6. Enter the Vertex sub-object mode and select the vertex at the very front tip of the rocket body (as shown in Figure 5.12).

7. With the body selected, go into the Modify panel. In the Soft Selection rollout, click on Use Soft Selection and set the Falloff to 6.0. Now switch to the Scale tool (R). We need to scale along the *XY*-axis, which is a nonuniform scale. Do the scale in the Front viewport, center your cursor over the Transform gizmo's *XY*-axis as shown in Figure 5.13, and scale while watching the top view. Scale down to create a more pointed front.

8. Selecting some of the front vertices section by section in the Top viewport, scale and/or move the rest of the front to match the front of the rocket in the Top View image plane, as shown in Figure 5.14.

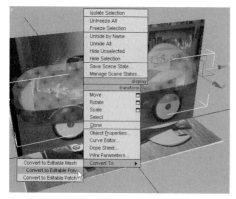

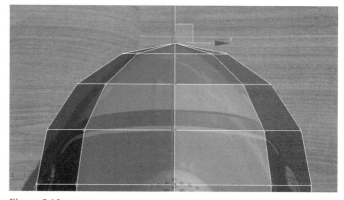

Figure 5.11

Convert to an editable poly.

Figure 5.12

Select the vertex at the very front tip.

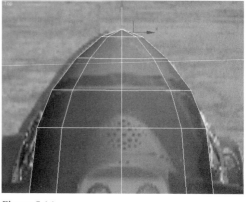

Figure 5.13

Center your cursor over the Transform gizmo.

Figure 5.14

Select some front vertices and scale and/or move to match.

9. Using vertices with or without soft selection (using a Falloff setting if needed), shape the rest of the body to the shape in the three image planes (you can also look at Figure 5.16). Don't worry about the back end of the rocket body just yet; we'll tackle that in the next step.

10. When you have the general shape of the body of the rocket, go into Polygon mode, select the polys at the rounded back end of your shape, as shown in Figure 5.15, and delete them by pressing Delete.

    Figure 5.16 will show you the result of the deletion.

Figure 5.15

Select the end polys to cut the end of the rocket body.

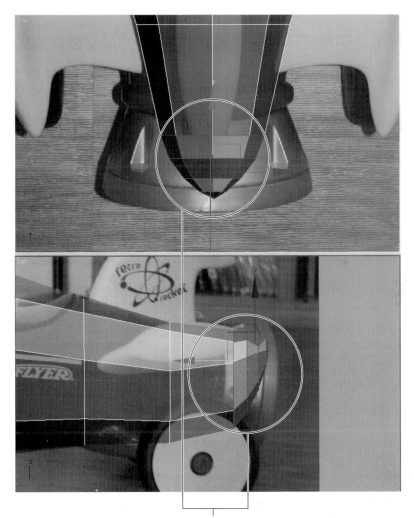

Select and delete the end polygons.

Smoothing the Body

The body looks very rough and chunky right now. To smooth out the rough model, we
will use Subdivision Surfaces as we did on the hand exercise in the previous chapter. As we
discussed earlier, a subdivision surface is a surface that has been divided into more faces
while retaining the object's general shape. You subdivide to add more detail to an object
or to smooth out the shape. In 3ds Max, Subdivision Surfaces is a rollout in the Modify
panel for an editable poly.

The following steps will guide you through the process of smoothing out the rocket's
body shape.

1. Go to the Modify panel to view the editable poly's parameters. Under the Subdivision
   Surface rollout, check the Use NURMS Subdivision box. This subdivides the polygons
   and relaxes the transition between polygons, smoothing the shape of the rocket's body.
   If you are still in Polygon mode, you will see the orange SDS cage appear. This cage
   allows you to continue editing the body's overall shape by just selecting the lower-res
   cage's polys and editing them. This lets you affect its broader form without having to
   select many more polys of the smoothed version.

2. Enter Poly mode (press 4) with the rocket's body selected, select the polygons on one
   side of the rocket body's right side (as shown in Figure 5.17), and delete them.

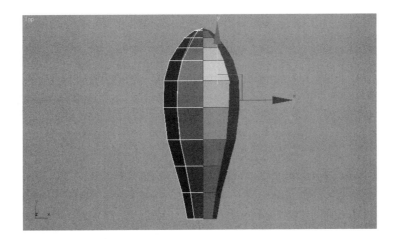

Figure 5.17

Select the polygons as shown.

3. Go to the top level of the editable poly (press 6). Go to the main toolbar and click on the Mirror tool ( ). In the Mirror dialog box, choose the *X*-axis. Under Clone Selection, choose Reference. This creates a mirrored copy of that half of the body. Using Reference allows you to make changes to the original side of the body and automatically have those changes mirrored to the other side.

4. Select the original side of the rocket and rename it **Rocket Body ORIG**. Select the reference side of the rocket that you just created and name it **Rocket Body REF**.

5. In the Layer Manager, create a new layer called **ROCKET**, and assign both halves of the rocket mesh to the new layer.

6. With Rocket Body REF selected, go to the Display panel ( ) and click Freeze Selected under the Freeze rollout to freeze the reference half of the mesh. Now when you work on the original, your changes will reference to the other side.

Freezing the reference half keeps you from accidentally working on the wrong half of the mesh.

Adding Detail to the Rocket Body

The wheel wells on the front sides of the body are the first details we will add to the body. To create the wheel wells, we need to add some more segments to the main body. To do this, we will use the Cut and Slice tools you used in the Hand and Dresser exercises in the previous chapter. You will be adding edges as shown in Figure 5.18 using the following steps.

Both the Cut and QuickSlice tool can be used in any of the sub-object modes. However, for the rocket's body, we will be in Vertex mode.

1. Go into the Layer Manager and hide the Image Plane layer. With the rocket's body selected, press the 1 key to enter Vertex sub-object mode. In the Modify panel, go to the Edit Geometry rollout and select QuickSlice, as shown in Figure 5.19.

2. To create the new cuts, you will need to use both the top view and the side view. You will create one cut along the top and down the length, and two cuts from the top to the bottom of the rocket (as shown in Figure 5.18).

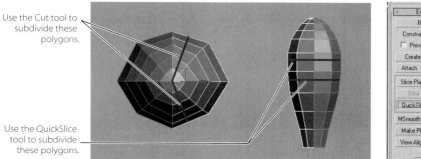

Use the Cut tool to subdivide these polygons.

Use the QuickSlice tool to subdivide these polygons.

Figure 5.18

Use the QuickSlice and Cut tools to add detail to these areas on the rocket's body.

Figure 5.19

Select QuickSlice.

3. QuickSlice creates straight lines of edges only, so you need to click where you want the slice to begin, move the pointer to where you want the line to end, and click again. Use Figure 5.18 to show you where to create the division line. When you first click, you will see the slice before it is created. You can set the direction and location of the inserted edges by moving the pointer, so you can be sure the position of the slice is where you want. To stop slicing, you can right-click in the viewport or click Quick-Slice again to turn off the tool. Once you lay down the QuickSlice lines, your rocket shape will have new divisions, as shown in Figure 5.20.

We will continue to add some detail using the Cut tool to where the wheel well detail will be added in the steps continued next. As you may recall from the Hand exercise in the previous chapter, the Cut tool works nearly the same way as QuickSlice. With the Cut tool, you can begin and finish the cut line at a vertex or at any point along an edge. The Cut tool also creates cuts from edge to edge in the same or another polygon.

The Cut tool has three modes: cutting to a vertex, cutting an edge, and cutting a polygon. Each mode displays a different pointer, as shown in Figure 5.21. The pointer's appearance will change according to where you click on the model.

4. Select the rocket's body. Select the Cut tool in the Modify panel under the Edit Geometry rollout, as shown in Figure 5.22.

Lay down a cut line along the body as shown in Figure 5.18 to create subdivisions in the model (Figure 5.23). (Remember that you are working on only the original side of the body.) The cut along the length of the body will start at the front at the vertex on the tip of the rocket (shown in the following graphic) and end between two vertices.

New QuickSlice Subdivisions.

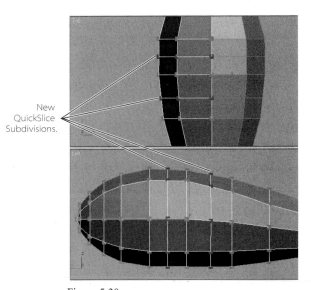

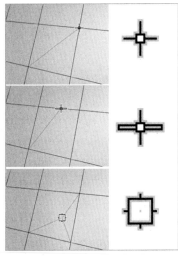

Figure 5.20

QuickSlice added divisions where the wheel well will be placed.

Figure 5.21

The Cut Tool modes

Figure 5.22

Select the Cut tool in the Modify panel.

Figure 5.23

Adding divisions with the Cut tool on the rocket's body mesh

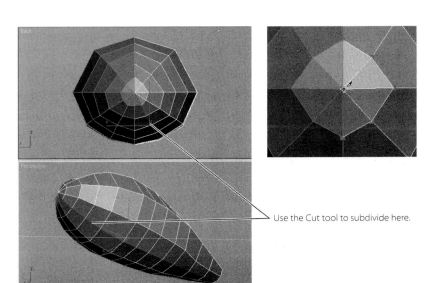

Use the Cut tool to subdivide here.

Creating the Wheel Well

Now that we have created more detail on the mesh, we can mold the wheel wells as shown on the actual rocket in Figure 5.24.

You can continue with your own scene file (just make sure to turn off NURMS smoothing before you continue), or pick up and use the scene file `Rocket_01.max` from the Scenes folder in the Red Rocket project that you copied to your hard drive.

Here are the steps to follow.

1. Select the Rocket Body ORIG mesh. Change to Poly mode (press 4) and select the three polygons in the middle of the body, as shown in Figure 5.25.

2. In the Modify panel under the Edit Polygons rollout, click the Extrude Settings button, as shown in Figure 5.26.

   In the Setting dialog box, set Extrusion Type to Group and Extrusion Height to 0.8, as shown in Figure 5.27. Click OK.

Figure 5.24

The rocket's wheel well

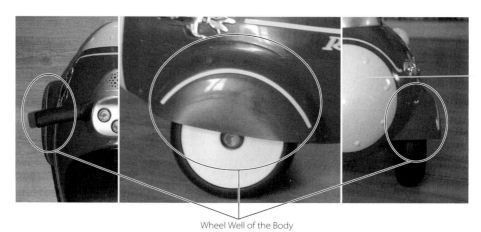

Wheel Well of the Body

Figure 5.25

Change the Poly mode and select the three polygons.

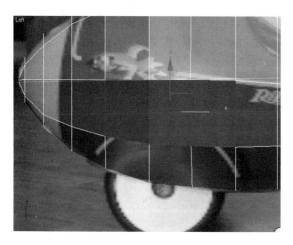

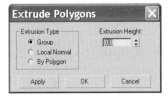

Figure 5.26

Click the Extrude button.

Figure 5.27

Setting the Extrusion parameters

3. Now select all the polygons that were created with the extrude operation shown in Figure 5.28 (on the left). Right-click in the Front viewport to activate it, press the V key, and select Back View to switch to the Back viewport. In the Back viewport, use the Rotate and Move tools to align the polygons so that they line up with the wheel well in the Front View image plane as shown in Figure 5.28 (on the right). (You can switch back to the Front viewport at any time by pressing F.)

4. With Rocket Body ORIG still selected, switch to Vertex mode. Select and move the second row of vertices from the bottom of the rocket body out to the right and slightly down as shown in Figure 5.29. This evens out the bottom part of the body to give it a more rounded look. If we left those vertices where they were, that part of the body would appear lopsided. And who wants that?

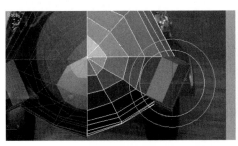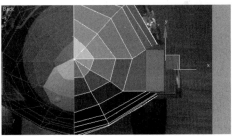

Figure 5.28

Use the Rotate and Move tools.

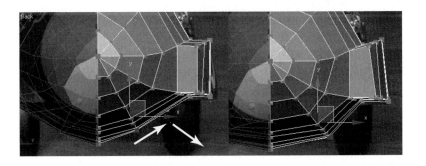

Figure 5.29

Round out the bottom of the rocket's body.

Let's apply Subdivision Surfaces to the model again to see how the wheel wells looks when smoothed. There are still several things that we need to do to improve the look of the body. The wheel well polygons need to be moved down and reshaped to have an arch on the top. Select Rocket Body ORIG. In the Modify panel, turn on Use NURMS Subdivision under the Subdivision Surface rollout. Now, when it is subdivided, it looks a bit better. Figures 5.30 and 5.31 show the rocket before and after NURMS have been enabled for the mesh.

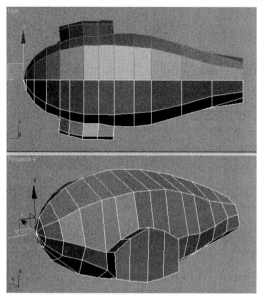

Figure 5.30

The rocket mesh before smoothing is enabled

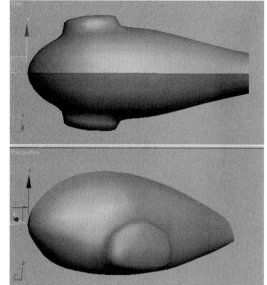

Figure 5.31

After smoothing is enabled, the smoothed rocket looks better.

Now we need to hollow out the wheel well. Follow these steps.

1. Disable NURMS smoothing by turning off the Use NURMS Subdivision check box.

2. Enter Polygon Selection mode. Select the polygons at the bottom side of the wheel well, as shown in Figure 5.32.

3. Go to the Edit Polygons rollout in the Modify panel and open the Inset Settings button. Set the Inset Amount to 0.1 and click OK. Then, with the newly created inset polygons still selected, extrude them with an Extrusion Height of –0.7 to push in the area. Finally, delete the inside polygon.

We don't need to create the inside of the wheel well because we are not going to see it. We extruded into the wheel well in step 2 to make a solid lip at the wheel well, but it only needs to go halfway up.

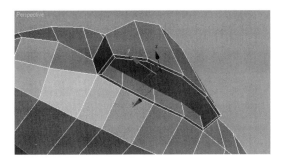

Figure 5.32

Select the polygons at the bottom of the wheel.

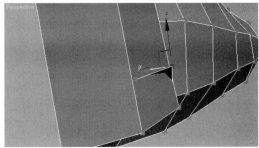

Figure 5.33

The geometry is poking through the outside!

4. Check to make sure that the new edges don't poke through the mesh (in Figure 5.33). If any do, select the vertex and move them inward.

5. Enable NURMS smoothing, and your rocket body should resemble the one in Figure 5.34. Make sure to disable NURMS smoothing before you continue with the rest of the exercise.

6. Save your work.

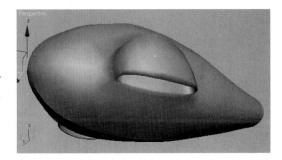

Figure 5.34

The smoothed wheel wells look pretty good.

Creating the Control Panel

We'll now create the control panel for the rocket, as shown in Figure 5.35. You can continue with your own scene file, or pick up and use the scene file `Rocket_02.max` from the Scenes folder in the `Red Rocket` project.

1. To create the control panel, we need to add one more cut along the top of the body for extra mesh detail, as you can see in Figure 5.36. To create this cut, we will try another method of creating new polygons: the Connect tool.

Figure 5.35

The control panel

The Connect tool creates new edges between pairs of selected edges. In the Connect Edges Dialog Settings box, shown in Figure 5.37, you can specify the number of edges to be created. Using the Pinch and Slide values, you can define the spacing between those new edges.

2. Switch to Edge mode (press 2). In the Top wiewport, select the edge at the top center of the Rocket as shown in Figure 5.38. Go to the Modify panel, and in the Selection rollout, click on the Ring button. This selects all the edges from top to bottom.

3. Stay in Edge mode and in the Edit Edges rollout, select the Connect button. This adds a single new edge.

Figure 5.36

Add a cut line using the Connect tool to create extra mesh detail for the control panel.

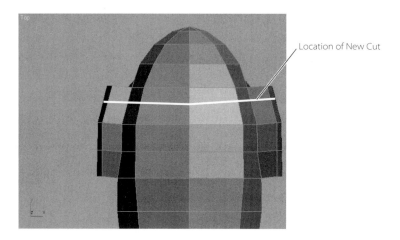

Figure 5.37

The Connect Edges dialog box

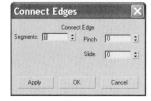

Figure 5.38

Select the edge at the top center.

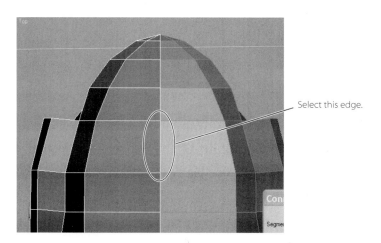

4. Now we are going to create a new cut line vertically down the length of the rocket body, as shown in Figure 5.39, using the same technique as in the previous exercise (the Connect tool).

5. This time, select one of the horizontal edges at the top of the rocket (as shown in Figure 5.40). Then in the Selection rollout, select Ring to automatically select all the horizontal edges above and below your initial selection. Go to Edit Edges and click Connect to create the new cut line shown in Figure 5.39.

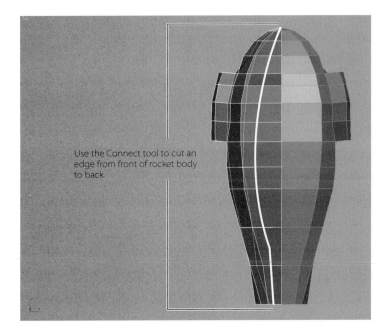

Figure 5.39

Add a lengthwise cut line to the rocket body.

Use the Connect tool to cut an edge from front of rocket body to back.

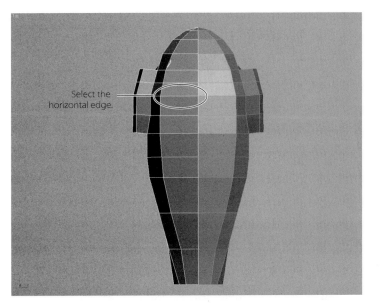

Figure 5.40

Select one of the horizontal edges at the top.

Select the horizontal edge.

Figure 5.41

The polygon at the tip does not have an edge to connect.

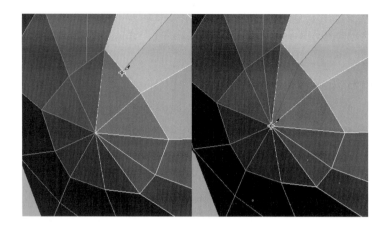

There is one little problem, however. The front end of the rocket doesn't connect to the newly added cut line. This is because the polygon at the tip, shown in Figure 5.41, does not have an edge for the new cut line to connect to, because all of those edges come to a point at the tip. We will continue the new cut line to the tip using the Cut tool in the next step.

6. Rotate the Perspective viewport so you can see the front end of the rocket clearly. Switch to Vertex mode and in Edit Geometry rollout, click the Cut tool. Center the cursor over where the new Connect Edge cut line ends and click. Then move to the tip of the rocket nose and click to finish the cut, as shown on the right in Figure 5.41.

7. With the new vertices along this lengthwise cut line, in the Top viewport, move the vertices to fit the shape of the control panel as shown in the Top View image plane. See Figure 5.42.

8. Switch to Poly Selection mode and select the control panel polygons shown in Figure 5.43.

9. Go to the Edit Polygons rollout and click the Extrude Settings icon. Extrude the polys with an Extrusion Amount of 1.0 and with the Extrude Type set to Group.

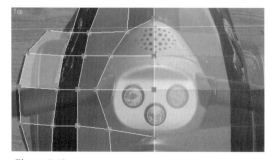

Figure 5.42

Shape the new vertices around the control panel in the Top viewport.

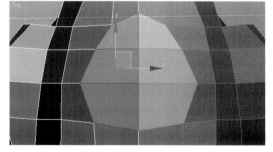

Figure 5.43

Select the control panel polygons.

If you look at the top view of the rocket, you will see the new extrude where it meets the reference half of the rocket body, as shown in Figure 5.44.

The two sides where you extruded should split away from each other. Remember that the two sides will eventually be stitched together to form the whole body, so all we need to do is make sure that all the vertices of the original side are aligned in the middle. For the original rocket half, you'll need to delete the polygons along the middle and move the vertices together. We'll do this in the following steps.

10. Select the middle inside polygons, as shown in Figure 5.45, and delete them.

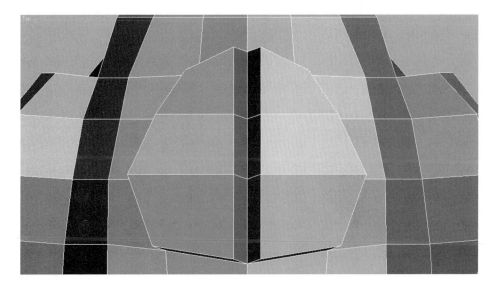

Figure 5.44

The top view of the rocket

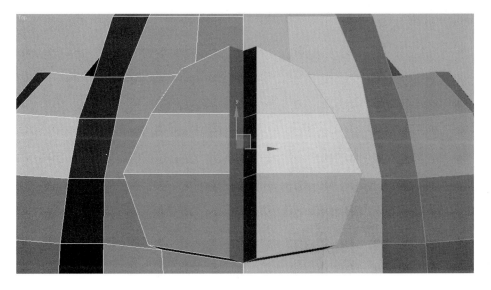

Figure 5.45

Select the middle inside polygons.

11. Switch to Vertex mode, select the vertices shown in Figure 5.46. Move them along the *X*-axis to the middle, where the original and the reference halves meet, as shown in Figure 5.47. The problem is fixed! When the body halves are stitched together later, the body mesh will look seamless.

12. Switch to Vertex mode, and using the Front, Side, and Top viewports, move the vertices of the control panel to line up with the real rocket's control panel in the image planes, as shown in Figure 5.48.

13. Let's look at this rocket body smoothed. Go to the Subdivision Surfaces rollout and check Use NURMS Subdivision to smooth the model again. It should look like the graphic shown in Figure 5.49.

14. Use the cage to further edit the control panel to better fit the real control panel in the reference image planes.

Figure 5.46

Select the vertices shown here.

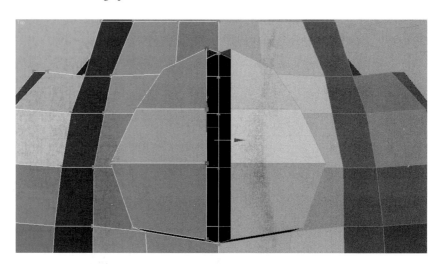

Figure 5.47

Line up the vertices to fix the split in the control panel between the two halves of the rocket body.

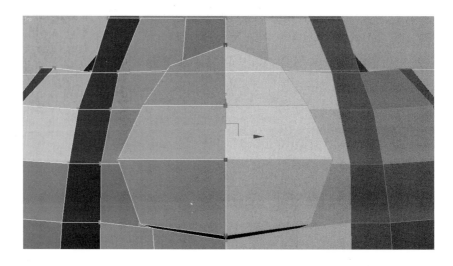

Figure 5.48

Shape the vertices of the control panel to the outline shown in the image planes.

Figure 5.49

Use NURMS Subdivision.

You will see the Subdivision Surfaces cage as long as you are in Polygon mode.

When you exit NURMS Smoothing, the polygons for the control panel will seem exaggerated, as shown in Figure 5.50, and will go beyond the outlines of the real control panel in the image planes.

That is because the lower-resolution cage model is a rough shape before smoothing is applied to it. Once you re-enable smoothing, Subdivision Surfaces will smooth the detail down, shrinking it back from the cage's shape a little. With NURMS smoothing enabled, the control panel will look like Figure 5.51 and will fit the real model.

Figure 5.50

The polygons appear exaggerated.

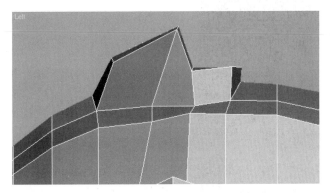

Figure 5.51

The smoothed control panel as seen in profile.

Creating the Back Wheel Axle

Let's turn our attention to the back wheels. In the following steps, we will create the back axle shown in Figure 5.52. You can use your own scene file or load the scene file Rocket_03.max from the Scenes folder in the Red Rocket project.

1. Disable smoothing by unchecking the NURMS option and switch to Polygon mode. Change your Top viewport to a Bottom viewport (press B).

2. Select the two polygons at the back bottom of the body shown in Figure 5.53, and extrude them with an Extrusion Amount of 0.6.

3. The extruded polygons will split at the middle where the original and mirrored reference halves of the body meet, as they did with the control panel earlier in this exercise. Move the vertices and fix the seam in the center the same way you did for the control panel. Make sure to delete the unneeded inside polygons as you did with the control panel. You can see the fixed result in Figure 5.54.

Figure 5.52

The back wheels

Figure 5.53

Select the two polygons at the back bottom of the body.

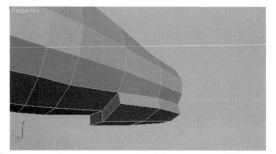

Figure 5.54

The fixed result

4. Go into Vertex mode and adjust the extruded polygons of the back axle so that they have the shape of the axle from the Side View image plane, as shown in Figure 5.55.

5. Select the polys on the side of the extruded polygons and extrude them with an Extrusion Amount of 0.6, as shown in Figure 5.56.

6. Rearrange the vertices to create a small delta wing coming off the bottom/side of the body, as shown in Figure 5.57.

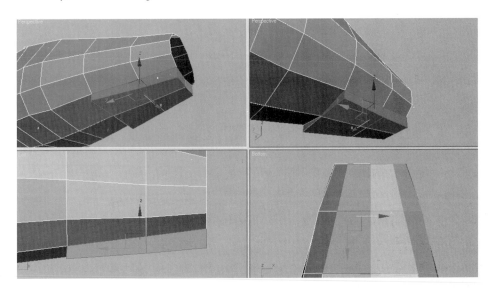

Figure 5.55

Adjust the extruded polygons to better fit the shape of the back.

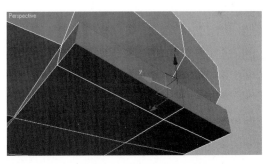

Figure 5.56

An Extrusion Amount of 0.6

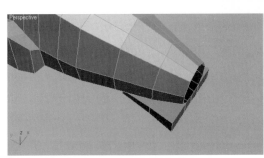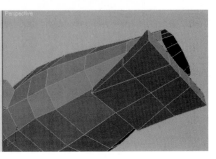

Figure 5.57

Create a small delta wing.

Figure 5.58

The rocket body is taking shape.

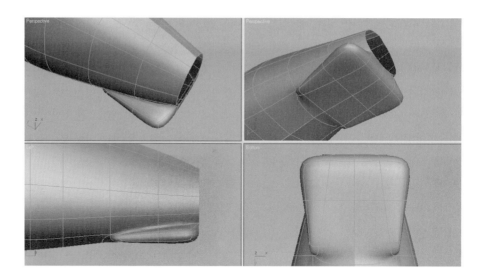

Figure 5.58

The rocket body is taking shape.

7. Turn on Subdivision Smoothing again to see the smoothed results shown in Figure 5.58.

8. While still in NURMS Subdivision mode, try moving the cage vertices to sculpt the back wheel axle. Save your work.

The body is finished for now. Later we will create the seat and add the small lip that connects the thruster to the back.

Creating the Fins

In this section, we will create the top and side fins for the Rocket body mesh shown in Figure 5.59. Load the scene file `Rocket_04.max` from the Scenes folder in the Red Rocket project, or continue to work with your own scene file.

Figure 5.59

The top and side fins

The fins have specific features—rounded corners and edges—that require us to create them as a modified primitive. There is a nice dip in the wing and a bulbous rounded end; so we will need extra segments across the top. Follow these steps to create the fins.

1. In the Create panel, click the Create Geometry icon and select Standard Primitives from the drop-down menu. Click to create a Box primitive. In the top view over the wing on the image plane, click and drag to create a box with the following parameters: Length 4.5, Width 3.2, Height 0.4, Length Segs 4, Width Segs 4, and Height Segs 2.

2. Press Alt+X to make the model see-through (if it isn't already). Now you should be able to see the image plane under the box you just created for the side fin shown in Figure 5.60.

3. Select and rotate the box –16 degrees in the Z-axis to line up with the side fin. Convert the box to an editable poly and enter Vertex mode.

4. Using the Top viewport, move the vertices to match the fin in the Top View image plane, as shown in Figure 5.61.

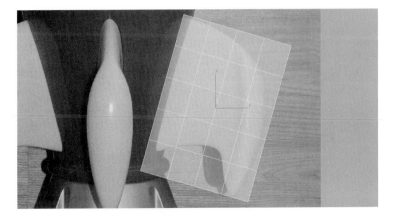

Figure 5.60

See the image plane under the box.

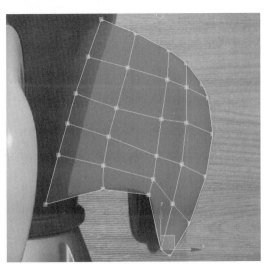

Figure 5.61

Move the vertices to match the fin.

5. On the side of the fin model, select the center row of vertices, go to the Edit Geometry rollout, and in the Constraints Group, turn on Normal. As shown in Figure 5.62, move the vertices, which are now constrained along their individual normal (meaning they will move only perpendicularly out from their current surface location), to create a nice round edge.

6. Select the vertices along the top and bottom rows at the edge of the fin model. The Constrain Group is still turned on for the Normal setting. Now move the vertices up along the X-axis, and they will move away from the center to create the bulbous rounded end of the fin (Figure 5.63).

7. Choose the row of vertices shown in Figure 5.64. (Make sure you select both rows on the top and bottom sides of the box.)

Figure 5.62

Move the vertices to create a nice round edge.

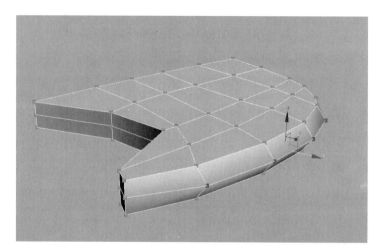

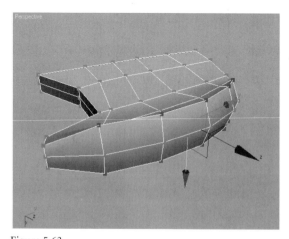

Figure 5.63

Create the rounded end of the fin.

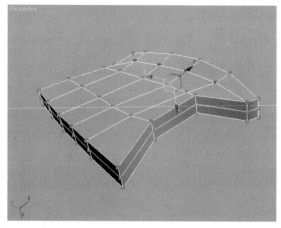

Figure 5.64

Choose the row of vertices here.

8. With Normal in the Constrain Group still turned on, move this set of vertices along the X-axis as you did in the previous step to increase the bulbous end of the fin, as shown in Figure 5.65. Move that row of vertices in the X-axis a little closer to the tip of the fin.

9. Select the row shown in Figure 5.66, and move the vertices closer to the tip of the fin to slightly narrow the bulbous end.

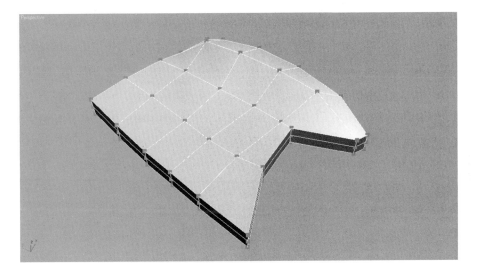

Figure 5.65

Scale up more vertices to create the rounded tip of the fin.

Figure 5.66

Refine the shape of the fin's bulbous tip.

10. Enable NURMS smoothing for the fin as you did for the Rocket body mesh itself, and check your work against the fin shown in Figure 5.67. Remember to disable smoothing when you're done.

> To set up a hot key for NURMS Sub Division Surfaces, go to Customize Menu → Customize User Interface → Main UI → Nurms (Poly) and assign a hot key combination such as CTRL+ALT+N. As a general rule, it is best to learn the default UI before assigning any hotkeys.

11. Select the fin and select the Move tool. Press and hold the Shift key and move the fin to create a copy of the fin. In the Clone Options dialog that opens when you release the mouse button, click Copy For The Object. You now have two fins. Clone one more fin so you have three fins. Select the fins and add them to the Rocket layer in the Layer Manager.

12. Select the first fin and line it up to the body of the rocket on the side on which you are currently working. Select a copied fin, and move and orient it to line up with the fin on the other side of the body.

13. Select the third fin and place it on top of the rocket body as the vertical fin. Line it up with the images of the real rocket. Figure 5.68 shows you the fins placed on the rocket. Save your work.

The Scenes folder of the Red Rocket project has a completed fin model. The "Merging Objects into a Scene" sidebar discusses how to import a finished model into an existing scene and merge it with the current objects.

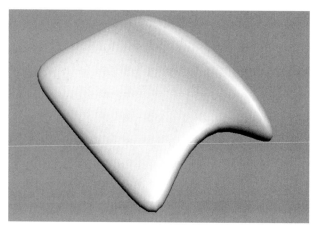

Figure 5.67

Smoothing makes the fin look more like the real fin in the red rocket.

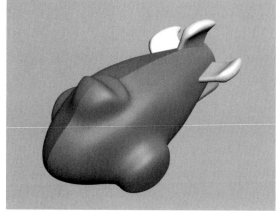

Figure 5.68

The fins are in place.

MERGING OBJECTS INTO A SCENE

Let's try to merge an external model into this scene. Pretend that you have created a fin model for the red rocket in a different scene file. You can import that fin into your current scene with the rocket body, instead of creating a whole new Fin object in this scene. In 3ds Max, this procedure is called *merging*.

1. Save your work.

2. Delete the three fins you've already created for your rocket.

3. Choose File → Merge and navigate to the `Fin.max` file in the Scenes folder in the Red Rocket project as shown here (below left).

4. Click Open. The Merge dialog window opens, as shown here (below right).

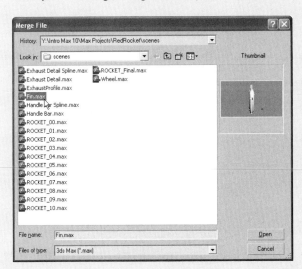
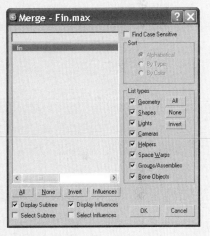

5. Select the Fin object from the dialog window and click OK. The Fin object will appear in your scene as the top center fin of the rocket.

Instead of creating the fins from scratch, you can clone and position the fin to create the side fins, or you can load your previous scene file and continue with the Rocket Model exercise. If you keep the merged fins, make sure to add them to the Rocket layer in the Layer Manager.

Creating the Thruster

The back end of the rocket toy is the round thruster shown in Figure 5.69. You can continue with your own scene file or load `Rocket_05.max` from the Scenes folder in the Red Rocket project.

Figure 5.69

The thruster seen from above and below

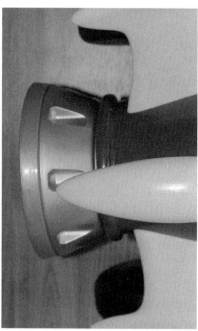

Top View

Bottom View

You will create the thruster using the Lathe modifier technique, which you used to create the knobs for the dresser model in the previous chapter. Using a lathe works only when the object to be modeled is round and has the same look and detail all the way around. Like the dresser knob we created in Chapter 4, we will use splines—more specifically the Line tool—to fashion the profile of the thruster. The Line tool in 3ds Max is like the Pen tool in Photoshop or the Mask tool in After Effects: it creates a 2D shape with no depth. The Lathe modifier then creates a 3D object by rotating that shape about one of the three axes (*X*, *Y*, or *Z*).

Using Lathe for the Thruster Shape

We need to identify the profile and draw it with the Line tool.

1. The profile shape we need to use is laid out in Figure 5.70. In the Create panel, click the Create Shapes icon. There you will find the Line tool button. Click Line and, in the Front viewport, lay out a profile similar in shape to Figure 5.70. The shape will make more sense once you see it lathed.

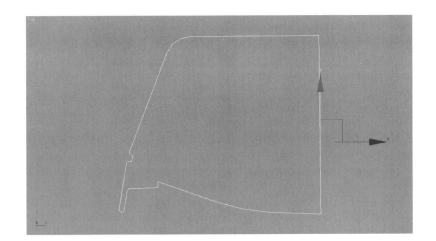

Figure 5.70

This shape will be used to lathe the thruster for the rocket.

If you prefer not to create the shape, you can merge in an existing shape for the thruster's profile. Click File → Merge, navigate to the Scenes folder of the Red Rocket project, and open the file called ThrusterProfile.max. Select the Exhaust Profile Line object and click OK. The profile shape will merge into your scene.

2. Once you have created the spline or merged the existing one into the scene, select the spline, go to the Modify panel, and add the Lathe modifier to the line.

Don't worry if you get something like the lathe shown in Figure 5.71, which is rotating about the wrong axis. Currently, the profile line is rotating about the axis at the center of the line shape. We need the axis of rotation to be at the inside edge of the profile shape.

3. Go to the Modify panel and select the lathe to display its parameters. Under the Parameters rollout, in the Align section, click the Min button (shown in Figure 5.72). This moves the rotation axis for the profile to the inside edge.

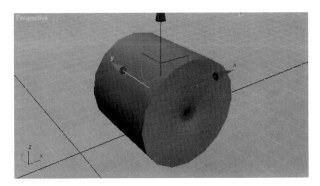

Figure 5.71

The lathe is rotating about the wrong axis.

Figure 5.72

Click the Min button.

The lathed object should look more like the thruster but will have a big hole in the middle (Figure 5.73). This is also an axis issue. You need to adjust the axis of rotation of the lathe to get rid of the hole.

4. Go to the Modifier Stack, expand the Lathe modifier (click the plus sign to the left of the Lathe entry in the Modifier Stack), and select Axis. We now are in the lathe's sub-object mode. Go to the Perspective viewport and move the Transform gizmo to the left until the hole is closed to the naked eye.

> Be cautious with step 4. You can't actually close the hole this way; you can only make it smaller. If you cross over the line, the normals will flip on the entire object. Get the hole as small as you can; when the thruster is finished, you can add a Cap Hole modifier from the Modifier List.

5. Go back to the Lathe parameters and change Segments to 20. This will help the thruster look less faceted than it does right now, but it will look a bit chunky on the edges. Don't be too concerned with that; the thrusters will not be seen that close in this scenario. Use the Segments parameter to make your lathes look only as smooth as needed for your shot, as shown Figure 5.74.

6. Name your thruster geometry **Thruster**, and add it to the Rocket layer in the Layer Manager.

7. Move it to the back of the rocket body, according to the reference images.

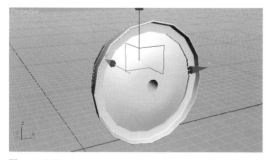

Figure 5.73
The lathe is starting to look more like the thruster.

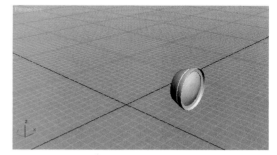

Figure 5.74
Using the Segments parameter

Using Booleans for the Thruster Detail

Take another look at Figure 5.69. The thruster has indented detail running around the side. We will create this in our model using a Boolean operation. A Boolean operation is a geometric operation that creates a shape from the addition of two shapes, the subtraction of one shape from another, or the common intersection of two shapes.

In theory, we will need to subtract the indented shape from the thruster mesh we have created so far. We'll start by creating the shape we need to use by cutting it out of the Thruster mesh. In Figure 5.69, you can see that the top of the shape indented into the thruster side has flat corners, the bottom corners are rounded, and the whole rectangle shape tapers.

You can continue with your own work or open Rocket_06.max in the Scenes folder of the Red Rocket project to catch up to this point.

1. Let's make the work area a little easier to navigate by hiding some of the rocket parts. Open the Layer Manager and click to hide the Image Planes layer, expand the Rocket layer, and click in the Hide column to hide the three fins. You can unhide them from the Layer Manager at any time.

2. Go to the Create panel and, under Shapes, select Rectangle. Click and drag in the Top viewport to create a rectangle with Length 0.74 and Width 0.42. Move the rectangle above the thruster geometry we just lathed, as shown in Figure 5.75.

3. Center you cursor over the wireframe of the rectangle and right-click; choose Convert To → Editable Spline as shown in Figure 5.76. Converting to an editable spline will give you access to the sub-object modes, as you saw in the previous chapter, and it will let you edit the shape for the detail we need in the thruster.

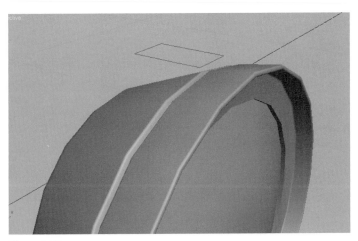

Figure 5.75

Move the rectangle above the thruster geometry.

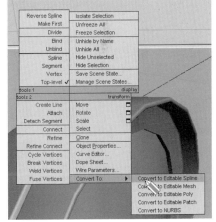

Figure 5.76

Convert the rectangle to an editable spline.

4. Go into Vertex mode for the rectangle spline and select the bottom two vertices. Go into the Geometry rollout, enter a value of **0.04** for Chamfer, and press Enter (Figure 5.77).

5. Select the two top vertices and move them closer together so that the rectangle tapers at that end. In the Geometry rollout, enter a value of **0.1** for Fillet. Click the Fillet button to round out the top of the cylinder, as shown in Figure 5.78.

> Watch carefully to make sure the chamfer and fillet in steps 4 and 5 don't create overlapping vertices. Too much of a good thing can cause trouble.

6. Exit Vertex mode by clicking on the editable spline in the Modifier Stack. When it is in sub-object mode, it is yellow. When it is at the top level, it is gray.

> If you don't want to create the splines, you can merge an already created spline from the scene file `Thruster Detail Spline.max` in the Scenes folder of the Red Rocket project.

7. With the spline selected, go into the Modifier List and choose Extrude. Set the Extrusion Amount to 0.4. We will use this to indent into the thruster sides.

8. Line up the Thruster Detail object to the thruster as shown in Figure 5.79.

There are eight indentations all around the thruster, so we are going to copy this one and array the indentation around the thruster eight times. To make it easier, move the pivot point of the Boolean object to the center of the thruster; this will enable the object to be copied nicely around the thruster.

Figure 5.77
Enter a value of 0.04.

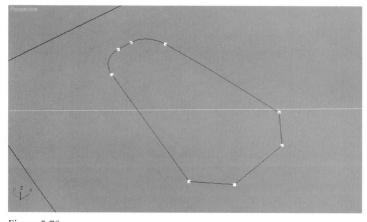

Figure 5.78
Click the Fillet button to round out the top of the cylinder.

Figure 5.79

Line up the Thruster Detail object to the thruster.

9. With the thruster selected, go to the Hierarchy panel ( ) and click Affect Pivot Only.

10. We want to make sure the pivot is in the center of the exhaust. In the main toolbar, select the Align tool ( ) and make sure Affect Pivot Only is active. Leave the dialog box settings at their default values and press OK.

> The pivot should be the only thing that moves. If the object moves, Undo (Ctrl+Z) and try the step again.

11. Click Affect Pivot Only again to disable it. Press A to turn on Angle Snap. Change to the Rotate tool while holding down the shift key and rotate 45 degrees in either direction around the thruster dish. When you release the mouse button, the Clone dialog should open. Select Copy, enter a value of **7** for Number of Copies, and press OK. This will place seven copies of the object, each at 45 degrees of rotation around the thruster, making a total of eight Boolean objects that are 360 degrees around, as shown in Figure 5.80.

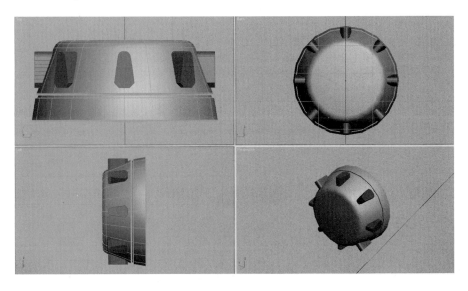

Figure 5.80

Seven copies of the object

Figure 5.81

Using ProBoolean to add detail to the Thruster object

12. Select the Thruster, go to the Create panel, and select to create Geometry. In the pull-down menu, select Compound Object and select ProBoolean. Click the Start Picking button, as shown in Figure 5.81. Move to the Detail objects and click on each one to subtract from the thruster.

> If you don't want to spend time creating the Thruster Detail objects, you can merge the pre-made model from the scene file `Thruster Detail.max` in the Scenes folder of the Red Rocket project.

Your thruster should now have the indentations shown in Figure 5.82.

13. Unhide the other parts of the rocket to see how everything looks so far. You can do this through the Layer Manager window. Save your work.

Figure 5.82

The thruster with its indentation detail

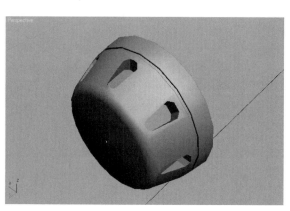

Further Body Work

We need to add some finishing touches to the body of the rocket. You can continue working with your own scene file or load `Rocket_07.max` from the Scenes folder in the Red Rocket project.

1. Select and delete the reference half of the body. You don't need it anymore.

2. Select the original body half and make sure Use NURMS in the Subdivision Surface rollout is turned on in the Modify panel.

3. Choose Symmetry from the Modifier List. This will copy the half of the rocket body to the other side. Depending on your settings, the rocket might disappear. If this happens, go to the Symmetry parameters in the Modify panel and, under Mirror Axis, choose X and check Flip.

You should see a seam running along the top middle of the body (Figure 5.83). To fix this, we need to bring those vertices in toward the center of the body until the seam disappears.

4. In the Modifier Stack, select Vertex from the Editable poly heading. This will take you into Vertex mode for the rocket's body. The mirrored side of the body will disappear because we are lower in the Modifier Stack.

5. Select the vertices that run along the middle. Select and move a few at a time. From the side view, you can see that those vertices stick up farther than the row below; this is what causes the ridge. Make the vertices level with the row of vertices below them by moving them along the Z-axis, as shown in Figure 5.84. (This step will be easier if you turn off the Use NURMS in the Subdivision Surface rollout.)

6. Go to Symmetry up in the Modifier Stack to view the whole body without the seam. Turn smoothing back on if necessary (Figure 5.85).

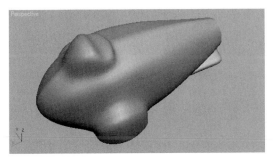

Figure 5.83

A seam runs down the middle of the rocket body.

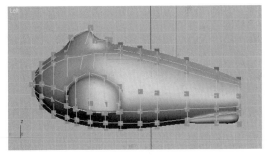

Figure 5.84

Make the vertices level with the row of vertices below them.

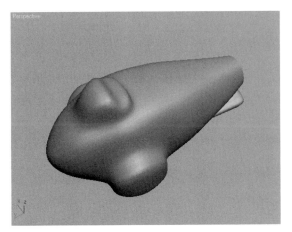

Figure 5.85

The seam is gone!

The next detail to manage is a small lip at the back end of the body (shown in Figure 5.86). We are doing the lip after we complete the body because this detail is easier to create after the body is stitched together. If you look in the Modifier Stack, the Symmetry modifier is on top and the Editable Poly modifier is on the bottom. If you go down a level to edit the body through the Editable Poly modifier, the mirrored side will disappear. That won't make things easy, will it?

One way around this dilemma is to convert the entire object into an editable poly, which will permanently stitch the two sides together. Another option is to add another Edit Poly modifier *over* the Symmetry modifier and edit the two sides of the body that way. It's not advisable to collapse into an editable poly until the very end of the model process, so we are going to use the Edit Poly modifier instead:

1. Turn off smoothing if it's currently enabled. Also, hide the fins and the thruster.

2. Make sure the body is selected (with the Symmetry modifier). Go to the Modifier List and select Edit Poly to add the modifier to the rocket.

3. In the Edit Poly modifier, go into Borders mode and select the edge in the back of the body, as shown in Figure 5.87.

4. Go to the Edit Borders rollout and click Cap, as shown in Figure 5.88. This will create a poly where the hole was.

5. Switch to Poly mode and select the new polygon. Go to the Edit Polygons rollout and open the Bevel Settings dialog box. We will do four bevels through open the dialog box. Between each bevel, make sure you click Apply and not OK. This will apply your bevel but keep the Settings dialog open for more.

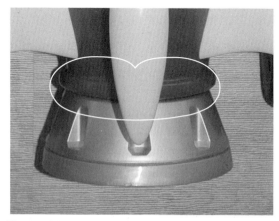

Figure 5.86

The lip between the thruster and the rocket body

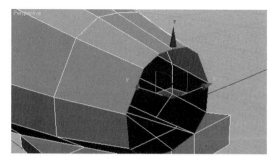

Figure 5.87

Select the edge in the back of the body.

6. Make four bevels with the following values:

BEVEL NO.	HEIGHT	OUTLINE AMOUNT
1st	0.05	0.3
2nd	0.2	0.1
3rd	0.2	−0.1
4th	0.05	−0.3

Figure 5.88

Click Cap in the Edit Borders rollout.

7. Click the Edit Poly name to go to the top level of the Edit Poly modifier.

To see how the rocket body looks when it is smoothed, you will have to do something other than turning on NURMS in the editable poly for the body as you have been doing. If you click back to the Editable Poly entry in the Modifier Stack and try to turn smoothing on, you will see the Warning dialog box shown in Figure 5.89. You do not want to continue turning on smoothing this way.

If you click the top Edit Poly modifier in the Modifier Stack, and look for the Subdivision rollout, you won't find it. The Edit Poly modifier doesn't have that feature; it is available only in a converted editable poly. Until we collapse the model into an editable poly, we will have to use another modifier: Turbo Smooth. Turbo Smooth is similar to Subdivision Surfaces in the editable poly, but it has fewer bells and whistles.

8. Select the rocket body and select Turbo Smooth from the Modifier List.

9. Unhide the exhaust and the fins. Make sure everything lines up, and render if you'd like (Figure 5.90). (See Chapter 11, "3ds Max Rendering," for more about rendering.)

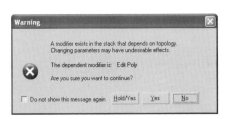

Figure 5.89

Warning!

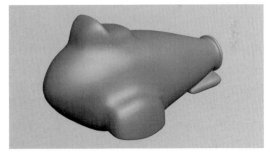

Figure 5.90

The finished rocket body

Making the Wheels

We are in the home stretch. The wheels, the handlebars, and the buttons for the control panel are all that are left to model. In this section, we will model the wheels, as shown in Figure 5.91.

Figure 5.91

The wheels of the rocket are next.

 You can continue with your own scene file or load `Rocket_08.max` from the Scenes folder in the Red Rocket project.

If you don't want to create the wheels, you can merge the wheels using an already created model from the scene file `Wheel.max` in the Scenes folder of the Red Rocket project.

Creating the First Wheel

The wheels are created using the same general technique as the body and fins: Select the polygons of a standard/extended primitive and edit them. This time we are going to use a Chamfer Cylinder.

1. If the Image plane is hidden, unhide it for the side view. In the Layer Manager, make sure the default layer is checked. This will ensure that the object you create for the wheel will not be in the layer that has the hidden Rocket objects.

2. Go to the Create panel. In the drop-down menu, select Extended Primitives and click to create a Chamfer Cylinder.

3. To get the side of the wheel to finish, click and drag the cylinder in the Side viewport. Go to the Modify panel and set the Chamfer Cylinder parameters as follows:

PARAMETER	VALUE
Radius	2
Height	1.2
Fillet	0.2
Height Segs	1
Fillet Segs	3
Sides	30
Cap Segs	1
Smooth	Checked
Slice	Unchecked

Set the parameters as shown in Figure 5.92.

4. Convert the Chamfer Cylinder to an editable poly and go into Vertex mode. Select the vertex on the front in the center, as shown in Figure 5.93.

5. Go to the Edit Vertices rollout in the Modify panel and select the Chamfer Settings dialog box. Set the Chamfer Amount to 0.4 and click OK.

6. Switch to Polygon mode and select the new center polygon, as shown in Figure 5.94.

7. Go to the Edit Polygons rollout and open the Bevel Settings dialog box. Set Height to -0.4 and Outline Amount to 0.0, and click Apply to create one bevel. Then set Height to 0.5 and Outline Amount to -0.12 and click OK to create a second bevel.

8. Now change the viewport so you can see the back of the wheel.

9. Go back into Vertex mode and select the center vertex. Go to the Edit Vertices rollout and click the Settings button for Chamfer. Set the Chamfer Amount to 0.2 and click OK.

Figure 5.92

Set the Chamfer Cylinder parameters as shown.

Figure 5.93

Select the vertex on the front in the center.

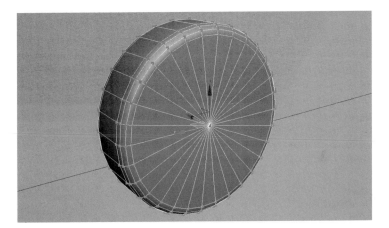

Figure 5.94

Select the new center polygon.

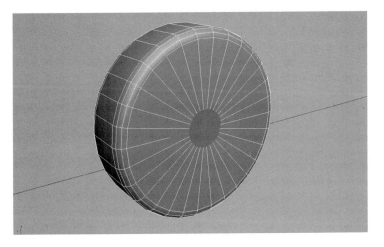

10. Switch back to Polygon mode and select the new center polygon. In the Edit Polygons rollout, extrude the polygon with an Extrusion Amount of 3.0. You can see the completed wheel in Figure 5.95.

Figure 5.95

The completed wheel

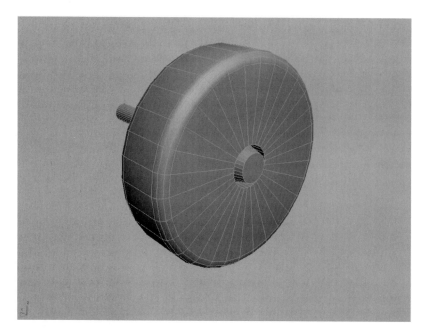

Placing the Wheels

One wheel is done! Now, make three clones for the front and back wheels. Place them at the wheel wells. Don't worry if the front wheels don't fit and penetrate the body. It was hard to tell how big to make the wheel wells until we had the wheels. We will fix that here:

1. In the Modifier Stack, click the Light Bulb icon next to TurboSmooth (Figure 5.96). This turns off the effect of the modifier.

2. The body of the rocket will appear low poly again, as you can see in Figure 5.97. It's usually easier to model in the low-poly version rather than the smoothed one.

3. Move down one level in the Modifier Stack to the Edit Poly modifier and go into Vertex mode.

Figure 5.96

Click the Light Bulb icon next to TurboSmooth.

4. Change any viewport to a bottom view. Select the vertices on the inside of the wheel well and move them to make the opening larger, so the wheels can fit, as shown in Figure 5.98.

5. Go back to the Modifier Stack and click the light bulb next to TurboSmooth to turn it back on. See if the wheels fit with the body when it is smoothed as shown in Figure 5.99.

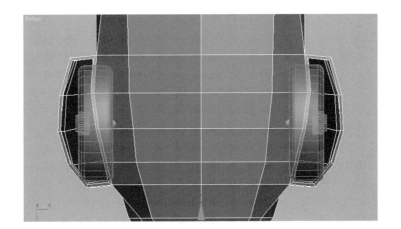

Figure 5.97

The body of the rocket in low poly

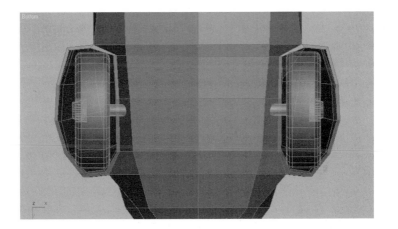

Figure 5.98

Select the vertices on the inside of the wheel well and move them.

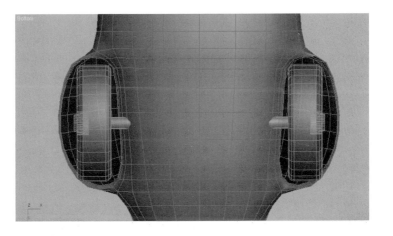

Figure 5.99

Make sure the wheels fit into the wheel wells.

Get a Handle on Things

The red rocket has a pair of handles just as a bike does. They help keep the driver (usually a child) from face planting every time he or she gets on it. As funny as that may be, a parent can only watch it so many times. This is why most grownups find the handles (shown in Figure 5.100) to be the most important part of the rocket. We will model them now.

The handlebars will be created using a modeling technique called *lofting*, which creates a shape that is extruded along a path. Each handlebar is a compound object that uses one shape as a profile and another as the path to form a 3D surface or object.

Figure 5.100

The handlebars help prevent calamities of the falling kind.

LOFTING

The Loft compound object has many features and only a few restrictions. The Shape object can be complex, consisting of several noncontiguous splines and even nested splines. A new Shape object can be selected at any point along the path, and the cross-section will automatically transition from one shape to the next. Any 2D shape can be used as the Shape object, but only a shape that consists of a single spline can be used as the Path object.

Creating the Path

Take another look at Figure 5.100 and imagine a straight line passing through the middle of one of the handlebars. This is the path we want to create.

You can continue with your own scene file or load `Rocket_09.max` from the Scenes folder in the Red Rocket project. You can hide the objects in the scene at this point to help keep an uncluttered workspace.

1. Start by going to the Create panel. Click the Create Shape icon and select the Line tool.

2. In the Back viewport, against the image of the front view of the rocket, click to place the line's first point where the handlebar meets the control panel. Move the cursor to where the handlebar has a bend in it and create another point. Place a final point where the handle ends, as shown in Figure 5.101, and right-click to create the line.

Figure 5.101

Place a final point where the handle ends.

3. Move to the Modify panel and enter Vertex mode for the line, as shown in Figure 5.102. Select the middle vertex, go to the Line Parameters/Geometry/Fillet, and enter **0.1**. This will add a smooth corner to the bend.

> Merge the scene file `Handle Bar Spline.max` from the Scenes folder of the Red Rocket project if you don't want to create the path yourself.

Figure 5.102

Enter Vertex mode for the line.

Creating the Shape

Now that we have the path for the loft, we need the profile shape, which is a cross-section of the handlebar. This shape is an oval with a flat top, as shown in Figure 5.103.

Figure 5.103

An oval with a flat top

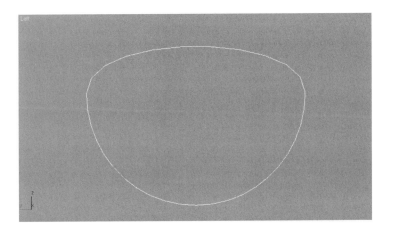

Figure 5.104

Select Get Shape from the Creation Method rollout.

To create this shape, follow these steps:

1. Use the right-click menu to create a Circle shape from the Create panel and convert it to an editable spline.

2. Go into Vertex mode, select the top vertex, and delete it to flatten the top.
   Next, we will create the Loft object.

3. Select the Handle Bar Path spline and go to the Create panel. Click to create geometry and select Compound Objects. Click the Loft icon.

4. Because we started the Loft process with the handlebar's path line, we only need to let 3ds Max know which shape to use. Go to the Creation Method rollout (Figure 5.104), and select Get Shape.

5. Select the handlebar shape in a viewport to use as the loft's shape.

Editing the Loft Object

In Figure 5.105, you can see the loft's path and cross-section shape as well as the resulting Loft object.

In this example, the shape is rotated 90 degrees along the path, putting the handle on its side so to speak, as you can see in Figure 5.106.

The Shape needs to be turned to make the broad flat side point up, as shown in Figure 5.107.

Figure 5.105

The loft lives!

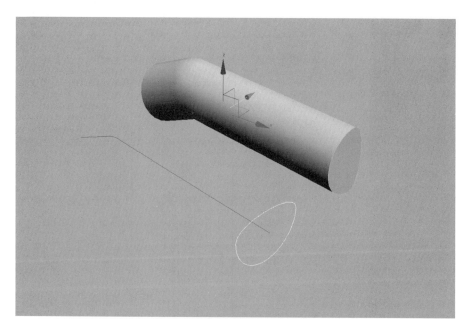

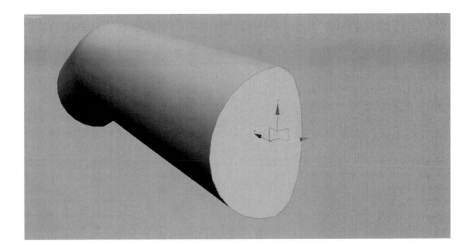

Figure 5.106

The handlebar is oriented incorrectly, with the broad flat side facing us.

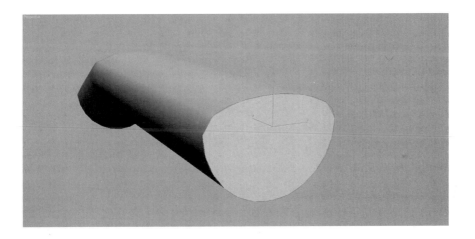

Figure 5.107

You need to rotate the shape with the broad flat side up.

To edit the loft, we will go into its sub-object mode. The sub-objects of a loft are the Path and the Shape.

The original splines were instanced when the loft was created, so they are still connected to the loft. This means changes made at the sub-object level on the splines will be transferred to the lofted object. If necessary, you can alter the shape of the path line or shape splines and the loft will change accordingly. You cannot, however, move or rotate the path or shape splines to affect the shape of the loft. You must use Move or Rotate at the sub-object level of the loft instead.

Figure 5.108

The Shape sub-object mode

1. Go to the Modify panel and select the Loft object.
2. Go into the Shape sub-object mode (Figure 5.108).

3. In a viewport, select the loft's shape at the end of the Loft object. The shape will turn red when it is selected, as shown in Figure 5.106. You should notice the shape spline is the smoother line in this figure.

4. Select the Rotate tool and rotate the shape on the loft –90 degrees. The entire loft will be updated as shown in Figure 5.107.

Adding Detail

The next step is to create the subtle curves and dips of the handlebars. The outside end of the real handlebar is curved. There is a groove toward the middle, and the handle tapers up where it meets the control panel. To look this good, the handlebar we've created needs more than one cross-section. With a Loft operation in 3ds Max, you can have any number of cross-sections for your loft, and they can be of varying shapes.

To edit a loft for these details, we are going to add more shapes along the path, and then edit those shapes to taste.

Figure 5.109

Reduce the Path Steps.

Figure 5.110

Make a copy of the loft shape.

1. Go back to the top level of the loft in the Modify panel, and go to the Skin Parameters rollout. This is where you can manage the Steps (subdivisions) in the loft. By default, there is a value of 5 for both the Shape Steps and the Path Steps. The Shape Steps here are fine, but the Path Steps value is too high. To fix this, turn Path Steps down to 1, as shown in Figure 5.109. If there are too many steps in your loft, it will get too heavy and dense to model.

2. Go back to Shape mode and select the shape. Take the cursor and center it over the Z-axis wire of the Transform gizmo that is connected to the shape.

3. We need to make copies of the Shapes so we can taper down the end of the handlebar. Shift+click and drag the gizmo to move the shape just a little bit up the body of the handlebar to make a copy of the loft shape, as shown in Figure 5.110.

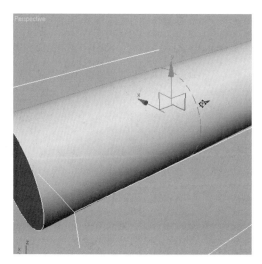

4. In the dialog box, choose Copy. Make three copies and place them close to the end of the handle, as shown in Figure 5.111. Switch to the Scale tool, and scale the outside shape down 30 percent and the middle shape down 10 percent. Leave the last inside shape alone, which should create a nice curved taper at the end of the handlebar.

5. Select the inside shape on the loft, and make four more copies in a row close to where the bar curves (Figure 5.112). Select the two inside copies and scale them both down 20 percent. This will create the groove toward the center of the handlebars.

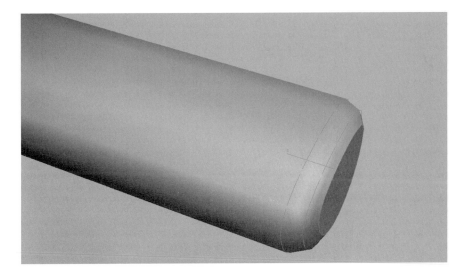

Figure 5.111

Place copies of the loft's shape close together at the end to taper them down.

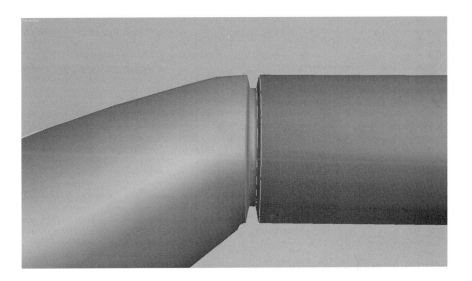

Figure 5.112

Creating the groove

6. Select the shape closest to the bend, and make a copy. Move it all the way to the other end of the object, away from the tapered tip. This is where it will meet the body of the rocket. Select the Scale tool, and scale this end shape up 50 percent. Exit the Loft's sub-object mode.

7. If any parts of the rocket are hidden, unhide them and see how the handlebars line up. You will probably agree that there is room for improvement (Figure 5.113).

8. Instead of rotating the Loft object, rotate the last shape at the end of the loft. Go back to sub-object mode and select the last shape to rotate to line up with the body, as shown in Figure 5.114.

9. Select the handlebar and mirror it for the other side of the rocket. Place it as needed. Figure 5.115 shows the rocket with its handlebars.

Figure 5.113

The handlebars will probably not line up with your rocket body right away.

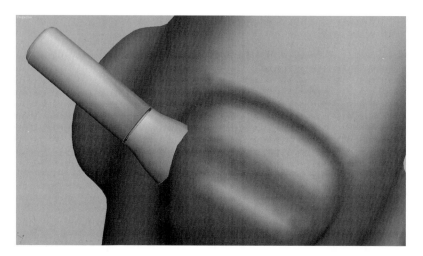

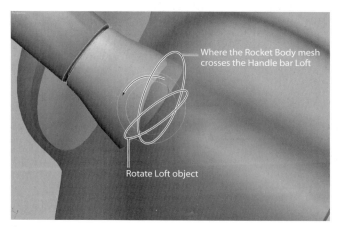

Figure 5.114

Rotate the end Shape object to line up with the rocket body.

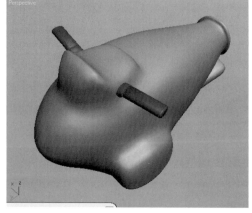

Figure 5.115

The rocket with the handlebars in place

If you prefer, you can merge the scene file `Handle Bar.max` from the Red Rocket project to complete the handlebars or check your own work.

Hold onto Your Seat

What fun would it be to ride a rocket standing up? Speaking from experience, it's not fun. So let's give our rocket model a nice comfy seat. Then we'll be finished with the model!

You can continue with your own scene file or load `Rocket_10.max` from the Scenes folder in the Red Rocket project.

1. If you are using your own scene file and not `Rocket_10.max`, in the Left view, create a cylinder with the following options.

PARAMETER	VALUE
Radius	3
Height	8
Height Segments	1
Cap Segments	1
Sides	40
Smooth	Checked

Use the parameters shown in the dialog box in Figure 5.116.

2. From the side view, line up the cylinder so it is over the part of the rocket body where the seat would be (as shown in Figure 5.117).

From the top view, the cylinder should be evenly spaced on both sides of the rocket (Figure 5.118).

Figure 5.116

The Parameters dialog box

Figure 5.117

Line up the cylinder with the seat area.

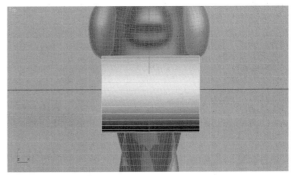

Figure 5.118

The top view of the cylinder

3. Select the rocket body, go to the Create panel, and click to create the geometry. Select Compound Objects from the menu and select ProBoolean. Choose Start Picking from the Pick Boolean rollout, and then select the Cylinder in a viewport. The cylinder will cut a seat into the rocket body as shown in Figure 5.119.

Because the Boolean operation will collapse all the modifiers on the body, it is important that it be the last operation we perform on this model. We won't want to make any changes to the body that would require access to its modifiers. Once any modifiers are collapsed, editing becomes difficult.

4. Convert the rocket body to an editable poly by right-clicking on the Rocket Body object.

5. The control panel of the rocket needs some buttons. To add them, create a few Chamfer Cylinders and place them there. Now you're really done! Figure 5.120 shows the completed red rocket with buttons in the control console.

6. Save your work, but that is second nature to you by now—right?

Figure 5.119

The seat is almost done.

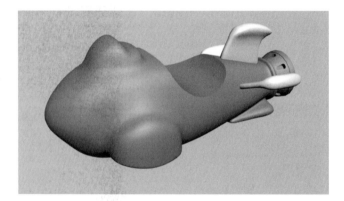

Figure 5.120

The rocket!

Unhide any parts of the rocket that you may have hidden to clear your workspace. Take it all in. As you can see, a fairly complex object is nothing more than a collection of simple shapes hammered, chiseled, cut, poked, and prodded into place. By learning how to dissect a complex object into its component shapes and learning how to view modeling an object as a series of steps, you will grow as a modeling artist.

Summary

When you built the red rocket, you employed several of the Editable Poly tools you learned about in the previous chapter. The more you use these tools, the faster they will become an instinctive part of your workflow. You also used the very handy Symmetry modifier to cut your work on the body in half.

After setting up the scene with background images, you were able to line up model parts and build them to fit the actual object as you worked in the scene.

In the next chapter, we will continue exploring the Editable Poly tools while creating a smoother, more organic model.

CHAPTER 6

Character Poly Modeling

Organic modeling is typically used when you create natural objects, such as a tree trunk, a hilly landscape, or a character. These models are generally of a higher polygon count than most, because organic models require smooth surfaces and need to be seamless. With a more mechanical model such as the dresser you modeled in Chapter 4, "Modeling in 3ds Max: Part I," there is little to no need for highly detailed, high-polygon-count surfaces. A human head model for a character, however, needs finely detailed surfaces because an organic model's parts need to flow together seamlessly. With the human head model, there should really be no clear distinction between where the geometry of the lower lip stops and the jaw starts, or where the top of the nose ends and the forehead begins. A basic knowledge of anatomy and an understanding of balance and proportion are important when you're designing a character that needs to be appealing and believable.

Realistic computer-generated (CG) characters are already very common in television and films; they appear as stunt doubles, as vast crowds of people, and even as primary characters to the scene or even the entire show. There are several situations where using a CG character works better for a show than using a real person. For example, CG stunt doubles are safer and sometimes cheaper than using an actual stunt person.

Another opportunity for organic character modeling arises when a storyline calls for an unusual or nonhuman character. Weird creatures can be created with better clarity using CG than using puppetry or special makeup effects. In any case, there is a large call for good character and organic modelers in both high and low poly counts.

This chapter introduces you to character modeling, focusing on using the editable poly toolset to create an organic alien model suitable for character animation. With the exception of the alien's eyes, the model will be a single object created from a very basic form. There are a few other tools, such as Surface tools, in 3ds Max that are also used in character modeling, but these are more advanced and beyond the scope of this introductory book. However, the concepts and practices talked about in this chapter will set you up with a solid foundation for any kind of character modeling.

Topics in this chapter include:

- **Setting Up the Scene**
- **Creating the Basic Form**
- **Adding Detail**
- **Final Touches**

Setting Up the Scene

As mentioned already throughout the previous chapters, acquiring and utilizing good reference material is essential for creating a successful character. At the minimum, sketches of the character's front and side features are necessary. You can import and use these views as background images as you create the character in 3ds Max. Additional perspective sketches of your intended character from several points of view and sketches of specific features, such as headgear, weapons, or other devices, can be very helpful during the modeling process for quick reference to your goal.

HIGH- AND LOW-POLY MODELING

High poly-count models are used when a model's level of detail needs to be impeccable, such as when the model is used in close-ups. In a case such as this, efficiency is overruled in favor of detail.

Low polygon-count modeling, or low-poly modeling, refers to a style of modeling that sacrifices some detail in favor of efficient geometry that places a very low load on the system on which it is being created or rendered. Because they require less memory, can be easier to animate, and can render quickly, low-poly models are especially useful in games, as well as being useful for filling in a scene's background without overly taxing the scene.

Creating Planes and Adding Materials

Like the toy rocket exercise in Chapter 5, "Modeling in 3ds Max: Part II," this exercise begins by creating crossed boxes and applying the reference images to them.

1. In a new scene, go to the Top viewport and create a tall, wide box oriented along the *X*-axis.

2. In the Parameters rollout of the Command panel, set the Length to a very small value, such as 0.05, Width to 66, and Height to 56. This essentially gives us a flat plane. If your computer display displays the plane improperly, change the Length value to something slightly higher. The point here is to have as flat a plane as possible without messing up your display.

When using certain displays, you may see artifacting with a very thin object such as this thin box you created in Steps 1 and 2. This is inherent in the display and not necessarily the geometry. Rendering the frame should show you if it's a display or an object problem.

3. Rename this box **Alien Front Image**.

4. With the box still selected, click the Move tool () in the main toolbar. In the Transform type-ins at the bottom of the user interface, move it to the origin by entering **0** in all three axis fields as shown.

The box will move to the origin, as shown here.

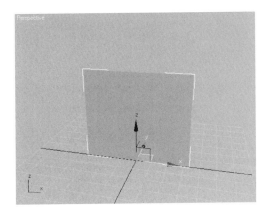

5. Create another box in the Top viewport. This rectangle should be oriented along the *Y*-axis (i.e., the Top viewport's vertical axis). Go to the Modify panel and set the Length to 20, Width to 0.05, and Height to 56, and then rename the box object **Alien Side Image**.

6. Move this box to the origin as well. The Perspective viewport should look similar to Figure 6.1. You will use these crossing boxes to outline the shape of your alien model.

Figure 6.1

The crossing boxes setup

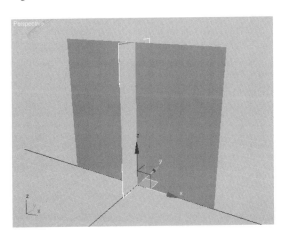

You may be wondering why the boxes were created in the Top viewport instead of the Front and Side viewports, which is how they end up being oriented. When the box is created in the Top viewport, the pivot point (or Transform gizmo) is positioned at the bottom of the box so the box is automatically aligned along the Home Grid, which saves you a step in the long run.

Adding the Materials

The reference materials are then texture mapped onto the crossing boxes to provide reference inside the scene itself while you model the character. Therefore, it's critical to ensure that the features of the character that appear in both reference images (the front and the side), are at the same height. For instance, the top of the head and the shoulders should be at the same height in both the front and side views to make the modeling process easier, eliminating as much guesswork as possible.

1. Click the Material Editor icon (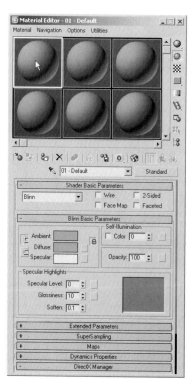) in the main toolbar to open the Material Editor.

2. Select the top-left sample sphere by clicking in it, as shown here. This is the sample slot where you will make the material that will map the front view reference of the alien character. For more on texturing and mapping, see Chapter 7, "Materials and Mapping."

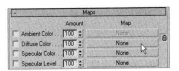

3. Expand the Maps rollout in the Material Editor, and click the Diffuse Color button (currently labeled None), as shown here. This will open the Material Map browser.

4. Double-click the Bitmap entry at the top of the Material/Map browser, as shown here. This allows you to import an image file to place onto the material to be mapped onto the box.

5. In the Select Bitmap Image File dialog box that opens, navigate to the Chapter 6 files on the companion CD and select the `Alien Sketch Front.jpg` file. Click the Open button to add the front alien image to the material as shown.

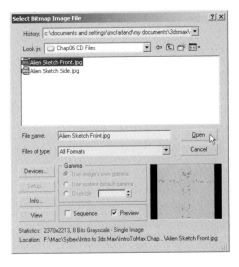

6. In the Material Editor's horizontal toolbar, click the Show Map in Viewport button, as shown here. This will allow you to see the image map in all the viewports that are using the Smooth + Highlights display once the material has been assigned to the box.

7. With the Alien Front Image box selected in the scene (shown here), click the Assign Material to Selection button in the Material Editor toolbar. The alien's front reference image will now be displayed on the face of the box.

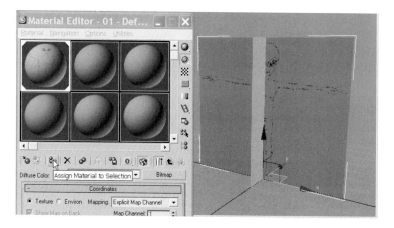

Reference images do not work very well in 3ds Max when they are drawn on white paper before they are scanned to a digital file. By default, white is the color of selected objects in 3ds Max, so scene objects can be visually lost when they are in front of a reference image that is drawn on a white background. If the drawings are on white background, use Photoshop, or another image-editing package, to process the images to make the background gray.

8. In the sample slot area of the Material Editor, select the sample slot to the right of the current slot, as shown here. Its boundary will turn white to indicate that it is the current material.

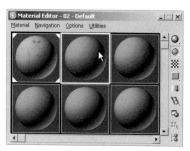

SEEING QUALITY BITMAPS IN THE VIEWPORTS

The Show Map in Viewport toggle () in the Material
Editor determines whether the maps in a material are
displayed in all viewports set to the Smooth + Highlights display mode. In many cases, the quality of the
images displayed is high enough to allow you to line up
major features in the reference image to the model's
corresponding feature, but not high enough to have a
very effective reference. The quality level of the bitmap
display can be set in the Preference Settings dialog box.
The following steps explain how to change the bitmap
viewport quality when using the DirectX video driver.
The steps to follow when using the OpenGL or Software
drivers are similar.

1. From the main menu, select Customize ➔
   Preferences.

2. Click the Viewports tab, and then click the Configure Driver button
   in the Display Drivers section.

3. In the Configure Direct3D dialog box that appears, select a resolution
   in the Download Texture Size section or select the Match Bitmap Size
   As Closely As Possible option, which will let you increase the displayed
   resolution of any maps shown in the viewports. This does not affect
   the actual size of the images used in the scene, only how they are
   shown in the viewports.

4. If necessary, repeat step 3 to increase the resolution of the background
   image in the Background Texture Size section.

5. Click OK in both dialog boxes to accept the changes. You must close
   and then reopen 3ds Max for the changes to take effect, however.

   Be aware that increasing the displayed resolution can decrease viewport performance and increase the system resources required to manage
the scene.

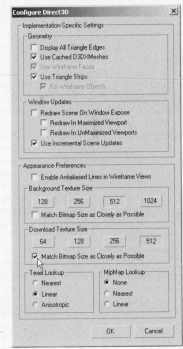

Figure 6.2

**The scene with the
reference images
applied to the boxes**

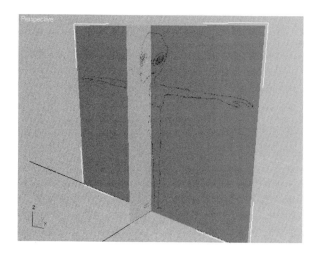

9. Repeat steps 2 through 5, this time choosing the `Alien Sketch Side.jpg` file in the Select Bitmap Image File dialog box to import the side view of the alien.

10. Select the narrower box and click the Assign Material to Selection button. Your Perspective viewport should look like Figure 6.2. If the images do not appear in the viewport, right-click the viewport's title and choose Smooth → Highlights from the pop-up menu to change the viewport rendering mode. Close the Material Editor.

Creating the Basic Form

The alien form we are modeling here is pretty common: one large head, one neck, two arms, a torso, and two legs. This is pretty standard for bipedal, humanoid 3D characters. You can always embellish this alien later on by adding facial features, for example, or modeling more detailed arms and legs.

When you create an organic character, you might be tempted to try to model one piece of the final product, such as the head or hands, to completion *before* you begin modeling another piece of the character. This is rarely a good idea because the scale and balance of the components must be built together from the beginning. A better practice is to block out the basic form of the character and focus on the size and crucial shapes of the major elements, and then add detail for the finer features. The following exercises describe the steps required to block out the alien's major features. When you feel you have gained enough confidence, we encourage you to step back into this alien exercise and redesign the alien with more intricate features, or even add an additional set of arms to the torso. Go wild!

Blocking the Torso

The basic structure for the torso will begin with a simple box primitive. After converting the box into an editable spline, you will add the Symmetry modifier to the object so that any manipulations performed on one side are instantly performed on the other. Is that cool or what?

Continue with the previous exercise's scene file, or open the Alien1.max scene file in the Alien Model folder on the companion CD.

1. Right-click on the name of each viewport that has Smooth + Highlights display enabled, and choose Edged Faces to display the rendered surfaces and the edges of each face.

2. In the Top viewport, create a box with Length, Width, and Height segments set to 2.

3. Rename the box **Alien** and change its display color, if necessary, to a color that contrasts well against the boxes that display the front and side reference images.

4. Move the box upward until it is centered on the torso in the reference images and modify its parameters to fit the torso. It's better if the box is slightly smaller than the sketched torso so that the image is visible beyond the box (similar to the box shown in Figure 6.3.)

5. Convert the box into an editable poly object.

Figure 6.3

Move and adjust the box to match the reference images.

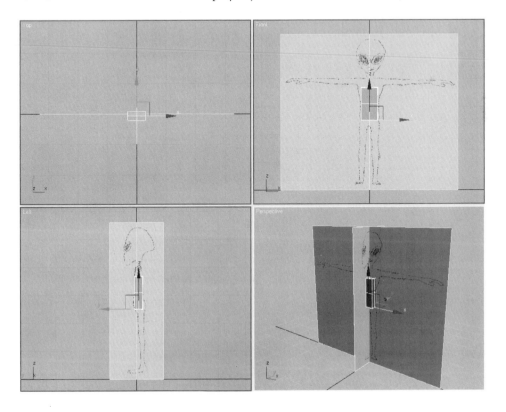

6. Access the Vertex sub-object level, and delete the left half of the box by dragging a selection region around the left-most vertices as shown and then pressing the Delete key.

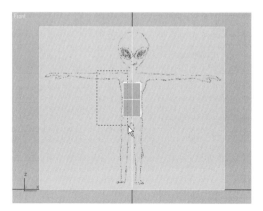

7. Exit the Vertex sub-object level. It's important that the next step occur at the object level.

8. Switch to the Modify tab of the Command panel and apply the Symmetry modifier to the box. The Symmetry modifier allows you to model only one side of the character while 3ds Max models the reciprocal side automatically. You can see the left half of the box return, as shown here.

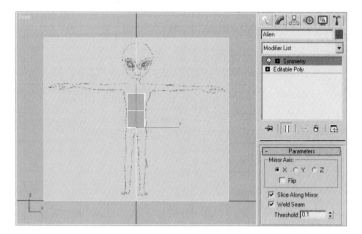

9. The box currently obscures the reference images and can make modeling more difficult. Turning on the See-Through mode in the object's properties will reduce this

problem. With the Alien object selected, right-click in the viewport and choose Object
Properties from the Quad menu, as shown here.

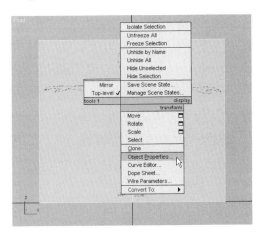

10. In the Object Properties dialog box—which should now be open—check the See-
    Through option in the Display Properties section shown here and then click the
    OK button. The object will become transparent in the viewports, and the edges will
    remain visible. Now, that's better.

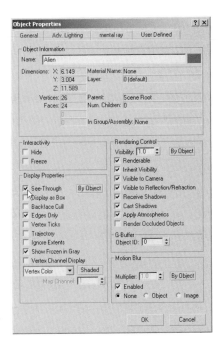

Forming the Torso

You will begin forming the basic shape of the torso by moving the editable poly's vertices and extruding its polygons in the following steps.

1. In the Modify panel, select the editable poly level of the Modifier Stack, as shown here. The left side of the object will disappear, but don't worry; the left side will still be there when you return to the Symmetry modifier. This allows you to select vertices with a selection region in the Right viewport without selecting the vertices on the opposite side as well.

2. Access the Vertex sub-object level and start to form the torso by moving the vertices in the Front viewport to match the background image, as shown in Figure 6.4. Use a selection region to select both the front vertices and the vertices directly behind them.

3. Switch to the Right viewport and move the vertices to match the side-view reference image.

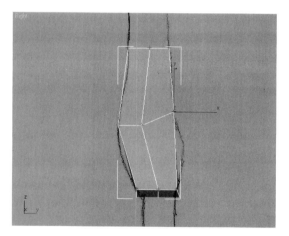

The alien's back has two curves; a concave curve at the lower part of the spine and a convex curve at his rear. The alien's front has a similar, more subtle compound curve. The editable poly object, however, does not have enough vertices to match the complexity of the image. We will use the Chamfer tool to refine or soften an edge by subdividing it into two colinear edges, with new polygons located between them. For more on the Chamfer tool, see Chapter 4. The angle between the new polys and the old polys is one-half the previous value. When the polys on both sides of the edges are coplanar, no new angle is introduced to the model, but a gap is created between two new edges.

4. In the Selection rollout, click the Edge button (◁) to switch to the Edge sub-object level.

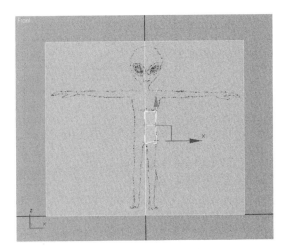

Figure 6.4

Adjust the editable poly's vertices to match the background image.

5. Select the four edges that go around the alien's belly horizontally like a belt. Switch viewports as necessary to select them all. You can also just select one of the edges, and use the Loop function to select the other edges that go all the way around the belly. For more on the Loop function, see Chapter 4.

6. In the Edit Edges rollout, click the Chamfer button, as shown here.

7. Click and drag on any of the selected edges to chamfer all of them, creating a new loop of edges around his belly as shown.

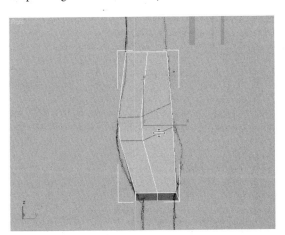

8. Release the mouse button. Click and drag again to add two more rings of edges and further refine the mesh. Make sure that you do not drag so far that the new edges overlap.

9. Switch back to the Vertex sub-object level and continue to move the vertices to match both the front and side reference images, as pictured here.

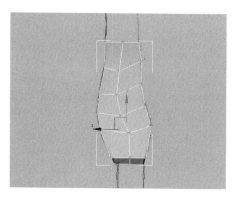 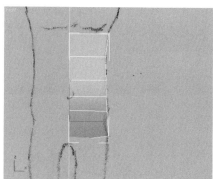

10. Switch to the Perspective viewport. Zoom and arc-rotate the view to see the top polygon in the model.

11. In the Polygon sub-object level, select the top polygons in the model and click on the Extrude tool in the Edit Polygons rollout. Be sure to select both the front polygon and the rear polygon hidden behind the flat box with the front reference image.

12. Click and drag the top polygons to extrude them approximately one-third the distance to the alien's armpit. Release the mouse button and repeat the process two more times until the top polygon is even with the top of the alien's armpit.

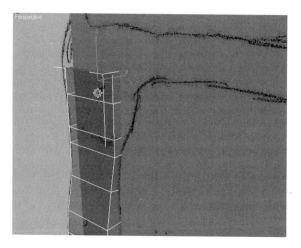

13. Switch back to the Vertex sub-object level and move the new vertices to match the reference images. The inner pair of vertices should be higher than the other pair, causing the top edges to no longer be parallel to the others, as shown here.

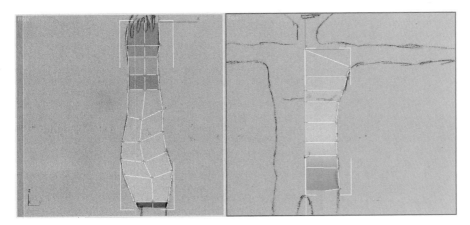

Cleaning Up the Geometry

When you create models with the editable poly toolset, you will often generate unnecessary or unwanted polygons. In this section, you will eliminate some internal polygons that the model doesn't need.

1. Continue from the previous exercise. Select all of the polygons in the model, right-click in the viewport for the Quad menu, and choose Isolate Selection. The two boxes will disappear, and the torso will remain.

2. Arc-rotate the viewport to look at the inner surfaces between the two halves of the model. You will be able to see the six internal polygons created with the Extrude tool, as shown in Figure 6.5. You might need to turn off the See-Through mode to see these polygons clearly, though. These, and the six additional polygons created by the Symmetry modifier, are undesirable because they make the model unnecessarily complex and can affect later results when you use several of the Polygon Editing tools. It's important to stay on top of any extra polys you create to keep your model efficient.

Figure 6.5

The internal polygons created with the Extrude tool

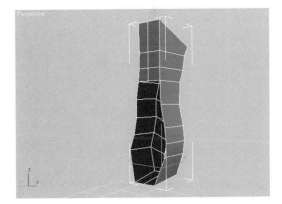

3. Select and delete the six internal polygons by pressing the Delete key.

4. In Edge sub-object mode, select all the edges, front and back, from the alien's shoulder to its hip and then chamfer these edges, as shown here. The new polygons created by the Chamfer tool will form the curvature around the sides of the alien.

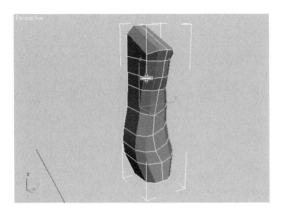

5. Exit the Edge sub-object level. Click the Symmetry entry in the Modifier Stack to see the full model of the torso so far. Both sides will display, as shown here.

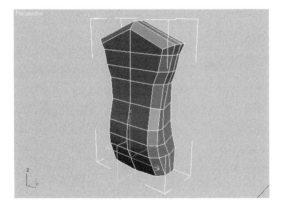

6. Exit Isolation mode by clicking the floating yellow Exit Isolation Mode button. Save your work—but you already knew that, right?

Adding the Arms

The next step in roughing out the basic form of the character is to add the alien's shoulders, arms, and hands. The arms will be partitioned into a shoulder/clavicle element and an upper and lower arm. Modeling a simple hand was already covered in Chapter 4's intro-duction to 3ds Max modeling, so we will only skim over it for this alien.

Continue with the previous exercise or open the Alien2.max scene file in the Alien Model folder on the companion CD.

1. Select the Alien object, click the Editable Poly entry in the Modifier Stack, and access the Polygon sub-object level by pressing 4 on the keyboard.

2. Select the four top polygons at the alien's shoulder area, including the chamfered polys, as shown here.

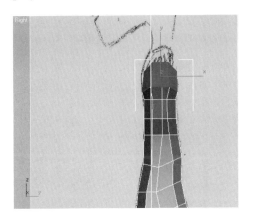

3. In the Edit Polygons rollout, click the Settings button next to the Hinge from Edge button to open the Hinge Polygons from Edge dialog box.

4. Click the Pick Hinge button and select either of the straight, horizontal edges near the armpit as the hinge for the tool, shown here. The selected polygons' new orientation will be previewed in the target orientation in the viewports.

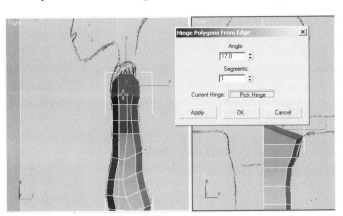

5. Set the Angle parameter value to 17, and click the Apply button. The previewed orientation will set into the model. Now, the selected polys will be previewed rotating another 17 degrees about the selected edge because you are still in the Hinge Polygons from Edge tool. Click the OK button to accept the second hinge action and exit the tool. Your model should look similar to Figure 6.6.

Figure 6.6

Hinge the shoulder area twice.

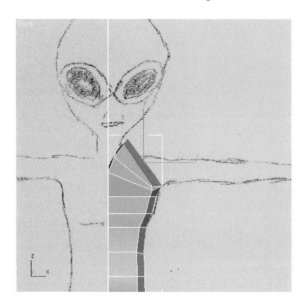

6. Switch to the Vertex sub-object level and adjust the vertices to define the clavicle and shoulder area, as shown here.

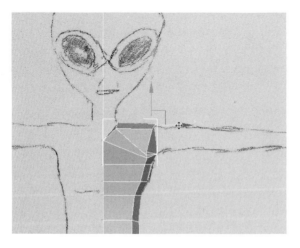

Throughout the modeling process, you may find yourself turning the See-Through mode on and off to hide and unhide the background images and to isolate the model. The images in this chapter switch between these modes as required. Press Alt+X to toggle See-Through on and off easily. Alt+Q will get you into (but not out of) Isolation mode. To exit Isolation mode, you will have to click the floating yellow button.

The Chamfer tool in the Edit Vertices rollout is similar to the Chamfer tool in the Edit Edges rollout. Rather than subdividing an edge into two colinear edges, it creates a new polygon by creating new vertices, projecting into all the polygons that share each selected vertex. For more on this, see Chapter 4. If the arm were extruded now, it would be very boxy and would require the edges to be chamfered. But by first chamfering the vertices, the resulting extrusion is more acceptable.

7. Zoom into the shoulder and select the four vertices at the corners of its perimeter. Click the Settings button (▣), next to the Chamfer button in the Edit Vertices rollout.

8. In the Chamfer Vertices dialog box that opens, increase the chamfer amount to divide the angle between the perpendicular edges, as shown here. Click the OK button when you are done.

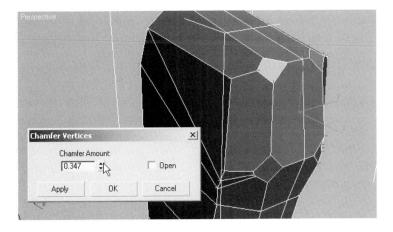

A vertical edge that bisects the polygons will be extruded to make the arm. If this vertical edging remains, it will create undesired internal polygons. However, selecting and deleting the offending edge would also delete the polygons that it contributes to the perimeter, which would leave a hole in the model. The Remove tool deletes the edge and combines the adjacent polygons into a single polygon, solving our problem.

9. In Edge sub-object mode, select the edge and click the Remove button in the Edit Edges rollout as shown. The edge will be deleted and the perimeter will remain intact. Yay!

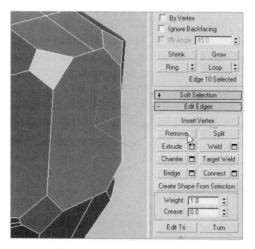

10. Select the polygon where the arm will be, and extrude it to about half the length of the upper arm.

11. Move the vertices to straighten the arm, and then select and scale all end vertices down slightly as shown.

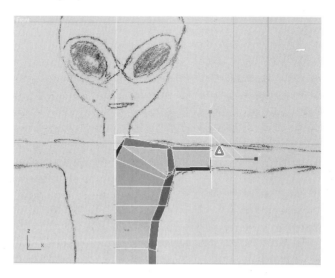

12. Repeat steps 10 and 11 two more times, scaling the vertices up at the elbow and then down at the wrist to resemble the following graphic.

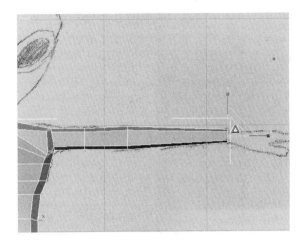

13. Similar to the extrusion modeling procedures described in Chapter 4's Hand exercise, block out the basic form for the alien's hand to have three long fingers and one thumb. You need not get into the smoothing details of the Chapter 4 Hand exercise using NURMS; however, the basic blocky hand for the alien will suffice. When completed, the hand and fingers should look similar to those shown in Figure 6.7. Save!

Adding the Legs

To create the legs and feet, you'll use methods similar to the ones you have used to build the Alien model so far. Extruding polygons, chamfering vertices and edges, and scaling vertices and polygons are all mainstays of polygonal modeling. In this section, you will also use the QuickSlice tool to add edges to polygons where additional detail is necessary, as you did in the Dresser exercise in Chapter 4. Continue with the previous exercise or open the Alien3.max scene file in the Alien Model folder from the companion CD.

Figure 6.7

The modeled hand and fingers

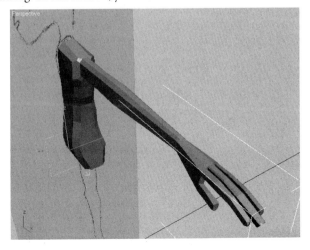

1. Hide the Alien Front Image object or move it behind the model so that it doesn't obstruct the view in the Perspective viewport.

2. Arc-rotate and zoom into the polygon that will be extruded to create the leg at the bottom of the model.

3. Select the edge that bisects the bottom polygons as shown here, and use the Remove tool to get rid of the edge. Do not just delete the edge.

4. Select the bottom polygon. In the Edit Geometry rollout, click the QuickSlice button, as shown here. The cursor will turn into an arrow.

5. The intent here is to add an additional polygon near the centerline of the model to accommodate the detail around the crotch. Click on the edge in the front of the model that runs from the center to the side, near the symmetry plane that divides the model in half.

6. Move the cursor. A thin line that projects from the initial point through the tip of the cursor to the edge of the selected polygon will be selected.

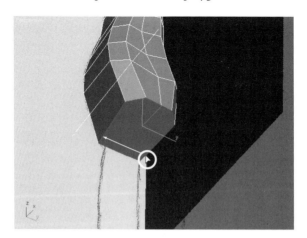

7. Click in a similar location on the opposite edge at the back of the model. A new edge will appear, and the single selected polygon will be divided into two coplanar polygons, as shown below left.

8. Click the QuickSlice button to turn it off.

9. Select the larger polygon and extrude it about half the distance to the knee.

10. Select and then move and scale the vertices at the knee of the leg to match the reference images, as shown here.

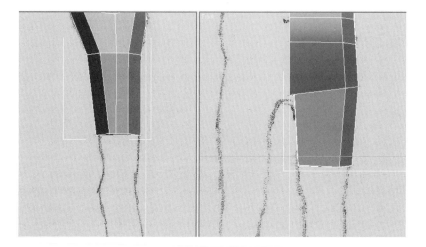

11. Repeat the leg extrusions at the alien's knee, mid-calf, and ankle. Adjust the vertices at each location, shown here.

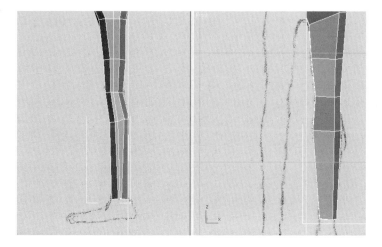

12. Arc-rotate so that you can see the inner portion of the leg. These edges are not chamfered like the edges on the outside of the leg. Select one inside-vertical edge at the front of the model and another at the back of the model.

13. In the Selection rollout, click the Loop button, as shown here. Loop expands the selection to include all edges that meet, end to end, and are aligned with the selected edges. See Chapter 4 for more on Loop.

> Instead of expanding the selection, you can use the spinner arrows next to the Loop button, to shift the edge selection to the next aligned edges. The Loop tools at the other sub-object levels work in a similar fashion.

14. All of the inside edges from the ankle to the crotch are selected. Use the Chamfer tool or the Chamfer Settings tool to subdivide the edges as shown here. Make sure to save you work if you haven't been doing so all along.

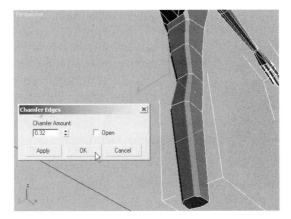

Adding the Feet

Now that the alien has a leg to stand on, you need to give him a foot. You'll continue using the Extrude and Chamfer tools along with the Hinge Polygons from Edge dialog box, as you did with the hand. You can continue the previous exercise for the following steps:

1. Extrude the polygon at the base of the leg, until it extends to the bottom of the foot.

2. Select the polygon at the back of the foot and use Hinge Polygons From Edge with an angle of 37.5 (as shown here) to create the polygons that make up the heel portion of the foot. Pick the edge at the top of the heel as the hinge. Click OK to close the dialog box.

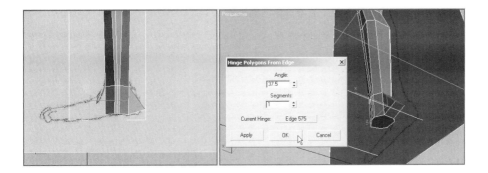

3. Chamfer the edges of the polygons created with the Hinge from Edge tool, and then adjust the vertices as required to fit the form of the reference.

4. Extrude the polygon, at the front of the ankle, twice to create the foot. The first extrusion is used to make the transition from the ankle to the foot, and the second extends the foot to the beginning of the toes, as shown here.

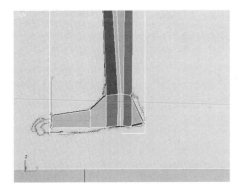

5. If the foot is pivoted incorrectly, select all of the vertices from the ankle down and rotate them until the foot points forward and slightly outward, as shown here.

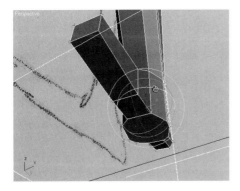

6. Continue to edit the vertices and edges of the feet to block out their basic forms to match the front and side reference images.

7. Use the QuickSlice and Extrude tools, along with the transforms, to create the alien's toes and complete the leg, as shown. Save—but I don't need to tell you that!

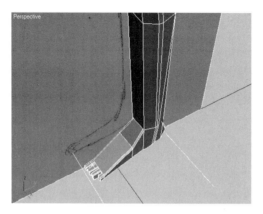

Modeling the Head

The last major component to add to the model is the alien's head. In addition to the tools that have already been covered, the Cut tool, the Soft Selection method, and the Shaded Face Toggle option are added to your 3ds Max modeling toolset options. You may continue with your work from the previous steps or open the Alien4.max scene file in the Alien Model folder from the companion CD.

1. Zoom into the top of the model, where the neck will be. Select the vertices at the base of the neck, along the symmetry plane, and move them vertically as shown here.

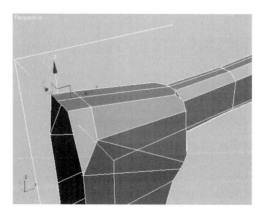

2. Select the two polygons at the top of the neck and click the *Z* button, next to the Make Planar button in the Edit Geometry rollout, as shown here. This will rotate all of the selected polygons to make them flush with the *Z* plane.

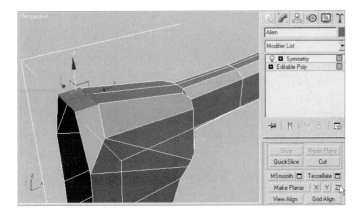

3. Select the edge that divides the top polygons, depicted here as a dark gray line (yours will be red when selected), and remove it with the Remove tool.

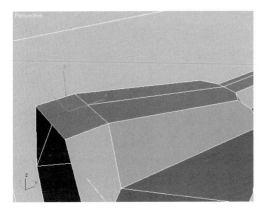

4. You will need to refine the edges of the neck that you will extrude to create the neck in the next step. The objective here is to reduce the angle of the corner edges of the top polygon by adding additional edges to cut the corners. Instead of chamfering the edges or vertices, click the Cut tool in the Edit Geometry rollout. Create a new edge at the first corner by clicking at each point where you want the vertices of that new edge to be (shown here). Right-click to begin a new cut line, and create a new

edge at the other corner (shown here as black lines). Click the Cut button when you are done.

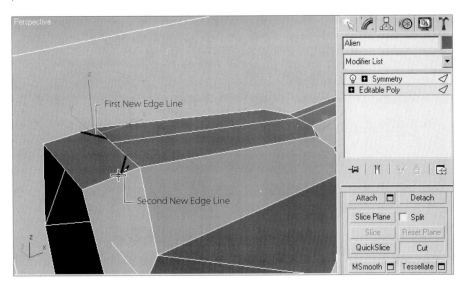

5. Extrude the neck polygon upward and adjust its vertices to match the front and side reference images, as shown here. With the neck geometry in place, you'll see that the alien's chin will be well below the top of the neck in the side image. This is fine, so don't worry about it—yet.

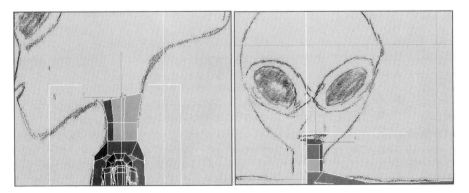

6. Using the Extrude tool, move the vertices as required to form the front and sides of the head so it will be similar to the model shown in Figure 6.8.

7. Extrude the polygons at the back of the head about half the remaining distance to the back of the head in the reference image, and then scale the vertices down a bit.

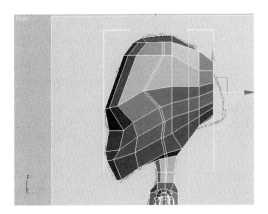

When sub-objects are moved, rotated, or scaled, the effect is applied explicitly and fully only to the selected sub-objects. This can result in a blocky, uniform appearance that is unappealing for an organic model. Soft selection lessens this effect by applying the transforms fully to the selected sub-objects and then, to a lesser degree, to the sub-objects that are in close proximity to the selection. The sub-objects that are closer to selection are more affected by the transform, and those that are farther away are less effective. When soft selection is used, 3ds Max color codes the selected sub-objects to provide a visual cue regarding how much of an effect the transforms will have. The colors range from red to orange to yellow to green to blue, with red sub-objects being fully affected and blue being unaffected. For more on soft selection, see Chapter 4. Let's try soft selection as we continue the alien model here.

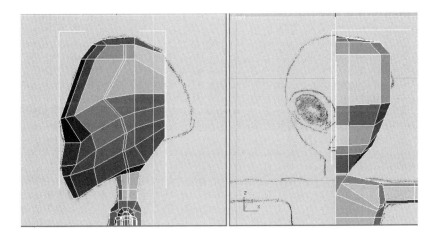

Figure 6.8

The modeled head after the front and sides are blocked out

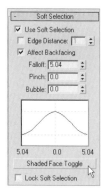

8. In the Soft Selection rollout, check the Use Soft Selection option and click the Shaded Face Toggle button as shown here.

9. Increase or decrease the falloff value until the non-blue colors extend to polygons at the side of the head.

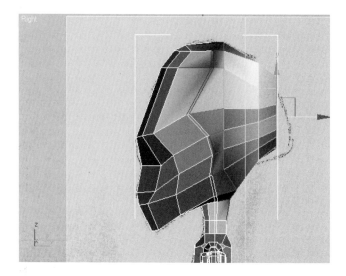

10. Move and scale the end polygons to match the reference image as neatly as possible with the current geometry.

Refining the Head

As you can see, the head needs additional segmentation to better match the reference image. We'll use the Connect tool to add that segmentation. The Connect tool adds edges to a model by subdividing pairs of selected edges. Continue from the previous exercise's steps and your current work.

1. Turn off Use Soft Selection and switch to the Edge sub-object level.

2. Select any of the nearby horizontal edges on the side of the head that need to be subdivided.

3. In the Selection rollout, click the Ring button as shown here. Similar to the Loop tool, the Ring tool selects all edges that are nearly parallel to the selected edge and lie along

the same plane (for more, see Chapter 4). All the horizontal edges that need to be subdivided are selected, as shown in Figure 6.9.

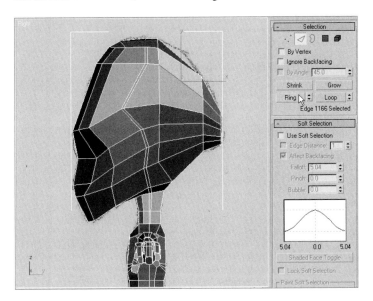

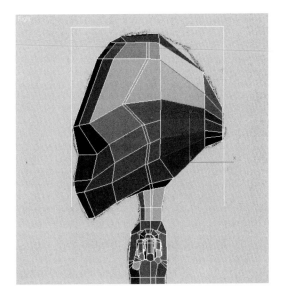

Figure 6.9

Figure 6.9

The horizontal edges to be subdivided are selected.

4. To open the Connect Edges dialog box, click the Settings button next to the Connect button in the Edit Edges rollout. Set the Segments value to 2 as shown, and click the OK button. All of the selected edges are subdivided into three edges each.

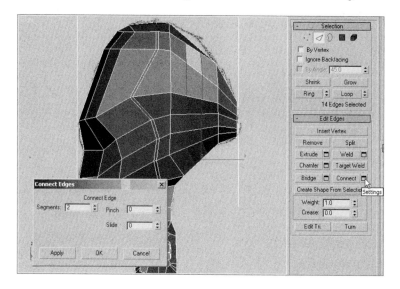

5. Turn Use Soft Selection back on and reduce the Falloff value until only two rings of polygons, outside of the selected edges, show any colors other than blue.

6. Move the selected edges upward as shown to match the reference image.

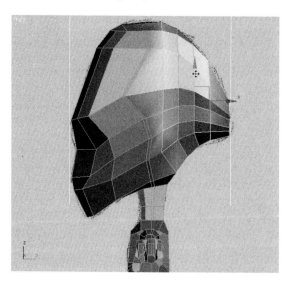

7. Continue shaping the head using the Connect, Remove, and Soft Selection tools, and by moving the sub-objects to block out the head as desired.

8. Many polygons were created with the previous steps on what will become the internal area of the head. They must be removed. Access the Polygon sub-object level. In the Front viewport, use a window selection to select all the unwanted polygons and then delete them, as shown. You saved your work already, right?

9. Access the Polygon sub-object level. In the Front viewport, use a window selection to select all the unwanted polygons and then delete them.

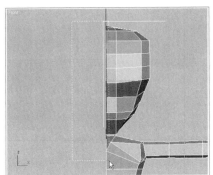 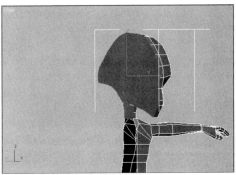

The basic form of the alien model is complete. The viewer can clearly see a humanoid character with a large head that slopes down in front and tapers in the back. In the next section, we'll cover adding details to the model, including a more-defined musculature, eyes, and a mouth.

Adding Detail

With the basic form blocked out, the alien needs to have detail added to define its appearance. You'll start by adding the TurboSmooth modifier to subdivide and smooth the mesh, and then you'll continue the modeling process by working on the legs, arms, torso, and finally the head. TurboSmooth creates a nonrendering framework around the mesh, with its own vertices that can be weighted to control the localized deformation of the mesh.

The TurboSmooth modifier has two iteration options: Iterations and Render Iterations. The Iterations option determines the amount of smoothing the model has in the viewports. If Render Iterations is unchecked, Iterations also determines the amount of smoothing in renderings. When Render Iterations is checked, the amount of smoothing in renderings can be different, usually higher, than the smoothing shown in the viewports. This allows you to work on a less-dense model for faster feedback on your computer system as you work, and it automatically renders the model at a higher density.

The TurboSmooth Modifier

In this section, you'll apply the TurboSmooth modifier to the alien model to smooth its surfaces. You can continue with the previous exercise or open the Alien5.max scene file in the Alien Model folder on the companion CD.

1. Exit any sub-object level, if necessary, and then select the Symmetry modifier in the Modifier Stack.

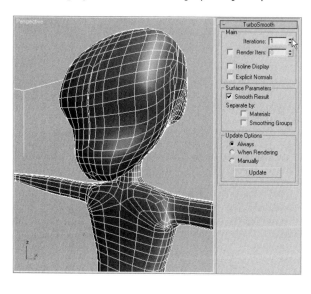

2. Expand the Modifier List and click the TurboSmooth modifier, as shown here. The modifier appears at the top of the Modifier Stack.

> To quickly locate a modifier in the Modifier List, repeatedly press the letter key that corresponds to the first letter in the modifier's name. 3ds Max will select the first modifier that starts with that letter and then cycle through the list, selecting the next modifier that starts with that letter each time the key is pressed. With 3ds Max 2008, you can also hold down the first letter's key and then press the key for the second letter of the modifier's name. 3ds Max will then select it for you.

3. Set Iterations to 1 and make sure that Isoline Display is unchecked in the main section of the TurboSmooth rollout. Isoline Display causes only the model's original edges to display, rather than all the edges in the newly subdivided mesh, for faster feedback in 3ds Max. When the Iterations parameter is set to a high value, enabling Isoline Display will reduce the display complexity on the model in the viewport.

Use caution when increasing the Iterations value in the TurboSmooth modifier. Dragging the Iterations spinner upward quickly, or directly entering a high value in the Iterations field, can cause 3ds Max to generate an enormous number of polygons that may exceed the memory capacity of your system, resulting in a crash. It is best to increase the Iterations parameter in increments of 1 until the minimum acceptable level of smoothing is obtained. You shouldn't really need to go above 3 iterations at worst.

While you are working in the editable poly level of the Modifier Stack, you will want to see the smoothed result of your character throughout the modeling process. This is easily accomplished by clicking the Show End Result toggle button (⏐ / ⏐) just below the Modifier Stack. This way you can see the end result of your model and the modifiers affecting it while you are working at an earlier modifier level.

Adding Detail to the Legs

The legs need more detail, especially around the knee, to allow them to deform properly when they are animated. Follow these steps to add leg detail:

1. Unhide any reference images and zoom into the area around the alien's leg. The knee is one area in particular that needs additional detail to accommodate any deformations caused by animating with Bones or Character Studio.

2. Select all of the polygons directly above and below the knee, and then use the Quick-Slice tool twice, once above and once below the knee, to add additional segmentation as shown. The angle of the Slice plane should match the angle of the edges above or below the new edges.

3. In Vertex sub-object level, select the vertices at the front of the knee. Turn on Use Soft Selection, and then reduce the Falloff value until only the vertices near the front of the knee are fully or partially selected.

4. Move the vertices forward to create the bulge of the knee cap, as shown.

5. Turn off Use Soft Selection and then use the Connect tool to further subdivide the edges in the calf area. Move the new edges so they are concentrated around the mid-calf area like this.

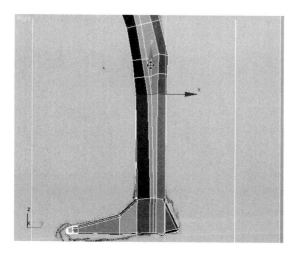

6. At the Vertex sub-object level, move and scale the vertices to sculpt the calf as shown here.

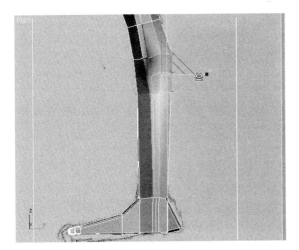

7. Adjust the vertices for the thigh area, making sure the vertices near the center do not cross the centerline of the model, as shown here.

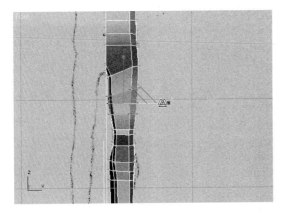

8. Use the tools discussed in this section to finish modeling the legs the way you want them to match the reference images. Using the Cut tool and then using the Bevel Polygons tool is an excellent method for modeling the calcaneus, the bone that protrudes from the side of the ankle, as shown here. To make sure the edits are effective

and generating the correct result, toggle the Show End Result button and render the scene frequently to check your progress.

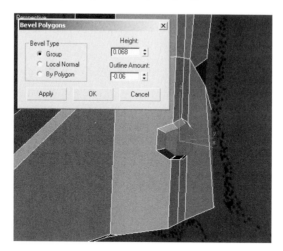

9. Zoom out and render the legs, and you should have legs that are similar to the graphic shown here. Save!

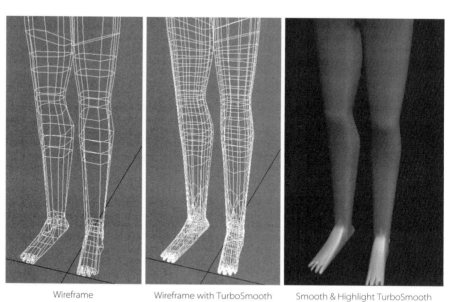

Wireframe   Wireframe with TurboSmooth   Smooth & Highlight TurboSmooth

Adding Detail to the Arms

To allow proper deformation, additional detail must be added to the elbow area, in a manner similar to the way you detailed the legs. Additional musculature is also required in the arms and at the shoulders. Be sure to toggle the Show End Result button back and forth to see how the low-polygon modeling affects the final, smooth object.

1. Select the vertical edges in the arm, from the bicep to the wrist, and use the Connect tool with Segments set at 2 to add additional vertical edges to the arm, as shown here.

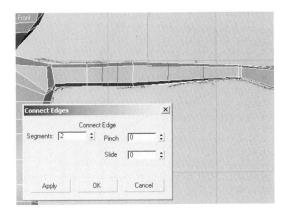

2. Move the new edges near the elbow, leaving one vertical loop of edges at the bicep and the forearm.

3. With Use Soft Selection turned on, move and scale the elbow until it is slightly larger than the arm, as shown here.

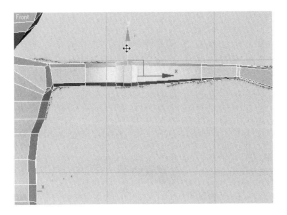

4. Select the edge in the middle of the bicep. We will use this edge to define the bulge of the bicep. With the character's hands oriented with the palms face down, the bicep should bulge forward and not upward, as shown here.

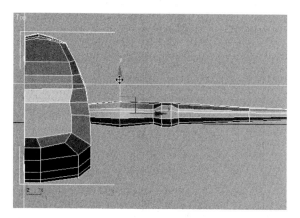

5. The character has long slender fingers that tend to look like tubes or tentacles when the diameter of each segment is similar in size. To help define the individual finger bones, you need to increase the size of the knuckles. Select all of the edges located at the alien's knuckles, including the thumb, and chamfer them twice. The second chamfer should concentrate two sets of edges closer to the centerline of the knuckles shown here.

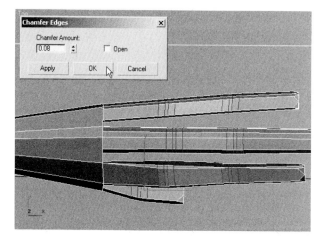

6. Select the inner pair of edges at each knuckle and scale the edges to increase their diameter to puff out the knuckles as shown.

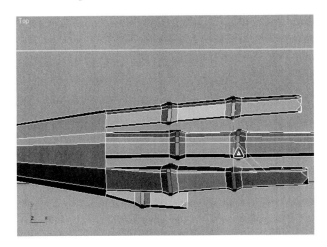

7. If the knuckles appear to change the fingers' diameters too abruptly, turn on Use Soft Selection and scale them again along the *X*-axis only.

8. The hand tapers too smoothly from the wrist to the fingers, so there is no clear line of delineation between the forearm and the fingers. Use the QuickSlice tool to add an additional edge vertically across the hand just above the wrist, and then move and scale it to better define the hand, as shown here.

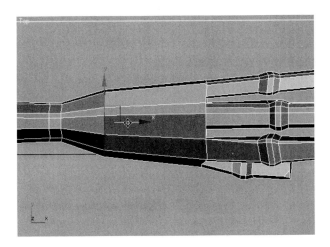

9. The thumb is tucked under the hand in an unnatural position. Select and move the vertices of the thumb and the inside heel of the palm forward and out from underneath the index finger as shown.

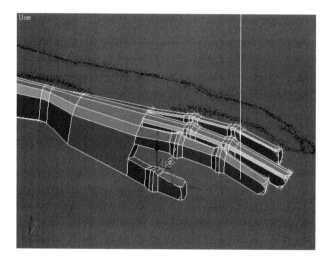

10. Make any additional changes to the hand to shape it as you wish. For instance, if the finger tips are too boxy in a smooth rendered image, move the vertices near the end of the fingers back a bit, or select and bevel the end polygons of the fingers.

TARGET WELDING VERTICES

Having multiple vertices in close proximity can result in long thin faces that are difficult to deform, unacceptable folds or creases in the surfaces, and undesirable results when using the Bevel or Inset tools. These modeling problems are all common. They can be reduced or eliminated by welding the vertices. Standard welding is covered in Chapter 4 and revisited later in this chapter. A standard weld replaces two or more selected vertices that are within a specified proximity to each other with a single vertex. This single vertex is located at the averaged locations of the original vertices selected.

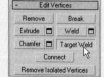

Target welding works somewhat differently and is generally preferred over regular welding With the Target Weld button activated in the Edit Vertices rollout, you click the vertex to be eliminated and then click the target vertex. The original vertex moves to the target vertex, adjusts its associated edges and polygons, and is welded to it. The original vertex and target vertex must be separated by only a single edge.

Make sure you save your work as you progress. Saving at every milestone as you work from one body part to another is a good idea.

Refining the Shoulder

We need more detail in the shoulder. As you can see, the shoulder is currently flat from the end of the arm to the neck. In this section you will add the detail required to place a bulge at the top of the shoulder that tapers into the clavicle. Let's start where you left off at the end of the previous exercise.

1. Select and chamfer the loop of edges that runs over the shoulder and under the armpit. Set Chamfer Amount to 0.25, as shown here. The selected edges around the armpit are shown in gray.

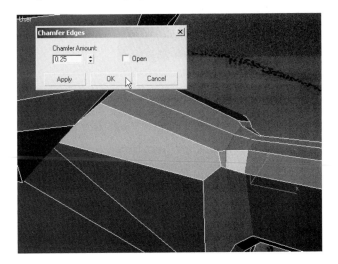

2. Select the three edges that run along the clavicle (the collarbone), and use the Connect tool to add two more sets of perpendicular edges.

3. When editable poly sub-objects are moved in a viewport, they adhere to the same transform coordinate system restrictions as any other object in a scene. Similar to using the local transform coordinate system, the Constraints option in the Edit Geometry rollout allows you to limit the movement of the sub-objects to be parallel to the associated edges or polygons. This diminishes any unnecessary deformations caused by moving a sub-object away from a surface of the model. With the four new edges selected, go to the Edit Geometry rollout, and choose the Edge radial button. This constrains the four edges to avoid unwanted movement as you place them.

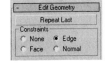

4. Move the edges closer to the shoulder, as shown here. Note that they do not leave the plane in which they lie due to the constraint in step 3.

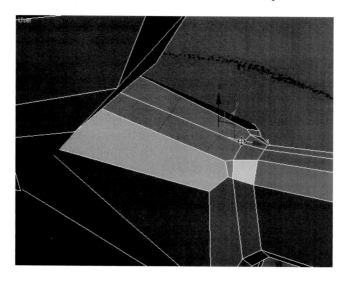

5. Change the Constraints option back to None to turn off the constraint.

6. Select the vertex at the top of the shoulder. Using Soft Selection, move it upward to create the shoulder bulge, shown here.

7. Zoom out and render the modeled arm; it should look similar to Figure 6.10.

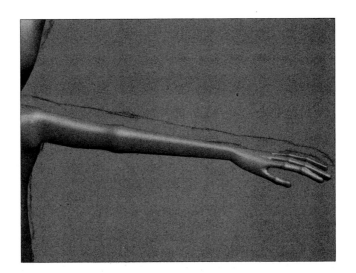

Figure 6.10

The model after adding detail to the arm, hand, and shoulder

Adding Detail to the Torso

The shape of the alien's torso is fairly plain, and decidedly not anatomically correct, so the detail added will be subtle. You will need to add some bulges for the wider hips and a belly button.

1. Zoom into the alien's hips, and select the three bands of horizontal edges that circle the alien at the waistline. As always, the selected edges are shown darker here.

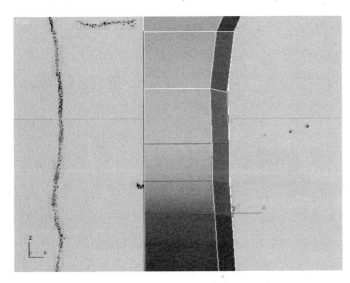

2. Chamfer the new edges. Using Edge Constraints, move the edges to concentrate them around the hip area as shown.

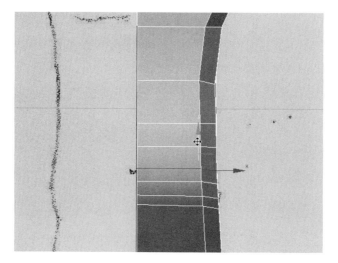

3. Turn the Constraints off and turn Use Soft Selection on. Move the hip vertices into place to create a wider hip as shown.

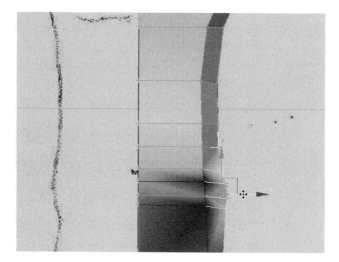

4. Use the Cut tool to create a perimeter around where the belly button will be and remove any internal edges that may occur.

5. Select the edges that encircle the intended belly button, omitting the edges along the center line of the model, and chamfer them with a Chamfer Amount of 0.01 as shown. The chamfer creates extra polygons to allow you to indent the belly button without affecting the polygons and edges further away from the belly button.

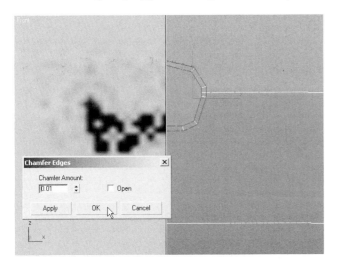

6. Select the polygon at the center of the belly button and move it into the alien's abdomen to create an "innie," as shown here.

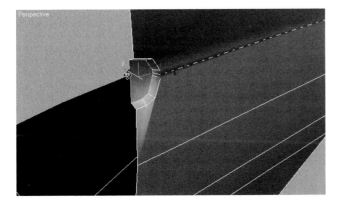

Adding Detail to the Head

Besides the overall shape of the head, the two main features that should be considered are the alien's eyes and mouth. Without lips, a tongue, or teeth to consider, the mouth is the simpler of the two features to model; the mouth simply consists of an appropriately shaped hole in the head. Who doesn't need one of those? Rather than deleting faces though, the mouth will need to be extruded into the head to prevent the appearance of a hollow skull.

The areas surrounding the eyes are going to be modeled using the Cut tool to define the shape of the eyes and then using Chamfer and Extrude to create the raised perimeter. The eyes themselves are spheres that are altered using the Hemisphere parameter. The following steps are a continuation of your work so far in this chapter.

Creating the Mouth

The mouth is going to be a simple extruded polygon, with the extrusion projecting into the alien's head. You'll begin by creating the perimeter of the mouth using the Cut tool.

1. Zoom into the mouth area to get a good working view.

2. Use the Cut tool to draw new edges around the perimeter of where you would like the mouth. You can roughly follow the mouth position in the front reference image as shown.

3. Use the Bevel Polygons dialog box to extrude and scale the polygon into the alien's head as shown. A negative value for the Height parameter causes the bevel to recess the polygon, rather than extrude it out from the head.

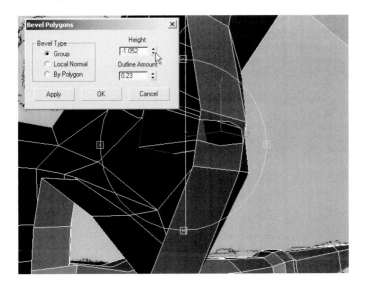

4. Select the edge at the center line of the mouth and delete it with the Delete key to open that side of the mouth and eliminate any internal faces, as shown here.

5. Start modeling the eye area by moving vertices around the eye in the reference so the vertices will run around the edges of the raised eye ridge.

6. To subdivide an edge at a particular location to create a better eye, switch to the Edge sub-object level. Click the Insert Vertex button in the Edit Edges rollout. Click on any edge to place a new vertex at that point, as we do here.

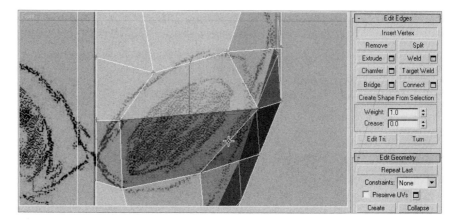

7. Continue to manipulate the vertices and edges until the eye area is a single, flat polygon. Then, select that single eye polygon and use the Inset Polygons dialog box to create a ring of faces to surround the eye as shown.

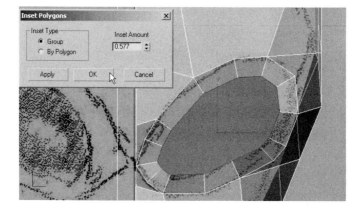

8. Select and delete the central eye polygon and then select all of the polygons that surround the new hole.

9. Bevel the selected polygons to create the eye ridge as shown.

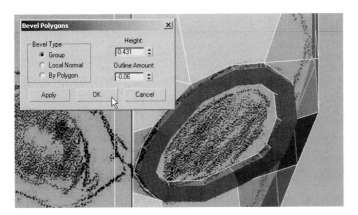

Creating the Eyes

Rather than creating the eyes as components of the alien mesh itself, you will make them as separate objects that will be linked to the model. This method allows for greater flexibility when applying materials to, or animating, the eyes.

1. Exit any sub-object level. Create a sphere with a radius of approximately 3 in the Front viewport where the alien's eye is.

2. Decrease the Hemisphere parameter value until the visible boundary of the sphere is slightly larger than the eyehole, as shown.

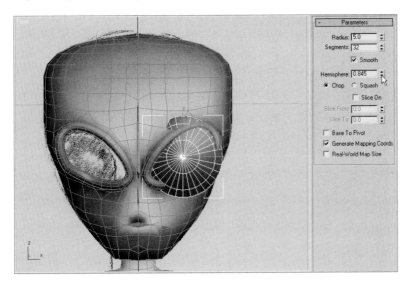

3. Convert the eye to an editable poly. Rotate and move it to position it correctly in the eye socket.

4. Make any necessary edits to the vertices or edges to hide any portions of the eyeball sphere that protrude through the surface of the alien's head.

5. Exit any sub-object level and rename the object **Eye Left**.

6. Click the Mirror tool (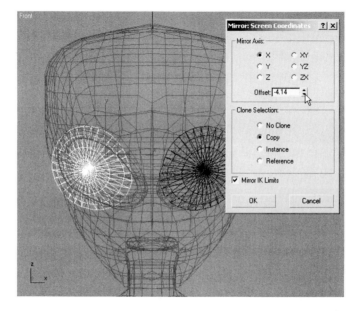) in the main toolbar to open the Mirror dialog box. Set the axis to *X* and set Clone Selection to Copy. Increase the offset amount until the new eye appears correctly in the other eye socket, as shown here.

7. Rename the new object **Eye Right** and make any changes required to make the eye fit in the socket.

8. Select both eye objects and link them to the Alien object with the Select and Link tool from the main toolbar to cause them to follow the alien's head movement.

Final Touches

The major portion of the modeling is complete. The only remaining tasks are to weld the seams, clean up any areas with unwanted sharp corners, and add a few asymmetrical features so that the model does not look quite so computer generated. You can continue with the previous exercise or open the Alien7.max scene file in the Alien Model folder from the companion CD.

1. Hide the reference images if necessary to have a better view of what you'll be working on. Save your scene before moving to the next step.

> When you've been using the Symmetry or TurboSmooth modifiers (as you have with the alien model), you should always save a copy of the model or entire scene before you convert any model to an editable poly. Do this first, just in case you need to edit it at the Symmetry or TurboSmooth level. You will lose access to those modifiers once you make the conversion.

2. Select the alien and convert it to an editable poly. This will set the actions of the modifiers into the mesh, and you will not be able to edit those modifiers. Saving the file as you did in the previous step gives you the chance to go back and make changes to the initial model if needed.

3. Select all of the vertices that share the center line of the model or border on an opening at the center generated now that you have converted to an editable poly. Make sure you don't select any of the vertices from the eye ridges that are close to the center line. You will notice gaps running down the middle seam of the alien in the following graphic. We plan to close these gaps to create a smooth mesh for the alien in the next steps.

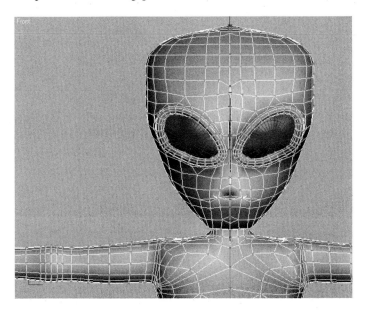

4. Click the Settings button, next to the Weld button in the Edit Vertices rollout, to open the Weld Vertices dialog box.

5. The Weld Threshold parameter is the maximum distance that selected vertices can be apart before they are welded. Slowly increase the value for Weld Threshold until the visible gaps are closed as shown here.

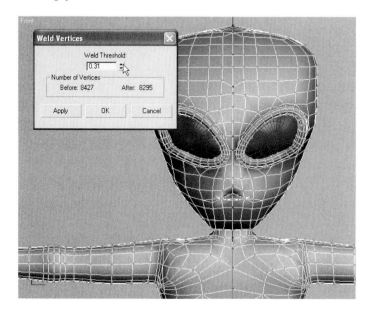

6. Examine the model closely, especially around the mouth and eyes. Make any corrections you like. In the next steps, we will use Paint Deformations to smooth and finesse the model.

3ds Max uses a paintbrush analogy to reduce the sharpness, or tension, between adjacent polygons. Adjust the size of the virtual brush and click and drag over the areas to be smoothed.

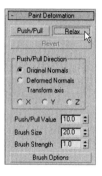

7. In the Paint Deformation rollout, click the Relax button.

8. A Brush icon will appear in the viewports as a circle with a line projecting from its center, as shown here. The circle always remains parallel to the surface of the model. Reduce the Brush Size parameter to about 1.0.

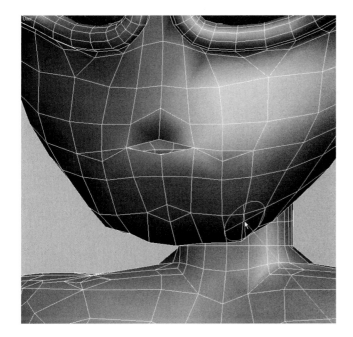

9. Click and drag the brush over the areas of the mesh you would like to smooth. This reduces the angle between the adjacent polygons, effectively smoothing the area.

Humans, animals, and many other living real-world creatures are basically, but not perfectly, symmetrical. Asymmetrical imperfections are natural and should be reflected in your character models. The vertices around the eyes, the brow, and the mouth are areas to consider altering to make them asymmetrical. The changes should be subtle and should not call attention to the varied area, unless that feature is significant to the character's makeup.

Summary

This chapter explored and explained several tools used to create organic models. From a simple box, a torso was formed to match the general shapes shown in the reference images. The Symmetry modifier required you to model only half of the character while it generated the reciprocal half. The legs, arms, and a head followed, all remaining in a simple boxy configuration. The TurboSmooth modifier was added to the top of the Modifier Stack to subdivide and smooth the polygons. Additional detail was added and then the model was collapsed and fine-tuned.

Although we used an alien character here, this toolset can be utilized for any type of organic model.

CHAPTER 7

Materials and Mapping

Applying materials is the phrase used in 3ds Max to describe applying colors and textures to an object. A material defines an object's look—its color, tactile texture, transparency, luminescence, glow, and so on. *Mapping* is the term used to describe how the textures are wrapped or projected onto the geometry (for example, adding wood grain to a wooden object). After you create your objects, 3ds Max assigns a simple color to them, as you've already seen. This allows them to render and display properly in your viewports.

How you see an object in real life depends on how that object transmits and/or reflects light back to you. Materials in 3ds Max simulate the natural physics of how we see things by regulating how objects reflect and or transmit light. You define a material in 3ds Max by setting values for its parameters or by applying textures or maps. These parameters define the way an object will look when rendered. As you can imagine, much of an object's appearance when rendered also depends on the lighting. Applying materials and lighting go hand in hand. In this chapter and in Chapter 10, "3ds Max Lighting," you will discover that materials and lights work closely together.

Topics in this chapter include:

- **Materials and the Material Editor**
- **Mapping a Pool Ball**
- **Mapping, Just a Little Bit More**
- **Using Opacity Coordinates**
- **Mapping the Rocket**

Materials

Materials are useful for making your objects appear more lifelike. If you model a table and want it to look like polished wood, you can define a shiny material in 3ds Max and apply a wooden texture, such as an image file of wood, to the diffuse channel of that material.

The first half of this chapter shows you the parameters and functions of the materials and the Material Editor window. If you want to skip ahead to work on a mapping exercise, go to the "Mapping a Pool Ball" section later in the chapter. Make sure you come back to skim over the hows and whys in the first half of the chapter.

Materials also come in handy when you want to add the appearance of detail to an object without actually modeling it. For instance, if you want a brick wall to look like real brick, but you don't want to model the bricks in the wall, you could use a brick texture. Using a texture would be a time-saving alternative. You can plainly see a brick wall in Figure 7.1.

However, in Figure 7.2, the wall shows the appearance of detail in each line of bricks using a texture map (called *bump mapping*). This texture map renders the appearance of dimension for each brick and the inset grooves between each of them, without the hassle of actually modeling the surface of the wall with that level of precision.

This shortcut is an easy trap to fall into. Using texture maps to accommodate too much detail can make your scene look fake and primitive. Don't depend on textures to do the work for you. A model that is not detailed enough for a close-up shot more than likely will not be saved by a detailed texture map. In the end, the level of detail that is needed boils down to trial and error. You have to see how much texture trickery you can use to keep a model's detailing at bay before the model no longer works in the shot. In the beginning, it's safe to assume you should model and texture as much detail as you can. You can work toward efficiency as you learn more about 3ds Max and CG.

Figure 7.1

A brick wall

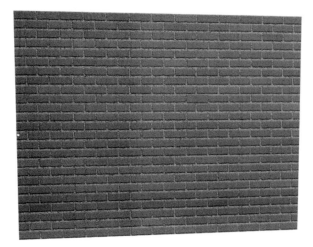

Like a model, a texture map needs to be as detailed as the scene calls for. You will want to gauge the detail of your texturing based on the use of the object in the scene. A far-away object won't need to have a massive texture map applied to its material. Textures mapped onto a material often add the final element of realism to a scene, and it takes a lot of experience to determine how detailed to make any textures for mapping. So let's start gaining some of that experience now.

Material Basics

What makes a material look the way it does? The primary force in a material is its color. However, there are several ways to describe the color of a material. In 3ds Max, three main parameters control the color of a material: ambient color, diffuse color, and specular color.

Figure 7.2

The same brick wall shown from an angle. The detail in the wall was created with bump mapping.

Ambient color is the color of a material when it is exposed to ambient light. This essentially means that an object will appear this color in indirect light or in shadow. Ambient gives you the very base color of the object, upon which you add the diffuse and specular colors.

Diffuse color is the color of a material when the object is exposed to direct light. Typically, ambient and diffuse colors are not too far apart. As a default they are locked together.

Specular color is the color of a shiny object's highlight. The specular highlight on an object can be controlled by factors other than its color—for example, its size and shape. The color, however, sets the tone of the object and, in some cases, the degree and look of its shine.

For example, in a new scene, open the Material Editor by choosing Rendering → Material Editor. The spheres you see in the Material Editor are sample slots where you can edit materials.

Each tile, or slot, represents one material that may be assigned to one or more objects in the scene. As you click on each slot, the material's parameters are displayed below. You edit the material through the settings you see in the Material Editor.

Select one of the material slots, and click it. Let's change the color of the material. Under the Blinn Basic Parameters, click on the gray color swatch next to the Diffuse parameter. This opens the Color Selector window, as shown here.

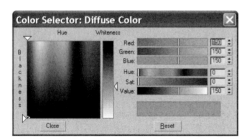

Using the sliders on the right, you can set the red, green, and blue values for the color, or you can control the color using the Hue, Sat (Saturation), and Value levels. For more on color and RGB/HSV values, see Chapter 1, "Basic Concepts."

You can also very easily select the desired color from the gradient on the left by dragging your mouse pointer over the colors until you find one you prefer. It's best to pick the general color you need from the swatch on the left and then tweak the exact color by using either the RGB or the HSV controls on the right. The Hue of a color represents the actual color itself. Saturation defines how saturated that color is. Value sets how bright the color will be.

Once you have a color you like, close the Color Selector. If you want to restart the color, press Reset to zero out any changes. You'll notice that the ambient color has changed as well as the diffuse color. You will see why in the next section on the Material Editor itself.

In addition, you can add textures to almost any of the parameters for a material. Notice the blank square icon next to the Diffuse color swatch. Click that icon, and you will get the Material/Map browser, as shown in Figure 7.3. The Material/Map browser is used throughout the chapter.

Figure 7.3

The Material/Map browser

The Material Editor

The Material Editor is the central place in 3ds Max where you do all of your material creation and editing. You create materials to assign to any single or group of objects in the scene. You can also have different materials assigned to different parts of the same object. In a full scene, it's customary to have many different materials

It is wise to get to know how the Material Editor works first, and then get to know the types of materials and shaders in 3ds Max. Open the Material Editor by choosing Rendering → Material Editor or by pressing the keyboard shortcut M. Figure 7.4 shows the Material Editor and its major parts.

The following list describes the functions of the Material Editor:

Sample Slot The sample slot provides you with a quick preview of your material. Each material is displayed on a sphere in one of the tiles (or slots) you see in the Material Editor dialog. Right-clicking on any of the materials will give you a few more options, including the ability to change how many sample tiles you can see in the Material Editor (as shown here). The fewer samples, the quicker the Material Editor will load.

Get Material This button brings up the Material/Map browser. Here you can browse from the scene or from a Material Library. The Material Library stores a collection of saved materials that you can bring into the current scene. You can use 3ds Max's default materials or create your own and store them in your own custom library.

Figure 7.4

The Material Editor

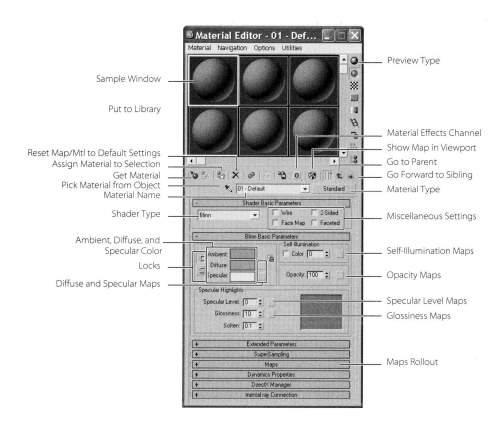

Assign Material to Selection You can use this button to assign the material to the selected object(s) in the scene. You can also apply materials by clicking and dragging the sample sphere from the Material Editor directly onto the object in the viewport; however, this can be less accurate, especially if you have a lot of objects.

Reset Map/Mtl to Default Settings This function resets the values for the map or material in the active sample slot.

Put to Library You can save your material to a library using this function. Building up a library of useful materials can save time, especially when you're trying to re-create complex materials. Once you've gotten a material just right, there's no reason you shouldn't save it to your library by using this button.

Material Effects Channel Here you can assign an effect ID to the material. Effects are used in the video post or Combustion for things such as glow, highlights, and so on. Some of these effects will be covered in Chapter 11, "3ds Max Rendering."

Show Map in Viewport This will display your texture map in the viewport. This means that you won't have to render every time you want to see how your material appears on a 3D object. However, displaying your map in a viewport has limitations. The limitations are basically those of your graphics card and your chosen method of displaying 3D in the viewport (Open GL, Direct 3D, or Software). The difference between viewing the map in the viewport and in its final rendered state may be quite different. However, seeing a map in the viewport is useful on many levels.

Go to Parent Just as you created objects that related to each other, materials in 3ds Max may have several components to them (such as texture maps) that work in a hierarchy, where information from one node is fed upstream into the parameter for the material. When you are working with sub-maps, this option will take you back to the base material. This makes it easier to navigate in the Material Editor when you are editing your materials.

Go Forward to Sibling This function is the reverse of Go to Parent. This option will take you into the next map channel.

Preview Type Sometimes the default sphere won't give you an adequate preview of the material. You can change the preview to a cube or a cylinder.

Pick Material from Object When you need to edit a material on an object, you can use this button to select the material from an object in the scene. The material is placed in the active sample slot.

Material Name This is the name you give a material. This should be a descriptive name for the material that will instantly tell you what the material is for. 3ds Max will automatically give new materials a default name, such as the name 03, but it's recommended that you change the material name from the default. You should do this before you apply it to an object when you are adjusting the parameters (color, etc.) to suit your needs.

Material Type Different materials have different uses. When called on to create a more complex material, for example, you can change the material type to Blend. A Blend material will mix the results from two different materials together for a compound effect. The default material type is Standard. Material types are explained in the next section.

Shader Type Shading types describe how the surface responds to light. How an object looks depends on how its surface reacts to light, so the Shader type for a material is very important. Shaders provide different options for specific materials. The default shader is Blinn. Shader types are covered later in this chapter. Not all material types let you specify different shaders.

Miscellaneous Settings These are fairly basic settings used to change the appearance of the material. Here are two important settings.

> **Wire** When you turn Wire on, the object attached to this material will render as a Wireframe object, as shown in Figure 7.5. This simple setting is very powerful; it's used when you need to render line art or wireframe views.

2-Sided This setting enables you to render both sides of a single surface. By default, only one side of a surface will render, and that is typically all you need. Sometimes, however, when you penetrate through a surface, you will have to see the other side. In this image (Figure 7.6), a hemisphere is rendered without 2-Sided turned on.

In this image (Figure 7.7), 2-Sided has been enabled. Notice the inside of the hemisphere.

Locks Here you can lock the Ambient parameter to the Diffuse parameter and lock the Diffuse to the Specular. Any changes made to one while the locks are enabled affect both.

Ambient, Diffuse, and Specular Color Changing the ambient color will affect the way the material appears for ambient light. Changing the diffuse color affects the overall color of the material. Changing the specular color changes the color of the highlighted light. You change the color by clicking on the color swatch next to the parameter.

Diffuse and Specular Maps These buttons provide shortcuts to the maps for Diffuse and Specular. A map applied in Diffuse (for example: bitmap, which is an image file) will affect the base appearance of the material. A map applied to Specular will use the mapped image to define the color of the shine. Mapping is covered in the Pool Ball exercise later in this chapter, as well as in the rocket that we'll texture.

Specular Level This setting determines how shiny the material appears. For something such as a metallic surface, the setting will be up around 180 to 220. You can also map a grayscale texture to determine which areas will appear shiny and which will appear dull.

Glossiness This setting determines the spread of the specular shine. A higher value means that it will look more plastic (high gloss across the surface of the model).

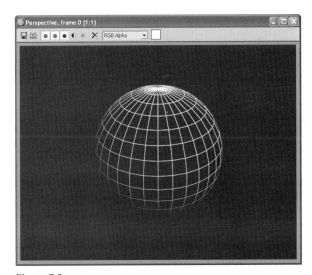

Figure 7.5

The render as a Wireframe object (Wire on)

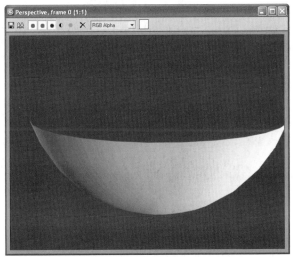

Figure 7.6

The render without 2-Sided turned on

Figure 7.7

**The render with
2-Sided enabled**

Figure 7.7

**The render with
2-Sided enabled**

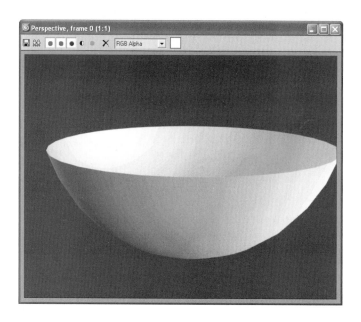

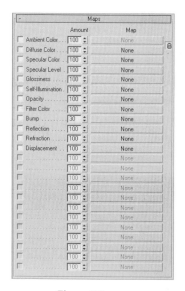

Figure 7.8

**Applying maps to
these parameters
further defines
the look of your
material.**

Self Illumination This slot defines how the material is affected by light. The more self illumination it is given, the less the material is affected by lighting, but the flatter it will become.

Opacity A material's opacity determines how transparent it appears. If it is set to 100 (the default), then the material is 100 percent opaque—that is, it's solid. If it is set to 0, then it is completely invisible. You can apply a grayscale opacity map here that uses a bitmap (or other map) to define which portions of the material are transparent. Areas of white on the map will be opaque, whereas the black areas will render transparent; the intermediate values of gray will have different levels of transparency.

Maps Maps allow you to apply bitmap or procedural textures, which help define the material beyond simple color and opacity settings. Common maps include bump maps (use grayscale values to simulate bumps and dents), displacement maps (use grayscale maps to mathematically calculate depth and height and redefine the mesh accordingly), reflections, glossiness, and so on, as shown in Figure 7.8.

Material Types

Different materials have different uses. The Standard material is fine for most uses. However, when you require a more complex material, you can change the material type to one that will fit your needs. To change a material type, click the Material Type button called out in Figure 7.4. By default, it displays Standard in the button. Once you click the button, the Material/Map browser opens (as shown in Figure 7.9) from which you can choose the material type.

Standard

Standard material is the default type for the materials in the Material Editor. This material has values for ambient, diffuse, and specular components. With it, you can imitate just about any surface type you can imagine. The more advanced surface types (see the following discussions) combine elements of different shaders for more complex effects.

Blend

Just as it sounds, this material type blends two materials together. Figure 7.10 shows the parameters for a Blend material type. Notice the controls for mixing two different materials. You assign the materials through the Material 1 and Material 2 parameters.

Figure 7.9

Choose the material type from the Material/Map browser

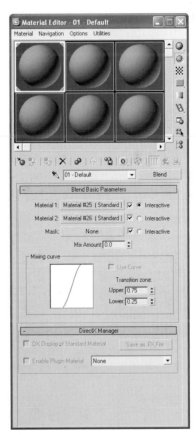

Figure 7.10

The Blend material type allows you to mix two different materials together.

Composite

Similar to the Blend, a Composite material combines up to 10 materials, using additive colors, subtractive colors, or opacity mixing (Figure 7.11).

Double Sided

The Double Sided material type divides the material into two sub-materials, one for the outward face and one for the inner face. Figure 7.12 shows the parameters for the material.

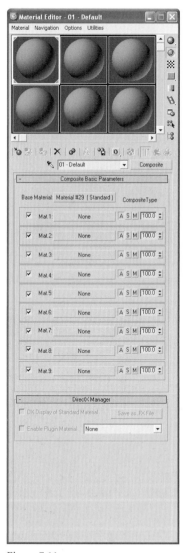

Figure 7.11

The Composite material type allows you to blend up to 10 materials.

Figure 7.12

A Double Sided material allows you to assign two materials to either side of a surface.

To set the Facing Material, you can click on the bar to create and edit a new material, or you can click and drag an existing material from the Material Editor onto the Facing Material bar. You set up the Back material in exactly the same way.

In the following graphic (Figure 7.13), one material is assigned to the outer face of an object and another one is assigned to the back of the surface. Here, a bowl has a solid blue material mapped to the outside, and the inside face is a checkerboard pattern map.

Neither the facing nor the back material need to have 2-Sided enabled for the Double Sided material to render both sides of the surface.

Ink 'n Paint

Ink 'n Paint is a powerful Cartoon material that creates outlines and flat cartoon shading for 3D objects based on Falloff parameters. Figure 7.14 shows the parameters for an Ink 'n Paint material.

Figure 7.15 shows you a sample render with the Cartoon shading material applied to a bowl and a cone.

Matte/Shadow

Use Matte/Shadow material when you want to isolate the shadow. The material will receive shadows, but it will remain transparent for everything else. It is useful for rendering objects onto a photo or video background because it creates a separate shadow that you can composite on top of the background. Rendering in separate passes, such as a separate shadow, is very useful because you can have total control of the image by compositing just the right amount of any particular pass.

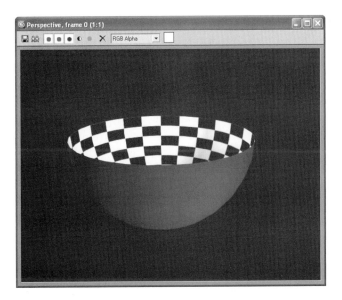

Figure 7.13

One material is assigned to the outer face and another material is assigned to the back.

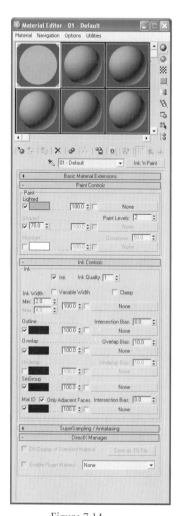

Figure 7.14

**The Ink 'n Paint
material's
parameters**

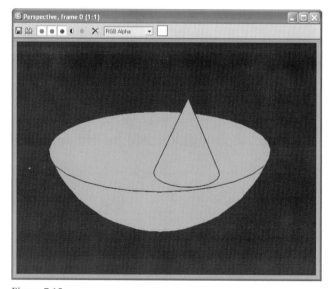

Figure 7.15

A Cartoon-shaded render using the Ink 'n Paint material

Multi/Sub-Object

Use this material when you need to apply different materials to polygons of a 3D object. Material IDs are assigned either manually or automatically, depending on how you create the material. (This is covered later in the chapter.) Material IDs determine which sub-material is applied to which polygon. This lets you assign different surface treatments to a single object. This keeps modeling simpler because you do not have to make separate objects for everything that needs a different material.

Raytrace

The Raytrace material is a powerful material that expands the available parameters to give you more control over photo-real renderings. The material uses more system resources than the Standard material at render time, but it can produce more accurate renders—especially when true reflections and refractions are concerned. You will use this material in Chapter 11.

Shellac

The Shellac material superimposes one material on another using additive composition. This allows you to create a material that is highly glossy, such as a finely varnished wood surface (Figure 7.16).

Top/Bottom

Top/Bottom divides the material into a top material and bottom material with an adjustable position (Figure 7.17). The material is in the first slot in the Material Editor in the figure. This material is useful for creating an object that has two different materials on either side, such as a cookie with chocolate on the top.

> The Standard material type has typically been the most commonly used material type. With the increasing use of the mental ray renderer and the use of mental ray Arch and Design materials, this is changing. Because this is an introductory text, we are going to stick to Standard materials. That will be sufficient to give you a foundation in the Standard materials and method of rendering. You will need to change the material type only for special needs. However, you will need to change the type of shader more often to achieve certain surface qualities. You will explore the types of shaders next.

Figure 7.16

The Shellac material allows you to superimpose a shiny layer on top of another material.

Figure 7.17

The Top/Bottom material type

Shader Types

The way light reflects from a surface defines that surface to your eye. In 3ds Max, you can control what kind of surface you work with by changing the shader type for a material. This option will let you mimic different types of surfaces such as dull wood or shiny paint or metal. The following descriptions outline the differences in how the shader types react to light.

Anisotropic

Most of the surface types that you will see in this section typically create rounded specular highlights that spread evenly across a surface. By contrast, *anisotropic* surfaces have properties that differ according to direction. This creates a specular highlight that is uneven across the surface, changing according to the direction you specify on the surface. The Anisotropic shader (Figure 7.18) is good for surfaces that are deformed, such as foil wrappers or hair.

Figure 7.18

The Anisotropic shader

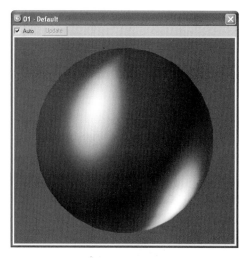

Figure 7.19 shows the Material Editor for an Anisotropic material. Notice the extra controls for the specular highlights. These allow you to control how the specular will fall across the surface.

Blinn

This is the default material in 3ds Max because it is a general-purpose, flexible shader. The Blinn shader (Figure 7.20) creates a smooth surface with some shininess. If you set the specular color to black, however, this shader will not display a specular and will lose its shininess, making it perfect for regular dull surfaces, such as paper or an indoor wall. Figure 7.21 shows the Blinn shader controls in the Material Editor.

Because this is the most-often used shader, let's take a look at its Material Editor controls. The ambient, color, and specular colors all work as you saw earlier in this chapter. You can set the color you want by clicking the color swatch, or you can map a texture map to any of these parameters by clicking the Map button and choosing the desired map from the Material/Map browser.

SPECULAR HIGHLIGHT CONTROLS

The parameters in the Specular Highlights section of the Blinn Basic Parameters rollout are interesting in this shader. The specular color, which defaults to white, controls the color of the highlight. Decreasing the brightness of that specular color, whatever the color may be, will decrease the brightness of the specular highlight on the object, making it seem less shiny. Changing the specular color to black will negate any surface shine.

The surface shine is also regulated by the Specular Level parameter. The higher the value, the hotter the specular highlight will render on the object. Figure 7.22 shows a

Figure 7.19

The Material Editor for the Anisotropic material

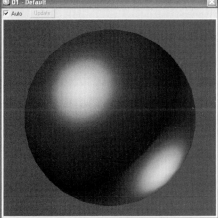

Figure 7.20

The Blinn shader

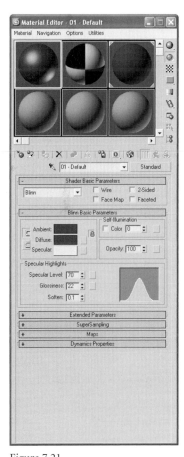

Figure 7.21

The Material Editor for the Blinn material

sphere with a Blinn with a Specular Level of 0 on the left, a Specular Level of 35 in the middle, and a Specular Level of 100 on the right.

The Glossiness parameter controls the width of the specular highlight. With the same sphere with a Specular Level of 35, Figure 7.23 shows you a Glossiness of 0 on the left (which creates a broad specular), a Glossiness of 35 in the middle (which creates a fairly tight, shiny specular highlight), and a Glossiness of 75 on the right (which creates a high gloss pinpoint specular highlight). The higher the value, the glossier the surface will appear.

Finally, the Soften parameter controls the softness of the specular highlight. Figure 7.24 shows a sphere with a Blinn material assigned with a Specular Level of 55, a Glossiness of 10, and with a Soften value of 0 on the left and a Soften value of 1 (the max) on the right.

Soften controls the specular breadth on specular highlights that are already broad—that is, they have lower Glossiness values. You may want to look at these parameters at work in a Max scene, as your monitor will display the specular highlights better than a printed page.

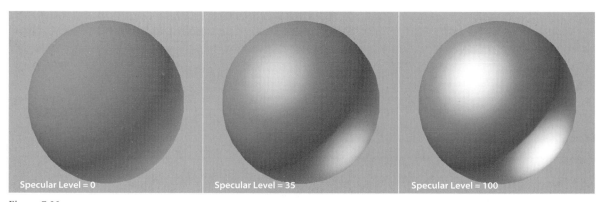

Specular Level = 0   Specular Level = 35   Specular Level = 100

Figure 7.22
The Specular Level of a Blinn controls the amount of highlight on the surface.

Glossiness = 0   Glossiness = 35   Glossiness = 75

Figure 7.23
The Glossiness parameter controls the width of the specular highlight.

Figure 7.24

The Soften parameter helps rein in broad specular highlights by softening their edges.

You've probably noticed the graph (shown here) in the Material Editor when you work with the Specular Level, Glossiness, and Soften parameters. This graph shows you the falloff of the specular you are editing for the material. The shorter the graph, the lower the level of specular highlight. The rounder the graph, the broader and softer the specular highlight.

For shiny objects, you will need to use a fairly sharp specular. For extremely shiny objects, such as polished metals, a pinpoint specular is best. Plastic objects will work best with a broad, diminished specular. Matte objects, such as paper or cloth, work great without a specular highlight, or at least a very darkly colored one.

SELF-ILLUMINATION

The Self-Illumination parameter creates the illusion of incandescence on an object, meaning the object seems to be self-lit. The object's darker areas (where it is not receiving direct light) will essentially take on the color specified for the Self-Illumination parameter.

The higher this value, the flatter the object will appear, because Self-Illumination will essentially negate any shadowing or ambient falloff on the material. The specular highlights on the material will still show up on a material with Self-Illumination turned all the way up to 1.0. You can also change the color of the Self-Illumination by clicking the Color check box and choosing a color in the swatch that appears when Color is enabled. This allows you to have a different self-illumination color than the color of the material itself. Figure 7.25 shows a Self-Illumination value of 0 on the left and a Self-Illumination value of 1.0 on the right. Notice how the sphere flattens out as Self-Illumination helps keep the shadow areas as bright as the diffuse.

A Self-Illumination value does not emit a light in the default scanline renderer—that is, the object will not illuminate other objects in the scene. For such an effect, you will need to use more advanced rendering techniques with mental ray, for example.

Figure 7.25

The Self-Illumina-
tion value sets the
incandescence of a
material.

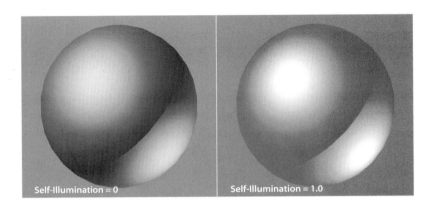

Figure 7.25

The Self-Illumination value sets the incandescence of a material.

Self-Illumination = 0

Self-Illumination = 1.0

OPACITY

The Opacity setting sets the transparency of an object. The higher the Opacity value, the more solid it renders. The lower the Opacity value, the more see-through the object will render.

Metal

The Metal shader is not too different from the Blinn shader. Metal creates a lustrous metallic effect, with much the same controls as a Blinn shader, but without the effect of any specular highlights. When you are first starting, it's best to create most of your material looks with the Blinn shader until you're at a point where Blinn simply cannot do what you need. The graphic (Figure 7.26) displays a sphere with a Metal shader with a Specular Level of 120 and a Glossiness of 60.

The black areas of the shader may throw you off at first, but keep in mind that a metal-lic surface is ideally black when it has nothing to reflect. Metals are best seen when they reflect the environment. As such, this shader requires a lot of reflection work to make the metal look just right.

Multi-Layer

With some surfaces, you need complex highlights. In some cases, while an Anisotropic might be useful, you may need further control in the complexity of your specular shape and falloff. A Multi-Layer shader will stack two Anisotropic highlights together to give you increased control over the highlights you can create.

Here you can see a Multi-Layer material assigned to a sphere (Figure 7.27).

The two layered specular highlights are created in such a way, as shown in Figure 7.28, to create an "X" formation for the highlight.

Figure 7.26

A sphere with a Metal shader

Figure 7.27

A Multi-Layer material assigned to a sphere

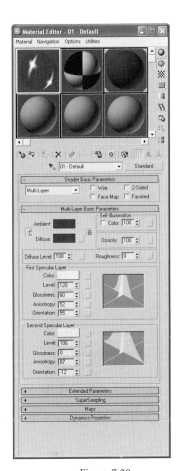

Figure 7.28

The Multi-Layer shader lets you create complex highlights.

Oren-Nayar-Blinn

The Oren-Nayar-Blinn shader (Figure 7.29) generally creates good matte surfaces such as cloth or clay. The shader has specular highlight controls very similar to those of the Blinn shader.

Phong

The Phong shader (Figure 7.30) is a legacy shader that was created before the introduction of the Blinn shading model The Phong shader looks very similar to the Blinn shader, and it has the same controls. Phong creates smooth surfaces with some amount of shininess, just as Blinn does. However, Phong does not handle highlights as well as Blinn. This is especially true for glancing highlights, where the edge of a surface catches the light. Phong is good for creating plastic objects, as well as many other surfaces.

Figure 7.29

The Oren-Nayar-Blinn shader

Figure 7.30

The Phong shader

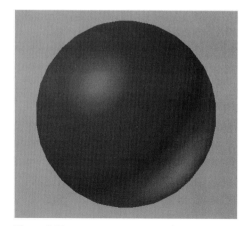

Figure 7.31

The Strauss material

Figure 7.32

The Translucent shader

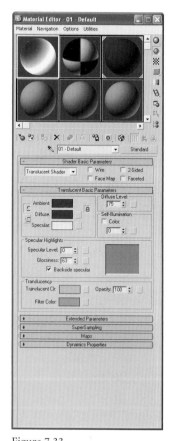

Figure 7.33

A Translucent shading material allows light to scatter through the object.

Strauss

The Strauss material (Figure 7.31) can create metallic and nonmetallic surfaces. Its main controls are Color, Glossiness, Metalness, and Opacity. The specular highlights, for the most part, are governed by the Glossiness of the material. The higher the Metalness value, the darker the unlit portions of the surface become, again relying on reflections for the metallic look.

Translucent

Translucence is where light is scattered as it passes through the material—for example, when a flashlight shines behind a sheet of parchment. The Translucent shader (Figure 7.32) is very similar to the Blinn; however, this shader adds a touch of translucency to the material.

You can also simulate frosted and etched glass by using translucency. Figure 7.33 shows the Material Editor for a Translucent shading material.

Mapping a Pool Ball

Let's put some of that hard-earned knowledge to work and map an object. You will be creating and texturing a pool ball. Although this may not seem the most exotic thing to texture, you can learn a lot about surfaces, shading, and mapping techniques by texturing it. You'll be able to flex your mapping muscles even more in exercises later in the chapter.

Starting the Pool Ball

If you have skipped to this section from the beginning of the chapter, have a run through and get a good taste of texturing in 3ds Max. Feel free to look at the earlier parts of the chapter for some of the hows and whys of what you will accomplish in the next exercise. Otherwise, roll up your sleeves and follow along with these steps to texture a pool ball.

You can begin with your own project, or you can copy the Pool Ball project found on the companion CD to your hard drive. It contains a texture image file you'll need for this exercise.

1. In a new scene, create a sphere. The size doesn't matter here. How's that for fast modeling?

2. Open the Material Editor by pressing the keyboard shortcut M or clicking the Material Editor icon () in the main toolbar.

3. In the Material Editor, select one of the sample slots. Go to the Blinn Basic Parameters rollout.

4. The most logical thing to start with is the color. The base color of an object is defined by the Diffuse parameter—although Ambient is also locked to Diffuse, which is fine. The Diffuse parameter is shown here.

5. Click on the color swatch to the right of the Diffuse parameter to open the Color Picker window. Pick any color at this point. Once you have chosen your color, click the Close button, and you will see that the sphere in the sample slot has changed to your color.

Choosing a Surface Type

The next step is to decide what the surface of your object is going to be. Will it be shiny or matte? You will need a shiny surface, because real pool balls are glossy. We will have to adjust the specular highlights using the Blinn's controls.

1. Go to Specular Highlights under Blinn Basic Parameters. Set the Specular Level to 98 and the Glossiness to 85. Keep Soften at the default. The specular graph here is quite sharp.

2. That is it for the Basic material. Now apply it to the object by dragging the material from the sample slot to your sphere in the viewport and release the mouse button. The sphere will change to the color you chose for the diffuse, and in the sample slots the corners will become outlined with white triangles as shown here.

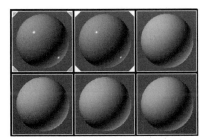

The corner triangles on a sample slot in the Material Editor mean the material is "hot" or applied. Before you apply the material, it is "cool" and there are no corners. This is the default. When the corner triangles are solid white, the material is "hot" and the object it is applied to is currently selected.

The material in the editor is now the material assigned to the object. If you were to change any of the parameters of the material, it would be instantly updated on the object. Once you assign a material, there's usually no need to return to the object's default color, although you may find yourself replacing the material with another material frequently.

Figure 7.34 shows you what the pool ball should look like, most noticeably its specular highlight. However, viewing in the viewport isn't the same as a rendered image. The viewport gives the lowest level of quality, and it should not be used to make final decisions on the look of your material. Instead, it should be used as a point of reference.

Figure 7.34

The pool ball in a viewport

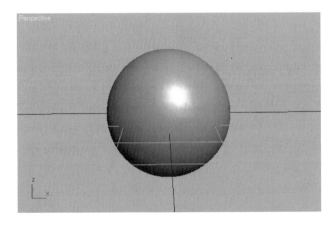

Figure 7.35 shows this pool ball rendered. Rendering (covered in detail in Chapter 11) combines the materials, lights, shadows, and environments within a scene to create the final look. Notice how much more detailed the specular highlight is in the render. To check your render, click the Quick Render icon (🌐) in the main toolbar.

Figure 7.35

The pool ball rendered

Mapping the Pool Ball

This simple material is only part of the story. Just creating a sphere and making it shiny and green doesn't make a realistic ball. Pool balls have a graphic strip or number in a circle. You still need to add the markings of a real pool ball, not just a solid color. Figure 7.36 shows some real pool balls. You can't create the needed detail using the basic parameters of the Standard material. What you need is a bitmap.

Figure 7.36
Pool balls

This step has to do with texture placement. As you gain more experience, you'll learn how to prepare your texture images for your models. A bitmap replaces the diffuse color with an image. The image you use can be hand drawn and scanned, created in a program such as Adobe Photoshop, or taken with your digital camera. The image we are going to use (Figure 7.37) was created in Photoshop. A white circle with a "2" is in the middle and one that is cut in half is on either side.

Figure 7.37
The proposed bitmap texture for the ball

The theory behind this image is quite simple. Pool balls have the number on opposite sides of the ball. In your texture map, you'll need to make two 2s in the blue backdrop. The two halves of the white circle and the 2 will simply tile together when the texture image wraps around the sphere, much like how a wrapper wraps around a piece of candy. This way you have two 2s on the ball, easy as pie. To apply this bitmap as a texture, follow along here:

1. Go to the Material Editor and select the sample slot that is applied to the sphere. Go to the Maps rollout and click on the bar to the right of Diffuse Color, which is currently marked None. The Material/Map browser will appear. See Figure 7.38.

2. Make sure the Browse From group is set to New. Select Bitmap and click OK, as shown here. An Explorer window (Figure 7.39) will appear. Navigate to the PoolBallColorTexture.tif file in the SceneAssets\Images folder of the Pool Ball project on the CD (or the one copied to your hard drive).

Figure 7.38

Apply bitmap as a texture from the Material/Map browser

Figure 7.39

Selecting a bitmap image for the material

3. The Material Editor has changed, and you are now in a separate module from the Material parameters. You are in the Bitmap parameter. There are several rollouts that we are going to ignore for now. The most important rollouts in the Bitmap section are Bitmap Parameter and Coordinates. The Bitmap Parameter rollout deals with the actual bitmap image; the Coordinate rollout controls how the bitmap image moves relative to the surface of the object. Leave all the settings at their defaults. See Figure 7.40

> If you ever need to change a bitmap image in a texture already applied, simply go to the bitmap's Material Editor and under the Bitmap Parameter rollout, click on the bar with the filename to the right of the Bitmap parameter. The file browser will reopen. Choose another image file, and it will replace the current bitmap file.

4. You will be able to see the bitmap in the sample slot, but not in the viewport. To fix this, click the Show Map in Viewport button (🎱) on the Material Editor's toolbar (just below the sample slots).

> Think of the Material Editor as a literary outline. The heading of the outline is the full material, and its parameters when they are mapped (like Diffuse or the entries in the Maps rollout) are like an outline's subheadings that all fall under the main material.

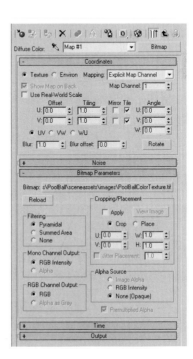

Figure 7.40

The Material Editor shows the parameters for your bitmap image.

5. Right now you can see only the Bitmap parameters. What if you want to go back and adjust the specular on the material itself? The Go to Parent button (🔼) is on the Material Editor's toolbar. The parent is the material. Clicking this icon will take you back to the material's own parameters, where you will find the Blinn Basic Parameters again. Any map that is added to a material is known as a *child* to that material, much the same way as the hierarchy worked in the Mobile project in Chapter 2, "Your First 3ds Max Animation."

As a matter of fact, you can have an outline view of your materials. Open the Material/Map Navigator (Figure 7.41) with the Material/Map Navigator button (🔳) located on the Material Editor's toolbar.

MAPPING COORDINATES

When you put a 2D image onto a 3D object, think of it as being "projected" onto the surface, as if you had a white object and a slide projector was projecting a picture onto the white surface. Mapping coordinates describe how the image is projected or wrapped around the surface. Coordinates are spelled out in terms of *U, V,* and *W. U* is the horizontal dimension, *V* is the vertical dimension, and *W* is the optional depth. All primitives have mapping coordinates, including our sphere. That doesn't necessarily mean the image will wrap itself correctly, although it works fine for our Pool Ball exercise (imagine that!). Merely having the mapping coordinates only means the map will show up. In order to edit the mapping coordinates, you need to use the Coordinate rollout. You will learn more about mapping coordinates later in the chapter.

The Material/Map Navigator is a floating dialog you can use to navigate through your material and maps. This is very useful for complex materials that use a lot of maps. It is a very simple dialog: The blue sphere represents the material and its main parameters and the parallelogram is for the bitmap. The parallelogram is green by default and red when Show Map in Viewport has been activated. Click the entry you need to show in the Material Editor to edit its contents.

6. Now render the ball to check the map's appearance. With your Perspective viewport active, click the Quick Render icon (the teapot). Figure 7.42 shows the pool ball with the mapping.

Figure 7.41

The Material/Map Navigator window displays your materials in an outline format.

Figure 7.42

The ball with the mapped image

Adding a Finishing Touch—Reflection Mapping

With the image applied, the pool ball looks pretty good at this point (Figure 7.42)—but it's not perfect. The small nuances are what really make a render look good. One thing this pool ball is missing is a reflection of its environment. Now, short of creating and texturing a pool table and several other pool balls, we need to make a cheat.

There are two ways to create reflections: the "faking it" method (using mapping) and the raytrace method. Both methods require us to go to the Maps rollout in the Material Editor. We are going to use the cheat and add a bitmap into the Reflections Map slot. We are going to use the "faking it" method.

> *Raytrace* is a rendering methodology that traces rays between all the lights in the scene with all the objects and the camera. It can provide true reflections of objects in the scene. Chapter 11 covers raytracing in more depth.

To fake the reflection, you'll need an image that looks like the "room" around the ball. We are going to use a photograph taken for this occasion and saved as the image file `ReflectionMap.tif` in the SceneAssets\Images folder of the Pool Ball project on the companion CD (Figure 7.43).

Figure 7.43

The reflection map used to "cheat" the reflections on the pool ball

This image has all the elements that you might see around a pool ball—specifically, more pool balls! To add this image as a reflection for the ball, follow these steps:

1. Go to the Material Editor and make sure you are at the material's parameters; use the Navigator or Go to Parent button if you are still in the diffuse bitmap area where you applied the image file.

2. Go to the Maps rollout and click on the bar currently marked None next to the Reflections parameter. Select Bitmap from the Material/Maps window, and then navigate to ReflectionMap.tif in the SceneAssets\Images folder of the Pool Ball project on the CD, or on your hard drive if you've already copied it.

3. Do a quick test render with the Quick Render icon (the teapot). The reflections are pretty strong (Figure 7.44).

4. You need to adjust how much reflection is on the ball. Click the Go to Parent button, and go to the Maps rollout. The type-in area next to the names lets you specify the amount of map applied to the material. Change the value next to Reflections from 100 to 10. Test-render the pool ball again. You should notice a much nicer level of reflection (Figure 7.45). Voilà!

If you have lost the view of your pool ball somehow, or if you simply want to center it in the Perspective viewport (or any other viewport), press the Z shortcut to focus the viewport on all the objects in the scene. In this case, it will center the pool ball.

Figure 7.44

The reflections are a bit heavy. If you could reduce the amount of reflection, they'd be better.

Figure 7.45

The reflections look much better and add a certain realism to the pool ball.

Background Color

You may notice that the background in the renders in Figures 7.44 and 7.45 are white, whereas your renders' backgrounds are (probably) black. There are many reasons why you would want to control the background color, which you can do with a simple setting change. You may want a specific color to offset your scene (for example, blue to represent the sky) or you may want a picture in your background.

To change the background of your renders, go to the main menu and choose Rendering → Environment (Figure 7.46). The Background parameter is at the top of the dialog box. Click on the color swatch and choose your color. That's it!

To add an image to the background, click on the bar marked None to add a bitmap, just as you did with the bitmaps on the pool ball. Once you do, the image will render in the background with your scene. To change the image, click that bar, which at that point should list the path and filename of the current image, to take you to the Material/Map browser where you can select a new bitmap and image.

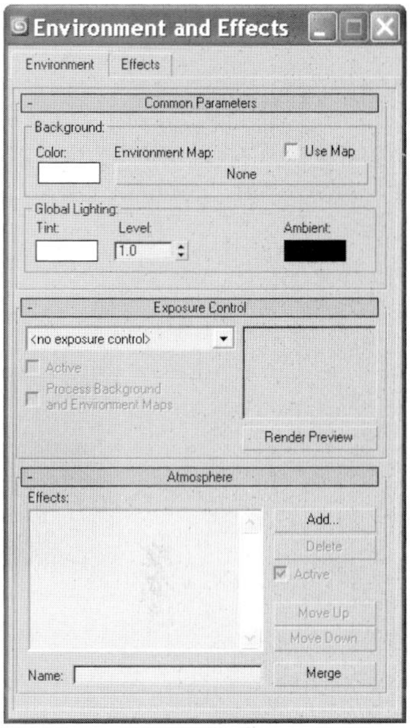

Mapping, Just a Little Bit More

Now that you know how to add maps to a material, removing them is very simple. In the Material Editor for the parent material's parameters (not the map's parameters), you can right-click on the map name, as shown in Figure 7.47, to select Clear from the context menu.

If you don't want to clear the map entirely, but just need to turn it off for a little while, you can just uncheck the box to the left of the parameter name, as shown in Figure 7.48. Check it back on to use that map again.

Figure 7.46

**Choose Rendering →
Environment.**

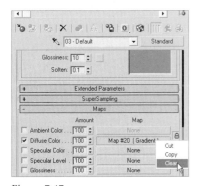

Figure 7.47

Removing a map from a parameter

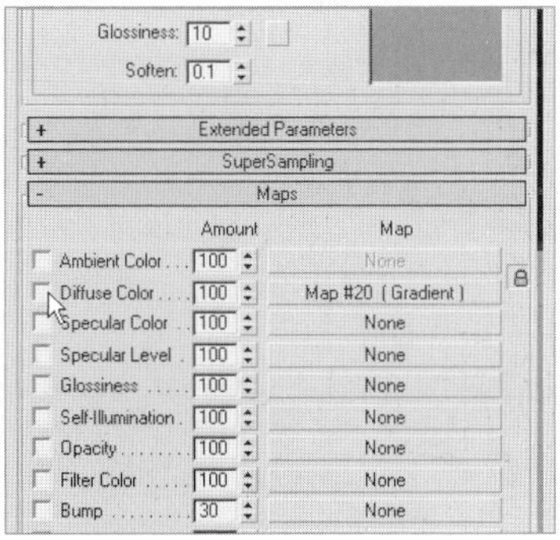

Figure 7.48

Unchecking the box next to a mapped parameter will temporarily remove the map from the parameter.

Seeing More Sample Slots

If you have a scene with several materials, and you need to see more sample slots than the default in the Material Editor, simply right-click on any slot and select either 5 × 3 Sample Windows or 6 × 4 Sample Windows from the context menu. This will help you navigate a heavy scene that has tons of materials that you need to modify. In the following graphics, you can see the sample slots multiply!

Here's what 5 × 3 Sample Windows looks like.

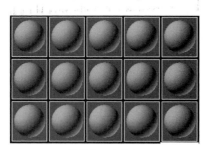

5 × 3 Sample Slots

And here's what 6 × 4 Sample Windows looks like.

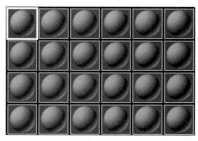

6 × 4 Sample Slots

As you've seen, the sample slots for any given material in the Material Editor constantly update to show you any changes you've made to that material. However, if you want a

Figure 7.49

Magnify gives you a larger view of your material.

larger image than the relatively small sample slot, double-click on the slot or right-click on the slot and select Magnify from the context menu, as shown in Figure 7.49.

3ds Max will open a larger window (Figure 7.50), which is resized by dragging the corners of the window, with a sample of that material. It will by default update automatically as you make changes to the material.

Figure 7.50

A larger view of your material sample

You've already noticed that there are only 24 sample slots in the Material Editor. This does not limit the number of materials you can use to 24. You should consider the Material Editor as a scratchpad of sorts. You can create as many materials as you'd like in a 3ds Max scene; however, only 24 can be loaded in the Material Editor window at the same time.

If you click the Get Material button in the Material Editor, you can list all the materials that are used in the scene. When the Material/Map browser is open, click the Scene radio button for the Browse From parameter, and all of the materials assigned in the scene will be listed. When an object's material is not shown in a sample slot, it does not mean it has been deleted. You can load it back into any sample slot for editing at any time.

Assigning Materials to Sub-Objects

You've seen several times how to assign a material to an object. You can, for instance, drag the material from the Material Editor to the object in a viewport. You can also select an object in the viewport, and then select a Sample Slot material and click the Assign Material to Selection button (![icon]) in the Material Editor.

You may want to assign materials to sub-object polygons as well as whole objects. One approach is to use the Multi/Sub-Object material type briefly discussed earlier in the chapter

There is a much easier way to assign materials to sub-objects, however. Just select the appropriate polygons on the surface (the object must be an editable mesh or poly, or have an Edit Mesh/Edit Poly modifier applied), and assign the material as you regularly would (using the Assign Material to Selection button or dragging the material to the selected polygons in the viewport). A sphere with several polygons assigned to different materials is shown in Figure 7.51.

Figure 7.51

Applying materials to a mesh's sub-object polygons is easy.

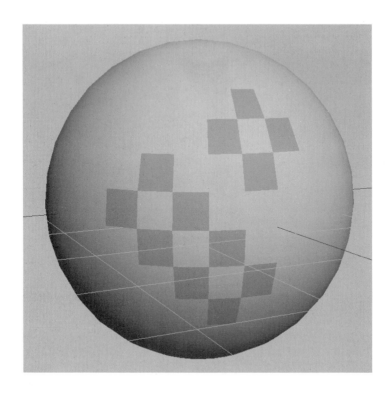

Once you apply a material to a sub-object, a new Multi/Sub-Object material is created in the scene automatically. You can load the new Multi/Sub-Object material by using the eyedropper to click on the object in the viewport to load the material into a sample slot.

Maps

By now you've noticed that the Material/Map browser has different maps you can access. These maps are divided into categories.

You've already used the bitmap map a few times. Let's take a look at the rest of the maps by category. Open the Material/Map browser. The categories are listed on the left. By default, All is selected as shown here.

The categories and their more important maps are explained in the following sections.

2D Maps

2D maps are two-dimensional images that are typically mapped onto the surface of geometric objects or used as environment maps to create a background for the scene. The simplest 2D maps are bitmaps; other kinds of 2D maps are generated procedurally.

Procedural maps are generated entirely within 3ds Max and rely on a set of parameters you set for their look. Images brought in the way the pool ball's color and reflection maps were brought in are not procedural maps. They are *bitmaps*—that is, raster image files. For more on raster image files, see Chapter 1.

Click on the 2D Maps category in the Material/Map browser to see the available 2D maps.

Bitmap

As you've already seen, a *bitmap* is an image file that you load into 3ds Max. It can be a photo, a scan, or any image that is readable by 3ds Max.

Checker

A procedural map, the checker map is a checkerboard pattern that is generated in 3ds Max. Its parameters in the Material Editor, which are shown in Figure 7.52, control the look of the checkerboard.

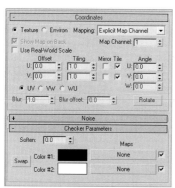

Figure 7.52

The checkerboard pattern

Parameters in the Material Editor   A Sphere with a Checker Applied to Its Color

The Tiling values under the Coordinates rollout determine the number of checkers. The higher the number, the more checkers. Color #1 and Color #2, of course, control the two colors of the checkerboard; black and white are defaults. You can either click the color swatch to change the color, or you can click the Map bars (labeled *None* until you assign a map) next to each color. The Blur parameter allows you to blur the edges of the checkers, and the Soften parameter under the Checker Parameters rollout blurs the checkers together.

Gradient

A *gradient is* a procedural map (the parameters are shown in Figure 7.53) that grades from one color to a second color that grades to a third color.

Figure 7.53

The Gradient map

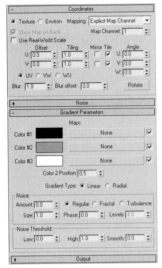

Gradient Parameters

A cylinder is shown grading from black (top) to white (bottom).

In the Coordinates rollout, the parameters are much the same as they are for the checker map. These coordinates are pretty much the same for all procedural maps, as they allow you to position the map as you need on the object by setting the options such as Tiling and Offset.

The colors for the gradient are set by Color #1, Color #2, and Color #3. You can also map these colors. The Color 2 Position parameter sets the *relative* location of the middle color to the upper and lower colors—i.e., 0.5 is the middle because the other colors are at 0 and 1.0.

Gradient Ramp

Similar to the Gradient map, but much more powerful, the Gradient Ramp is a procedural map that allows you to grade from and to any number of grayscale shades. Gradient Ramps are perfect for creating maps that fall off (for example, for opacity effects where the opacity fades away). See Figure 7.54.

Use the sliders along the ramp in the Material Editor to set the position of the gray value. Click in the ramp to create a new slider at that grayscale value. The Black and White sliders at the very ends do not move. To delete a slider, right-click on it, and choose Delete from the context menu that appears. Notice the value and position readout above the ramp.

3D Maps

Similar to 2D maps that are generated in two dimensions, 3D maps are patterns generated procedurally in all three dimensions. For example, Marble has a grain that goes through the assigned geometry in *X, Y,* and *Z*. If you cut away part of an object with Marble assigned as its texture, the grain in the cutaway portion matches the grain on the object's exterior.

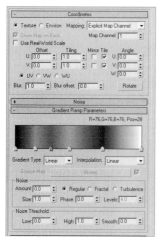

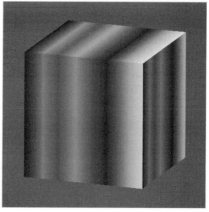

Figure 7.54
The Gradient Ramp

Here is how a gradient is shown in the Material Editor.

Here's what happens when it is applied to a cube.

When you create a 3D map, notice that the Coordinates rollout has Tiling and Offset parameters in three axes, whereas the 2D maps only have *X* and *Y*.

Try using some of the 3D maps (such as Marble, Wave, Stucco, and Wood) to see how they work on a simple object in your scene. They all have basically the same Coordinates rollout; however, each has its own Parameters rollout to control the color and other settings.

Marble

A Marble map creates veins of colors that run through an object. The 3D aspect of the map allows it to spread across all three dimensions, creating a more realistic texture. Color #1 and Color #2 control the two colors of a Marble map, while the third color is a grainy blend of the two together, shown in Figure 7.55.

Figure 7.55
The Marble map

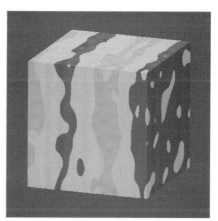

The Marble Map Parameters

The Marble map's parameters are shown here applied to a cube.

Noise

Noise is a great way to easily add some randomness to a parameter or to add a bit of randomness to a surface's color or specular highlight, for example. See Figure 7.56.

Figure 7.56

The Noise effect

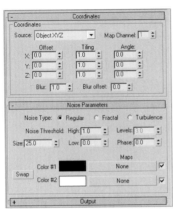

Noise Parameters

The parameters have been applied to this cylinder.

Used sparingly, noise can add great detail to highlights for any shiny object when mapped to the specular color. In this case, just make sure the colors in the noise do not contrast too much against each other, which would make the map faint.

Wood

Wood is a quick way to add wood grain to a material. See Figure 7.57.

Figure 7.57

The Wood effect

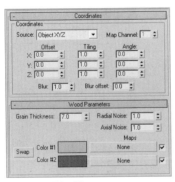

Wood Parameters

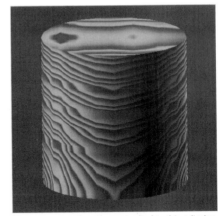

The parameters have been applied to this cylinder.

Just like with the Marble map, you can set the color of the wood grain with Color #1 and Color #2. Adding Radial Noise and Axial Noise will make the wood appear to have more burls.

Compositor and Color Modifier Maps

In image processing, *compositing images* refers to superimposing two or more images to combine them in a variety of ways. In CG, compositors are meant specifically for compositing colors or maps together for some advanced effects. Color Modifier maps alter the color of pixels in a material for some advanced effects. Color modifiers and compositor maps will not be covered in this book.

Using Opacity Maps

Opacity mapping allows you to cut out parts of an object by making those parts invisible. You can also create wonderful fading effects using opacity maps. With opacity mapping, you don't have to model certain details, which can be a real time saver. In this example, you will create a chain-link fence. However, you will not model a fence. You will create it entirely from mapping. To make a chain-link fence, follow these steps:

Figure 7.58

The chain-link texture

1. Open the Chain Link Opacity Map.max file in the Texture Scene Files folder on the companion CD. Open the Material Editor and select a sample slot. First, you are going to add a bitmap to the diffuse color, so go to the Maps rollout. Select the bar next to Diffuse Color. Pick Bitmap from the Material/Map browser and navigate to the Texture Scene Files folder on the CD. Choose Chain Link.tif (shown in Figure 7.58).

2. Go to the Coordinates rollout and change both the U and V Tiling parameters to 3.0. This will scale down the image because the image repeats three times.

3. Apply the material to the Plane geometry in the scene. Click the Show Map in Viewport button. Render and you will see something similar to Figure 7.59. As you can see, the chain-link image appears on the plane, but you can't see the objects on the other side.

Figure 7.59

The chain-link fence is rendered.

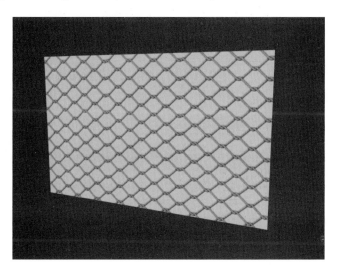

4. Go to the Material Editor. Click the Go to Parent button to get to the Maps rollout for the parent material. Click on the bar next to Opacity and select Bitmap from the Material/Map browser. In the Explore window, navigate to the Texture Scene Files folder on the CD and select `Chain Link OP.tif` (shown here).

5. The tiling values for the opacity map must be the same as the diffuse map; otherwise, the transparency of the fence will not line up with the links of the fence. Go to the Coordinates rollout, and change both the U and V Tiling to 3.0. Render to see the results shown in Figure 7.60.

Figure 7.60

The render when both the U and V Tiling are set to 3.0

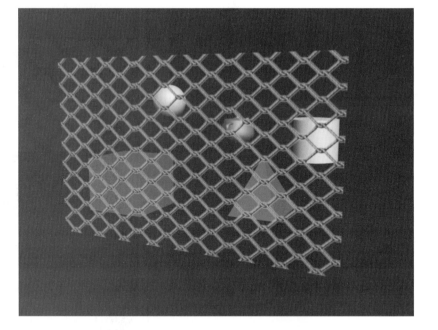

You can see immediately how useful opacity mapping can be. 3ds Max uses the white portions of the image map to display full opacity, whereas the black areas become transparent. If you did not have an opacity file such as the one in this exercise, you could easily create one by painting a black-and-white matte of the color image that you are using for the material.

Mapping the Rocket

In a previous exercise, you turned a boring sphere into an exciting pool ball using Diffuse and Reflection maps. Now let's dive into mapping the rocket we modeled in Chapter 5 to get it ready for lighting and rendering in Chapters 10 and 11, respectively.

Study the full-color image of the rocket shown in Figure 7.61. (It's also shown in the Color Section of this book.) That will give you an idea of how the rocket is to be textured. Let's begin with the wheels.

Figure 7.61

Let's texture the rocket!

The Wheels

The wheels of the real toy rocket are made of plastic that is fairly smooth, shiny and reflective. The black tires are different from the wheels: they have a rough, bumpy surface (Figure 7.62). The bumpiness breaks up the shininess, similar to what happens when you throw a handful of sand into a pool of water. The surface is still shiny and reflective but is distorted by the bumpiness, giving an appearance of a slightly matte finish.

Since the tire was created from a single primitive, and then modified, we don't have separate objects to which to apply materials. One option is to break apart the object so it has distinct areas (distinct objects), but this method adds an extra complication because we have to manage more objects. To avoid this, we are going to use a texturing technique using Multi/Sub-Object (MSO) materials. This material was explained earlier in the chapter; now let's put it into practice.

Black part of the tire has a slight bumpiness which changes the shininess, making the surface appear more matte.

Figure 7.62

The tire is a rough black plastic

A Simple, Shiny Red Plastic   A Simple, Shiny White Plastic

Selecting Polygons and Named Selection Sets

With a Multi/Sub-Object material, you select the polygons on the objects you want to assign a particular type of material, as opposed to selecting the entire object. The hardest part of creating an MSO material is selecting those polygons. However, there are a few things that will make selecting at a sub-object level easier.

Selecting by region (see Chapter 3, "The 3ds Max Interface," under the Selection Tools Icons) allows you to use the mouse to select one or more objects by defining an outline or area, instead of simply clicking them. There are five different types of regions from which to choose; the default is a rectangle marquee. For this task, your best bet is probably to use the Lasso region selection (which works just like the Lasso tool in Adobe Photoshop) to select the polygons around the wheel that demarcate the tire portion of the wheel.

Start by opening your final rocket model from your work in Chapter 5, or open the `Rocket_Material_Wheel_Start.max` file from the Scenes folder of the Red Rocket project on the CD. This file has hidden the rest of the rocket using the Layer Manager. To unhide the other parts of the rocket, use the Layer Manager. Keep the other body parts hidden for now.

1. Press F4 so you can see the edges on the shade model. Press F2 so that when you select the polygons, they will be shaded and easier to see.

2. Select the wheel and open the Modify panel. In the Modifier Stack, select Polygon to enter Polygon Selection mode (you can also press 4 for Polygon mode).

3. Click the Select Region flyout, shown here, and select the Lasso Selection Region icon from the flyout. (Feel free to try the other region selection methods, too). Using Lasso, click and drag in the viewport around the polygons you want to select to defining a lasso region.

Holding down the Ctrl key lets you add polygons to your selection, and holding down the Alt key lets you remove polygons from your selection.

4. Click the Select tool ( ). Now, select the polygons that make up the tire portion of the wheel, as shown in Figure 7.63.

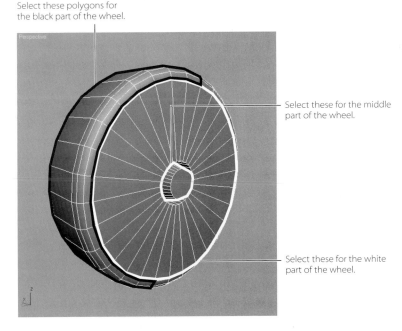

Select these polygons for the black part of the wheel.

Select these for the middle part of the wheel.

Select these for the white part of the wheel.

Figure 7.63

The wheel is composed of three distinct sections.

Be careful to use the Select tool, not the Select and Move tool. You do not want to accidentally move any of the polygons while you are trying to select them.

5. Another method to try in selecting the polygons for the black part of the Wheel is to use Edge mode. Go to Edge Selection. Arc rotate so you are viewing the back side of the wheel. Select a single edge on the perimeter of the wheel (Figure 7.64).

Single Edge Selection

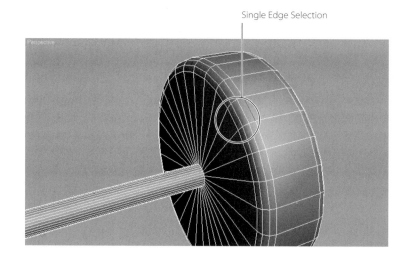

Figure 7.64

Select a single edge on the perimeter of the wheel.

6. Click Loop from the Selection Rollout, which will select all the edges that are touching head to toe. Then click Grow four times. Hold down the Ctrl key and click the Polygon icon in the Selection rollout.

7. Once you have selected all the tire polygons on the wheel object as shown in Figure 7.65, save the selection as a Selection Set.

8. With the polygons selected, enter the name **Wheel_Black** in the Named Selection Set (shown here) field and press Enter.

Figure 7.65

Select all the tire polygons.

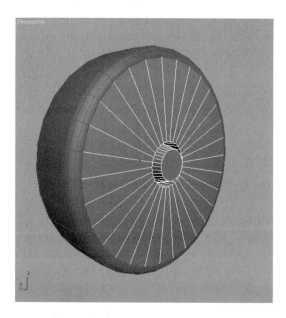

From here on, you can select all those polygons quickly by selecting them from the Named Selection Set pull-down menu shown in Figure 7.66.

Figure 7.66

Using Named Selection sets

9. Once you have saved the selection set, select the white portion of the wheel, as shown in Figure 7.67 as well as in Figure 7.63. Save a Named Selection set called Wheel_White.

10. Finally, select the middle part of the wheel (the bolt) as called out in Figure 7.63 and shown in Figure 7.68, and create a Named Selection set called Wheel_Bolt.

Creating a Multi-Sub Object Material

Now that you have made your selections for the wheel, you will create the Multi/Sub-Object material for the wheel, consisting of three distinct parts: black tire, white hubcap, and red bolt.

1. Open the Material Editor and select a sample sphere. We will start with the Red material for the bolt. Name the material **Red Bolt**, as shown in Figure 7.69.

2. In the Blinn Basic Parameters rollout, select the color box next to the Diffuse Color that controls the base color of an object; a Color Selector dialog will open. Create a red color with the values of Red: 200, Green: 0, Blue: 0, as shown in Figure 7.70.

3. Change the Specular Highlights to make the surface appear shiny. Set the Specular Level, which controls the intensity of the highlight, to 90 and set the Glossiness, which controls the size of the highlight, to 80.

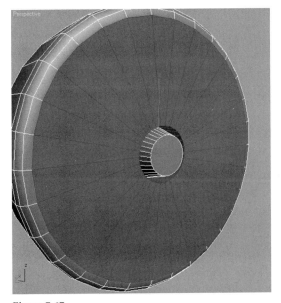

Figure 7.67

Select the white part of the wheel.

Figure 7.68

Select the middle part of the wheel, the bolt.

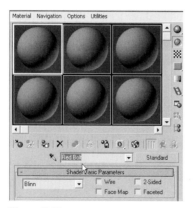

Figure 7.69

Name the material Red Bolt.

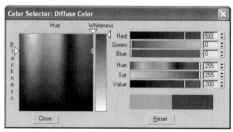

Figure 7.70

Create a red color.

4. Select another sample sphere and set its name to Wheel White. Change the Diffuse Color to White. Set Specular Level to 90 and Glossiness to 80, as with the Red material.

5. Select a third sample sphere in the Material Editor and name it **Wheel_Black**. Change the diffuse color to black. Because the highlights on the tire will be different, set the Specular Level to 50 and Glossiness to 20.

6. Make sure you are in Poly mode. If the wheel bolt isn't already selected, go to the Selection Set drop-down list and select Wheel_Bolt. This will select all the polygons you selected for the bolt part of the wheel.

7. Press F2 so that the selected polygons are no longer shaded full red and you can just see the edges around the poly colored red, instead. This makes it easier to see the applied material in the viewport.

8. Go to the Material Editor, select the Red Bolt material, and drag it to the selected polygons to assign it to those polygons.

9. Go to the Named Selection Set list and choose Wheel_White, and then go to the Material Editor and grab the Wheel White material and drag it to the selected polygons, assigning the material.

10. In the Named Selection Set list, choose Wheel_Black to select those polygons. Drag the Wheel_Black material from the Material Editor to the selected polygons.

11. Your wheel now has three distinct materials applied to its appropriate parts. Save your work!

Although there are different ways to create a Multi/Sub-Object material, this method of creating an MSO material is perhaps the most straightforward and the easiest to implement in this scenario.

Loading the MSO Material into the Material Editor

Congratulations! You have created a Multi/Sub-Object material, even though it may not appear that way. What you did was create three separate materials and apply them to sub-objects on the Wheel object. What 3ds Max did was work behind the scenes to create the MSO material. How mysterious! The three materials you see in the Material Editor are now just instances of the main or *parent material* called the Multi Sub-Object material. We will load this material into the ME so you can see it in the following steps.

1. In the Material Editor, select a sample sphere that isn't being used.

2. Next to the material title is an eyedropper icon ( ). Click the eyedropper, and then click on the wheel. The MSO material should be loaded into the Material Editor, as shown here.

3. The Material Editor parameters for the wheel's MSO material are shown in Figure 7.71. Change the name of the MSO material to **Wheel**.

Fine-Tuning the Materials

Continue with your own scene file. Select the Perspective View and press F9 for a Quick Render of the wheel (F9 is the shortcut key for a Quick Render). Keep in mind that the rest of the rocket is hidden and accessible through the Layer Manager.

Materials originally applied to the wheel are now instanced to the MSO material.

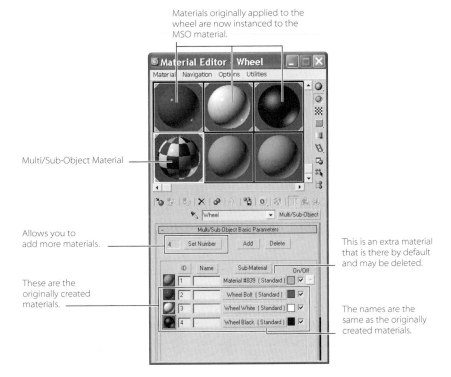

Multi/Sub-Object Material

Allows you to add more materials.

These are the originally created materials.

This is an extra material that is there by default and may be deleted.

The names are the same as the originally created materials.

Figure 7.71

The Multi/Sub-Object material for the wheel

The rendered result (shown in Figure 7.72) looks a bit flat. Specular highlights help make a 3D object look real, but highlights don't show up on flat surfaces.

Figure 7.72

The rendered wheel is a bit flat looking.

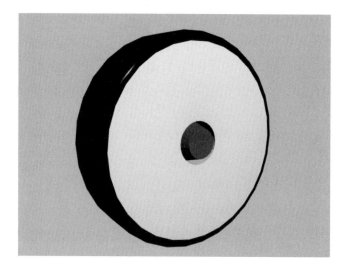

For example, in Figure 7.73, you can see three cylinder objects of varying flatness. The cylinder with the most rounded sides shows the highlight the most.

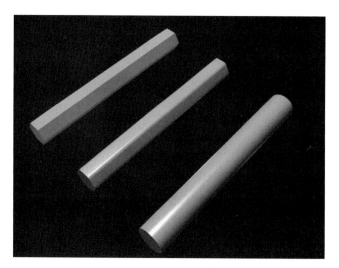

You can see a highlight on the black tire part of the wheel, but there's no highlight anywhere on the white hubcap and only a little highlight on the red bolt. One solution is to add more curves to your model to try to bring out the specular; another solution is to change your material somehow. This decision can be made depending on how close you will see the wheel in any of your shots. If the wheel is only seen from a distance, there is no need to further detail the model. Because we will only be seeing the wheel from a distance, we will alter the material. We can add a few things to bring out the shine in the material.

Usually shiny objects are also reflective, so if we add reflections to the flat hubcap surface, the render would look more convincing. As with the Pool Ball exercise earlier in the chapter, you can fake the reflections for a very convincing result, especially when you do not have a full CG environment built for the rocket that would allow true raytraced reflections (for more on raytracing, see Chapter 11).

To assign a reflection map to the wheel, follow along.

1. In the Material Editor, select the `Wheel Bolt` material. In the Maps rollout, click None (to the right of Reflections). Choose Bitmap from the Material/Map browser, navigate to the SceneAssets\Images folder in the Red Rocket project, and select the rocket `Rocket_Refmap_Blur.jpg` image file. If you don't see this map, make sure the Files of Type field is set to JPG.

2. Render a frame of the wheel bolt. Now the wheel's bolt will look like a perfect mirror, because the reflection amount is being used at 100 percent.

3. In the Material Editor, navigate up a level to the Maps rollout and change the Reflection Amount to 30.

4. Repeat the preceding steps for the other two wheel materials. Figure 7.74 shows the wheel rendered with the mapped reflection. You should notice a subtle difference between Figure 7.74 and Figure 7.72, which shows the wheel with no reflections. You can adjust the Reflection Amount to taste.

Figure 7.74

The wheel rendered with mapped reflections

The mapped reflection helps give the wheel more substance as it makes the material more convincing when rendered. A true reflection, as you will see with raytracing in Chapter 11 "3ds Max Rendering", will give you more accurate reflections, provided you are rendering in a created environment, which we are not. Figure 7.75 shows an example of a raytraced reflection and rendered in a simple 3D room. The wheel on the left is the fake mapped reflection; the wheel on the right is the raytraced reflection showing the accurate environment.

Figure 7.75

The wheel on the left has a mapped reflection, and the wheel on the right has a raytraced reflection.

Applying a Bump Map

We are almost but not totally done with the wheel. The black part of the wheel is only halfway there. One important feature of the wheel is the bumpiness on the surface (refer to Figure 7.62 on page 334). This bumpiness changes all the Specular and Reflective properties on that part of the wheel. Bump mapping is very common in CG. It adds a level of detail to an object fairly easily by creating bumps and grooves in the surface and giving the object a tactile element. Bump mapping uses the intensity values (aka the brightness values) of an image or procedural map to simulate bumpiness on the surface of the model, without changing the actual topology of the model itself. You can create some surface texture with a bump map; however, you will not be able to create extreme depth in the model. For that, you may want to model the surface depth manually or use displacement mapping instead. To add a bump map to the tire, follow these steps:

1. In the Material Editor, you should have the Wheel Black material selected and the Maps rollout open from the previous step.

2. Click the None button next to the bump map. In the Material/Map browser, choose Noise.

Noise is a map of color patterns that is generated procedurally in three dimensions so you don't have to fuss with mapping coordinates. (Mapping coordinates specify the location of an image on your object, as discussed later in the chapter.)

3. When you place the noise map in the bump map slot, you will automatically be taken to the Parameters for the Noise Map in the Material Editor (shown here). Change the size to 0.02. Click the Go to Parent icon (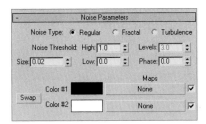) to move up a level to the main Material parameters.

4. Go to the Maps rollout and increase the Bump Amount from 30 (the default) to 60.

5. Render; you should now see a texture on the tire (Figure 7.76) that resembles the real bumpiness of the tire in Figure 7.62.

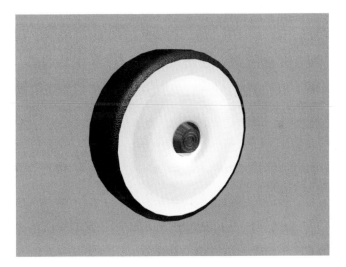

Figure 7.76

Add a bump map to the tire.

The wheel is complete!

Now you'll need to apply the MSO material you created to the other three wheels. There's a hard way to do this—and an easy way. The hard way is to select the polygons for the tire, the hubcap, and the bolt for each wheel , and apply the MSO material The easy way is to copy the finished wheel, place it where the other three wheels are located, and delete the original wheels. Just make sure to unhide the rest of the rocket using the Layer Manager.

Creating Material Libraries

While a material is in the Material Editor or applied to an object, it is part of the scene and is saved with the scene, whether it is displayed in a sample slot in the Material Editor or not. However, for complicated scenes, it is inconvenient to have all the materials active in the Material Editor, because you are limited to only 24 sample slots. Once you get to your twenty-fifth material, you will have to store some of the materials elsewhere, such as a material library, to make available slots for editing in the Material Editor. You can later bring those stored materials back into the Material Editor easily.

To create a material library:

1. In the Material Editor, select the sample sphere with the Wheel Multi/Sub-Object material.

2. Click on the Get Material button in the Material Editor (🔘).

3. In the Material Map browser, go to Browse From and select Mtl Library, as shown in Figure 7.77.

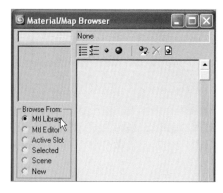

Figure 7.77

The Material Map browser

4. If default Library is loaded, go to the Library Management Tool icons at the top of the Material/Map browser (Figure 7.78) and use the Clear Library button. Don't worry; nothing will be permanently deleted.

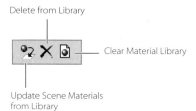

Figure 7.78

The Library Management tools

Delete from Library

Clear Material Library

Update Scene Materials from Library

5. Drag and drop the MSO material (and any other material from your scene) from the Material Editor to the Material/Map browser. This automatically loads it into the current Library.

6. Go to the File section to the left of the Material/Map browser, and click the Save As button (shown here).

7. Save the Library in the MaterialLibraries folder in the Red Rocket project. Name it **rocket1.mat**. (There already is a file in that folder called rocket.mat for your reference.)

> You can also load a library from a 3ds Max scene file, instead of a material library file (*.mat). When browsing from the Material Library in the Material/Map browser, choose Open, and then choose 3ds Max (*.max) from Files of Type. Select and load the .max scene file. All materials assigned in that scene are then listed in the browser. To convert the collection of materials to a library file, click Save and save it as a MAT file (.mat).

You can load the scene file Rocket_Material_Wheel_Final.max from the Scenes folder of the Red Rocket project to skip to this point or to check your work.

Mapping the Fins: Introduction to Mapping Coordinates

An image map is two-dimensional; it has length and width but no depth. Geometry in 3ds Max, however, extends in all three axes. How is a material that contains 2D image maps applied properly to a 3D scene object? Are the maps projected in a single direction onto the object's surfaces or do they envelop the object cylindrically or spherically? The answer depends on the type of mapping coordinates applied to the object. Mapping coordinates define how and where image maps are projected onto an object's surfaces and whether the maps are repeated across those surfaces.

Mapping coordinates can be applied to objects in several ways. The Generate Mapping Coords option is on by default. When primitive objects are created and the Generate Mapping Coords option is checked at the bottom of the Parameters rollout, the appropriate mapping coordinates are created automatically.

Loft objects, which are covered in Chapter 5, "Modeling in 3ds Max: Part II," control mapping in the Mapping section of the Surface Parameters rollout. The Length Repeat value determines how many times the material's maps are repeated along the length of the Path object, and the Width Repeat value determines how many times the maps are repeated around the scene object.

> If any part of your rocket is hidden in the scene file, especially if you started with the scene files from the CD, unhide those parts in the Layer Manager.

The Base Material

The top vertical fin on the rocket's tail is nothing special as far as materials are concerned. It is a white plastic that is just a bit shiny and has a decal, as you can see in Figure 7.79. At this point, you easily can create the material itself:

1. Open the `Rocket_Material_Fin_Start.max` file from the Scenes folder of the Red Rocket project, or continue with the `Rocket_Material_Wheel_Final.max` file from the previous exercise.

2. Open the Material Editor and select an available sample sphere. In the Blinn Basic Parameters, click the color swatch next to the Diffuse, and make it white.

3. Name the Material **Fin_Decal**. Unlike the side fins, the top fin has a decal on its side, so it will have its own material. Apply the material to the Fin object by dragging and dropping the sample sphere from the Material Editor to the fin.

4. Back in the Material Editor, in the Specular Highlights group of the Basic Blinn Parameters set the Specular Level to 80 and the Glossiness to 60. When you render, the base color may look a bit gray; that is just the basic lighting in the scene.

5. We need to add reflections for the fin. Go to the Maps rollout in the Material Editor, click None next to the Reflection map, and select Bitmap from the Material/Map browser. Navigate to the SceneAssets\Images folder in the Red Rocket project and select the `Rocket_Refmap_Blur.jpg` to assign it as the reflection map.

6. The Material Editor window will display the Bitmap Parameters section. Go up a level by clicking on the Go to Parent icon. Go to the Map rollout and turn the Reflection Amount down to 35.

7. Render. You'll see a plain, white shiny fin, as shown in Figure 7.80.

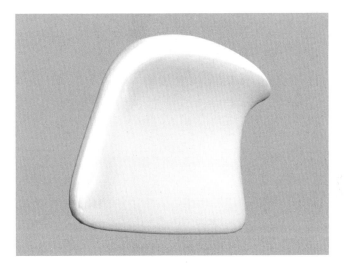

Adding the Decal

The main feature of this vertical fin is its decal. This is an image that we need to add to the material. The image is a 2D image and won't be as easy to apply as the 3D noise map we used earlier for the bump map of the tire. The decal will become a part of the Diffuse color; we will replace the color we created for Diffuse with the image itself.

1. In the Material Editor, select the Fin Decal sample sphere.

Make sure you are at the top level of the material and can see the Maps rollout.

2. Click None next to the Diffuse Color map. Choose Bitmap from the Material/Map browser, navigate to the SceneAssets\Images folder in the Red Rocket project, and choose RedRocketDecal.tif.

3. In the Material Editor toolbar, click the Show Map in Viewport button ( ). This will display the decal in the viewport. Figure 7.81 shows the mapped decal on the top fin.

> Don't panic just yet. Every object in 3ds Max has a set of *mapping coordinates* that tell the program how to place a 2D image onto your geometry. Honestly, 3ds Max gets it wrong most of the time the first time you try to map a 2D image.

Figure 7.81

The decal isn't mapping properly to the top fin.

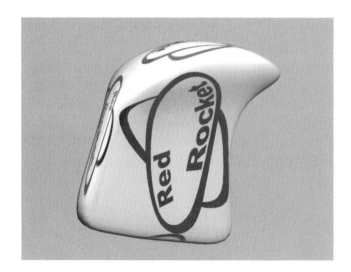

4. In the Material Editor's Bitmap parameters for the decal, go to the Coordinates section (shown in Figure 7.82); this area is where you adjust the map. Details about the parameters in this section are discussed in the Coordinates Rollout Explanation sidebar.

5. The decal needs to be rotated, scaled, and positioned. In the Material Editor, under the Bitmap parameters in the Coordinates section, change Angle W to 90.

6. Set the Tiling to U: 1.6 and V: 2. With Bitmap Coordinates, the higher the number, the smaller the map will become, in order to allow it to repeat or tile. In this case, we do not want the bitmap to repeat; we're just using the values to shrink the size of the decal on the surface. To turn off the tiling, simply uncheck the Tile boxes.

Figure 7.82

The Coordinates section of the Bitmap parameters

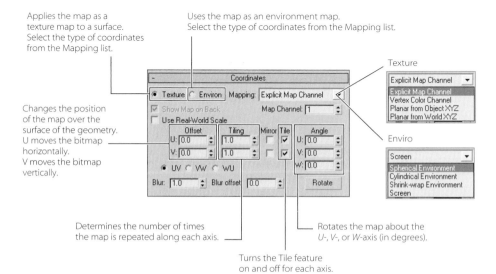

7. Set the Offset to U: –0.11 and V: 0.05.

The size and placement of the decal are not bad, but there are still copies of the decal on all the sides of the top fin, as shown in Figure 7.83.

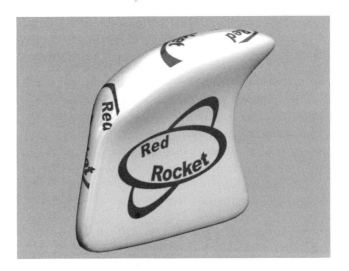

Figure 7.83

Copies of the decal are still on all sides of the top fin.

This happened because the model for the top fin started out as a box with six sides, so the Material Editor put a decal on each side of the geometry. This method works if the bitmap image has a random pattern, and you don't mind having that image on all sides of the object. Here, the mapping coordinates inherent in the top fin geometry will not allow us to place the decal on *just* the sides of the fin.

In the next section, we will use a modifier to change the mapping coordinates on the Top Fin object.

COORDINATES ROLLOUT EXPLANATION

The Coordinates rollout in the Bitmap parameters for a 2D image has several options, as you can see in Figure 7.82. Here is a brief explanation of the settings:

Applies the Map as a Texture Map or Environment You can select the type of coordinates from the Mapping pull-down menu. As you can see in Figure 7.82, there are different coordinate choices for Textures or Environments.

Offset UV Changes the position of the map over the surface of the geometry. U moves the bitmap horizontally, and V moves the bitmap vertically on the surface.

Tiling UV Determines the number of times the map is repeated along each axis.

Angle UVW Rotates the map about the *U-, V-, or W*-axis in degrees.

Figure 7.84

The UVW Modifier's parameters

Using a UVW Modifier

Instead of dealing with the surface's own mapping coordinates as we have tried here, we are going to use a modifier to replace those coordinates on the geometry. The *UVW Map modifier* makes the decal act more like a real decal that we can control by moving a modifier gizmo around to place the coordinates as we please. (For more on UVW Mapping, see the sidebar "Understanding UVW Mapping" later in this chapter.)

The UVW Map modifier is a common method for applying and controlling mapping coordinates. You select the type of mapping projection, regardless of the shape of the object, and then set the amount of tiling in the modifier's parameters. The mapping coordinates applied through the UVW Map modifier override any other mapping coordinates applied to an object, and the Tiling values set for the modifier are multiplied by the Tiling value set in the assigned material. Figure 7.84 shows the parameters for the UVW modifier.

CREATING THE UVW MAP MODIFIER

To use the UVW Map Modifier to properly map the decal to the fin, follow these steps.

1. Set the coordinates in the Bitmap parameters for the decal back to their default values:

    Offset: U: 0.0 V: 0.0

    Tiling: U: 1.0, V: 1.0

    Angle: W: 0.0

    UV Tile boxes: Check Off to turn the Tiling feature off

2. Select the Fin and go to the Modify panel. From the Modifier drop-down list, choose UVW Map modifier.

3. In the Modifier Stack, you can see the UVW Mapping modifier stacked on top of the editable poly. You will also see an orange gizmo next to the top fin geometry.

    When you apply the UVW Map modifier to your object, the gizmo always conforms to the shape of the object. Because this is a decal, we want the image to keep its original proportions.

4. Go to the UVW Map Modifier parameters and, in the Alignment section, click the Bitmap Fit button (shown in Figure 7.85).

Figure 7.85

The Alignment section for the UVW Map parameters

5. This will take you to an Explorer window. Navigate to the SceneAssets\Images folder in the Red Rocket project and select the file `RetroRocktDecal.tif`. This will change the size of the UVW Map gizmo to the size and aspect of the image rather than the geometry. See Figure 7.86.

Figure 7.86

Select the file
`RetroRocktDecal`
`.tif`.

ADJUSTING THE UVW MAP GIZMO

Now we will adjust the UVW Map Gizmo in the following steps:

1. In the Modifier Stack, click the plus sign in the black box next to UVW Mapping modifier, and select the gizmo. The gizmo entry will turn yellow, which means you are in sub-object mode for that modifier, as shown here.

2. Now look at the top Fin in the viewport, and you should see the plane-shaped Modifier gizmo. You will now be able to transform it to suit where you need the decal placed.

3. Switch to the Rotate tool, go to the Transform field at the bottom of the 3ds Max interface, and enter **75** in the *X*-axis as shown here.

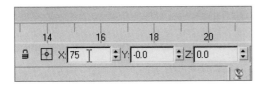

4. Switch to the Scale tool (press R), and scale down the gizmo to 40 percent. Then switch to the Move tool (W) and center the decal on the fin as shown in Figure 7.87.

Figure 7.87

Center the decal on the fin.

5. In the viewport, the decal looks like a bright white rectangle, while the rest of the top fin is gray. That is okay. Render and you will see something similar to Figure 7.88.

Figure 7.88

Render and the decal will look much better on the fin.

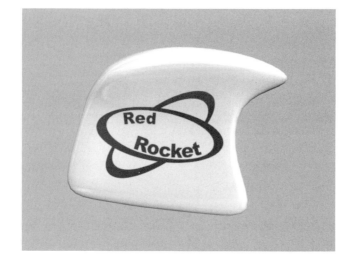

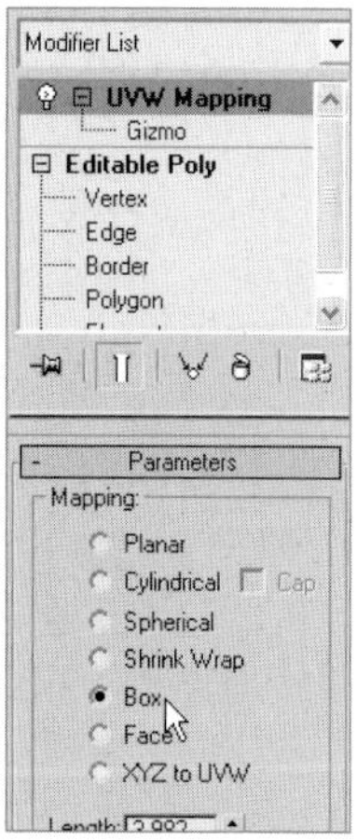

Figure 7.89

The UVW Mapping Modifier parameters

CORRECTING THE PROJECTION

While the decal on this side of the fin looks fine, if you look on the other side of the fin, the decal is flipped. The type of UVW Map modifier projection we are using (Planar projection) is useful only when one side of an object needs to be mapped. In this case we need the decal to show up correctly on the other side of the Fin. What do we do now?!?

1. Go to the UVW Mapping Modifier parameters, and select Box under Mapping, as shown in Figure 7.89.

2. This works, but now we have the decal in places we don't want, as shown in Figure 7.90. This is because Box Mapping projects the image from six sides, using a planar map for each side, but uses the sided-surface *normal* (a vector that defines which way a face or vertex is pointing) to decide the mapping direction. So, we are going to trick the modifier and remove the depth.

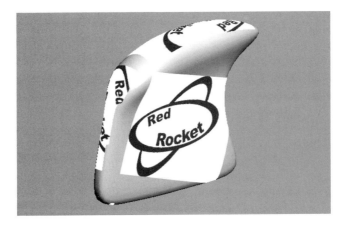

Figure 7.90

The decal as seen with the sided-surface normal

3. In the parameters for the UVW Map modifier, change the Height parameter to 0.01, as shown in Figure 7.91.

4. The copies of the decals we don't want on the fin should disappear. In the sides we don't want, we have scaled the Box Projection gizmo down to almost nothing; the projections for those sides are actually still there but now they are very small and not noticeable on the fin. This isn't the most sophisticated way to fix the issue, but it works for our needs. In CG, whatever works is the best course of action.

> We can't change the Height parameter of the UVW Map Modifier gizmo to 0 because then the modifier won't work properly. A very small value such as 0.01 works very well instead.

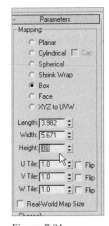

Figure 7.91

Change the Height parameter to 0.01.

ADDING THE MATERIAL TO THE MATERIAL LIBRARY

This is a good time to add this decal material to the Material Library.

1. Select the Fin_Decal material in the Material Editor and click the Get Material button ( ).

2. In the Material Map browser, go to the Browse From section and select Mtl Library.

3. In the File section in the Material/Map browser, click Open and navigate to the MaterialLibraries folder in the Red Rocket project (or wherever you saved the previous Library) and click Open.

UNDERSTANDING UVW MAPPING

The UVW Map modifier consists primarily of a yellow gizmo that determines how the image maps are projected onto the surfaces of an object. The images are projected outward or inward from the gizmo and extend through the assigned objects to all surfaces. The size and orientation of the gizmos affect how the maps are projected onto the relevant objects. The properties of the different mapping types are listed here:

Planar Projects the image map perpendicular to the perimeter of the rectangular gizmo.

Cylindrical Projects the map outward from the center of a cylindrical gizmo as if the map were wrapped around the object in two axes.

Cap Projects the map to the end caps of the cylindrical gizmo in a planar fashion.

Spherical Projects the map outward from the center of a spherical gizmo as if the map were completely enveloping the object. The top and bottom of the image maps are gathered at the poles of the gizmo and may cause some distortion.

Shrink Wrap Similar to the Spherical method, except that the four corners of the image map are gathered at a single location.

Box Projects the image in six perpendicular planes from the center of the gizmo.

Face Applies the image map to each face of an object regardless of its size or orientation.

XYZ to UVW Used with procedural maps, such as Noise or Smoke, to control the maps when the object changes size.

4. Drag and drop the Fin_Decal material into the Material Map browser to add it to the Library. Click Save.

5. Render out the fin and check your work. Save your scene file.

You can load the scene file `Rocket_Material_Fin_Final.max` in the Scenes folder of the Red Rocket project to skip to this point or to check your work.

Mapping the Body

The rocket body is made up of three texturing areas:

- **The main body**— red with a white decal
- **The Control panel**—a gray metallic material
- **The nose**—white plastic with teardrop embossed features

The easiest way to texture is to use the Multi-Sub Object Material technique you used on the wheel. The body has a logo on it, so it will have the same issue as the Fin: The logo image will appear on the opposite side of the object when you use Planar mapping. Another way of dealing with the logo-flipping issue is to apply the material to each side separately. You would apply the same material to specific selected polygons on each side of the object, but 3ds Max lets you apply two maps and two UVW Map modifiers instead of one. This gives you independent control over each side of the rocket body.

Use this technique if you want to put a different design on the other side of your model.

1. Open the Rocket_Material_Body_Start.max.

2. Select the rocket and go to the Modify panel. Go to Polygon mode and select the polygons on one half of the rocket. This is accomplished most easily in the top view.

   The Seat and Control Panel polygons are also selected now. We want to deselect them for now. To do this, go to the Modify panel and, in the Selection rollout, check Ignore Backfacing. This allows you to select only the polygons facing you. Hold down Alt while you select what you want to subtract from any selection. This can be a bit tedious, but it must be done. Once finished, your selection should resemble Figure 7.92.

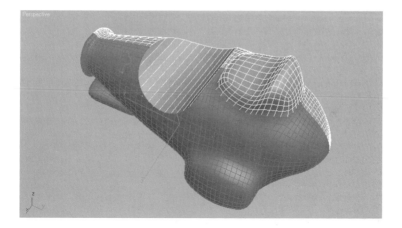

Figure 7.92

Select one half of the rocket's body, without the seat or control panel polygons.

Creating the Material

We'll begin by creating a material for the red body.

1. Open the Material Editor, select a sample sphere, and click on the color swatch next to Diffuse. Change the color to red (with values of R: 200, G: 0, B: 0). Name the material **Rocket Body Right.**

2. Drag and drop the new material onto the selected polygons of the rocket to assign the material to that half of the rocket.

3. Go to the Material Editor. On the toolbar, click the Show Map in Viewport button (🖼). Don't worry if the map doesn't look correct.

4. In the Specular Highlights section of the Material Editor, change the Specular Level to 90 and Glossiness to 80.

5. Go to the Maps rollout and change the Amount value next to Reflections to 20, and then click the None button. In the Material/Map browser, choose Bitmap to place an image file for the reflection map.

6. Navigate to the SceneAssets\Images folder in the Red Rocket project and select the file `Rocket Refmap blur.jpg` for the reflection.

7. Click the Go to Parent button to return to the Maps rollout, and click the None button next to Diffuse Color. In the Material/Map browser, choose Bitmap.

8. Navigate to the SceneAssets\Images folder in the Red Rocket project and select the file `RocketBodyRight.tif`. Click the Show Map in Viewport button.

9. Press the F9 key to do a Quick Render. The decal will probably be tilting (Figure 7.93), so we see part of it toward the front and seat of the rocket.

Figure 7.93
The decal is tilting.

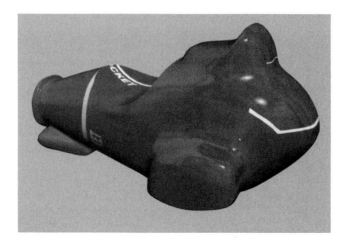

10. Go back to the Material Editor, and in the Coordinate rollout uncheck the Tiling UV boxes to turn off tiling, as shown here. Don't worry if the map doesn't look quite right yet. The map on the rocket may appear in a strange layout, such as shown previously, or may even be a strange color (in some rare cases).

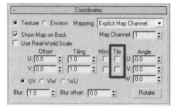

The model still needs mapping coordinates. We will get to them later.

Flipping the Decal

In the following steps, we will create a copy of the one side's material and flip it for the other side.

1. Go back to the Modifier panel, go to Polygon mode, and select the polygons on the opposite side of the rocket. Remember to deselect the Seat and Control Panel polygons.

2. In the Material Editor, drag and drop the Rocket Body Right material sample sphere onto an available sample sphere to make a copy of the material. Rename the material **Rocket Body Left**.

3. Go to the Maps rollout for this new material and click the button next to Diffuse Color to take you to the Bitmap parameters. Select the bar with the image path and in the file selection window, select the `RocketBodyLeft.tif` for a flipped version of the previous color map (Figure 7.94). Click the Show Map in Viewport button.

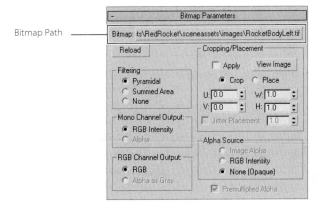

Bitmap Path

Figure 7.94

Replace the previous map with a flipped version for the opposite side of the rocket.

4. In the Coordinate rollout, change the Map Channel to 2, as shown here. This lets you have many different sets of coordinates on the same object simultaneously. Don't worry that the Red Rocket graphic disappears, it will return when we add the UVW map for the left of the rocket.

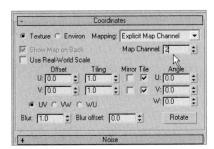

5. Drag and drop the flipped material onto the selected polygons of the rocket (representing the other side of the rocket).

We are now adding the mapping coordinates. We have two materials for each side of the rocket. The Right side of the rocket has Map Channel 1 and the Left side has Map Channel 2. We are going to start by adding and editing the mapping for the Right side with Map Channel 1.

6. Go into the Modify panel and click the Editable Poly entry to leave sub-object selection level. Then, from the Modifier List, choose the UVW map modifier. We are going to keep it on the default mapping setting, which is Planar. In the Alignment parameters of the modifier change to the X-axis, as shown here.

7. Click the Bitmap Fit button, navigate to the SceneAssets\Images folder in the Red Rocket project, and select the file `Rocket_Body Right`. This will change the Modifier gizmo to make it the same size as the bitmap image, keeping the image's scale proportional.

8. In the Modify panel, go to the Modifier Stack and click on the black box with the plus sign next to the UVW Mapping modifier, shown here. Click on Gizmo to allow you to transform the image (via the gizmo) without affecting the object.

9. Move the Modifier gizmo so the white stripe in the decal is lined up approximately to the front of the rocket, as shown in Figure 7.95.

10. Exit the UVW Map Modifier gizmo sub-object mode by clicking the modifier in the stack.

Figure 7.95

Line up the stripe in the material to the real rocket's stripe.

11. Add a second UVW Map modifier onto the rocket, and change the Map Channel to 2.

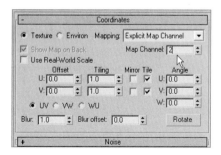

This UVW Map modifier is for the Left side of the rocket. Remember, we changed the Map Channel in the Bitmap Coordinate; now we need to reflect that in the modifier.

12. In the Alignment parameters of the second UVW Map modifier, change the axis to *X*. Click on the Bitmap Fit button, and navigate to where the `Rocket Body Left.tif` bitmap is found and click Open.

13. Go to the Modify Stack, click the Gizmo sub-object, and move the Bitmap gizmo to line up the image with the map on the opposite side of the rocket, as shown in Figure 7.96.

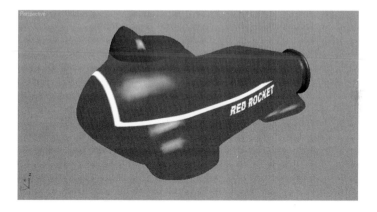

Figure 7.96

Align the "flipped" bitmap image on the other side of the rocket.

If you render, you should now see the stripe decals on the side of the rocket as shown in Figure 7.97.

Adding a Seat

We don't have to worry about mapping the polygons of the seat for the rocket because we have a model of a seat to add.

Choose File → Merge, navigate to the Scenes folder in the Red Rocket project, and select the file `Seat.max` to merge in the seat geometry, as shown in Figure 7.98. The extra geometry adds detail to the model by giving it a nicer seat. If you had to, you could forego the seat geometry, instead selecting the seat polygons and assigning a glossy black material to them.

Figure 7.97

A render of the rocket shows how the decal is mapped on the body.

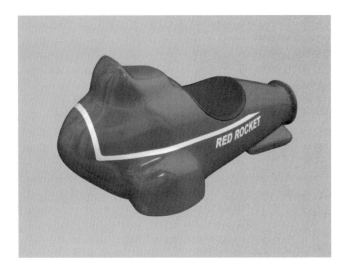

Figure 7.98

Adding the seat

The Control panel and Nose materials still need to be created and added to the model.

The Control Panel

In this section, we will texture the Control panel.

1. As you have done before, create a new material in an available sample sphere in the Material Editor and set its color to gray. If you prefer, you can just use the default grey (R150, G150, B150).

2. Set the Specular Level to 50 and the Glossiness to 20.

3. Name this new material **Control_Panel**.

For the Control panel, we should add just a little bit of bump to the surface to give the panel some tactile feel.

4. Select the Control_Panel material in the Material Editor. In the Maps rollout, change the Bump Level to 20 and click None to create a map.

5. Select Noise from the Material/Map browser to add a Noise texture to the bump map.

6. In the Noise parameters for the Noise map, change the Size to 0.02.

Finally, let's add a reflection map to the Control panel, as we did with the body of the rocket.

7. In the Material Editor, select the Maps rollout, set the Reflection Amount to 10, and click None next to Reflection to add a map.

8. Select Bitmap from the Material/Map browser and navigate to the Red Rocket project's SceneAssets\Images folder to select `RocketRefmapBlur.tif`.

9. In a viewport, select the rocket, enter into Polygon Selection mode (by selecting the Editable Poly entry in the Modifier Stack in the Modify panel), and select the polygons that make up the Control panel, as shown in highlight in Figure 7.99. Drag the Control_Panel material onto the selected polygons to assign the material.

10. Click on the Editable Poly Object Level when you are finished. If you don't, the two UVW Mapping modifiers will be applied only to the Control panel polygons.

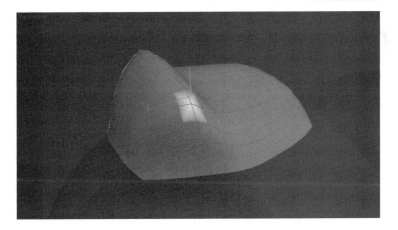

Figure 7.99

Select the polygons of the Control panel.

Because the buttons of the Control panel are separate objects, you easily can create colorful materials for them, using more or less the same settings from the previous materials. Simply assign each button its own material for its own distinctive color.

Voilà! All that remains now are the thruster and the nose of the rocket.

Bring on the Nose, Bring on the Funk

The material for the nose is pretty similar to the material we just created for the Control panel, except the Diffuse color should be white.

1. Copy the Control_Panel material by dragging it onto an empty sample sphere in the Material Editor and changing its Diffuse color to white. Feel free to adjust the Specular settings as you see fit. (A Specular level of 90 and a Glossiness value of 80 work very well.) Name the new material **Nose**.

   The Control panel had a slight bump map on the material. Let's remove that from the Nose material.

2. Select the Nose material and its Material Editor. Right-click on the map bar next to the Bump parameter, and select Clear from the context menu, as shown here.

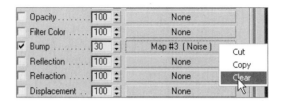

   The Nose material now has no bump map, but it retains the reflection map from the Control panel's material, saving us a little bit of work.

3. Select the polygons of the nose, as shown here in a box (Figure 7.100), and drag the material from the Material Editor to the selected polygons to assign the material. When you're finished, click Editable Poly to return to object mode.

Figure 7.100

Select the polygons of the nose.

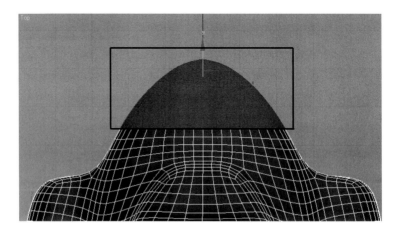

4. Save your work, and make sure to version up the file as not to overwrite your previous scene file.

The Thruster

The final part of the rocket model to texture is the Thruster. Using the experience you've already gained from texturing the rest of the rocket, this will be a breeze. If you prefer, you can load the `Rocket_Material_Thruster_Start.max` file from the Scenes folder of the Red Rocket project, or just continue with your own scene.

Figure 7.101 shows the thruster. Notice the round bulbous section in the left of the image. This is the middle yellow part of the thruster.

Figure 7.101

The Thruster object has a yellow part, the circle in the middle, and the outside housing.

In this section, we'll experiment with a selection technique to make it easier to isolate the middle, yellow part of the thruster. Also remember to use the Layer Manager to unhide any parts of the rocket that may be hidden in your scene

1. Select the thruster and enter Polygon mode. Select the center ring of polygons of the thruster, as shown here in white (Figure 7.102).

If the Thruster object is not an editable polygon in your scene, first add an Edit Poly modifier to the object before continuing.

2. In the Modify panel's Selection rollout, click the Grow button five times to enlarge your selection to include all the polygons that make up the yellow round inside of the thruster, shown here in white (Figure 7.103).

3. Open the Material Editor and select an available sample sphere. Name this material **Thruster Yellow Light**.

4. In the Blinn Basic Parameters, click on the color swatch next to Diffuse and change the color to yellow (R: 255, G: 210, and B: 0).

Figure 7.102

Select the center
ring of polygons of
the thruster.

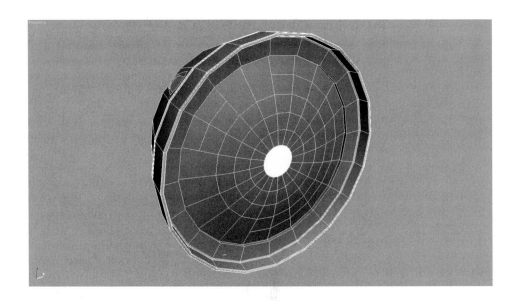

Figure 7.103

Click the Grow but-
ton in the Modify
panel's Selection
rollout.

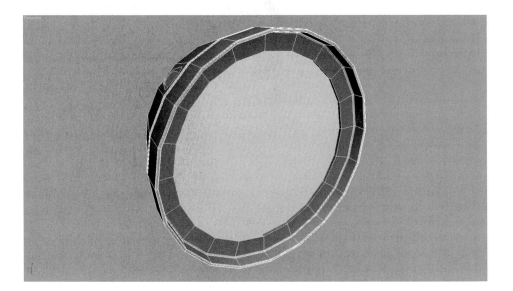

5. In the Specular Highlights section, change Specular Level to 90 and Glossiness to 80.

6. To give the yellow material a bit of a lightness, change Self Illumination to 50 and Opacity to 90.

7. Go to the Maps rollout and change the Reflection Amount to 50 and add a bitmap to Reflections. Navigate to the SceneAssets\Images folder in the Red Rocket project and

select the file `RocketRefmapBlur.tif` to add a reflection map similar to the rest of the rocket.

8. Drag and drop the material to the selected polygons.

9. To save a lot of time, we can easily select the other polygons of the thruster. With the round center polygons still selected, choose Edit → Select Invert.

10. Drag and Drop the Control_Panel material onto the selected polygons. Done! Figure 7.104 shows the textured thruster.

Figure 7.104

The textured thruster

11. Unhide all the other parts of the rocket using the Layer Manager, as needed, and render a frame of the fully textured rocket, as shown in Figures 7.105 and 7.106.

Figure 7.105

The rocket!

Figure 7.106

The rocket from behind

Figure 7.106

The rocket from behind

12. Save your work, pat yourself on the back, and have a nice smoothie to celebrate. You can load the scene `Rocket_Material_Thruster_Final.max` from the Scenes folder in the Red Rocket project to check your work.

All the parts of the rocket now have materials applied.

If you are in the `Rocket_Material_Thruster_Start.max` or the `Rocket_Material_Thruster_Final.max` file, open the Layer Manager and unhide all the other parts of the body. They should all be textured as well. You can also open the scene file `Rocket_Material_Final.max` to check your work. You may find all these scene files in the Scenes folder in the Red Rocket project.

Summary

Creating materials for your objects is usually the next step after modeling them. Creating materials can give you a sense of accomplishment because it is essentially the last step in making the object look as you envisioned—aside from lighting and rendering, of course.

There are several ways to create materials, from simple colors to complex mappings on distinct parameters. Finding the right combination of maps, shader types, and material types can make a world of difference in the look of your scenes. It's important to remember that like everything else in CG, applying materials takes time, and gaining wisdom with your materials and maps will come with practice.

In this chapter, you learned the basics of materials, what kinds of materials are in 3ds Max, and how to create and edit them in the Material Editor. Then, you learned how choosing the right type of shader will make your surface look right, and how to apply your knowledge to mapping a pool ball, reflections and all. Next, you learned a few more tricks with the

Material Editor and found out about the different kinds of maps available in 3ds Max. With that knowledge, you mapped the entire rocket you modeled in Chapter 5, and readied it for its next step, lighting in Chapter 10.

If you'd like some additional practice, go back and adjust all the materials on the rocket with different types of materials, colors, and settings to see how they affect the render of the rocket. So far we've done all this with a minimal lighting setup. As you will see in Chapter 10, "3ds Max Lighting," lighting plays a vital role in how you texture your model. Soon you'll find yourself tweaking settings for the specular highlights, reflections, color, and so on as you change your lighting environment to gain the best render.

CHAPTER 8

Introduction to Animation

The best way to learn how to animate is to jump right in and start animating. You will begin this chapter by picking up the Mobile exercise from Chapter 2, "Your First Max Animation," and adding animation to the shapes of the mobile. You'll take a good look at 3ds Max's animation tools so you can start editing animation and training your timing skills.

Topics in this chapter include:

- Hierarchy in Animation: The Mobile Redux
- Using Dummy Objects
- The Bouncing Ball
- Using the Track Editor–Curve Editor
- Track View
- Anticipation and Momentum in Knife Throwing

Hierarchy in Animation: The Mobile Redux

Do you remember way back when you were reading Chapter 2? Those were good times, weren't they? After setting up the mobile in that exercise, you animated only the bars to rotate, but you left the rotation of the shapes for later. In this chapter, you'll pick up where you left off with the mobile from Chapter 2 and finish the animation using the hierarchies that were set up in that exercise.

> If you skipped the Mobile exercise in Chapter 2, you may want to try it now before you move on with this animation exercise. Understanding hierarchies and how they work in animation is extremely important.

You can begin this exercise by using your own Mobile file from Chapter 2, or you can open Mobile_v05.max from the Scenes folder in the Mobile project on the companion CD. This scene file is the same as the file you ended up with in Chapter 2 (Mobile_v04.max), except this version takes the animation of the bars to frame 100 instead of frame 50 as in version 4 of that file.

If you haven't already done so from the previous Chapter 2 exercise, copy the Mobile project from the companion CD to your hard drive. Set your Max project folder by choosing File → Set Project Folder and selecting the Mobile project that you copied from the CD to your hard drive.

Animating the Shapes

With the Mobile_v05.max scene open (or your own file), scrub through the animation to become familiar with the scene. The intent here is to create a hierarchy in the mobile and animate the bars. Now you will add rotation to the shapes hanging from the bars. Figure 8.1 shows the mobile in mid-animation.

To add animation to the shapes under the bars, follow these steps:

1. Go to frame 0 of the animation, and click the Auto Key button (Auto Key) at the bottom of the UI.

2. Select the triangle hanging from the bottom bar, and go to frame 50. Rotate the triangle in the Z-axis in either direction at least a full turn of 360 degrees, if not a lot more, as shown in Figure 8.2. Don't scrub your animation yet.

3. Still at frame 50, select the square on the bar above, and rotate that shape in the Z-axis several hundred degrees in either direction. Figure 8.3 shows the rotation of the square. The bottom bar goes along with the square's rotation because this is how they were linked in Chapter 2. Don't scrub your animation yet.

4. Still at frame 50, select the star and rotate it several hundred degrees on the Z-axis in either direction (Figure 8.4).

Figure 8.1

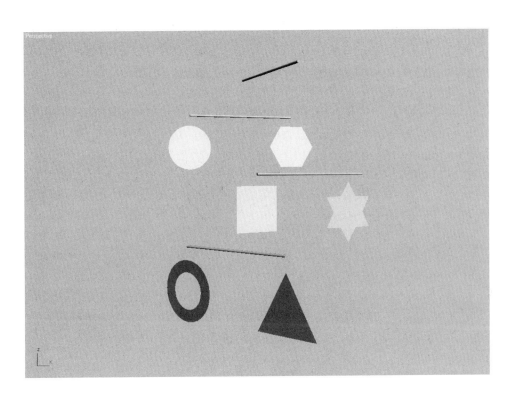

The mobile is back!

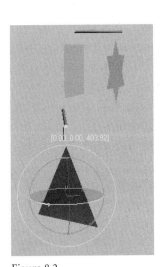

Figure 8.2

Rotate the triangle 360 degrees or more in *Z*.

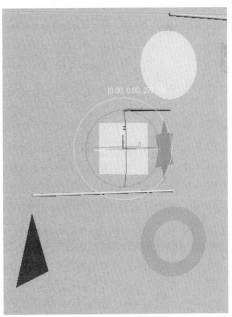

Figure 8.3

The square is rotated, and its child bar goes along for the ride.

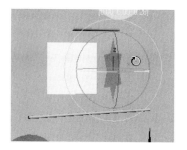

Figure 8.4

Rotate the star in Z.

Now scrub your animation and check the results. In theory, all the bars should rotate and so should the shapes hanging on the bars. When you scrub, however, the mobile will seem to have lost its mind. The shapes will rotate completely off axis, as if you have set rotation keyframes on the *X*- and *Y*-axes as well as the intended *Z*-axis. The same will occur with the lower bar. It will go off its axis and rotate in an unpredictable manner. This behavior is explained in the next section, with easy solutions to fix the issue.

Making a Mistake

Why would we purposely show you an incorrect workflow? Because learning from missteps is as important to learning CG as learning the correct steps. Being able to troubleshoot is essential to becoming good in CG, and the more trouble you get yourself into, the better you will become at digging your way out.

This example of strangely rotating hierarchies is an isolated issue that is called *gimbal lock* in many CG circles. Different CG packages have different ways of interpreting exactly how an object rotates when it is rotating along more than one axis. Imagine three cars all staring each other down at a three-way intersection—with the traffic light out. Who goes first in this situation is important to the flow of traffic at the intersection. When a 3D package calculates rotations, it needs to know which axis to rotate first before tending to the rotation of the other axes. In 3ds Max, the *animation controller* is the traffic light directing the animation. With gimbal lock, you have an incorrect interpretation of the rotations, so the resulting animation seems off axis.

In this exercise, the multiple rotations inherited by the children shapes and bars from their parents caused havoc with their own rotations, so the axes became confused and everything looks just plain wrong. The easiest way to fix this issue is to reassign the animation controllers in charge of the rotations for those objects to one that will not lock up.

Animation Controllers

By default, 3ds Max assigns a Euler XYZ controller to the rotations of objects. This is the best controller to use in the majority of circumstances. In this example, however, it doesn't quite work. To assign a different controller, follow along here:

Figure 8.5

The Assign Controller rollout in the Motion panel

1. Select the square; you will start with that object. Switch to the Motion panel (click the Motion Panel tab (⊛) in the Command panel, as you see in Figure 8.5. Open the Assign Controller rollout. You'll see that the Rotation controller for the square is set to Euler XYZ.

2. Select Euler XYZ from the list in the Motion panel, as shown in Figure 8.5. Click the Assign Controller button ([?]) to open the Assign Rotation Controller window (Figure 8.6). Choose TCB Rotation from the list. If you do not first select the controller from the Controller List, the Assign Controller button will be grayed out and unusable.

3. The square and the bar linked beneath it should snap back into axis. Scrub the animation, and you'll see that the square and the bar beneath it are not behaving as you would expect: They are rotating on the *Z*-axis only, as they should. Figure 8.7 shows the resulting animation. Notice that the star and triangle are still rotating off axis.

4. Select the triangle and repeat steps 2 and 3 to assign a TCB Rotation controller to the triangle. Do the same for the star. Figure 8.8 shows the proper rotations of the shapes and the bars—but looks are deceiving. We're not done yet!

If Euler XYZ caused such a ruckus, why isn't TCB Rotation the default for rotating objects? For one thing, the editing options you have with a Euler XYZ controller are head and shoulders above what you get with TCB Rotation. With the Euler XYZ, 3ds Max splits the *XYZ* rotation animation into three separate tracks to give individual control over each axis. This is ideal.

In addition, the TCB Rotation has taken the several hundred degrees of rotation you have animated, and cut it down to within 180 degrees of rotation at most. The square, triangle, and star don't seem to be rotating the several hundred degrees you intended.

> **Assign Rotation Con...**
>
> AudioRotation
> >Euler XYZ
> Linear Rotation
> LookAt Constraint
> Motion Clip SlaveRotation
> Noise Rotation
> Orientation Constraint
> Rotation List
> Rotation Motion Capture
> Rotation Reaction
> Rotation Script
> SlaveRotation
> Smooth Rotation
> TCB Rotation
>
> Default: Euler XYZ
>
> Make Default   OK   Cancel

Figure 8.6

Choosing TCB Rotation limits your options and the rotation.

It is not a good idea to change the default animation controllers based solely on your experience with this exercise. On the other hand, if you run into a gimbal lock situation in the future, you'll have a good idea what caused it, and you'll be able to troubleshoot it quickly.

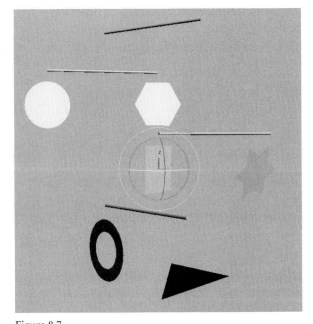

Figure 8.7

You've fixed the rotation of the square and its children.

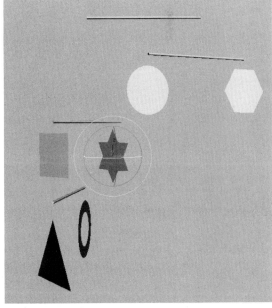

Figure 8.8

The mobile seems to rotate properly, but does it really?

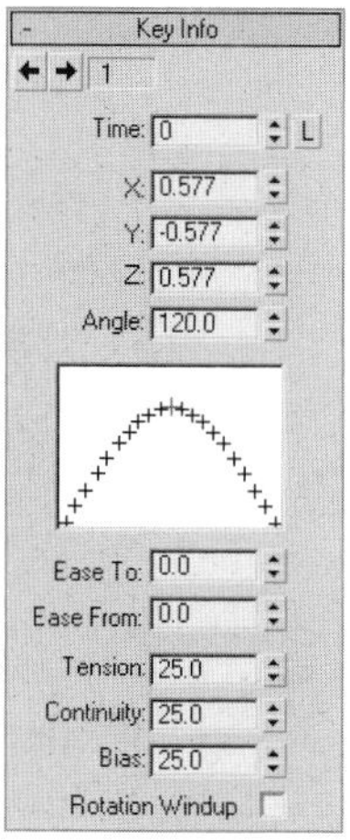

Figure 8.9

Edit your controller in the Key Info rollout.

Figure 8.10

Adding more rotation to the square in the Key Info rollout

Editing the TCB Rotation Keyframes

To fix the problem that the objects do not rotate the several hundred degrees you want, you will have to manually edit the controller to allow a greater degree of rotation:

1. Select the square and open the Key Info rollout (Figure 8.9).

2. The Key Info rollout shows you the properties of the animation on the selected object on a key-by-key basis. If everything is grayed out, use the arrows at the top of the rollout to move through the keyframes. Go to the first keyframe at frame 0 (shown as Time: 0 in the rollout). The Angle displays the orientation of the square at the beginning of the animation: 120. Use the arrows again to move to keyframe 2 (Time: 50).

3. The Angle parameter should change to a value of 117.643 (your value may differ slightly). The X parameter value reads –1.0. The X, Y, and Z parameters represent the direction in the respective axes. The value –1 means the square is rotating backward. Don't get confused because this value is now in X and not Z. Remember, you gave up the individual controls for X, Y, and Z when you changed from the Euler XYZ controller. While at this second keyframe, click Rotation Windup at the bottom of the rollout, and enter the value **500** for Angle. You must first turn on Rotation Windup to enter **500** for the Angle (Figure 8.10).

4. Scrub your animation, and the square will rotate more, as you first intended. Repeat steps 2 and 3 for the triangle and star to fix their rotations with the TCB Rotation controller. At this point, you can save the 3ds Max file for use in the next section.

Any parameter that is animated has a controller. A controller essentially deals with all the animation functions in the scene for 3ds Max, such as storing keyframe values. Interpolating in-betweens is handled by the controllers. By default, the Position XYZ controller is assigned to an animation on an object's position and a Euler XYZ is assigned to its rotation. These controllers are the most useful as they split the X, Y, and Z into separate tracks to give individual control over each axis. You will have the opportunity to work with and edit individual tracks later in this chapter.

Using Dummy Objects

Another way to circumvent this particular issue of rotation confusion is by using helper objects in 3ds Max called *dummy objects*. Changing the controller for an object is not always the best solution—particularly if the range of movement will be changed. You saw this problem when you changed to TCB Rotation before you had to fix it in Key Info to add more rotation. Using dummy objects, you can insert a helper in the hierarchy that will negate the gimbal lock issue and make it very clear to 3ds Max how the rotations should proceed. As a matter of fact, it's common for animators to make copious use of dummies as controllers for their animation *rigs*. A rig is essentially any setup in the scene that helps you animate objects in the scene.

Dummies (called *null nodes* in other CG applications such as Maya) are very useful nonrendering objects that can be used in several ways. In this case, they serve as place-holders and are used directly in the hierarchy to straighten out the rotation confusion. They serve as parents to the mobile shapes that may come down with rotation confusion or gimbal lock.

Placing Dummies in the Mobile

You can begin this exercise by either using your own Mobile file from Chapter 2, or by opening Mobile_v05.max from the Scenes folder in the Mobile project on the CD or your hard drive.

To create dummy objects for the animation hierarchy, follow these steps:

1. Go to the Create panel. In the Helpers ( ), click Dummy (Figure 8.11).

2. There are no Parameter rollouts or settings for the dummy. Move your cursor to the Front viewport, center it over the circle, and then click and drag to create. Create a dummy that is slightly larger than the shape.

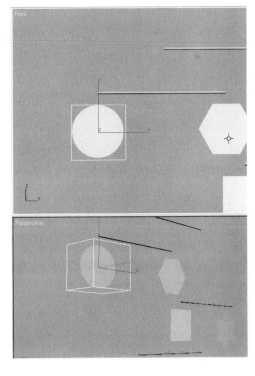

Figure 8.11

Create a dummy object to fit over the circle.

Linking the Dummies

If you scrub the animation, you will notice that the circle moves along with the rotation of its parent bar, as it did before. This is because the dummy is not part of the hierarchy yet. You are going to change the structure of the hierarchy in order to break the relationship of the circle with its parent object and restructure it to add the dummy between the bar and the circle. This is done by relinking the new order.

3. Make sure the Time slider is at frame 0. Go to the main toolbar and click on the Select and Link tool ( ). Use the Select and Link tool to select the circle, and then click and drag it to the dummy object. Make sure you don't let go until the cursor changes to the icon to make the proper link, as shown in Figure 8.12.

Figure 8.12

Drag the circle to the dummy object, and then drag the dummy to the cylinder.

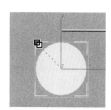 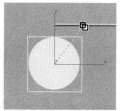

To jump to the beginning of an animation, just press the Home key on your keyboard; this is a shortcut to jump to the start. Likewise, pressing the End key will take you to the end of an animation.

4. You're not done yet. If you scrub the animation, the circle will no longer move with its parent bar. You have to link the dummy to the bar. Select the dummy, and click and drag to the Parent cylinder (Figure 8.12). This completes the new hierarchy. Now the circle is the child of the dummy, and the dummy is the child of the parent bar above it. Play the animation, and you will see the dummy moving along with the mobile, with the circle in tow.

5. Fantastic! Now it is time to animate the circle shape itself. Move to the end of your timeline (frame 100, press the End key), and click the Auto Key button at the bottom of the interface (you can also press the N key to toggle Auto Key on and off). Select the circle, and rotate a few hundred degrees on the Z-axis in either direction. Do not rotate the dummy, just the circle. Figure 8.13 shows how the circle rotates within the dummy, which then follows with the bar's rotation.

6. Repeat steps 1 and 2 to create dummies for the other shapes in the mobile. Relink the shapes to their dummies, as you did in steps 3 and 4. Animate the shapes themselves to your heart's content. If you see funky rotation on the dummies and shapes, either

you have made an error in the linking order, or you have animated the dummies rotating and not the shapes themselves.

Play the animation. As you can see, the funky rotation is gone and now you have a perfectly normal rotation. The bar's rotation moves the dummy below it, and the dummy pulls the circle. Because the bar is not directly pulling the circle, the circle is free to rotate without rotation confusion.

Once you feel confident with how this exercise works, you should have a pretty solid idea of how hierarchies work in animation. Feel free to go through this entire exercise another time before moving on.

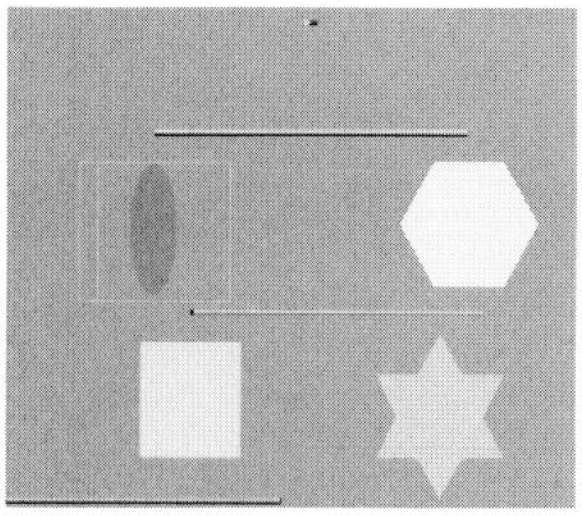

Figure 8.13

Success! The circle is now rotating properly.

Editing Dummies

Each dummy gets its orientation from the viewport in which you create it. When you place one of the mobile's dummies, you don't need to have it aligned perfectly with the shape for which the dummy is being used. However, it is a good idea to match things up as best as you can to keep track of which dummy goes with which shape.

Let's say you created a dummy and it is nowhere near its shaper. The Align tool can move the dummy so it is centered on the shape. To see how the Align tool works, follow along with these steps:

1. Create a dummy of any size anywhere in the mobile scene (Figure 8.14).

2. Make sure the dummy is selected. Go to the main toolbar and select the Align tool (◈). Move your cursor to the shape to which you want to align the dummy and click it. The Align Selection dialog window will open (Figure 8.15).

3. The Align Selection dialog gives you the choice of aligning an object along any axis, orienting the object (this feature is for rotations), and aligning for the object's scale. Keep the checks in the *X,Y,Z* position, but change the Current and Target Object to Center and then press OK. The dummy will match up with the shape as shown in Figure 8.16.

Figure 8.14

Create a dummy.

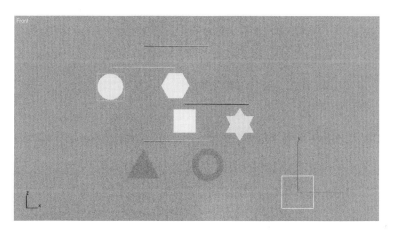

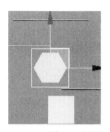

Figure 8.15

The Align Selection dialog window

Figure 8.16

Aligned to center

Although it may seem like more work, using dummies is a great workflow for animation. It keeps the scene's animation neater and better defined. As you gain more experience, you will begin to learn when you should use dummies in your hierarchy to make the animation workflow smooth.

The Bouncing Ball

A classic exercise for all animators is creating a bouncing ball. As a matter of fact, you will find bouncing ball tutorials almost everywhere you look. Although you will see it as a straightforward exercise, there is so much you can do with a bouncing ball to show character, that the possibilities are almost limitless. Animating a bouncing ball is a good exercise in physics, as well as cartoon movement. You'll first create a rubber ball, and then you'll add cartoonish movement to accentuate some principles of the animation techniques discussed in Chapter 1, "Basic Concepts." Aspiring animators can come use this exercise for years and always find something new to learn about bouncing a ball.

In preparation, copy the Bouncing Ball project from the CD to your hard drive. Set your current project by choosing File → Set Project Folder and selecting the Bouncing Ball project that you copied from the CD to your hard drive.

Animating the Ball

Your first step is to keyframe the positions of the ball. As introduced in Chapter 1, *keyframing* is the process—borrowed from traditional animation—of setting positions and values at particular frames of the animation. The computer interpolates between these keyframes to fill in the other frames to complete a smooth animation.

Open the `Animation_Ball_00.max` scene file from the BouncingBall folder you just copied to your hard drive.

You'll start with the *gross animation*, or the overall movements. This is also widely known as *blocking*. First, move the ball up and down to begin its choreography.

Follow these steps to animate the ball:

1. The first thing you need to do in this scene is to move the pivot point for the ball. Go to the Hierarchy panel ( ). Choose Pivot, and under the Adjust Pivot rollout, click the Adjust Pivot Only button. Zoom in on the ball and move the pivot so that it is at the bottom of the ball. Then click on the Affect Pivot Only button again to deactivate— but you already knew that.

2. Turn on the Auto Key button (keyboard shortcut N) and move the timeline to frame 10. Select the ball and move it along the *Z*-axis down to the ground plane. That will be 0 units in *Z* when you release the mouse button in the Transform type-ins on the bottom of the interface. You can also just enter the value and press Enter (Figure 8.17).

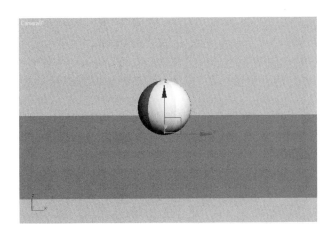

Figure 8.17

At frame 10, move the ball to meet the ground plane.

This has created two keyframes, one at frame 0 for the original position the ball was in, and one at frame 10 for the new position to which you just moved the ball.

Copying Keyframes

Now you want to move the ball up to the same position in the air as it was at frame 0. Instead of trying to estimate where that was, you can just copy the keyframe at frame 0 to frame 20.

You can see the keyframes you created in the timeline. They are red tick marks in the timeline. Red keys represent Position keyframes, green keys represent Rotation, and Blue keys represent Scale. When a keyframe in the timeline is selected, it turns white. In Figure 8.18, the keyframe at frame 0 is selected and is white.

Figure 8.18

Selected keys in the timeline are white.

1. Select the keyframe at frame 0; it should turn white when it is selected. Hold down the Shift key on the keyboard (this is a shortcut for the Clone tool), and click and drag the selected keyframe to move it to frame 20. This will create a keyframe with the same animation parameters as the keyframe at frame 0.

2. Click and drag on the Time slider to *scrub* through the keyframes.

Using the Track Editor–Curve Editor

Right now the ball is going down and up.

To continue the animation for the length of the timeline, you could continue to copy and paste keyframes—but that would be very time-consuming, and you still need to do your other homework and clean your room. A better way is to loop or *cycle* through the keyframes you already have. An *animation cycle* is a segment of animation that is repeatable in a loop. The end state of the animation matches up to the beginning state, so there is no hiccup at the loop point.

In 3ds Max, cycling animation is known as *Parameter Curve Out-of-Range Types.* This is a fancy way to create loops and cycles with your animations and specify how your object will behave outside the range of the keys you have created. This will bring us to the Track View, which is an animator's best friend. You can go through the Track View's UI in the "Track View" section later in this chapter at any time, or you can hang tight and see how you work with Track Editor first using the Bouncing Ball exercise. You will learn the underlying concepts of the Track Editor throughout this exercise as well as its basic UI. Feel free to reference the "Track View" section as you continue.

The Track View is a function of two animation editors, the Curve Editor and the Dope Sheet Editor. The Curve Editor allows you to work with animation depicted as curves on a graph that sets the value of a parameter against time. The Dope Sheet Editor displays keyframes over time on a horizontal graph, without any curves. This graphical display simplifies the process of adjusting animation timing because you can see all the keys at once in a spreadsheet-like format. The Dope Sheet is similar to the traditional animation exposure sheets or X Sheets.

> Navigation inside a Track View–Curve Editor is pretty much the same as navigating in a viewport; the same keyboard/mouse combinations work for panning and zooming.

You will use the Track View–Curve Editor (or just Curve Editor for short) to loop your animation in the following riveting steps:

1. With the ball selected, in the main menu, choose Graph Editor → Track View → Curve Editor. In Figure 8.19, the Curve Editor displays the animation curves of the ball so far.

Figure 8.19

The Curve Editor shows the animation curves of the ball.

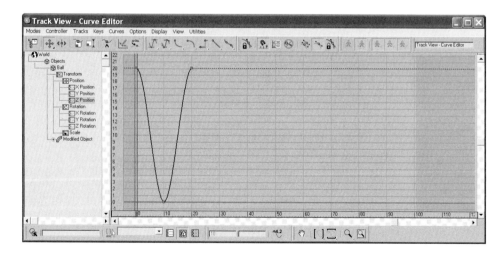

2. A toolbar runs across the top of the Curve Editor under the menu bar. In that toolbar, click the Parameter Curve Out-of-Range Types button (▣) shown in Figure 8.20.

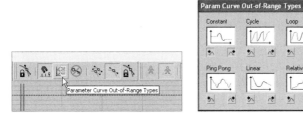

Figure 8.20

Choosing to loop your animation

3. This will open the Param Curve Out-of-Range Types dialog box (Figure 8.20). Select Loop from this window by clicking its thumbnail. The two little boxes beneath it will turn orange. Click OK. To read up on the other Parameter Curve Out-of-Range Types available, see the "Parameter Curve Out-of-Range Types" sidebar later in this chapter.

4. Once you set the curve to Loop, the Curve Editor displays your animation as shown in Figure 8.21. The out-of-range animation is shown in a dashed line. Scrub your animation in a viewport and see how the ball bounces up and down throughout the timeline range.

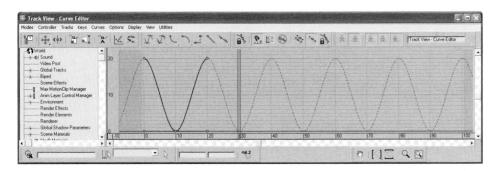

Figure 8.21

The Curve Editor shows the animation loop.

Reading Animation Curves

As you can see, the Track View–Curve Editor (from here on called just the Curve Editor) gives you control over the animation in a graph setting. Curves allow you to visualize the interpolation of the motion. Understanding what animation curves do in the Curve Editor is critical to getting your animation to look right. Once you are used to reading animation curves, you can judge an object's direction, speed, acceleration, and timing at a mere glance.

The Curve Editor's graph is a representation of an object's parameter, such as position (values shown vertically) over time (time shown horizontally). Every place on the curve represents where the object is; a keyframe does not need to be on the curve. So, the shape of the curve makes a big difference in the motion of the object.

Here is a quick primer on how to read a curve in the Curve Editor.

In Figure 8.22, an object's Z Position parameter is being animated. At the beginning, the curve quickly begins to move positively (that is, to the right) in the *Z*-axis. The object shoots up and comes to an *ease-out*, where it decelerates to a stop, reaching its top height. The ease-out stop is signified by the curving beginning to flatten out at around frame 70.

Figure 8.22

The object quickly accelerates to an ease-out stop.

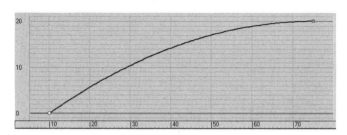

PARAMETER CURVE OUT-OF-RANGE TYPES

There are several ways to interpret the curves of an animation when they are out-of-range, meaning when they extend before your first keyframe and beyond your last keyframe. The Parameter Curve Out-of-Range Types is opened through the Curve Editor with this toolbar button ([icon]). The types are the following:

Constant Used when you do not want any animation out-of-range. This curve type will hold the value of the end and or beginning key of the range for all frames. Constant is the default out-of-range type.

Cycle Used when you need the animation to loop or cycle by repeating the same animation that is within the range. If the first keyframe does not line up with the last keyframe of the curve range, there will be an abrupt "jump" from the last key to the first with every cycle. If the start and end values do not need to match, and that hiccup in the cycle is desired, use Cycle.

Loop Used when you need the animation to loop or cycle smoothly despite any differences in the start and end keyframe values. Loop repeats the same animation in the curve range, but it also interpolates between the last and first keyframes in the range to create a smooth loop in the cycle. Loop's ability to create a smooth loop can only go so far before it acts like a Cycle (e.g., when the key values at the start and end are too disparate).

Ping Pong Used when you want your animation to oscillate back and forth. Ping Pong repeats the same animation in the range, but it plays it front to back and then back to front, and so forth, to alternate the playback, as shown here.

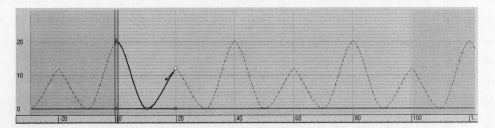

Linear Used when you need your animation to continue at the same velocity as its beginning or end. The animation curve is projected out from the range in a straight line, picking up the trajectory from the shape of the start or end of the curve, as shown here.

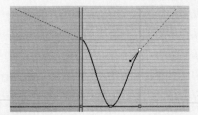

Relative Repeat Used when you need your animation to repeat as in a cycle and to continue building on itself as it cycles. Each repetition is offset by the value at the end of the range, as shown here.

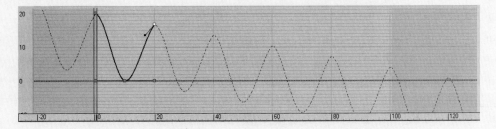

You can select any one of these types for either the before or after by clicking one of the smaller boxes below the thumbnails. You can set both the before and after out-of-range type by clicking the thumbnail of the type itself.

In Figure 8.23, the object slowly accelerates in an *ease-in* in the positive *Z* direction until it hits frame 75, where it suddenly stops.

Figure 8.23

The object eases in to acceleration and suddenly stops at its fastest velocity.

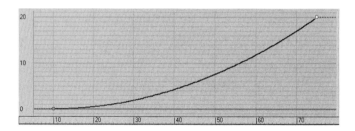

In Figure 8.24, the object eases in and travels to an ease-out where it decelerates starting at around frame 69 to where it slowly stops at frame 75.

Figure 8.24

Ease-in and ease-out

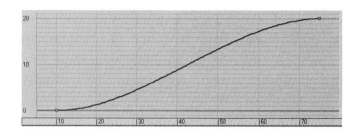

Finally, in Figure 8.25, the object jumps from its Z Position in frame 24, to its new position in frame 25.

Figure 8.25

Step interpolation makes the object "jump" suddenly from one value to the next.

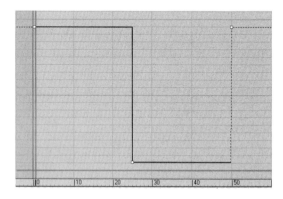

Figure 8.26 shows the Track View–Curve Editor, with notes on its major aspects called out for your information. See the "Track View" section later in this chapter for a more thorough explanation of the UI and toolset for the Track View.

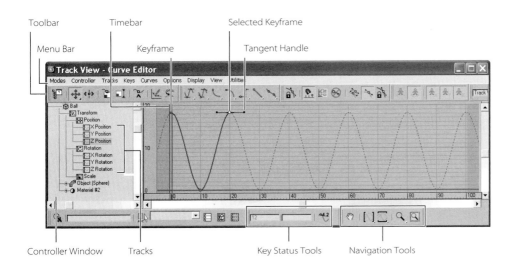

Toolbar Timebar Selected Keyframe

Menu Bar Keyframe Tangent Handle

Controller Window Tracks Key Status Tools Navigation Tools

Figure 8.26

The Curve Editor

Refining the Animation

Now that you've played back the gross animation of the bounce, how does it look? Not like a ball bouncing, really, but the framework is getting there. Notice how the speed of the ball is consistent. If this were a real ball, it would be dealing with gravity; the ball would speed up as it gets closer to the ground and there would be "hang time" when the ball is in the air on its way up as gravity takes over to pull it back down.

This means you have to edit the movement that happens between the keyframes. This is done by adjusting *how* the keyframes shape the curve itself using tangents. When you select a keyframe, a handle will appear in the UI, as shown in grayscale in Figure 8.26 and shown up close here.

This handle adjusts the tangency of the keyframe to change the curvature of the animation curve, which in turn changes the animation. There are different types of tangents, depending on how you want to edit the motion. By default the Smooth tangent is applied to all new keyframes. This is not what you want for the ball, although it is a perfect default tangent type to have.

Editing Animation Curves

Let's edit some tangencies to better suit your animation. The intent is to speed up the curve as it hits the floor and slow it down as it crests its apex. Instead of opening the Curve Editor through the menu bar, this time you are going to use the shortcut. At the bottom of the interface, click the Mini Curve Editor button shown here.

Mini Curve Editor

This Mini Curve Editor is almost exactly the same as the one you launch through the main menu bar. A few tools are not included in the Mini Curve Editor toolbar, but you can find them in the menu bar of the Mini Curve Editor. Figure 8.27 shows the Mini Curve Editor open in the 3ds Max UI.

Figure 8.27

The Mini Curve Editor

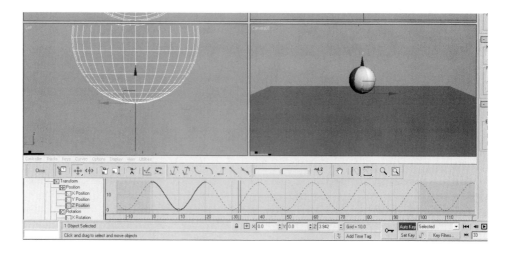

To edit the curves, follow these steps:

1. Scroll down the List Controller window on the left of the Mini Curve Editor by dragging the Pan tool (the hand cursor) to find the Ball Object/Position XYZ. Click on the Z Position track. This will bring only those curves to the Key window that you want to edit, as you saw in Figure 8.27.

2. The Z Position curve is blue, as is almost everything relating to the Z-axis. The little gray boxes on the curves are keyframes, as you saw in Figure 8.26. Select the keyframe at frame 10. You may need to scrub the Time Ruler out of the way if you are on frame 10. The key will turn white when selected. Remember, if you need to zoom or pan in the Curve Editor's Key Editing window, you can use the same shortcuts you would use to navigate in the viewports. You will change this key's tangency to make the ball fall faster as it hits and bounces off the ground.

3. In the Mini Curve Editor toolbar, change the Tangent type for the selected keyframe from the Auto default to Fast by selecting the Fast Tangent icon ( ). When you do this, you will see the Animation Curve change shape as shown in Figure 8.28.

Figure 8.28

The effect of the new tangent type

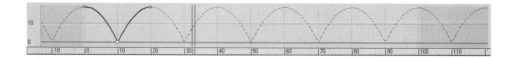

4. Select the perspective view and play the animation. You can easily correlate how the animation works with the curve's shape as you see the timeline travel through the Mini Curve Editor as the animation plays.

Finessing the Animation

Although the animation has improved, the ball has a distinct lack of weight. It still seems too simple and without any character. In situations such as this, an animator can go wild and try several different things as he or she sees fit. This is where creativity helps hone your animation skills, whether you are new to animation or have been doing it for fifty years.

Animation shows change over time. Good animation conveys the *intent,* the motivation for that change between the frames.

Squash and Stretch

The concept of *squash and stretch* has been an animation staple for as long as there has been animation. It is a way to convey the weight of an object by deforming it to react (usually in an exaggerated way) to gravity, impact, and motion.

You can give the ball a lot of flare by adding squash and stretch to give your object some personality. Follow along with these steps:

1. The Auto Key Animation button should still be active. If it isn't, press N to activate. In the Mini Curve Editor, drag the blue double-line time bar (called the Track Bar Time slider) to frame 10. (See the following graphic.) Click and hold the Scale tool to access the flyout. Choose the Select and Squash tool ( ). Center the Scale gizmo over the *Z*-axis of the Transform gizmo in the Perspective viewport. Click and drag down to squash down about 20 percent

   This will scale down in the *Z*-axis and scale up in the *X*- and *Y*-axes to compensate (Figure 8.29).

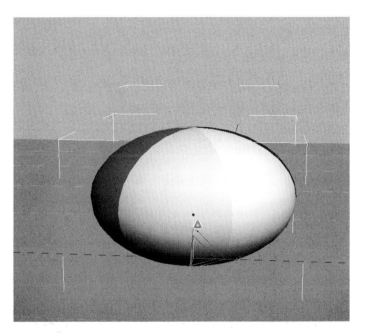

Figure 8.29

Use the Squash tool to squash down the ball on impact.

2. Move to frame 0. Click and drag up to stretch the ball up about 20 percent (so that the ball's scale in *Z* is about 120), as shown in Figure 8.30. When you scrub through the animation, you will see that at frame 0 the ball stretched and then the ball squashes and stays squashed for the rest of the time. You'll fix that in the next step.

Figure 8.30

Stretch the ball when it is at its apex.

You need to copy the Scale key from frame 0 to frame 20 first, and then apply a Loop for the Parameter Out-of-Range Type. Because the Mini Curve Editor is open, it obstructs the timeline; therefore, you should copy the keys in the Mini Curve Editor. You can just as easily do it in the regular Curve Editor in the same way:

3. In the Mini Curve Editor, scroll in the Controller window until you find the Scale track for the ball. Highlight it to see the keyframes and animation curve. Click and hold the Move Keys tool in the Curve Editor toolbar (⊹) to roll out and access the Move Keys Horizontal tool (Figure 8.31).

Figure 8.31

Use the Move Keys Horizontal tool to drag the keyframes.

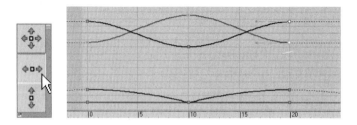

4. Click and drag a selection marquee around the two keyframes at frame 0 in the Scale track to select. Hold the Shift key, and then click and drag the keyframes at frame 0 to frame 20 (Figure 8.31).

5. In the Mini Curve Editor's menu bar, select Controller → Out-of-Range Types. Choose Loop, and then click OK. Play the animation. The curves are shown in Figure 8.32.

Figure 8.32

The final curves

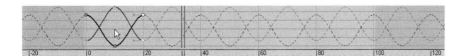

Setting the Timing

Well, you squashed and stretched the ball, but it still doesn't look right. That is because the ball should not begin to squash too long before it hits the ground. It needs to return to 100 percent scale and stay there for a few frames. Immediately before the ball hits the ground, it can squash into the ground plane to heighten the sense of impact. The following steps are easier to perform in the regular Curve Editor rather than in the Mini Curve Editor. Close the Mini Curve Editor by clicking the Close button.

Open the Curve Editor to fix the timing, and follow these steps as if they were law:

1. Move the Time slider to frame 8; Auto Key should still be active. In the Curve Editor, in the Controller window, select the ball's Scale track so that only the scale curves appear in the Editing window. In the Curve Editor's toolbar, select the Add Keys button (🔧). Your cursor will change to an arrow with a white circle at its lower right. Click on one of the Scale curves to add a keyframe on all the Scale curves (*X, Y,* and *Z*).

2. Because they are selected, the keys will be white. In the Key Status tools, you will find two text type-in boxes. The box on the left is the frame number, and the box on the right is the selected key(s)' value. Because more than one key with a different value is selected, there is no number in that type-in box. Enter **100** (for 100 percent scale) in the right type-in box, and 3ds Max will enter a value of 100 for the scale in *X, Y,* and *Z* for the ball at frame 8, as shown in Figure 8.33.

Figure 8.33

Enter a scale of 100.

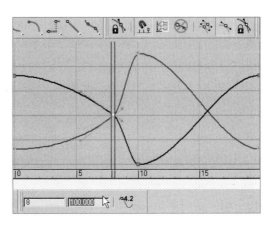

3. Move the Time slider to frame 12, and do the same thing in the Curve Editor. These settings are bracketing the Squash so that the Squash happens only a few frames before and a few frames after the ball hitting the ground, as shown in Figure 8.34. Press N to deactivate Auto Key. Save your work.

Figure 8.34
Much less Squash!

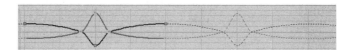

Once you play back the animation, the ball will begin to look a lot more like a nice cartoonish one, with a little character. Experiment with changing some of the scale amounts to have the ball squish a little more or less, or stretch it more or less to see how that affects the animation. See if it adds a different personality to the ball. If you can master a bouncing ball and evoke all sorts of emotion with your audience, you will be a great animator indeed.

Moving the Ball Forward

Make sure you set your current project to the Bouncing Ball project. Then you can load the Animation_Ball_01.max scene file from the Bouncing Ball project folder on your hard drive (or from the CD) to catch up to this point, or to check your work.

Now that you have worked out the bounce, it's time to add movement to the ball so that it moves across the screen as it bounces. Layering animation in this fashion, where you settle on one movement before moving on to another, is common. That's not to say you won't need to go back and forth and make adjustments through the whole process, but it's generally nicer to work out one layer of the animation before adding another. The following steps will show you how:

1. Move the Time slider to frame 0. Select the ball with the Select and Move tool, and move the ball in the Perspective viewport to the left so it is still within the camera's view. That would be about −30 units in the X-axis (Figure 8.35).

2. Move the Time slider to frame 100. Press N to activate the Auto Key again. Move the ball to the right to about 30 units along the X-axis.

3. Don't play the animation yet; it isn't going to look right. Go to the Curve Editor, scroll down in the Controller window, and select the X Position track for the ball (Figure 8.36).

When you created the keyframes for the up and down movement of the ball (which was the Z-axis), 3ds Max automatically created keyframes for the X and Y Position tracks, both with essentially no value. To fix it, keep following with these steps:

4. Select the keyframes on the X Position track at frame 10 and frame 20, and delete them by pressing the Delete key on your keyboard.

Figure 8.35

At frame 0, move the ball to the left of the viewport.

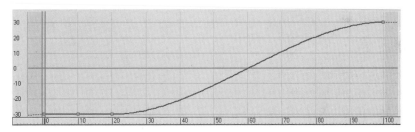

Figure 8.36

The X Position of the ball does not look right.

5. Select the Parameter Curves Out-of-Range Types button (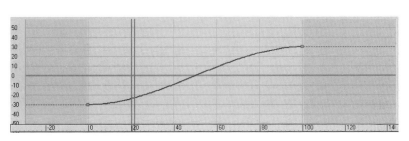), and select Constant. This will remove the *Loop* from the X Position Track but won't affect the Z Position track for the ball's bounce (Figure 8.37). Press N to deactivate Auto Key. Play the animation. You can use the / button (slash) as a shortcut for play animation.

Figure 8.37

The X Position curve for the ball's movement

6. There is still a little problem. Watch the horizontal movement. The ball is slow at the beginning, speeds up in the middle, and then slows again at the end. It eases in and eases out, as you can see in the curve in Figure 8.37. This is caused by the default tangent, which automatically adds a slowdown as the object goes in and out of the keyframe. In the Curve Editor, select both keys for the X Position and click on the Linear Tangent (![icon]) to create a straight line of movement so there is no speed change in the ball's movement left to right.

Figure 8.38 shows the proper curve.

Figure 8.38

The X Position curve for the ball's movement now has no ease-in or ease-out.

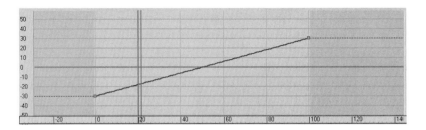

Adding a Roll

You need to add some rotation, but there are several problems with this. One, you moved the pivot point to the bottom of the ball in the very first step of the exercise. You did that so the squashing would work correctly, that is at the point of contact with the ground. If you were to rotate the ball with the pivot at the bottom, it would look like Figure 8.39.

Figure 8.39

The ball will not rotate properly because the pivot is at the bottom.

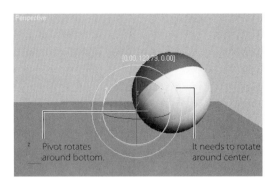

Using the XForm Modifier

You need a pivot point at the center of the ball, but you can't just move the existing pivot from the bottom to the middle—it would throw off all the squash and stretch animation.

Unfortunately, an object can have only one pivot point. To solve the issue, you are going to use a modifier called *XForm*. This modifier has many uses. You're going to use it to add another pivot to the ball in the following steps:

1. At this point, double-check that AutoKey is deactivated. The button is red when it is active.

   Select the ball. From the main menu bar, select Modifiers → Parametric Deformers → XForm. You may also select it from the Modifier List from the Modify panel. XForm will be added to the ball in the Modifier Stack, and an orange bounding box will appear over the ball in the viewport. XForm has no parameters, but it does have sub-objects, as you can see here.

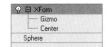

2. Expand the Modifier Stack by clicking the black box with the plus sign next to Xform. Then click Center. You will use the Align tool to center the XForm's *center point* on the ball in the next step.

3. Click the Align tool, and then click on the ball. In the dialog box, make sure the check box for the *X, Y,* and *Z* are checked, which means those axes are active. Now click Center under Target Object, and then press OK. The XForm's center will move, as shown here.

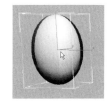

   Now to be clear, this isn't a *pivot point.* This is the *center point* on the XForm modifier. If you go to the Modifier Stack and click on the Sphere, the pivot point will still be at the bottom, as shown here.

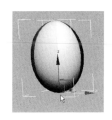

   Now, the XForm modifier allows the ball to rotate, without Squash and Stretch getting in the way. By separating the rotation animation for the ball's roll into the modifier, the animation on the sphere object is preserved.

Animating the XForm Modifier

To add the ball's roll to the XForm modifier, follow along with these illuminating and incredibly insightful steps:

1. Turn on Auto Key and select the Select and Rotate tool.

2. In the Modifier Stack, click on Gizmo for the sub-object of XForm. This is a very important step because it tells the Modifier to use the XForm's *center* instead of using the pivot point of the ball.

3. Move the Time slider to frame 100 and rotate the Ball 360 degrees on the *Y*-axis (you can use Angle Snap to make it easier to rotate exactly 360 degrees). Click on the XForm to deactivate the sub-object mode. Play the animation.

   The ball should be a rubbery cartoon ball at this point in the animation. Just for practice, let's say you need to go back and edit the keyframes because you rotated in the wrong

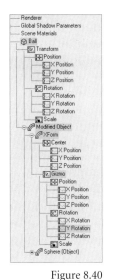

Figure 8.40

The XForm's gizmo selected in the Curve Editor window

direction and the ball's rotation is going backward. Fixing this issue requires you to go back into the Curve Editor as follows:

Open the Curve Editor (mini or regular). Scroll down in the Controller window until you see the Ball tracks. Below the Ball's Transform track is a new track called *Modified Object*. Expand the track by clicking on the plus sign in the circle next to the name. Go to the gizmo and select Y Rotation Track (Figure 8.40).

You will see the Function curve in the Edit Key work area. You want the keyframe at frame 0 to have the value 0 and the keyframe at frame 100 to be 360 degrees. Select both keyframes and change the Tangent to Linear, as shown in Figure 8.41.

Close the Curve Editor and play the animation. Play the Bounce Ball.mov QuickTime movie file located in the RenderOutput folder of the Bouncing Ball project on your hard drive (or on the CD) to see a render of the animation. You can also load the Animation_Ball_02.max scene file from the BouncingBall project folder on your hard drive (or on the CD) to check your work.

Bouncing Ball Summary

Working with the bouncing ball gave you quite a bit of experience with the 3ds Max's animation toolset. There are several ways to animate a bouncing ball in 3ds Max. It is definitely a good idea to try this exercise a few times at first, and then to come back to it later—after you have learned other 3ds Max techniques.

> If you are interested in seeing the differences in workflow between 3ds Max and Maya, you can see how to animate the bouncing ball with a similar ball exercise in *Introducing Maya 2008: 3d for Beginners*.

Track View

As you have already seen, the Track View–Curve Editor is a powerful tool for creating and editing your animation scenes. In this section, the user interface for the Track View is laid out and explained as a brief reference for you. Figure 8.42 shows the Track View–Curve Editor.

Figure 8.41

Setting the rotation of the ball

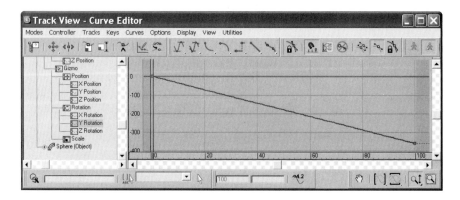

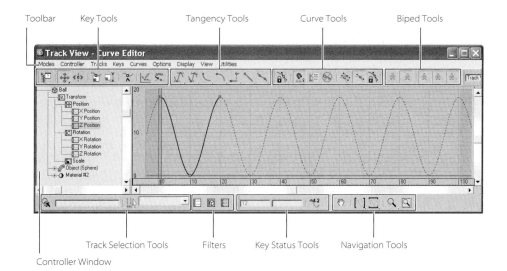

Figure 8.42

**The Track
View–Curve Editor**

The Curve Editor window can be a bit daunting at first. Now that you've had some experience with it in this chapter, it should seem pretty straightforward. The left side of the window (called the Controller window) displays the objects in the scene in an outline format. These objects have subheadings called *tracks* under them when they are animated. Each track will define animation on one axis of movement or rotation or scale, or one parameter that is keyframed. When you click on a track, its animation information will display in the graph area on the right. In the Curve Editor, you can access the curves and keyframes to edit the animation. In the Dope Sheet version of the Track View, you can access keys in a different manner, as discussed in the next chapter.

You can switch between the Curve Editor and the Dope Sheet by selecting the desired window in the Modes menu in the main menu bar. Most of the tools discussed here are also accessible through the menu bar and the toolbar. The toolbar is divided into function sets.

Key Tools Toolbar

The following table lists the tools used in editing keys in the Curve Editor window. You used a few of these tools in the Bouncing Ball animation.

ICON	NAME	FUNCTION
	Filter	Filters the display in the Curve Editor to make viewing complicated scenes easier.
	Move Keys	Lets you select a keyframe and move it freely in the graph.
	Move Keys Horizontal	Lets you select a keyframe and move it horizontally, to change its timing only.

continued

continued

ICON	NAME	FUNCTION
	Move Keys Vertical	Lets you select a keyframe and move it vertically, to change its value only.
	Slide Keys	Lets you select keyframes and move the group and slide the adjacent keys away as you move the group.
	Scale Keys	Lets you select keys and scale them to expand or compress the amount of time between them.
	Scale Values	Lets you select keys and increase or decrease the values of the keys proportionally without moving them in time.
	Add Keys	Add keys to an existing animation by clicking a curve.
	Draw Curves	Draw new curves, or revise existing curves, by drawing directly on the animation curve graph.
	Reduce Keys	Reduce keys when you have more keys than necessary on a curve.

Key Tangency Toolbar

As you saw with the bouncing ball, changing the tangency on a few keys can dramatically alter the look of your animation. By default, new keys are set to Auto Tangents, which generally keep the curve smooth. 3ds Max sets an appropriate tangency automatically; however, you can easily change the tangency by manually moving the handles on the keyframes. Once you select an Auto Tangent's handle, 3ds Max will automatically shift the handle to a custom handle, allowing you to move it. The following table lists the icons for the tangency tools.

ICON	NAME	FUNCTION
	Set Tangents to Auto	This rollout icon boasts three tools for controlling Auto tangents. The top icon sets both handles to Auto, the middle sets the In tangent, and the bottom icon sets the Out tangent to Auto.
	Set Tangents to Custom	Custom tangents allow you to move the handles to form your own curvature. If you hold the Shift key as you drag a tangent handle, it will break continuity with the other handle, allowing you to have a different In tangency than Out tangency.
	Set Tangents to Fast	Sets the tangent to accelerate in or out of a keyframe quickly, or both.
	Set Tangents to Slow	Sets the tangent to go slowly into or out of the keyframe, or both.
	Set Tangents to Step	Sets the tangent to "jump" from one value to the next in a single frame. The animation will be frozen until the next keyframe when it will jerk to that position or value.
	Set Tangents to Linear	Sets the tangency to a straight linear progression into or out of the keyframe, or both.
	Set Tangents to Smooth	Attempts to keep the curve smooth across all values to achieve a more realistic motion in many cases.

Beginners' Gallery

On the following pages, you will find a combination of images from the book as well as images created by a few artists fairly new to 3ds Max, all of whom are students at The Art Institute of California–Los Angeles, where one of the authors teaches. We hope these images will inspire your own creativity as you become more familiar with 3D in general and 3ds Max specifically. On the Internet, you can find a wealth of information about schools and programs such as The Art Institute of California–Los Angeles, where you can continue your education in CG work.

Some of these artists have been using 3ds Max for only a short period of time, and already they've been able to use the tools and techniques they've learned, to channel their artistic eye and creativity into some beautiful and interesting imagery.

ABOVE: The toy rocket that we modeled in Chapter 5, "Modeling in 3ds Max: Part II," is textured in Chapter 7, "Materials and Mapping." Use this photo to study how the surface of the rocket reflects its environment and how its coloring reacts to light, especially as you light and render the rocket in Chapter 10, "3ds Max Lighting," and Chapter 11, "3ds Max Rendering."
BELOW: By the end of Chapter 7, "Materials and Mapping," your rocket will look like this color image. By applying materials, you set a look for the model that is further refined in the lighting and rendering stages of production.

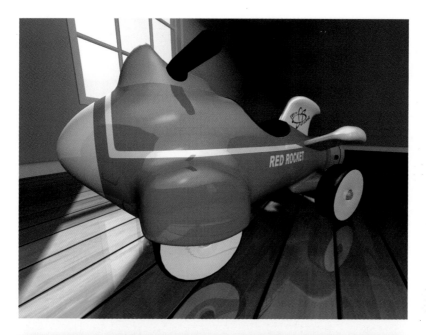

ABOVE: As you finish with the rocket example in Chapter 11, your rocket will take on a whole new life. Reflections of its environment and lighting touches will bring your model to life.

BELOW: The chess set, frequently used throughout Chapters 10 and 11 to illustrate lighting and rendering topics, is rendered in color for your reference.

ABOVE: Shane Sternstein created this moody and ominous kitchen for a lighting and texturing course. His use of volume lighting and moody shadows reinforces the suggestion that the "Dark Kitchen" is actually a morgue.

BELOW: Shane Sternstein created this still life image using mental ray with meticulous textures and obsessive attention to lighting. What sells this image most is Sternstein's attention to detail; notice the cracks in the wall, the distressed materials of the cabinet, and the subtle nature of the incense smoke.

ABOVE: For this piece, Ronald N. Howard used mental ray along with daylight lighting in order to get the proper "morning" lighting. He also used mental ray Sky within the Daylight system to color the scene because most of the textures in it were gray. The textures themselves were created in Photoshop, referencing some examples provided by his teachers in his game-creation courses.

BELOW: Ronald N. Howard created this library for his Materials and Lighting course. The scene uses a base Daylight lighting system in mental ray with some Omni lights added to make more of the scene visible. The textures were painted in Photoshop, based on photographs of rocks and marble, and were used for the color as well as bump maps.

A B O V E : The Game Wizards Production Team at the Art Institute of California–Los Angeles created the game "Mythos" as an exercise in game production as they would encounter it in the professional world. 3ds Max was used to create this game efficiently using low-polygon-count models and resourceful texture maps. In this image, you can see how detail is created in the textures. This circumvents the need to create unnecessary models that would bog the game down during play.
B E L O W : In another scene from the "Mythos" game, a small fleet of low-poly-count ships approaches the beach. Like many professional game designs, this render relies heavily on textures to convey atmosphere and detail.

ABOVE: When he modeled this Stormblade vehicle, Colin Mills was inspired by vehicles from the game *Warhammer 40,000*. The model uses polygons and was rendered using mental ray. Colin made sure to create maps for his render for diffuse, specular level, specular color, bump, and ambient occlusion.

BELOW: Colin Mills designed this peculiar robot character for a modeling class. He added several maps to the robot's materials to make sure there was enough detail when he rendered through mental ray.

ABOVE: This corridor was created by Andrew Prince using polygon modeling and texture maps created in Photoshop. His floor and stone wall maps are quite successful; you don't see tiling or seams easily, which is always a plus when you are texturing a model.
BELOW: Andrew Prince created this simple pistol model and used Planar mapping for its materials. He rendered the gun through mental ray using indirect lighting for a soft, lighted feel.

ABOVE: Nelson Mendez created this dumpster model out of a surprisingly low 526 polygons for a game art class. The detail lies within the textures Nelson used. Textures are an important tool for game development.

BELOW: The payphone was created for Torrence T. Trotter's Game Modeling and Animation class as an example of an *asset model*, a model used as an prop or set piece (for example) in a game. The model consists of only 178 polygons. Two texture pages were used on this model: a diffuse map and a bump map to give it detail.

ABOVE: Ruben Morales created this exterior scene and rendered it to a background photograph of a setting sun. To keep the polygon count low, the warehouse relies on mapping for its details. It was created for a game-modeling class.

BELOW: Using different architectural- and design-type materials in 3ds Max, Sean Dunny created the plane and rendered it with mental ray. He used particle effects to simulate the muzzle flashes on the guns and the vapor trails left behind by the plane, as well as the smoke from the exhaust vents. The plane was lit using the Daylight system, with mental ray Sun and an IES sky (a type of light system found in 3ds Max and used in conjunction with the Daylight system used in Radiosity renders).

ABOVE: Charles Ptacek created this model of Central Music Hall in Chicago for a Hard Surface and Organic Modeling class. It is created with polygons and some basic NURBS converted back to polygons. The scene is lit with a Standard Sky Light.

BELOW: Danika VanAlstyne is a student in the Interior Design Department. This department's curriculum is geared to further the students' skill sets and work with AutoCAD projects. This scene is a loft space with a meditation corner. Its muted reds and blacks are a soothing environment for its dweller.

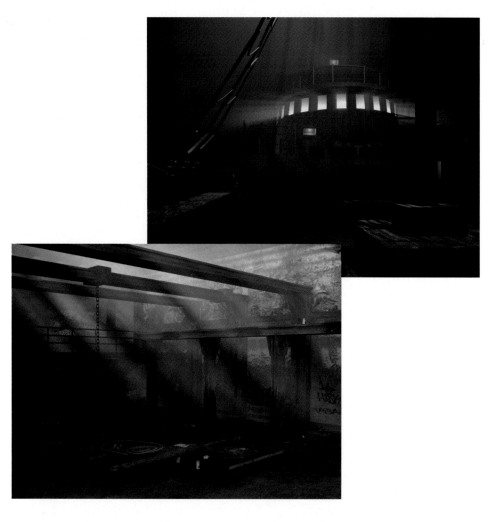

ABOVE: By referencing a few fishing boats and crabbing boats, Brian F. Lee was able to get a pretty good idea of the "Foggy Ship" he wanted to build. After building the model, he used a series of textures, lights, and a foggy environmental effect to really bring the scene to life. The textures came from pictures of rotted wood and rusty metal that Brian took at the marina and edited in Photoshop. Brian painted in some extra details and made them ready to tile. The volume lights, combined with the fog, give a very natural look, and the Omni lights from within the hull of the ship and on the dock give a more mechanical appearance.

BELOW: Joshua Palacios used just 4,463 polygons to create this model. He made the beams, bottles, rope, rails, and spray cans with extruded splines; used some bevels to put dents and holes in the floor; and used regular planes (with alpha channel maps) for the chains, walls, and ceiling. Joshua then painted some paint splatters near the cans and tried to make the graffiti look as real as possible by placing it where graffiti artists would paint. For the lighting, Joshua used four omni lights on the lower floor to give it some light inside. Then he used a Target spotlight from above to give the room an exterior light effect, rendered with a touch of fog.

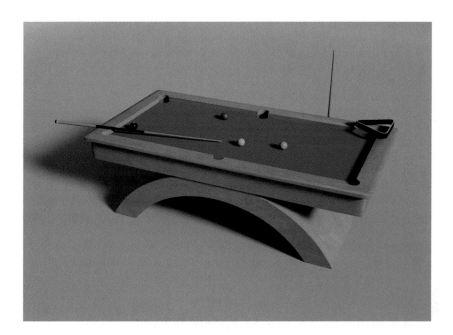

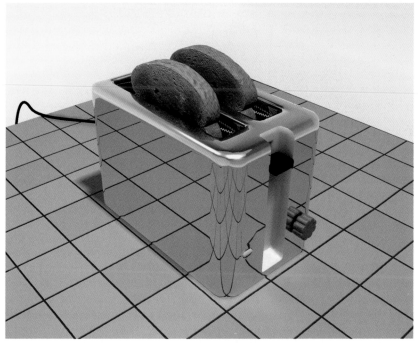

ABOVE: Jua Harmon created this image for his portfolio. The model is accented by simple materials rendered with soft shadows in mental ray.
BELOW: Jua Harmon's toaster was rendered with raytraced reflections to give the chrome a more believable look. The textures on the face of the toast are quite nice.

ABOVE: Joshua Palacios was given a polygon count limit of 500 to create a game asset for his game-modeling class. He used 473 for his design, again relying on textures to give the most detail bang for the buck. Joshua started out using splines to get the figure of the gun, and then he extruded them to convert the model to an editable poly, where he was able to clean up the edges of the object. He next broke out the different parts of the pistol and shaped them up as low poly as possible. He lit and rendered the image using the Skylight in 3ds Max.

BELOW: Chun Jay Hwang's "Sword of Omens" is a homage to the Thundercats cartoon that one of this book's authors grew up on. The low-poly model was created for a game-texturing class and was created to be used as a game asset prop. The render lays out the sword in a nice manner, showing you just one way you can present your models for review.

ABOVE: The school's Game Wizards Production Team worked on the game "Detox" in a production course to teach the students the ins and outs of a typical professional game production. This crane model was created by Ruben Morales and is rendered with a typical gray material using soft shadows from Final Gather's renderer. The crane has a few nice details in the hydraulic hoses and cables running along its "fingers" that give the model believability. Imagine how the fingers will animate when the crane moves!

BELOW: In another semester, the Game Wizards Production Team created the "Thunder Flash" game. Here you can see a dilapidated car in front of a majestic church façade. Because the production team was tasked with creating assets for a game, they had to rely on well-painted texture maps. The rust on the front of the car and the dirt and grime on the chassis give the car a very interesting look and beg further study.

ABOVE: Ronald N. Howard's 5,500 poly-count model was created for his game modeling and texturing courses. The throne room itself is just a box with some pillars in it and some really cool axes on the wall. He relied heavily on the textures and lighting to make the image pop. For the lighting, Ronald used the Daylight system from mental ray but also added some volume lights shining through the window to give that faint dust effect you see. He also added three Omni lights near the top of the room to brighten things up a little. On the floor, nice mapping work brings out the specular of the glossy tiles.

BELOW: Shane Sternstein created this kitchen counter for his 3ds Max class. The use of raytraced reflections goes a long way to make this image believable. His use of soft lighting and indirect lighting through mental ray's Final Gather gives the room a warm morning glow.

Curves Toolbar

The Curves tools act on the animation curves themselves, allowing you to easily make changes to an animated track. You will run into some of these tools as you become more experienced with Max. Don't worry about memorizing all these functions.

ICON	NAME	FUNCTION
	Lock Selection	Locks the current selection so you don't accidentally select something else.
	Snap Frames	Snaps keys to frames when you move them. When off, you can move keys to sub-frames (i.e., in-between frames).
	Parameter Out-of-Range Curves	Allows you to set the behavior of your animation before and beyond the keyframed range.
	Show Keyable Icons	Toggles an icon to tell you whether a track is keyable or not. Red is keyable; black is not.
	Show Tangents	Toggles the display of tangent handles on individual curves.
	Show All Tangents	Toggles the display of tangent handles on all curves in the graph.
	Lock Tangents	Locks a selection of tangent handles so you can adjust them all at once. When off, however, you only have access to one tangent handle at a time.

Biped Toolbar

These new Curve Editor Biped tools make the process of using the Curve Editor for biped animation much more streamlined than before. Biped tools will be covered in the next chapter. The following table lists the icons and their names for your reference. The Biped toolbar is visible only if you have a biped in your scene.

ICON	NAME
	Show Biped Position Curves
	Show Biped Rotation Curves
	Show Biped X Curves
	Show Biped Y Curves
	Show Biped Z Curves

Navigation Toolbar

These tools are for Track View navigation. Tools such as Pan, Zoom, and Zoom Region work the same as in the Viewport Navigation tools. Some of the tools are designed specifically for the Track View. A few often-used icons are listed in the following table:

ICON	NAME	FUNCTION
Pan	Pan	Use this tool to drag the key window. You can also use the middle mouse button.
[ ]	Zoom Horizontal Extents	Adjusts the display so that the entire active time segment is shown.
	Zoom Value Extents	Adjusts the display so that the full heights of the curves are visible.
	Zoom	Zooms both time and value proportionally together. This is a rollout with two other Zoom options nested.
	Zoom Region	Lets you drag a region to scale the display to fit.

Anticipation and Momentum in Knife Throwing

This exercise will give you more experience animating in 3ds Max. In it, you'll animate a knife being thrown at a target. You will edit more in the Curve Editor and be introduced to the concept of anticipation in animation, as well as momentum and secondary movement.

In preparation, copy the Knife project from the CD to your hard drive. Set your 3ds Max project folder by choosing File → Set Project Folder and selecting the Knife project that you copied from the CD to your hard drive.

Blocking Out the Animation

To begin this exercise, open the Animation_Knife_00.max file in the Knife project and follow along here:

1. Move the Time slider to frame 30 and activate the Auto Key button.

2. Move the knife to the target object, as shown in Figure 8.43.

3. Move the Time slider to frame 15, where the knife is halfway between its start and the target, and move the knife slightly up in the Z-axis, so that the knife moves with a slight arc (Figure 8.44).

Figure 8.43

Move the knife to the target at frame 30.

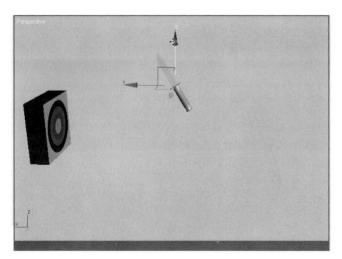

Figure 8.44

Move the knife up slightly at frame 15.

Figure 8.45

Change the frame range in the Time Configuration window.

4. For now, change the frame range in the Time slider so you're working between frame 0 and frame 30. Click the Time Configuration button () at the bottom of the UI next to the navigation controls. Figure 8.45 shows the Time Configuration window. In the Animation section, change the End Time to 30 from 100. The Time slider will reflect this change immediately.

5. Scrub your animation, and you should see the knife move with a slight ease-in and ease-out toward the target with a slight arc up in the middle. You want the position of the knife to start at frame 10, so open the Curve Editor and scroll down in the Controller window until you see the three X, Y, Z Position tracks for the knife. Hold the Ctrl key and select all three tracks to display their curves (Figure 8.46).

6. Drag a selection marquee around the keyframe at frame 0 (Figure 8.47). In the Curve Editor toolbar, select and hold the Move tool ( ) to access the Flyout icons, and select the Horizontal Move tool in the flyout ( ). Use this tool to move the keyframes to frame 10.

7. This will compact the curve, as shown previously, so you will need to move the keys at frame 15 to the new middle, frame 20 (Figure 8.48).

Figure 8.46

The Initial Curve Editor for the knife

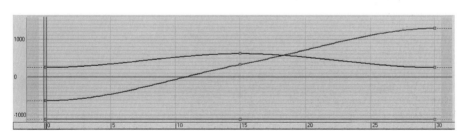

Figure 8.47

Marquee-select the keyframe at frame 0.

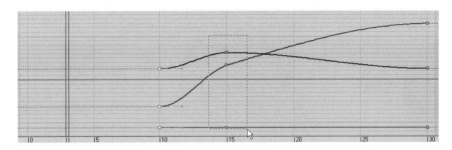

Figure 8.48

Move the keys to the new middle.

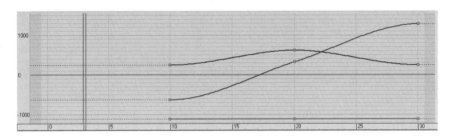

That's it for the gross animation or blocking of the shot. Did you have fun?

Trajectories

When it comes to animation, it is very helpful to be able to see the path your object is taking over time. These paths are known as *trajectories* in Max. The easiest way to see the trajectories is to select the knife object, go to the Motion panel, and click Trajectories, as shown in Figure 8.49. Your viewports will display a red curve to show you the path of the knife's motion as it arcs toward the target, as shown in Figure 8.50.

The trajectory will remain displayed until a moving object is selected. The large hollow square points on the trajectory curve represent the keyframes set on the knife so far. Let's adjust the height of the arc using the trajectory curve. Turn on the Sub-Object button at the top of the Motion panel (Figure 8.51).

Figure 8.49

Turning on trajectories for the knife

Figure 8.50

The curve shows the trajectory for the knife's motion.

Keys are your only sub-object choice in the pull-down menu to the right of the button. Select the middle keyframe and move it up or down to suit your tastes, as shown in Figure 8.52. Once you settle on a nice arc for the path of the knife, turn off the Trajectories button.

As you can imagine, the Trajectories panel can be useful in many situations. It not only gives you a view of your object's path, but it also allows you to edit that path easily and in a visual context, which can be so important.

Adding Rotation

The next step is to add a bit of rotation to the knife. As an animator, you need to research and gather as much information about your subject matter as you can. Throwing knives is usually a bad idea, but you can throw something else—ideally something that is shaped and weighted like a knife—at a target (the inanimate kind) to see how to animate your knife. Almost invariably, you'll find that the object will have to rotate once or twice before it hits its target. To add rotation to your CG knife, follow these steps:

1. Move to frame 30, and press E for the Select and Rotate tool. Auto Key should still be active. Rotate in the *Y*-axis 443 degrees, as shown in Figure 8.53.

2. Open the Curve Editor, scroll down to find the X, Y, and Z Rotation tracks, and select them. Use the Horizontal Move tool to shift the keyframes at 0 to frame 10. Press N to deactivate the Auto Key. Figure 8.54 shows the Curve Editor graph for the knife.

3. Play the animation, and you will see that the knife's position and rotation eases in and eases out. A real knife would not ease its rotations or movement. Its speed would be roughly consistent throughout the animation.

4. Go back to the Curve Editor, select the X Position track, and then select all the keyframes and switch the Tangent to Linear. Now select the Z Position track; you'll need to finesse this one a bit more than the X Position. You are going to use the handles on the tangents that appear when you select a keyframe. These handles can be adjusted; just center your cursor over the end and click and drag. Figure 8.55 illustrates how you want the Z Position animation curve to look. This will give the trajectory a nice arc and a good speed of travel.

Figure 8.51

Choose the sub-object level.

Figure 8.52

Raise the arc of the knife by altering its trajectory.

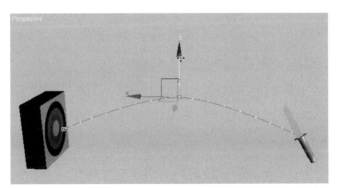

Figure 8.53

Rotate in Y.

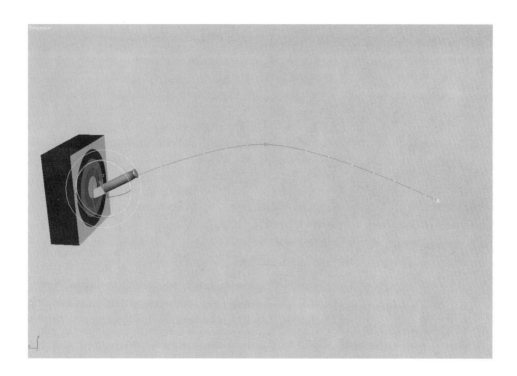

Figure 8.54

Move the first rotation keyframes to frame 10.

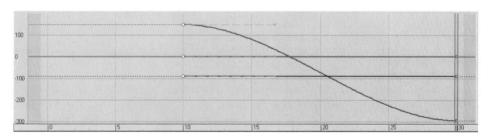

Figure 8.55

Adjust the curve for the knife's arc through the air.

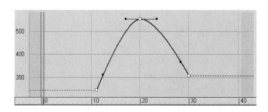

5. Now it is time to edit the Rotation keys. In the Curve Editor scroll to find the X, Y, and Z Rotation tracks. The first thing you can do is add a bit of drama to the knife to make the action more exciting. To this end, you can say that the rotation on the knife is too slow. Select the X Rotation track and select its keyframe at frame 30. In the Key

Stats, change the value to –52. The higher the value, the faster the knife will rotate. This will add one full revolution to the animation and some more excitement to the action.

6. Adjust the tangent handles to resemble the curve shown in Figure 8.56. The knife will speed up just a little bit as it leaves the first rotate keyframe. The speed will be even as it goes into the last keyframe.

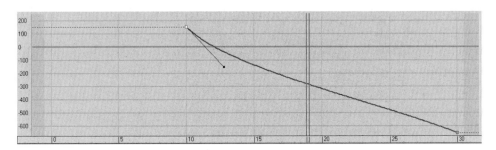

Figure 8.56

Match your curve to this one.

With just a little bit of fast rotation as the knife leaves frame 10, you give the animation more spice. A little change in the curve can make a big difference in an animation—every little bit counts. The knife should now have a slightly weightier look than before when it rotated with an ease-in and ease-out.

Adding Anticipation

Instead of making the knife just fly through the air toward the target, you should animate it to move back first to create *anticipation*, as if an invisible hand holding the knife pulled back just before throwing it to get more strength in the throw. This anticipation, although it's a small detail, can add a level of nuance to the animation that enhances the total effect. Follow these steps:

1. Move the Time slider to frame 0. Go to the Curve Editor, scroll the Controller window, and select X Rotation track for the knife. In the Curve Editor toolbar, click the Add Keys button ( ), bring your cursor to frame 0 of the curve, and click to create a keyframe. This creates a key at frame 0 with the same parameters as the next keyframe, as shown in Figure 8.57.

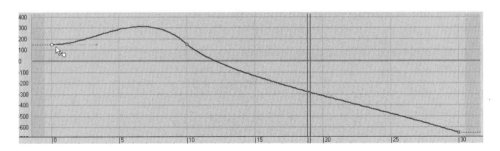

Figure 8.57

Adding a key to the beginning to create anticipation for the knife throw

2. Select the Move tool and select the key at frame 10. In the Key Stats type-in, change the value of that key to 240. If you play back the animation, it will look weird. The knife will cock back really fast and spin a bit. This is due to the big hump between frames 0 and 10.

3. Keep the tangent at frame 0 set to the default, but change the tangent on the key at frame 10 to Linear. Play back the animation. You'll have a slight bit of anticipation, but the spice will be lost and the knife will look less active and too mechanical.

4. To regain the weight you had in the knife, press Ctrl+Z to undo your change to the tangency on frame 10 and set it back to what you had (just like Figure 8.57). You may have to undo more than once. Now, select the Vertical Move tool and select the In tangent for keyframe 0. This is the tangent handle on the left of the key, as shown in Figure 8.58.

Figure 8.58

The In tangent is the one on the left.

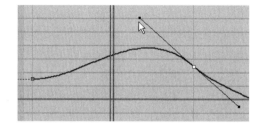

It's very common to try something in the course of your work, and rely on Undo to get back to the starting point. You can sometimes expect to Undo several times when you find yourself at a dead end.

5. Press Shift and drag the tangent handle down to create a curve that is similar to the one shown in Figure 8.59. By pressing Shift as you dragged the tangent handle, you broke the continuity between the In and Out handles, so that only the In handle was affected. Play back the animation. It should look much better now.

Remember, the smallest tweaks in the Curve Editor can have a huge positive or negative impact on your animation.

Figure 8.59

To create a believable anticipation for the knife throw, set your curve to resemble this one.

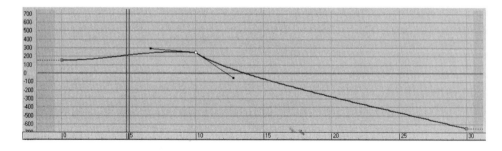

Follow-Through

The knife needs more weight. A great way to show that in animation is by adding follow-through. This is part of the animation concept of secondary movement that was mentioned in Chapter 1. The follow-through for the knife would be having the knife sink into the target a little bit and push back the target as it transfers momentum to the target. For more on momentum, see the sidebar later in this chapter.

Knife Follow-Through

To add follow-through to your animation, follow these steps:

1. You want to sink the knife into the target after it hits. Select the Time Configuration button (shown in the following graphic), and change the End Time to 40 to add 10 frames to your frame range. This will not affect the animation; it will merely append 10 frames to the current frame range.

2. Select the knife and go to frame 30, where it hits the target. In the Curve Editor, select the X Position of the knife. Add a keyframe with the Add Keys tool at frame 35.

3. Note the value of the key in the type-in boxes at the bottom of the Curve Editor window (*not* the type-in boxes at the bottom of the main UI). In this case, the value in this scene is about –231. You will want to set the value for this key at frame 35 to about –224 to sink it farther into the target. If your values are different, adjust accordingly so you don't add too much movement. Also make sure the movement flows *into* the target and not back out of the target as if the knife were bouncing out.

4. Keep the tangent for this new key set to Auto. With these relative values, scrub the animation between frames 30 and 35. You should see the knife's slight move into the target. The end of your curve should look like the curve in Figure 8.60.

5. You still need to add a little bit of follow-through to the rotation of the knife to make it sink into the target better. In the Curve Editor, select the X Rotation to display its curve. Add a key to the curve at frame 35. The value of the key at frame 30 should already be about –652. Set the value of the keyframe at frame 35 to be about –655 (Figure 8.61). Keep the tangent set at Auto.

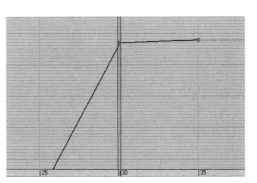

Figure 8.60

Your animation should end like this.

Figure 8.61

Set −655 at frame 35.

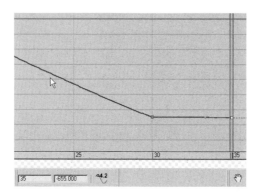

Be careful about how much the knife sinks into the target. Although it is important to show the weight of the knife, it is also important to show the weight of the target; you do not want the target to look too soft. Make sure your keys at frame 35 for the X Position and X Rotation are not too much.

Transferring Momentum to the Target

To make the momentum work even better for the Knife animation, you will have to push back the target as the knife hits it. The trouble is, if you animate the target moving back, the knife will float in the air. You have to animate the knife *with* the target. However, animating them separately in the hopes they will match up will frustrate you and will more than likely look bad.

If you think that hierarchy has to be involved here, you are absolutely right. Basically, the knife will have to be linked to the target so that when the target is animated, the knife will follow precisely, because it is stuck in the target.

This won't mess up the animation of the knife. Because the knife will be the child in the hierarchy and can have its own animation separate from the target, you can link it after you are finished with the knife animation. Just follow these steps:

1. Go to frame 30, where the knife impacts. Select the Select and Link tool. Select the knife and drag it to the target as shown in Figure 8.62. Nothing should change until you animate the target object.

2. Move the Time slider to frame 34 and press N to activate the Auto Key tool. With the Select and Rotate tool, select the target object and rotate it back about 5 degrees as shown in the second image in Figure 8.62. The pivot of the target has already been placed properly, at the bottom back edge.

3. Go to the Curve Editor, scroll to find the Y Rotation track for the target object, select the keyframe at frame 0, and move it to frame 30. Then hold the Shift key, and click and drag the keyframe (which will make a copy of it) to frame 37. Your curve should resemble the curve in Figure 8.63.

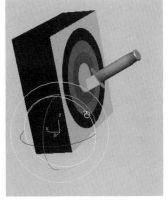

Figure 8.62

Move the knife to the target, and then rotate the target back slightly.

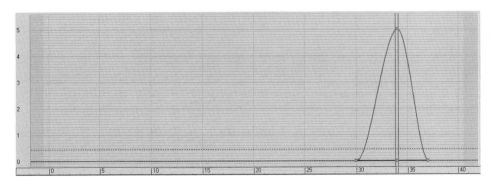

Figure 8.63

The target will rock back and forth on impact.

4. Change the Tangent at frame 0 to Fast and leave the other keyframe tangents alone.

5. Add a little wobble to the target to make the animation even more interesting. This can be done very easily in the Curve Editor. Select the Y Rotation of the target to display just that curve. Use Add Key to add two keyframes at frames 40 and 44. Using the Vertical Move tool, give the key at frame 40 a value of about 1.7. Your curve should resemble the one in Figure 8.64.

6. Finally, add a little slide to the target. Get the Select and Move tool, move the Time slider to frame 37, and move the target just a bit along the *X*-axis. Go to the Curve Editor, scroll to the X Position of the target object, select the keyframe at frame 0, and move it to frame 30 so the move starts when the knife hits the target. Change the tangent for frame 30 to Fast and leave the other tangent at Auto.

Done! Play back your animation. Experiment and change some of the final timings of the target's reaction to the impact, as well as some of the values, to see how small changes can make big differences in how the weights of the knife and target look to the viewer.

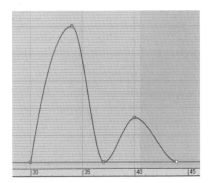

Figure 8.64

The target animation curve

MOMENTUM

Understanding what momentum is and how it works is pretty important for an animator. When an object is in motion, it has momentum. The amount of momentum is calculated by multiplying the mass of the object by its velocity. The heavier something is, or the faster it is moving, the more momentum it has and the bigger the bruise it will leave if it hits you.

That's why a tiny bullet can cause such a great impact on a can of stew, for example. Its sheer speed greatly increases its momentum. Likewise, a slow-moving dump truck can bash in your car, relying on its sheer mass for its tremendous momentum.

Basically, when one moving object meets another object that is moving or not, momentum is transferred between them. That means when something hits an object, that target is somehow moved if there is sufficient momentum transferred to it.

It follows that the more weight an object has, the more momentum will transfer to the target. Also, the more velocity an object has, the more momentum will be transferred to the target on collision. You will be able to show the weight of an object in animation by showing how much momentum it transfers when it impacts another object. This could be as simple a as knife hitting a target and moving it back, as you animated in the exercise in this chapter, or as complicated as a heavyset man walking down the street. In the latter case, because the pavement can't give way underneath the man, the momentum that is transferred is reflected back to the man and absorbed by his body. That makes his body bend and flex and his big belly jiggle up and down with each step.

Impact is a perfect opportunity for an animator to show his subject's weight in motion, and it is always intrinsic in good animation.

You can see a sample render of the scene in the `knife_animation.mov` QuickTime file in the RenderOutput folder of the Knife project on the CD (or copied onto your hard drive). You can also load the `Animation_Knife_01.max` scene file from the Scenes folder of the Knife project to check your work.

A similar exercise where you throw an ax teaches you much the same animation practice in Maya in *Introducing Maya 2008: 3d for Beginners,* if you are curious about how 3ds Max and Maya animate similar scenes.

Summary

In this, the first of two chapters on animation in this book, you learned the basics of creating and editing animation. You learned how to fix hierarchy problems in animation and how to use dummy objects to help you animate properly. You bounced a ball to learn timing issues and how to edit animation curves through the Curve Editor. You then learned the ins and outs of the Track Editor–Curve Editor before moving on to a thrown knife to learn about trajectories and the concepts behind using secondary movement to help give your animation weight.

Animation can be a lot of fun, but it is also tedious and sometimes aggravating. A lot of time, patience, and practice are required to become good at animation. It all boils down to how the animation makes you think. Is there enough weight to the subjects in the animation? Do the movements make sense? How does nuance enhance the animation? These are all questions you will begin to discover for yourself. This chapter merely introduced you to how to make things move in 3ds Max. It gave you some of the basics of animation techniques to help you develop your eye for motion. Don't stop here. Go back into the chapter and redo some of the exercises. Try different variations on the same themes. Keep working.

CHAPTER 9

Character Studio and IK Animation

At one time or another, almost everyone in the 3D community wants to animate a character. This chapter examines the 3ds Max toolsets used in the process of character animation. In this chapter, you will learn about two of the three components that make up Character Studio, a full-featured package incorporated into 3ds Max for mostly animating bipedal characters, including humans, aliens, robots, and anything else that walks on two feet, though you can have characters with more than two feet in certain situations.

Although Character Studio (CS) creates an instant structure for a character, you will also work with Inverse Kinematics (IK), which creates hierarchical structures for animating individually linked objects.

Character animation is a broad and complex field that everyone wants to experiment with at some point. This chapter introduces you to the basics of using Character Studio and Bones. Further investigation into these tools is a must if you want your animation to be full of life and character.

Topics in this chapter include:

- **Character Animation**
- **Character Studio Workflow**
- **Creating a Biped**
- **Animating a Biped**
- **Associating a Biped to a Character**
- **Using Inverse Kinematics**

Character Animation

The character animation CG specialty is easily one of the toughest specialties to master. It takes an exceptional eye and a special insight to become an amazing animator. To use one word, good character animation comes down to *nuance*. Because we as people move ourselves and are surrounded by other people who move, we are innately critical when a character is not well animated. That is because the detail and nuance in movement is so inherent, so ingrained in our experience, that we never really think twice when we see someone move. We just intrinsically *know* how they move the way they do. However, we do notice when that nuance is missing in an animation of a person. As observers, we may not know exactly what is missing, but we instinctively know that something is wrong and it looks funny.

When you character animate, you have to have a keen eye for detail and an understanding of how proportions move on a person's body. Setting up a CG character to walk *exactly* like a human being is amazingly complicated. You must account for muscles, bone structures, and a host of other details that most 3D software does not begin to address.

However, good animation for a character is actually not that difficult right out of the box. Character systems such as Character Studio make it a breeze to set up characters and have them moving in a walk cycle very quickly. Don't limit your character animation studies to Character Studio, though. While learning and mastering *how* CS works and how to animate with it, you mustn't lose sight of the fact that you are trying to learn *how to animate* as opposed to learning how to run a piece of software. Never let mastery of a software program be your primary mission. You will quickly limit yourself that way.

In other words, once you gain a solid grasp of how CS and other character tools work, use them to learn how to really animate. Character Studio is just a means to an end. You're here to learn to animate, not to learn how to run CS. Now that we have that out of the way, we can concentrate on getting you comfortable with CS. Have fun!

Character Studio Workflow

Character Studio is a system built into 3ds Max to help automate the creation and animation of a character, who may or may not be exactly a *biped* (two-footed creature). Character Studio comprises three basic components: the Biped system, the Physique modifier, and the Crowd system. Biped and Physique are used to pose and animate a single character, and the Crowd utility is used to assign similar movements and behaviors to multiple objects in your 3ds Max scene. This chapter covers the Biped and Physique features, but Crowd is beyond the scope of this book.

The first step in the Character Studio workflow is to build or acquire a suitable character model. The model should be *bipedal,* meaning it stands on two feet. In the future, however, you needn't limit yourself to strictly humanoid models; CS is perfectly useful for animating anything from a human to a dinosaur to a bumblebee, as long as the model's configuration allows it. The second step in the process is to *skin* (bind) the character model to the skeleton, so the animation drives the model properly.

> Models should typically be in the reference position known as the "da Vinci pose," where the feet are shoulder width apart and the arms are extended to the sides with the palms down, as shown in Figure 9.1. This allows the animator to observe all of the model's features, unobstructed by the model itself, in at least two viewports. This layout of a model is a standard in the CG industry because it facilitates skinning the model to its skeleton.

Figure 9.1

A bipedal character in the reference position

Again, the term *bipedal* refers to an animal or character with two feet. So, in 3ds Max, a *biped* is a predefined, initially humanoid, structure. It is important to understand that you animate the biped that is associated with your model and not the model itself. Once the model is bound to the skeleton, the biped structure *drives* the model. You would use the Physique modifier in CS to create that relationship between the skeleton and the model.

Using the Physique modifier ensures that your model follows the biped's animation. You will work with attaching a model to a biped using Physique later in this chapter. You can also use another 3ds Max methodology, the Skin modifier, to attach the model to the biped skeleton. The differences between the two methodologies are explained next.

Physique versus Skin

Currently, 3ds Max has two modifiers that essentially do the same thing. Physique and Skin can both be used to transfer the movement of a skeletal system such as a biped to a mesh, making the character move with the skeleton rig. Of the two, Physique is the older modifier. Historically in 3ds Max's first releases, Character Studio, which included Physique in its package, was developed by Unreal Pictures as the first major plug-in for 3ds Max and was sold as a separate program.

Over time, however, users demanded that a program similar to Physique be included as part of the base 3ds Max package. Autodesk, responsive to the needs of its users, developed the Skin modifier to satisfy the customers' need. However, when CS was bundled free of charge with 3ds Max, Physique was included, and so the base 3ds Max package included two modifiers to do the same character-skinning task.

Over time, Skin has had numerous improvements that add to its capabilities, while Physique has more or less remained the same. Because both can accomplish the same work, you can choose which one you want to learn. It comes down to personal taste; some users swear by Physique, others swear at it—and the same goes for Skin. Physique is covered in this chapter and will be your introduction to how to attach a model to a biped skeleton. Once you feel you understand the methodology, try your hand at using Skin the next time.

General Workflow

The default biped, shown in Figure 9.2, consists of legs, feet, toes, arms, hands, fingers, pelvis, spine, neck, and head. After your model is ready, you will create a biped and, using its parameters and the Scale transform, fit the biped closely to the model. The better the biped to model relationship, the easier the animation will be.

Figure 9.2

The default biped

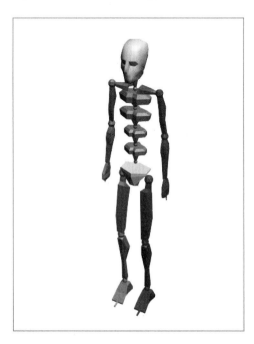

BONES AND SKIN

The Bones system and Skin modifier are similar to Character Studio. Bones is a series of linked, hierarchical components that are used, in conjunction with the Skin modifier, to control the displacement of a model similar to the Biped and Physique method. Many animators swear by Bones. They appreciate the finer control they are able to achieve over the character's motion and motion restrictions. With finer control comes more work; Bones requires a more tedious setup process to create a skeleton than Biped.

Once the biped is fit snugly to the model, you select all of the components of the model, not the biped skeleton, and apply the Physique or Skin modifier in a process often referred to as *skinning*. It may take a while to properly test and refine the relationship between the model and the biped to get it to an acceptable level.

The final step is animating your character. You can accomplish this by adding any combination of default walk, run, and jump cycles included with CS to the biped, then applying any freeform animation to the character, and finally refining the animation keyframes in the Dope Sheet. Don't expect the default walk, run, and jump cycles to create realistic motion though. They are just a starting point and must be tweaked to achieve acceptable movements. Character animation is about nuance and subtlety, and those artistic touches take a significant amount of time and effort to master.

In a student or prospective employee's work, I can immediately spot default or "canned" animations that are straight out of the program's library of motions. Default cycles are a great place to get your start. Don't let yourself stop with canned motions, though. You will have to imbue your own sensibility into a character to really make it as a good animator.

The best way to start is to jump in and examine the tools available. In the next section, you will work with a biped and adjust the parameters and components to modify it, unless you close the book and watch TV instead.

Creating a Biped

As stated previously, you should create your model first and then create and modify your biped to fit the model. In this section, however, you are going to examine the procedure for creating and modifying a biped first to provide an understanding of its capabilities. Later in this chapter, we will revisit the methods for adjusting your biped specifically to match a model.

Placing a Biped in a Scene

Let's create a Biped system for your scene to get a feel for how CS works. Unlike many of the objects that you've created so far, Biped is located under the Systems category of the Create tab in the Command panel, as shown here.

Follow these steps to create and adjust a biped:

1. From the Command panel, select Create → Systems → Biped.

2. Click and drag in the Perspective viewport to create the biped shown in Figure 9.3.

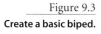
Figure 9.3
Create a basic biped.

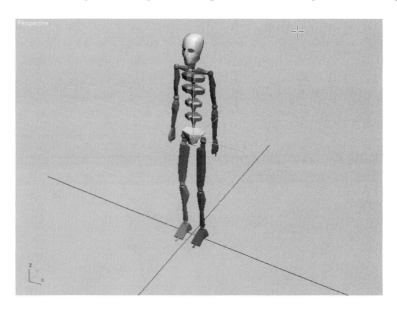

The first click sets the insertion point. Dragging defines the height of the biped system and defines all of the components. All of the biped's components are sized relative to the biped's Height parameter.

With this action, you created 30 visible and 5 hidden objects arranged in a linked hierarchy, not just a single object. All of the elements on the left side of the biped's body are blue, and all of the elements on the right side are green. This coloring scheme is carried throughout 3ds Max.

3. Go to Tools → New Scene Explorer, which opens up a *modeless* dialog (one that floats so you can still edit your scene while it is open; Figure 9.4 shows the Select from Scene dialog that opens when you invoke the New Scene Explorer command); it is for viewing hierarchies, among other things. All of the objects are indented from the edge of the dialog box, indicating that they are subordinate to, or children of, the objects above them in the list.

4. Close the Scene Explorer dialog box.

5. While the biped is still selected, scroll the Command panel to display the Create Biped rollout. This rollout is where changes to the biped's structure are made. You can increase the number of fingers and toes and the number of links in each to match your model. You can add a tail or ponytails by increasing the number of links for these parameters. You can even discard the arms altogether.

> Adding neck links will make your biped taller, but adding spine links won't—it will only subdivide the torso area for more control in the midsection.

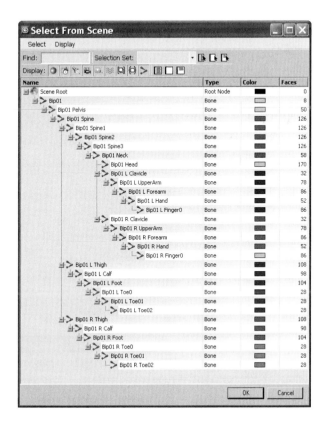

Figure 9.4

The Select from Scene dialog opens when you open a new Scene Explorer window

6. Change the parameters as you like. The biped in Figure 9.5 includes additional fingers and toes, as well as a tail and a ponytail.

Figure 9.5

**A biped with modi-
fied parameters**

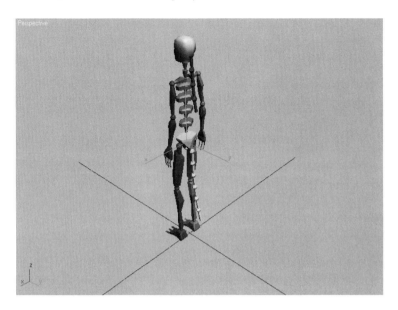

The root object of the hierarchy is named Bip01, for the first biped that you create in a scene, and all the associated objects will have a Bip01 prefix. Changing the name of the object in the Name and Color rollout changes only the name of the root object and does not cascade throughout the hierarchy. Changing the name in the Root Name section of the Create Biped rollout, however, affects all of the objects in the biped.

Modifying a Biped

Bipeds are very generic in appearance. You will rarely, if ever, use the default biped in an actual animation beyond learning CS. Luckily, bipeds have a complete set of tools available for modifying their structure and their behavior to match a model. You will have to select an appropriate editing mode to access the appropriate tools to adjust your biped. This section covers the tools used to adjust the size of a biped's individual elements.

If you haven't already, create a biped in your scene as discussed earlier. To begin modifying the biped, follow along here:

1. Clear your selection set by clicking the Select Object button ( ) in the main tool-bar and then clicking on any blank area of a viewport. Nothing in your scene should be selected.

2. Click any part of your biped to select it. Bipeds react differently than other objects. Selecting any single component of the biped opens the entire Biped object for editing.

3. Click the Motion tab of the Command panel (Figure 9.6). The purpose of a biped is to create an animation, so all of the biped's parameters, including those that control animation as well as appearance, are consolidated under the Motion tab of the Command panel, and not under the Modify tab as you may initially think.

4. In the Biped rollout, click the Figure Mode button (shown here) to display the rollouts that pertain to the biped's configuration, not its animation or footstep control. The Figure Mode button turns blue to indicate the current mode that the system is using.

5. Expand the Structure rollout to access the same parameters that were used when you first created the biped to adjust its basic configuration. Make any additional modifications that you choose.

> In the Body Type area at the bottom of the Structure rollout, you can change the overall appearance of the biped from the default Skeleton to Male, Female, or Classic. The body type has little to do with the biped's capabilities and is more a matter of preference.

Figure 9.6

Biped parameters are on the Motion tab of the Command panel.

6. Select the biped's left upper arm. In the main toolbar, click the Select and Rotate button.

7. In the main toolbar, set the reference coordinate system for the current Rotate tool to Local, as shown here. Most transforms that are applied to a biped are applied in the Local coordinate system so they are relative to the object, rather than the world or the current viewport.

8. Place your cursor over the green *Y*-axis ring of the Rotate Transform gizmo and drag upward to rotate the upper arm upward, as shown in Figure 9.7. Notice that the arm rotates at the shoulder as it's supposed to. The pivot point is already placed correctly.

   All of the pivot points for the biped elements are already placed at the top of the objects. For example, the upper arm pivots at the shoulder, the lower arm pivots at the elbow, and the hand pivots at the wrist. This is one of Character Studio's great time savers.

9. Click the Scale transform in the main toolbar. The reference coordinate system automatically switches to Local and grays out as shown here to indicate that the parameter cannot be altered. All Scale transforms applied to biped components must be applied in the Local Reference coordinate system.

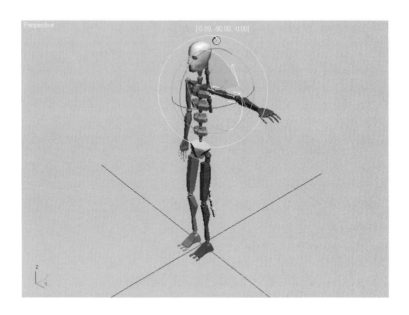

10. Click and drag the *X*-, *Y*-, and *Z*-axis handles of the Scale Transform gizmo individually, as shown in Figure 9.8. The Y and Z handles make the upper arm large or small, causing your biped to bulk up or thin out. Dragging the X handle changes the length of the upper arm. For the best reference, you should observe the changes in all of the viewports while you're adjusting the scale.

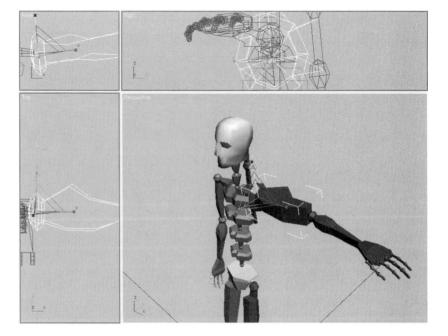

11. Select and adjust the left lower arm, hand, and fingers to suit yourself. Don't worry about the right side yet; we will discuss that shortly.

12. Select each of the spine links and scale them to give your biped a nice, tapered torso. Dragging the X handle upward will scale the links vertically and push the elements above them upward, increasing the height of the biped. Scaling the top spine link in the positive Z-direction will push the clavicles and all other arm components outward, as shown in Figure 9.9. The clavicles are linked to the middle of the top spine link and can be protruded by that link. If necessary, scale the clavicle to extend beyond the top spine link.

Figure 9.9

Scaling the top spine link pushes the arms outward.

13. Select and scale the pelvis to spread the hips out further.

14. Similar to what you did in steps 11 and 12, use the Scale transform to adjust the scale of the biped's left upper and lower leg and foot to your liking (Figure 9.10).

As you can see, creating a biped is fairly simple. You simply click and drag to place the system, and drag to set the biped's height and proportionate size. You then adjust the parameters of the structure in the Motion panel. Finally, you position and adjust the size of each of the biped's components using the transforms to fit the needs of your intended character model.

Copying and Pasting Postures

Most characters are basically symmetrical, with some variations in their surface appearance to make them look less perfect and a bit more natural. Character Studio allows you to set the structure and form—called the *posture*—for elements on one side of a biped's

body and then paste those features to the elements on the other side. For instance, when the length, width, and pose of the left arm, hand, and fingers are tweaked to your satisfaction, you can paste the same dimensions and orientations to the relative components on the right side. You don't need to model the opposite side independently.

You can continue with the previous exercise or open CSBiped1.max from the Biped Scene Files folder on the companion CD to follow with these steps:

1. Select the biped and access Figure mode.

2. Double-click the left upper arm. Double-clicking an object selects that object as well as all the objects below it in the hierarchy. In this case, you are also selecting the lower arm, hand, and all finger joints when you double-click the upper arm (Figure 9.11).

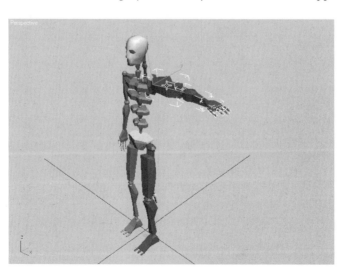

3. Open the Copy/Paste rollout.

4. Postures must be saved as collections prior to being pasted. Click the Create Collection button (shown here) and then rename the collection from the default Col01 to **Left Arm**.

5. Click the Copy Posture button just below the blue Posture button to copy the selected posture to the Clipboard. A preview of the copied posture will appear in the Copied Postures area of the Command panel, as shown here.

6. Click the Paste Posture Opposite button (shown here). The size, scale, and orientation of the selected objects will be applied to the reciprocal objects on the opposite side of the biped, as shown in Figure 9.12.

Copied postures are not limited to being pasted within a single biped; they can also be pasted to other bipeds. Simply copy the posture, select any part of another biped, and then click the Paste Posture button.

7. Repeat steps 2 through 6 to copy the posture of the left leg to the right side leg of the biped.

As you've seen in this section, modifying a biped's appearance and posture is pretty easy! You select any of the biped's components, use the Rotate and Scale transform tools, and change the components' size and orientation as needed for your character. In the "Associating a Biped to a Character" section later in this chapter, you will explore the procedures for fitting a biped to a specific model to ensure a smooth animation setup.

Now is a good time to save your scene before you proceed to the next section.

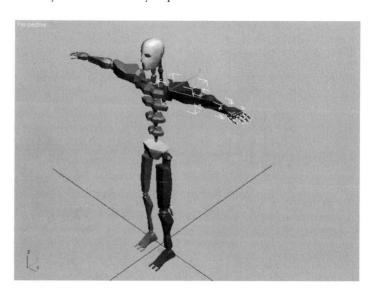

Figure 9.12

Pasting a posture to the other side of a biped

Animating a Biped

Bipeds can be animated in several ways, including footstep-driven animation and freeform animation. Just as it sounds, with *footstep-driven animation* you add visible Footstep objects to your scene and direct the biped to step onto those footsteps at particular points in time to suit your animation intent. Footsteps can be added individually or as a set of walk, run, or jump steps; they can be moved or rotated to achieve the desired result and direction. When using footstep-driven animation, the legs and feet of the biped are not the only things animated; the hips, arms, tails, and all other components are animated too. A short animation sequence can generate hundreds, or even thousands, of animation keys.

Footstep-driven animation is often a good starting point, but it is rarely the complete solution to your animation needs. For example, there is no method for turning a biped's head or raising its arms using footsteps.

Even when footsteps are used to create the initial movement of a biped, freeform animation must be used to augment and tweak the character's motion. Freeform animation is when you animate the components of the biped manually, as you would animate any other object, such as the bouncing ball. To refresh yourself, you can refer back to Chapter 8, "Introduction to Animation," which includes using the Auto Key method and the Track View in Curve Editor mode.

Animation keys that are added to the selected Biped objects appear in the track bar, just like other objects, where they can be moved, modified, or deleted to adjust the animation. Some character animators forgo footstep-driven animation altogether and use freeform animation exclusively. They enjoy the finer control freeform animation gives them when they create keys only where they choose and not throughout the automated footsteps. In this section, you will explore both the footstep-driven and freeform methods for animating a biped.

Moving the Biped into Place

As a system, bipeds can't be moved by using the Move transform in the main toolbar. To position a biped correctly, you must first select and move the root object using the Body Vertical and Body Horizontal buttons. We will go over this in the following steps.

Continue with the previous exercise or open CSBiped2.max from the Biped Scene Files folder on the companion CD. If you open the CD file, select the biped and enter Figure mode.

1. In the previous exercise, when you scaled either of the leg elements along the *X*-axis, the feet of the biped moved off the construction plane—or the Home Grid—as shown in Figure 9.13. The Home Grid (aka the construction plane) is where the new footsteps will be placed, so you will want the biped's feet to be at that elevation.

2. Maximize the Right viewport and zoom so that you can see the dark, horizontal line indicating the construction plane, the feet, and the pelvis. The pelvis isn't really important at this point, but the root object located inside of it is.

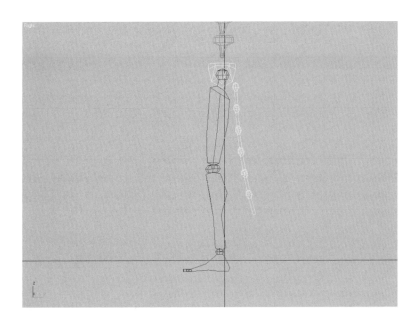

Figure 9.13

Keep track of the position as you scale.

3. In the Track Selection rollout, click the Body Vertical button. This selects the diamond-shaped Bip01 object, which is the root object of the hierarchy, and activates the Move Transform gizmo.

4. Use the Move Transform gizmo to move the biped until the feet rest on the Home Grid, as shown in Figure 9.14.

5. Switch back to a four-viewport display.

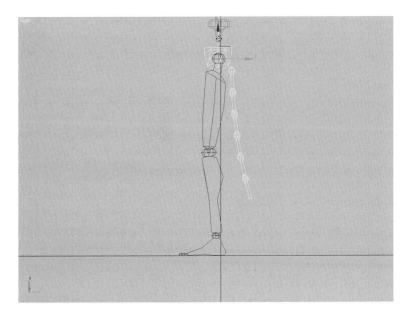

Figure 9.14

Moving the biped to the construction plane

Adding Footsteps

Adding footsteps is as simple as adding a specified number of steps with a particular gait, or clicking the mouse button to place footsteps individually. We'll try both methods in this chapter. First, let's begin by placing a series of footsteps. Here's how:

1. With the biped selected, click the Footstep Mode button in the Biped rollout, as shown here. The rollouts change to display the tools for adding and controlling a biped's motion. The Footstep mode and Figure mode are exclusive; you cannot be in both modes at the same time.

2. In the Footstep Creation rollout, make sure that the Walk gait is selected and then click the Create Multiple Footsteps button to open the Create Multiple Footsteps dialog box.

3. In the dialog box that appears, you will assign Footstep properties for the number of steps you want, the width and length of each step, and which foot to step with first. Set the number of footsteps to 8 and leave the other parameters at their default values, as shown in Figure 9.15. Click the OK button.

Figure 9.15

Creating multiple footsteps

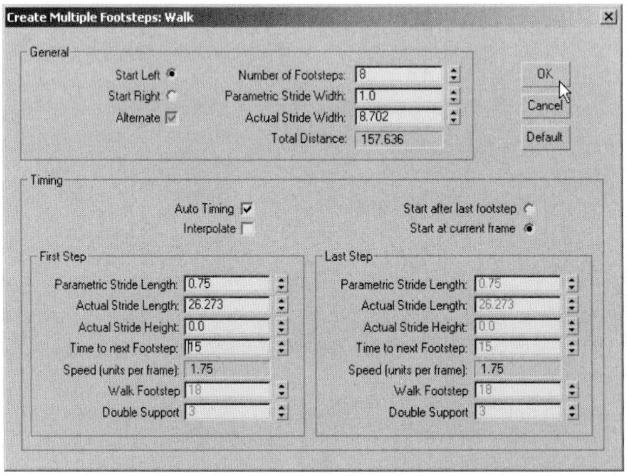

4. Zoom out in the Perspective viewport to see the footsteps you just created (Figure 9.16). Look at the Time slider, and note that the scene now ends at frame 123; that's 23 more frames than the 100 frames the scene had at the beginning of this chapter. 3ds Max

recognized that it would take the biped 123 frames, or just over 4 seconds, to move through the eight steps that it was given.

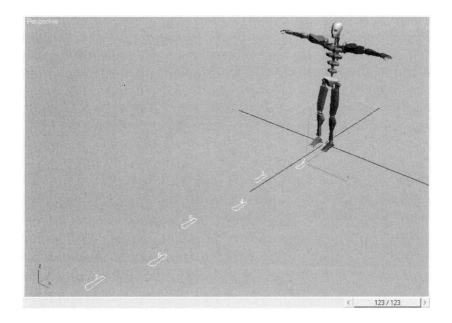

Figure 9.16

Zoom out to review the footsteps.

5. Click the Play Animation button (▶) in the Playback Controls area. What happens? Nothing. The biped must be told explicitly to create animation keys for the steps that you have just added to the scene. Drag the Time slider back to frame 0.

6. In the Footstep Operations rollout in the Command panel, click the Create Keys for Inactive Footsteps button shown here. The biped will drop its arms and prepare to walk through the footsteps that are now associated with it.

7. Click the Play Animation button again. This time the biped walks through the footsteps with its arms swinging and its tail swaying back and forth. Sweet!

Controlling the View

Now the problem is that the biped walks off the screen so you cannot see the end of the walk cycle. What good is that? Motion cycles can be very linear and difficult to track, so Character Studio contains the In Place mode to follow a biped's animation. While in the In Place mode, the biped will appear to stay in place while the scene moves around it in relation. The In Place mode cannot be used in a Camera viewport, however.

1. In the Biped rollout, click the Modes and Display text with the plus sign to the left of it, as shown here. This is actually a small rollout located inside of another rollout that expands to show additional display-related tools.

2. In the Modes and Displays rollout, click the In Place Mode button.

3. Click the Play Animation button again. This time the biped will appear to be walking in place while the footsteps move underneath it, as shown in Figure 9.17. Stop the animation playback when you're ready.

Figure 9.17

The biped does not change position in the viewport when it is in the In Place mode.

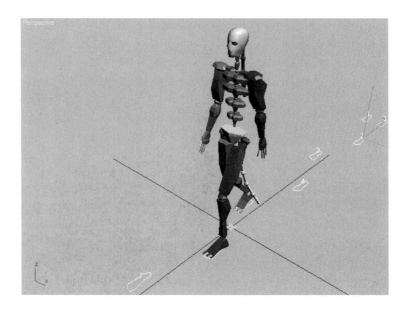

Using the In Place mode helps you work out the way a character moves without having to navigate throughout 3D space with your viewport; so you won't need to hunt down your biped. It is important to closely watch the cycle movement and try to finesse parts to suit the character, to make it the best animation you can.

The In Place mode is great for tweaking your animation cycle because the viewport moves with the character in 3D space and you can concentrate on how its body is moving.

WALK, RUN, OR JUMP?

What is the difference between a walk, run, or jump gait in 3ds Max? The difference is not speed or length of stride; it's the number of feet that the biped places on the ground at any given moment. In a walk gait, the biped has either one foot or both feet on the ground at all times. During a run sequence, the biped has either one foot on the ground or, in midstride, zero feet on the ground. When the biped is executing a jump sequence, it has either both feet on the ground or zero feet on the ground while it is airborne. You can use any of these gaits or mix and match them to begin your character's motion.

Adding a Run and Jump Sequence

Creating a footstep cycle does not limit you to these footsteps. Any extra footstep sequences can be added to a biped. These new footsteps are appended to any existing footsteps. This, in turn, extends the length of the animation, if necessary, to accommodate the additional footsteps. In the next exercise, you will add footsteps to the existing animation cycle.

Continue with the previous exercise or open CSBiped3.max from the Biped Scene Files folder on the companion CD, select any biped component, and access Footstep mode from the Motion panel.

1. Click the Run button ( ) in the Footstep Creation rollout. This will apply a run gait to any footsteps you will add to your current footsteps in the Create Multiple Footsteps dialog box.

2. Click the Create Multiple Footsteps button to open the Create Multiple Footsteps dialog box.

3. Change the number of footsteps to 10 and click the OK button.

4. In the Footstep Operations rollout, click the Create Keys for Inactive Footsteps button to associate the new footsteps with the biped.

5. Click the Play Animation button. The biped walks through the first 8 steps and then runs through the next 10. As you can see, the run sequence meets the definition of a run, but it is far from realistic. In the next section in this chapter, you'll learn how to add to or modify a biped's motion with freeform animation to make a better cycle.

6. Click the Jump button in the Footstep Creation rollout, and then click the Create Multiple Footsteps button.

7. In the Create Multiple Footsteps dialog box, set the number of footsteps to 4 and click the OK button. Because a jump is defined as a sequence with either two feet or zero feet on the ground at a time, four jump steps will equal two actual jumps.

8. Click the Create Keys for Inactive Footsteps button to associate the new jump footsteps with the biped.

9. Press the Play Animation button. The biped will walk, run, and then end the sequence with two jumps. If only it were this easy to control your kids.

> The Actual Stride Height parameter in the Create Multiple Footsteps dialog box determines the height difference from one footstep to the next. For example, to animate your biped walking up a flight of stairs, you would set the actual stride height to the same value as the riser height of each stair, so each footstep would correspond to a stair-step.

Adding Freeform Animation

Good animation rarely if ever comes from a first try. When you set your keys initially, you will need to edit them to suit good timing and form, as well as to fix any issues that may come up. Character animation is relational: When one part of the body is in one movement, another part of the body is in an accompanying or supportive or even opposite form of movement. When you are walking and your right leg swings forward in a step, your right arm swings back and your left arm swings out to compensate. With character work, you have to remain cognizant of the entire body of the character and how it moves.

As with everything that is automated, the walk, run, and jump cycles that CS creates definitely need some work before they will be acceptable as good animation; they definitely lack the human touch, which is the earmark of good animation. For example, based on a standard CS cycle, the biped's head never turns, the torso is very stiff, and the arms swing similarly regardless of the gait type selected. When animating using CS, you will need to add the little nuances of movement that make animation interesting and personable. You will need to add animation to the biped to gain personality. Luckily, you can easily add or modify the biped's existing animation keys with freeform animation using the Auto Key button and the Dope Sheet. The following exercises contain examples of freeform animation.

Moving the Head

Any character's head will move along while the character walks. The following steps will guide you through the process of creating head movement for your biped. Continue with the current project scene or open the CSBiped4.max file from the Biped Scene Files folder on the companion CD.

1. Select one of the biped's components and, if necessary, exit the Footstep mode by clicking the Footstep Mode button.

2. Drag the Time slider to frame 50, approximately the point when the biped lifts its left foot off of footstep number 2.

> Footsteps are numbered, starting with the number 0 and initially alternating from the left to the right side. They are also color-coded, corresponding to the biped, with blue footsteps on the left and green footsteps on the right.

3. Select the biped's head and note the animation keys that appear in the track bar, as shown in Figure 9.18.

4. In the track bar, select the two keys on either side of the current frame and delete them.

5. Click the Auto Key button (Auto Key) to turn it on.

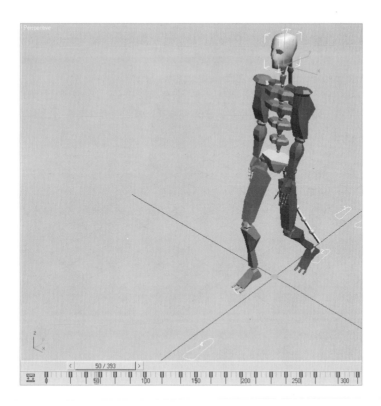

Figure 9.18

**Selecting a compo-
nent of the biped
reveals all of that
object's animation
keys in the track bar.**

6. Click the Rotate Transform button and rotate the head as shown here to the left and
   up, as if the character sees somebody in a second floor window offscreen. A new key
   will be created at frame 50, recording the time and value of the head's rotation.

7. Scrub the Time slider back and forth. Watch the head rotate from a neutral position
   to the orientation that you created and then rotate back to the neutral position.

8. Select all the keys between frame 50 and frame 100 (but not keys at frames 50 and 100).
   Delete them by pressing the Delete key. This will make room for the new key that
   you are about to create. If animation keys are too close together, the animation could
   appear jerky.

9. Select the key at frame 50, hold the Shift key down, and drag a copy of the key to
   frame 90 as shown here. Use the readout at the bottom of the 3ds Max window to
   drag the key with precision. Copying the key will cause your biped to hold that neck
   pose for 40 frames or about one and one-third seconds. Scrub the Time slider to
   review the animation.

10. Select the biped's left upper arm.

11. In the track bar, select and delete all keys between frames 50 and 100. The animation keys for the arms define their swing motion and the biped walks. If you scrub the Time slider or play the animation, the biped will hold its arm unnaturally stiffly for 60 frames because you deleted the animation keys between two points where it holds its hand forward. That's OK; we're just making room for some new keys.

12. Move the Time slider to frame 60. This is the location for the first new animation key.

Moving the Arms

Now it's time to animate the arms, which are essential components in any walk cycle. To do so, follow these steps:

1. Rotate the upper arm upward, so that it points to the same location at which the head is looking.

2. Continue adjusting the biped's left arm, hand, and fingers until they appear to be pointing at something, as shown in Figure 9.19.

3. Double-click on the left upper arm to select it and all of the components below it in the hierarchy.

4. In the track bar, select the key at frame 60, hold the Shift key down, and drag it to frame 85 to create a copy of that key.

5. Drag the Time slider and watch the Perspective viewport. The biped will walk for bit, notice something off-screen, point at it, and drop its arm while looking forward again before breaking into a run and then a jump.

6. Click the Auto Key button to turn it off.

Figure 9.19

Rotate the biped's arm, hand, and fingers to assume a pointing posture.

Completing the Motion Sequence

The CSBiped5.max file on the Biped Scene Files folder on the companion CD contains the completed scene to this point.

For additional practice, add keys to the animation of the biped's arms when it jogs through the run cycle. For example, when the left foot is fully extended and the heel plants on the ground, the right arm should be bent at the elbow and swung forward and slightly in front of the biped's body. As the right foot swings forward during the next step, the right arm should swing backward and assume a nearly straight posture. Bend each of the spine links and swing both arms backward to prepare the biped for each of the jumps. Use the Body Vertical button in the Track Selection rollout to lower the pelvis into a pre-launch position, as shown in Figure 9.20, before the biped launches into its upward motion. Remember to make sure the Auto Key button is turned on to record all the changes that you make as animation keys.

Modifying Animation in the Dope Sheet

What if you need to change the animation that is generated with CS? To that end, you will need to edit the keyframes of the biped once you are happy with the base animation cycle. For this, you need to use the Track View–Dope Sheet. The Track View–Curve Editor, as you have already seen, is used to edit the function curves between animation keys; however, the Track View–Dope Sheet interface is cleaner and is used to edit the specific value and position of the keys. It is not a different set of keyframes or animation; it's just a different way of editing them. Furthermore, access to editing the footstep keys is available only in the Dope Sheet. In this exercise, you will add individual footsteps and modify the footstep timing in the Dope Sheet to make the biped dance and jump.

Figure 9.20

Use the Body Vertical button to position the biped for a jump.

Control of footstep animation is not available in the Track–View Curve Editor. You can, however, convert footstep animation to freeform animation using the Convert button ( ) in the Biped rollout. All existing animation will be retained, but the footstep-driven feature will be replaced by simple function curves that can be edited in the Curve Editor.

Adding Footsteps Manually

With the following steps, you will manually add footsteps to your biped character:

Create a new scene with a biped or open CSBiped6.max from the Biped Scene Files folder on the companion CD. This is a biped with no footsteps applied.

1. Enter the Footstep mode.

2. In the Footstep Creation rollout, click the Walk Gait button and then the Create Footsteps (at current frame) button as shown here.

3. In the Top viewport, click in several locations to place alternating left and right footsteps to your liking.

4. Change the gait to Jump, and then click the Create Footsteps (Append) button (shown here) to create additional footsteps. Create about 12 footsteps in all.

5. When you are done, use the Move and Rotate transforms to adjust the footstep locations and orientations as desired. Your Top viewport should look similar to Figure 9.21.

6. In the Footstep Operations rollout, click the Create Keys for Inactive Footsteps button and then play the animation.

Figure 9.21

Manually place the footsteps in the Top viewport.

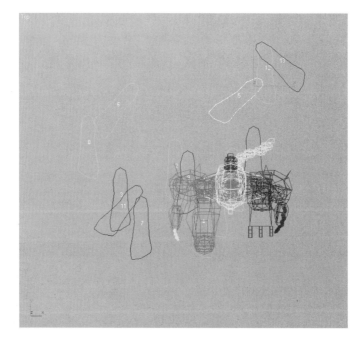

7. Character Studio doesn't have a collision detection feature, so it is very possible that limbs will pass through one another, which is quite uncomfortable in real life. If this happens, the footsteps must be modified to eliminate these conditions. If necessary, move any footsteps that cause collisions or other unwanted conditions during the playback.

Using the Dope Sheet

In Chapter 8, you experimented with the Track View–Curve Editor and learned how to adjust the values of animation keyframes while observing the values between keyframes displayed as a function curve. When the Track View is in Dope Sheet mode, frames are displayed as individual blocks of time that may or may not contain keys. Although you cannot see the flow from key to key that the Curve Editor displays with its curves, the Dope Sheet mode has its advantages. For one the Dope Sheet has the ability to add Visibility tracks to control the display of an object as well as Note tracks for adding text information regarding the keys. Notes are helpful when you are working with other animators, or even when you want to remind yourself of something later on regarding that animation.

Using the Track View–Dope Sheet, you can adjust the point in time when a foot plants on or lifts off the ground, how long the foot is on the ground, and how long the foot is airborne. Rather than appearing as single-frame blocks in the Dope Sheet, like other keys do, footstep keys appear as multiframe rectangles that identify each foot's impact time with the footstep. Let's try the Dope Sheet on for size here:

1. Exit the Footstep mode.

2. In the main toolbar, choose Graph Editors → Track View → Dope Sheet. The Dope Sheet will open.

3. In the Navigation pane on the left, scroll down until you find the Bip01 entry. Expand the Bip01 and Bip01 Footsteps entries. The footstep keys appear as rectangles in the Key pane. As expected, the left keys are colored blue and the right keys are colored green. If necessary, click the Zoom Region button (🔍) in the lower-right corner of the Dope Sheet window and drag a zoom window around the footstep keys, as shown in Figure 9.22. The region will expand to fit the key pane.

Figure 9.22

Zoom to the Footstep keys.

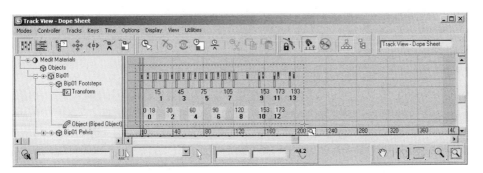

4. Select a few Footstep keys in the Navigation pane (the panel on the left).

The white dot on the left side of a selected key identifies the frame when the heel of the biped's foot first impacts the footstep. Similarly, the white dot on the right side of a selected key identifies when the biped's foot lifts off a footstep (Figure 9.23). A blue key overlapping a green key indicates that both feet are on the ground. A vertical gray area with no footstep indicates that the biped is airborne and neither foot is on the ground.

Figure 9.23

The dots indicate when contact begins and ends. You can drag a dot to change the duration of contact.

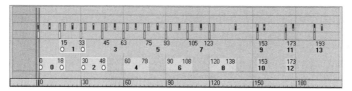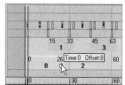

5. Select the first key (numbered 0), place the cursor over the right-side white dot (as shown in the second image in Figure 9.23), then drag the dot to the right to extend the length of time that the biped's foot is on the ground.

You can't move the end of one footstep key beyond the beginning of another one, and you must maintain a one-frame gap between same-side footsteps. You can't move a key to a point in time beyond the active time segment nor can you modify keys for footsteps that have been created, but not yet associated to the biped. In addition, footsteps must be at least two frames long.

Figure 9.24

Drag the Time slider until the biped is airborne.

6. The double vertical line in the Dope Sheet's key pane is another Time slider that allows you to scrub through the animation. Drag the Dope Sheet's Time slider to a point in time when the biped is airborne, as shown in Figure 9.24. Scrub the Time slider, and the foot will remain planted on the ground and then quickly move to the next footstep. The shorter the gap between footstep keys, the faster the movement between them.

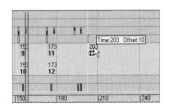

Figure 9.25

Create a key gap to get your biped airborne.

A biped's airborne time is calculated using the standard physics values for acceleration due to gravity: 32 ft/s² or 9.8 m/s².The biped does not simply hover at a user-defined altitude by moving it in the Z-axis and setting a key, as you would do with most other 3ds Max objects. Therefore, increasing the airborne time by increasing the gap between footsteps will boost the height to which the biped rises, acting against the gravitational force pushing it downward.

7. Select the next-to-last Footstep key and drag it to the right to create a gap approximately 30 frames wide between any frames, as shown in Figure 9.25. This will cause the biped to be airborne for about one second.

It is possible to move a footstep beyond the limits of the active time segment in the Dope Sheet. For example, in a 100-frame animation, you can move the last footstep to start at frame 105 and end at frame 123. When you play the animation, it will begin to loop at frame 100, and you will never see the animation created by the last keys. Use the Alt+R key combination to extend the active time segment to include all existing keys.

8. Move the Time slider to the frame when both feet are planted before the jump starts. Turn on the Auto Key button.

9. To prepare the biped to leap, select the Bip01 object and move it downward, causing the biped to bend its knees more. Rotate the spine links, neck, and head to bend the torso forward and tuck the chin. Rotate both arms backward into a pre-jump posture, as shown in Figure 9.26. Be sure to choose Local as the reference coordinate system for the Rotate transform.

10. Move the Time slider forward until the biped is at the apex of the jump. Rotate the biped's components into positions you like, such as the split shown in Figure 9.27. Delete any animation keys that may interfere with your desired motion.

The CSBiped7.max file on the Biped Scene Files folder on the companion CD contains the completed exercise so you can check your work.

As you saw in this section, there are several ways to animate a biped including the footstep-driven method, the freeform method, and a combination of techniques. You can also modify the animation in the track bar, with the Auto Key button, and with the Track View–Dope Sheet Editor. The next section addresses the methods for associating your biped to a 3D model, aka skinning.

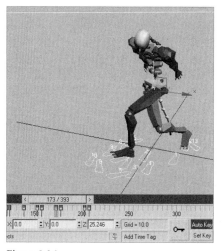

Figure 9.26

Prepare your biped to jump!

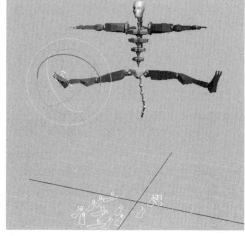

Figure 9.27

Position your biped in mid-jump.

Associating a Biped to a Character

The purpose of a biped is to be the portal through which you add animation to your model, rather than animating the model itself using direct vertex manipulation or deforming modifiers. Any motion assigned to a biped is passed through it to the nearest vertices of the associated model, essentially driving the surfaces of the model. For this reason, it is important that the biped fit as closely as possible to the model.

Creating and Modifying the Biped

In the following steps, you'll create and adjust a biped to fit to a character model. You can open the CSAlien.max file from the Biped Scene Files folder on the companion CD. It contains a completed alien model in the reference position:

1. With the alien model file open, select all of the model's components, right-click in a viewport and choose Freeze Selection. This will prevent you from inadvertently selecting the alien instead of the biped.

2. Create a biped with a height about the same as the alien's. This will size most of the biped's parts similar to those of the alien already, as shown in Figure 9.28.

3. With the biped still selected, click the Motion tab of the Command panel and enter Figure mode. Changes to the biped's features or pose must be made in Figure mode to be retained by the system.

4. Use the Body Vertical and Body Horizontal buttons in the Track Selection rollout and the Move Transform gizmo to position the biped's pelvis in the same location as the

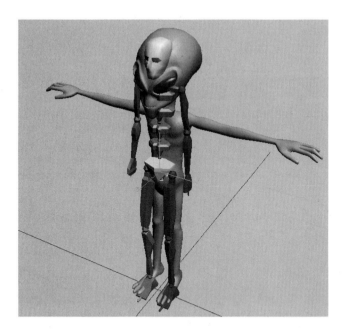

Figure 9.28

Create a biped about the same height as the alien model.

model's pelvis, as shown in Figure 9.29. With the pelvis located properly, scaling the legs or spine to match the model's proportions will be much easier. Check to make sure the location is correct in all of the viewports.

As you did in a previous exercise, you will modify one side of the biped to fit the model and then paste that posture to the other side.

5. In the Front viewport, select the pelvis and scale its width so that the biped's legs fit inside the alien's legs. Scale the pelvis in the Right viewport so that it roughly encompasses the alien's lower region. See Figure 9.30.

VIEWING FROZEN OBJECTS

If your background color is similar to the default shade of gray that Max uses to depict frozen objects, the model may seem to disappear against the background. There are several solutions to this situation:

1. You can go to Object Properties, turn off Show Frozen as Gray, turn on See-through, and set all viewports to Smooth + Highlights mode.

2. You can change the shaded color in the Customize User Interface dialog box (Customize → Customize User Interface → Colors).

3. You can change the viewport background color in the Customize User Interface dialog box (Customize → Customize User Interface → Colors).

Figure 9.29

Match the positions of the biped pelvis and the model pelvis.

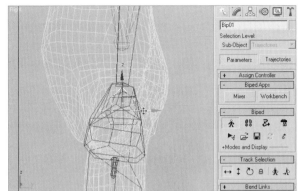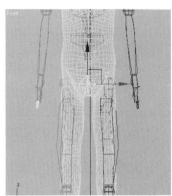

Figure 9.30

Scale the pelvis to fit.

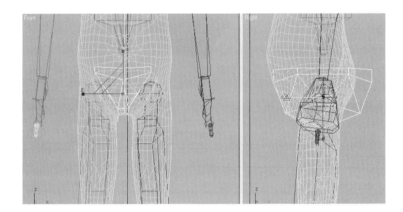

6. Select the biped's left upper leg, and then scale it along the *X*-axis until the knee aligns with the alien's knee. Scale it in the *Y*- and *Z*-axes until it is similar in size to the alien's thigh, as shown in Figure 9.31.

Figure 9.31

Scale the length, width, and depth of the biped's upper leg to match the alien's thigh.

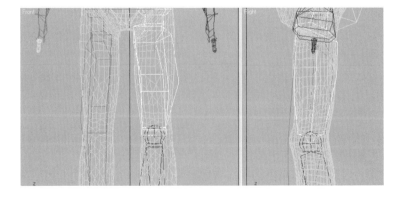

7. Select the biped's left calf. In the Right viewport, rotate the calf to match the model and then scale it in the *X*-axis until the biped's ankle matches the alien's ankle. You may need to select the left foot and use the Move transform, in the Front viewport, to orient the calf to the model. Scale the calf to match the proportions of the alien's calf.

> Modifying a biped to match a model can be a time-consuming task that requires continual tweaking and modification. Moving the foot as described in the previous step may require that the upper leg's proportions be readdressed. Don't expect to perform this task quickly without making any revisions to components on which you have previously worked. The better the biped matches the model now, the easier the animation will be later.

8. Continue working down the leg by scaling the biped's foot to match the alien's. Be sure to check the orientation of the foot in the Top viewport. In the Structure rollout, use the Ankle Attach parameter to move the biped's ankle slightly backward, as shown in Figure 9.32.

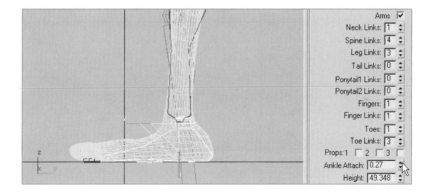

Figure 9.32

Increasing the Ankle Attach parameter to move the ankle

9. In the Structure rollout, change the number of toes to 3 and toe links to 2.

10. Scale and move the biped's toes to match the model's. Be sure to select the first toe link and use the Local Transform coordinate system to move the toes, as shown in Figure 9.33.

11. Double-click the left upper leg to select it and all of the objects below it in the hierarchy. Create a collection and then copy/paste the posture of the left leg to the right as you did in the Copy and Paste Postures section in this chapter. The model is not perfectly symmetrical; make any necessary changes to the right side of the biped.

Figure 9.33

**Match the model
and biped toes.**

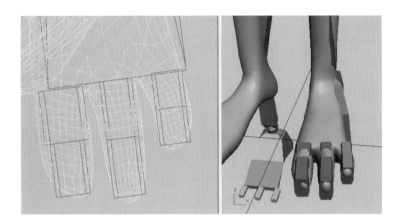

Adjusting the Torso and Arms

Similar to the method used to adjust the legs, you will use the Scale and Rotate transforms to fit the biped to the model. The locations of the arms rely on the scale of the spine links. You can continue with your file from the previous exercise or open CSAlien2.max from the Biped Scene Files folder on the companion CD

1. In your scene (or the one from the CD), select the biped, and then access Figure mode, if you need to.

2. Select each of the spine links in turn, and then rotate and scale them to fit the alien's torso. Only the lowest spine link can be moved, and this will move all of the links above it as well. Each spine link should be scaled down slightly in the *X*-axis to lower the biped's clavicles to match the model's, as shown in Figure 9.34.

3. Move, rotate, and scale the left clavicle as required to place the biped's shoulder socket in the proper location.

4. Scale and rotate the left upper arm and left forearm using the same techniques you used to adjust the biped's legs.

Figure 9.34

**Match the biped's
clavicles to the
model**

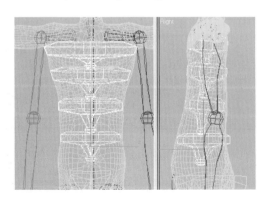

5. Scale and rotate the left hand as required to fit the model, as shown in Figure 9.35.

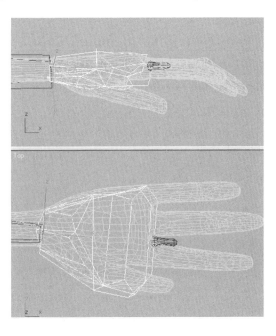

Figure 9.35
Adjust the hand to fit the model

6. In the Structure rollout, increase the number of fingers to 4 and finger links to 2.

Once the fingers have been adjusted, you cannot go back and change the number of fingers or finger links. If you do, all modifications to the fingers will be lost.

7. Adjust the biped's fingers to match the model's fingers, as shown in Figure 9.36. This can be one of the more tedious tasks in character animation, depending on the complexity and orientation of the model's fingers. Take your time and get it right. (Would you rather do it right or do it over?)

8. When you are done, paste the posture to the right side of the biped and make any required changes.

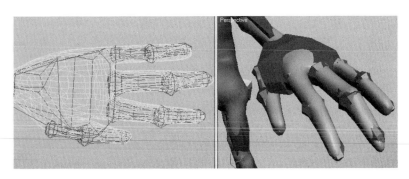

Figure 9.36
Match the biped to the model's fingers

Adjusting the Neck and Head

The head and neck will seem easy to adjust when compared to the hands. You need to make sure the neck links fill the alien's neck area and scale the head to fit. Follow along here:

1. In the Structure rollout, increase the number of neck links to 2.

2. Move, scale, and rotate the neck links to match the proportions of the model's neck, as shown in Figure 9.37.

Figure 9.37

Adjust the neck links to match the model's neck

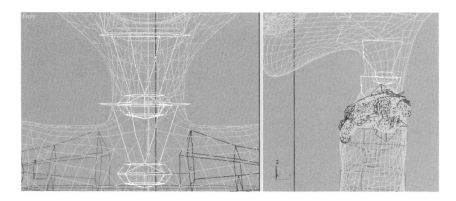

3. Move and scale the head to the approximate size of the alien's head, as shown in Figure 9.38.

Figure 9.38

Matching the head

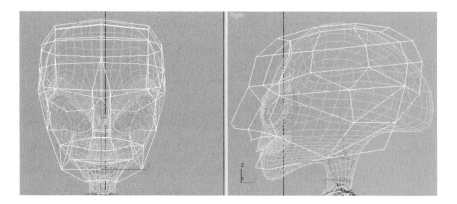

That's it. The biped has been created and adjusted to fit the 3D model, and half the battle is over. In the next section, you will tie the biped to the model and make adjustments to the skinning process. Now would be a good time to save your work and have some lemonade. Just don't spill it on your computer.

Applying the Physique Modifier

The Physique modifier is the tool used to skin the 3D model to the biped so that all of the biped's animation is passed through to the model. It's important to remember that the modifier is applied to the model and not to the biped. Continue with the previous exercise or open CSAlien3.max from the Biped Scene Files folder on the companion CD to follow these steps:

1. Right-click in any viewport and select Unfreeze All from the Quad menu to unfreeze the alien model, as shown here.

2. Select all three of the alien components: the body and both eyes.

3. In the Named Selection Sets field in the main toolbar, enter the name **Alien** to save the alien meshes as a named selection set, as shown here. This makes it easier to select all the components for the alien in one fell swoop by selecting its name from the drop-down list on the main toolbar.

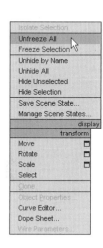

> By creating named selection sets, you can quickly access all of the desired components by selecting the named selection set from the drop-down list on the main toolbar. For reference, see Chapter 3, "The 3ds Max Interface," for the icons and functions of the named selection sets.

4. Repeat the Named Selection Sets process for the biped by selecting all of the biped's components and naming the selection set **Alien Biped.**

5. Select the Alien selection set from the main toolbar drop-down and click the Modify tab of the Command panel.

6. Expand the Modifier List and select the Physique modifier, as shown here.

7. In the Physique rollout, click the Attach to Node button (). The button will turn yellow and wait for you to identify the root object in the hierarchy that controls the mesh.

8. Press the H key to open the Pick Object dialog box. This method will be easier than trying to click on the object directly in a cluttered scene. Select the Bip01 Pelvis object and click the Pick button, as shown in Figure 9.39.

9. In the Physique Initialization dialog box, accept the defaults and click the Initialize button. The cursor will briefly turn into a coffee cup to indicate that the initialization is in progress. It will return to normal when the process is complete.

Figure 9.39

Use the Pick Object dialog box to select the root object in a cluttered scene.

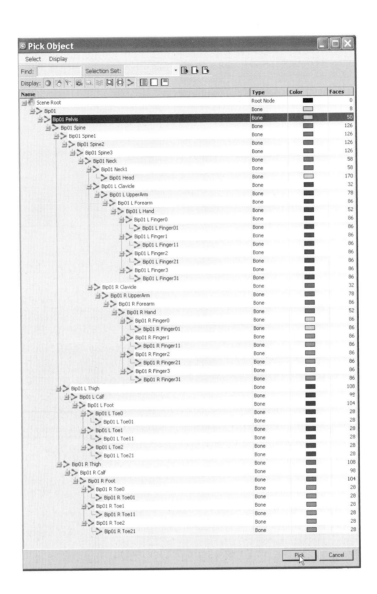

Testing the Model

The most time-consuming part of the process is complete. You have created a biped, adjusted all of its component parts to fit your model, and applied the Physique modifier to link the model to the biped. The final step is to test the model by adding animation such as with the following:

1. Select any element of the biped and click the Motion tab of the Command panel.

2. Enter Footstep mode.

3. Add a footstep sequence as you did in the "Animating a Biped" section of this chapter. Don't forget to create keys for the inactive footsteps. Exit the Footstep mode when you are done.

4. Activate the In Place mode, and then zoom and pan the Perspective viewport to get a good view of the action.

5. To select the entire biped, select the Alien Biped named selection set from the drop-down list on the main toolbar.

6. Right-click in any viewport and choose Hide Selection from the Quad menu to hide the biped and obtain an unobstructed view of the model.

7. Click the Play Animation button. Your alien will walk through the scene. It should be similar to the rendered alien shown in Figure 9.40.

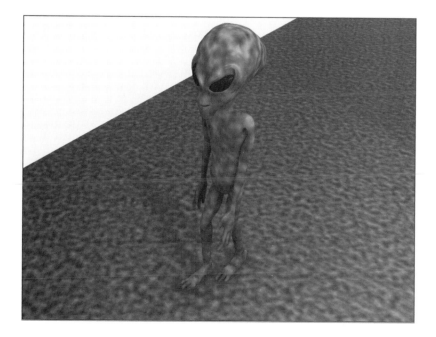

Figure 9.40

The rendered alien during a walk cycle

The completed Character Studio Alien exercise can be found in the CS Alien Complete .max file on the Biped Scene Files folder on the companion CD.

As we mentioned at the beginning of the chapter, Character Studio is a very complete character animation package, and we've barely scratched the surface here. There are tools for saving biped configurations and sequences of animation. You can mix animation sequences from different files to create an entirely new motion. When the model does not skin as well as you need, you can use envelopes to refine the skinning process further, define vertices to be excluded from a specific biped object's influence, or include bulge conditions to define the model's behavior depending on the angle between subsequent biped elements. The list goes on, but the good news is that the CS tutorials and help system that ship with 3ds Max are very thorough and you should find the information in those places to expand your Character Studio skills once you have a solid footing with the basics of CS. It's important to realize that animation requires nuance, and the best animation with the simplest rig and setup will beat a mediocre animation created with the more wonderful, complicated, ingenious setup.

Using Inverse Kinematics

When a hierarchy is set up through linking, the result is a kinematic chain. As you saw in Chapter 2, "Your First Max Animation," transforms are passed from a parent object to all of the children objects down the chain. Imagine your arm is a system of linked 3ds Max objects; when you pivot your forearm (the parent) at the elbow, your hand (the child) and your fingers (the descendants) are also transformed to maintain the relationship between the objects. This is known as Forward Kinematics (FK) and is the default method of passing transforms in a hierarchy.

When Inverse Kinematics (IK) is used, the child object is transformed while the parent and ancestor objects maintain their relationships throughout the chain. Using the same arm analogy, lifting your arm by grabbing and pulling up on a finger would raise the hand, which would raise the forearm, causing a curl at the elbow. With IK, the end of the chain, the child, is positioned in your animation and rest of the chain upstream rotates and pivots to fit the new layout of the chain to achieve a possible pose. IK setups require the use of an IK solver to determine how the parent objects react to the child transforms and joint constraints to prevent unnecessary twists in the motion.

In the following exercise, we will play some more with toys of war by linking a machine gun mounted on a tank model. Here, the goal is to arrange the IK setup so that the gun pivots vertically at the joints only and then pivots at the turret.

Linking the Objects

The machine gun unit consists of the gun itself, two two-component pivot assemblies, two shafts, and the turret ring. The gun is at the top of the hierarchy, and the turret is at the bottom.

1. Open the IKGun1.max file from the Biped Scene Files folder on the companion CD.

2. Begin by linking the Gun object to the PivotTop object, the cylindrical object near the gun. The PivotTop object will flash briefly to signify that is has been linked. If you are having difficulty selecting the proper object directly, press the H key to open the Select Parent dialog box.

3. Continue creating the hierarchy by also linking the PivotTopRing to PivotTop, PivotTop to Shaft1, and then Shaft1 to PivotBottom.

4. Complete the setup by linking PivotBottomRing to PivotBottom, PivotBottom to Shaft2, and Shaft2 to Turret. If you open the Select From Scene dialog box and make sure the Display Subtree is checked, you hierarchy will look like Figure 9.41.

Figure 9.41

The Select From Scene dialog box showing the hierarchy

Creating Joint Constraints

The gun assembly should only be able to rotate in certain ways. The gun itself should only pivot perpendicular to the PivotTop object, for example. This is accomplished by constraining the Rotate transform for the PivotTop object, the parent of the gun, to a single axis. The transforms can further be restricted by limiting the range of motion an object can rotate within an acceptable axis. This method is used to prevent the gun barrel from rotating to the point where it disappears within the tank body. Both of these tasks are accomplished under the Hierarchy tab of the Command panels, as you will see in the following steps:

1. In the Command panel, click the Hierarchy tab (![icon]).

2. Click the IK button and then, in the Inverse Kinematics rollout, click the Interactive IK button, as shown here. The IK button will turn yellow to signify which family of rollouts is displayed. The Interactive IK button will turn blue to indicate that this feature is active and any transforms applied to objects in the hierarchy are applied in IK mode.

3. In the Perspective viewport, select and move the Gun object along the X-axis. The gun's orientation changes and all of the hierarchy elements, including the turret, change to maintain the connection, but they all rotate oddly. This is because the orientation at the joints is not constrained to a single axis or limit of degrees.

Figure 9.42

Drag the To spinner to –40

4. Undo any transforms that were applied.

5. Select the PivotTop object. In the Rotational Joints rollout, uncheck the X Axis and Z Axis Active check boxes.

6. Check the Limited check box in the *Y*-axis section. Increase the From parameter to approximately –65 by dragging the spinners. The Pivot and its children will rotate in the viewport and then snap back to their original orientations when the mouse is released. Drag the To spinner to approximately –40, as shown in Figure 9.42. Limiting the orientation restricts how far the object can rotate in a particular axis, and dragging the spinners instead of typing in the values gives visual feedback regarding the axis about which the object is rotating.

7. Select Shaft1 and uncheck the Active option for the the *X*-, *Y*-, and *Z*-axes in the Rotational Joints rollout. Repeat the process for the Shaft2 and Gun objects. None of these objects needs to rotate on their own; they just need to follow their parent objects.

8. Select the PivotBottom object. Check the Active and Limited options in the *Y*-axis area. Set the From value to –4 and the To value to 30. Uncheck the *X*-axis and *Z*-axis Active options.

9. Select the Turret object. Only the *Z*-axis option should be checked so the Turret can only rotate laterally and not flip over. Do not check the Limited option; the Turret should be able to rotate freely.

10. In the Object Parameters rollout, check the Terminator option to identify the Turret as the top object in the IK structure, as shown here.

11. Select the Gun object and then click the Link Info button at the top of the Hierarchy panel. In the Rotate section of the Locks rollout, check the X option, as shown here. The Gun should now not rotate in any axis except the local *X*-axis.

12. As shown here, select the Turret object and check the *X*-, *Y*-, and *Z*-options in the Move section, to lock any movement for the Turret. The turret should be fixed in place. In a complete 3ds Max scene, the Turret would be linked to a larger structure to define its transforms.

13. Click the IK button at the top of the Hierarchy panel, and then click the Interactive IK button again to turn it on if necessary. Test your IK chain by moving the gun. As it moves, the other objects in the chain will reorient to maintain the proper relationships with their parent objects. Turn off the Interactive IK button when you are done.

Applying the IK Solver

An IK solver calculates the controls required to position and orient the members of an IK chain when one or more members is moved or rotated. The IK solver defines the top of the chain and identifies the goal, or the base of the chain. The IK solver precludes the need to activate the Interactive IK mode in the Hierarchy panel whenever IK is required.

The two appropriate IK solvers for this situation are the HI (History Independent) solver and the HD (History Dependent) solver. The HI solver is better suited for long animation sequences and character animation, and the HD solver is better suited for machine animation. Because the goal for this animation for this setup is for a machine, in this case a tank, the HD solver will be used here.

Continue with the previous exercise or open the IKGun2.max file from the Biped Scene Files folder on the companion CD.

1. Undo any transforms that were applied in your own scene during the previous exercise if necessary. You can undo a string of commands easily by right-clicking the Undo button in the main toolbar.

> Right-click the Undo button in the main toolbar to see a list of the recent changes to the scene, with the most recent changes at the top of the list. Click on the entry in the list that defines the last command that you want undone. That command and all of the commands above it will highlight. Press the Enter key to undo all the selected commands.

2. Choose Edit → Hold from the main menu. A few IK operations, including applying an IK solver, are not always undoable through the Undo command. If the result of the IK solve is not correct, choose Edit → Fetch to restore your scene to the point just before you executed the Edit → Hold.

3. Turn off Interactive IK.

4. Select the Gun and choose Animation → IK Solvers → HD Solver. A rubber band line will stretch from the gun's pivot point to the cursor, as you can see in Figure 9.43. Place the cursor over the Shaft2 object and click to define it as the end of the IK chain. The IK chain should now be bound to the object that has been designated as the Terminator.

> When the cursor is moved over the other viewports while an IK solver is being assigned, the view will update to show the rubber banding line projecting from the object to the cursor in that particular viewport. The viewport does not have to be the active viewport for this viewport change to occur.

Figure 9.43

A line stretches from
the gun's pivot to
the cursor

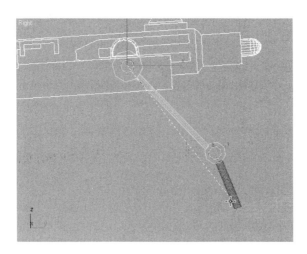

5. The End Effector acts as the pivot point of the Terminator object and can be used to straighten out the chain without actually moving the child object. On the Motion panel, in the IK Controller Parameters rollout, click the Link button in the End Effectors area and then click on the Turret. Turret appears in the End Effector Parent field.

6. Select the Gun and use the Move Transform to test your IK setup. Moving the Gun forward, backward, up, or down will now cause the two pivots to rotate within their limits.

The HD solver's IK components are not listed in the Select Objects dialog box because they act on behalf of the objects to which they are assigned. To modify any of its properties, select the object and open the Motion panel of the Command panels. The IK Controller Properties rollout contains the options for modifying the IK chain.

Summary

This chapter introduced you to two powerful tools for reducing the time and effort required to animate objects and characters. Character Studio is a fantastic tool that speeds up the process of character animation. Using the Biped system, you can quickly create and adjust the substructure that controls a 3D model. Once the Physique modifier associates or skins the model to the biped, character animation can be added using footstep-driven or freeform animation.

IK is used throughout mechanical design and character animation, and it is another 3ds Max tool that you may find invaluable once its workflow becomes second nature to you. The exercises in this chapter examined the basics of an IK setup and the basic use of an IK solver for a mechanical animation of the tank. The IK setups can include several IK chains controlling the transforms for different components of the same model. Easily selected controls can be placed in the scene for simple selection and manipulation of a complex model's components. IK can also be used for organic character animation, because 3ds Max has different types of IK for character work as well (such as the HI IK or Limb Solver IK). This chapter covered only one type of IK (using the HD solver) for a simple use of IK. Most practical applications will use the HI system; however, for the purposes of this book, familiarizing you with the simpler HD solver primes you for further study in 3ds Max IK systems.

CHAPTER 10

3ds Max Lighting

Light is everything. By light we see, and by light we show. Light shapes the world around us and defines shape, color, and texture. Computer graphics hang on every word light has to whisper. Without faithful lighting, any good computer graphic will fall to its knees and fail. Lighting is the most important aspect of CG, and it just simply cannot be mastered at a snap of the fingers. The trick to correctly lighting a CG is understanding how light works and seeing the visual nuances it has to offer.

In this chapter, you will study the various tools used to light in 3ds Max. This chapter will serve as a primer to this most important aspect of CG. It will start you on the path by showing you the tools available and giving you opportunities to begin using them.

Topics in this chapter include:

- **Basic Lighting Concepts**

- **Three-Point Lighting**

- **3ds Max Lights**

- **Common Light Parameters**

- **Ambient Light**

- **Lighting the Red Rocket**

- **Creating Shadows**

- **Atmospheres and Effects**

- **Light Lister**

Basic Lighting Concepts

On a conceptual level, the lighting in 3ds Max mimics the real-world direct-lighting techniques used in photography and filmmaking. Lights of various types are placed around a scene to illuminate the subjects as they would for a still life or a portrait. Your scene and what's in it dictate, to some degree at least, which lights you put where. A number of considerations must be kept in mind when settling on a methodology and light types for CG, but the overall concept of lighting is strikingly similar between a real-world set lighting and CG.

At the basic level, you want your lights to illuminate the scene. Without lights, your cameras have nothing to capture. Although it seems rather easy to throw your lights in, turn them all on, and render the scene, that couldn't be further from the truth.

Lighting is the backbone of CG. Although it is technically easy to insert and configure lights, it is *how* you light that will make or break your scene. That skill really only comes with a good deal of experience and experimentation, and it requires a good eye and some patience.

In this chapter, you will learn the basic procedures for lighting a scene in 3ds Max. No single chapter could explain everything about lighting, and no beginner or intermediate CG student should expect to quickly master the art of lighting CG. In short, lighting touches every single aspect of the CG pipeline. A strong *lighter* understands modeling form and is able to make adjustments to enable efficient lighting. Lighters understand motion and how to light for it. They understand textures and materials, and they frequently are tasked with creating or adjusting materials to work perfectly with their lights. Strong lighters are also rendering experts. When it's time to render, they must know what is and is not doable in a scene. They must diagnose problems and overcome obstacles to make sure every frame is rendered faithfully and with artistic merit.

Develop Your Eye

As corny as it sounds, to be an artist, you must learn to see. This is especially true for CG lighting. There are so many nuances to the real-world lighting around us that we take them for granted. We intuitively understand what we see and how it's lit, and we infer a tremendous amount of visual information without much consideration. With CG lighting, you must re-create these nuances for your scene. That amounts to the work of lighting.

The most valuable thing you can do to improve your lighting technique is to relearn how you see your environment. Simply put, you must refuse to take for granted what you see. If you question why things look the way they do, you'll find that the answers almost always come around to lighting.

Take note of the distinction between light and dark in the room you're in now. Notice the difference in the brightness of highlights and how they dissipate into diffused light and then into shadow.

When you start understanding how real light affects objects, you'll be much better equipped to generate your own light. After all, the key to good lighting starts with the desire to simply create an interesting image.

Your Scene and Its Needs

Your scene needs a careful balance of light and dark. Too much light will flatten your image and lose details in form. This is the first mistake many beginners make; they tend to over-light to make sure everything is lit. Figure 10.1 is a rendering of a chessboard that has too many bright lights. The lighting only flattens the image and removes any sense of depth and color.

On the other hand, under-lighting a scene will make it muddy and gray and pretty lifeless. Your details will end up covered in darkness, and everything will flatten out as well. Figure 10.2 shows you the same chessboard that is under-lit. You hardly notice the details in the mesh.

Your first job as a lighter is to find the balance between over-lighting and under-lighting. It sounds simple, and it is—although it requires lighting a shot several times and test rendering it to check the outcome. Like a photographer, you want your image to have the full range of exposure. You want the richest blacks and the brightest whites in your frame to give it a deep sense of detail. Figure 10.3 shows you a fairly well-balanced lighting for the same chessboard. The light and shadow complement each other, and the lighting works to show off the features of the objects in the scene.

Figure 10.1
An over-lit chessboard

Figure 10.2
An under-lit still life

Figure 10.3

When the lighting is balanced, the image is more interesting.

Three-Point Lighting

Three-point lighting is a traditional approach to lighting a television shot. After all these years, the concepts still carry over to CG lighting. In this setup, three distinct roles are used to light the subject of a shot. More than one light can be used for each of the three roles, but the scene should in effect seem to have only one primary or *key* light, a softer light to fill the scene, and a back light to make the subject pop out from the background.

Figure 10.4

A three-point lighting schematic

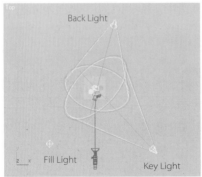

This does not mean there are only three lights in the scene. Three-point lighting suggests that there are three primary angles of light for your shot, dependent on where the camera is located.

Three-point lighting ensures that your scene's main subject is well lit and has highlights and a sense of lighting direction using shadow and tone. Figure 10.4 shows you a plan view of the three-point lighting layout. The subject is in the middle of the image.

Key Light

A *key light* is placed in front of the subject for the primary light. The key is placed off to one side to give a sense of direction to the light, because one side will be brighter than the other. Shadows will fall from this light to heighten the sense of direction and increase the depth of the shot.

Although it is possible for several lights to fulfill the role of key light in a scene—for example, three overhead ceiling lights—one light should dominate, creating a definitive direction. Figure 10.5 shows the subject being lit by a single key light.

Here, the key light produces a moody still life. It may be composed of more than one 3ds Max light, although the intent would be that all the lights that comprise the key should come from roughly the same angle.

Fill Light

A more diffused light than the key light, the *fill light* seems directionless and evenly spread across the subject's dark side. This fills the rest of the subject with light and decreases the dark area caused by the key light.

The fill light shouldn't necessarily cast any shadows onto the subject or the background. In fact, the fill light is actually used to help bring up the darkness and soften the shadows created by the key light. Figure 10.6 shows the same still life with an added fill light in the scene. The fill light clearly softens the shadows and illuminates the dark areas that the key light misses by design.

In most cases, you'll need to place the fill light in front of the subject. The fill, however, is aimed so that it shines from the reverse side of the key light. This angle intentionally targets the dark side of the subject. Even though the still life in Figure 10.6 is still a fairly moody composition, much more is visible than with only the key light in Figure 10.5.

Back Light

The *back light,* also called a rim light, is placed behind the subject to create a bit of a halo, which helps make the subject pop out in the shot. As a result, the subject has more presence against its background. Figure 10.7 shows how helpful a back light can be.

Figure 10.5
Key light only

Figure 10.6
A fill light is now included.

Figure 10.7

A back light makes the subject pop right out.

The back light brings the chess pieces out from the background and adds some highlights to the edges, making the composition more focused.

Don't confuse the back light with the background light, which lights the environment behind the subject.

Three-Point Lighting in Action

The focus of a three-point lighting system is the primary subject of the shot. This means the lighting is based on the position and angle of the subject to the camera. When a camera is moved for a different shot, even within a scene of the same subject, a new lighting setup is more than likely required. This makes three-point lighting shot-specific and not scene-specific. Of course, once you have a shot set up with the lighting you like, changing it slightly to suit a new camera angle is much easier than starting from scratch.

When the lighting is completed for the subject of a shot, the background will probably need to be lit as well. For the background, you would typically use a directed primary light source that matches the direction of the key light. This becomes your background's main light. Then you would use a softer fill light to light the rest of the background scene and to soften the primary shadows.

Practical Lighting

Practical lighting is a theatrical term describing any lights in a scene that are cast from lighting objects within the scene. For example, a shaded lamp on a nightstand in the background of a scene set in a bedroom would need practical lighting when the light is turned on. The practical lighting shouldn't interfere with the main lighting of the scene, although if the scene's lighting is explicitly coming from such a source, you will have to set up your key light to match the direction and general mood of the practical light in the shot.

Not every light-emitting object in your CG scene automatically calls for its own light in 3ds Max. Rendering tricks such as *glow* often are used to simulate the effect of an active scene light. This way, you don't need to actually use a 3ds Max light. Of course, if you need the practical light to illuminate something in the scene, you need to create a light for it.

3ds Max Lights

3ds Max has two types of light objects: photometric and standard. *Photometric lights* are lights that possess very specific features to enable a more accurate definition of lighting, as you would see in the real world. Photometric lights have physically based intensity values that closely mimic the behavior of real light. They are rather advanced and will not be covered in this book.

Standard lights are still extremely powerful and capable of realism, but they are more straightforward to use than photometric lights and less taxing on the system at render time.

A chessboard scene is included on the companion CD. To practice the lighting techniques as you read through this chapter, load the `Chess_Board_Start.max` file in the Lighting Scene Files folder.

Default Light

What happens if you have no lights at all in your 3ds Max scene? In this case, the scene is automatically lit by *default lighting*. When you add light objects, the default lighting is replaced entirely by the new lights. There is very little you can do with the default lighting; it is there for your convenience so you easily can view an object in Shaded mode and test render without creating a light first.

One or Two Default Lights

When you use default lighting, there is only one light. However, you can customize the configuration so that you can have two lights for default lighting.

To change to two default lights, in the main menu bar choose Customize → Viewport Configuration. In the Rendering Method tab, you can choose whether you want one light or two lights in your default lights under the Rendering Options heading. Figure 10.8 shows the Viewport Configuration's Rendering Method tab.

Figure 10.8

You can choose one or two lights for your default lighting.

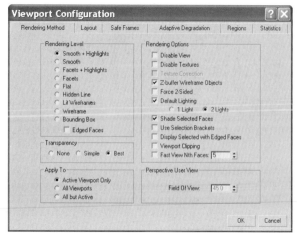

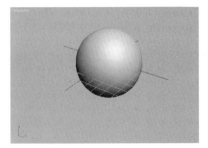 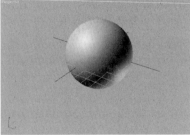 

Figure 10.9

The default light and the viewpoint

In a single default light, you have a single key light. This light is linked to the viewport, and it moves with the point of view. Setting up the default lighting to have two lights adds a single fill light that is placed opposite the key light. The key is always placed in front of the scene's object being viewed, on its upper-left side. The default fill light, if added, is created behind the object and to the lower right. The link between the default light and the viewport is broken when you have two default lights. In the above images (Figure 10.9), there is a sphere on the left with a single default light. The same sphere is in the middle with two default lights. In the image on the right, the two default lights are no longer connected to the viewport.

In Figures 10.10 and 10.11, you can see how the second default fill light works for the chessboard. Figure 10.10 has the single default light, and Figure 10.11 has two default lights. You can see the addition of a second set of highlights on the chess pieces in Figure 10.11 due to the added fill light.

Converting Default Lights

Remember that the default lights have no parameters and cannot be edited. You can, however, convert the default lighting into light objects that can be edited. To do this, the 2 Lights default lighting option must be selected in the Viewport Configuration.

Figure 10.10

A single default light provides a key light.

Figure 10.11

Two default lights provide a key light and a fill light.

To add the default lighting to your scene, choose View → Add Default Lights to Scene. If you only have 1 Light default lighting, this menu option will be grayed out and the following dialog box will open, giving you the option to add either one or both default lights to the scene.

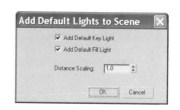

3ds Max will bring the default lights in as Omni lights (which you will learn about soon). Once you add the default lights, you can edit them like any other light. However, it's always best to just begin lighting the scene with your own lights created from scratch.

Using Default Lights

Once you add a light, any default lighting that has not been added to the scene will be removed. Likewise, if you remove all the lights in a scene, 3ds Max will re-create the default lighting. Figure 10.12 shows the two default lights inserted as Omni lights (the diamond shapes) in the sphere's scene.

Use default lighting as a temporary solution. It gives you an easy way to have a constant light that travels with the viewport's point of view—provided it's the single default light. This helps you see the detail in your modeling, animation, and texturing without having to worry about creating and placing lights, especially lights that would follow the viewport.

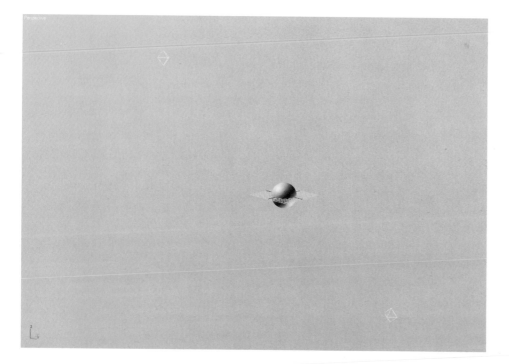

Figure 10.12

Default lights are created in the scene as Omni lights.

Standard Lights

Standard lights will be the staple of your lighting diet for some time to come. They are the only lights covered in this book. The lights in 3ds Max try to mimic the way real lights work. For example, a light bulb that emits light all around itself would be an Omni light in 3ds Max. A desk lamp that shines light in a specific direction in a cone shape would be a spotlight. Each of the different Standard lights cast light differently. We will look at the most commonly used lights.

3ds Max has a total of eight light types in its Standard Light collection. The following lights are in the collection:

Target Spotlight

Free Spotlight

Target Direct Light

Free Direct Light

Omni Light

Skylight

mr Area Omni Light

mr Area Spotlight

The last two on this list have the prefix "mr" to signify that they are mental ray–specific lights. mental ray is an advanced renderer that is commonly used in production today. It offers many sophisticated and frequently complex methods of lighting that enhance the realism of a rendered scene. Because mental ray is fairly complex, it will not be covered in this book, so its lights will not be covered in this chapter.

After you read this chapter, you should be familiar enough with lighting to get started and try new things without using any advanced lighting and rendering methodologies. You will get the chance to light a radiosity effect in the next chapter.

Target Spotlight

A *Target spotlight,* as shown in Figure 10.13, is one of the most commonly used lights because it is extremely versatile. A spotlight casts light in a focused beam, similar to a flashlight. This type of lighting allows you to light specific areas of a scene without casting any unwanted light on areas that may not need that light. You can control the size of the *hotspot.* This is the size of the cast beam.

The light is created with two nodes, the light itself (*light source*) and the Target node, at which the light points at all times. This way you are able to animate the light following the subject of the scene easily, as a spotlight would follow a singer on stage. Select the target and move it as you would any other object in 3ds Max. The Target spot will rotate to follow the target. Similarly, you can animate the light source, and it will orient itself accordingly to aim at the stationary target. (You may also animate both if you prefer.)

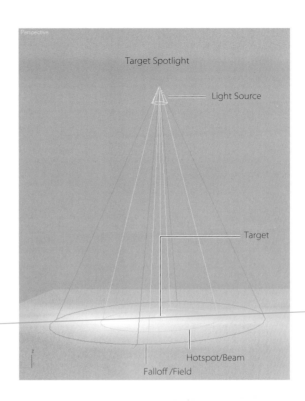

Figure 10.13
A Target spotlight

Target Spotlight

Light Source

Target

Target

Hotspot/Beam

Falloff /Field

CREATING A TARGET SPOT

Create a Target spot by going to the Create panel and clicking the Lights button () to access the light creation tools shown here.

Click the Target Spot button, and in the Top viewport, click and drag to create a Target spotlight, as shown here.

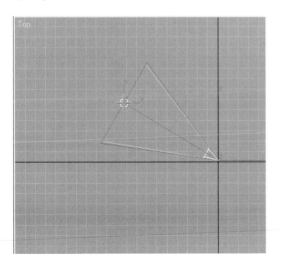

FALLOFF/FIELD

Select the light source of the Target spot. Go to the Modify panel, and open the Spotlight Parameters rollout as shown in the graphic.

The falloff, which pertains to Standard lights in 3ds Max, is represented in the viewport by the area between the inner light-blue cone and the outer dark-blue cone. The light diminishes to 0 by the outer region.

The *falloff* is the area in which the intensity of the beam falls off, or dissipates, creating a soft area around the Hotspot circle, as shown in Figure 10.14.

Field parameter is a function for Photometric lights, which are not covered in this introductory text.

SPOTLIGHT SHAPE

You can also change the shape of a spotlight from circular to rectangular by selecting either Circle or Rectangle in the Spotlight Parameters rollout. In addition, using the aspect value, you can set the height-to-width ratio for the hotspot for either Circle or Rectangle spots. Figure 10.15 shows a rectangular spot with an aspect of 4.0.

Figure 10.14

The falloff of a hotspot

When rendered, the rectangular spot looks like the image in Figure 10.16.

SELECTING THE LIGHT

You can move (and animate) the entire light, including the light and the target, by select-ing the light object in the viewport in the middle of its display, as shown in the following graphic on the left (Figure 10.17). To access the parameters of the light, you have to select the light, as shown on the right (Figure 10.17). The target does not list any parameters for the light.

INTERACTIVE CONE SETTINGS

3ds Max has the ability to control the Hotspot/Beam and the Falloff/Field parameters in the viewport. Follow these steps to interactively change a spotlight's hotspot and falloff.

1. Select the spotlight's source.

2. Click the Select and Manipulate tool in the main toolbar ( ).

3. Click and drag the green circles at the end of the spotlight cone to set the hotspot and falloff ranges, as shown in Figure 10.18.

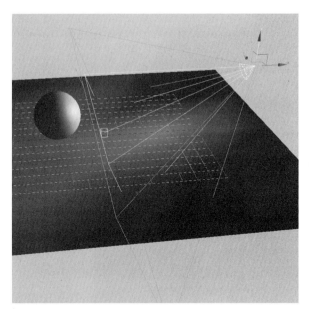

Figure 10.15

A spotlight can also be rectangular.

Figure 10.16

The rendered image

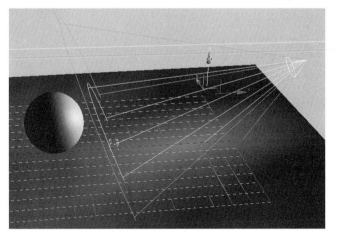

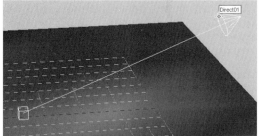

Figure 10.17

Selecting the Light

Target Direct Light

A *Target Direct light* has Target and Light nodes to help you control the direction and animation of the light. It also has a hotspot and beam, as well as a falloff much like the Target spot. However, where the Target spot emits light rays from a single point (the light source) outward in a cone shape, the Target Direct light casts parallel rays of light within its beam area. This helps simulate the lighting effect of the sun, because its light rays (for all practical purposes on Earth) are parallel. Figure 10.19 shows a Target Direct light in a viewport.

Figure 10.18

**Setting the hotspot
and falloff ranges**

Figure 10.18

**Setting the hotspot
and falloff ranges**

Figure 10.19

A Target Direct light

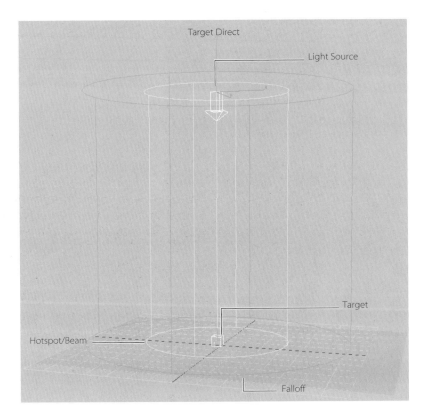

Because the directional rays are parallel, the Target Direct lights have a beam in a straight cylindrical or rectangular box shape instead of a cone.

You can create a Target Direct light much the same way as a Target spot.

1. Select Target Direct from the Create panel and click in an Orthographic window to set the light and define the target direction and length of the light by dragging.

2. Select the light for the Target direct and open the Modify panel.

In the Directional Parameters rollout, you'll find the same parameters for the Target Direct light that you had for the Target spot. The procedure to select the light is the same as for the Target spot as well. You can select the middle of the light for the whole object, or you can select either the target or light. You have to select the light to bring up the parameters for the light object.

Although the spotlight and the directional light don't seem to be very different, the way they light is strikingly different, as you can see in the following graphics (Figure 10.20).

The spotlight rays cast an entirely different hotspot and shadow than the directional light, despite having the same values for those parameters.

> It's preferable to create lights in the Orthographic viewports because they give you a better idea of size and direction than a Perspective or Camera viewport.

Free Spotlight

A *Free spotlight* is virtually identical to a Target spot, except that this light has no target object. You can move and rotate the free spot however you want, relying on rotation instead of the target to aim it in any direction. A Free spotlight is shown in Figure 10.21.

Figure 10.20

A Target spot and a Target direct

Figure 10.21

A Free spotlight does not have a target.

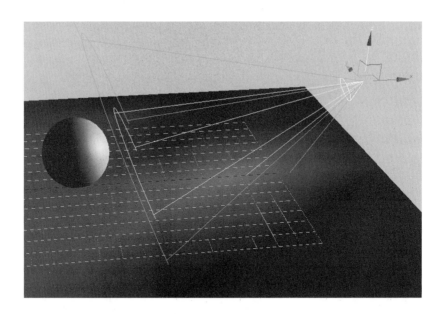

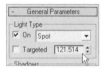

To create a Free spotlight, choose Free spot in the Create panel, click in a viewport, and drag to set its initial direction and length. The one other difference between a Free spotlight and a Target spotlight is that whereas the length of the Target spotlight is controlled by its target, a Free spot has a parameter in the General Parameters rollout of the Modify panel, as shown here. You set the length by adjusting this unmarked value next to the Targeted check box.

You will study the General Parameters rollout later in this chapter.

Adjusting the length of a spotlight will not matter when the light is rendered; however, seeing a longer light in the viewports can help you line up the light with objects in the scene. Likewise, you can shorten the length of the light to clear some wireframe clutter from your viewports.

Spotlights (including Target spots) are great for key lighting because they are very easy to control and give a fantastic sense of direction.

Free Direct Light

The *Free Direct light* is identical to the Target Direct light, but it doesn't have the Target node. Its parameters are the same as the Free spot's, and it is selected and moved in the same way. Figure 10.22 shows a Free Direct light.

Directional lights (including Target directs) are also great lights to use as key lights. You can also use them for fill lights, although the hotspot size must be large to avoid seeing the edges of the hotspot.

Directional lights are also used frequently to simulate sunlight, although their beams must be quite wide to avoid any chance of seeing the hotspot or falloff area.

Omni Light

The *Omni light* in 3ds Max is a point light that emanates light from a single point in all directions around it. Figure 10.23 shows an Omni light.

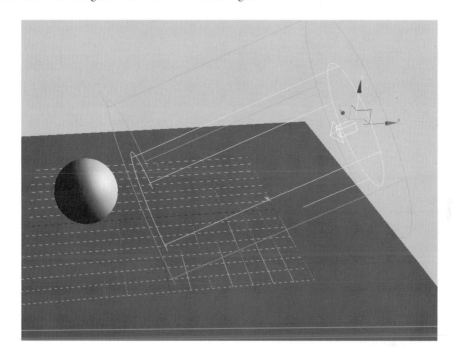

Figure 10.22
A Free Direct light

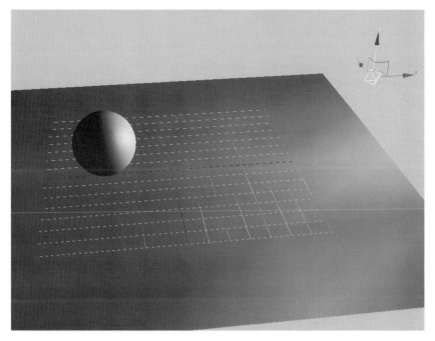

Figure 10.23
An Omni light is a single-point source light.

Figure 10.24
Omni light General Parameters

Unlike the spot and directional lights, the Omni light does not have a special rollout, and its General Parameters rollout is much simpler, as shown in Figure 10.24.

An Omni light is shown rendered in Figure 10.25. Notice how the ground plane is brighter directly below where the light sits.

Omni lights are not as good for simulating sunlight as directional lights are. The Omni light's rays spread from a single point source, so by the time they reach their subjects, the light direction and shadows will be too disparate across the scene. In this graphic (Figure 10.26), the Omni light in the image on the left creates different shadow and lighting directions for all the objects in the scene, and the directional light in the image on the right creates a uniform direction for the light and shadow, as would the sun here on Earth.

Figure 10.25
An Omni light lights the sphere and floor.

Omni Light

Directional Light

Figure 10.26
Omni light and directional light

> Try to avoid casting shadows with Omni lights because they will use a lot more memory than a spotlight when casting shadows.

Omni lights are good for fill lights as well as for simulating certain practical light sources that have a brighter center and fall off evenly around that bright spot in all three axes. You could even use Omni lights for all three points in your three-point lighting system, as shown in Figure 10.27 on the chessboard scene. This lighting gives the scene a nice soft feel.

Figure 10.27

Using Omni lights for all three points in a three-point lighting system

Skylight

Skylight is a special 3ds Max light used with an advanced rendering method to quickly generate a scene rendered in a soft outdoor light. We will not be covering this more advanced lighting and rendering methodology; however, here is a quick introduction to the light itself.

Figure 10.28 shows a skylight high above the scene with the three spheres. It is created by selecting the Skylight button in the Create panel and clicking to place it in a viewport.

The skylight's Skylight Parameters rollout is shown in Figure 10.29.

The skylight is used to create a soft, global lighting to simulate light from the sky. This look is often seen with renders using Global Illumination or Radiosity. In these lighting/rendering solutions, the skylight creates a sky dome that sits around the objects in the scene. Light is emitted

Figure 10.28

A skylight placed over the spheres and ground plane

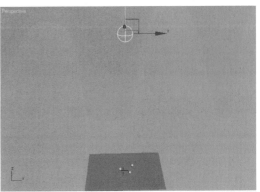

Skylight Parameters

☑ On   Multiplier: 1.0 ↕

Sky Color
○ Use Scene Environment
● Sky Color...
☐ Map: 100.0 ↕
None

Render
☐ Cast Shadows
Rays per Sample: 20 ↕
Ray Bias: 0.005 ↕

Figure 10.29

The Skylight Parameters rollout

from the entire surface area of the dome to cast an even light throughout the scene, much as a sky lights an outdoor area.

The rendering of a Skylight scene, as shown in Figure 10.30, is flat and bright. There is no definition because shadows are not enabled.

Turning on shadows gives you a beautiful render, as shown in Figure 10.31, with soft shadows and contact shadows that really make the spheres look as if they are sitting outside in afternoon light.

The render time for this frame, however, is significantly longer than any of the other renders so far in this chapter. Calculating soft light such as this is quite intensive, unless a lighting plug-in such as Light Tracer is enabled in the render setup.

> The Skylight light is not intended to be used without some other light source(s) in the scene. It is designed to be used only with Radiosity, Light Tracer, or mental ray rendering techniques. These techniques are more advanced, so they will not be covered in this book. It is important to learn traditional lighting and rendering methods before moving into advanced techniques.

Common Light Parameters

Most of the parameters for the Standard lights are the same for all the lights and will be described in this section. You may want to create a spot or directional light so you can follow along with the information about light parameters given here.

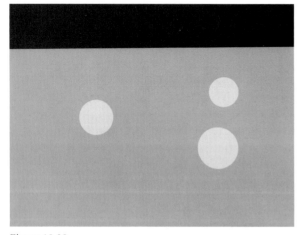

Figure 10.30

The skylight flattens the spheres and blows them out.

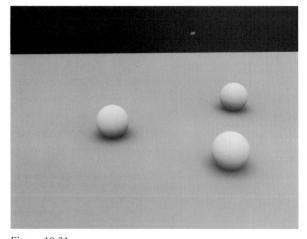

Figure 10.31

Turning on shadows for the skylight dramatically increases render times, but it gives a nice effect with soft shadows mimicking a radiosity effect.

General Parameters Rollout

The General Parameters rollout for all the Standard lights (except for Skylight) is shown in Figure 10.32. In the Light Type section, you can change the type of light that is currently selected. Simply choose the type (Spot, Directional, Omni) from the drop-down menu. 3ds Max will replace the light with the new light type; it won't change its position or orientation. This can be immensely helpful when you are deciding which light will work best for a scene. Otherwise, you would have to delete and re-create lights to find the solution that best suited your scene.

You can turn a Free spot or Free directional to a target of the same kind by checking the Targeted check box. Of course, the On check box controls whether the light is on or off in the scene.

In the Shadows section of the General Parameters rollout for these lights, you will find the controls for the shadow-casting properties of the selected light. Use the drop-down menu to select the type of shadows to cast. The two most-frequently used shadow types, Shadow map and Raytraced, are discussed later in the chapter.

The Use Global Settings toggle can be very useful. When it is turned on, all of the lights in your scene will be set to use the same Shadow parameters of the light you have selected and for which you have enabled Use Global Settings. This is useful in the event you need the same type of shadows cast from all the lights in the scene. It can save you the hassle of specifying the settings for all the lights. It does, however, limit you to the same shadow settings for all the lights. While you are learning, you should leave Use Global Settings off and set each light manually as needed. Again, shadows are covered a little later in this chapter.

Figure 10.32

The General Parameters rollout for all the Standard lights is the same.

Intensity/Color/Attenuation Rollout

The Intensity/Color/Attenuation rollout, shown in Figure 10.33, is used to adjust your light's brightness and color settings.

Figure 10.33

The Intensity/Color/Attenuation rollout

Light Intensity

The Multiplier parameter works like a dimmer switch for a light. The higher the value is, the brighter the light will be. The Multiplier can go into negative values. A negative amount will subtract light from your scene, allowing you to create dark areas within lit areas or to remove excess light from a surface that has unwanted spill light.

Light Color

The Color Swatch next to the Multiplier is used to add color to your light. Simply click on the color swatch to open the Color Selector. The darker the color is, the darker the light will be.

Light Decay

Under the Decay section, you can set the way your light fades across distance. This is not the same as falloff with spots and directional lights, though. Falloff occurs on the sides of a hotspot, whereas *decay* happens along the path of the light as it travels away from the light. Figure 10.34 shows a light with no decay type set. Figure 10.35 shows the same light with its decay Type set to Inverse Decay. Figure 10.36 shows the same light with decay Type set to Inverse Square Decay. Notice the decay rate increases with each successive figure.

Figure 10.34

A light with no decay evenly illuminates all the numbers.

Figure 10.35

A light with Inverse Decay illuminates the back numbers less.

Figure 10.36

A light with Inverse Square Decay illuminates the first two numbers and begins to lose the remaining three.

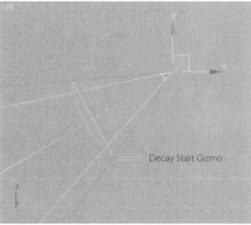

Figure 10.37

Seeing the start of a light's decay helps you see how it will illuminate your scene.

If no decay is set for a light, its intensity remains at full strength from the light to infinity. An Inverse Decay diminishes the intensity of the illumination over distance traveled according to some brainy formula. An Inverse Square Decay more closely resembles the decay of real-world light, and it is a stronger rate of decay than Inverse Decay. Use this decay rate to drop off the effect of a light quickly before it reaches too far into the scene; however, you will need a stronger Multiplier value to increase your light's intensity to compensate for the much faster decay.

In Figure 10.37, you can quickly see and set the start of a decay in spot and directional lights by changing the Start value in the Decay section of the rollout.

In the following image (Figure 10.38) you can see a decay start that is closer to the light and its effect on the render in the top-left corner.

The start of the decay is moved closer to the spheres in Figure 10.39.

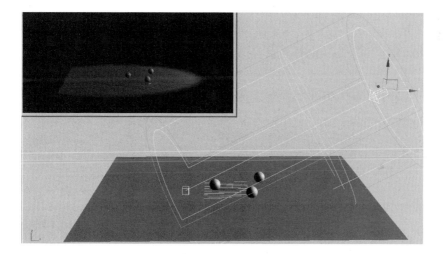

Figure 10.38

A decay start

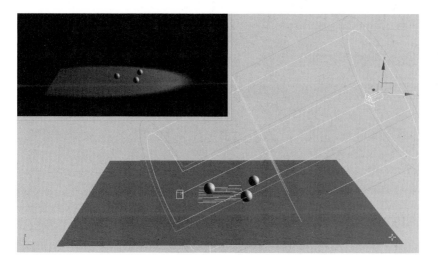

Figure 10.39

A decay start closer to the spheres

Light Attenuation

Light attenuation is another way to diminish the intensity of a light over distance. With attenuation, however, you have more implicit control on the start and end of the fade, and you can specify an area where the light fades in and then fades out. To do this, set the Attenuation distances to the desired effect.

NEAR ATTENUATION GROUP

The following values set the distances where the light fades into existence:

Start The distance at which the light starts to fade in.

End The distance at which the light reaches its full intensity.

Use Toggles on/off the use of near attenuation for the light.

Figure 10.40 shows a render of near attenuation at work. The first numbers are darker, the back numbers are brighter.

Figure 10.41 shows a spotlight and the Attenuation display in the viewport.

FAR ATTENUATION GROUP

The following values set the distances where the illumination fades out of existence:

Start The distance at which the illumination starts to fade away.

End The distance at which the illumination has faded to nothing.

Use Toggles on/off the use of far attenuation for the illumination.

Figure 10.42 shows a render of the far attenuation on the same set of numbers, using the same light as before. Now the lights fade into darkness the farther back they are in the scene, which is similar to decay.

Figure 10.43 shows the Far Attenuation display for the spotlight.

Figure 10.40

Near attenuation fades in the light.

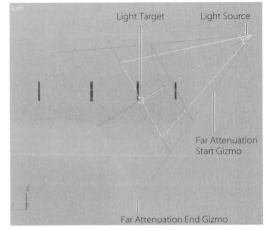

Figure 10.41

The spotlight displays the attenuation distances.

Figure 10.42

Far attenuation fades out the light.

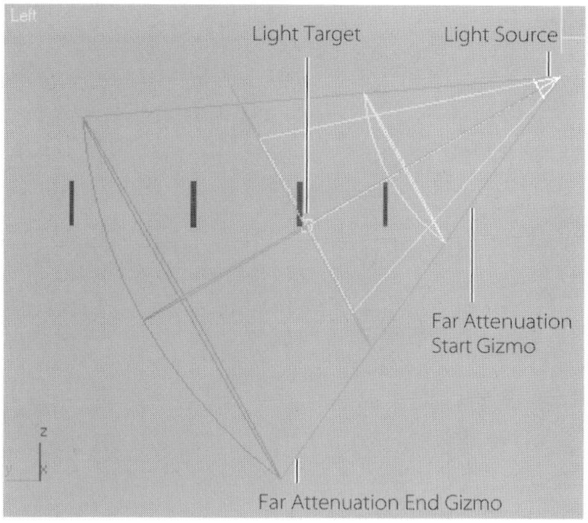

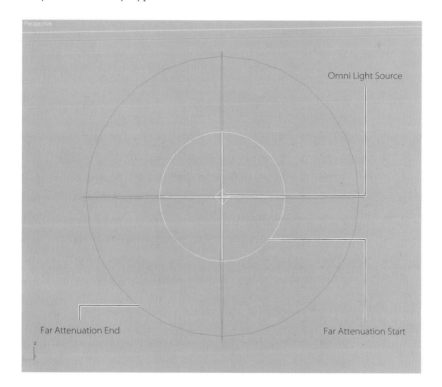

Figure 10.43

The spotlight displays the attenuation distances.

Figure 10.44 shows the Attenuation display for an Omni light in a viewport.

You can always use both near and far attenuation to set a sliver of light in your scene, as shown in Figure 10.45. As you can see, attenuation is a more precise way to set a diminishing light intensity over the Decay Type.

Figure 10.44

The Attenuation display for an Omni light

Figure 10.45

Using both near and far attenuation gives you a slice of light where you need it.

Both decay and attenuation are important to use when the light needs to be realistic. Light decays in real life; your renders will assume a higher fidelity when the lights in them decay. The effect may be subtle, but it can make a large difference.

Advanced Effects Rollout

The Advanced Effects rollout (shown in graphic on the left) enables you to control how a light affects the surfaces it illuminates. You can increase or decrease the contrast and softness of a light's effect on a surface. You can also dictate which lighting component of the light is rendered on the surface.

Contrast and Soften

By adjusting the Contrast and Soften Diffuse Edges values, you can alter the way the light hits your surface. The following image (Figure 10.46) was rendered with default Contrast and Soften Diffuse Edges values,

This image (Figure 10.47) was rendered with a Contrast of 25 and a Soften Diffuse Edges value of 50. It has deeper contrast, but with slightly softer values leading from the diffuse color.

Contrast Changes the contrast level between the diffuse and ambient areas of the surface when lit.

Soften Diffuse Edge Controls the softness of the edge between the diffuse and ambient areas of the lit surface.

Light Components

Light in a CG program is differentiated into an *ambient*, a *diffuse*, and a *specular* component. The ambient component of light is the general ambient light in a scene. There is no

Figure 10.46

Using default Contrast and Soften Diffuse Edges values

Figure 10.47

Using a Contrast of 25 and a Soften Diffuse Edges of 50

direction to ambient light, and the light itself is cast evenly across the extent of the scene. The diffuse component of light is the way it illuminates an object by spreading across its surface. The specular component of light is how the light creates highlights on a surface, especially when that surface is glossy. (You may want to review the discussion of these components in Chapter 7, "Materials and Mapping.")

In the Affect Surfaces section of the Advanced Effects rollout, you can toggle the check boxes that will render only those components of the light on the surfaces they illuminate. This is a good way to separate your renders into lighting components that you can later control in compositing, although it leads to a longer workflow.

Figure 10.48 is rendered with the diffuse component of the lights in the scene.

Figure 10.48

Only the diffuse component of the lights are rendered.

Figure 10.49 shows only the specular highlights rendered.

Figure 10.49

Only the specular component of the lights are rendered.

Figure 10.50 shows only the ambient light rendered on the objects.

Figure 10.50

Only the ambient light in the scene is rendered.

Ambient Light

Ambient light in 3ds Max is not a light per se; it is a global setting in the render environment. Ambient light, in short, is an even light with no direction or source. It is a way to globally brighten the entire scene to add an even light to all objects. Using too much ambient light will wash out your objects and give you flat renders.

To set an ambient light level in your scene, in the main menu select Rendering → Environment to open the Environment and Effects window shown in Figure 10.51.

To set an ambient light, click on the Ambient color swatch under the Global Lighting section and pick an appropriate color. The brighter the color value, the brighter the ambient light will be throughout the scene.

> You can also create an ambient light in your scene by creating an Omni light and toggling on the Ambient Only check box under the light's Advanced Effects Parameters rollout.

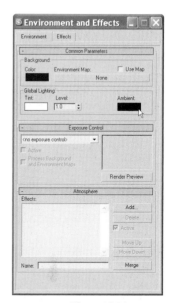

Figure 10.51
The Environment and Effects window

Lighting the Red Rocket

Now that we have an overview of how lights work in 3ds Max, let's put them to good use and light the Red Rocket textured model from Chapter 7. Because lighting goes hand in hand with rendering, we will create the basic lighting setup based on the three-point system discussed earlier in this chapter. We'll work more with the lighting and settings when we get to Chapter 11, "3ds Max Rendering."

> Occasionally, setting a project and opening a scene file fails to open all the appropriate image files used in the scene. In these cases, you will have to reconnect the image files needed by navigating to their folders (usually in the project's SceneAssets/Images folder) and picking the files manually. 3ds Max will give you the error message and give you a chance to replace the file when you first open the scene.

Set your current project to the Red Rocket project you've copied to your hard drive from the CD. Open `Rocket_Light_Start.max` from the Scenes folder of the Red Rocket project.

This scene is very simple (Figure 10.52). It is the final rocket from Chapter 7. (If you prefer, you can use your own rocket file.).

The rocket, with all its many parts, has been frozen in the scene on the CD so you can work freely without worrying about selecting objects other than the lights. The rocket and the room it is in can be unfrozen by going to the Layer Manager and clicking the Unfreeze icon next to the Rocket layer (as shown in Figure 10.53).

Figure 10.52
The rocket set into a simple room

Figure 10.53

Use the Layer Manager to unfreeze parts of the scene.

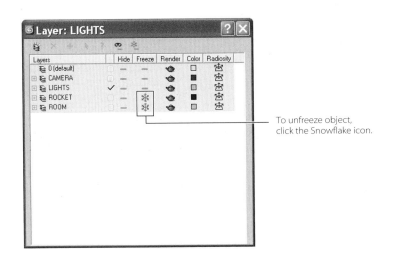

To unfreeze object, click the Snowflake icon.

Figure 10.54

The selection of lights you can create

To begin lighting the rocket, follow along here:

1. Go to the Create panel and select the Lights icon () to bring up the selection of lights you can create, as shown in Figure 10.54.

2. Click to create a Target spot. Go to the Top viewport, and click and drag from the right side of the viewport toward the middle, as shown in Figure 10.55. The first click will create the camera; the drag places the target.

When you create your first light, the scene will turn black momentarily. This is because when you create a light, the default lights are removed from the scene.

3. Move to the Front viewport, select the light, and move it up as shown in Figure 10.56. If your front view is not visible, simply select one of the viewports and press F for the Front viewport.

Figure 10.55

Click and drag from the right side toward the middle.

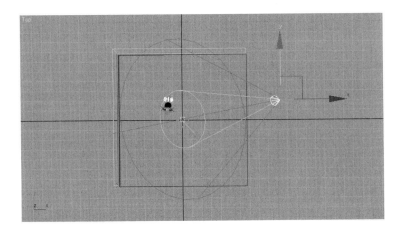

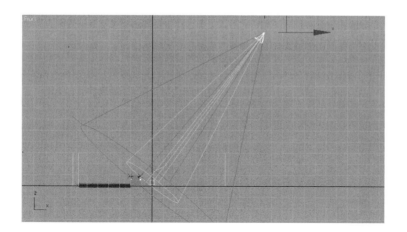

Figure 10.56
Move the light.

4. Name the light **Key Light**. This light will have shadows and give the scene its main source of light and direction.

5. Go to the Modify panel, check the On box under Shadows, and set the Shadow Type to Shadow Map, as shown in Figure 10.57. This is the default shadow type. Later in the chapter, we will expand on all the shadow types and their uses in 3ds Max.

6. Go to the Intensity/Color/Attenuation rollout in the Modify panel, and set the Multiplier to 0.8. As you learned earlier in the chapter, the Multiplier acts like a dimmer switch and controls the light's brightness.

7. In the Spotlight Parameters rollout, change the Hotspot/Beam parameter to 18 and the Falloff/Field value to 38, as shown in Figure 10.58. Both these parameters affect the width of the cone of light. The closer the two values are, the sharper the edge of the light will be; the farther they are from each other, the softer the light will be.

Figure 10.57
The Parameter settings in the Modify panel

Try a render (press F9 for a Quick Render) and you will see the rocket as shown in Figure 10.59.

Not bad, but look at how dark the shadow is. Once we add a fill light, the shadows will be better. For the fill we'll use an Omni light. You may also notice that the rocket looks a bit like it is floating above the ground. Let's address that issue first, in the following steps:

Figure 10.58
The Parameter settings in Spotlight Parameters

1. Select the key light (the Target spot), and in the Shadow Map Params rollout (Figure 10.60), change the Bias to 0.1. Bias moves the shadow toward or away from the object. The shadow is too far away from the rocket, and that is why in Figure 10.59 it appears to be floating.

2. In that same rollout, change the Size parameter to 1500. Size specifies the amount of resolution in the shadow; the more the pixels the more crisp the edge of the shadow will appear.

Figure 10.59

Rendering the rocket with the first light in place

Figure 10.60

The Shadow Map Params rollout

3. Go back to the Create panel to create another light. Click to create an Omni light. In the Top viewport, click in the bottom-left corner to place the Omni as shown in Figure 10.61.

4. In the Front viewport, move the light up about half the height of the backdrop.

5. The Omni is just a fill light in this scene, so we don't want any shadows from it. Furthermore, we will turn off specular highlights on the rocket from this light to make sure the render looks as if there is only one light in the room. By default, shadows are always off, but not the specular, so we will turn it off manually. With the Omni light selected, go to the Modify panel and under the Advanced Effects rollout, uncheck Specular as shown in Figure 10.62.

Figure 10.61

Place an Omni light in the scene.

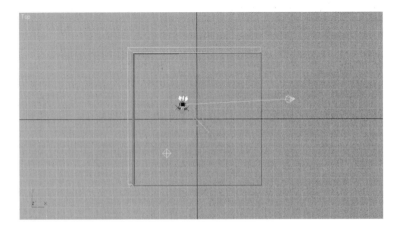

6. Go to the Intensity/Color/Attenuation rollout for the Omni light, and change the Multiplier to 0.3.

7. Render again (press F9) and you'll see the render looks better, but that the rocket's shadow is still dark (Figure 10.63).

8. To fix the darkness of the shadow in Figure 10.63, we could add more lights to the scene, but then the scene would get too bright. The solution is to adjust the density of the shadow (you will see more on shadows in the next section in the chapter). Select the key light, go to the Modify panel and in the Shadow Parameters rollout, change the Object Shadow's Dens parameter to 0.8 (Figure 10.64).

Figure 10.62

Advanced Effects parameters

Figure 10.63

The rocket with a key and fill light

9. Press F9 for another Quick Render (or press the Teapot icon in the main toolbar), and you will see that the rocket's shadow looks much better (Figure 10.65).

This exercise used what is arguably the most popular shadow-casting method. There are other ways to cast different types of shadows, each with its own advantages and distinct look. In the following section, we will explore different shadowing techniques.

When creating shadows don't be too quick to smother your scene with light or too eager to show off your careful modeling work and textures. Leaving objects in shadow and darkness is as important as revealing them in light. You can say a lot visually by not showing parts of a whole and leaving some interpretation to the audience.

Using shadows intelligently is very important in lighting your scenes. Without the shadows in the rocket scene, the rendered image would look weird. The rocket would float in the scene and have no contact with its environment. You would also lose a great deal of the sense of direction without shadows.

Figure 10.64

The Shadow Parameters rollout

A careful balance of light and dark is important for a composition. The realism of a scene is greatly increased with the simple addition of well-placed shadows. Don't be afraid of the dark. Use it liberally, but in balance.

You can create the following types of shadows in 3ds Max:

Advanced Raytraced

mental ray Shadow Map

Area Shadow

Shadow Map

Raytraced Shadows

Each type of shadow has its benefits and its drawbacks. The two most common types used are Shadow maps (which you've already seen) and Raytraced shadows.

When you use shadows, controls in the Shadow Parameters rollout and the shadow type-specific rollouts are available when you select the shadow type.

Shadow Parameters Rollout

The settings in the Shadow Parameters rollout govern the common parameters for all shadow types discussed here. In this rollout, you can adjust the color of your shadow as well as its density (i.e., how dark it appears).

You should always check your light's Multiplier values first to make sure your fill light does not wash out your shadows before you adjust the shadow parameters themselves. For instance, the fill light(s) generally has a lower intensity than the key light(s).

Click on the Color Swatch to pick a color for your shadows. More often than not, you will have your shadow colors at black, if not close to black. You can also control the density of the shadows by adjusting the Density value. As you can see in Figure 10.66, adjusting

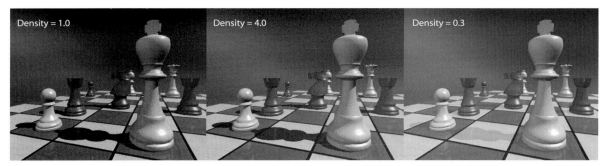

Figure 10.66

Shadow Density

the density changes how much of the shadow is rendered. A Density of 0 will turn off your shadows in essence.

Interestingly enough, you can also apply a map to your shadow by checking the Map box and clicking on the button bar currently labeled None. From there, you can choose a map. In Figure 10.67, a checker map was mapped to the shadow on a fruit arrangement. Notice how the checker pattern shows up just in the shadows between and on the fruit.

Figure 10.67

You can map a texture to the shadow, as shown on this fruit still-life render.

Selecting a Shadow Type

For the most part, you will be more than happy with the results from a Shadow Map shadow in your scenes. However, to get shadows to respond to transparencies, you will need to use Raytraced shadows. Additionally, if you need to soften your shadows the farther they are cast from the object, you will need to use Area Shadows. These shadow types are discussed next.

Shadow Maps

The Shadow map generates a bitmap file during a pre-rendering pass of the scene. This map is used to place the shadows in the final render. It is often the fastest way to cast a shadow. However, Shadow Map shadows do not show the color cast through transparent

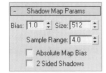

or translucent objects. Once you select Shadow Maps in the General Parameters rollout for a light, the Shadow Map Params rollout appears. It is shown here.

Because this shadow type relies on maps, it is important to be able to control the resolution of the generated maps. When you are close to a shadow, the resolution needs to be higher for the cast shadow than if it were farther from the camera in order to avoid jagged edges around the shadow.

The following parameters are useful for creating Shadow maps:

Bias The shadow is moved, according to the value set, closer or farther away from the object casting the shadow. Figure 10.68 shows how the bias moves the shadow away the higher the value is set.

Figure 10.68

The Bias offsets the shadow from the casting object.

Size Detailed shadows will need detailed Shadow maps. Increase the Size value, and 3ds Max will increase the number of subdivisions for the map, which in turn increases the detail of the shadow cast. Figure 10.69 compares a low Shadow Map Size to render the chessboard with one four times larger. Notice how the shadows on the left (Size = 1024) are somewhat mushy and less noticeable and the shadows on the right (Size = 4096) are crisp and clean. You don't want to set your Shadow Map size to be too high, though. It will increase render time for little to no effect. A range around 2048 is usually good for most cases. Larger scenes like this chess board that have a large scale to them will require higher Size values such as the 4096 used. The rule of thumb is to use the lowest Size value that will get you the best result for your scene.

In some scenes, you may discover that no Shadow Map size will give you good results (for instance in large outdoor scenes). In these cases, you will have to revert to a different shadow method, such as Raytraced shadows.

Figure 10.69
The Shadow Map size affects the shadow detail.

Sample Range This creates and controls the softness of the edge of shadow-mapped shadows. The higher the value is, the softer the edges of the shadow will be. Figure 10.70 shows you how a soft edge (on the left) can make the lighting seem weaker or farther away from the subject than crisp shadows (on the right).

Figure 10.70

Soft-edge shadows

Raytraced Shadows

Raytracing involves tracing a ray of light from every light source in all directions and tracing the reflection to the camera lens. You can create more accurate shadows with raytracing. However, the render takes significantly longer to calculate. Raytraced shadows are always hard edged, yet they are realistic for transparent and translucent objects. Figure 10.50 shows a pair of chess pieces rendered with a plane casting a shadow over them. The plane has a checker mapped to its opacity, so it has alternating transparent and opaque squares defining the checkerboard. On the left side of the image in Figure 10.71, the light is casting Shadow Map shadows, while on the right the light is casting Raytraced shadows.

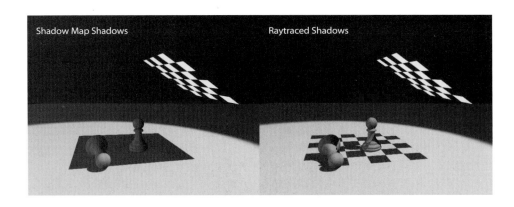

Use Raytraced shadows when you need highly accurate shadows or when Shadow Map resolutions are just not high enough to get you the crisp edges you need. You can also use Raytraced shadows to cast shadows from wireframe rendered objects.

The Raytraced Shadow rollout, shown here, controls the shadow. The Ray Bias parameter is the same as the Shadow Map Bias in that it controls how far from the casting object the shadow is cast.

Creating Soft Shadows Due to Distance

The only way you will be able to create a natural shadow that softens the farther it gets from the casting object is to use Area shadows. These types of shadows are natural. If you notice a telephone pole's shadow, the farther the shadow is from the pole, the softer the shadow becomes. Adding such a shadow to a render can greatly increase the realism of the scene.

To enable a soft shadow such as this, select Area Shadows as your shadow type. By default, the Area Shadow will work for you. Figure 10.72 shows a regular Raytraced shadow.

Figure 10.73 shows an Area shadow at the default settings.

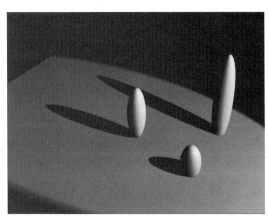

Figure 10.72

A Raytraced shadow is too hard-edged.

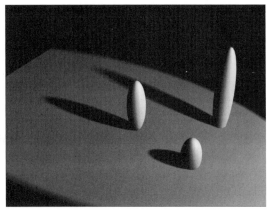

Figure 10.73

An Area shadow begins to soften at the ends.

Go to the Area Shadows rollout shown in Figure 10.74. To adjust the softness of the shadows, you will not want to increase the Sample Spread because that parameter, just like the Sample Range of the Shadow Map shadow, softens the entire shadow. A true shadow is crisp where it meets the casting object and softens as it casts away.

To further soften the ends of the shadows, in the Area Light rollout, set the Length to 80 and the Width to 60. This will increase the softness of the shadow in a realistic way, while keeping the contact shadow crisp. However, the render, shown in Figure 10.75, does not look very good. The soft ends are very grainy.

You will need to increase the quality of the shadow, so set the Shadow Integrity to 6 and the Shadow Quality to 10. The render will take longer, but you will get a beautiful shadow, as shown in Figure 10.76.

Figure 10.74

The Area Shadows rollout

Figure 10.75

Render with the Length set to 80 and Width set to 60.

Figure 10.76

Increase the shadow quality to obtain a very realistic shadow.

Atmospheres and Effects

Creating atmospheric effects with lights, such as fog or volume lights, is accomplished through the Atmospheres and Effects rollout in the Modify panel for the selected light, as shown here.

Using this rollout, you can assign and manage atmosphere effects and other rendering effects that are associated with lights. In the following exercise, you will learn how to create a volumetric light (similar to a flashlight shining through fog). You will also learn how to exclude objects from a light, so that the light does not illuminate them. This is an important trick to know.

Creating a Volumetric Light

Let's create a fog light now.

1. Open the Rocket_Amosphere_Start.max scene file in the Lighting Scenes folder on·the companion CD. Go to Create Panel → Lights and click on the Target Direct light.

Move your pointer to the Top viewport, and click and drag from the top of the viewport down toward the rocket.

As shown in Figure 10.77, the light begins outside the room the rocket is in. This scene is already equipped with two Omni lights to act as fill lights in the room.

Figure 10.77

The light begins outside the room the rocket is in

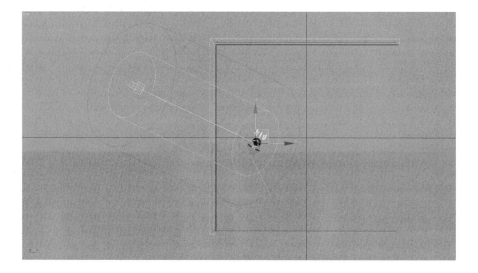

2. Move to the Front viewport and move the light up along the *Y*-axis, and then move the target so it is centered to point the light directly on the rocket, as shown in Figure 10.78. Make sure the light is shining into the room from outside through the window.

3. If you do a Quick Render (F9), you will see that the scene is being lit from the direction of the light (Figure 10.79).

Figure 10.78

Move the light up and move the target.

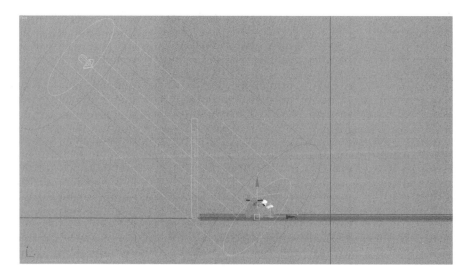

Figure 10.79
A test render of the rocket

This first render probably looks very odd. The rocket and floor have reflections on them; so they show up even if there is no light in the scene at all. That is the way reflections work.

Adding Shadows

Now you need some shadows in the scene.

1. In the General Parameters rollout for the light, go to the Shadows section and check the box to enable shadows. Select Shadow Map from the drop-down menu. This will turn on Shadow Maps shadows for this light.

2. Go to the Shadow Map Params rollout and set the size to 2048; this will add some sharpness to the shadow's edge and make it more like a daylight shadow. Also change the Bias to 0.1, which will move the shadow so it is under the rocket. If you do a Quick Render, you won't see any shadows (as shown in Figure 10.80).

Figure 10.80
You won't see any shadows if you do a Quick Render.

This is because the window is blocking the light. The window glass object has a Material that has the Opacity turned down to 0. However, Shadow Map shadows don't recognize transparency in materials. To solve this problem, you need to exclude the Window Glass object from the Light.

Excluding Object from a Light

1. The Exclude button is in the General Parameters rollout for the light, just below the Shadows. Click the Exclude button to bring up the Exclude/Include window shown in Figure 10.81.

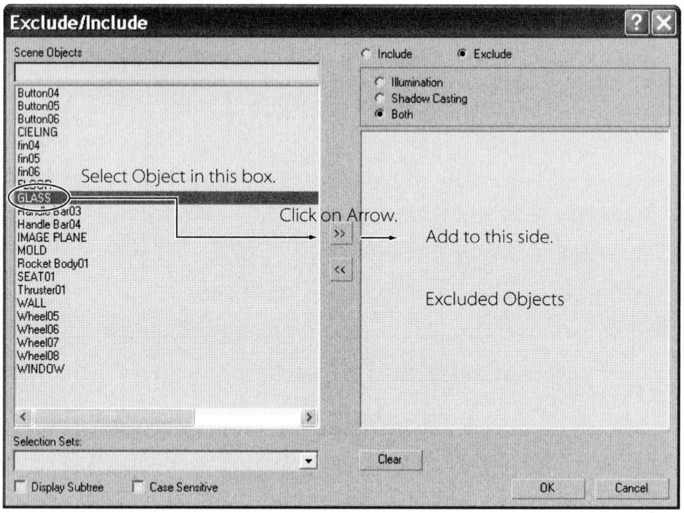

Figure 10.81

The Exclude/Include window allows you to exclude certain objects from being lit by the light in the scene.

2. Click on the Glass object and press the right arrows in the middle of the window (Figure 10.81) to add the Glass to the other side, excluding the object from receiving light and casting light. Click OK.

3. Quick Render your scene to take a look. Now you can see shadows. We didn't exclude the whole window with its frame because the inside frame is a nice detail to cast shadows. Figure 10.82 shows the render with the shadows.

Adding a Volumetric Effect

The whole point of this exercise is to add volume to the light. This will give this scene some much needed atmosphere.

1. Go to the Atmosphere and Effects rollout for the light. Select Add from the rollout to open the Add Atmosphere or Effect window, which is shown in Figure 10.83.

2. In the window, select Volume Light and click OK to add the effect to the light.

Figure 10.82

Shadows!

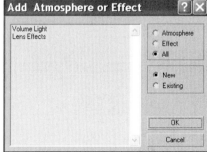

Figure 10.83

The Add Atmosphere or Effect settings

3. Volume Light will be added to the rollout, as shown in Figure 10.84.

4. Render the scene. You should see a render similar to Figure 10.85.

To adjust the volume light, select the Volume Light entry in the rollout and click the Setup button. This will bring up the Environment and Effects dialog window. Scroll down to the *Volume Light Parameters* section to access the settings for the volume light, shown in Figure 10.86. Experiment with different settings to see how the volume light renders.

Figure 10.84

Add Volume Light to the rollout

Volume Light Parameters

The default parameters for a volume light will give you some nice volume in the light for most scenes, right off the bat. If you want to adjust the volume settings, you can edit the following parameters:

Exponential The density of the volume light will increase exponentially with distance. By default (Exponential is off), density will increase linearly with distance. You will want to enable Exponential only when you need to render transparent objects in volume fog.

Density This value sets the fog's density. The denser the fog is, the more light will reflect off the fog inside the volume. The most realistic fogs can be rendered with about 2 to 6 percent Density value.

Most of the parameters are for troubleshooting volume problems in your scene if it is not rendering very well. Sometimes you just don't know what that problem is and you have to experiment with switches and buttons. The Noise settings are another cool feature to add some randomness to your volume:

Noise On This toggles the noise on and off. Render times will increase slightly with Noise enabled for the volume.

Figure 10.85

Volume light!

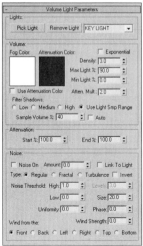

Figure 10.86

The Environment and Effects window displays the Volume Light parameters.

Amount This is the amount of noise that is applied to the fog. A value of 0 creates no noise. If the Amount is set to 1, the fog renders with pure noise.

Size, Uniformity, Phase These settings determine the look of the noise and let you set a Noise Type (Regular, Fractal, or Turbulence).

Adding atmosphere to a scene can heighten the sense of realism and mood. Creating a little bit of a volume for some lights can go a long way to improving the look of your renders. However, adding volume to lights can also slow your renders; so use it with care. Also be aware that adding too much volume to a scene may look peculiar; so use volumetric light sparingly and with good reason. Reserve it for when it is called for in the scene and will add ambience to the image.

Light Lister

If several lights are in your scene and you need to adjust all of them, selecting each light and making one adjustment at a time can become tedious. This is where 3ds Max's Light Lister comes in handy. Accessed through the main menu bar by choosing Tools → Light Lister, this floating palette gives you control over all of your scene lights, as shown in Figure 10.87.

This is the perfect tool to edit your lights once you have them set up initially. You can choose to view/edit all the lights in your scene or just the ones that are selected. Using this easy dialog window gives you instant access to almost all the important light parameters in one place. When you adjust the values for any parameter in the Light Lister window, the changes are reflected in the appropriate place in the Modify panel for that changed light.

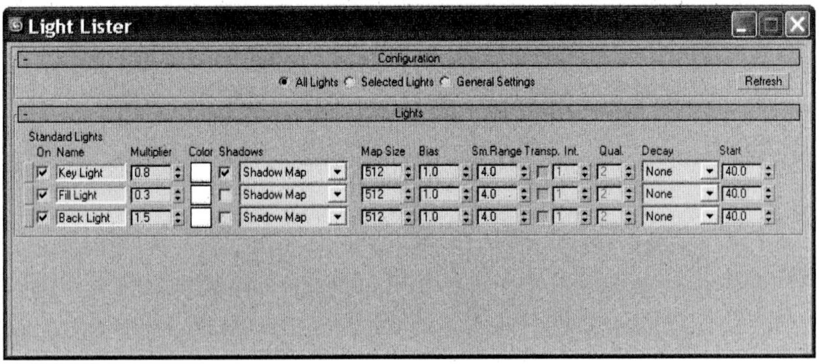

Figure 10.87

The Light Lister window

Summary

Lighting is the aspect of CG that is arguably the most difficult to master (some users think it's even harder than character animation), and it is the most easily criticized. People in the CG industry can tell very quickly when lighting is done poorly.

In this chapter, you began by reviewing some key concepts in CG lighting, including three-point lighting. Then you learned the different types of lights that 3ds Max has to offer, from default lights to Target spots, and how to use them. You dove into the common light parameters to gauge how best to control the lights in your scene before you moved on to creating all different types of shadows. You ran through a set of short exercises in which you created a volumetric light for a fog effect and finished with a tour of the Light Lister window.

Several books are devoted to CG lighting. It is a craft that takes getting used to. This chapter introduced you to the concepts and tools you need to begin. Now it's your turn to take the models you have created (and the ones you will create in the future), texture them, and light scenes with them to develop an eye for the ins and outs of lighting.

There really is no quick way to learn how to light. It would be quite a disservice to pretend that a chapter, or even an entire book, will give you everything you need to know. Take the information and references in this chapter and apply them on your own. Working on your own may not sound like fun, and it may not seem as easy as being guided step by step, but it is the best education you will get.

CHAPTER 11

3ds Max Rendering

Rendering is the last step in creating your CG work, but it is the first step to consider when you start to build a scene. During rendering, the computer calculates the scene's surface properties, lighting, shadows, and object movement, and then it saves a sequence of images. To get to the point where the computer takes over, you'll need to set up your camera and render settings so that you'll get exactly what you need from your scene.

This chapter will show you how to render your scene using 3ds Max's scanline renderer and how to create reflections and refractions using raytracing.

Topics in this chapter include:

- **Rendering Setup**

- **Motion Blur**

- **Previewing with Active Shade**

- **Cameras**

- **Safe Frame**

- **Render Elements**

- **Rendering Effects**

- **Raytraced Reflections and Refractions**

- **Bringing It All Together: Rendering the Rocket**

Rendering Setup

In a manner of speaking, everything you do in CG can be considered setup for rendering. More specifically, how you set up your render settings and what final decisions you make about your 3ds Max scene ultimately determine how your work will look. In many ways, you should be thinking about rendering all along—especially if you are creating 3D assets for a game, where the 3D scenes are rendered in real time by the game engine. If you create models and textures with the final image in mind and gear the lighting toward elegantly showing off the scene, the final touches will be relatively easy to set up.

To set the proper settings, begin with the Render Scene dialog box.

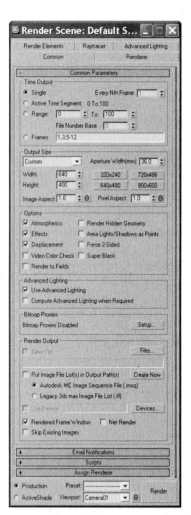

Figure 11.1

The Common tab in the Render Scene dialog box

Render Scene Dialog Box

The Render Scene dialog box is where you define your render output for 3ds Max. You can open this dialog box by clicking the Render Scene icon () in the main toolbar, by selecting Rendering → Render, or by pressing F10. You've already seen how to Quick Render (🖌) a frame in your scene to check your work. The settings in the Render Scene dialog box are used even when the Quick Render button is invoked; so it's important to understand how this dialog box works. Figure 11.1 shows the Common tab in the Render Scene dialog box.

Common Tab

The Render Scene dialog box is divided into five tabs; each tab has settings grouped by function. The Common tab stores the settings for the overall needs of the render—for example, image size, frame range to render, and the type of renderer to use.

In the Common Parameters rollout, you will find the most necessary render settings. They are described in the following sections.

TIME OUTPUT

In this section, you can set the frame range of your render output by selecting one of the following options (shown here):

Single This option renders the current frame only. The frame range is set to single by default.

Active Time Segment This option renders the frame range in the timeline.

Range This option renders the frame range specified in the text boxes.

Frames This option renders the frames typed in the text box. You can enter frame numbers separated by commas or specified as ranges, such as 3–13, to render only the specified frames.

Every Nth Frame This option is enabled when you are rendering more than one frame. It allows you to render every *n*th frame, where *n* is a whole number, so you can specify how many frames to skip.

Typically, you will be rendering single frames as you model, texture, and light the scene. The closer you are to final rendering, especially for scenes with moving cameras or lights, the more likely you will need to render a sequence of images to check the animation of the scene and how the lighting works. This is where the Every Nth Frame function comes in very handy. Using it, you can render every fifth frame— for example, to quickly see a render test range of your scene without having to render the entire frame range.

You should always test render at least a few frames of an animation before you render the entire frame range, because the smallest omission or error can cost you hours of rendering and effectively bottleneck production flow and get several people annoyed at you. This practice is a good habit to start. Whenever you want to launch a render of the entire scene, render at least one frame to check the output. If you have animated lights or cameras, use the Every Nth Frame option to test a few frames.

OUTPUT SIZE

The image size of your render, which is set in the Output Size section (shown here), will depend on your output format—that is, how you want to show your render. Chapter 1, "Basic Concepts," explains the popular resolutions used in production.

By default, the dialog box is set to render images at a resolution of 640 × 480 pixels, defined by the Width and Height parameters respectively. This resolution has an image aspect of 1.333, meaning the ratio of the frame's width to its height. Changing the Image Aspect value will adjust the size of your image along the Height parameter to correspond with the existing Width parameter to accommodate the newly requested aspect ratio. Different displays have different aspect ratios. For example, regular television is 1.33:1 (simply called 1.33) and a high-definition (HD) television is a widescreen with a ratio of 1.78:1 (simply called 1.78). The resolution of your output will define the screen ratio.

Pixel aspect affects the image because it actually changes the shape of the pixel from a square to a rectangle. This reflects how TV screens (standard definition, not HD) display images. When output is displayed on a TV screen, the image will be squeezed slightly horizontally. Therefore, renders are created a bit wider so that when they are displayed on a TV screen, they will appear normal. This is especially visible when you render a round object as shown in the following graphic (Figure 11.2). On the left, the sphere is rendered with a pixel aspect of 1.0 (i.e., 1:1 ratio). On the right, the sphere is rendered with a pixel aspect of 0.9 (i.e., 0.9:1 ratio). However, when the sphere on the right is displayed on a standard TV, it will appear round and not stretched in this manner.

Figure 11.2

Rendering a round object for display on a TV screen

You hardly ever have to worry about Pixel Aspect ratios. They are mentioned only for those who may be outputting directly to DV tape or DVD. Luckily, in the Output Size section of the Render Scene window there is a drop-down menu for choosing presets from different film and video resolutions. Custom is the default, and it allows you to set your own resolution. You can also select one of the Preset Resolution buttons. For DVD or TV output, you should select the NTSC D-1 (video) preset. For output to a DV tape, you should select the NTSC DV (video) preset. They both have a pixel aspect ratio of 0.9 to account for the TV "squeeze." Of course, if you (or your client) are in Europe or in another place where the PAL standard is used, you will need to select the PAL equivalents of the aforementioned presets, because TV resolutions and frame rates differ internationally. For more on aspect ratios and frame rates, see Chapter 1

The higher the resolution, the longer the scene will take to render. Doubling the resolution might quadruple the render time. To save time when you're working with large frame sequences, you can render tests at half the resolution of the final output and render every fifth frame or so.

The image quality of a render also affects how long a render will take. In addition to turning down the resolution for a test, you can use a lower-quality render and/or turn off certain effects, such as Atmospherics (light fog). Quality settings are explained in the following section.

OPTIONS

The Options section (shown in the following graphic) lets you access several global toggles. Three boxes are checked by default. You can toggle the rendering of specific elements in your scene. For example, if you are using Atmospherics (Volume Light) or Effects (Lens Flare) and don't want them to render, you can uncheck the appropriate box(es). This is a shortcut to turn off the Effect or Atmosphere.

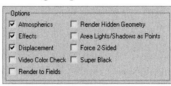

RENDER OUTPUT

What good does it do to render a scene if you don't save the files? When you are done setting up the dialog for your image output, you need to tell 3ds Max where to render the images and what file format to use. Use the Render Output section shown here to indicate that the file should be saved.

The Image Format can be selected to be a single image file or sequence of image files that form a sequence or it can be a movie file such as a QuickTime. In fact, 3ds Max supports many image file formats. The most common movie format is arguably QuickTime. A sequence of frames is typically rendered to Targa or TIFF files.

Choosing a Filename

To specify a location and file type to render to, click the Files button to open the Render Output File dialog box shown in Figure 11.3. Select the folder to which you want to render, and set the filename. You can set the file type using the Save As Type pull-down menu.

Figure 11.3

The Render Output File dialog box defines how the render saves to disk.

Proper file naming is very important when you render a scene, particularly when you are rendering a sequence of images and have hundreds of frames. Saved images are usually identified by a filename, a frame number, and an extension in the form `filename_####.ext`—for example, `stillife_0234.tif`. This format is used in production facilities and accepted by most compositing programs, such as Combustion or After Effects.

When you enter the filename for an image sequence, as shown here, you can include an underscore (the _ character) *after* the filename and before the frame number to help differentiate the two. This is especially useful if you use version numbers in your scene names. If you don't use an underscore (or similar character) between the filename and frame number, your rendered image files can be confusing, as shown in the file list in Figure 11.4.

> It's a good idea to name your rendered images according to the scene's filename. This way you can always know from which scene file a rendered image was produced without rooting through several files and/or guessing.

The extension portion of the image filename is a three-letter abbreviation that corresponds to the type of file you are rendering. By specifying a file format in the Save As Type drop-down menu, you automatically set the extension for the file in its filename. This way you ensure that you can identify the file type.

Figure 11.4

Image filenames without a separator between the filename and frame number are confusing to look at and might play out of sequence.

Name ▲	Size	Type
testrange_v010000.tif	1,013 KB	TIF Image
testrange_v010002.tif	1,013 KB	TIF Image
testrange_v010004.tif	1,013 KB	TIF Image
testrange_v010006.tif	1,013 KB	TIF Image
testrange_v010008.tif	1,013 KB	TIF Image
testrange_v010010.tif	1,013 KB	TIF Image
testrange_v010012.tif	1,013 KB	TIF Image
testrange_v010014.tif	1,013 KB	TIF Image
testrange_v010016.tif	1,013 KB	TIF Image
testrange_v010018.tif	1,013 KB	TIF Image
testrange_v010020.tif	1,013 KB	TIF Image
testrange_v010022.tif	1,013 KB	TIF Image
testrange_v010024.tif	1,013 KB	TIF Image
testrange_v010026.tif	1,013 KB	TIF Image
testrange_v010028.tif	1,013 KB	TIF Image
testrange_v010030.tif	1,013 KB	TIF Image
testrange_v010032.tif	1,013 KB	TIF Image
testrange_v010034.tif	1,013 KB	TIF Image
testrange_v010036.tif	1,013 KB	TIF Image
testrange_v010038.tif	1,013 KB	TIF Image
testrange_v010040.tif	1,013 KB	TIF Image
testrange_v010042.tif	1,013 KB	TIF Image
testrange_v010044.tif	1,013 KB	TIF Image
testrange_v010046.tif	1,013 KB	TIF Image
testrange_v010048.tif	1,013 KB	TIF Image
testrange_v010050.tif	1,013 KB	TIF Image
testrange_v010052.tif	1,013 KB	TIF Image
testrange_v010054.tif	1,013 KB	TIF Image
testrange_v010056.tif	1,013 KB	TIF Image
testrange_v010058.tif	1,013 KB	TIF Image
testrange_v010060.tif	1,013 KB	TIF Image
testrange_v010062.tif	1,013 KB	TIF Image
testrange_v010064.tif	1,013 KB	TIF Image

Image File Type

You can save your images in a wide range of formats when you render with 3ds Max. The format you choose depends on your own preference and your output needs. For example, JPEG (Joint Photographic Experts Group) files may be great for the small file sizes preferred on the Internet, but their color compression and lack of alpha channel (a feature discussed later in this chapter in the "Image Channels and the Rendered Frame Window" sidebar) make them undesirable for professional film or television production work beyond test renders and *dailies*, a meeting where the day's (or week's) work on a production is looked at and discussed for direction.

Furthermore, it's best to render a sequence of images rather than a movie file for two reasons. First, you want your renders to be their best quality with little to no image compression. Second, if a render fails during a movie render, you must re-render the entire sequence. With an image sequence, however, you can pick up where the last frame left off. The best file type format to render to is Targa or TIFF (Tagged Image File Format), though it can come down to personal preference. For example, OpenEXR is an incredibly robust file to work with in compositing and is preferred by many professional artists.

These file formats enjoy universal support, have little to no image quality loss due to compression, and support an alpha channel. Almost all image-editing and compositing packages can read Targa and TIFF formatted files, so either is a safe choice most of the time. For more on image formats, see Chapter 1.

IMAGE CHANNELS AND THE RENDERED FRAME WINDOW

Image files are composed of red, green, and blue channels. Each channel specifies the amount of that primary additive color in the image. (See Chapter 1 for more on how computers define color.) In addition, some file formats can also save a fourth channel, called the alpha channel. This channel defines the transparency level of the image. Just as the red channel defines how much red is in an area of the image, the alpha channel defines how transparent the image is when layered or composited on another image. If the alpha channel is black, the image is perfectly see-through. If the alpha channel is white, the image is opaque. The alpha channel is also known as the matte. An object that has a transparency in its material, such as the wine bottle shown rendered here, will render with a gray alpha channel.

The alpha channel is displayed in the Rendered Frame window. You have seen this window display your test renders several times throughout this book. It is shown here.

To view an image's alpha channel in the Rendered Frame window, click the Display Alpha Channel icon. To reset the view to RGB (full-color view), click the Display Alpha Channel icon again. You can also see how much red, green, or blue is present in the frame by clicking any one of the red, green, and blue disc icons that are the Enable RGB Channel icons.

To save an image you like in the Rendered Frame window, click the Save Bitmap button. The Clone Rendered Frame button is quite useful in that it creates a copy of this window for you so you can compare a newer render to an older render without needing to save the images.

To copy a rendered image into another program, click the Copy Bitmap icon, which will copy the image into the Windows Clipboard. This image will then be available when you open other programs. You can paste it quickly into another application in fewer steps than before by using this new feature.

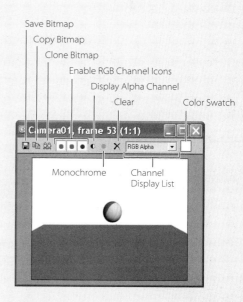

Figure 11.5

**The Render Process-
ing dialog box
shows you every-
thing you want to
know about your
current render.**

Render Processing

When you click the Render button in the Render Scene dialog box, the Render Processing dialog box pops up (Figure 11.5). This dialog box shows the parameters being used, and it displays a process bar indicating the render's progress. You can pause or cancel the render by clicking the appropriate button. Rendering can consume most, if not all, of your system's resources. (It may also consume more than your system's resources, which usually results in a crash!) Pausing a render will not let you access your scene in 3ds Max, but it will stop the process on your system momentarily so that you can tend to another PC task.

Assign Renderer

The Assign Renderer rollout displays which renderers are assigned to your scene. Two types of renderers are available in 3ds Max by default (without any additional plugins installed):

Default Scanline Renderer The scanline renderer renders the scene as a series of horizontal lines.

mental ray Renderer This is a general-purpose renderer that can generate physically correct simulations of lighting and material effects.

mental ray is not covered in this book because it is an advanced renderer. All of the renders in this book are accomplished using the default scanline renderer. mental ray is a powerful high-quality renderer that you should try once you've mastered scanline rendering.

Rendering the Bouncing Ball

Seeing is believing, but doing is understanding. In this exercise, you will render the Bouncing Ball animation from Chapter 8, "Introduction to Animation," to get the feel for rendering an animation in 3ds Max. Just follow these steps:

1. Set your Project folder to the Bouncing Ball project that you copied to your hard drive from the CD. Open the `Animation_Ball_02.max` file in the Scenes folder. Let's render a movie to see the animation.

2. Open the Render Scene dialog box. In the Time Output section, select Active Time Segment: 0 to 100.

3. In the Output Size section, select the 320 × 240 preset button and leave Image/Pixel Aspect as is.

4. Leave the Options group at the default, and skip down to the Render Output section. Click the Files button to open an Explorer window. Navigate to where you want to save the output file, preferably into the RenderOutput folder in your Bouncing Ball project. Name the file **Bounce Ball**, and click the drop-down menu next to Save As

Type to choose MOV Quick Time File (*.mov) for your render file type. Normally, we would render to a sequence of images rather than a movie file like this; however, for short renders, a QuickTime works out fine.

By default, 3ds Max will render your file(s) to the RenderOutput folder in the current project directory.

Apple's QuickTime movie file format gives you a multitude of options for compression and quality. The quality settings for the QuickTime file are not the same as the render quality settings.

5. After you select MOV Quick Time File and click the Save button, the Compression Settings window, shown in Figure 11.6, opens. Set the parameters for the QuickTime as indicated:

Compression Type: Photo–JPEG

Frames per second: 30

Compressor Depth: Color

Quality: Best

Click OK.

If you are concerned about the file size of your renders, you can slide the Quality bar to a lower quality setting for the compressor. The Photo-JPEG compressor makes fairly good images with small file sizes. However, you'll want to deliver your renders at the highest quality you can muster. To improve quality, use a different Compressor Type. For example, Animation is lossless and makes big files, but those big files look much better.

6. Skip down to the bottom of the Render Scene dialog box, and verify that Production is selected. Select the viewport you want to render in the Viewport drop-down menu. You need to render Camera01.

7. Click Render. The Rendered Frame window will show you a preview of the render as it goes through the frames, and the Rendering Process dialog box will appear.

After the render is complete, navigate to your render location (by default it is set to the RenderOutput folder for the Bouncing Ball project). Double-click the Quick-Time file to see your movie, and enjoy a latte.

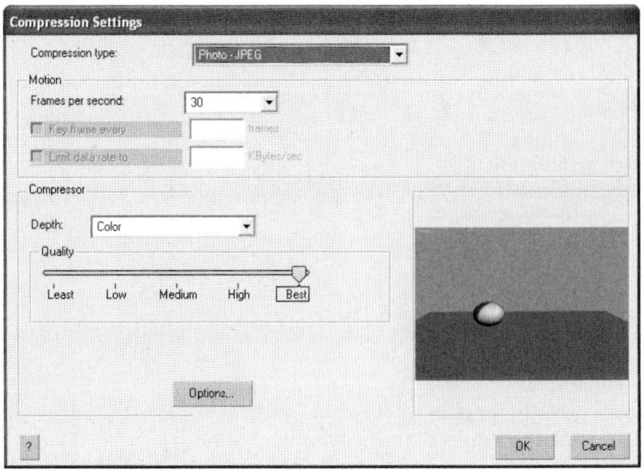

Figure 11.6

QuickTime compression settings affect the quality of the rendered QuickTime video file.

Renderer Tab Basics

The Renderer tab, found in the Render Scene dialog box, has options that determine the look and quality of the render. The options that are displayed in this tab depend on which renderer you assigned to render your scene. We are going to cover the default scanline only. This rollout sets the parameters for the default scanline renderer.

Most of the features in Options (shown here) are used to make rendering a scene more efficient. If you want to do a quick render of an animation, for example, turn off Mapping and Shadows. You will still see the movement, but the processing will go faster.

Antialiasing

Aliasing is the staircase effect you see in an image just at the edge of a line or area of color, particularly when that edge is at an angle, as shown in Figure 11.7.

Antialiasing can smooth this stepped effect on diagonal or curved lines. It blurs and mixes the color values of pixels adjacent to the jagged line or curve, as shown in Figure 11.8. Turning this feature off will speed up your renders, but the quality loss will be noticeable.

Filters

Filters are the last step in antialiasing. You can use them to access different methods of calculating the antialiasing at the subpixel level in order to sharpen or soften your final output. You don't need to worry about which filter to use until you have much more rendering experience under your belt. The Area filter, which is the default filter, will work great.

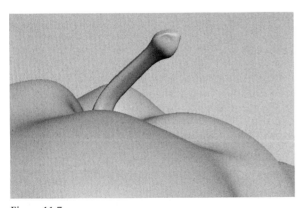

Figure 11.7

Aliasing is the stepped effect on diagonal and curved lines. Notice the top ridges of the fruit and its stem.

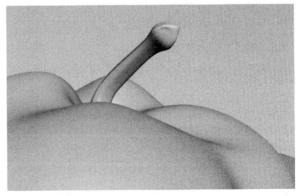

Figure 11.8

Antialiasing helps smooth jagged diagonal and curved lines.

If you are curious about the different filter types, select a filter. A short description of it will appear in the box below the Filter Maps check box.

Motion Blur

With *motion blur,* a renderer can simulate how the eye or a camera sees an object in motion. When an object moves relatively fast, your eye (or a camera) perceives a blur on the object. Using motion blur for an animation can greatly enhance the fidelity of your render, although it adds more processing time. Use motion blur sparingly in most scenes. It takes a careful eye to choose the right blur amount for an object.

The Renderer tab in the Render Scene dialog box has two sections used for setting the type of motion blur you need.

Object Motion Blur

The Object Motion Blur section (shown here) lets you access the motion blur settings.

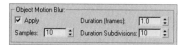

The Object Motion Blur settings are as follows:

Duration (Frames) The higher the Duration number, the more blur you get. You can see the difference in the motion blur for the ball in Figure 11.9.

Samples This setting determines how many duration subdivision copies are sampled. The higher the Samples number, the better the motion blur quality.

Duration Subdivisions This setting determines how many copies of each object are rendered within the duration. The higher the Subdivisions number, the smoother the motion blur will look.

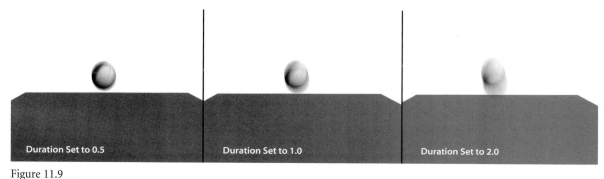

Figure 11.9

Different durations give different motion blur lengths.

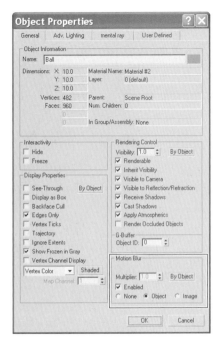

Figure 11.10

Choose the type of motion blur for an object through its Object Properties window.

Setting the Duration very high and the Samples and Duration Subdivisions low will give you a ghosting effect that will kill the look of the motion blur. You will need to find the right balance to achieve a believable blur. Remember that more is less. Just a touch of motion blur may be all a scene needs.

Image Motion Blur

As you'll notice in the Render Scene dialog box, Object Motion Blur is turned on by default. However, you still need to enable motion blur on a per object basis; this means you have to toggle motion blur on for any object that you want to render with blur.

To turn on motion blur, select the object and right-click on it in a viewport. From the Quad menu, choose Object Properties. Select the type of motion blur (shown in Figure 11.10) you want, and then adjust the parameters in the Renderer tab.

The difference between Object and Image motion blur types can be seen in Figure 11.11. The bouncing ball on the left is rendered with Object motion blur, and the one on the right is rendered with Image motion blur. Both are rendered with the same Duration. The Image motion blur renders smoother, although it may not be as accurate because it is a smearing effect created *after* the object is rendered into the image. The Object blur renders the blur during the scanline rendering process itself.

For now, you only need to be concerned with the Duration parameter for an Image motion blur. This setting, as with the Object motion blur, sets the amount (and therefore the length) of the blur. Remember not to go overboard with motion blur. A little goes a long way.

Figure 11.11

Different motion blur types give you different results. The one on the left is Object motion blur, and the one on the right is Image motion blur.

Previewing with ActiveShade

ActiveShade is a fantastic 3ds Max feature that lets you interactively preview a render as you make changes in the scene. This is particularly helpful for texturing and lighting because the floating ActiveShade window updates whenever you make a light or material change in the scene.

> ActiveShade doesn't render Atmospheric effects.

To enable ActiveShade, open the Render Scene dialog box (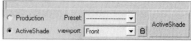). At the bottom of the window, click to toggle on the ActiveShade rendering, as shown in the following graphic. Pick your viewport, and either click the ActiveShade button in the Render Scene dialog box or click the Quick Render button in the main toolbar. The icon in the main toolbar changes ( ) as you switch from Production rendering to ActiveShade rendering.

> You can have only one ActiveShade window open at a time. If you try to open another window, an alert will ask whether you want to close the other window.

You can also turn a viewport into an ActiveShade window. Select the view where you want to enable ActiveShade, and right-click the viewport's name. Select Views → ActiveShade from the context menu as shown in Figure 11.12.

That viewport will then become an ActiveShade window and will update a render every time you make changes to the scene. This helps keep the clutter of open windows to a minimum.

Cameras

Cameras in 3ds Max, as shown in the Perspective viewport in Figure 11.13, capture and output all the fun in your scene. In theory, the cameras in 3ds Max work as much like real cameras as possible. Hence, the more you know about photography, the easier these concepts are to understand.

The *camera* creates a perspective through which you can see and render your scene. You can have as many cameras in the scene as you want. However, it's a good idea to position the camera you're planning to render with where you want it for your final framing. You can use the Perspective viewport to move around your scene as you work, leaving the render camera alone.

Figure 11.12

Select ActiveShade from the context menu.

Figure 11.13

A camera as seen in a viewport

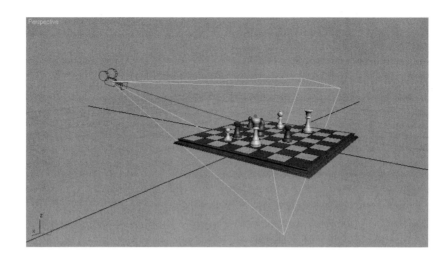

Creating a Camera

There are two types of cameras in 3ds Max: Target and Free. A *Target camera*, much like a Target spotlight, has a Target node that allows it to look at a spot defined by where the target is placed (or animated). A Target camera is easier to aim than a Free camera because once you position the target object at the center of interest, the camera will always aim there.

On the other hand, *Free cameras* have only one node, so they must be rotated to aim at the subject, much like a Free spotlight. If your scene requires the camera to follow an action, you will be better off with a Target camera.

You can create a camera by clicking on the Cameras icon (📷) in the Create panel and selecting either of the two camera types, as shown here.

To create a Target camera, click in a viewport to lay down the Camera node, and then drag to pull out and place the Target node. To create a Free camera, click in a viewport to place it.

Using Cameras

Figure 11.14

Stock lenses make it easy to pick the right lens for a scene.

A camera's main feature is the *lens,* which sets the *focal length* in millimeters and the *field of view* (FOV), which determines how wide an area the camera sees, in degrees. By default, a 3ds Max camera lens is 43.456mm long with an FOV of 45 degrees. This default lens will most likely meet all your camera needs, but in case you need to change the lens, you can use the Lens or FOV parameters to create a new lens using the spinner or by entering a value. To change a lens, you can also pick from the stock lenses available for a camera in its Modify Panel parameters, as shown in Figure 11.14.

The 3ds Max Lens and FOV are tied together. One drives the other because the focal length of a real lens sets the field of view.

The most interactive way to adjust a camera is to use the Viewport Navigation tools. You can then place the camera while you see its field of view in that viewport. The Camera viewport must be selected for the Viewport Camera tools to be available to you in the lower-right corner of the UI. You can move the camera or change the Lens or FOV. Chapter 3, "The 3ds Max Interface," has a complete list of the tools in the "Viewport Navigation Controls" subsection. You can also change a camera by selecting the camera object and moving and rotating it just as you would any other object.

Talk Is Cheap!

The best way to explain how to use a camera is to create one, as in the following steps:

1. Set your project to the Rendering Scene Files project you have copied to your hard drive from the CD. Open the `Camera Create.max` scene file in the Rendering Scene Files folder on the CD. This is the chessboard from the lighting chapter, but without a camera. Creating a camera is the same as creating a light. It's easier to create a camera in the Top viewport, so you can easily orient it in reference to your scene objects. Figure 11.15 shows the intended position of a camera for this scene.

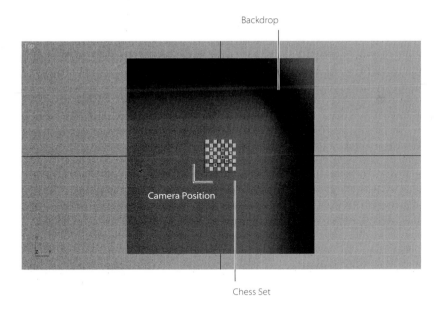

Figure 11.15

The camera would go here.

2. In the Create panel, click the Cameras icon ( ). Select the Target camera and go to the Top viewport. Click from the bottom of the viewport and drag to the chessboard as shown in Figure 11.16. The first click creates the Camera object. The mouse drag and release sets the location of the target, just like creating a target light.

Figure 11.16

Create a camera to look at the chessboard.

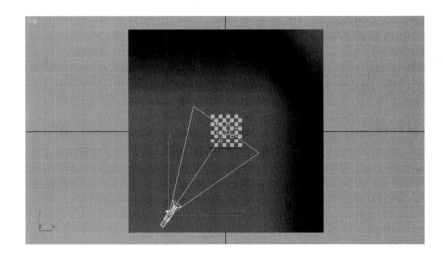

3. The camera was created along the ground plane. You need to move the entire camera up using the Front viewport. The easiest way to do this is to select the camera and target using the line that connects the camera and target. That will select both the target and camera so you can move them as a unit. Use the Move tool to relocate the camera higher in the scene to place it at the level of the chess pieces.

4. To see the Camera viewport, select a viewport and press the C key. This changes the viewport to whatever camera is currently selected. If there are multiple cameras in your scene and none are selected, when you press C, you will get a dialog that gives a list of the cameras in the scene from which you can choose, as shown in Figure 11.17.

5. Now Quick Render the scene (press F9 or click the Teapot icon) through the camera you just created and positioned. Find a good framing for the chessboard and set your camera.

Figure 11.17

The Select Camera dialog box will list the cameras in the scene.

When the camera is set up, take some time to move it around and see the changes in the viewport. Moving a camera from side to side is known as a *truck*. Moving a camera in and out is called a *dolly*. Rotating a camera is called a *roll*. Also change the Lens and FOV settings to see the results.

Zooming a lens (changing the Lens parameter) is not the same as a dolly in or dolly out. The field of view changes when you zoom, and it stays constant when you dolly. They will yield different framings.

Animating a Camera

Now that the camera is in the scene, let's add some animation to the camera. Camera animation is done in the same way as animating any object. You can animate the camera or the target or both. You can also animate camera parameters such as the lens or FOV.

1. In the scene you just worked in, select the camera.

2. Move the Time slider to frame 30.

3. Press N to activate Auto Key, or click its icon.

4. Use the Move tool to move the camera farther away from the still life. The idea is to create a dolly out of the still life.

5. Now scrub through the animation and make any edit you desire.

> If you are comfortable using the Perspective viewport, you can convert it to a Camera view by pressing Ctrl+C. Cool trick!

Clipping Planes

You can limit what your camera sees in a scene. For example, in a huge scene, you can exclude or *clip* the geometry that is beyond a certain distance by using *clipping planes*. This helps minimize the amount of geometry that needs to be calculated. Each camera has a clipping plane for distance (far) and foreground (near), as shown in Figures 11.18 and 11.19 respectively. The near clipping plane will clip geometry within the distance designated from the camera lens.

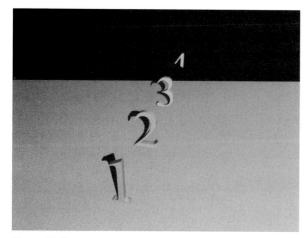

Figure 11.18

A far clipping plane cuts off the distant extents of a scene.

Figure 11.19

A near clipping plane cuts off the extents directly in front of a camera.

Figure 11.20

Click the Clip Manually check box and set the distances.

You can also use clipping planes to create a cutaway look for a model. Set your near clipping plane to a distance into the object, and the object will render as if it were sliced, giving you a perfect cutaway look.

Likewise, if you find that a model or scene you have imported looks odd or is cut off, check to make sure your clipping planes are adjusted to fit the extent of the scene, especially with imported models.

To enable clipping planes, click the Clip Manually check box and set the distances needed, as shown in Figure 11.20.

Once you turn on manual clipping planes, the camera will display the near and far extents in the viewports with a red plane marker, as shown in grayscale in Figure 11.21.

Figure 11.21

When Clip Manually is enabled, a camera will display its manual clipping planes in a viewport.

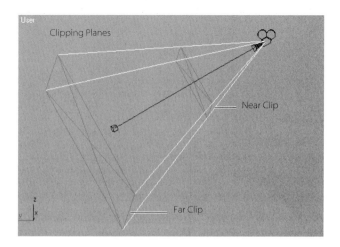

Safe Frame

Because every TV is different, what you see on one screen may look somewhat different on a different screen. To help make sure the action of your scene is contained within a safe area on all TV screens, you can enable the Safe Frame view in any viewport. This will, as shown in Figure 11.22, show you a set of three boundaries in your viewport.

The Live area is the extent of what will be rendered. The Action Safe area is the boundary where you should be assured that the action in the scene will display on most if not all TV screens. Most TVs will display somewhere between the Action Safe and the Live areas. Finally, the Title Safe boundary is where you can feel comfortable rendering text in your frame. Because some TVs distort the image slightly at the edges, any text that falls outside the Title Safe area may not be readable. Although they are based on TV technology from years ago, these conventions hold true in professional production to this day. The Safe Frame areas are still good guidelines to use when framing your shot.

To view Show Safe Frame in the chosen viewport, right-click on the name in the viewport to access the context menu, and then choose Safe Frame from the list.

Title Safe

Action Safe

Live Area

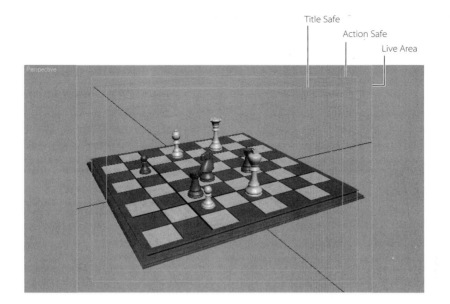

Figure 11.22

Safe Frame gives you a suggested boundary for the action of your framing.

Render Elements

The Render Elements tab is another tab in the Rendering Scene dialog box. You might not need this feature as a beginner, but you will be surprised at the control you get when you render your scene into separate passes to composite later. As a beginner, you should concentrate on becoming familiar with rendering and lighting. As the months pass and you feel more comfortable rendering, you should discover that most CG is layered.

This means that separate passes are rendered outside of 3ds Max and layered or composited together with finer control in a program such as Photoshop for still images, and Combustion, After Effects, or Shake for image sequences. The ability to layer is another reason why rendering to image files is preferred over rendering to movie files.

However, you will need to understand compositing to be able to control and layer the elements back together.

Shadows and reflections are the main elements that you might consider rendering separately, especially when you are first learning. When these elements are separate, you gain a greater degree of control in compositing because you can affect the shadows or reflections any way you want (soften, color, transparency, etc.) as you composite them back on top of the image. For example, if you render a scene of a tree casting a shadow across a lawn, you will have to render the entire scene again if you decide to lighten the shadow color. If you have the shadow as a separate pass, you can very easily and interactively change the darkness of the shadow as you composite it in Shake, for instance.

The following list describes common elements to render:

Alpha Renders a black-and-white matte to be used in compositing. This is especially helpful when you need different mattes for different objects in your scene. In Figure 11.23, the chessboard is shown rendered Alpha only.

Figure 11.23
The Alpha element

Reflection Renders only the reflections so you can composite them separately onto the color render to have control over the amount of reflections in the final composited image, for example. Figure 11.24 shows the chess pieces' reflections in the chessboard rendered as an element.

Figure 11.24
**The Reflection
element**

Refraction Renders only refracting elements in transparent or translucent objects so they may be layered in the composite at a later time.

Self-Illumination Renders the incandescence of an object's material separately, so its intensity may be controlled in composite.

Shadow Renders only the shadows cast in the scene into the Alpha channel of the image. Figure 11.25 shows the chess piece's shadow element. Keep in mind that you will have to render to an image format that has an Alpha channel, such as TIFF.

Figure 11.25

The Shadows element as shown in the Alpha channel of the image

Specular Renders only the highlights on an object's glossy material. Figure 11.26 shows the specular highlights on the chess pieces. Look at how the nicks and scratches on the pieces are so noticeable in this element.

Figure 11.26

The Specular element

Z-Depth Renders a grayscale image that responds to the depth of a scene. The closer an object or a part of an object is, the whiter it renders. The farther from the camera an object or its parts are, the darker the render. This pass is then used in a compositing program, such as Combustion, to create a sense of haze or blur to add a depth of field to the image. Figure 11.27 shows a Z-Depth pass generated for the chessboard scene.

Figure 11.27

The Z-Depth element

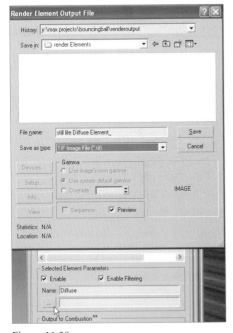

Figure 11.28

In the Selected Element parameters type-in box, enter where you want to save the bitmap elements.

Now, let's try rendering something. Follow along with these steps.

1. Select the Render Elements tab in the Rendering Scene window, click the Add button, and select the element you want to render.

2. Once you select a render element, it will be added to the Element Rendering List. Then you'll need to go down to the Selected Element parameters to input where you will save the bitmap elements, as shown in Figure 11.28. The dialog box will name the element automatically. However, when you go into the Explorer window to save it, you should name it again.

3. If you want each element to be rendered in its own Rendered Frame window, check the Display Elements box. If it is unchecked, the program will render the elements to a file and the Render Frame window will not show you the progress of each element.

4. Click the Render button to begin a render. 3ds Max will render the entire scene, and then output the elements as needed.

Rendering Effects

Rendering Effects offers a variety of special effects such as lens effects, film grain, and blur to add to your render. Rendering Effects allows you to create effects without having to render to see the results. They are rendered after your scene is rendered, and they are added to the rendered image automatically.

Lens Effects: Glow

You will add a glow effect to a light bulb hanging over the chessboard in a scene.

For this scene, we've chosen to glow the Light Bulb object. You can also glow a light; this property can only be set through Object Properties.

You will glow the Light Bulb object in the following steps:

1. Set your project to the Rendering Scenes project you copied from the CD. Load the Chess_Glow.max scene file from the Rendering Scene Files project's Scenes folder.

2. Select the light bulb, and then right-click on the Light Bulb object. From the context menu, select Object Properties, as shown in Figure 11.29.

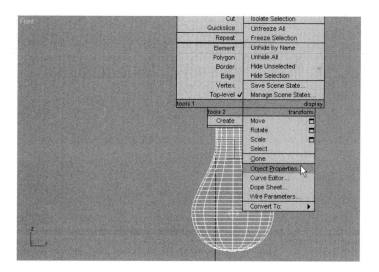

Figure 11.29

Select Object Properties from the context menu.

3. In the dialog box, go to the G-Buffer section and assign 2 as the Object ID number for the glow effect, as shown in Figure 11.30. This tells 3ds Max which object gets the glow. The number you assign doesn't matter unless you want different glows on different objects. In that case, each glow object would receive its own Object ID number.

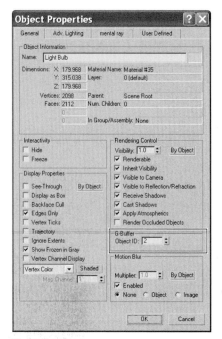

Figure 11.30

Set a unique number for the Object ID.

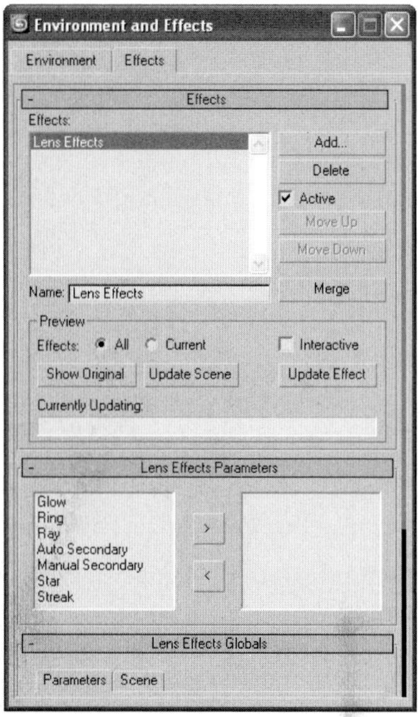

Figure 11.31

Adding the Lens Effects to the Environment and Effects window

Another way you can assign glow is through the object's material. Go to the Material Editor, and in the toolbar, click and hold on the Material ID channel. The benefit of using the material for the glow is that you can glow any object that has the material applied.

4. In the menu bar, choose Rendering → Effects to open the Environment and Effects window. Click the Add button. Then pick Lens Effects from the Add Effect dialog box. Figure 11.31 shows that the Lens Effects have been added.

5. Scroll down to Lens Effects Parameters and select Glow to add to the box on the right, as shown in Figure 11.32.

6. While still in the Environment and Effects window, scroll down to Glow Element. This is where you create the settings for the Glow Effect. There are two tabs:

Parameters This tab is where you set the size and color of the glow, as shown in Figure 11.33.

Options This tab is where you can assign the glow to the object desired. Under Image Sources, you have to choose how the glow will be applied to the object, through the material or object properties.

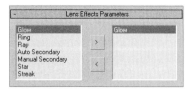

Figure 11.32

Select Glow in the Lens Effects Parameters.

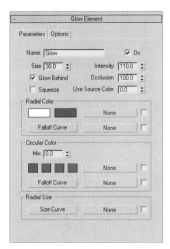

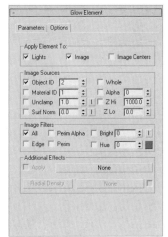

Figure 11.33

Set the size and color of the glow.

Figure 11.34

Set the Object ID parameter to 2.

7. Click the Options tab. Because you are creating the light bulb's glow through the Light Bulb object's Object ID, set the Object ID parameter to 2, as shown in Figure 11.34. Leave the other parameters at their default values.

8. Click over to the Parameters tab to set the glow's size. Setting the size for the glow can be a bit tricky because the size of the glow depends on the size of your object. Set the Size value to 5. Leave the Intensity set at the default; once you render the effect, you can adjust the Intensity.

9. To add color to the glow, you can use two methods: You can set the Use Source Color parameter to set the glow color to a percentage of the object's material color. You also can use the Radial Color parameter to set the colors for the inside of the glow (on the left in the Radial Color parameter) and the outside of the glow (on the right in the Radial Color parameter). In this case, set the Use Source Color to 65 because the light bulb has a yellow material applied. If you have Interactive Preview enabled (see the note in this section), you can see how the glow looks. Otherwise, run a Quick Render to check the look.

10. The default intensity looks okay, but it could be brighter. Change the Intensity to 165. Render. Okay, it looks good. See Figure 11.35.

Using the Preview in the Environment and Effects window as shown here (in the Effects tab) provides a much easier way to view the Effects than rendering a frame does. You can select whether you want to preview all of the effects (All) in the scene or just the one you are working on (Current). Toggling Interactive updates the preview when you change the Effects parameters by opening a Render window and updating it as you make changes. Enabling Interactive may cause your computer to slow down, so leave it unchecked and use the Update Effect button when you want to see an update.

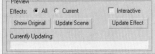

Figure 11.35

Glow!

Raytraced Reflections and Refractions

In this section, you will learn how to create realistic reflections and refractions in your renders. As you saw in Chapter 7, "Materials and Mapping," you can apply an image map to an object material's Reflection parameter to add a fake reflection to the object. To get a true reflection of the other objects in the scene, you will need to use raytracing methodology. There are essentially two ways to create raytraced reflections in a scene: by using a Raytrace map or by using a Raytrace material.

The Raytrace material is a more detailed solution; however, it can take twice as much time as using a Raytrace map, because the Raytrace material requires more calculation.

As you learned in Chapter 4, "Modeling in 3ds Max: Part I," determining the level of detail you need for a reflective surface is important. There is no reason to use the Raytrace material for a reflection unless your camera is right up on the object. In many cases, the Raytrace map looks great and saves tons of rendering time. Keep in mind though, the amount of control you will have with a Raytrace map is significantly less than with the Raytrace material.

First, you will try using the Raytrace material.

Raytrace Material

In the following steps, you will learn how to use the Raytrace material to create reflections in a scene with a fruit still life arrangement.

Creating the Raytrace Material

1. Set your project to the Rendering Scene Files project you copied from the CD. Open the `Still Life_Raytrace.max` file found in the Scenes folder of the Rendering Scene Files project on the companion CD. Change the Camera view to Camera01 in one of the viewports if it isn't already.

2. Open the Material Editor and select a sample slot. Click the Get Material button (Figure 11.36) and select the Raytrace material (materials have a blue sphere icon on the left) from the Material selections, as shown in Figure 11.37.

3. The parameters to create reflections are available through the Raytrace Basic Parameters rollout, as shown in Figure 11.38. Leave most of these parameters at their default values, but change the Reflect color swatch to white from black. This will set the reflection of the material all the way to the maximum reflectivity.

4. Change the Diffuse Color swatch to black to turn the column black. This will make the column appear as a reflective black glass material in the render.

5. Apply the Raytrace material to the Column in the scene. Render. Figure 11.39 shows the result.

Tweaking the Render

The render will show the Raytrace material on the column reflecting like a flat mirror. It looks very convincing, but you may notice the jagged edges or artifacts around the reflected objects. What you're seeing is aliasing in the reflections. The antialiasing filters set by default may not be enough. Clone this rendered image by pressing the Clone Rendered Frame Window icon (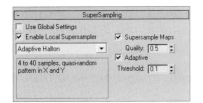), which is found in the Rendered Frame Window toolbar, to make a copy of this rendered image in another window.

When the defaults aren't enough, it is time for the heavy artillery: *SuperSampling*. SuperSampling is an extra pass of antialiasing. By default, 3ds Max applies a single SuperSample over all the materials in the scene. However, if a specific material needs more antialiasing, you can apply a separate SuperSample method to that material.

In the current Still Life scene, select the material slot for the column's Raytrace material. Go to the SuperSampling rollout and uncheck Use Global Settings. Check Enable Local Supersampler. In the pull-down menu, choose Adaptive Halton, as shown here.

Figure 11.36

Click the Get Material button.

Figure 11.37

Select the Raytrace material.

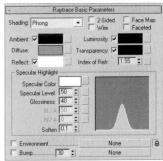

Figure 11.38

The Raytrace Basic Parameters rollout

The Adaptive Halton method performs well in this case. However, always try the regular patterns first; they tend to render faster. Quick Render the scene, and you will notice a marked improvement in the quality of the reflections (Figure 11.40).

Figure 11.39

The Raytrace material renders reflections.

Figure 11.40

Reflections with the Raytrace material with SuperSampling enabled

Raytrace Mapping

You can apply raytracing only to a specific map; you can't apply it to the entire material. Because raytracing typically takes longer to render, this can save time. In this case, you will assign a Raytrace map to the Reflection map of a material to get true reflections in the scene, at a faster render time than using the material as you just did. Follow these steps:

1. In the scene you just worked in, open the Material Editor and select an unassigned sample slot. Keep the Material set to Standard Material.

2. In the Map*s* rollout, click the mapping bar labeled None next to Reflections. Choose the Raytrace map in the Material/Map browser, as shown in Figure 11.41.

    Leave the Raytrace Map parameters at the default, as shown in Figure 11.42.

3. Click the Go to Parent button ( ) in the Raytrace Map Parameters view to return to the material's parameters.

4. Go to the Blinn Basic parameters and change the diffuse color to black to match the black column from the previous render.

5. In the Specular Highlights section, change the Specular Level to 98 and Glossiness to 90, as shown in Figure 11.43.

6. Apply the material to the column object in the scene and Quick Render.

7. You will notice the same aliasing in the reflections as in the previous example. Set the SuperSampling as you did with the prior example, and render again.

Take a look at both the images created with reflections created using the Raytrace material and the Standard material with the Raytrace map applied to Reflections. They look almost the same. This is good to know because it takes about half the time to render the Raytrace map. However, you will notice slightly better detail in the reflections created with the Raytrace material. You and the requirements of your scene will determine which reflection method works best in a particular situation. However, it's good always to start with the Raytrace map to see if it creates enough detail without too much bother.

Figure 11.41

Choose the Raytrace map.

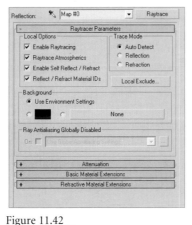

Figure 11.42

The Raytrace Map parameters

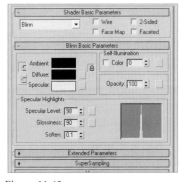

Figure 11.43

The Specular Highlights parameters

Refractions Using the Raytrace Material

Creating raytraced refractions in glass can be accomplished using the same two workflows as raytraced reflections. The same conditions apply here. The Raytrace material renders nicer, but it takes longer than using a Raytrace map for the Refraction map in a material.

Keep in mind that render times are much slower with refractions, especially if you add SuperSample to the mix—so don't freak out. Next you will create refractions using the Raytrace material:

1. In the same scene, change the Camera01 viewport to Camera02. This gives you a better view of the wine glass through which we will refract, as shown in Figure 11.44.

Figure 11.44

Changing Camera01 to Camera02

2. In the Material Editor, select an unassigned sample slot and click the Get Material button. This material will be for the wine glass.

3. Choose the Raytrace material from the Material/Map browser.

4. Go to the Raytrace Basic Parameters rollout, and change the color swatch for Transparency to white from black. (Black is opaque and white is fully transparent.)

5. Uncheck the box next to Reflect and change that spinner to 20. This sets a slight reflection for the material.

6. Take a look at the Index of Refr parameter. This value sets the *Index of Refraction* (IOR) value that determines how much the material should refract its background. For more on IOR, see the Refraction sidebar in this chapter. The value is already set to 1.55. Leave it at that value.

7. Go to the Extended Parameters rollout (Figure 11.45). The Reflections section of the parameters is at the bottom. Select Additive and change Gain to 0.7. This gives a bit of reflection brightness for the clear wine glass.

8. Go to the SuperSampling rollout and uncheck Use Global Setting. Enable Local SuperSampler and keep it set to Max 2.5 Star.

9. In the Specular Highlights group, change the Specular Level to 98 and Glossiness to 90, as shown in Figure 11.46.

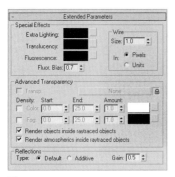

Figure 11.45

The Extended Parameters rollout for the Raytrace material

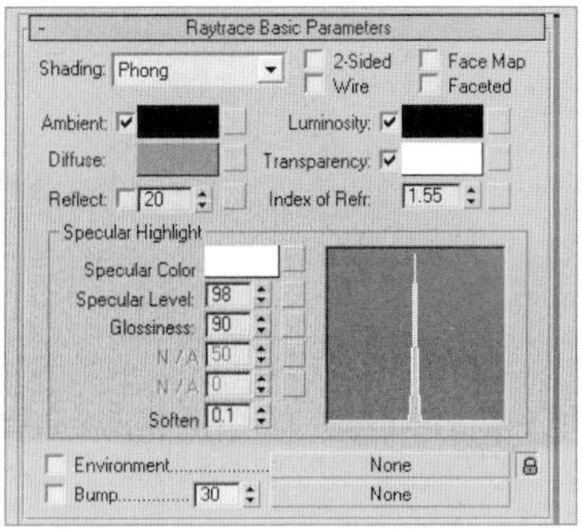

Figure 11.46

The Specular Highlights group parameters

10. Apply the material to the wine glass. The glass will turn transparent in the viewport. Quick Render. Figure 11.47 shows the result.

Figure 11.47

The wine glass refraction is rendered with the Raytrace material.

You will notice a very nice wine glass render, with the bell pepper refracting through it slightly. Change the Index of Refr parameter on the material to 8.0 and you will see a much greater refraction, as shown in Figure 11.48. That may work better for a nice heavy bottle, but it is too much for the glass. An Index of Refr parameter between 1.5 and 2.5 works pretty well for the wine glass, particularly at the bottom of the glass where it rounds down to meet the stem.

Refractions Using Raytrace Mapping

Just as you did with the reflections, you will now use a Raytrace map on the Refraction parameter for the Wine Glass material. In the following steps, you will create another refraction render for the wine glass:

1. While still in the same scene, open the Material Editor and select an unassigned sample slot. You are going to keep the material set to Standard.

2. Go to the Maps rollout and click the bar labeled None, which is next to Refraction. Choose the Raytrace map from the Material/Map browser. The material in the sample slot will turn transparent.

3. Click the Go to Parent button to return to the material's parameters.

4. Go to the Maps rollout and click the bar labeled None next to Reflection. Choose the Raytrace map from the Material/Map browser. Be warned that this setting will take a long time to render the image. If you have a slower computer or perhaps are in a rush, uncheck the Reflection Map box to turn off the reflection entirely.

5. Click the Go to Parent button to return to the material's parameters.

6. Go to the Maps rollout and change the amount of the Reflection to 6. This will reduce the amount of reflection.

7. Go to the Blinn Basic Parameters rollout and change the Opacity value to 0.

8. Go to the SuperSampling rollout and uncheck Use Global Setting. Enable Local SuperSampler and keep it as Max 2.5 Star.

9. In the Specular Highlights group, change the Specular Level to 98 and Glossiness to 90.

10. Apply the material to the Wine Glass object in the scene and render (Figure 11.49).

Figure 11.49

Use Raytrace map on the Refraction parameter to create a refraction in the wine glass.

You can control the IOR through the material's parameters in the Extended Parameters rollout, in the Advanced Transparency section, shown in Figure 11.50. Set the IOR to different numbers to see how the render compares to the Raytrace Material renders.

The render will take quite some time to finish. The raytracing reflections and refractions slow down the render quite a bit. You can leave out the reflections if you'd like, but that will reduce the believability of the wine glass. You can also map a reflection as you did with the pool ball in Chapter 7; however, having true reflections will make the wine glass look much more realistic. When you raytrace both the reflection and the refraction, using the Raytrace material seems to be the better way to go.

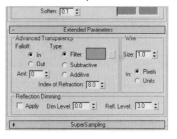

Figure 11.50

The Advanced Transparency section in the Extended Parameters rollout

REFRACTIONS

Refraction is the bending of light that creates a distortion of an image seen through a transparent or translucent object, such as glass. How light passes through from one medium, such as air, and into another medium, such as glass, determines how much light is bent and therefore how much refraction is seen. This phenomenon is simulated in a material using the Index of Refraction parameter (IOR). When there is no refraction, the IOR is set to 1; that is, there is no difference in the medium into and out of which the light is traveling. With an IOR higher than 1, the background distorts inside the object, such as when viewing a table through a crystal ball. With an IOR lower than 1, the refraction occurs at the edge of the transparent object, such as an air bubble in water.

The typical IOR value for glass is about 1.5. Because IOR relates to an object's density, you may need to adjust the IOR to get the best possible result for different types of glass, for instance. The denser the object, the higher the IOR needs to be set. Of course, refractions require that an object be semitransparent so that you can see through it to the object(s) behind it that are being refracted.

Bringing It All Together: Rendering the Rocket

Now that you have some experience with the rendering workflow in 3ds Max, let's take a quick look at rendering a short 45-frame sequence of the rocket. You will essentially take the rocket scene laid out (with the atmospheric fog light through the window we setup) in the previous chapter. You'll need to tweak a few of the scene settings, such as setting the rocket's and environment's materials to have raytraced reflections for maximum impact. You'll also animate a camera move so you can render out a sequence you can pin to your refrigerator door. Let's go!

Creating the Camera Move

We'll begin by animating the camera.

1. Set your project to the Red Rocket project from the CD. Start by opening Rocket_ Raytrace_Start.max.

This file is the same one we used at the end of the Chapter 10, "3ds Max Lighting," but all the Reflection maps have been taken out because we will be raytracing everything (Figure 11.51).

Figure 11.51

The rocket in its room, ready to go

2. To begin animating click the Auto Key button while at frame 0 (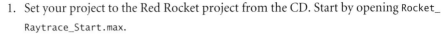) to activate it. Go to the timeline at the bottom of the Interface and move the Time slider to 45. Now when changes are made, key frames will be created for any selected objects.

3. Select the Camera Viewport because we are going to create a simple camera animation. As you saw in Chapter 3, when the Camera viewport is selected, the Viewport

Navigation tools change, as shown here. These Navigation tools make animating the camera easier.

4. Select the Dolly Camera tool ( ), to move the camera closer to the rocket. Click and drag the Dolly Camera tool in the Camera viewport until you see only the front of the rocket, as shown in Figure 11.52.

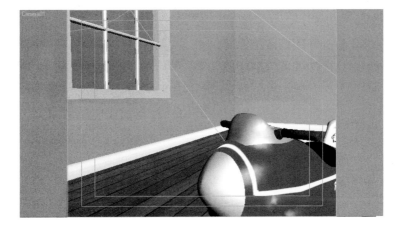

Figure 11:52

Dolly the camera closer to the rocket.

5. Select the Truck Camera tool ( ), which allows you to pan the camera. Click and drag up and to the left in the Camera viewport to center the rocket in the viewport to match the framing you see in Figure 11.53.

Figure 11.53

Truck the camera to match this framing.

6. Back to the Camera Navigation tools, select the Orbit Camera tool ( ). Center the tool in the middle of the viewport, and click and drag to the left until you get a better view of the side of the rocket as shown in Figure 11.54.

Figure 11.54

Orbit to the side of the rocket.

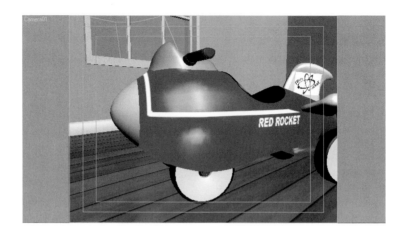

7. Use the Truck Camera tool again to move the camera more to the left and to center the rocket in the viewport. Figure 11.55 should be the final position of the rocket in the camera view. Your camera move will end at this position at frame 45 of the animation.

Figure 11.55

The final framing for your rocket at frame 45

8. Go to the Animation Player section shown here, and play the animation you created. Make any adjustments you would like to personalize the camera move. Turn off the Auto Key button and save your file. Remember to version up your file so you don't overwrite your current work.

Adding Raytraced Reflections

In Chapter 7, we used reflection bitmaps to fake the reflections on the rocket by using a bitmap to create the illusion of reflection. This technique usually looks very good, but there are circumstances where you need the reflections to look more accurate within the scene. This is when you use Raytrace map instead of a bitmap image. The Raytrace map calculates reflections as they work in the real world, reflecting the object's environment. Of course, in order for raytraced reflections to work, your object needs to be in an environment, much like the rocket's simple room. There has to be something around the object to reflect. To demonstrate this, we are going to add Raytrace to the rocket and the room.

The Rocket

To add raytraced reflections to the rocket, begin here:

1. Open the Material Editor, and you will see all the materials that were created earlier for the rocket.

2. In the Material Editor, select the first sample sphere at the top left, this is the texture for the left side of the rocket body.

   This is the only side of the rocket that will be visable in our renders, so that is the only side we will change.

3. Go to the Maps rollout, and you will see that the bitmap reflection from Chapter 7 has already been removed. If you are continuing with your own scene file, simply remove the current bitmap before continuing. To do so, just drag None from another map slot onto the Reflection channel.

4. Change the Amount value for Reflections to 20, and click None to add a map. In the Material/Maps browser, choose Raytrace.

5. Quick Render a frame, and you should see some reflections of the room. If you want the rocket to have a higher amount of reflection, you only have to go back to the Maps rollout and make the Reflection value higher than 20.

6. Go through the materials in the Material Editor for the rocket's remaining parts to add Raytrace to their reflections as well. For those materials in the `Rocket_Raytrace_Start.max` scene, you will notice that the reflection bitmaps have already been removed from the following parts of the body to make them ready for the Raytrace map:

   - Both sides of the rocket's body (Although you only see one side of the body in these renders, you may opt to put Raytrace on both.)
   - The nose
   - The fins
   - The hubcaps (white part of the wheels)
   - The tires (black part of the wheels)
   - The seat

7. Go through the Material Editor and add Raytrace to those materials. If you are continuing with your own scene, replace the reflection bitmap on the above list of materials with the Raytrace map.

We aren't adding Raytrace to everything on the rocket because Raytrace Reflections take a lot more time to render. Don't bother adding them to parts of the scene that won't make a difference. Figure 11.56 shows a render of the rocket with the Raytrace map applied to the aforementioned materials.

Figure 11.56

The rocket with ray-traced reflections

The Room

In the room, the floors and the glass on the window should also have raytraced reflections, since reflections would look very good raytraced on these objects, especially with the camera move. Let's start with the hardwood floor.

The floors have one issue with which we have to deal. The grooves between the wood panels should not have reflections, only the panels should reflect. We need to apply a mask to the reflections to block the Raytrace from the grooves in the floor. The floor already has a bump map to mark out the grooves, so that is what we will use as the mask as well.

> If the textures we are talking about do not display in the viewports, simply select the material in the Material Editor and click on the Show Map in Viewport icon in the Material Editor. If the bitmap files' paths are not connected when you open the scene file, 3ds Max will open an error dialog, allowing you to browse for the missing image(s). This can occur when sharing projects and scenes between computers, as is a common occurrence. In this case, simply navigate to that project's SceneAssets/Images folder to find the disconnected bitmap image(s).

1. Go to the Material Editor and select the sample Sphere material for the floor (the material is called FLOORS).

2. Go to the Maps rollout, change the reflections amount to 50, and click on None to add a map. Instead of selecting Raytrace, select Mask as shown here.

3. Click on Map, and select Bitmap from the Material/Map browser. Navigate to the SceneAssets\Images folder of the Red Rocket project and choose `WoodFloorREF.tif`.

4. When the bitmap is applied, you will be in the Bitmap Parameters section. Go to the Coordinate rollout and change from Environ to Texture. Whenever you apply a bitmap to reflections by default, 3ds Max changes the bitmap to Environ because it is trying to behave like a real reflection. We need the mask bitmap to behave like a normal bitmap and look to the UVW map modifier applied to the floor for its coordinates (Figure 11.57).

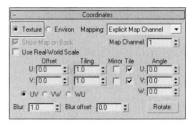

Figure 11.57

Change the bitmap back to a Texture instead of an Environ.

5. Now click the Go to Parent tool in the Material Editor toolbar to get back to the Mask parameters. Click Mask from the Material/Map browser, and select Raytrace.

6. Quick Render the frame and you'll notice the reflections are pretty high. But you can also see how the grooves have no reflection, so the mask works! For a better reflection, turn the reflection amount in the Maps rollout down to 20 for the floor. Figure 11.58 shows a render of the rocket.

Figure 11.58

The reflections in the floor look great!

Turning On the Environment Effects

Any Raytrace maps added to your scene can make the render time very slow. If you are just trying to check an animation, it is wise to deactivate Raytrace while you do your test renders. To do so, open the Render Scene dialog box (press F10 or click on its icon in the main toolbar) and click on the Raytracer Tab/Global Raytrace Engine Options to uncheck Enable Raytracing, as shown in Figure 11.59. Just remember to turn it back on when your test renders are finished.

To round off the scene, we need atmosphere: Volume light was already added to the key light in the previous chapter, so we just need to turn it on. The Render Scene dialog has a deactivate button for Atmosphere, so you can easily turn it on and off as you test render. To re-enable Atmosphere in the render, go to the Common tab of Render Scene dialog and, under the Options section, check the Atmospherics box as shown here.

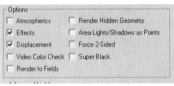

Quick Render the frame (Figure 11.60).

Figure 11.59

The Raytrace Global Parameters options

Outputting the Render

This scene has an animation on the camera, so doing a Quick Render just won't do. We need to render out the entire 45 frames of the camera move. As you saw with the Bouncing Ball render earlier in the chapter, rendering out a sequence of images is done through the Common tab of the Render Scene dialog.

Figure 11.60

The rocket is rendered with the volume light through the window.

In the Time Output section, click to select Active Time Segment: 0 to 45, as shown here. The scene file you started with from the Red Rocket project will have its time segment set properly to 1 to 45. If you are working from your own scene file, however, you can either set the Active Time Segment in your scene to 1 to 45, or you can set the Range in the Render Scene dialog manually to render from frame 1 to frame 45.

The resolution of the render is set in Output Size. The default resolution is 640 × 480, as shown here.

On a good computer, this render takes about 1 minute 20 seconds per frame with environments turned on; that means the whole 45-frame sequence will take just over one hour to render. If you want to render faster and you don't mind it being smaller, you can render out at a smaller resolution. Half the default size is 320 × 240 and will cost you one-fourth of that time (15 to 20 minutes or so or so) to render.

To change to the lower resolution, in the Output Size section, click on the preset button 320 × 240 as shown here. Now it should take just about 20 seconds per frame to render.

Go to the Render Output section of the Render Scene dialog and click Files to open the Render Output File dialog shown in Figure 11.61. Typically, animations are rendered out in a sequence of images, but for simplicity's sake, we will render out to a QuickTime movie as we did with the bouncing ball earlier in this chapter.

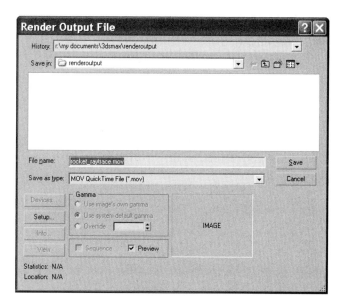

Figure 11.61

Name your output render image files.

In the Render Output File window (Figure 11.44), select where you want to store the rendered file, and pick a name for the QuickTime movie (rocket_raytrace.mov, for example). Then, in the Save As Type drop-down menu, choose MOV QuickTime file (.mov) and click Save. The Compression Settings window will appear, as shown in Figure 11.62. Again, it is generally preferable to render to a sequence of images rather than a movie file; however, in this case, a QuickTime will be best.

Figure 11.62

The Compression Settings dialog

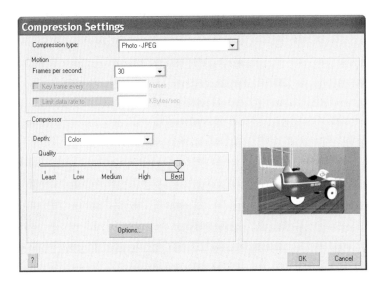

In the Compression Settings window, select Photo—JPEG for the Compression type, set Frames per second to 30, and set the Quality to Best, just as you did with the Bouncing Ball exercise. You can set the Quality slider to a lower value for a smaller QuickTime file. But remember, this Quality setting applies only to the compression of the QuickTime file and not to the render itself. Click OK to return to the Render Output File dialog, and click Save to return to the Render Scene dialog window.

Save your scene file, and you are ready to render! Just click Render in the Render Scene dialog, and go outside to play catch with your kids or hassle your spouse or sibling into a needless argument for a little while. In about 20 minutes (or one hour if you chose to render at 640 × 480), run back inside and play the QuickTime file saved in the location you chose earlier. Then take a huge magnet and stick your monitor to your fridge door. Voilà! You are now ready to enter the world of 3ds Max dynamics.

Summary

Rendering is the way you get to show your finished scene to the world, or whoever will stop and look. It enables the vector-created scene to be displayed in bitmap images or movie files on any monitor. Getting to this point in your scene takes quite a bit of work, as you can see, but once you see the results playing back on your screen, it all seems worth it.

Nothing is more fulfilling than seeing your creation come to life, and that's what rendering is all about. However, don't consider the rendering process merely the last thing to do—the point where you press a button and then go kill time bickering until the render is finished. Rendering may be the last step of the process, but you should travel the entire journey with rendering in mind, from design to models to animation to lighting. Always allow enough time to ensure that your animations render properly and at their best quality. Most beginners seriously underestimate the time needed to properly complete this step in CG production and don't allow enough time for the render. Lighting and rendering is so important, as a matter of fact, that lighting professionals (who also handle rendering) are among the most sought-after and highest-paid workers in the entertainment CG field.

In this chapter, you learned the basics of rendering with Autodesk 3ds Max 2008. You began by learning about render output and the types of files to which you can render. You rendered the Bouncing Ball exercise from Chapter 8 and enabled motion blur for heightened effect. Then you learned about cameras and rendering separate passes with Render Elements. Finally, you learned how to render glows and how to use raytracing to render true reflections and refractions in a scene. You put all that to good use in rendering the Red Rocket project that you've worked on throughout the book to a 1.5 second Quick-Time file.

After you have rendered many more scenes, you'll have a much better understanding of how to set up your scene from the very beginning to efficiently achieve a great result. It won't hurt to go over the examples in this chapter more than once and try to render your own scenes in different ways.

CHAPTER 12

Particles and Dynamics

Animating large numbers of similar objects can be an arduous task to say the least. With hundreds, if not thousands, of individual objects and all of their animated parameters and transforms to consider, this is a task that, one object at a time, could quickly become overwhelming. Luckily, 3ds Max has several tools for animating large numbers of objects in a scene including instanced objects, externally referencing objects, instanced modifiers, the Crowd utility for characters, and particle systems for controlling any number of particles. *Particles* are usually small objects, often in large numbers, that can represent rain, snow, a swarm of insects, a barrage of bullets, or anything else that requires a large quantity of objects that follow a similar action or are part of a larger system of movement.

Yet another method of creating simultaneous animations for several objects is through the use of *reactor*, the physics engine contained within 3ds Max. Using reactor, you can calculate the interactions between many rigid and soft body objects or simulate fluids or rope dynamics.

Topics in this chapter include:

- **Understanding Particle Systems**
- **Setting Up a Particle System**
- **Particle Systems and Space Warps**
- **Using Rigid Body Dynamics**
- **Using Soft Body Dynamics**

Understanding Particle Systems

Particle systems are a means to manage the infinite possibilities encountered when controlling thousands of seemingly random objects in a scene. The particles can follow a tight stream or emanate in all directions from the surface of an object, for example. The particles themselves can be pixel-sized elements on the screen or instanced geometry from an object in the scene. Particles can react to forces called *space warps,* such as wind and gravity, and bounce off objects called *deflectors* to give them a natural flow through a scene. Particles can even spawn new particles upon collision. There is a wide base of options when you are animating particle systems, especially when you are trying to simulate real-world effects such as smoke or rain.

All particle systems have two common, yet distinct components: the emitter and the particles. The *emitter,* as the name suggests, is the object from which the particles originate. The location and, to a lesser extent, the orientation of the emitter are vital to the particles' origination point in the scene. However, emitters are nonrendering objects, making their size and color unimportant.

Particles themselves are the elements that spew from the emitter. The number of particles can range from a few (to simulate a burst from a gun) to thousands (to simulate smoke from a burning building). As you would imagine, the number of particles visible in a viewport can adversely affect the viewport refresh speed and your ability to quickly navigate within the viewports. By default, far fewer particles are shown in the viewports than actually render in the scene. This helps maintain a reasonable system performance level.

Particle System Types

Two types of particle systems are available in 3ds Max: event-driven and non-event-driven particle systems.

Event-Driven Particle Systems

Event-driven particle systems use a series of tests and operators grouped into components called *events.* An operator affects the appearance and action of the individual particles and can, among many other abilities, change the shape or rotation of the particles, add a material or external force, or even delete the particles on a per-particle basis. Tests check for conditions such as a particle's age, its speed, and whether it has collided with a deflector. Particles move down the list of operators and tests in an event and, if the particles pass the requirements of a test they encounter, they can leave the current event and move to the next. If they do not pass the test, the particles continue down the list in the current event. Particles that do not pass any test in an event commonly are deleted or recycled through the event until they do pass a test. Events are wired together in a flowchart style to clearly display the path, from event to event, that the particles follow.

Particle Flow is the event-driven particle system in 3ds Max, and it is a very comprehensive solution to most particle system requirements. The upper-left pane in the Particle View window in Figure 12.1 shows a partial layout of the events in a Particle Flow setup.

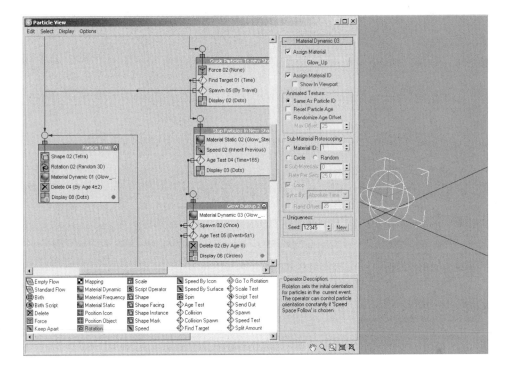

Figure 12.1

The Particle View window and a Particle Flow emitter

Events are the named boxes, operators are the gray boxes, and tests appear as yellow diamonds. To the right of the Particle View window is a common example of one of the several emitter types that a Particle Flow can utilize. Using Particle Flow, you can create almost any particle-based effect, including rain, snow, mist, a flurry of arrows and spears, and objects assembling and disassembling in a blast of particles. Unfortunately, an in-depth examination of Particle Flow is beyond the scope of this book. However, we will familiarize you with the fundamentals of particles in the hopes you will be inspired to learn more in the course of your own work—which, when you think about it, is the best way to learn any program.

Non-Event-Driven Particle Systems

Non-event-driven particle systems rely on the parameters set in the Modify panel to control the appearance and content of the particles, as opposed to passing through events that may alter some of the particles. All particles are treated identically by the system's parameters as a whole; there are no tests to modify the behavior for certain particles within the system.

These particles can be bound to space warps to control apparent reactions to scene events, and they can be instructed to follow a path.

Non-event-driven particle systems have been around for a long time; they are stable, easy to learn, and an acceptable solution for many particle requirements. Non-event-driven particle systems are the focus of this chapter and will familiarize you with the workings of 3ds Max's particle workflow.

Six different non-event-driven particle systems are available in 3ds Max; each has its own strengths.

- The Super Spray particle system
- The Particle Array particle system
- The Particle Cloud particle system
- The Blizzard particle system
- The Spray particle system
- The Snow particle system

They all have similar setups and, after you understand one type, the others are easy to master.

The Super Spray particle system is the most commonly used non-event-driven particle system in Max. It features a spherical emitter with a directional arrow to indicate the initial direction of the particles. It has eight rollouts containing the parameters that control the appearance and performance of the particles. The particles can emerge over a specified range of time or throughout the length of the scene's duration. When rendered, they can appear as one of several 2D or 3D shapes, as instanced scene geometry, or as interconnecting blobs that ebb and flow as they near each other. The particles can even spawn additional particles when they collide and load a predesigned series of parameters called a *preset*. The Super Spray particle system essentially replaced the older, less-comprehensive Spray particle system, and it will be the main focus of this chapter. The graphic shown in Figure 12.2 displays a Super Spray particle system created in a viewport.

Rather than being the emitter, the Particle Array particle system, as shown in Figure 12.3, is only a visual link to the particle system emitter itself. The PArray uses an object in the scene as the emitter for the particles. While the parameters are adjusted with the PArray selected, the particles are emitted from the vertices, edges, or faces of the designated scene object. When used in conjunction with the PBomb space warp and the Object Fragments setting, acceptable object explosions can be created.

The Particle Cloud particle system, as shown in Figure 12.4, contains particles within a volume defined by the emitter or by selecting a 3D object in the scene to act as the constraining volume. When instanced geometry is used as the particle type, an array of space cruisers or a school of fish can be represented by the PCloud system. The PCloud object does not render, and any object used to constrain the particles can be hidden to give the illusion that the particles are not held in place by an external force.

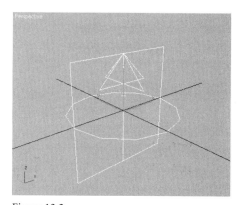

Figure 12.2

The Super Spray particle system

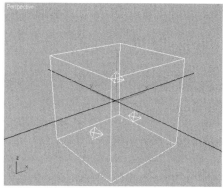

Figure 12.3

The Particle Array particle system

Instanced geometry takes instanced copies of an object and assigns one instance to the particles in a scene. You can animate a school of fish, for example, by assigning an instanced fish model to particle locations and then animating the particles to school together and swim along.

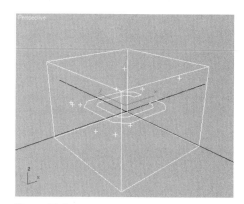

Figure 12.4

The Particle Cloud particle system

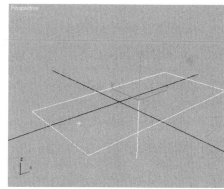

Figure 12.5

The Blizzard particle system

The Blizzard particle system, which is similar to the Super Spray particle system in its toolset and capabilities, is shown in Figure 12.5. The presets that ship with Blizzard are designed to simulate the particle motion of rain, snow, or mist. The Blizzard particle system has replaced the less-capable Snow particle system.

The Spray and Snow particle systems, shown in Figure 12.6, are the original particle systems that shipped with the initial release of 3D Studio Max, the first Windows release after four DOS-based versions of 3D Studio. At the time, they were cutting edge and beneficial, but they have not been improved significantly since their implementation. Spray and

Snow do not offer primitive or instanced geometry as particles, presets, or particle spawning. The concepts used with these two systems are similar to the other more-advanced systems, but they are seldom used anymore.

Figure 12.6

The Spray and Snow particle systems

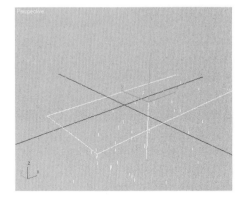

Figure 12.7

The particle system's parameters

Setting Up a Particle System

Particles are renderable objects in Max and are created in the Geometry tab of the Command panel. Like most other objects in 3ds Max, the particle system's parameters can be changed immediately after they are created in the Create panel. Once you deselect the system, however, their parameters must be changed in the Modify panel, just like any other object in 3ds Max. To set up a particle system, follow these steps.

1. Click Create → Geometry → Particle Systems from the Command panel and then click on the Super Spray button in the Object Type rollout. The particle system's parameters appear in the Command panel (Figure 12.7).

2. Click and drag in the Perspective viewport to create the Super Spray emitter. The emitters do not render, so the size does not matter; the arrow will point in the positive *Z* direction, as shown in Figure 12.8.

Figure 12.8

The Super Spray emitter created in the Perspective viewport

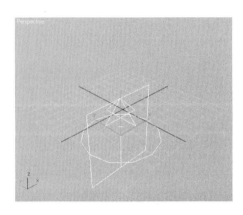

3. Drag the Time slider to the right until the particles extend beyond the limits of the viewport. Frame number 10 should be sufficient. To see the mass of particles, click Zoom Extents to expand your Perspective viewport to show everything in the scene.

   The Basic Parameters rollout controls how the particles spread as they exit the emitter, the size of the emitter, and how they display in the viewports.

4. In the Basic Parameters rollout, set both Spread values to 30 to spread the particles out 30 degrees in both the local X- and local Y-axes of the emitter. The Off Axis parameter rocks the emission direction along the X-axis and the Off Plane parameter rotates the angle of emission around the Z-axis. Both of these should remain at zero. See Figure 12.9.

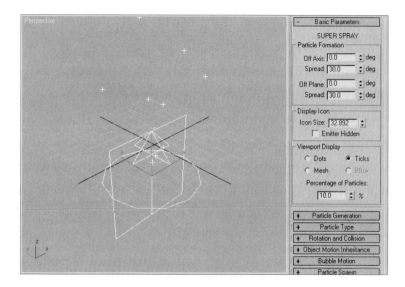

Figure 12.9

The Basic Parameters rollout

5. In the Viewport Display area, make sure Ticks is selected and the Percentage of Particles is set to 10. This ensures that the particles appear as small crosses in the viewports, regardless of the type of particle used, and that only 10 percent of the particles that are actually emitted are displayed in the viewport. Both of these parameters are used to ensure a minimal loss of performance in the viewport when particles are used.

6. Click the Quick Render button ( ) in the main toolbar. The particles appear as small dots in the Rendered Frame window. If you cannot see them, try changing the object color in the Name and Color rollout. In the next section, you will increase the size of the particles in the Rendered Frame Window by increasing the particle's Size parameter. More particles are visible in the rendering than in the viewport because the Percentage of Particles value affects only the viewports and not the renderings.

The Particle Generation Parameters

The parameters in the Particle Generation rollout control the emission of the particles including the quantity, speed, size, and life span. If you can't see any particles in your scene, the first place to look should be the Particle Generation rollout.

1. Expand the Particle Generation rollout (Figure 12.10).

   In the Particle Quantity area, the Use Rate value determines the number of particles emitted at each frame and the Use Total value determines how many particles are emitted over the active life of the system. Only one of these options can be active at a time. Increase the Use Rate value to 12.

2. Increase the Speed value to 15 to increase the velocity of the particles.

3. In the area of the UI, click the Play Animation button (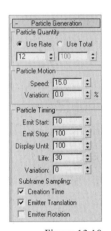 ...). The particles spew from the emitter briefly and then stop. The particles have a distinct beginning and ending time that controls when the emitter can eject any particles.

4. In the Particle Timing section of the Particle Generation rollout, change the Emit Start value to 10, change the Emit Stop value to 100, and then click the Play Animation button again. The particle system will pause for 10 frames at the beginning of the active time segment and then emit 12 particles every frame for the remaining 90 frames.

5. Drag the Time slider to frame 50 or so and then zoom out in the Perspective viewport until the limits of the particles extents are visible. Play the animation again. The particles increase their distance from the emitter until frame 45 and then travel no farther.

   There are several parameters that determine when a particle is visible. The Emit Start and Emit Stop parameters mentioned earlier bracket the frames when the particles are emitted. The Display Until parameter in the Particle Timing area defines the last frame when any particle is visible. Regardless of whether this frame falls within the Start and Stop values, when the Display Until frame is reached, no more particles appear in the viewports or in any renderings. Another parameter that controls the display of particles is the Life value. The Life value determines how long each particle exists in a scene from when it is emitted until it disappears. Currently, the Life value is set to 30 so that at frame 45, which is 30 frames after the emission begins at frame 15, the particles disappear. Particles that are emitted after frame 10 also live for 30 frames, moving the same distance from the emitter before dying.

   Figure 12.10

   The Particle Generation rollout

6. Change the Life value to 40, allowing the particles to travel one-third farther from the emitter, and change the Variation to 20, adding randomness to the particle's lifespan.

7. Play the animation. The particles now travel farther from the emitter and die between 32 and 48 frames after being emitted.

8. In the area of the Particle Generation rollout, change the Size value to 10 and then render one frame of the scene at some point after frame 30. The result should look similar to Figure 12.11.

Notice that the particles are smaller very near the emitter and also very far away from the emitter. By default, the Grow For value causes the particles to grow from a size of zero to full size over the first 10 frames of their lives. The Fade For parameter causes those same particles to shrink from full size to zero size during the last 10 frames of their lives.

9. Change the Fade For value to 0, so the particles retain their size at the end of their lives, and leave Grow For at its default.

10. Render the Perspective viewport again and notice how the particles grow, but never shrink. See Figure 12.12.

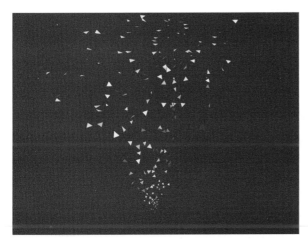

Figure 12.11

The Super Spray particle system rendered in the Perspective viewport

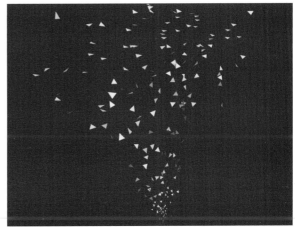

Figure 12.12

The particle system with the Fade For value changed to 0

VARIATION

In many situations utilizing particle systems, the particles are intended to appear as many similar but random objects. When the particles all have identical parameters (such as speed, life span, or rotation), the illusion of randomness disappears, which can greatly detract from its sense of reality. To alleviate this situation, in many of the parameter areas of the Super Spray particle system's rollouts, you will find a Variation parameter. The Variation settings modify their related parameters on a per-particle basis to add seeming randomness to the system. For example, changing the Variation parameter (below the Speed parameter) to 20 will assign a velocity to each particle within 20 percent of the Speed value. When the Speed parameter is set to 10 and Variation is set to 20, each particle is assigned to a random speed between 8 and 12 to 20 percent on either side of 10.

Putting It Together

Now that you have a basic understanding of particle systems, you will continue to work with them by creating a system that represents the bullets fired from a gun and the brass expelled from the ejection port. This will require two particle systems, one for each type of object leaving the gun. We will also examine the different particle types that can be emitted.

Creating the Particle Systems

The basic process of creating a particle system is fairly simple; you place the emitter in the scene, fine-tune its location and orientation, and then adjust the system's parameters. The third item mentioned is the one that will take the most experimentation to perfect.

1. Open the Particle Gun.max file from the companion CD. This file is similar to the completed IK gun file created in Chapter 9, "Character Studio and IK Animation," with a target, floor, materials, lights, and a camera added. The lights and camera have been hidden for clarity.

2. In the Top viewport, create a Super Spray particle system. Move and rotate it so that the emitter is recessed slightly into the barrel of the gun, similar to Figure 12.13. Turn on the Angle Snap toggle (⊿) to rotate the system precisely 90 degrees.

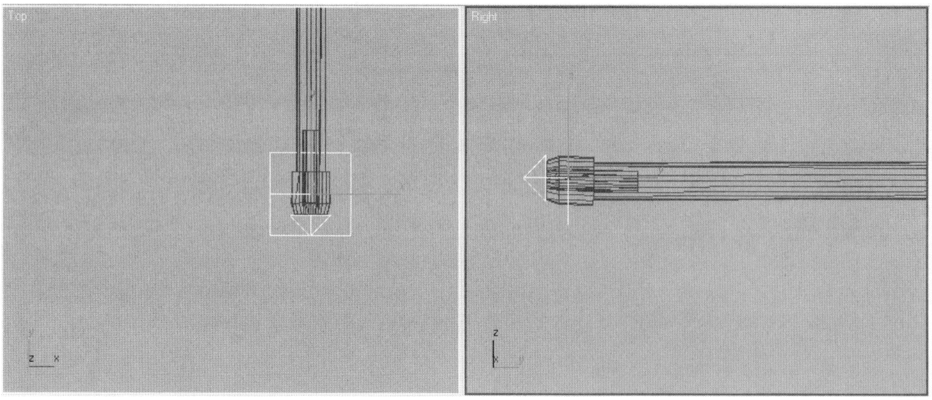

Figure 12.13

The Top and Right viewports showing the proper placement of the Super Spray particle emitter

3. Click the Select and Link button (⬚) in the main toolbar.

4. Click on the particle system; a rubber-banding line stretches from the emitter to the cursor. Place the cursor over the gun barrel and then click again. The gun flashes white to indicate that the linking is complete. Any changes in the gun's orientation or position are now passed down to the particle system, keeping it co-located and oriented with the gun. See Figure 12.14.

5. Rename this particle system **Super Spray Bullets**.

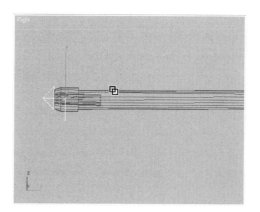

Figure 12.14

Changes in the orientation or position are passed down to the particle system.

6. Create a second Super Spray particle system and place it on the right side of the gun body. Orient the emitter so that the particles are ejected upward and away from the gun, as shown in Figure 12.15. In the figure, the target and its supports have been hidden for clarity.

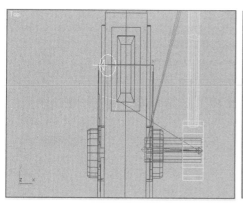
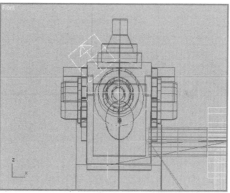

Figure 12.15

The Top and Front viewports showing the proper placement of the second Super Spray particle emitter

You may see a random particle or two already emitted by the particle systems. They are caused by the Emit Start time being set to the initial frame of the scene. This anomaly is corrected in the next section.

7. Link this particle system to the gun, just as you did with the other in steps 3 and 4.

8. Rename this system **Super Spray Brass**.

Configuring the Particle System Timing

The amount of particles emitted over time defines the density of the particles in the scene. The speed of the particles also factors into the proximity of the particles.

1. In the Time Controls area, click the Time Configuration button (▣).

2. In the Time Configuration dialog box, change the Length value to 300, as shown in Figure 12.16, and then click the OK icon. At 30 frames per second (fps), the scene is now 10 seconds long.

3. Select Super Spray Bullets and then click the Modify tab of the Command panel.

4. In the Particle Generation rollout, set the Use Rate to 10, the Speed to 10.0, the Emit Start value to 45, and the Emit Stop value to 300. After a one-and-a-half second pause, the gun will fire then die off quickly.

5. Change the Display Until value to 300, as shown in Figure 12.17, so that the particles appear in the scene for the entire active time segment. Set the Life value to 300 so the particles do not die out in the scene.

6. In the Particle Size section, change the Size value to 4. Drag the Time slider to approximately frame 80 and then render the Camera viewport. The scene should look similar to Figure 12.18.

The particles appear as triangles that grow as they travel away from the emitter. When you are creating a traditional gun, this is not the look you want for the particles; the rounds should all appear the same size for the life of the particles. The particle type is covered in the next section and in the "Particle Systems and Space Warps" section later in this chapter. The conditions that allow the particles to pass through the Target object are also addressed.

Figure 12.16

The Time Configuration settings

Figure 12.17

Change the Display Until value to 300.

Figure 12.18
The rendered Camera viewport showing the particles

Selecting the Particle Type

There are several types of particles that can be emitted by a particle system. Standard particles consist of eight different 2D and 3D particles including cubes, spheres, and six-pointed stars.

The Facing Standard particle type is a square, 2D particle that maintains a continuous orientation perpendicular to the viewport. Using opacity mapped materials in conjunction with Facing particles can give the illusion of smoke or steam without using a massive number of particles. Facing particles are sometimes referred to as *sprites.*

MetaParticles use what is known as *metaball technology,* where each particle appears as a blob with a sphere of influence surrounding it. Whenever the two spheres of influence from two particles in close proximity overlap, the particles meld together in an organic manner similar to mercury or the wax in a lava lamp. Using MetaParticles can be computationally intensive, so caution should be a priority when that is the selected particle type. Start with a quantity of particles fewer than you would expect to use and then increase the amount, as required, after test rendering the scene.

Geometry that exists in the scene can also be substituted for the particles at render time. Using instanced geometry, a particle system can emit any objects from jet fighters to fire fighters, or nearly any other geometry in the scene, using the material from the object that is instanced. The original scene object can be hidden so as not to appear in the render of the scene, while still being instanced by the particle system.

To resume the Particle System exercise, continue with the following steps:

1. With the Super Spray Bullets particle system selected, expand the Particle Type rollout.

2. In the Particle Types section, select MetaParticles.

3. From the menu bar, choose Edit → Hold to temporarily save the scene. If rendering the scene causes a system crash, it can be restored to this point using Edit → Fetch. 3ds Max is a stable program, but rendering MetaParticles can significantly task a computer system.

4. Render the scene. The particles that are near to each other combine to form blobs of meshes, as shown in Figure 12.19.

Figure 12.19

The rendered scene with the MetaParticles effect

5. In the MetaParticle Parameters section, decrease the Tension to 0.1. Tension controls a particle's effort to maintain a spherical shape while in proximity to another particle. Lowering the Tension increases the amount of interparticle combining.

6. Render the scene again to see the effect of the lower Tension value, as shown in Figure 12.20.

Figure 12.20

The rendered scene with the lower Tension value

7. MetaParticles would be the solution if this gun were shooting out gobs of melted cheese, rather than a conventional machine gun. In this case, instanced geometry is the appropriate particle choice. Mmmmm, melted cheese.

8. Right-click on a blank area of the Active viewport and choose Unhide by Name from the Quad menu. Select the Bullet and Brass objects from the list in the Unhide Objects dialog box and then click the Unhide button. Two small objects, a bullet and a brass casing, appear below the gun.

9. At the top of the Particle Type rollout, select Instanced Geometry for the particle type, as shown in Figure 12.21. In the Instancing Parameters section, click the Pick Object button.

10. Select the Bullet object in the scene. If necessary, press the H key to open the Pick Object dialog box to select the object by name. The bullet flashes white briefly to indicate that the selection is successful and the object name is now identified in the Instancing Parameters section as the instanced geometry object.

11. Render the Camera viewport. There are still a few problems that need to be corrected. The particles are growing as they leave the emitter, the particles grow to be too large for the gun barrel, and the bullets rotate in several axes, rather than maintaining a forward orientation, as you can see in Figure 12.22. The bullets also display their object color, the color used by the particles system, rather than the material applied to the Bullet object.

12. In the Particle Size section of the Particle Generation rollout, set the Grow For and Fade For parameters to 0. This will cause the particles to maintain a constant size throughout their life spans.

Figure 12.21

The Particle Type parameters

Figure 12.22

The rendered scene showing the large particles and rotating bullets

13. When using standard or metaparticles, the Size parameter defines the size of the particle. When using instanced geometry, however, it becomes a multiplier of the object's actual size. With the current Size value set to 4, the bullets are scaled to four times their modeled size. That's a little big, so set the Size value to 1.

14. Expand the Rotation and Collision rollout. In the Spin Axis Controls section, select Direction of Travel/Mblur to make each bullet's orientation follow its direction of travel, as shown in Figure 12.23.

Figure 12.23

The Rotation and Collision settings

15. At the bottom of the Particle Type rollout, make sure that the Instanced Geometry radio button is selected and then click the Get Material From button.

16. Render the Camera viewport again. All of the particles are now oriented properly, as you can see in Figure 12.24.

Setting Up the Other Particle System

We have a particle system set up to emit the bullets, and now we need one that ejects the brass casings from the machine gun. In many cases, the same parameters must be maintained among the two systems so these parameters will be wired together, ensuring a common value between them. This way the casings will shoot out with the bullets.

1. Continue with the previous exercise or open the `Particle Gun1.max` file from the companion CD.

2. Select the Super Spray Brass particle system.

Figure 12.24

The rendered scene with all of the particles oriented properly

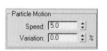

3. In the Particle Generation rollout, set the Size to 1 and set both the Grow For and Fade For values to 0. Set Emit Start to 45, Emit Stop to 300, Display Until 300, and Life to 300.

4. In the Particle Motion section, reduce the Speed value to 5. The rate of particles emitted is still set to 10; the Speed value just determines the velocity of the particles as they leave the emitter.

5. In the Particle Type rollout, choose Instanced Geometry in the Particle Types section and then click the Pick Object button. Select the Brass object as the geometry to be instanced.

6. Select the Instanced Geometry option in the Mat'l Mapping and Source section at the bottom of the Particle Type rollout, and then click the Get Material From button to define the material applied to the particles.

7. In the Rotation and Collision rollout, select the Direction of Travel/Mblur option.

8. Select the Bullet and Brass objects and hide them.

9. Drag the Time slider, and your bullets and brass should emit together.

Wiring the Parameters Together

The values that define the parameters unique to each particle system in the scene have been set properly. Several values, such as the Use Rate, must maintain the same value for both particle systems so that, for example, the amount of brass ejected matches the number of bullets fired. These parameters can always be adjusted manually; however, the Parameter Wiring tool forces one object's parameters to drive another's. In the following exercise, the parameter values of the Super Spray Bullets particle system are used to define the parameter values of the Super Spray Brass particle system. By wiring parameters together, you can control more than one system by manipulating only one of them.

1. Continue with the previous exercise or load the `Particle Gun2.max` file from the companion CD.

Figure 12.25

Choose Wire Parameters from the Quad menu.

2. Select the Super Spray Bullets particle system. Right-click in the viewport and choose Wire Parameters from the Quad menu. See Figure 12.25.

3. From the small pop-up menu that appears, choose Object (SuperSpray) and then Birth Rate from the cascading menu. A rubber-banding line connects the particle system to the cursor. At this point, the object to be wired to the Super Spray Bullet's Birth Rate parameter must be selected (Figure 12.26).

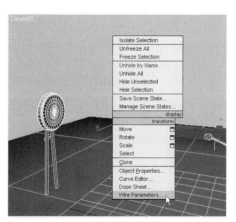

Figure 12.26

Select the object to be wired to
the Super Spray Bullet's Birth Rate
parameter.

Figure 12.27

Select Super Spray Brass in the Pick Object dialog box.

4. Press the H key to open the Pick Object dialog box, select Super Spray Brass, and then click the Pick button (Figure 12.27).

5. From the small pop-up menu that appears, choose Object (SuperSpray) and then Birth Rate from the cascading menu (Figure 12.28).

6. The Parameter Wiring dialog box opens, as shown in Figure 12.29. The Birth Rate parameters are highlighted in both the left and right windows. The left side of the dialog box displays the Super Spray Bullets particle system's parameter, and the right side displays the parameters for the Super Spray Brass particle system.

7. The control direction, defining which parameter controls the other, can be set so that either one of the parameters controls the other, or bidirectional control can be set so that either parameter can change the other. In this case, the bullet rate is used to control the brass rate. Click the right arrow between the two parameter windows, as shown in Figure 12.30.

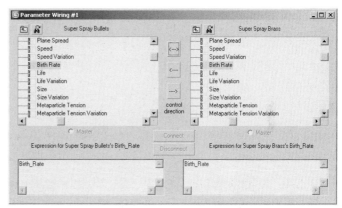

Figure 12.28

Select Object (Super-Spray) and then Birth Rate.

Figure 12.29

The Parameter Wiring dialog box with the Birth Rate parameters highlighted

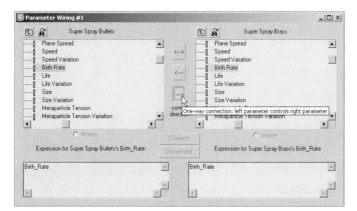

Figure 12.30

Click the right arrow between the two parameter windows.

8. Complete the wiring process by clicking the Connect button. The parameters in each window will turn a color to indicate that they are wired.

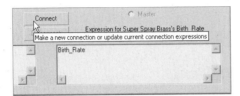

9. Select the Super Spray Bullets particle system and change the Use Rate to 12.

10. Select the Super Spray Brass particle system and examine its Use Rate. It is now set to 12 as well.

You can try to change the Use Rate for the Super Spray Brass particle system, but it won't work. The related spinners simply do not work, and they shouldn't because the particle system's Use Rate is defined by the Use Rate of the Super Spray Brass particle system. You can highlight and change the value manually; however, nothing will really happen. When you deselect the system and then select it again, the Use Rate reverts to the value set by the other system.

11. Select the Life parameter in both windows; click the right arrow and then the Connect button. The Life parameters are now wired together as well.

Unfortunately, the Emit Start, Emit Stop, and Display Until parameters are not exposed to the Parameter Wiring dialog box. These values must be changed for each particle system manually.

12. Close the Parameter Wiring dialog box.

13. Drag the Time slider. The two particle systems emit equal numbers of particles at the same time. The brass ejects in a straight line from the gun body, as shown in Figure 12.31. The straight-line emission is corrected in the next section. You can now change the rate at which the bullets fire, and the brass will eject properly automatically!

The particle systems have been created and linked to the gun so that they maintain the proper position and orientation when the gun moves or rotates. The systems have been adjusted to fire bullets from the barrel and eject brass from the side at an equal and wired rate. In the next section, the processes of adding space warps to interject gravity into the scene and to cause the particles to collide with scene objects are covered.

Figure 12.31

The straight-line emission

Particle Systems and Space Warps

Space warps are nonrendering objects that can modify or manipulate the objects in a scene. Modifier-based space warps, for example, deform objects based on the object's proximity to the space warp. In this section, the focus is on the Forces and Deflectors categories of space warps, the space warps that affect particle systems.

The Forces space warps affect particle systems by altering the trajectory of the particles as they move through the scene. Each space warp displays as an icon in the viewports that must be bound to each object that it is designated to affect. The bindings appear as wide gray lines at the top of the Modifier Stack.

The Forces space warps are listed here:

Motor Applies a directional spin to the particles, creating a circular movement. The orientation of the Space Warp icon defines the direction of the rotation.

Vortex Similar to the Motor space warp, Vortex causes the particles to move in a circular motion but also decreases the radius of the motion over distance, creating a funnel-shaped motion.

Path Follow Requires the particles to follow a spline path. The particle timing is controlled by the Path Follow's parameters.

Displace Changes the particle trajectory by pushing them based on the space warp's Strength and Decay values. Image maps can also be used to define the amount of displacement.

Wind Adds a directional force to the particles based on the space warp's orientation. Randomness can be added to increase the realism of the simulation.

Push Applies a constant, directional force to the particles.

Drag Rather than changing the direction of the particles, Drag slows the speed of the particles as they pass through its influence.

PBomb Disperses particles with a linear or spherical force. This can be effective when used with the Particle Array particle system.

Gravity Applies a constant acceleration used to simulate the affect of gravity on the particles. Gravity can be applied in a linear fashion.

Adding Gravity to a Scene

When looking at the particle systems in the previous exercises, especially the Super Spray Brass system in our machine gun scene, it's evident that the motion of the particles is not realistic. The particles are emitted at approximately a 45-degree angle up and away from the gun body. The particles maintain a perfectly straight trajectory and never fall to the earth as they should. In this exercise, gravity is added to both particle systems to cause the bullets and brass to drop. To begin the exercise, follow these steps:

1. Continue with the previous exercise or load the `Particle Gun3.max` file from the companion CD.

2. Drag the Time slider to frame 100.

3. Click Create → Space Warps. Choose Forces from the drop-down menu if necessary, and then click the Gravity button.

4. Click and drag in the Top viewport to place and size the Gravity Space Warp icon. The size and the location are unimportant, but the orientation of the icon defines the direction of the gravitational force. See Figure 12.32.

5. Select the Super Spray Brass particle system. Click the Bind to Space Warp button ( ) in the main toolbar.

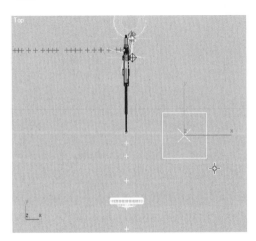

Figure 12.32

Click and drag in the Top viewport to place and size the Gravity Space Warp icon.

6. Click on the Particle System emitter or the particles themselves and drag the cursor toward the Gravity Space Warp icon. A rubber-banding line connects the particle system to the cursor.

7. Place the cursor over the Gravity space warp, the cursor's appearance changes to identify it as a valid object for binding, and then release the mouse button. The space warp flashes briefly to indicate a successful binding, and the particles drop through the floor as shown in Figure 12.33.

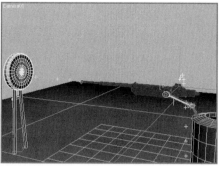

Figure 12.33

After the Gravity is bound to the particle system, the particles drop through the floor.

8. Select the Super Spray Bullets space warp and bind it to the Gravity space warp as well.

9. Play the animation. The particles from both systems are affected by the gravity, but the bullets drop too far for their distance from the gun to the target. Reducing the amount of gravity isn't appropriate because the brass would fall too slowly and the gravitational force should be consistent throughout the scene. This situation is fixed by increasing the velocity of the bullets as they leave the barrel.

10. The Bind to Space Warp button is still active. Click the Select Object button, and then select the Super Spray Bullets particle system.

11. Make sure the Time slider is at a frame well into the animation so that changes to the system are reflected in the viewports.

12. In the Modify panel, click the SuperSpray entry in the Modifier Stack to expose the particle system's parameters.

13. In the Particle Generation rollout, increase the Speed value to 50. The visible trajectories of the particles will flatten out.

> At the bottom of the Rotation and Collision rollout, you will find the Interparticle Collisions section. Enabling this parameter causes Max to calculate and determine the result of any situation where two particles impact each other. This can add a measure of realism to the way the particles react, but it can also consume a significant amount of system resources. Use this feature with caution and always Hold the scene prior to enabling or testing the feature.

Controlling the Particles with Deflectors

As you saw in the previous exercises, particles travel through a scene, guided by space warps but unaffected by geometry. *Deflectors* are a type of space warp that causes the particles that impact it to bounce as if they have collided with an unmovable surface. The amount of Bounce assigned to a deflector is a multiplier that defines the velocity of a particle after it impacts the space warp. A Bounce value of 0.5 results in the particle's speed being reduced to 50 percent of the speed it was when it hit the deflector. Most deflectors have Time On and Time Off parameters that control when the deflector is active.

Deflecting the Brass at the Floor

To get the spent casings to collide with the ground, follow these steps:

1. Continue with the previous exercise or load the `Particle Gun4.max` file from the companion CD.

2. Drag the Time slider to frame 100.

3. Click Create → Space Warps. Choose Deflectors from the drop-down menu and then click the POmniFlect button.

4. In the Top viewport, click and drag to define the two opposite corners of the deflector. The deflector should be similar in size to the Floor object in the scene. Unlike the Forces space warps, deflectors must be positioned in the stream of the particles, as shown in Figure 12.34.

UNDERSTANDING DEFLECTOR NAMES

The names assigned to the different deflectors distinguish the shapes and properties of those deflectors. Understanding the deflector naming convention is key to selecting the correct deflector for the task at hand.

- If the deflector name begins with a P or an S, the deflector is Planar or Spherical in shape.

- If the deflector name begins with a U, this is a universal deflector and any scene geometry can be assigned as a deflector, instead of the Deflector icon itself.

- If the deflector name ends with "OmniFlect," this deflector affects all particles that impact it. The OmniFlect deflectors are more advanced than the simpler space warps that end with "Deflector."

- If the deflector name ends with "DynaFlect," this deflector affects all particles that impact it and, when used with dynamic simulations, can affect other objects in the scene.

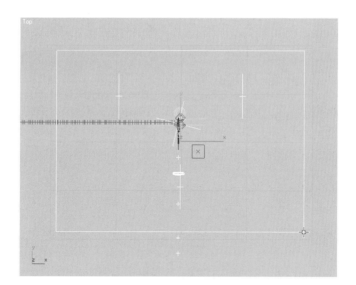

Figure 12.34

The deflector must be positioned in the stream of the particles.

5. Move the deflector 0.3 units in the positive Z direction. The impact point is based on the particle location. When using instanced geometry, the particle location is defined by the center point of the geometry. The bullets and brass are about 0.3 units in radius; so moving the deflector up 0.3 units prevents the particles from sinking into the floor.

6. Select the Super Spray Brass particle system and then click the Bind to Space Warp button in the main toolbar. Click on the particle system, or particles, drag to the perimeter of the deflector, and then release to bind the deflector to the particle system.

7. Activate the Camera viewport and then play the animation. The particles initially bounce equal in height to their highest point after being ejected, but they discontinue shortly afterward.

8. Select the Deflector object in the viewport, not the deflector binding in the Modifier Stack.

9. In the Timing section of the Parameters rollout, set the Time Off value to 300, as shown in Figure 12.35, to leave the deflector on during the entire active time segment.

10. In the Reflection section, set the Bounce value to 0.25 and the Variation to 10 percent. Increase Chaos to 50 percent so the particles' directions are not constrained to a straight line.

11. In the Common section, increase the Friction value to 4.0 to prevent the particles from spreading too far along the deflector's surface.

12. Play the animation. The brass is ejected from the side of the gun, falls to the floor, and spreads a bit from the point of impact.

Figure 12.35

Set the Time Off value to 300.

Deflecting the Bullets at the Target

The brass is handled, and now the bullet collisions need to be addressed equally as well.

1. Click Create → Space Warps, and then click the UOmniFlect button.

2. In the Top viewport, click and drag to place and size the universal deflector. The size and position do not matter. This is just a visible icon. A scene object will be selected to act as the deflector. See Figure 12.36.

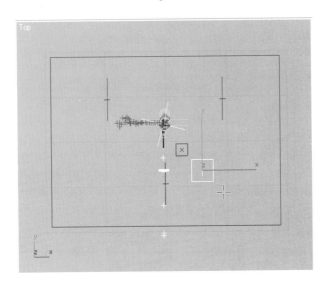

3. Select the Super Spray Bullets particle system, and bind it to the UOmniflect icon, not the Target object. Bind the particle system to the POmniFlect deflector as well.

4. Click the Select Object button and then select the UOmniFlect icon.

5. Click the Pick Object button and then select the Target object in the scene.

6. In the Timing section, set the Time Off value to 300.

7. In the Reflection section, set Bounce to 0.01, Variation to 10, and Chaos to 4.

8. Play the animation. The particles hit the target, fall to the floor, and then spread out a bit.

As you can see, the proper use of Force and Deflector space warps, in conjunction with particle systems, can successfully animate thousands of small objects within the constraints of a scene. The completed scene can be examined using the `Particle Gun Complete.max` and `Particle Gun.avi` files on the companion CD. In the remaining sections in this chapter, we will look at the implementation of rigid and soft body dynamics in physics simulations.

Using Rigid Body Dynamics

Part of the core package of 3ds Max is the physics engine known as *reactor*. With reactor, complex physical conditions are accurately animated showing the interaction of the scene objects with each other and with external forces such as wind or gravity. Objects are assigned mass, elasticity, and friction properties, and designated as movable or immovable objects. Rigid body dynamics, soft body dynamics, rope, and cloth simulations are all within the limits of reactor's toolset. The Real Time Preview window displays a lower-resolution, unrendered example of the animation to be created to make it much easier to visualize how your dynamic simulation will run without a lot of wait. The reactor engine calculates the animation, but the standard practice of creating keyframes is the final output of the simulations. These keyframes can be edited and manipulated; however, the integrity of the simulation could be compromised.

Creating the Simulation Objects

In this exercise, a series of primitive objects are dropped onto a complex inclined object to examine the interaction of the scene objects, as shown in Figure 12.37. Although this is a simple example of the use of the physics simulator, reactor can be used to simulate the interactions of very complex scenes with many colliding objects and external forces.

1. Open the `Rigid.max` file from the companion CD. This consists of an inclined box with additional boxes, cylinders, and a hemisphere placed on its surface to make the simulation more complex.

2. Create two rows of spheres above the inclined board. Make sure they are all over the top edge of the board and fit between the two angled rails on the sides, as shown in Figure 12.38.

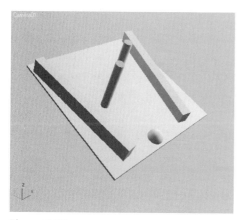

Figure 12.37

A series of primitive objects are dropped onto a complex inclined object.

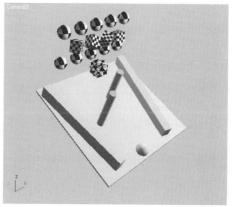

Figure 12.38

Create two rows of spheres above the inclined board.

3. Create a row of small boxes between the rows of spheres as shown, and rotate them each about all three axes to offset them.

4. From the Extended Primitives category of geometry objects, create a Star2 hedra and position it near the other objects. The scene should look similar to Figure 12.39.

Figure 12.39

The scene after creating additional objects for the simulation

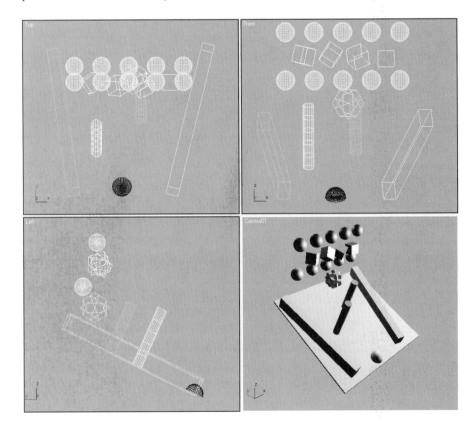

5. Open the Material Editor and then apply the Checker material to all of the objects you created. The Checker Diffuse Color map helps discern the rotation of each object in the simulation.

Assigning the Physical Properties

Each object in the scene must be assigned the correct properties to define their reactions during the simulation. Note that any objects that are to be stable and immovable are assigned a Mass value of 0.

1. Select all of the objects that make up the inclined board in the scene.

2. Go to the main toolbar and place the cursor to the far right of the bar until the cursor changes to an arrow with what appears to be white boxes behind it. Right-click, and

Figure 12.40

Open the Rigid Body Properties dialog box.

from the menu choose reactor. This will bring up the floating toolbar. Right-click on the title bar and choose Dock → Left.

3. From the reactor toolbar, click the Open Property Editor button () to open the Rigid Body Properties dialog box shown in Figure 12.40.

4. Make sure Mass is set to 0 in the Physical Properties rollout and Mesh Convex Hull is selected in the Simulation Geometry rollout.

5. Select all of the spheres that you created. Set their Mass value to 1.0 and choose Bounding Sphere in the Simulation Geometry rollout, as shown in Figure 12.41. When using a spherical object, Bounding Sphere is more accurate and calculates faster than Mesh Convex Hull.

> Most 3D geometry works as expected during a reactor simulation. However, reactor contains its own Plane object for use whenever flat, 2D surfaces are required. When a 3ds Max plane is used instead of a reactor plane, Concave Mesh must be chosen as the Simulation Geometry type.

6. Select all of the boxes that you created, assign a Mass value of 1.0, and choose the Bounding Box option.

7. Select the hedra. Increase its mass to 1.0 and select Mesh Convex Hull for the simulation.

You have now assigned dynamic parameters to the scene objects; however, there is more to do to set up the simulation.

Figure 12.41

Choose the Bounding Sphere in the Simulation Geometry rollout.

THE SIMULATION GEOMETRY ROLLOUT

-   The Simulation Geometry rollout defines how reactor defines the surfaces of an object during the simulation. The Bounding Box and Bounding Sphere options place the extents of the objects, as far as the simulation is concerned, at the limits of the smallest possible box or sphere that could encompass them.

-   Mesh Convex Hull closely follows the extents of the object, with all vertices included within the simulation volume, while spanning any concave areas. Complicated meshes can increase the calculation time when using Mesh Convex Hull, so the Proxy Convex Hull options allow a less dense substitution object to be used to define the simulation parameters.

-   When Concave Mesh is used, the actual surface of the geometry is used. This can drastically increase the calculation time and should only be used when necessary. Using the Proxy Concave Mesh option can reduce the simulation time when using a complicated object.

-   3ds Max assigns the Not Shared option to the selected geometry when multiple objects are selected that do not utilize the same Simulation Geometry setting.

Creating the Collection

Scene objects must be members of a collection to be included in any simulations. The collections appear as simple icons in the viewports that are selected to access the simulation's parameters, including editing the list of included objects.

1. Continue with the previous exercise or open the `Rigid1.max` file from the companion CD.

2. Click the Create Rigid Body Collection button (🎲) in the reactor toolbar.

3. Click in any viewport to place the Rigid Body Collection icon, as shown in Figure 12.42. The location does not matter.

Figure 12.42

Click in any viewport to place the Rigid Body Collection icon.

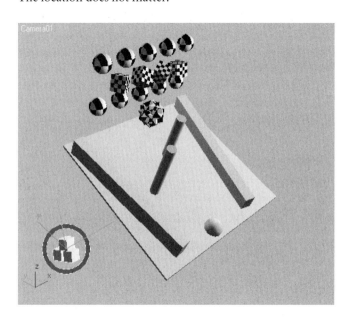

4. In the Command panel, click the Add button at the bottom of the RB Collection Properties rollout (Figure 12.43).

5. In the Select Rigid Bodies dialog box that opens, select all of the objects in the scene except for the collection itself and then click the Select button, as shown in Figure 12.44. The object names will appear in the Rigid Bodies field in the Command panel.

Figure 12.43

Click the Add button in the RB Collection Properties rollout.

In most cases, not every object in a scene is required to be in a simulation. An object should be omitted if its impact on the simulation is not required. For example, in a scene where marbles spill across a table and onto a floor, the marbles, table, and floor must be included, but the nearby lamp or the ceiling should be omitted.

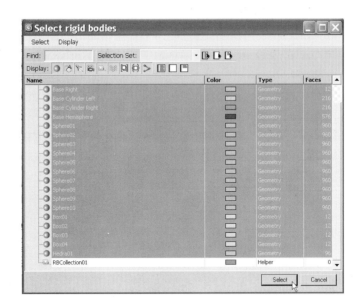

Figure 12.44

The Select Rigid
Bodies dialog box

Testing the Simulation

The reactor engine provides the Real-Time Preview window where you can view the simulation. Materials and lighting are not considered for this preview; therefore, it is much faster, but less accurate, than rendering the animation.

1. Click the Preview Animation button (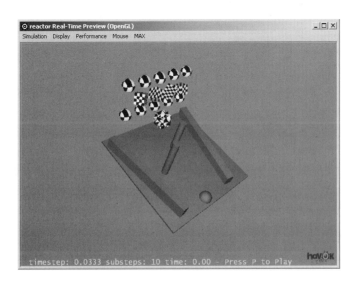) in the reactor toolbar. The reactor engine analyzes the simulation and then opens the reactor Real-Time Preview window shown in Figure 12.45.

Figure 12.45

The reactor Real-
Time Preview win-
dow showing the
scene

2. Press the P key to begin the preview, and then press P again to stop it.

3. After the preview runs its course, choose Simulation → Reset to place the objects at their starting points and review the animation.

> You can click and drag in the Preview window to arc-rotate around the simulation objects.

4. The hedra is large for the scene and may cause a bottleneck. Close the Preview window.

5. Select the hedra and reduce its Radius value.

6. Select all of the objects of the inclined board, and then open the Rigid Body Properties dialog box.

7. Set the Friction property to 0.1.

8. Select the remaining objects in the scene, and set the Friction to 0.1 as well.

9. Rearrange the objects to change the simulation to your liking. See Figure 12.46.

10. Continue to preview the animation and rearrange the objects until the simulation meets your liking.

Figure 12.46

Rearrange the objects to change the simulation to your liking.

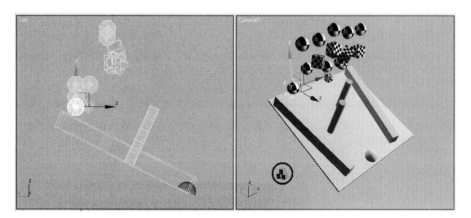

Creating the Animation

The Preview window showed what the animation will be like, but the animation keys have not been created from the simulation. The next exercise creates keys for all the objects in the collection. Creating the keys is not undoable, so it is recommended that an Edit → Hold be performed prior to creating the animation. This will create a return point in the scene in case something goes awry. This way, you can use Undo to come back to this place in your workflow.

1. In the Time Configuration dialog box, increase the length of the scene's animation to 200 frames.

2. Click Edit → Hold from the main menu.

3. Click the Create Animation button () from the reactor toolbar.

4. Click OK in the reactor dialog box that opens and warns you that the action cannot be undone, as shown here.

5. 3ds Max creates keys at every frame for every object in the simulation.

The process of creating keys with reactor cannot be undone, but the objects can be selected and their keys can be deleted in the track bar, the Dope Sheet, or the Function Curve dialog boxes.

6. Play the animation. The scene animates through frame 100 and then stops. The default value for all simulations is 100 frames.

7. To restore the scene to its state before 3ds Max created the animation, click Edit → Fetch from the main menu and then click the Yes button in the dialog box that opens.

8. Click the Utilities tab (T) of the Command panel.

9. Click the reactor button in the Utilities rollout.

In reactor, solvers provide the algorithms that determine each object's reactions in the simulation. The two available solver options in 3ds Max 2008 are Havok 1 and Havok 3. The Havok 1 solver has more functionality and can handle all types of simulation objects. Havok 3 is faster and more accurate, but it can solve only for rigid body objects. If only rigid body objects are used in a simulation, Havok 3 is usually the better choice.

10. In the About rollout, select Havok 3 from the Choose Solver drop-down menu. Havok 3 is the better choice when using only rigid body objects.

11. Expand the Preview & Animation rollout and change the End Frame value to 200.

12. Click Edit → Hold again, and then click the Create Animation button shown in Figure 12.47.

13. 3ds Max creates keys based on the simulation. You can fetch the scene and rearrange the objects as you want to change the simulation parameters and rerun the animation. Remember to hold the scene before creating the animation each time, so you can easily go back to your hold point.

Figure 12.47

Click the Create Animation button.

The completed exercise is available as the `Rigid Complete.max` file in the Dynamics Scene Files folder on the companion CD and the final rendering as `Rigid Complete.avi`.

Using Soft Body Dynamics

Soft body objects differ from rigid body objects in that they can deform upon impact with other objects in the scene. To be included in a simulation as soft body objects, scene objects must have the Soft Body modifier applied and be members of a soft body collection. Soft body objects can interact with rigid body objects in the same simulation. Physical properties are assigned to soft body objects in the same manner that they are assigned to their rigid counterparts.

Creating the Collections

Before you can simulate the reactions between soft body objects, all objects considered in the simulation must be contained in a collection.

1. Open the `Soft.max` file from the Dynamics Scene Files folder on the companion CD. As you can see in Figure 12.48, this is a simpler version of the project used in the previous exercises with the Mass and Simulation Geometry options already selected.

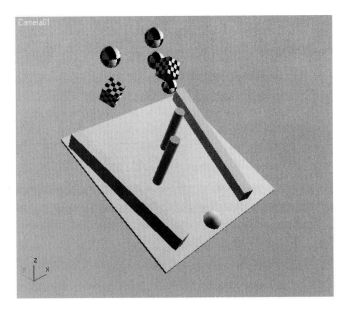

Figure 12.48

This is a simpler version of the project.

2. Select all of the base objects, and then click the Create Rigid Body Collection button in the reactor toolbar. The icon is placed at the center of the selection, and the selected objects are added to the collection.

3. Select the spheres and boxes with the Checker material applied.

4. Click the Apply Soft Body Modifier button (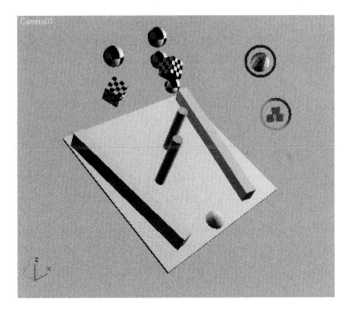) in the reactor toolbar.

In 3ds Max 2008, the Soft Body modifier is applied incorrectly when it is applied to instanced objects. It is applied to each instance for the total number of instances selected. For example, if you have eight instanced objects and apply the Soft Body modifier to them, each object will have the modifier applied to it eight times. For this exercise, the objects used are not instances.

5. With the objects still selected, click the Create Soft Body Collection button ( ) in the reactor toolbar. The dropping objects are automatically added to the soft body collection.

6. Move the Collection icons away from the scene geometry. Your Perspective viewport should look similar to Figure 12.49.

Figure 12.49

The Perspective viewport with the rigid and soft body collections

Creating the Animation

In the previous exercise, the Havok 3 solver was selected because of its capabilities when using rigid body objects exclusively. With the combination of both soft and rigid objects in this exercise, the Havok 1 solver is the better choice.

1. In the Utilities panel, click the reactor button and then choose Havok 1 from the drop-down menu in the About rollout as shown here.

2. Click the Preview Animation button in the reactor toolbar and play the animation in the reactor Real-Time Preview window, shown in Figure 12.50. The animation plays slower than the rigid body preview due to the more complex animation required by the deforming meshes.

Figure 12.50

Click the Preview Animation button.

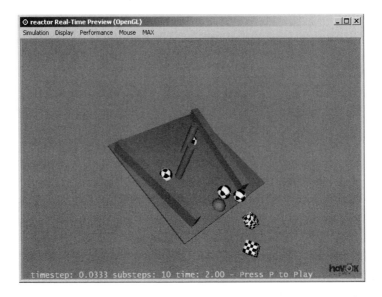

In a complex scene, or on a slower computer, the reactor Real-Time Preview may display the scene at a rate that is too slow to easily determine the effectiveness of the simulation. In these cases, you need to create the animation and then, if revisions are required, delete all of the simulation objects' animation keys before making any changes and re-creating the animation.

3. Close the Preview window.

4. Select one of the spheres and then, in the Modify panel, change its Mass to 2, Stiffness to 4, and Friction to 0.1, as shown here. Repeat this step with one more sphere and one of the boxes. The parameters of individual objects can be set in the reactor Soft-Body Modifiers settings. The larger mass value will cause the object to impact with a greater force.

5. Test the animation again. Continue to make changes and then, when you are satisfied, Hold the scene.

6. Click the Create Animation button in the reactor toolbar to create the animation using the properties assigned to the objects.

The completed exercise can be found on the companion CD as `Soft Complete.max` and `Soft Compete.avi`.

Summary

This chapter introduced you to both Max's non-event-driven particle systems and the reactor physics simulation engine. Using particles, thousands of seemingly random or purposeful objects can be animated by effectively manipulating the particle system's parameters. Particles can appear as primitive shapes, interconnecting blobs, or any instanced geometry object from the scene. Particle systems can be affected by external forces, such as gravity, wind, or vortex, and they can bounce off many types of deflectors positioned within the flow of particles.

The reactor component of Max is a powerful tool for creating accurate animations based on the interactions of scene objects. Rigid or soft body objects in collections can impact each other and deform, bounce, or slide away based on the objects' physical properties. Animations can be previewed and then thousands of animation keys can be created quickly to fulfill a scene's physics-based animation requirements.

So Long, and Thanks for All the Fish

And that's about it for us. (Awkward pause. Do you lean in for a hug, or go for a simple handshake?) We hope you found this text illuminating and helpful in priming you for a fruitful and exciting education in Autodesk's 3ds Max. There are so many resources to be found in bookstores and on the Internet that you should feel confident and secure in jumping into the next step of your CG education.

By now, you should be familiar with the workings of 3ds Max and know what parts of the CG process you find appealing. Whether it's modeling or lighting, animating or dynamics, you now have a firm grasp of how to get things done. If you feel shaky in some areas, we strongly recommend going back to those chapters and redoing the exercises to build your confidence.

We hope the most important idea you take with you from this book is the notion that proficiency in and mastery of a CG program such as 3ds Max takes patience and practice. The best way to learn is to experience the software in pursuit of your own artistic endeavors. Don't be afraid to throw yourself into your own personal projects, challenging yourself to get better with every effort. Treat this text as a formal introduction to all that 3ds Max has to offer your artistic work, and forge on ahead. Enjoy, have fun, and good luck!

About the Companion CD

Topics in this appendix include:

- What You'll Find on the CD

- System Requirements

- Using the CD

- Troubleshooting

What You'll Find on the CD

If you need help with installing the software provided on the CD, refer to the installation instructions in the "Using the CD" section of this appendix. Note that *trial, demo,* or *evaluation* versions of software are usually limited either by time or functionality (for example, not letting you save a project after you create it).

Tutorial Files

For Windows

The CD is organized into folders for the major tutorials in the book, such as Alien Model, Hand, etc. Each folder contains all the files and support materials for that project. The CD also contains several .zip files, which contain scene files for the following: Biped Scene Files, Dynamics Scene Files, Lighting Scene Files, Rendering Scene Files, and Texture Scene Files. You will need to copy the .zip files onto your hard drive and unZip them to reveal the respective scene files, which are referenced throughout the book. If you do not have software to unzip the .zip files you can go to `http://www.winzip.com/`.

Before you load a scene file, make sure you set the project folder through the File menu to that exercise's project, as directed in the book. As you work through the exercises in the book and load the required scene files, if 3ds Max gives you the Missing External Files dialog (telling you it cannot find a path to the texture images) you can browse for the texture files' path manually by clicking Browse. You will be able to find all the texture images inside that particular project's sceneassets\images folder.

3ds Max Trial Version

Trial version. For Windows.

The Autodesk 3ds Max 2008 30-day trial provides free access to the software for noncommercial use. Animation and 3D graphics students, industry professionals, or anyone interested in breaking into the world of computer graphics (CG) now has the opportunity to explore all aspects of the 3ds Max software. This product is subject to the terms and conditions of the end-user license agreement that accompanies the software.

Autodesk and 3ds Max are registered trademarks of Autodesk, Inc., in the USA and other countries. For more information and software updates, visit `www.autodesk.com/3dsmax`.

System Requirements

Make sure that your computer meets the minimum system requirements shown here. If your computer doesn't match up to most of these requirements, you may have problems using the software and files on the companion CD. For the latest information, please refer to the `ReadMe` file located at the root of the CD-ROM.

At a minimum, for the 32-bit version of 3ds Max, you'll need a laptop or desktop PC running Windows XP Professional or Windows Vista with at least 512MB of RAM,

500MB swap space, and an Intel Pentium IV or AMD Athlon XP or higher processor. You'll also need a hardware-accelerated OpenGL or Direct3D video card. The requirements for the 64-bit version are higher. See the Autodesk website for the most up-to-date requirements: `http://usa.autodesk.com/3dsmax`.

Using the CD

To install the items from the CD to your hard drive, follow these steps:

1. Insert the CD into your computer's CD-ROM drive. The license agreement appears.

2. Read through the license agreement, and then click the Accept button if you want to use the CD.

> *Windows users:* The interface won't launch if you have autorun disabled. In that case, click Start → Run (for Windows Vista, click Start → All Programs → Accessories → Run). In the dialog box that appears, type **D:\Start.exe**. (Replace **D** with the proper letter if your CD drive uses a different letter. If you don't know the letter, see how your CD drive is listed under My Computer.) Click OK.

The CD interface appears. The interface allows you to access the content with just one or two clicks.

Troubleshooting

Wiley has attempted to provide programs that work on most computers with the minimum system requirements. Alas, your computer may differ, and some programs may not work properly for some reason.

The two likeliest problems are that you don't have enough memory (RAM) for the programs you want to use, or you have other programs running that are affecting installation or running of a program. If you get an error message such as "Not enough memory" or "Setup cannot continue," try one or more of the following suggestions and then try using the software again:

Turn off any antivirus software running on your computer. Installation programs sometimes mimic virus activity and may make your computer incorrectly believe that it's being infected by a virus.

Close all running programs. The more programs you have running, the less memory is available to other programs. Installation programs typically update files and programs; so if you keep other programs running, installation may not work properly.

Have your local computer store add more RAM to your computer. This is, admittedly, a drastic and somewhat expensive step. However, adding more memory can really help the speed of your computer and allow more programs to run at the same time.

Customer Care

If you have trouble with the book's companion CD-ROM, please call the Wiley Product Technical Support phone number at (800) 762-2974. Outside the United States, call +1(317) 572-3994. You can also contact Wiley Product Technical Support at `http://sybex .custhelp.com`. John Wiley & Sons will provide technical support only for installation and other general quality control items. For technical support on the applications themselves, consult the program's vendor or author.

To place additional orders or to request information about other Wiley products, please call (877) 762-2974.

Index

Note to the Reader: Throughout this index **boldfaced** page numbers indicate primary discussions of a topic. *Italicized* page numbers indicate illustrations.

A

About rollout, 577, *577*
absolute values, 28
Academy Flat aspect ratio, 22
Academy Standard aspect ratio, 22
Action Safe area, 518
Active Time Segment option, 503
ActiveShade window, **513**, *513*
Actual Stride Height
    parameter, 429
Adaptation Degradation button, **81**
adaptive degradation, 94–95
Adaptive Halton method, 527–528
Add Atmosphere or Effect
    window, 496, *497*
Add Default Lights to Scene dialog
    box, 463, *463*
Add Effect dialog box, 524
Add Keys tool, 396
Add Selected Objects to
    Highlighted Layer icon, 98
additive color, **20**
Advanced Effects rollout,
    480–481, *480–482*
Affect Pivot Only option, 218
Affect Surfaces section, 481, *481*
airborne time, footsteps, *436*, 437
aliasing
    purpose, **510**, *510*
    Raytrace material, 527, *528*
alien character
    arms
        details, **277–280**, *277–280*
        modeling, **254–259**,
        255–259
    eyes
        area, **288–289**, *288–289*
        creating, **289–290**, *289–290*
    feet, **262–264**, *263–264*
    final touches, **290–293**,
    291–293

form, **246**
head
    detail, **286–290**, *286–290*
    modeling, **264–271**,
    264–271
legs
    detail, **273–276**, *273–276*
    modeling, **259–262**,
    259–262
mouth, **286–289**, *286–288*
planes for, **240–242**, *241*
reference materials, **242–246**,
    242–246
scene setup, **239**
shoulder
    modeling, **254–256**,
    255–256
    refining, **281–282**, *281–283*
smoothing, **271–273**, *272*
torso
    blocking, **247–249**, *247–249*
    cleaning up, **253–254**,
    253–254
    detail, **283–285**, *283–285*
    forming, **250–253**, *250–253*
Align icon, **70–71**, *71*
Align Selection dialog box, 377,
    378
alpha channel, 18, 507, *507*
Alpha element, rendering, 520,
    520–521
Always Arrange tool, 103, *103*
ambient color and light, **297–298**
    contrast levels, 480
    function, 481, *482*
    pool ball, 315
    setting, 301, 309, **482–483**, *483*
Amount parameter, volumetric
    lights, 498
Anamorphic Ratio standard, 22
Angle parameter, 374

Angle Snap option, 554
Angle UVW setting, 349
animation, **24**, **369**
    bouncing ball. *See*
        bouncing ball
    cameras, **517**
    character animation. *See*
        Character Studio
    controllers, **372–374**, *372–373*
    controls, **81–83**, *81–83*
    dummy objects, **374–378**,
    375–378
    ease-in and ease-out, **26**
    follow-through and
        anticipation, **26–27**
    frames, keyframes, and in-
        between frames, **24**, *25*
    hierarchies, **370–374**, *371–374*
    Inverse Kinematics, **448–452**,
    449–450
    knife throwing. *See* knife
        throwing
    Mobile project, **58–59**, *58–59*
    rigid body dynamics, **576–578**,
    577
    soft body dynamics, **579–580**,
    579–580
    squash and stretch, **26**
    weight in, **26**
    in workflow, **11**
animation cycles, 379–380
Animation menu, 65
animators, **13**
Anisotropic shader, **308**, *308*
ankles
    alien, 261–263, *261–263*
    biped, 441, *441*
    calcaneus, 275
antialiasing
    purpose, **510**, *510*
    Raytrace material, 527, *528*

anticipation, **26–27**, **403–404**, *403–404*
Applies the Map as a Texture Map or Environment setting, 349
Arc Rotate tool, 40, 85, **89**
Arc Rotate Selected tool, 85, **89**
Arc Rotate Subobject tool, 85
Arc Rotate Viewport Navigation tool, 186
architectural modeling, **10**
Area Shadows feature, **492–493**, *492–493*
Area Shadows rollout, 493, *493*
areas in vector images, 16
arms
  alien character
    details, **277–280**, *277–280*
    modeling, **254–259**, *255–259*
  bipeds
    associating to models, 442, *442*
    Dope Sheet for, 437, *438*
    in walking, **432**, *432*
Aspect parameter, 466
aspect ratio
  output size settings, 503–504
  spotlights, 466
  standards, **22**
Assign Material to Selection button, 299
Assign Renderer rollout, **508**
Assign Rotation Controller window, 372, *372*
associating biped to characters, **438–448**, *439–447*
Atmospheric & Effects rollout, 493, *493*, 496
atmospheric effects, **493–497**, *494–497*
attenuation, lighting, **478–480**, *478–480*
Auto Key Animation Mode icon, 54, 81
Auto Keyframe feature, 58
Auto Tangents setting, 396
AVI files, 19
axes in viewports, **37–38**, *38*
axles in Red Rocket, **206–208**, *206–208*

back lights, **459–460**, *460*
back wheel axle in Red Rocket, **206–208**, *206–208*
Backface Culling, 48
background color, **323**, *323*
background images, **184–186**, *184–186*
balls
  bouncing. See bouncing ball
  pool. See pool ball
bars, Mobile project
  animating, **58–59**, *58–59*, **370–374**, *371–374*
  copying, **45–46**, *45*
  creating, **41–43**, *42–43*
  positioning, **44**, *44*
Basic Parameters rollout, 551
belly button, alien character, 285, *285*
Bend modifier, 76, *76*, 119–120, *119*
Bevel Settings window, 134, *134*, 222, *222*
Bevel tool, 130, **134**, *134*
bevels
  dresser, 142–145, *142–144*
  Red Rocket model, **222–223**, *222*
Bezier vertex, 164
Bezier Corner vertex, 164
Bias parameter, 490, *490*
Bind to Space Warp option, 567, 569
biped animation. See Character Studio
Biped rollout, 419, *419*
Biped system, 412–413
Biped toolbar, **397**
Birth Rate parameter, 561–562, *562–563*
Bitmap Fit button, 350, *350*
bitmap images, **14–16**, *15*
  in mapping, **316–320**, *317–318*, 327
  in viewports, **245**, *245*
Bitmap Parameter rollout, 318–319
Bitmap parameters, 318–319, **348–349**, *348*

B

Blend material, 303, *303*
Blinn Basic Parameters rollout, 309, 532
Blinn shader, **308–309**, *309*
  Opacity setting, **312**
  Self-Illumination parameter, **311**, *312*
  Specular Highlights section, **309–311**, *310–311*
Blizzard particle system, **549**, *549*
blocking, 378
  alien torso, **247–249**, *247–249*
  knife throwing, **398–399**, *398–400*
blur, **511–512**, *512–513*
bodies
  Red Rocket, **188–191**, *189–192*
    details, **193–195**, *194–195*
    finishing, **220–223**, *221–223*
    mapping, **354–359**, *355–359*
    smoothing, **192–193**, *193*
  rigid. See rigid body dynamics
  soft body dynamics, **578**
    animating, **579–580**, *579–580*
    collections, **578–579**, *578–579*
Body Horizontal button, 424
Body Type rollout, 419
Body Vertical button, 424–425
Bones system, 415
Bookmark Name Field, 104
Boolean operators, **216–220**, *217–220*
borders
  Editable Polys, 125, 137
  object state, 101
Bounce parameter, 568–570
bouncing ball, **378**
  animating, **378–379**, *379*
  cycling, **379–384**, *380–385*
  forward motion, **390–392**, *391–392*
  refining, **385–386**, *385–386*
  rendering, **508–509**
    motion blur, **511–512**, *512–513*
    Renderer tab, **510–511**, *510*
  roll, **392–394**, *392–394*

squash and stretch, **387–389**, *387–389*

summary, **394**

timing, **389–390**, *389–390*

Bounding Box option, 573

bounding boxes

    rendering level, 94, *94*

    rigid bodies, 573

Bounding Sphere option, 573

box modeling techniques, 166

Box parameter, 354

boxes for scene setup

    alien character, **240–242**, *241*

    Red Rocket, **184–186**, *184–186*

brick wall texturing, **296–297**, *296–297*

brightness of specular color, 309

Bubble parameter, 127

bullets. *See* gun and bullets simulation

bump mapping, 108, **296–297**

bumps maps, Red Rocket wheels, **342–343**, *343*

By Angle option, 126

By Polygon option, 172, *172*

By Vertex option, 126

C

calcaneus, alien character, 275

calf area

    alien character, 274–275, *274*

    bipeds, 441

cameras, **513**, *513*

    animating, **517**

    clipping planes, **517–518**, *517*

    controls, **85–87**, *86–87*

    creating, **73–74**, *74*, **514**, *514*

    navigation for, 83, *83*

    Red Rocket, **534–536**, *534–536*

    working with, **514–516**, *514–516*

Cap parameter, 354

Cap Segments parameter, 43

Cap tool, **137–138**, *137–138*

Cartesian coordinates, 23, **36**, 38

Cartoon material, 305, *306*

center pivot icons, 68

center points, XForm, 394, *394*

CGI. *See* Computer-Generated Imagery (CGI)

chain link fence, **331–332**, *331–332*

Chamfer Cylinders, 224–225, *225*

Chamfer Settings dialog box, 132, *132*

Chamfer tool

    alien arms, 257

    Editable Polys, **132–133**, *132–133*

Chamfer Vertices dialog box, 257, *257*

channels, 18, **507**, *507*

character animation, **411–412**

    Character Studio. *See* Character Studio

    Inverse Kinematics, **448–452**, *449–450*

character animators, **13**, 412

character modeling, **9–10**

character sheets, 5

Character Studio, 411

    bipeds

        animating, **424**

        associating, **438–448**, *439–447*

        creating, **415–418**, *416–418*

        Dope Sheet, **433–437**, *435–438*

        footsteps, **426–428**, *426–428*

        freeform animation, **430–433**, *431–433*

        modifying, **418–421**, *419–421*

        positioning, **424–425**, *424–425*

        postures, **421–423**, *422–423*

        run and jump sequence, **429**

    Physique and Skin modifiers, **413–414**

    workflow, **412–415**, *413–414*

checker maps, **327**, *327*

Checker Parameters rollout, 327

chess board

    cameras, **515–516**, *515–516*

    effects, **523–525**, *526*

lighting, 462

    components, **480–482**, *481–482*

    contrast and edges, 480, *481*

    default, 462, *462*

    Omni lights, 472

    Raytrace material, 527, *528*, *530–533*

    safe areas, 518, *519*

    shadows

        density, 489, *489*

        raytraced, 491, *492*

        shadow maps, 489–490, *489*

chest of drawers, **139**

    bottom, **145–152**, *145–153*

    drawers, **154–160**, *154–160*

    knobs, **160–165**, *160–165*

    references for, **139–140**, *140*

    top, **141–145**, *141–144*

children objects

    in hierarchies, **41**, **52–55**, *52–55*

    Inverse Kinematics for, **448**

    materials, 319

chin, alien character, 266, *266*

circles

    creating, **46–50**, *46–50*

    extruding, **47–49**, *49*

circular Target spotlights, 466

clavicles

    alien character, 281

    biped, 421

Clip Manually option, 518

clipping planes, **517–518**, *517–518*

Clone Options window, 45, *45*

Clone Rendered Frame button, 507

CMYK color, 20

Collapse Selected icon, 103

collections

    hard body dynamics, **574**, *574–575*

    soft body dynamics, **578–579**, *578–579*

collisions, 546, 567

color, **20**

    background, **323**, *323*

    changing, 42, *42*

    channels, 18, **507**, *507*

    computer representation, **20–21**

depth, **17–18**
glow, 524, *525*
gradient, 298, **327–328**, *328–329*
highlight, 309
layers, 99, 187
lighting, 475
Marble maps, 329
materials, 297, *297*
particles, 551, 559
shadows, 488–489
Strauss material, 314
subtractive and additive, **20**
viewing, **21**
color banding, 18
Color Modifier maps, 331
Color Selector window, 297, *297*
color wheels, 20
coloring time, **14**
Command panel, 36, *36*, **72–73**, *72*
Create panel, **73–75**, *73–75*
Display panel, **78**, *79*
Hierarchy panel, **76–78**, *76–77*
Modify panel, **75–76**, *76*
Motion panel, **78**, *78*
Utilities panel, **79**, *79*
Common Parameters rollout, 502
Common tab, **502–505**, *502*
Communication Center button, **81**
Composite material, 304, *304*
compositing
images, 331
in postproduction phase, **7**
Compositors maps, 331
Compression Settings window, 509, *509*, 542, *542*
computer basics
aspect ratio, **22**
color, **20–21**
frame rate, **23**
image output, **17–19**
raster images, **14–16**, *15*
resolution, **21–22**
vector images, **16–17**, *17*
Computer-Generated Imagery (CGI), **2–3**
animation concepts, **24–27**, *25*
computer basics. *See* computer basics

coordinate systems, **23–24**, *24*
production phases, **4–8**, *5*
specialties, **13–14**
workflow, **8–13**
Concave Mesh parameter, **573**
concept art, **5–6**
cone spotlight settings, **466**, *467*
Configure Direct3d dialog box, 245, *245*
Configure Modifier Sets option, 119
Connect Edges dialog box, 200, *200*, 270
Connect tool, 102, **200–201**, *200–201*
Constant out-of-range type, 382
constraints
alien character, **281–283**, *283*
joint, **449–450**, *450*
Contrast setting, 480, *481*
control direction in parameter wiring, 562, *563*
control panel for Red Rocket, **199–205**, *199–205*, **360–361**, *361*
converting
default lights, **462–463**, *463*
vs. modifiers, **121–122**, *121–122*
primitives to meshes, **112–115**, *112–114*
cool colors, 20
Coordinate Display button, 80
coordinates and coordinate systems
bitmaps, 319–320, 348, *348*
mapping, 319–320, 328, **345–354**, *346–353*
overview, **23–24**, *24*
vector images, 16
Coordinates rollout, **349**
bitmap images, 319–320
checker maps, 327
gradient maps, 328
tools, **68**, *68*
copying
keyframes, **379**, *379*
objects, **45–46**, 166, *166*
postures, **421–423**, *422–423*
corner triangles for materials, 316
Corner vertex, 164

Create Biped rollout, 417–418
Create Key dialog box, 79, *79*
Create Keys for Inactive Footsteps button, 429, 434
Create menu, 64
Create Multiple Footsteps dialog box, 426–427, *426*, 429
Create New Layer icon, 98, 100
Create panel, 41–42, *42*, **73–75**, *73–75*
Create Rigid Body Collection button, 574
Create Soft Body Collection button, 579
crossing boxes setup
alien character, **240–242**, *241*
Red Rocket, **184–186**, *184–186*
Crowd system, 412
Current Frame control, 82
Current Layer Toggle column, 99
Curve Editor, **379–381**, *380–381*, **394**
animation curves
editing, **385–386**, *385–386*
reading, **381–384**, *382–385*
forward motion, **390–392**, *391–392*
knife throwing. *See* knife throwing
roll, **392–394**, *392–394*
squash and stretch, **387–389**, *387–389*
timing, 389–390, *389–390*
toolbars, **395–396**, *395*
Biped, **397**
Curves, **397**
Key Tangency, **396**
Navigation, **397–398**
Curve Editor icon, 72
Customize menu, 65
Cut tool, 176, **194–195**, *194–195*
Cycle out-of-range type, 382
cycles
animation, 379–380
bouncing ball, **379–384**, *380–385*
footstep, **426–428**, *426–428*
cylinders, 42–43, *42–43*
Cylindrical parameter, 354

D

da Vinci pose, 413, *413*
dailies, 506
decals, **347–354**, *348–353*,
  357–359, *357–359*
decay, lighting, **476–477**, *476–477*
default lighting, **461–463**, *461–463*
Default Scanline Renderer, 311,
  508
deflectors, 546, **568–570**, *569–570*
deformers, 75
Delete Highlighted Empty Layers
  icon, 98
Delete Objects tool, 102
Density parameter
  shadows, 489, *489*
  volumetric lights, 497
diffuse color and lighting,
  297–298
  contrast levels, 480
  function, 481, *481*
  in mapping, 317
  pool ball, 315
  Raytrace material, 527
  setting, 301
Diffuse Color button, 243
Direction of Travel/Mblur option,
  560–561
directional lights, **467–469**, *468*
Directional Parameters rollout, 469
Displace space warp, 565
displacement maps, 108
Display Alpha Channel icon, 507
Display Floater tool, 102
Display panel, 73, **78**, *79*
Display Subtree option, 449
Display Until parameter
  particle systems, 552, 556
  wiring, 564
dividing edges, **177**, *177*
dollies, 40, 516, 535, *535*
Dolly Camera icon, 86, 535, *535*
Dolly Camera + Target icon, 87
Dolly Target icon, 86
Dope Sheet, 395, **433–437**,
  435–438
Dope Sheet Editor, 380
Double Sided material, **304–305**,
  304–305

Down Arrow state, 102
Drag space warp, 566
Draw Curves tool, 396
drawers, **154–160**, *154–160*
dresser. *See* chest of drawers
dummy objects, **374–378**, *375–378*
Duration (Frames) setting, *511*,
  512–513
Duration Subdivisions setting,
  512–513
DynaFlect deflectors, 568
dynamics
  rigid body. *See* rigid body
    dynamics
  soft body, **578**
    animating, **579–580**,
      579–580
    collections, **578–579**,
      578–579

E

ease-in
  animation, **26**
  curves, 384, *384*
ease-out
  animation, **26**
  curves, 382, 384, *384*
Edge option, **178–180**, *179*
Edge Settings window, 136
Edged Faces rendering level, 94, *94*
edges
  chamfering, 133, *133*
  dividing, **177**, *177*
  Editable Polys, 125
  polygon, 109
  shadow maps, 491, *491*
  tessellation, **178–180**, *179*
Edit Borders rollout, 137
Edit Edges rollout, 200
Edit Geometry Rollout, **130**, *130*
Edit menu, 64
Edit Mesh modifier, 121
Edit Poly modifier, 121–123, *123*
Edit Poly tools, **124–131**, *125–131*
Edit Polygons rollout, 129
Edit (Sub-Object) rollout,
  128–130, *129–130*
Edit Vertices rollout, 257

Editable Poly tools, **124–131**,
  125–131
  Bevel, **134**, *134*
  Cap, **137–138**, *137–138*
  Chamfer, **132–133**, *132–133*
  Extrude, **131**, *131–132*
  Extrude Along a Spline,
    138–139, *138–139*
  Hinge from Edge, **136**,
    136–137
  Inset, **135**, *135*
  Outline, **135**, *135*
  Weld, **134**, *134*
editing
  animation curves, **385–386**,
    385–386
  dummy objects, **377–378**,
    377–378
  postproduction phase, **7**
effects
  atmospheric, **493–497**,
    494–497
  Red Rocket, **540**, *540–541*
  rendering, **523–525**, *523–526*
effects TDs, **13**
8-bit image files, **18**
elbow area, alien character,
  277, *277*
elements, Editable Polys, 125–126
Emit Start parameter
  particle systems, 552, 556
  wiring, 564
Emit Stop parameter
  particle systems, 552, 556
  wiring, 564
emitters. *See* particles and particle
  systems
Enable Local Supersampler
  option, 527, 531
Enable Raytracing option,
  540, *540*
End Effector, 452
End light attenuation setting, 478
Environment and Effects window
  ambient light, 483, *483*
  glow effect, 524–525, *524*
  volumetric lights, 497, *498*
environmental modeling, **10**
Euler XYZ controller, 372–373

event-driven particle systems, **546–547**, *547*
Every Nth Frame option, **503**
Exclude/Include window, 496, *496*
Expand icon, 103
explosions, 548
Exponential parameter, 497
Extended Parameters rollout, 530, *531*
extensions, filename, 506
Extrude Along a Spline tool, **138–139**, *138–139*
Extrude Polygons dialog box, 196, *197*
Extrude Settings dialog box, 170–172
Extrude tool, **131**, *131–132*
Extrude Vertices dialog box, 131, *131*
extruding
   circles, **47–49**, *49*
   fingers, **170–173**, *170–173*
   along splines, **138–139**, *138–139*
   thumb, **173–174**, *173–174*
   vertices, **131**, *131–132*
Extrusion Height option, 172
eyes, alien character
   area, **288–289**, *288–289*
   creating, **289–290**, *289–290*

F

Face option, **178–179**, *179*
Face parameter, 354
faces
   mesh, 124
   polygon, 109
   tessellation, **178–179**, *179*
   UVW mapping, 354
Facets rendering level, 92, *92*
Facets+Highlights rendering level, 92, *92*
Facing Standard particle type, 557
Fade For parameter, 553, *553*, 559, 561
falloff
   cartoon shading, 305
   selection, 127
   Target spotlights, **466**, *466*

far clipping planes, 517, *517*
far light attenuation, **478–479**, *478–479*
feet
   alien character, **262–264**, *263–264*
   associating to models, 441, *442*
   biped, 421
FFD (free-form deformation), 75
Field of View (FOV), 514
Figure mode, 438
File menu, 64
files
   formats, **19, 506–507**
   names, **505–506**, *505–506*
   workflow management, **32–35**, *33–35*
fill lights, **459**, *459*, 462, *462*
Fillet button, 218, *218*
film frame rates, 23
film production, 6
Filter tool, 395
filters
   antialiasing, **510–511**
   Curve Editor, 395
fingers
   alien character, 259, *259*, 278, *278*
   associating to models, 443, *443*
   creating, **170–173**, *170–173*
   modeling, 168, *168*
fins, Red Rocket, **208–212**, *208–212*
   base material, **346–347**, *346–347*
   decals, **347–354**, *348–353*, **357–359**, *357–359*
   mapping, **345–354**, *346–353*
FK (Forward Kinematics), 448
flat object specular highlights, 340, *340*
Flat rendering level, 92, *92*
floating point image files, **18**
floating toolbars, 65, *66*
flyouts, 27, 66
focal length, 514
fog lights, **493–497**, *494–497*
foley sound, 8
follow-through, **26–27, 405–406**, *405–406*

Footstep Creation rollout, 426, 429, 434
footstep-driven animation, **424**
Footstep Mode button, 426
Footstep Operations rollout, 429, 434
footsteps
   adding, **426–428**, *426–428*
   Dope Sheet for, **435–437**, *435–438*
   manual process, **434–435**, *434*
Forces space warps, **565–566**
formats, file, **19, 506–507**
forward bouncing ball motion, **390–392**, *391–392*
Forward Kinematics (FK), 448
4K Academy resolution, 22
FOV (Field of View), 514
fps (frames per second), 23
frame range options, 503
frame rate, **23**
frames
   overview, **24**, *25*
   on Time slider, **53–54**, *53*
frames per second (fps), 23
Free cameras, 85–86, **514**
Free Direct lights, **470**
free-form deformation (FFD), 75
Free Spotlight icon, 87
Free spotlights, **469–470**, *469–470*
freeform animation, **430–433**, *431–433*
Freeze column, 99
Freeze icon, 187, *187*
Freeze/Unfreeze All Layers icon, 99
freezing objects, 78
Friction parameter, 569
Front view
   Red Rocket, 185–186, *185*
   viewports, 36–37, *36*, 89
frozen objects, **439**
fruit arrangement, 530–533, *530–533*

G

G-Buffer section, 523
General Parameters rollout
   lighting, **475**, *475*
   spotlights, 470
   volumetric lights, 495–496

generalists, **14**
Generate Mapping Coords
    option, 345
geometry, instanced, 549, 560–561
Geometry category, **73–74**, *74*
Get Material From option, 560
Get Material function, **298**
gimbal lock, 372
Gizmos rendering level, **95–97**,
    95–97
Glossiness parameter, 301
    Blinn shader, 310–311, *310*
    Metal shader, 312
    Strauss material, 314
glow effects, **523–525**, *523–526*
Go Forward to Sibling control,
    function, 300
Go to End control, 82
Go to Frame control, 82
Go to Parent control, **300**
Go to Start control, 82
gradient color, 298, **327–328**,
    328–329
Gradient Ramp maps, **328**, *329*
Graph Editors menu, 65
gravity
    footsteps, 437
    space warp, **566–567**, *566–567*
grayscale images, **17**
Grid dialog box, 90
grids
    Home Grid, 28, *28*, 38, *38*, 90
    Status Bar settings, 80
    units, 90, *90*
gross animation, 378
Group extrusions option, 171, *171*
Group menu, 64
Grow For parameter, 553, 559, 561
Grow option, 126
gun and bullets simulation
    IK for, **448–450**, *449–450*
    particle systems, **554–555**,
        554–555, **560–561**
    particle types, **557–560**,
        558–560
    space warps, **565–566**
        deflectors, **568–570**,
            569–570
        gravity, **566–567**, *566–567*

timing, **556**, *556*
wiring parameters together,
    561–564, *561–565*

H

handlebars, Red Rocket, **228**, *228*
    details, **232–234**, *232–234*
    lofting, **230–232**, *230–231*
    paths, **228–229**, *229*
    shapes, **229–230**, *229–230*
handles, rotate, 44
hands, **167**
    alien character, 259, *259*
    associating to models, 442, *442*
    detail, **176–181**, *177–181*
    fingers
        alien character, 259, *259*,
            278, *278*
        associating to models,
            443, *443*
        creating, **170–173**, *170–173*
        modeling, 168, *168*
    palm, **167–170**, *167–170*
    Subdivision Surfaces, **175–176**,
        175–176
    thumb, **173–174**, *173–174*
Havok 1 solver, 577, 579
Havok 3 solver, 577
HD (History Dependent) solver,
    451–452
HDTV (High Definition TV)
    resolution, 22
head
    alien character
        detail, **286–290**, *286–290*
        modeling, **264–271**,
            264–271
    associating to models, **444**, *444*
    movement in walking,
        430–432, *431*
height
    aspect ratio, 22
    cylinders, 43
    extrusions, 172
    output size settings, 503
Height Segments parameter, 43
Help menu, 65
helper objects, **374–378**, *375–378*
Helpers category, **74**, *75*
hexagons, 50

HI (History Independent)
    solver, 451
Hidden Line rendering level,
    93, *93*
Hide by Category rollout, 78
Hide column, 99
Hide/Unhide All Layers icon, 99
hiding objects, 78
hierarchies
    Mobile project, **41**, *41*,
        370–374, *371–374*
    parent-child relationships,
        52–55, *52–55*
Hierarchy Mode tool, 102
Hierarchy panel
    pivot points, 56–57, *56*
    sections, **76–78**, *76–77*
Hierarchy panel icon, 73
Hierarchy tool icons, **66**, *66*
high color 5-bit image files, **18**
High Definition TV (HDTV)
    resolution, 22
high-poly modeling, **240**
high polygon-count modeling. *See*
    alien character
Highlight Selected Objects' Layers
    icon, 99
Hinge from Edge tool, **136**,
    136–137
Hinge Polygons from Edge
    dialog box
    arms, 255–256, *255*
    feet, 262–263
hip area, alien character, 283–284
History Dependent (HD) solver,
    451–452
History Independent (HI)
    solver, 451
Home Grid, 28, *28*, 38, *38*, 90
horizontal bars, Mobile project
    animating, **58–59**, *58–59*,
        370–374, *371–374*
    copying, **45–46**, *45*
    creating, **41–43**, *42–43*
    positioning, **44**, *44*
hot materials, 316
hotkeys, 90
hotspots, Target spotlights, 464
HSV (hue, saturation, and value)
    channels, 21, **298**

I

Ignore Backfacing option, 126
IK (Inverse Kinematics), **448**
    IK solver, **451–452**, *452*
    joint constraints, **449–450**, *450*
Image Aspect parameter, 503
Image Format setting, 505
Image motion blur, **512**, *512*
images, **17**
    background, **184–186**, *184–186*
    channels, **18**, **507**, *507*
    color depth, **17–18**
    file formats, **19**, **506–507**
    filenames, **505–506**, *505–506*
    in mapping, **316–320**, *317–318*
    movie files, **19**
    raster, **14–16**, *15*
    vector, **16–17**, *17*
impact, knife throwing, 406
in-between frames, **24**
In/Out Tangent for New Keys
    button, 82
In Place mode, **427–428**
incandescence, 311
incremental saves, 35
Index of Refraction (IOR),
    530–531, *532*, 533
Ink 'n Paint material, 305, *306*
Inset tool, **135**, *135*
instanced geometry, 549, 560–561
instances, object, **166**, *166*
intensity
    glow, 525
    lighting, 475
Intensity/Color/Attenuation
    rollout, **475–480**, *475–480*
intent
    animation, 387
    scripts for, 5
interface. *See* user interface (UI)
interparticle collisions, 567
Inverse Decay option, 476
Inverse Kinematics (IK), **448**
    IK solver, **451–452**, *452*
    joint constraints, **449–450**, *450*
Inverse Kinematics (IK)
    category, **77**
Inverse Kinematics rollout,
    449, *449*

Inverse Square Decay option,
    476–477, *476*
IOR (Index of Refraction),
    530–531, *532*, 533
Isoline Display option, 176,
    176, 272
Iterations parameter
    Subdivision Surfaces, 176
    TurboSmooth, 271–273, *272*

J

jagged lines, antialiasing
    purpose, 510, *510*
    Raytrace material, 527, *528*
joint constraints, **449–450**, *450*
JPEG (Joint Photographic Experts
    Group) format, 19
jump gait, 428
jumping
    Dope Sheet for, 437, *438*
    jump sequence, **429**

K

Key Filters icon, 82
Key Info rollout, 374, *374*
key lights
    default, 462, *462*
    three-point lighting,
        458–459, *459*
Key Mode control, 83
Key Status tools, 389
Key Tangency toolbar, **396**
Keyboard Entry rollout, 46, *46*,
    185, *185*
keyboard shortcuts, 90
keyframes, **24**, *25*
    copying, **379**, *379*
    purpose, 378
    setting, **53–54**, *53*
knees
    alien character, 273–274, *273*
    associating to models, 440
knife throwing
    anticipation, **403–404**, *403–404*
    blocking out, **398–399**,
        398–400
    follow-through, **405–406**,
        405–406

rotation, **401–403**, *401–403*
    targets, **406–408**, *407*
    trajectories, **400–401**, *400–401*
knobs, **160–165**, *160–165*
knuckles
    alien character, 278–279,
        278–279
    modeling, **178**, *178*

L

Lasso Selection Region icon, 335
Lathe modifier
    knobs, 160, 165, *165*
    for Red Rocket thruster,
        214–216, *215–216*
Layer Manager, 72
    Red Rocket lighting, 483–484,
        484
    scene files, 187, *187*
layout
    screen, **62–63**, *63*
    viewports, **36–37**
Layout Manager, **98–100**, *98–100*
leaping action, 437, *438*
Left view, 36–37, *36*, 89
legs
    alien character
        detail, **273–276**, *273–276*
        modeling, **259–262**,
            259–262
        associating to models, 441, *441*
Length parameter, 556
lens effect, **523–525**, *523–526*
lenses
    overview, 514–515, *514*
    zooming, 516
letterboxing, 22
libraries, material, **344–345**,
    344–345
Library Management Tool icons,
    344, *344*
Life parameter, 552, 564
Light Bulb icon, 119
Light Lister, **498**, *499*
lighters, **13–14**
lighting, 3, **455**
    Advanced Effects rollout,
        480–481, *480–482*
    ambient, **482–483**, *483*

attenuation, **478–480**, *478–480*
concepts, **456–457**, *457–458*
controls, **87**, *87–88*
decay, **476–477**, *476–477*
default, **461–463**, *461–463*
General Parameters rollout, **475**, *475*
Intensity/Color/Attenuation rollout, **475–480**, *475–480*
Light Lister, **498**, *499*
navigation for, **83**, *83*
practical, **460–461**
Red Rocket, **483–487**, *483–488*
shaders. *See* shaders
shadows. *See* shadows
standard. *See* standard lights
three-point, **458–461**, *458–460*
volumetric. *See* volumetric lights
in workflow, **11–12**
Lights category, **73–74**, *74*
Line tool, 160
Linear out-of-range type, 383, *383*
lines, vertex type, **164**
Link Info category, **77–78**, *77*
linking objects
dummy, **376–377**, *376–377*
machine gun unit, **448–449**, *449*
tools, **66**, *66*
lip-sync, 8
Lit Wireframes rendering level, **93**, *93*
Live area, 518
loading materials, **339**, *339*
Local Coordinate System, 23
Local Normal extrusion option, 171, *171*
Lock Selection tool, 80, 397
Lock Tangents tool, 397
Locks function, 301
Loft object mapping, 345
lofting, **228**, **230–232**, *230–231*
Loop out-of-range type, 382
loops
animation, 380
edges, 126
lossless compression, 19
low-poly modeling, 110, **240**

machine gun unit. *See* gun and bullets simulation
main toolbar tools, **65–66**, *65–66*
Align and Mirror, **70–71**, *71*
coordinate system, **68**, *68*
editing window, **72**, *72*
Linking and Hierarchy, **66**, *66*
named selection set, **70**, *70*
Selection, **67**, *67*
snapping, **69**, *69*
transformation, **68**, *68*
Undo/Redo, **66**, *66*
Make Unique option, 118
manipulators, 68
maps and mapping, **295**, **326**
2D, **326–328**, *327–329*
3D, **328–330**, *329–330*
coordinates, **320**, **345–354**, *346–353*
materials, 302
Opacity, **331–332**, *331–332*
pool ball. *See* pool ball
Red Rocket, **333**, *333*
body, **354–359**, *355–359*
fins, **345–354**, *346–353*
wheels, **333–343**, *334–343*
reflections, **321–322**, *321–322*
removing, **323**, *323*
shadows. *See* shadows
Maps rollout
alien character, 243, *243*
Raytrace maps, 529
reflections, 321
refractions, 532
Marble maps, **329**, *329*
mass
in momentum, 408
rigid body dynamics, 573
weight for, 26
Match Bitmap Sizes as Closely as Possible option, 245
Material Effects Channel function, 299
Material ID channel, 524
Material Map browser, 344, *344*
Material/Map Navigator, 319–320, *320*
Material Name function, **300**

M

materials and Material Editor
adding, **353–354**, *354*
alien character, **242–246**, *242–246*
basics, **297–298**, *297–298*
creating, **355–356**, *356*
functions, **298–302**, *299–300*, *302*
glow effect, 524
icon, 72
libraries, **344–345**, *344–345*
mapping. *See* maps and mapping
overview, **296–297**, *296–297*
Raytrace, 306, 527
creating, **527**, *527*
mapping, 528–529, 532
refractions, **530–533**, *530–533*
tweaking, **527–528**, *528*
sample slots, **324–325**, *324–325*
shaders. *See* shaders
sub-objects, **325–326**, *326*
types, **302–307**, *303–307*
matte, 507
Matte/Shadow material, **305**
Max Units setting, 90
maximizing viewports, **39**
MaxLens parameter, 514
MAXScript menu, 65
MAXScript Mini Listener button, 80
mental ray Renderer, 508
menu bar, 35, **63–65**, *64*
Merge File dialog box, 213, *213*
merging objects into scenes, **213**, *213*
Mesh Convex Hull parameter, **573**
meshes
modeling, **111–115**, *112–114*
vs. polygons, **122–124**, *123–124*
metaball technology, 557
Metal shader, **312**
Metalness parameter, 314
MetaParticles, 557–559
Min/Max Viewport tool, 89
Mini Curve Editor, **385–386**, *385–386*

Mirror dialog box, 70, *71*
Mirror icon, **70–71**, *71*
miscellaneous material settings,
    300–301
missteps, learning from, **372**
Mobile project, 32, 41
    dummy objects, **374–378**,
        375–378
    hierarchies, **41**, *41*, **54–55**,
        54–55, **370–374**, *371–374*
    horizontal bars
        animating, **58–59**, *58–59*,
            370–374, *371–374*
        copying, **45–46**, *45*
        creating, **41–43**, *42–43*
        positioning, **44**, *44*
    objects for, **46–51**, *46–51*
    pivot points, **56–57**, *56–57*
    planning, **40**
    Schematic View, **100–105**,
        101–105
modelers, **13**
modeling, **107**
    alien. *See* alien character
    chest of drawers. *See* chest of
        drawers
    converting vs. modifiers,
        121–122, *121–122*
    Edit Poly tools, **124–131**,
        125–131
    Editable Poly tools, **124–131**,
        125–131
        Bevel, **134**, *134*
        Cap, **137–138**, *137–138*
        Chamfer, **132–133**, *132–133*
        Extrude, **131**, *131–132*
        Extrude Along a Spline,
            138–139, *138–139*
        Hinge from Edge, **136**,
            136–137
        Inset, **135**, *135*
        Outline, **135**, *135*
        Weld, **134**, *134*
    hand. *See* hands
    meshes and sub-objects,
        111–115, *112–114*
    meshes vs. polygons, **122–124**,
        123–124
    modifier application, **115–117**,
        115–118

organic. *See* alien character
    planning, **108–109**, *109*
    polygons, **109–110**, *109–110*
    primitives, **110–111**, *111*
    in workflow, **8–10**
modeling windows, 37
modes, viewport, 45, 47,
    427–428, *428*
Modes and Display rollout,
    428, *428*
Modifier List, 47, *48*
Modifier Stack, 47–48, *48*,
    115–117
    options, **118–119**, *119*
    order in, **119–120**, *119–120*
modifiers, 47, **75–76**
    applying, **115–117**, *115–118*
    vs. converting, **121–122**,
        121–122
    options, **118–119**, *119*
    ordering, **119–120**, *119–120*
    for spheres, **112–115**, *112–114*
Modifiers menu, 64
Modify panel, 42, *42*, 73, **75–76**, *76*
Modify tab, 419
momentum
    knife throwing, **406–408**, *407*
    overview, **408**
motion blur, **511–512**, *512–513*
Motion Capture utility, 79
motion in vector programs, 16
Motion panel, 73, **78**, *78*
Motion tab, 419, *419*
Motor space warp, 565
mouth, alien character, **286–289**,
    286–288
Move Children icon, 103
Move Keys tool, 395
Move Keys Horizontal tool, 395
Move Keys Vertical tool, 396
movie files, **19**
Multi-Layer shader, **312**, *313*
Multi/Sub-Object materials, **306**,
    325–326
    creating, **337–338**, *337–338*
    loading, **339**, *339*
    polygons and named selection
        sets, **335–337**, *335–337*
Multiplier parameter
    lighting, 475, 477
    shadows, 488

N

Name and Color rollout, 418
Name and Color Type-In, 160, *160*
named selection sets
    purpose, **70**, *70*
    Red Rocket wheels, **334–337**,
        335–337
names
    conventions, **33**
    deflectors, **568**
    filenames, **505–506**, *505–506*
    objects, **44**
National Television System
    Committee (NTSC) standard
    color, **21**
    frame rates, 23
    resolution, 22
navigating viewports, **39–40**,
    83–89, *83–88*
Navigation toolbar, **397–398**
near clipping planes, 517, *517*
near light attenuation, **478–479**,
    478, 481
neck
    alien character, 264–266,
        264–266
    associating to models, **444**, *444*
New Scene Explorer option, 105
Next Key button, 83
NGons, 50
node-based editing workflow, 75
nodes
    hierarchy, 76
    null, 375
Noise maps
    bump maps, 343, *343*
    overview, **330**, *330*
Noise parameter, 497
non-event-driven particle systems,
    547–550, *549–550*
Normal Align icon, 71
normals
    defined, 27
    extruding along, 131
    Red Rocket, 353
nose for Red Rocket, **362**, *362*
Not Shared option, 573
NTSC (National Television
    System Committee) standard
    color, **21**

frame rates, 23
resolution, 22
NTSC DV standard
pixel aspect, 504, *504*
resolution, 22
nuance, 412
null nodes, 375
Number of Footsteps
parameter, 429

O

Object Color dialog box, 42, *42*
Object Fragments setting, 548
Object ID channels, 524, 526, *526*
Object Motion Blur settings,
511–512, *511*
Object Properties dialog box
glow effect, 523–524, *524*
image planes, 188, *188*
Object Space modifiers, 76
Object Type rollout, 550
objects, 27
copying, **45–46**, **166**, *166*
creating, **46–51**, *46–51*
dummy, **374–378**, *375–378*
freezing, 78
frozen, **439**
hierarchies
Mobile project, **41**, *41*,
370–374, *371–374*
parent-child relationships,
52–55, *52–55*
linking, **448–449**, *449*
merging into scenes, **213**, *213*
names, **44**
particle systems, 550–551
rotating, **44**, *44*
Scene Explorer, 106
in viewports, **37–38**, *38*
Off Axis parameter, 551
Off Plane parameter, 551
Offset parameter
3D maps, 329
bitmaps, 349
gradient maps, 328
Offset UV setting, 349
Omni lights, **471–473**, *472–473*
attenuation, 478, *479*
as default lights, 463, *463*

OmniFlect deflectors, 568
1K Academy resolution, 22
opacity
Blinn shader, **312**
mapping, **331–332**, *331–332*
materials, **302**
Strauss material, 314
Options section
glow effect, 524–525, *525*
Render Scene dialog box,
505, *505*
Orbit icon, 87
order, Modifier Stack, **119–120**,
119–120
Oren-Nayar-Blinn shader, **313**, *313*
organic modeling. *See* alien
character
organizing objects, **44**
origins, 38, 90
Orthographic viewports
navigation in, 83, *83*
rotating in, 40
tools in, **84–85**, *84–85*
out-of-range types, **381–383**, *381*,
383–384
Outline tool, **135**, *135*
output, 17
channels, **18**
color depth, **17–18**
file formats, **19**
movie files, **19**
raster, **14–16**, *15*
Red Rocket, **540–542**, *541–542*
size settings, **503–504**, *503–504*
time settings, **502–503**,
503–504
vector, **16–17**, *17*
over-lighting, 457, *457*

P

PAL (Phase Alternation Line)
standard
frame rates, 23
resolution, 22
palm, **167–170**, *167–170*
Pan Camera icon, 87
Pan tool, 397–398
panning, 39, 88

Param Curve Out-of-Range Types
dialog box, **381–383**, *381*,
383–384
Parameter Curve Out-of-Range
Types animation, 380
Parameter Out-of-Range Curves
tool, 397
Parameter Wiring dialog box,
562, *563*
Parameter Wiring tool, 561
parameters
object, **44**
wiring, **561–564**, *561–565*
parametric objects, 74
parent materials, 339
parent objects
in hierarchies, **41**, **52–55**,
52–55
Inverse Kinematics for, **448**
Particle Array particle system,
548, *549*
Particle Cloud particle system,
548, *549*
Particle Flow emitter, 547, *547*
Particle Generation rollout,
552–553, *552–553*, 556,
560–561
Particle Motion section, 561, *561*
Particle Quantity area, 552
Particle Size area, 552
Particle Type rollout,
558–560, *559*
Particle View window,
546–547, *547*
particles and particle systems, **545**
event-driven, **546–547**, *547*
gun and bullets. *See* gun and
bullets simulation
non-event-driven, **547–550**,
549–550
overview, 546
Particle Generation rollout,
552–553, *552–553*
selecting, **557–560**, *558–560*
setting up, **550–551**, *550–551*
space warps, **565–566**
deflectors, **568–570**,
569–570
gravity, **566–567**, *566–567*

pasting postures, **421–423**, *422–423*

Path Follow space warp, 565

paths for Red Rocket handlebars, **228–229**, *229*

PBomb space warp, 548, 566

PCloud object, 548

pelvis
associating to models, 439–440, *440*
biped, 421

per object motion blur, 512

Percentage of Particles parameter, 551

Perspective icon, 87

Perspective viewports, 36–38, *36*, 89
navigation in, 83, *83*
tools in, **84–85**, *84–85*

Phase Alternation Line (PAL) standard
frame rates, 23
resolution, 22

Phase parameter, 498

Phong shader, **313–314**

photometric lights, 74, 461

Physical Properties rollout, 573

Physique Initialization dialog box, 445

Physique modifier, **412–413**
for associating biped to models, **445–448**, *446–447*
vs. skin, **413–414**

Pick Material from Object function, 300

Pick Object dialog box, 445, *446*, 559, 562, *562*

Pin Stack option, 118

Pinch parameter, 127

Ping Pong type, 383, *383*

pipelines, 44

Pivot category, **76**, *76*

pivot points, 76
bouncing ball, 393–394, *394*
setting, **56–57**, *56–57*

pixel aspect, 504, *504*

pixelated images, 15

Place Highlight icon, 71

Planar deflectors, 568

Planar parameter, 354

planes
alien character, **240–242**, *241*
Red Rocket, **184–186**, *184–186*

planning
Mobile project, **40**
models, **108–109**, *109*

Play/Stop control, 82

playback controls, **82–83**, *82*

plugins, 79

polygons, 9, **109–110**, *109–110*
Editable Polys. *See* Editable Poly tools
high-poly and low-poly modeling, **240**
vs. meshes, **122–124**, *123–124*
organic. *See* alien character
Red Rocket wheels, **334–337**, *335–337*

pool ball, 314
background color, **323**, *323*
mapping, **316–320**, *317–320*
reflections, **321–322**, *321–322*
starting, **315**, *315*
surfaces, **315–316**, *315–316*

Position XYZ controller, 374

postproduction phase, **6–8**

postures, copying and pasting, **421–423**, *422–423*

practical lighting, **460–461**

Preferences icon, 103

prejump position, 437, *438*

preproduction phase, **4–5**, *5*

presets
resolution, 504
Super Spray particle system, 548–550

Preview & Animation rollout, 577

Preview Type function, 300

previewing
material, 300
rendering, **513**, *513*
rigid body dynamics, 575–576

Previous Frame/Key control, 82

Previous Key button, 83

primary colors, 20

primitives, 27
meshes from, **112–115**, *112–114*
overview, **110–111**, *111*

procedural maps, 327

production phases, **4–8**, *5*

projects
creating, **34**
saving, **34–35**, *35*
workflow, **32–35**, *33–35*

Prompt Line, **81**

props modeling, **10**

Proxy Convex Hull parameter, 573

Push space warp, 566

Put to Library function, 299

Q

Quad menu, 37

Quick Align icon, 71

Quick Render icon, 72

Quickslice tool, **194–195**, *194–195*

QuickTime files
Compression Settings window, 509, *509*
output to, 19

R

Radial Color parameter, 525

radiosity, 74, 99

radius
circles, 46, *46*
cylinders, 42–43
spheres not here??, 28

random particles, 553

Range option, 503

raster images, **14–16**, *15*

rasterization, 16

Ray Bias parameter, 492

Raytrace Basic Parameters rollout, 527, *527*, 530

Raytrace material, 306, 526–527
creating, **527**, *527*
mapping, **528–529**, *529*
refractions, **530–533**, *530–533*
tweaking, **527–528**, *528*

raytracing
reflections, 321, **536–540**, *538–540*
shadows, 488–489, **491–492**, *492*

RB Collection Properties rollout, 574, *574*

Reactor menu, 64

reactors. *See* rigid body dynamics
reading animation curves,
  381–384, *382–385*
Real-Time Preview window
  rigid body dynamics,
    575–576, *575*
  soft body dynamics, 580
rectangular Target spotlights, 466,
  466–467
Red, Green, and Blue (RGB)
  color, 20, **298**
Red Border state, 101
Red Rocket model
  body, **188–191**, *189–192*
    details, **193–195**, *194–195*
    finishing, **220–223**, *221–223*
    mapping, **354–359**, *355–359*
    smoothing, **192–193**, *193*
  cameras, **534–536**, *534–536*
  control panel, **199–205**,
    199–205, **360–361**, *361*
  effects, **540**, *540–541*
  fins, **208–212**, *208–212*
    base material, **346–347**,
      346–347
    decals, **347–354**, *348–353*,
      357–359, *357–359*
    mapping, **345–354**, *346–353*
  handlebars, **228**, *228*
    details, **232–234**, *232–234*
    lofting, **230–232**, *230–231*
    paths, **228–229**, *229*
    shapes, **229–230**, *229–230*
  lighting
    overview, **483–487**, *483–488*
    volumetric, 493–497,
      494–497
  mapping, **333**, *333*
  material libraries, **344–345**,
    344–345
  nose, **362**, *362*
  output, **540–542**, *541–542*
  planes for, **184–186**, *184–186*
  reflections, **536–540**, *538–540*
  rendering, **534–542**, *534–536*,
    538–542
  scene files, **187–188**, *187–188*
  seat, **235–237**, *235–236*,
    359–360, *360*

thruster, **214–220**, *214–220*,
  363–366, *364–366*
wheel wells, **196–199**, *196–199*
wheels, **223–224**, *224*
  axles, **206–208**, *206–208*
  bumps maps, **342–343**, *343*
  creating, **224–226**, *225–226*
  fine tuning materials,
    339–342, *340–342*
  mapping, **333–343**, *334–343*
  Multi/Sub-Object materials,
    337–339, *337–339*
  placing, **226**, *226–227*
  polygons and named
    selection sets, **334–337**,
    335–337
Redo icon, 35, **66**, *66*
Reduce Keys tool, 396
reference materials, 108
  alien character, **242–246**,
    242–246
  chest of drawers, **139–140**, *140*
  da Vinci pose, 413, *413*
References Mode tool, 103, *103*
reflections
  deflectors, 569
  mapping, **321–322**, *321–322*
  raytraced, **526–533**, *527–533*
  Red Rocket, 341, *341*, **536–540**,
    538–540
  rendering, **520**, *521*
  shaders for. *See* shaders
Reflections parameter, 322
Reflective parameter, 342
refractions
  raytraced, **526–533**, *527–533*
  rendering, 521
Relative/Absolute Transform
  button, 80
Relative Repeat type, 383, *383*
relative values, 28
Remove Modifier option, 118
removing maps, **323**, *323*
Render column, 99
Render Elements tab, **519–522**,
  520–522
Render Iterations option, 271, *272*
Render Output File dialog box
  Red Rocket, 541–542, *541*
  for saving scenes, **505–506**, *505*

Render Output section, **505**, *505*
Render Processing dialog box,
  508, *508*
Render Scene dialog box, 72, **502**,
  508–509
  ActiveShade feature, 513
  Options section, **505**, *505*
  output size settings, **503–504**,
    503–504
  Render Elements tab, **519–522**,
    520–522
  Render Output section,
    505, *505*
  Renderer tab, **510–511**, *510*
  time output settings, **502–503**,
    503–504
Rendered Frame window, 507
Renderer tab, **510–511**, *510*
rendering, 3, **501**
  bouncing ball animation,
    508–509
    motion blur, **511–512**,
      512–513
    Renderer tab, **510–511**, *510*
  cameras. *See* cameras
  effects, **523–525**, *523–526*
  filenames in, **505–506**, *505–506*
  image formats in, **506–507**
  to movies, 19
  in postproduction phase, **6–7**
  previewing, 513, *513*
  process, **508**, *508*
  raytraced reflections and
    refractions, **526–533**,
    527–533
  Red Rocket, **534–542**, *534–536*,
    538–542
  renderer assignment, **508**
  safe areas, **519**, *519*
  setup. *See* Render Scene
    dialog box
  vector images, 16
  viewport, **91–95**, *91–94*,
    461–462, *461*
  in workflow, **12–13**
Rendering menu, 65
Rendering Method tab,
  461–462, *461*
Reset Map/Mtl to Default Settings
  function, 299

resizing
  polygons, 135
  viewports, 89
resolution
  output size settings, 503
  raster images, 15
  standards, **21–22**
RGB (Red, Green, and Blue)
  color, 20, **298**
riggers, **13**
rigid body dynamics, **571**
  animating, **576–578**, *577*
  collections, **574**, *574–575*
  objects, **571–572**, *571–572*
  properties, *572–573*, **573**
  testing, **575–576**, *575–576*
Rigid Body Properties dialog box,
  572–573, *572*, *576*, *576*
rigs, 11, 374
rim lights, **459–460**, *460*
Ring option, 127
rocket model. *See* Red Rocket
  model
roll
  bouncing ball, **392–394**,
    392–394
  camera, 516
Roll icon, 87
room reflections, **538–539**, *539*
rotate handles, 44
Rotate tool, 96
Rotate Transform gizmo, 419, *420*
Rotation and Collision rollout,
  560–561, *560*
Rotation Windup option, 374
Rotational Joints rollout, 450, *450*
rotations
  bipeds, 419, *420*
  controllers, **372–374**, *373*
  knife throwing, **401–403**,
    401–403
  Mobile project, **58–59**, *58–59*
  objects, **44**, *44*
  views, 40
run and jump sequence, **429**
run gait, 428

S

safe areas, **519**, *519*
Safe Frame view, **519**, *519*

Sample Range parameter, 491, *491*
Sample Slot function, **298**
Samples
  Material Editor, 298, **324–325**,
    324–325
  Object Motion Blur, 512–513
  Raytrace maps, 529
  Raytrace material, 527, *528*,
    531–532
  shadows, 491, *491*
Save File As dialog box, 34–35, *35*
saving projects, **34–35**, *35*
Scale tool, 96
Scale Keys tool, 396
Scale Transform gizmo,
  419–420, *420*
Scale Values tool, 396
scaling
  keys, 396
  raster images, 15, *15*
  vector images, 16, *17*
Scene Explorer, **105–106**, *105*
scenes, **97–98**
  Layout Manager, **98–100**,
    98–100
  merging objects into, **213**, *213*
  Red Rocket, **187–188**, *187–188*
  Schematic View, **100–105**,
    101–105
  storyboard, 5
scenics, 10
Schematic View, **100–105**, *101–105*
Schematic View icon, 72
Schematic View Name Field,
  103, *104*
screen layout, **62–63**, *63*
scripts, **5**
scrubbing animation, 54, 79
seams, **221**, *221*
seat in Red Rocket
  adding, **359–360**, *360*
  creating, **235–237**, *235–236*
See-Through mode
  alien arms, 257
  frozen objects, 439
segments
  adding, 116
  lines, 164
Select and Link tool
  dummy objects, 376
  hierarchy, 52–55

Select Bitmap Image File dialog
  box, 243, *243*
Select Camera dialog box, 516, *516*
Select Highlighted Objects and
  Layers icon, 98
Select Objects dialog box, *449*, 452
Select Objects by Name dialog
  box, **67**, *67*
Select Parent dialog box, 448
Select Region flyout, 335, *335*
Select Rigid Bodies dialog box,
  574, *575*
Select tool, 102, 335
selecting
  particles, **557–560**, *558–560*
  viewport objects, **38**, *38*
  viewports, 37
Selection icons, **67**, *67*
Selection List icon, 82
Selection rollout, **125–127**,
  125–127
selection sets icons, **70**, *70*
Self-Illumination parameter
  Blinn shader, **311**, *312*
  materials, 302
  rendering, 521
Set Key Animation Mode icon, 82
Set Key Filters window, 81, *82*
Set Key icon, 81
Shaded mode, 46–47
Shader Type function, 300
shaders, **308**
  Anisotropic, **308**, *308*
  Blinn, **308–309**, *309*
    Opacity setting, **312**
    Self-Illumination
      parameter, **311**, *312*
    Specular Highlights section,
      309–311, *310–311*
  Metal, **312**
  Multi-Layer, **312**, *313*
  Oren-Nayar-Blinn, **313**, *313*
  Phong, **313–314**
  Translucent, **314**, *314*
Shadow Integrity parameter, 493
Shadow Map Parameters
  rollout, 495
shadow maps, **488–491**, *490–491*
Shadow Parameters rollout,
  488–489, *488*
Shadow Quality parameter, 493

Shadow Spread parameter, 493
shadows
  area, **492–493**, *492–493*
  creating, **488**
  General Parameters rollout, 475
  Matte/Shadow material, **305**
  Omni lights, 472
  raytraced, 489, **491–492**, *492*
  rendering, **521**, *521*
  shadow maps, **489–491**,
    490–491
  Shadow Parameters rollout,
    488–489, *488*
  skylights, 474, *474*
  volumetric lights, **495–496**,
    495–496
shapes and shape objects
  Red Rocket handlebars,
    229–230, *229–230*
  Target spotlights, **466**, *466–467*
  vector images, 16
Shapes category, **73–74**, *74*
Shellac material, 306, *307*
shiny objects, specular highlight
  for, 311
shots, storyboard, 5
shoulders, alien character
  modeling, **254–256**, *255–256*
  refining, **281–282**, *281–283*
Show All Tangents tool, 397
Show End Result option, 118
Show Frozen as Gray option, 439
Show Keyable Icons tool, 397
Show Map in Viewport button,
  244–245, **299–300**, 319, 347
Show Safe Frame option, 518
Show Tangents tool, 397
Shrink option, 126
Shrink Wrap parameter, 354
Sides parameter, 43
Simulation Geometry rollout, **573**
Single frame range option, 502
16-bit color display, **18**
size
  output settings, **503–504**,
    503–504
  particles, 552, 556, 559–560
  polygons, 135
  shadow maps, **490**, *491*

viewports, 89
volumetric lights, 498
Skin modifier, **413–414**
skinning, 415
Skylight Parameters rollout,
  473–474, *474*
skylights, **473–474**, *474*
Slice Plane tool, **149–154**, *150–153*
Slide Keys tool, 396
smoke, 557
Smooth rendering level, 91, *91*
Smooth + Highlights rendering
  level, 91, *91*, 245–246
Smooth vertex, 164
smoothing
  alien character, **271–273**, *272*
  Red Rocket body, **192–193**, *193*
  Subdivision Surfaces, 175
Snap Frames tool, 397
snapping icons, **69**, *69*
Snow particle system, 549–550, *550*
soft body dynamics, **578**
  animating, **579–580**, *579–580*
  collections, **578–579**, *578–579*
Soft Body modifier, 579
Soft Selection rollout, **127–128**,
  127–128
soft shadows, **492–493**, *492–493*
Soften Diffuse Edge setting,
  480, *481*
Soften parameter, 310–311, *311*
softness, shadow maps, 491, *491*
solvers
  IK, **451–452**, *452*
  rigid body dynamics, 577
sound in postproduction phase, **8**
Space Warp category, 73, **75**, *75*
space warps, 546
  creating, 73, **75**, *75*
  deflectors, **568–570**, *569–570*
  Forces, **565–566**
  gravity, **566–567**, *566–567*
special effects
  atmospheric, **493–497**, *494–497*
  rendering, **523–525**, *523–526*
specular element
  lighting, 481, *482*
  materials, 297, 301
  rendering, 521, *521*

Specular Highlights group
  Blinn shader, **309–311**,
    310–311
  flat objects, 340, *340*
  Raytrace maps, 532
  Raytrace material, 531
Specular Level parameter
  Blinn shader, 310–311, *310*
  bump maps, 342
  materials, 301
  Metal shader, 312
Specular Maps function, 301
speed
  in momentum, 408
  particles, **552–556**, *556*, 561
spheres, modifying, **112–115**,
  112–114
Spherical deflectors, 568
Spherical parameter, 354
Spin Axis Controls section, 560
spinners, 27
splines, 47
  components, 164
  extruding polygons along,
    138–139, *138–139*
spotlights
  attenuation, 478, *478–479*
  Free, **469–470**, *469–470*
  Target, **464–468**, *465–468*
Spray particle system, 549–550,
  550
Spread parameter, 551
sprites, 557
squash and stretch, **26**, **387–389**,
  387–389
standard lights, 74, 461, **464**
  Free Direct, **470**
  Free spotlights, **469–470**,
    469–470
  Omni, **471–473**, *472–473*
  skylights, **473–474**, *474*
  Target Direct, **467–469**, *468*
  Target spotlights, **464–468**,
    465–468
Standard material, **303**
standard welding, 280
Status Bar, **80–81**, *80*
Status Line, 80
steam, 557
stock lenses, 514, *514*

storyboards, **5**
Strauss material, **314**, *314*
stretch and squash, 74, **387–389**, *387–389*
Structure rollout, 419
Sub-Object icon, 119
sub-objects, 27
    Editable Polys, 125, *125*
    materials for, **325–326**, *326*
    meshes, **111–115**, *112–114*
Subdivision Surface rollout, **130–131**, *131*, 175–176, *175*
Subdivision Surfaces (SubDs), **175–176**, *175–176*
subdivisions, 48
subtraction process, 217
subtractive color, **20**
Sun lighting, 467
Super Spray emitters, 549, *550*
Super Spray particle systems, **548**, *549*
    creating, **554–555**, *554–555*
    Particle Generation rollout, **552–553**, *552–553*
SuperSampling
    Raytrace maps, 529
    Raytrace material, 527, *528*, 531–532
surface shine, 309–310, *310*
surfaces
    pool ball, **315–316**, *315–316*
    subdivision, **175–176**, *175–176*
Systems category, 73, **75**, *75*

T

Tagged Image File Format (TIFF), 19, 506–507
tangency, key, **396**
Taper modifier, 120, *120*
tapered polygons, 135
Targa (TGA) format, 19, 506–507
Target cameras, 85, **514**
Target Direct lights, **467–469**, *468*
Target spotlights, **464**, *465*
    cone settings, **466**, *467*
    creating, **465**, *465*
    falloff, **466**, *466*
    selecting, **466**, *467*
    shape, **466**, *466–467*

target welding, **280**
targets, knife throwing, **406–408**, *407*
TCB Rotation controller, **372–374**, *373*
teapot object, **77–78**, *77*
technical directors (TDs), **13**
television properties
    aspect ratio, 503
    color, **21**
    frame rates, 23
    pixel aspect, 504, *504*
    resolution, 22
Tension parameter
    MetaParticles, 558
    tessellation, **179–180**, *179*
Tessellate Selection window, 178, *178*
Tessellate tool, **178–180**, *178–180*
testing
    biped model, **446–447**, *447*
    rigid body dynamics, **575–576**, *575–576*
texture maps, 297
texturing. *See also* materials and Material Editor
    brick wall, **296–297**, *296–297*
    for detail, 108
    in workflow, **10–11**
thigh area
    alien character, 275, *275*
    associating to models, 440, *440*
three-point lighting, **458–461**, *458–460*
3D maps, **328–330**, *329–330*
3d space, **3–4**, *3*
32-bit image files, **18**
throwing. *See* knife throwing
thruster in Red Rocket
    creating, **214–220**, *214–220*
    texture, **363–366**, *364–366*
thumb
    alien character, 280
    creating, **173–174**, *173–174*
TIFF (Tagged Image File Format), 19, 506–507
Tiling parameter
    3D maps, 329
    bitmaps, 348
    checker maps, 327

gradient maps, 328
    UVW modifier, 350
Tiling UV setting, 349
time and timing
    bouncing ball, **389–390**, *389–390*
    deflectors, 569
    output settings, **502–503**, *503–504*
    particle systems, 552, **556**, *556*, 576
Time Configuration dialog box
    particles, 556, *556*, 576
    purpose, 83, *83*
Time Off parameter, 568–570
Time On parameter, 568–570
Time slider
    for keyframes, **53–54**, *53*
    overview, **79–80**, *79*
Time Tag button, 81
Title Safe area, 518
toes
    alien character, 263, *263*
    associating to models, 441, *442*
toolbars
    Curve Editor, **395–396**, *395*
        Biped, **397**
        Curves, **397**
        Key Tangency, **396**
        Navigation, **397–398**
    main. *See* main toolbar tools
Tools menu, 64
Top/Bottom material, **307**, *307*
Top view, 36–37, *36*, 89
torso
    alien character
        blocking, **247–249**, *247–249*
        cleaning up, **253–254**, *253–254*
        detail, **283–285**, *283–285*
        forming, **250–253**, *250–253*
    associating to models, 442
    biped, 421
Track Bar, **79–80**, *79*
Track View-Curve Editor, **379–380**, *380*, 394–395, *394–395*
    Curve Editor. *See* Curve Editor
    Dope Sheet version, 395, **433–437**, *435–438*
    navigation tools, **397–398**

tracks, object, 28, 395
trajectories
  knife throwing, **400–401**,
    400–401
  Motion panel, 78, *78*
Trajectories option, 78, *78*
transformation tools, **68**, *68*
translating parent objects, 41
translucence, 314
Translucent shader, **314**, *314*
transparency
  alpha channel, 18, 507, *507*
  opacity. *See* opacity
  Raytrace maps, **532–533**, *533*
  Raytrace material, **530–531**, *531*
  See-Through mode
    alien arms, 257
    frozen objects, 439
Truck Camera tool, **535–536**, *535*
Truck icon, 87
trucks, 516, 535, *535*
tumbling, 40, 89
TurboSmooth modifier,
  271–273, *272*
TurboSmooth rollout, 272, *272*
Twist modifier, 115–116, *115–116*
2-Sided material, 301, *301*
2D maps, **326–328**, *327–329*
2K Academy resolution, 22

U

U mapping coordinates, 320
U parameter, 348
U Tiling parameter, 331–332
under-lighting, 457, *457*
Undo tool, 35, **66**, *66*, 404
Unhide Objects dialog box, 559
Uniformity parameter, 498
units, 90
Units Setup option, 184
universal deflector, 568
Unlink Selected tool, 102
Up Arrow state, 101–102
Use Global Settings option, 475
Use light attenuation settings, 478
Use Rate parameter, 552, 556, 564
Use Source Color parameter, 525
Use Total parameter, 552

user interface (UI), **32**, **61–62**
  animation controls, **81–83**,
    81–83
  Command panel. *See*
    Command panel
  main toolbar. *See* main toolbar
    tools
  menu bar, **63–65**, *64*
  project and file management
    workflow, **32–35**, *33–35*
  scenes, **97–98**
    Layout Editor, **98–100**,
      98–100
    Scene Explorer,
      105–106, *105*
    Schematic View, **100–105**,
      101–105
  screen layout, **62–63**, *63*
  Status Bar, **80–81**, *80*
  Time slider and Track Bar,
    79–80, *79*
  viewports. *See* viewports
Utilities panel, 73, **79**, *79*
UVW Map Gizmo, **351–353**,
  351–352
UVW map modifiers, **350–354**,
  350–353

V

V mapping coordinates, 320
V parameter, 348
V Tiling parameter, 331–332
Variation parameter, 552–553
vector images, **16–17**, *17*
velocity in momentum, 408
version numbers
  filename, 506
  projects, **33–34**
vertical fins, Red Rocket, **208–212**,
  208–212
  base material, **346–347**,
    346–347
  decals, **347–354**, *348–353*,
    357–359, *357–359*
  mapping, **345–354**, *346–353*
vertices
  chamfering, **132–133**, *132–133*
  Editable Polys, 125
  extruding, **131**, *131–132*

lines, **164**
polygon, 109
welding, **134**, *134*
Video Graphics Array (VGA)
  resolution, 22
Viewport Configuration dialog
  box, 89–90, *89*, 461–462, *461*
Viewport Display area, 551
Viewport Navigation tools, 514
viewports, **36**
  bitmaps in, **245**, *245*
  changing views, **39**, *39*, **90**, *90*
  layout, **36–37**
  maximizing, **39**
  modes, *45*, *47*
  navigating, **39–40**, **83–89**,
    83–88
  object selection in, **38**, *38*
  objects and axes in, **37–38**, *38*
  overview, **89–90**, *89–90*
  rendering levels, **91–95**, *91–94*
Views menu, 64
volumes for vector images, 16
volumetric lights
  creating, **494–495**, *494–495*
  parameters, **497–498**, *498*
  shadows, **495–496**, *495–496*
  volumetric effect, **496–497**, *497*
Vortex space warp, 565

W

W mapping coordinates, 320
walk gait, 426–427
Walk Gait button, 434
walking
  footsteps, **426–428**, *426–428*
  freeform animation, **430–433**,
    431–433
wall, texturing, **296–297**, *296–297*
warm colors, 20
weight
  in animation, **26**
  in momentum, 408
  squash and stretch for, 387
Weld tool, **134**, *134*
Weld Vertices window, 134, *134*
welding target, **280**
wheel wells, Red Rocket, **196–199**,
  196–199

wheels, Red Rocket, **223–224**, *224*
  axles, **206–208**, *206–208*
  bumps maps, **342–343**, *343*
  creating, **224–226**, *225–226*
  fine tuning materials, **339–342**, *340–342*
  mapping, **333–343**, *334–343*
  Multi/Sub-Object materials, **337–339**, *337–339*
  placing, **226**, *226–227*
  polygons and named selection sets, **334–337**, *335–337*
White Border state, 101
White Fill state, 101
Widescreen aspect ratio, 22, 503
width
  aspect ratio, 22
  output size settings, 503
  specular highlight, 310
Wind space warp, 565
wine glass, 530–533
Wire material, 300, *301*
Wireframe rendering level, 93, *93*
Wireframe View mode, 48

wiring parameters, **561–564**, *561–565*
wobble, 407
Wood maps, **330**, *330*
workflow, **8**
  animation, **11**
  Character Studio, **412–415**, *413–414*
  lighting, **11–12**
  modeling, **8–10**
  project and file management, **32–35**, *33–35*
  rendering, **12–13**
  texturing, **10–11**
World Coordinate System, 23, *24*
World Space modifiers, 76
wrists, alien character, 277, 279, *279*

X

X axes, 3, 24, 36, 38
X coordinates, 23
X Position track, 401
X rotation parameter, 374

XForm modifier, **392–394**, *394*
XYZ-axis, 95
XYZ to UVW parameter, 354

Y

Y axes, 3, 24, 36, 38
Y coordinates, 23
Y rotation parameter, 374

Z

Z axes, 3, 24, 36, 38
Z coordinates, 23
Z-Depth element, 522, *522*
Z Position curve, 386
Z Position parameter, 382, 384, *384*
Z Position track, 401
Z rotation parameter, 374
Zoom tool, 397–398
zooming
  Curve Editor, 397–398
  lenses, 516
  viewports, 40, 88